PURPLSOC

Richard Sickinger
Peter Baumgartner
Tina Gruber-Mücke

PURPLSOC 2017 - PURSUIT OF PATTERN LANGUAGES FOR SOCIETAL CHANGE

A comprehensive perspective of current pattern research and practice

Editors: Richard Sickinger, Peter Baumgartner, Tina Gruber-Mücke

Book Design and Page Layout: Wolfgang Rauter, Stephan Längle

www.purplsoc.org

info@purplsoc.org

Edition Donau-Universität Krems

ISBN Paperback: 978-3-903150-43-0

ISBN eBook: 978-3-903150-44-7

Printed on demand in many countries. Distributed by tredition

Krems, Ocotber 2018

Dear Reader,

We live in a time of social and cultural change. Old patterns are losing their validity and relevance - new patterns are needed and in demand. We need a new approach which can formulate, generate and engage such patterns. The pattern language approach of Christopher Alexander serves this purpose - The interdisciplinary and participatory building blocks for societal change.

In the last two decades, the pattern approach of Christopher Alexander - which originated from architecture but has gone far beyond since – has been successfully implemented in a growing number of different domains, such as design, media, arts, IT, management, pedagogy, health care, linguistics, sociology, social activism, social innovation and grassroots movements. It has become a powerful interdisciplinary and participative tool for collecting and communicating informal knowledge with the purpose of creating morphological coherence through the things which we design, make or put into practice. Lastly, as Alexander states, with the objective to build a society which is alive and whole.

The Second World Conference PURPLSOC 2017 In Pursuit of Pattern Languages for Societal Change offers an overview of the newest developments in the application of the pattern language approach of Christopher Alexander in different domains, such as education, media, software development, management, pedagogy, health care, politics, social innovation, integration, art, personal development and design. Altogether 21 domains – from anthropology and automation to political science and systems science – were represented at the conference. The pattern language approach – a common language for a fragmented world.

This anthology of papers aims to disseminate Alexander's ground-breaking ideas and provoke further use and discussion of his methods.

Richard Sickinger
richard.sickinger@donau-uni.ac.at

Peter Baumgartner
peter.baumgartner@donau-uni.ac.at

Tina Gruber-Muecke
tina.gruber-muecke@fh-krems.ac.at

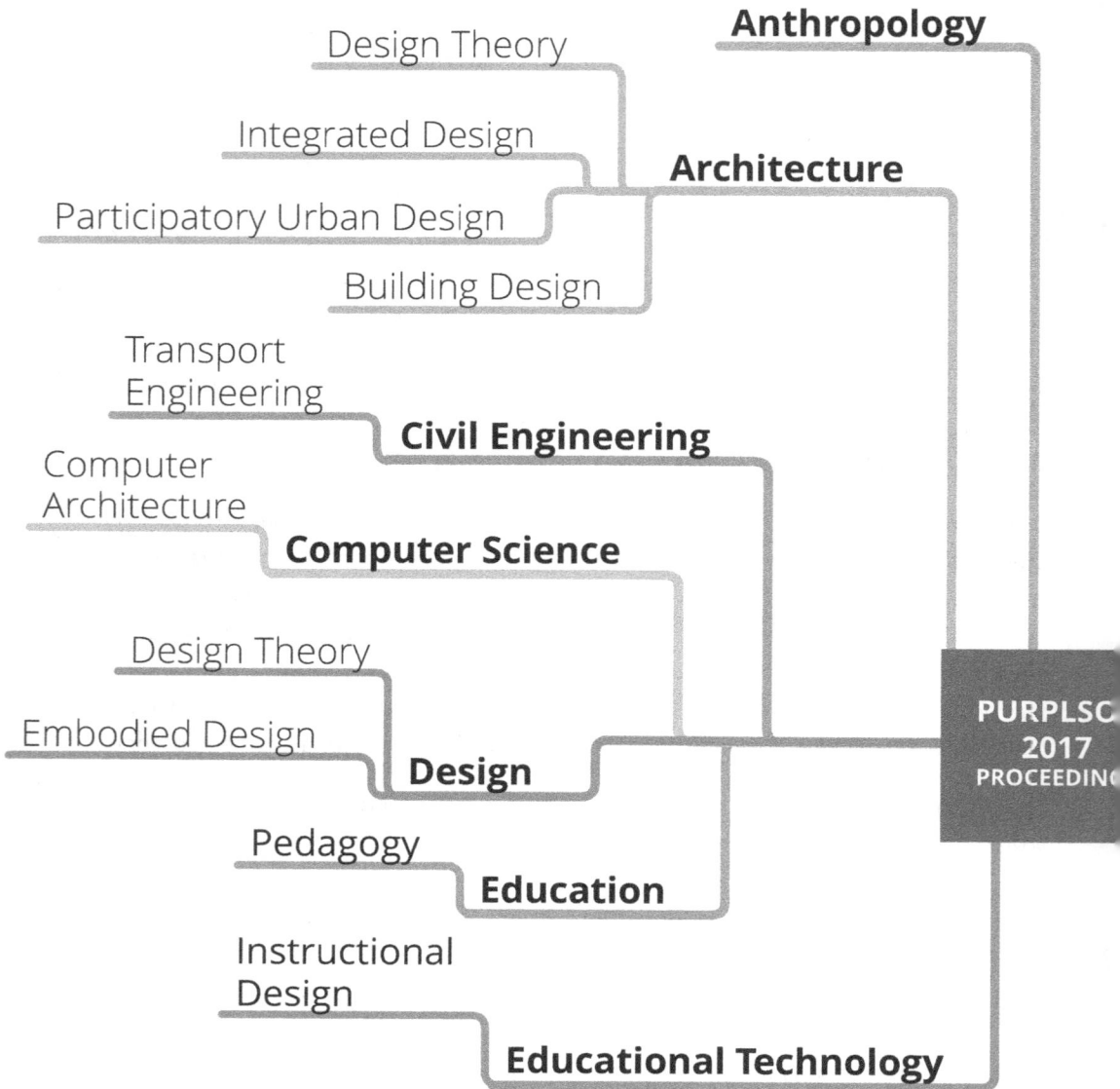

Design Theory

Integrated Design

Participatory Urban Design

Architecture

Building Design

Anthropology

Transport
Engineering

Civil Engineering

Computer
Architecture

Computer Science

Design Theory

Embodied Design

Design

Pedagogy

Education

Instructional
Design

Educational Technology

**PURPLSO
2017
PROCEEDIN**

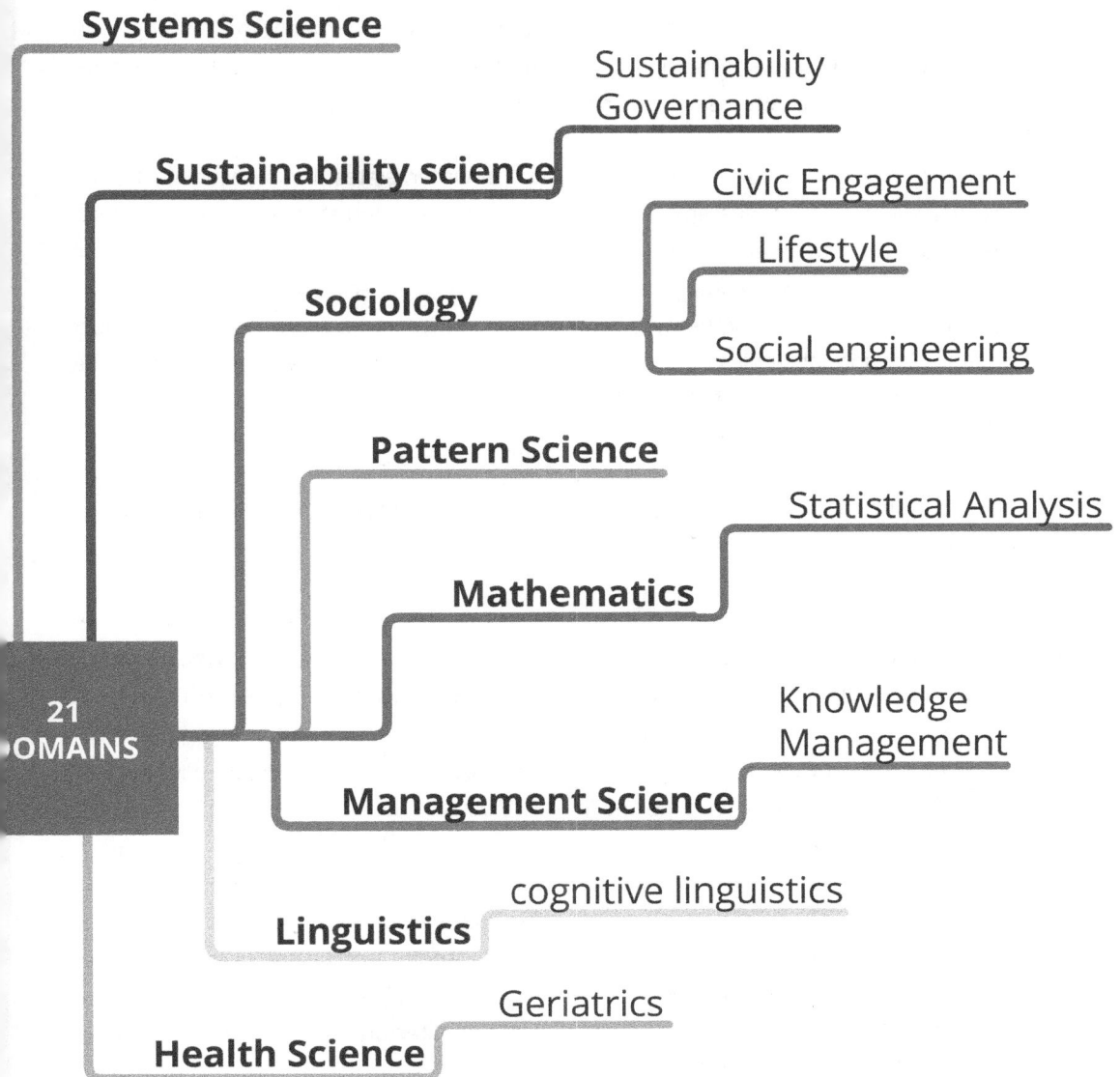

Systems Science

Sustainability
Governance

Sustainability science

Civic Engagement

Lifestyle

Sociology

Social engineering

Pattern Science

Statistical Analysis

Mathematics

Knowledge
Management

Management Science

cognitive linguistics

Linguistics

Geriatrics

Health Science

21
OMAINS

01 Are there patterns which globally link humanity? Patterns of Humanity looks at humanity, individually and collectively, to explore the question if there are patterns in the sense of a generalization or abstraction that are constant across cultures, although each culture might interpret that pattern differently. The author states "In our efforts to build large-scale habitable complex systems it is essential that our efforts be informed with knowledge and understanding of human beings and the cultures they have instituted the past tens of thousands of years. Only Patterns of Humanity will provide any hope of success."

02 Christopher Alexanders treatise, The Nature of Order, states that a shift away from a mechanistic mind-body dualism into a more holistic, integrated stance is essential for society today. Do, otherwise identical, design projects that are developed in the mechanistic (drafting and computer) or integrated (modeling) modes respectively truly display measurable divergent formal properties when completed? Method Shapes Morphology conduct several such formal studies on a small scale to observe any objective delta between the physical outcomes of these two contrasting methods of building.

03 A Pattern Language for Designing Regenerative Refugee Camps utilizes systems-thinking, permaculture design and a pattern language to offer regenerative solutions to the global refugee crisis.

04 The Central Role of Artifacts in Processes of Knowledge Production argues that artifacts, and pattern languages in particular, can act as containers and displayers of knowledge and thereby ground ideas and design principles into an intelligible form to enable non-experts to participate meaningfully in a design process. Such artifacts empower citizens with the capacity to sustain dialogue with experts, while providing an environment where local knowledge can emerge and influence design

05 Alexander's Patterns in Contemporary City and Transport Planning Processes – A Comparison of Theory and Practice shows the relevance of Alexander's essay "Nature of Order" as a central element in human-compatible transport planning due to its system-analytic character. A concrete example for the implementation of "A Pattern Language" in public participation, awareness building processes and in architectural competitions for community buildings is described and evaluated.

06 Although pattern languages are a powerful means to preserve and reuse expertise, a clear definition is missing about what a pattern language actually is. The Nature of Pattern Languages seeks to provide a clear and unambiguous mathematical foundation. It reveals

the nature of pattern languages by presenting a formal notion of pattern languages as node-coloured and edge- weighted directed multigraphs and shows how this model can be used to sharpen Alexander's idea of pattern languages.

07 Illuminating Egoless Creation with Theories of Autopoietic Systems examines one of the most important but overlooked concepts in pattern language theory: creation processes without the self (ego). Christopher Alexander, the inventor of the pattern language concept and methodology, focused on a generative mechanism beyond the individual designer level and claimed that creation originated from this basis. The authors illuminate this egoless creation concept from a systems theory perspective.

08 When Thievery Isn't an Option or An Overview of Embodied Making describes a nascent pattern craft: Embodied Making. This process, an art of sense-making, solutioning, and patterning, draws deeply and respectfully from preceding traditions (notably Alexandrian pattern languages, phenomenology, and Kaizen), but, perforce, engages in its own pathfinding, devising patterns for today's world from scratch.

09 Pedagogy of Wholeness: Accounting for the Missing Heart in Educational Research argues that Alexander's theory of centers and wholeness can be utilized for understanding and creating inspiring and nurturing learning environments. The centers-based approach assists in revealing design elements which reflect experiences that are "momentary perhaps, something we consider a haze of emotion... a feeling we recognize as deep, as vitally important... it lasts for a few seconds, perhaps even for a few minutes... and then our rude cosmology dismisses it" (Alexander), accounting for the 'missing heart' in current educational research.

10 How can teachers support students in becoming active learners? **Active Learning Patterns for Teachers** is a pattern language which describes good teaching practices for teachers, classified into three different categories: "Identify the seeds of curiosity, help them grow", "Lift them up to the next level" and "Enhance each other and keep changing". The authors also describe tools for teachers-workshops to promote the introduction and application of these patterns in schools.

11 Designing Hybrid Spaces for Creative work deals with the planning and design of hybrid spaces for innovation and learning processes using a design pattern language, an important contribution in the planning of three innovation rooms at TH Köln (Campus Gummersbach). The authors present three example patterns: hybrid learning space, physical to digital, and digital to real. The patterns aim to provide important design guidelines for similar projects at other universities.

12 Patterns for Hybrid Pedagogy aims at dissolving the dichotomies within education such as physical-digital, academic-nonacademic, online-offline, formal-informal, learning-teaching and individual-collective. It takes a more holistic view and takes the diversity of students and teachers into account. The 85 patterns are clustered into different categories: Hybrid Learning Space, Student Agency, Hybrid Production, Collaboration, Hybrid Assessment, Outside In, Inside Out, Sharing is Caring, Performance. This paper presents one pattern of each category and reflects about the process of finding and applying these patterns.

13 In the last decades, pedagogues all over the world have mined many patterns as well as pattern languages and communities of practices have emerged, like the pedagogical patterns project. **A Pattern Language Remix for ATS2020** makes use of existing pedagogical patterns and adapts them for teachers in specific learning and teaching settings. Through the example of the EU project "ATS2020 – Assessment of Transversal Skills", the authors show how existing pattern languages can be remixed and how new configurations can be found between patterns from different languages.

14 How can people who have never engaged in pattern languages, but are interested in using patterns, make effective use of patterns? **Patterns for Utilizing Patterns Towards Dementia-Friendly Communities** provides a collection of 12 patterns, called 'Patterns for Utilizing Patterns', which help utilize a select pattern language 'Words for a Journey', a pattern language for living well with dementia and forming Dementia-Friendly Communities.

15 Christopher Alexander's four volume "The Nature of Order" presents a metaphysical vision by which all of life, in the broadest sense, is brought forth by relentless application of a single fundamental transformation which manifests itself through 15 properties of life. **Six Investigations for Clarifying Alexander's Properties of Life** seeks to define the properties through six investigations and so to clarify Alexander's properties of life as metaphysically sound and scientifically usable.

16 How can the practical knowledge of elderly care in nursing homes, possessed by individual staff members and not necessarily shared, be acquired and put into practice as an effective means for creating a better environment for elderly people? **A Pattern Language Shaping a Desirable Environment for the Elderly** describes the research method and resulting pattern language consisting of 66 patterns obtained through conversations with staff members of Benesse Style Care Co., Ltd. In Japan.

17 Statistics as a subject is becoming increasingly important for academic and professional capacity. On the other hand, students of non-mathematical subjects confront statistics with great reservation. **Patterns of Statistical Analysis – Guiding Students Using Christopher Alexander`s Pattern Language Principles** show how the proximity of statistical structures to living structures identified by Christopher Alexander is taken up to develop a constructivist didactic concept that evades frequently negative attitudes to statistics by offering an approach to statistical models via known, non-mathematical patterns.

18 The pattern approach demonstrates the power of 'implicit and tacit knowing' in many fields and complements and recharges ,rational knowing' with experiential wisdom. Nevertheless, there still are open questions to be solved in order to understand and use pattern languages as dynamic systems. Resonating Patterns and Resonating Spaces. Potential Steps for Dynamic Pattern Technology and Digital Pattern Practice suggests to link the space-oriented concept of ,A Pattern Language' by Christopher Alexander with Latour´s time-oriented ,Actor-Network-Theory' to address challenges faced when creating a dynamic pattern language.

19 **Arrival City: Refugees In Three + One German Cities** not only has the intent to study the refugee crisis in various spatial and architectural settings and aspects but also to actively try to help refugees with their problems. The authors present three case studies in three different cities in Germany. In these cities the life of refugees from their original escape country/city to their arrival in their new cities and new countries is analyzed. Furthermore, how refugees can assimilate or integrate into their host countries, cities and neighborhoods and start a new life.

20 **A Refugee Pattern Language Cluster One - The Refugee Family** shares a draft pattern language for refugee integration, beginning with the larger refugee family domain. The formation of a 'Refugee Pattern Language' (RPL) is one of the key building blocks of PUARL's Initiative Refugee Integration in Europe.

21 In civic collaboration activities, it is important to involve people who are indifferent to such activities so that local government can take diverse values into consideration. **Patterns for Community Innovation by Empowering Indifferent People: Practice of Sabae City Office JK-section** shows how local high school girls in Sabae, Japan, who are indifferent to community design, can be motivated by patterns to participate and to achieve local innovations, therefore enabling civic collaboration.

22 Today, many young people feel insecure about having and raising children while working. The pattern language **Ways of Everyday World-Making: Living Well with Working and Parenting** helps young people reduce their anxiety over becoming a working parent and shows ways how young people can live well while both working and parenting by discovering that by doing daily chores, raising children, working and interacting with one's social network, we personally build the daily life that we live in.

23 How can young people be encouraged to cook, in response to the declining cooking population especially among young people in Japan? **Cooking Fun Language: Sharing the Hidden Fun of Cooking** proposes a Cooking Fun Language that documents the hidden enjoyment of cooking. Fun language is a collection of Fun Words, each showing a way of enjoying a certain cooking related activity that are unknown to those who have little experience. The authors present the creating process, a list of the Fun Words, the function of Cooking Fun Language, and future work.

24 How can one best describe the qualities of Washoku, the traditional cuisine of Japan? **A Cooking Language: A Pattern-Based Tool for Discovering and Applying History-Based Cooking Ideas** proposes the cooking language method, along with its first sample created from the Japanese cuisine: the Washoku Language. The authors briefly cover philosophical aspects of the method, describe its creation method, introduce the first instance of a cooking language and show results and analyses from two test cases of cooking using a cooking language.

25 Can a pattern language be expressed in a different way as with reading material? **Pattern Song: Auditory Expression for Pattern Languages** introduces the concept of the 'pattern song' as an auditory expression of a pattern language and presents the first such song. The authors discuss the auditory expression of a pattern language and analyze the relation between lyrics and patterns, as well as feedback from listeners.

26 Modern education makes great demands on young people in regard to decision-making and responsibility when forging one's own career path. **Life Transition Patterns: A Pattern Language for Shaping Your Future** presents a pattern language that supports young people in making life decisions about subjects such as school and career and enables high school and university students to make career choices in light of their preferred style of living. The authors present a summary of all 27 patterns and also provide examples of the usage of the pattern language.

27 Due to the widespread availability of restaurants, take-out options, and ready-made foods, many people have fewer opportunities to cook. Therefore, they have less familiarity with the activity, and can consequently feel intimidated or reluctant about cooking. **Cook-That-Dish Patterns for Tacos: A Tool for Collaborative Cooking** is a pattern language that aims to remove this fear and invites people to enjoy the cooking experience.

28 Developing a supportive social environment within local government agencies or companies is a key to improving general welfare. **Welfare Pattern Languages by a Local Government** presents two pattern languages, "Employment of the Disabled Patterns" and "Welfare Innovation Patterns", designed to disseminate tacit knowledge and experiential know-how to enrich co-creative interaction relating to welfare issues among stakeholders in the city of Kawasaki, Japan.

29 What might be a language that not only describes "the whole" of sustainability but is also generative of the solutions and actions we need? **Closing the Gap Between Concern and Action: Tools and Lessons from Exploring a Pattern Language** on Sustainability describes research that explored the nature of such a language using the aspirations of Alexander's "pattern languages" and the everyday experiences of a group of households seeking to "live more sustainably". Thirteen proto-Patterns were developed around one aspect of this experience – the need, as identified by the households, to maintain a "mindfulness" to the task.

30 Systemic design methods in the 21st century have roots in systems theory developed in the 20th century. During this period, the design profession has evolved with changes in technology. The rise of information technology has resulted in a turn towards interaction and materiality. **Multiparadigm Inquiry Generating Service Systems Thinking** proposes a generative pattern language coming through multiparadigm inquiry that builds on the history of systems theories developed from the 1960s into the 1990s.

Keynote

31 **A Building is not a Turkish Carpet – Patterns, Properties and Beauty** is a review by Max Jacobson of the historical development of Christopher Alexander and his various associate's work with particular attention to the developing concept of "beauty" in the various books. While it is illustrated that the actual word rarely if ever appears in the bulk of the work, it becomes a central focus of the latest 4-volume The Nature of Order. This eventual concept of beauty, derived initially from an intense analysis of ancient Turkish carpets, turns out to constitute the characteristics of Nature. As such, this 'natural' form of beauty omits other forms, such as the Sublime, Euclidean geometry, and the beauty of noble social ideals expressed in architecture.

Contents

Anthropology

01 Patterns of Humanity — 32
David West

02 Method Shapes Morphology — 50
David Getzin, Bryan Mock

Architecture

03 A Pattern Language for Designing Regenerative Refugee Camps — 82
Gregory Crawford, Nick Tittle, Maina Sulzbach-Petry, Geoffroy Godeau, Brecht Deriemaeker

04 The Central Role of Artifacts in Processes of Knowledge Production: an Empirical Investigation of Three Projects of Participatory Urban Design using Pattern Languages — 100
Aurelio David

Civil Engineering

05 Alexander's Patterns in Contemporary City and Transport Planning Processes – A Comparison of Theory and Practice — 120
Harald Frey, Robert Krasser

Computer Science

06 The Nature of Pattern Languages — 130
Michael Falkenthal,
Uwe Breitenbücher,
Frank Leymann

Design

07 Illuminating Egoless Creation with Theories of Autopoietic Systems — 152
Takashi Iba, Ayaka Yoshikawa

Contents

Design

08 When Thievery Isn't an Option or An Overview of
Embodied Making   **180**
Jenny Quillien

09 Pedagogy of Wholeness: Accounting for the Missing   **194**
Heart in Educational Research
Ana Pinto

Education

10 Active Learning Patterns for Teachers   **216**
Takashi Iba, Yoshihiro Utsunomiya

11 Designing Hybrid Spaces for Creative Work   **242**
Christian Kohls, Guido Münster

12 Patterns for Hybrid Pedagogy   **266**
Christian Kohls, Christian Köppe, Rikke Toft Nørgård

Educational Technologies

13 A Pattern Language Remix for ATS2020   **288**
Isabell Grundschober,
Andrea Ghoneim,
Peter Baumgartner,
Tina Gruber-Muecke

Health Sciences

14 Patterns for Utilizing Patterns Towards   **318**
Dementia-Friendly Communities
Tomoki Kaneko,
Takashi Iba

Linguistics

15 Six Investigations for Clarifying Alexander's   **334**
Properties of Life
Andrius Jonas Kulikauskas

Management Science

16 A Pattern Language Shaping a Desirable   **366**
Environment for the Elderly
Masaaki Yonesu,
Io Kato

Mathematics

17 Patterns of Statistical Analysis – Guiding Students using Christopher Alexander`s Pattern Language Principles — **380**
Valerie Larsen, Cornelia Eube, Sebastian Vogt

Pattern Science

18 Resonating Patterns and Resonating Spaces. Potential Steps for Dynamic Pattern Technology and Digital Pattern Practice — **404**
Wolfgang Stark, Stefan Tewes, Christina Weber

19 Arrival City: Refugees in Three + One German Cities — **430**
Hajo Neis, Briana Meier, Tomoki Furukawazono

20 A Refugee Pattern Language, Cluster One - The Refugee Family — **450**
Hajo Neis, Briana Meier, Tomoki Furukawazono

Sociology

21 Patterns for Community Innovation by Empowering Indifferent People: Practice of Sabae City Office JK-section — **478**
Norihiko Kimura, Yujun Wakashin, Takashi Iba

22 Ways of Everyday World-Making: Living well with Working and Parenting — **490**
Iroha Ogo, Takashi Iba, Kimie Ito, Seiko Miyakawa

23 Cooking Fun Language: Sharing the Hidden Fun of Cooking — **510**
Hitomi Shimizu, Ayaka Yoshikawa, Takashi Iba

24 Cooking Language: A Pattern-Based Tool for Discovering and Applying History-Based Cooking Ideas — **532**
Taichi Isaku, Takashi Iba

Contents

25 Pattern Song: Auditory Expression for Pattern Languages   **560**
Takashi Iba, Mayu Ueno, Ayaka Yoshikawa

26 Life Transition Patterns: A Pattern Language for Shaping Your Future   **580**
Takashi Iba, Tomoko Kubo

27 Cook-That-Dish Patterns for Tacos: A Tool for Collaborative Cooking   **600**
Ayaka Yoshikawa, Hitomi Shimizu, Takashi Iba

28 Welfare Pattern Languages by a Local Government   **618**
Kazuo Takiguchi, Naohiro Kitamura, Makoto Okada, Takashi Iba

29 Closing the Gap Between Concern and Action: Tools and Lessons from Exploring a Pattern Language on Sustainability   **650**
Greg Paine

30 Wicked Problems, Systems Approach, Pattern Language, Ecological Epistemology, Hierarchy Theory, Interactive Value: Multiparadigm Inquiry generating Service Systems Thinking   **678**
David Ing

Keynote   736
31 A Building is not a Turkish Carpet –
Patterns, Properties and Beauty
Max Jacobson

Sociology

Sustainability science

Sustainability science

Architecture

15

We would like to thank all authors, contributors and participants of the PURPLSOC Conference 2017

The objective of the PURPLSOC 2017 world conference was to stimulate the attention for pattern related work, both in the scientific community and the wider public, by showing its broad applicability and richness and bringing application/best practice examples from outside the scientific community into research.

The PURPLSOC platform provides a forum for scholars from a variety of fields as well as for a broad audience of practitioners and students to come together and discuss topics such as:

» Architecture, Urbanism and Regional Development
» Design, Media, Arts & IT
» Pedagogy, Education and Learning
» Social Activism, Social Innovation and Grassroots Movement
» Everyday Applications and Additional Disciplines

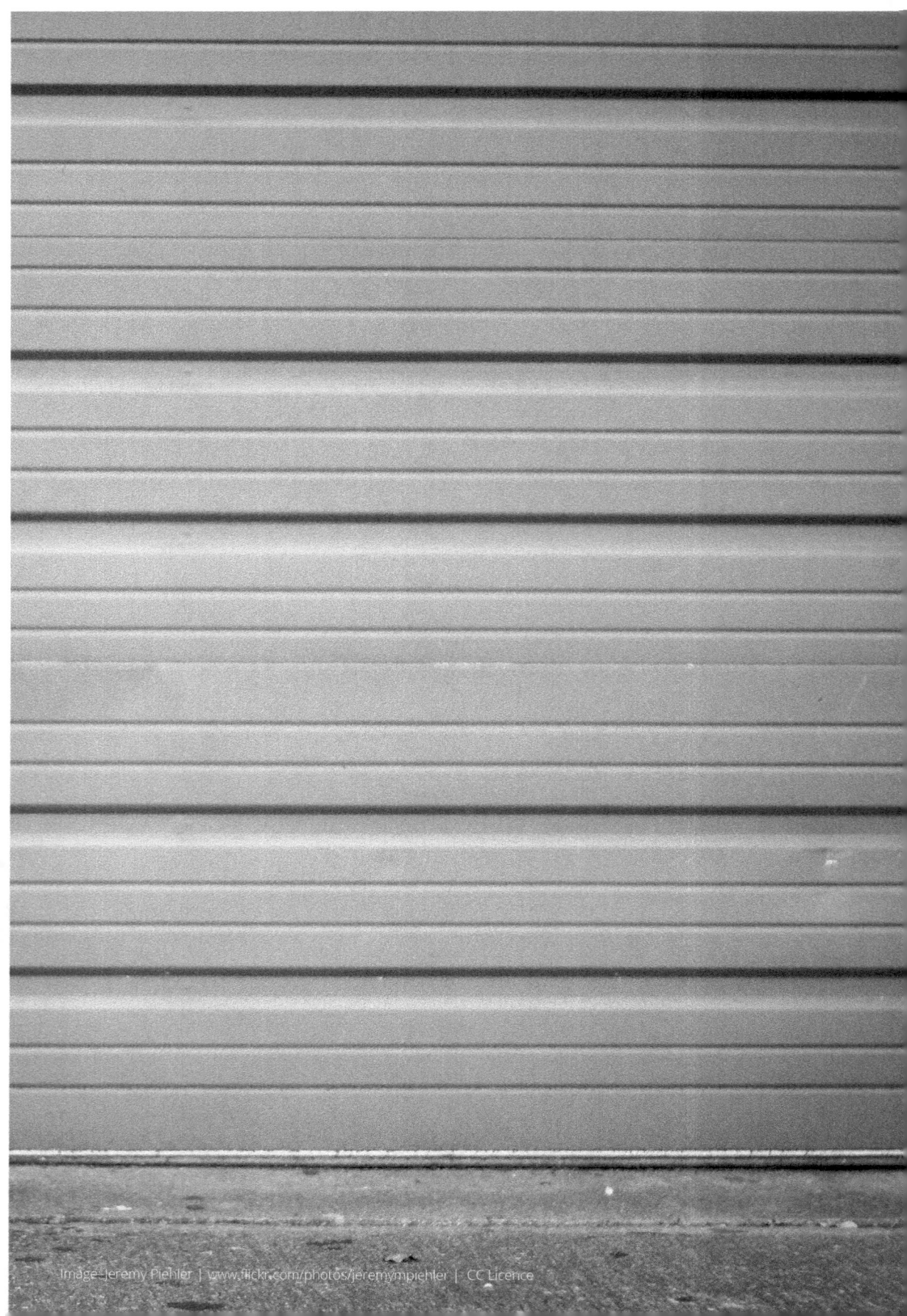

About the Authors

Peter BAUMGARTNER is full Professor for Technology Enhanced Learning and Multimedia at Danube University. He graduated in sociology and received his habilitation with a thesis on "Background Knowledge – Groundwork for a Critique of Computational Reason". His recent research focuses on (Higher Education) didactics, theory of teaching and learning, e- Education and distance education, e-Learning implementation strategies and the evaluation of learning environments. He has been key speaker at various TEL conferences and has published 8 books and over 120 articles. His blog "Gedankensplitter" is available at http://peter.baumgartner.name/.

Uwe BREITENBÜCHER is a research staff member and postdoc at the Institute of Architecture of Application Systems (IAAS) at the University of Stuttgart, Germany. His research vision is to improve cloud application provisioning and application management by automating the application of management patterns. Uwe was part of the CloudCycle project, in which the OpenTOSCA Ecosystem was developed. His current research interests include cyber-physical systems, patterns, and microservices.

Gregory CRAWFORD is the COO of Surplus Permaculture Design, CEO of Win/win Reactor and Creative Director of the Panya Project. Gregory is a systems thinker specializing in regenerative urban design, neighborhood skill-building and permaculture design. He is currently based in Detroit, Michigan, USA.

Aurelio DAVID is an Architect and a final-year Ph.D. Student at the Institute of Urban Planning and Design at the University of Dusiburg-Essen in Germany. He obtained a double master's degree with distinction in Sustainable Architecture Design from the Politecnico di Torino and Milano (Italy). He was also selected to take part in the multidisciplinary program "Alta Scuola Politecnica", where he studied Design Thinking, Innovation and Society, and Complexity Theory. Prior to his Ph.D., he worked at an NGO in Italy, where he dealt with issues of low- cost retrofit of social housing. His current activity of research addresses topics of architecture, public participation, and collaborative design. He is actively involved in several experiments of community participation in Germany.

Brecht DERIEMAEKER is a founding member of Surplus Permaculture Design, field engineer for Aqueous Solutions, core member of the Blueprint Alliance and lead designer for Terra Genesis International. Brecht works as a regenerative systems designer and electromechanical engineer. He currently works across the EU.

Cornelia EUBE received a Diploma (equiv. M.Sc.) in Electrical Engineering from the RWTH Aachen (1992, Germany) and a Bachelor of Arts in Educational Science from the FernUniversität in Hagen (2014, Germany). She worked as a development engineer in the field of RFIC design for many years. At present her scientific interest and work concern innovative teaching and learning in higher education.

Michael FALKENTHAL is a research associate and Ph.D. student at the Institute of Architecture of Application Systems (IAAS) at the University of Stuttgart, Germany. He studied business information technology at the Universities of Applied Sciences in Esslingen and Reutlingen focusing on business process management, services computing and enterprise architecture management. Michael gained experience in several IT transformation and migration projects at small- to big-sized companies. His current research interests are fundamentals on pattern language theory, cloud computing and the internet of things.

Harald FREY works at the Institute for Transportation at the Vienna University of Technology. He is a civil engineer and holds a PhD in the field of transport and infrastructure planning. His scientific output focuses i.a. on the interdependencies between transport system and city planning, transport modelling and future transport systems and is proofed by more than 200 articles and presentations. He is also member of several expert committees and is supporting communities and politicians in transport planning and transport policy.

Tomoki FURUKAWAZONO is a Ph.D. candidate in the Graduate School of Media and Governance at Keio University. He earned a Master of Media and Governance at the Graduate School of Media and Governance, Keio University. He is a visiting scholar of the University of Oregon.

David GETZIN is an independent researcher and analytic historian, currently working in Italy. He holds a master's in design studies from the Harvard Graduate School of Design with a concentration in the History and Philosophy of Design. While there, he spearheaded the ADPD digital publishing project. He coursed PhD studies at McGill University, and holds a B.F.A. in Theatre Arts from Illinois Wesleyan University. In architectural practice, he has been Project Manager for handcraft bronze-work in the NYC area, for water-features in the same, and has served as an architectural design consultant in Peru. He wrote and produced The Fundamental Process, a podcast on iTunes about architectural morphology and history.

Andrea GHONEIM is researcher at the Department of Interactive Media and Education Technologies at Danube University Krems. Her contributions to the EU funded projects ICT-go-girls, EUfolio and ATS2020. Assessment of Transversal Skills show her focus on competence acquisition in technology enhanced learning scenarios as well as on criteria for self- and peer assessment and quality assurance for (formative and summative) assessment strategies. She also edits the ePortfolio of WP2 of ATS2020, collecting artefacts, research findings and deliverables on Technology and Tools for ATS2020 (http://mahara.ats2020.eu/view/view.php?id=178). (Andrea Ghoneim's personal ePortfolio is accessible via http://www.mahara.at/user/andreaghoneim/index.

Geoffroy GODEAU is the CEO of Roots Culture, co-founder of Apples and People, and Technical Supervisor of the Panya Project. Geoffroy specializes in perennial polyculture food systems, natural building, and holistic education. He is currently based in Ittre, Belgium.

Tina GRUBER-MUECKE is full Professor for Entrepreneurship at the Department Business at IMC University of Applied Sciences Krems. She graduated in Business Administration and her research regarding pattern languages focuses on Pedagogical Patterns in Entrepreneurship and Usage of Patterns in Business Model Innovation.

Isabell GRUNDSCHOBER graduated at the Vienna University of Economic and Business with a major in Socio-Economics and at the University College for Teacher Education Vienna with a focus on elementary school education and digital literacy. Currently, she is finishing a Master in Applied Knowledge Management at the University of Applied Sciences Burgenland. Since January 2015 she is a researcher at the Department for Interactive Media and Educational Technologies at Danube University. Her fields of expertise are learning outcome-oriented education and its implementation, the recognition of prior learning and educational technology. Ms. Grundschober conducted several training sessions on the implementation of learning outcomes in Higher Education and coordinated the EU-project VALERU. She currently works on national and international funded projects in the area of educational technology and LLL research, e.g. assessment of transversal skills (ATS2020) validation for the inclusion of new citizens of Europe (VINCE), supporting bonds between labor market and higher education through higher apprenticeships (ApprEnt). More about Isabell Grundschobers' work and research can be read in her blog "Isabell goes EduTech".

Takashi IBA is a professor in the Faculty of Policy Management at Keio University. He received a Ph.D. in Media and Governance from Keio University in 2003. He is the president of CreativeShift Lab, Inc. and a board member of The Hillside Group. Collaborating with his students, he has created many pattern languages concerning human actions: Learning Patterns (2014), Presentation Patterns (2014), Collaboration Patterns (2014), Words for a Journey (2015), as well as academic books in Japanese, such as the bestselling Introduction to Complex Systems (1998) and Pattern Language (2013).

David ING is a doctoral candidate in Industrial Engineering at the Aalto University School of Science. He is a trustee and past-president of the International Society for the Systems Sciences (2011-2012). In 2012, he graduated from a 28-year career in IBM Canada. He resides in Toronto, Canada, and can readily be found on the Internet at coevolving.com.

Kimie ITO graduated from Rikkyo University with a degree in psychology and currently works at the Lifestyle Research Center at Kao Corporation. The main task at this research center is to understand consumer needs through qualitative surveys. In 2015, she became a member of the departmental project 'Lifestyle and Attitude Toward the Working Life'. Currently, she is working with other members at Kao Corporation to implement a workshop utilizing the 'Ways of Everyday World-Making' with the purpose of realizing a society in which working people can work contently and in ways that suit themselves.

Max JACOBSON retired in 2015 from his architectural firm Jacobson Silverstein Winslow Degenhardt, Berkeley, California, after 35 years of practice. Concurrently he taught in the architecture departments of UC Berkeley, Diablo Valley College, and the University of San Francisco. He was a co-author of A Pattern Language and later with his architectural partners co-authored The Good House and Patterns of Home. His latest book was Invitation to Architecture.

Tomoki KANEKO is a student of Keio University and studies at Iba Laboratory. His research field is ultra-ageing society. He works at a non-profit organization called Dementia Friendship Club and is also a member of the Dementia-Friendly Japan Initiative. He conducts events and workshops in the welfare field throughout Japan. He creates pattern languages and researches ways to use them. He is one of the co-authors of the book "Words for a Journey", a Pattern Language for Living Well with Dementia (2015). He is also a co-author of Parenting Patterns (2015) and Pattern Mining Patterns (2016).

Io KATO graduated from Tokyo University of the Arts, Faculty of Fine Arts, Department of Architecture. After graduation, first, he worked at Office of Kumiko Inui (http://www.inui-uni.com), and second, Established Archichi office (http://www.archichi.jp). At the same time, he taught at Kyoto University of Art and Design, Correspondence Education, Department of

Design, Architectural Design Course. Now he is working as Staff at Benesse Style Care Co., Ltd., Architectural Design Division.

Norihiko KIMURA is master course student of Graduate School of Media and Governance, Keio University, in Japan. He studies a methodology creating future visions based on Social Systems Theory, proposed by German sociologist Niklas Luhmann, and presents some papers. He also researches community design method based on pattern language method. He is interested in methodology or theory of communication that makes participation and creative activities.

Norihiro KITAMURA is a director of the Association of Hataraku Shiawase JIN-EN-DO. After graduating from the School of Business at Aoyama Gakuin University, he worked at an employment agency and as store management at a nail salon. During this time, he became interested in the work-life of persons with disabilities and in 2012, along with his friends, he founded an association called "Hataraku Shiawase JINEN-DO" to support the employment of people with mental problems. At present, he is managing the training center of the employment support for persons with mental disabilities and creates his own know-how to support them.

Christian KOHLS is a professor for computer science and sociotechnical systems at the University of Applied Science Cologne (TH Köln). He has mined patterns in several fields, including interactive graphics, e-learning, online training, and creativity methods. His PhD theses covered psychological and epistemological views on pattern theory. As a pattern enthusiast he has published many papers on design patterns and organized international workshops and conferences on the topic. He is also president of the Hillside Europe pattern community.

Robert KRASSER is responsible for Village and Town Development at the Salzburg Institute for Regional Planning and Housing (SIR). He graduated at the department of architecture at Technical University of Graz followed by advanced studies at the University of Cape Town in city planning & urban design and the ETH-Zürich in regional planning. His recent work focuses on urban re-development, life-sized cities, street design, integrated urban development strategies, everyday-cycling infrastructure and documentary photography of complex urban traffic patterns.

Tomoko KUBO is the Chief of the Survey Planning Team, Department of Educational Planning and Development, Division of Educational Innovation, at Kawaijuku Educational Institution.

Andrius Jonas KULIKAUSKAS is affiliated with the Self Learners Network. As a child, he dedicated himself to knowing everything and applying that knowledge usefully. He has a B.A. in Physics from the University of Chicago and a Ph.D. in Mathematics from UCSD. From 1998 to 2010, he led Minciu Sodas, an online laboratory for serving and organizing independent thinkers around the world. He teaches Philosophy, Ethics and Creative Writing. He is currently investigating How do people behave? and How should they behave?

Christian KÖPPE is a senior lecturer in Software Engineering and researcher at the HAN University of Applied Sciences in Arnhem/Netherlands. He gives lectures in different disciplines like Software Architecture, Programming, Object-Oriented Analysis and Design, Databases and others. His research is mainly on the use and value of (educational) design patterns, innovations in computer science education, but also on software architecture topics. He is board member of the Hillside group, an active member of Hillside Europe, and also member of the program committee of different conferences. He was the program chair of the 20th PLoP conference and conference chair of the VikingPLoP'16.

Valerie LARSEN is a research fellow with the Department of Mathematics and Technology of the University of Applied Science in Koblenz, Germany, where she develops didactic concepts to improve student learning within an innovative project to facilitate accessibility of higher education. After practicing as a midwife for 9 years, Valerie decided to embark on a second career in adult education. She studied educational sciences at the FernUniversität in Hagen.

Frank LEYMANN is a full professor of computer science and director of the Institute of Architecture of Application Systems (IAAS) at the University of Stuttgart, Germany. His research interests include service-oriented architectures and associated middleware, workflow- and business process management, cloud computing and associated systems management aspects, and patterns. Frank is co-author of more than 300 peer-reviewed papers, more than 40 patents, and several industry standards. He is on the Palsberg list of Computer Scientists with highest h-index.

Briana MEIER is a participant in the Portland Urban Architecture Research Lab and a doctoral candidate in the Environmental Sciences, Studies, and Planning program at the University of Oregon in the United States. An American Institute of Certified Planners accredited planner, Briana worked for several years in community-based urban planning and development prior to beginning her doctoral work. She holds a master's degree in urban and regional planning, and graduate certificates in urban design and real estate development from Portland State University.

Seiko MIYAKAWA graduated from International Christian University's College of Liberal Arts in 1986, and in 1988 she graduated from Nagoya University's Graduate School with a master's degree in Science in Biology. In 1988 she began working at Kao Corporation's Household Research Institute. She is responsible for the product development research, planning, and marketing research of household goods. Since 2014, her position has been Vice President of the Marketing Research & Development-Lifestyle Research Center. We cooperate with consumers to develop daily-necessity products in order to realize an affluent living culture. I have a four-person household, consisting of my husband, my son, my daughter, and myself.

Bryan MOCK is an artist and designer exploring the nature of the sacred through beauty and generative principles. His diverse background includes computer engineering, advanced mathematics, and he holds a degree in Architecture from Iowa State University. His obsession for the past year has been an independent art project called the Milkweed Mandala which has pushed him into new territories of exploration in materials, form making, vulnerability, and the latent pictographic world of his unconscious mind. Bryan attended the inaugural class of Building Beauty in October 2017.

Guido MÜNSTER is a researcher at the University of Applied Science Cologne (TH Köln) in the department for computer science. His Master thesis covered the pattern mining process for the patterns presented in this paper. He is also responsible for installing and running the innovation rooms. His work focusses on testing new tools and devices systematically.

Hajo NEIS, Ph.D. Director of Portland Urban Architecture Research Lab PUARL and co-director of CIU. Professor Neis teaches architecture design and urban theory. He previously taught at the University of California, FH Frankfurt, Prince of Wales UDTF, TU Dresden, Duisburg-Essen, and Meiji University. His main interest in research and design include the question of quality and value in architecture and urban structure and the question of process and sequence that create quality. He works together with Chris Alexander (CES) since 1978 and also heads his own architecture office (HNA), with projects in the US, Japan, and Germany. Dr. Neis has published in English, German, Japanese, Spanish and Greek Journals, and he is also a co-author of several books including: ,A New Theory of Urban Design' 1987, and ,Battle for the Life and Beauty of the Earth,' 2012.

Rikke Toft NØRGÅRD is associate professor at the Center for Teaching Developments and Digital Media, Aarhus University, Denmark. Her field of research lies within 'futuremaking through design thinking and new technologies in education,' new educational potentials with new technologies and media, and development of the concept of 'educational design thinking' (merging educational philosophy, design thinking and practices with new technologies). Her work particularly focus on value-based vision-driven design thinking for future HE and new HE futures. Rikke holds a PhD in digital gameplay with a focus on the gameplayer's interaction with and experience of gameplay design and technology.

Iroha OGO studies in the Faculty of Policy Management at Keio University. While studying under Professor Takashi Iba, she explores methods for communities and individuals to be more creative. She is challenged to describe the spirit of communities and has presented that method as Community Language (2015). She also worked at a private organization called 'manma', aiming to create a good environment involving family, and conducted 'Family Internship' which is a one-day hands-on program for young people.

Makoto OKADA is an expert researcher in the R&D Strategy and Planning Office, Fujitsu Laboratories, Ltd.; a visiting research fellow at the Centre for Global Communications, International University of Japan; and a Senior Researcher at the Keio Research Institute at SFC. He is also a founder member and the current co-director of the Dementia-Friendly Japan Initiative and an advisory board member of the Dementia Friendship Club. He is a co-editor of Words for a Journey (2015).

Greg PAINE PhD is an environmental planner with extensive experience in government. He is currently with the City Wellbeing Program, City Futures Research Centre, University of New South Wales Australia. His work on pattern is being developed into a book and a forthcoming website (revealingpattern.com).

Ana PINTO obtained a Masters in information technology in education and a PhD degree from the University of Sydney, Australia. Her PhD thesis, Pedagogy of Wholeness, has been attracting widespread praise for its consistent and comprehensive use of pattern language theory. Ana's research interests revolve around 'holistic' educational design for networked learning and critical literacies development. Her professional experience has included literacy teaching and learning, and designing, developing and delivering training for teachers.

Jenny QUILLIEN is the Curator at the newly founded Embodied Making Institute in Amsterdam, Holland. Prior to that she had a long university career with New Mexico Highlands, University, Boston University, and The University of Maryland. An abiding interest in the psychology of spaces led to a six-year collaboration with Christopher Alexander on The Nature of Order. Along with numerous articles, she authored Delight's Muse (an introductory overview of Alexander's magnum opus and Clever Digs: how workspaces can enable thought.

Hitomi SHIMIZU studies in the Faculty of Policy Management at Keio University. As a member of Takashi Iba's Laboratory, she explores methods to invite people to start cooking, for example, Cooking Fun Language. She is interested in using words as a tool to change human behavior, and aims to use words as a tool for living better with our planet.

Maina SULZBACH-PETRY is the Team Curator of Surplus Permaculture Design and maintains the big picture of many of our projects. Maina is currently based in Detroit, Michigan, USA.

Kazuo TAKIGUCHI is a local government official who has no academic or theoretical expertise in the field of social welfare. On the other hand, he has been actively engaged for about 10 years in an administrative department and has gained extensive practical experience in planning policies for sensitive social problems that occur to people in real life situations. Some examples of his responsibilities include case work on welfare protection, child abuse, and issues involving the mistreatment of people with disabilities. In other words, Kazuo Takiguchi's proficiency stems from providing direct support in the field and in planning programs for the welfare system.

Nick TITTLE is the CEO of Surplus Permaculture Design, Educational Director of the Panya Project and core member of the Blueprint Alliance. Nick works as an international Permaculture teacher, designer and practitioner. He is currently based in Charleston, South Carolina, USA.

Mayu UENO is a singer-songwriter belonging to Keio University's Iba Lab. Her pop compositions include titles such as, 'Akarui Uta,' 'Kuroi Namida', 'Sandwitch', and others. A student of pattern language, she joined the 'Ways of Everyday World-Making' project, and has created songs with Takashi Iba.

Yoshihiro UTSUNOMIYA is a developer and editor at Benesse Corporation, a leading company of the Japanese education sector. He graduated from the University of Tokyo with a Master of Science. He is also qualified to teach in Japanese junior high and high schools. His research covers both coral reef science and education. He has been involved in the development of many products for high school students and teachers such as GPS, an assessment tool of the students' general skills. He has also been one of the main developers of Active Learning Patterns for Teachers (2016) along with Takashi Iba.

Sebastian VOGT holds a Ph.D. in media and communication science from Ilmenau University of Technology (Germany). His (scientific) life is driven by technical innovation and its impact on media and education. Sebastian Vogt was fixed term professor in educational technology, in educational research and in empirical education research at the FernUniversität in Hagen (Germany). As of 2015 he is professor in media production and media technology at the "THM" in Friedberg (Germany).

Yujun WAKASHIN is an Adjunct Associate Professor of Graduate School of Media and Governance, Keio University, in Japan. He majored organizational psychology and communication theory. He produced many unique projects, such as JK-section in Sabae municipal office composed of high school girls, and NEET Co., Ltd. composed of people who are NEET (not in education, employment or training).

David WEST, Ph.D. is a retired professor of software development and systems design. His education — BA in Asian Philosophy, MS in Computer Science, MA in Cultural Anthropology, and PH.D. in Cognitive Anthropology — is reflected in the diversity of his published work. He has published two books, Object Thinking and Design Thinking (the latter with co-author Rebecca Rikner), and will have two more published in 2018, including his first work of fiction.

Masaaki YONESU graduated from Kobe University, Faculty of Environment Planning, and Department of Engineering. He got master's degree both from Kobe University and Massachusetts Institute of Technology in architectural study. Now he is working as Executive Operating Officer at Benesse Style Care Co., Ltd., Development Division.

Ayaka YOSHIKAWA studies in the Keio University Faculty of Environment and Information Studies. As a member of Takashi Iba's laboratory, she creates pattern languages about cooking, and also researches different ways of using patterns. She is the co-author of several pattern languages, including 'Cooking Patterns', a pattern language for everyday cooking. She has also convened various cooking workshops as well as idea generation workshops using patterns as a trigger for thought.

PURPLSOC Conference 2017

Patterns
of Humanity

West, David
Transcendence Corporation
profwest@fastmail.fm

The patterns community has been prolific: writing patterns of use in almost every domain imaginable, from architecture to software to design to education. In doing so they constantly refer to, involve, and discuss human beings and the role they play within the patterns and how they use, or are affected, by use of the patterns. This paper looks at humanity, individually and collectively, to explore the question: "Are there patterns of humanity?"

People, Culture, Patterns, Complex Systems

1. Background

The year is 1969. I am traveling with three other students and one faculty member on our way to San Francisco to attend the annual meeting of the American Anthropological Association. The Vietnam War is in full fury. The psychedelic counter-culture is in full flower. The anti-war movement is on the march.

Tensions ran high in the conference hall because of a developing schism between those that believed anthropology, especially ethnography, was an academic endeavor, independent of and above mere politics; and those who feared that anthropological research was being used, unethically, by the military and government to advance and support war objectives.

A rupture in the ranks occurred with about a third of the attendees forming their own organization — Society of Concerned Asian Scholars.

The "concerned scholars" were concerned about how their work, their insights into the values, practices, worldview, and organization of the people they studied, might be exploited and misused by the U.S. Military to harm those very people. An exemplary of how they feared this might happen was the work of Ruth Benedict in World War II.

During World War II, Benedict worked for the Bureau of Overseas Intelligence, studying the Japanese on behalf of the U.S. government and military. Her findings were later published as a book, **The Chrysanthemum and the Sword**. Although Benedict did predict previously unseen behavior — like the kamikaze suicide bombers — her work probably had little or no impact on the overall war effort.

The point made by SCAS, was that it could have. And, if it did it would have been immoral and unethical.

The work that motivated the recruitment of Benedict to government service was best captured in her book, **Patterns of Culture**. The central thesis of that book: culture is a *"consistent pattern of thought and action"* chosen from *"the great arc of human potentialities."* Further she thought that the observed patterns could be summarized in a label: Apollonian for the Zuni culture in the American Southwest; Dionysian for the plains Indians; paranoid for the Dobu of the South Pacific; or megalomaniacal for the Kwakiutl of the U.S. northwest coast.

Benedict's "patterns" are regarded by most contemporary anthropologists to be overly simplistic but most agree that they are more than simple stereotypes. They do provide a certain degree of insight into and a basis for analysis of cultures and how culture is manifest in individual and group behavior.

Elsewhere in the anthropology community can be found a related topic of interest — the search for "cultural universals." A belief, a practice, a technology, a value would be deemed "universal" if it was found in all cultures, including prehistoric, studied by anthropologists.

Religious people, mired in their ethnocentric perspective, imagine that their values are grounded in 'natural law' and therefor universal across all cultures. That is far from the case. I used to teach at a religious university — the only class they offered in cultural anthropology — and it was amazing to see those students come to the realization that not everyone believed as they did.

Although there are no discrete cultural universals, there are 'patterns'. I use pattern in the sense of a generalization or abstraction that is constant across cultures although each culture interprets that pattern differently.

This is not the precise definition of a pattern as stated by Alexander and most in the patterns community, but it is not inconsistent with that definition. If a pattern is a "general solution to a problem in context," is has the same purpose: to provide an abstraction or generalization that can be interpreted and applied differently in different contexts.

It seems plausible that we could "mine" patterns of humanity just as we mine patterns in business or education. We observe a multitude of cultural examples looking for commonalities among them (bottom up analysis) at the same time we review "patterns of culture" offered by anthropologists to see how the various implementations extend and modify those patterns (top down analysis).

If we can do this, and I believe we can, of what value is such an exercise. Patterns of Humanity will not contribute to writing more elegant or efficient code. They will not (directly) make us better change agents. They will not (directly) help us build buildings with QWAN.

Patterns of humanity might provide value in two ways.

The first is to provide foundational knowledge that would help us understand and improve more domain specific patterns. For example: a cultural pattern dealing with 'exchange behavior' might help us understand and improve patterns of collaboration. Understanding human communication pattern(s) might enhance our ability to craft pedagogical patterns.

The second, and probably more profound, contribution arises from our efforts to build large-scale complex systems. One example.

Mark Zuckerberg stated his vision for Facebook:

> *"Our goal is to strengthen existing communities by helping us come together online as well as offline, as well as enabling us to form completely new communities, transcending physical location. ... The path forward is to recognize that a global community needs social infrastructure ... and our community [Facebook] is uniquely positioned to prevent disasters, help during crises, and rebuild afterward."*

AT&T gave us Bell Labs who gave us the transistor and the laser. Xerox spawned Xerox PARC where most of today's computing infrastructure was invented. IBM is offering artificial intelligence (Hello Watson) that will change the future of humanity, for the immeasurable better — or worse.

Deep pocket companies have always funded innovation and that innovation has changed everything. Google is delivering self-driving cars, ubiquitous smart phone software and applications, and even "cures for death." As noted above, Facebook intends to build a global community safety net.

All of these 'systems' are ultra-large, highly dynamic, adaptive, and complex. It is almost certain that they will not be successful if the only, or even primary, worldview of those developing them remains the kind of algorithmic, "engineering," "scientific" mindset that dominates today's software world.

Forgive any hyperbole, but our technology, and the systems we are building and intend to build with it, present an existential threat to humanity. Simultaneously they present a potential to realize a utopian vision of human experience and life. In either case, with either outcome, it is essential that our efforts be informed with knowledge and understanding of human beings and the cultures they have instituted the past tens of thousands of years.

The following five patterns are intended as a tiny step towards developing such an understanding.

2. The Patterns

2.1. Reciprocity

Context: Humans are codependent — they need each other. Procreation, parent and child, group survival, defense, social and economic collaboration — are some of the ways that humans depend upon one another. Each and every one of these examples hinges of some sort of exchange: like good for good or service for service. An X for X exchange exists at each tier of Maslow's Hierarchy of Needs. Maslow's hierarchy is simple but reasonably comprehensive, and useful to illustrate the point that exchange is ubiquitous across every aspect of individual and collective existence.

Problem: Participation in exchange activity / behavior is "optional" in the sense that there is no innate imperative within individuals that mandates participation. So, how can participation be assured, as "appropriate," or, stated differently, how can exchange be "regulated."

Note: the problem includes quoted terms that are quite ambiguous. The lack of precision, in both definition and valuation, makes the problem complex and highly dynamic. This is a perfect ground for a general pattern amenable to myriad discrete solutions within the domain established by the pattern.

Solution: utilize one, or more, of the four types of reciprocity patterns observed across human culture. The four types being: general, balanced, negative and the subset of negative, market.

General reciprocity is exemplified within the parent-child relationship. Parents give a lot to their children with no concrete expectation of receiving anything in return. Another example: teachers who give a lot to students with no expectation of repayment. (When a graduate from Harvard gave his professor, who had told all his classes he wanted one when they went on to be hugely successful and affluent, a Mercedes it made national news because it was so incongruent with the pattern of general reciprocity.)

Balanced reciprocity can be readily observed among groups of friends or close colleagues. With balanced reciprocity there is no overt or explicit "accounting" but there is a deep tacit awareness of whether or not everyone in the group is contributing fairly, that if there were a ledger it would be in balance. Studies have shown that groups are aware of imbalances acutely and precisely — to the penny. Everyone in the group knows f each of the others is participating fairly or if one or more is "freeloading."

The only sanction for violating the norm of balanced reciprocity is exclusion from the group.

Balanced reciprocity can be a foundation for a market economy, and is, in many peasant markets. But most markets, especially in first world contexts are grounded in negative reciprocity.

Negative reciprocity is present when each party in an exchange attempts to maximize their own benefit at the expense of the other. Negatively reciprocal exchanges are further characterized by asymmetric information and/or power.

Market reciprocity is negative reciprocity made abstract and covert. There can be no balanced reciprocity in a market because value/price is determined by only one of the parties involved in the exchange. All kinds of factors further inhibit balance in a market exchange: "rent seeking" where one party can bring to bear the power of the government to protect and enhance their interests and 'marketing' used to convince one party of the existence of "value" when, in fact, none exists; are but two examples.

Discussion: very few, if any, intentionally designed systems get reciprocity right. Anthropological studies (ethnographies) provide consistent evident that the only truly sustainable form of exchange is grounded in balanced reciprocity. An extremely small number of systems have ever been grounded in general reciprocity — which only works if the social distance among participants is very small, e.g. parents and children or in communes or communities like the Amish. Negative reciprocity inevitably leads to breakdown of social ties — all parties to the exchange become isolated and alienated from each other. Market economies inevitably lead to extreme asymmetry in wealth distribution and the social tensions that arise therefrom.

A concrete example of these general statements is PLoP. Self consciously designed as a "gifting economy," a from of generalized reciprocity[1]. Authors contribute their work and offer their assistance to other authors in order that all may improve; shepherds offer their expertise and experience to help authors enhance their efforts; professionals offer writing education and assistance; and organizers "make things happen."

Unfortunately, general exchange ultimately depends on minimal social distance for it to be sustainable and members of the PLoP community have, collectively, less than average social connections.

Lacking the necessary social ties, you would expect a system like PLoP to succumb to pressures arising from the other forms of reciprocity. Negative reciprocity would exhibit itself if (when) some parties attempted to maximize their own value (prestige, influence, power) at the expense of the rest of the community; and, when failing, to withdraw.

More serious threats come when participants "tire" of altruism and seek an exchange that is more "balanced." Author's would diminish in number and enthusiasm as soon as they perceive the benefit of "benign editing" to be of less value than substantive feedback as to ideas and viewpoints presented in their work[2]. Shepherds should be harder and harder to

---

1   Typical academic conferences are exemplars of negative reciprocity.
2   Workshops conducted in the past few years seem to address this particular force; allowing interactive participation of authors and discussion of ideas as well as editing.

come by, the overall pool shrinking and the difficulty of recruiting replacements increasing. Organizers would begin to expect "compensation" for their efforts, even if limited to reimbursement for costs, e.g. free attendance, travel reimbursement, etc.

Could the admirable objectives that motivated PLoP founders have been realized in a more sustainable manner?

Possibly.

Anthropologists tell us that the only balanced reciprocity pattern is stable enough to be long term sustainable. But, like generalized, balanced reciprocity, is dependent on appropriate social distance. This suggests the need for shared participation in a "patterns community" that transcended the discrete event of a PLoP conference.

To use an analogy: the PLoP conference needs to be an event, an instance of generalized reciprocity, like a 'barn raising' within the context of an Amish community. Balanced reciprocity dominates the community and works because the social distance among members of that community is established and maintained by shared activities and values.

Unfortunately, modern society is not particularly amenable to the formation of sub-cultures, especially those incorporating balanced reciprocity. You see some instances in "affinity groups" like motorcycle clubs, but instances are rare.

Another issue arises from questions of scale.

All large-scale societies known to us are economically grounded in negative reciprocity. Should we infer from this that negative reciprocity is the only economic pattern that scales. Hopefully not.

There are societies that are grounded in a mix of balanced and general reciprocity, three with which I am familiar: Amish, the Mennonites, and the "Mormons." All three are centered in religion, but the most salient feature of each society is that the religion is leveraged to define and support community. It is the community and all of the community-centric, technically non-religious, activities that establish the minimal social distance required to make intra-community balanced reciprocity work. Within the context of overall balanced reciprocity, incidents of general reciprocity, e.g. a barn raising, are possible.

Even with religion as an anchor point, scale can interfere. There is no such thing as a "Christian Community" — or Islamic, Judaic, and not even Catholic. You find communities within those religions co-extensive with subsets, e.g. Charismatic Catholics or Ultra-Orthodox Judaism.

The earlier discussion of PloP suggests the possibility of establishing a smaller community based on balanced reciprocity with episodic instances of general reciprocity. But is it possible to scale this model? The Amish and Mennonites thrive in partial seclusion from the society around them and are therefore constrained as to the total membership of their society.

The LDS community is global, millions of members, while small compared to Catholic, Islamic, and even Buddhist communities, and continues to grow. It is also interleaved with surrounding communities and cultures and not limited by the same constraints as the other two communities.

This is not to say that Mormonism provides an adequate model for those wishing to establish new communities or enhance existing ones, ala Facebook; but it does suggest a rich field for exploration. As one explores the Mormon community — as opposed to the religion — you quickly notice just how many and how varied are the mechanisms for establishing and maintain minimal social distance. Sports leagues, little theatre activities, scouting, communal dinners, an extensive social welfare system, etc. all of which relies on voluntary participation and leadership.

The reciprocity patterns provide less in the way of guidance on "how to do something" than criteria for evaluating the QWAN of something done or built — or planned. If Facebook (Zuckerberg) is serious about strengthening existing communities and forming new ones, the role of reciprocity cannot be ignored. This could be particularly challenging for Facebook, as their entire business and community model is so solidly grounded in negative reciprocity that they are unaware of the alternatives.

It is evident that negative reciprocity is only short term stable. That pattern, applied at large scale societies inevitably leads to inequitable distribution of wealth and violent social upheaval leading only to another cycle of wealth concentration.

Alternatives must be understood and then applied if there is to be any hope of enhancing, reshaping, or creating social systems that support the humans within them.

2.2. Essence (aka God)

Context: Every culture: contemporary, historic, and prehistoric shows evidence of believing in the "supernatural." Evidence of this assertion includes intentional burial, often with the inclusion of artifacts of value; "magic;" shamans; or their more abstract incarnation, priests; and organized religion. The field of Neurotheology has found substantial evidence supporting the assertion that our brains are 'hardwired' to "believe."[3] Belief in the supernatural need

---

3   Examples include the "white light at the end of the tunnel" reported in so many near death experiences; the "feeling of 'oneness with the universe' characteristic of so many mystical experience reports; even the fundamental sense of 'self' versus 'other'. All of these and more can be induced and/or mitigated with simple application of electrical current to the appropriate areas of the brain.

not take the form of overt religion, deism, polytheism, magic, etc. — it can be as fundamental as the belief that something can be real, can be experienced, but cannot be explained; or, something can be known but cannot be expressed — the ineffable.

The ground of this context is the belief in a metaphysical reality for an essence, a spirit, an 'other', that transcends and complements the ordinary physical reality we all live within.

Problem: Since the "Age of Reason," aka "The Enlightenment," Western and all industrialized (now digitalized) societies have taken on the mien of militant anti-supernaturalism. "God is dead!" Everything can be explained, measured, and predicted — at least "in principle." Even those pesky quanta will someday be incorporated into neat simple equations via some kind of "string theory" or "loop quantum gravity." Systems we design and build, including social systems, are sterile, machinelike, constructs that only Herbert Simon could love.[4]

Solution: Admit the reality of complex adaptive, living, systems and stop "building machines." Admit that human beings are more than "meat machines," and human minds are other than "physical symbol systems." Leverage the ineffable. Incorporate the "essential" in your designs.

Discussion: this pattern is intimately and inextricably linked with both the Story and Divided Labor patterns presented below.

Google provides a classic example on how the 'supernatural' could be incorporated into software design — and, simultaneously, how that 'magic' was lost. Google search page is famous for its simplicity: a text entry field, a link to advanced search, and the "I'm feeling lucky" button. Luck is an epitome of the "supernatural" and, as such, offers a small bit of humanizing whimsy to the search process. Most of that whimsy has been lost. If you enter a search string, the button disappears. In some cases — e.g. sexually explicit searches — it cannot be found at all; in others it will link directly to the highest ranked paid ad and not the one "most likely relevant," as previous algorithms did. If you are lucky enough to be given a list of possible searches (a side effect of the text completion feature of the entry bar) you can find the 'lucky' link but you have to hover over a choice line and then move the select cursor to the right for the link to appear.

 "Magic" was supplanted by clear-eyed economics and/or politically correct censorship.

Humans recognize within themselves something other than mere biology, chemistry, and neural signal processing — a "soul," or "spirit," or "self." Designers of systems, especially

---

4   Herbert Simon is author of The Sciences of the Artificial, arguably the most influential design treatise for computer science, software engineering, and by extension almost all systems development.

computer grounded systems, deny the reality of this transcendent essence.

Interestingly, in a Carnegie Mellon Study of "Ultra-Large Scale" systems — the very kind of system that will dominate future design — human beings are seen as an essential and unavoidable "computational element;" one that cannot be reduced to a deterministic 'black box' with precisely defined inputs yielding predictable outputs. If we are to be at all successful with efforts to build complex systems we cannot treat humans as if they were machines devoid of soul.

2.3. Story

Context: John Donne asserted that "no man is an island," but in point of fact we are. Each consciousness exists within its own isolated space. Our senses provide our 'selves' with massive amounts of data, but the integration and interpretation of that data occurs within a discrete 'mind'.

Individuals are also capable of 'generating' data; of emitting signals and signs. Abstracted and generalized via consensus building, these signals can become language. When "you understand" what "I said" we have communication.

Appropriate and meaningful communication is essential to establish any kind of social, or cultural, system; essential for any kind of cooperative and collaborative interaction among groups of individuals.

Problem: The most effective means of communication is almost unknown, mostly because it is so ubiquitous that we are seldom aware of it, like the fish is unaware of the water, only the lack of it. Making things worse, as our analytical 'left brain'[5] keeps inventing more abstract, convoluted, and formal means of communication that simply makes things worse.

Software developers are among the most egregious offenders in this regard; primarily because they must convey meaning and intent to the *idiot savant* computer that cannot understand "stories." So they invent calculi of requirement specifications, use cases, entity relation diagrams, BNF notations, etc. etc., that try, and fail, to capture the meaning of a common story about a system and a user's dissatisfaction with that system. They even fool themselves, as the Agile community has, by redefining "user stories" as mere verbose "requirement specifications."

Solution: Effective Story Telling. A story is a narrative in a rich, implicit and explicit, context, rife with ambiguity and imprecision. Although the 'narrative' conveys the "meaning" of the

5   Perhaps the best discussion of how our analytical left brain usurped the fundamental power of our much older right brain is found in, The
     Master and His Emissary, by Iain McGilchrist. Yale University Press; Reprint edition (October 9, 2012)

story, that meaning is determined by the context rather than anything intrinsic to the narrative, e.g. grammatical structure.

The ability to engage in a sequence of story exchanges among human beings leads to the emergence [critical term] of a shared understanding, or theory in the sense suggested by Peter Naur, about some aspect of our common existence. It might be a theory of where thunder comes from (e.g. gods playing ninepins, or equalization of electrical potential) or a theory of why Microsoft Word insists that my grammar is wrong when I am saying exactly what I intend to say in the way I want to say it with little chance of being misunderstood by my reader.

For Peter Naur, the essential[6] difficulties of software development could be resolved only when the team engaged in collective theory building by exchanging stories about "an affair of the world and how the program would handle it." He called this effort, "Theory Building."

Discussion: Human beings have been using story to communicate, very effectively, since our animalistic grunting signals began to standardize and form the foundations of words and eventually language.

Ninety-percent of what you have come to know and understand was communicated to you via story. The lessons you learned in a formal setting, like school, were most effective and long lasting when you learned them via story and not rote memorization. The most memorable professor was the one that told the best stories about the subject matter.

Story telling is the mutual exchange of stories, listening to stories, responding with modified or alternative stories, until understanding held in common. Stories and story telling **always** work; unless rules are broken, e.g. lying or failing to listen, or there is intentional deceit (politician speaking).

The power of story is directly proportional to the amount of context, especially implicit context, evoked by the telling of the story. For example: consider how much context is evoked by the imaginary first line of a joke; "A *penguin*, a *Rabbi*, and a *Freudian Psychologist* walk into a *bar* ..." Four words recall to mind all that you know about penguins (real and cartoon), Judaism and the role of a Rabbi plus all the associated cultural stereotypes, and the study of psychology and the particular interpretations of Freud versus, for example, Jung. Not to mention all the stereotypical presentations of bar scenes coupled with your own experiences in multiple varieties and subtypes of such establishments.

---

6   *Fred Brooks divided the challenge of software development into the easily resolved, "accidental" problems and the incredibly difficult "essential" problems — for which there was "No Silver Bullet."*

But context leads to ambiguity to the exact extent that evoked context is not shared. Different languages, and more importantly different cultures, inevitably result in a lack of shared context, at least superficially. The idea that there are patterns of culture, implies that commonality, a common pattern, can be found across cultures even when the specifics seem to vary. All that is required is a process of story telling.

In software and system design, and even the most complex social systems will inevitably include some non-complex components like computers, you will eventually reach a point where it is necessary to convey a story to an entity incapable of understanding story and where there can be no possibility of shared cultural context.

In those circumstances there will be a need to "translate" the story into a "program." How might this be done?

The real power of object-oriented thinking derives from story. Stories have 'characters' who are expected to perform or speak in a certain manner in certain circumstances. An object (concept not programming construct just yet) is something that performs or speaks in a certain manner in certain circumstances.

To understand, refine, and design an object you tell stories about how in interacts with other objects in varied situations and circumstances. You think of the interaction and communication among a group of objects in the same way as you would characters on stage or in film and create the program as "screenplay." Screenplays, like stories are infinitely modifiable, including the potential for "ad libs" without breaking the program.

If you can use story and anthropomorphic objects to define your needs, programming a computer to accept inputs and return appropriate outputs becomes almost trivial — in the sense that, (and this is demonstrable) no object programming construct requires more than fifty lines of code to implement and no program requires more than a few thousand lines of easily modifiable — including during execution — code.

To better understand and to extend this discussion see almost anything that the author has written about objects and patterns: www.davewest.us. To extend the discussion about story specifically see "Patterns for Story Craft," David West and Jenny Quillien, SugarLoaf PLoP, 2010.

2.4. Divided Labor

Context: Individual differences.

Problem: That which must be done seldom is doable, equally in every aspect, by a single individual.

Solution: Apportion work in an equitable fashion according to individual abilities, expertise, interest, and predilections.

Discussion: This pattern is seemingly trivial, as evidenced by the terseness of the context-problem-solution statements.

However ...

Although patterns of divided labor exist in even the most 'primitive' societies, there is seldom any kind of 'rational', e.g. resolution of forces, explanation for the patterns.

For instance, in hunter-gatherer societies – the oldest and least sophisticated, least complex, societies of which we are aware there appears to be a universal pattern — Men Hunt and Women Gather. Why, no one has come up with a reasonable explanation, and not for lack of trying. It has been argued that men are bigger and stronger and better able to handle the rigors of hunting big animals. But the reality is that big animals, like mammoths, were always hunted and killed by groups – men and women. The pattern of hunting, wounding an animal and then running it down for miles and miles before it died, requires stamina, not muscle mass and guess which gender has greater stamina.

Child care has been advanced, but women give birth and within hours are back at hard labor gathering and preparing food while child rearing is a collective activity by those that are not immediately productive, the old and the young and women in advanced stages of pregnancy.

In modern times, no one can point to a set of skills or attributes that are unique to CEOs, ones that would justify their position in comparison to anyone else. The exception is experience, those with the right experience are clearly better at the job, but why is it that they were given the opportunity to have those experiences?

In the United States, the "World's Greatest Democracy", the elected office of Senator, since roughly the 1960s, has been a de facto hereditary office! The kinship involved is not agnate/cognate but 'virtual', grounded in affinity relationships. Jack Weatherford once did a kinship diagram of the US Senate in his work, *Tribes of the Senate*.

Efforts to eliminate gender, racial. and sexual-orientation based discrimination reveals how little justification there is for the assignment of work to any one person or group.

The pattern is clear and imperative: in every social system, every system involving human beings, there will be a distribution of labor. Exactly what mechanism or rationalization is used to enforce and justify that distribution is, at present, purely arbitrary.

We also know that the existing examples of labor distribution are fraught with exceptions, injustices, inconsistencies, and that, in general, the work poorly if at all. And no one is happy — except maybe the queen.

The ill conceived and militantly enforced effort, in the U.S. to literally make everyone equal ensures nothing except the dominance of the lowest common denominator and meticulously eliminates any possibility of excellence is guaranteed to bring about social disaster.

If we are to design human(e) systems we must understand a lot more about Divided Labor, hopefully grounded in a theory of individual differences, in cognitive, anthropological, psychological, and social terms.

This pattern is intimately related to **Rank** and to **Stereotypes**.

2.5. Stereotypes

Context: Human beings generalize. It is a necessary survival skill. We categorize, taxonomize (not a word), and label the highly variable world around us to reduce the cognitive burden of making sense. There are two different ways we do this, formally as a kind of set theory and naturally using embedded metaphor (re: the work of Lakoff and Johnson among others).

Problem: Most of our most intractable social problems, racism, sexism, genderism, ethnocentrism, and religious intolerance stem from the indiscriminate and erroneous use of classes and types and generalizations.

Solution: Define and constrain the use of stereotypes at the group level while simultaneously recognizing their absolute impotence when applied to the individual.

Discussion: Stereotypes exist and are useful – essential even. As human beings we lack the cognitive bandwidth to process the world absent their use. Inter-cultural and cross-cultural design would be impossible without the use of cultural stereotypes.

However, some things, especially individual human beings, cannot be stereotyped.

In software we attempt to design for the "typical user" even though we know that no such entity exists. Maybe we get real sophisticated and allow for customization of an interface so that it better suits the "novice" "competent" and "advanced" user – but usually not and certainly not in any way that actually maps to an individuals increasing mastery.

Another limitation of stereotypes is that they are caricature – they abstract only the most obvious characteristics and ignore every nuance. A "joke" tagline suggests that the "worst culture in the world be one that incorporates English cooking, Italian efficiency, and German romance while the best would integrate French cooking, Italian romance and German efficiency." The caricatures of these cultures supports the supposed humor but transcending the caricature, even to the extent of understanding the cultural stereotypes reveals the ridiculous nature of the caricature.

Most importantly of all, no stereotype of a group or of a culture is ever applicable to individual members of that group or culture.

A related issue is how cultural stereotypes apply only to everyone else, never to myself or to my culture. Ethnocentrism is the innate bias for seeing our own culture as "normal" "correct," and obvious while everyone else's is weird, suspect, or wrong and totally captured in the stereotype of each culture. We have a very hard time applying the same lens of stereotyping and caricature to Our culture.

Horace Mitchel Miner wrote a wonderful paper that exemplifies the way we use artificial perspectives and biases to think of other cultures but not our own. His paper was "Body Ritual Among the Nacerima" in 1956.

2.6. Rank

"All animals are equal, but,some animals are more equal than others."

George Orwell, Animal Farm

Context: Every society, every human system imposes among its membership some form of ranking, hierarchy, and/or differential status. Rank may be individual versus individual or group versus group.

Problem: with very few exceptions, Rank has become abstract and separated from humanity causing, with even fewer exceptions, inhumane, unfair, and alienating systems within which human beings chafe. A corollary problem: the more dynamic the system the greater the inefficiency and detrimental effects of 'fixed' rank.

Solution: Establish a form of dynamic rank: ephemeral, grounded in circumstance, and instantiated based on individual differences and abilities.

Discussion: In democracies there is a form of such dynamic rank associated with elective office. Power and authority of rank is transient and is coextensive with the term of office. In business, the senior most rank is usually transient as well, but determined by politics and stock prices. Elsewhere in the organization rank is divorced from the human and associated exclusively with the position.

In contrast, there are instances where rank is determined at birth and relinquished at death: royalty and caste are examples.

The less fluid / dynamic the mechanism for assigning and enforcing rank the greater the risk of system failure. This is especially true in complex social systems.

A foundation for beginning to establish a dynamic system of rank, "ephemeral, grounded in circumstance and based on individual differences and abilities" is evidenced in some forms of tribal organization, especially nomadic bands. Unlike sedentary groups tied to land cultivation, nomadic tribes constantly face new situations and new demands. Each situation requires its idiosyncratic solution based on skills, knowledge, or abilities not universally shared among the group.

For instance if the piñon harvest has been bad on the east side of the valley and the tribe over there decides to come and pick yours, you might need a "War Chief" and you would select the bravest, fiercest, and most strategic thinker to assume that office until the threat was past. Maybe you need to decide on where the group should go next and you might turn to the oldest or most experienced member of the group and appoint them "Trip Director."

Another foundation for developing a system of merit-based rank is found in gaming with the notion of reputation. People you play with are able to assess and publish their opinion of your skills. You become a level-6 warrior only when enough people who have fought virtual battles with you state that they believe you merit that status.

Yet another source of inspiration is found in the Agile culture and the Quality culture exemplified by the Maclcom Baldridge Award — transparency. In a group, a development team or a classroom, everyone already knows everyone else's abilities, limitation, and achievements.

If you want to have two well balanced sports teams, you take advantage of this tacit knowledge by appointing two captains and allow them to make alternate selections from the pool of available players.

Unfortunately, this means that the least able person is picked last and even though that is not news to that person, he or she might feel bad and therefore we cannot allow that to happen. Our tacit knowledge is ignored and we use some sort of artificial method for assigning teams which are, inevitably, less balanced and less fair.

In both Agile and Baldridge systems, all the tacit knowledge about the team and individual performance is 'published' — up there, on the wall, in the information radiators and big visible charts. Once this tacit information is made explicit the team is better able to manage itself and even improve the performance of the weakest members of the team.

It also becomes overtly obvious (it was always obvious) which individual possesses the greater skills in coding, analyzing, modeling, coaching, etc. and who should take the lead at different times in the development or learning cycle. [Unfortunately, this only works within the team because HR will not acknowledge individuals, only job titles.]

3. Conclusion

If you build a habitable structure you WILL need to deal with windows and doors. Architectural patterns ala Alexander will assure your design has the potential for QWAN.

If you build a habitable complex system involving human beings, you WILL need to deal with Rank, Stereotypes, Divided Labor, Story, Essence, and Reciprocity. Only Patterns of Humanity will provide any hope of success.

Method Shapes Morphology: How world-picture via the 15 properties impacts built projects

Getzin, David
Building Beauty, Sorrento, Italy
david.getzin@buildingbeauty.net

Mock, Bryan
Building Beauty, Sorrento, Italy
bryan.mock@buildingbeauty.net

This paper by designer Bryan Mock and analytic historian David Getzin is a case-study investigating the impact of design method on the morphology of built objects via computer, drafting and integral modeling respectively. The Nature of Order is architect Christopher Alexander's exposition of a method that when applied to built works. That book aims to assist makers in generating the most beautiful, well-adapted results possible. At core, is his theoretical framework of 15 fundamental properties of geometric form, applied through an iterative process of wholeness-extending transformations.

This system of morphogenesis was discovered and developed largely in response to observations of pattern-language-based approaches to design having yielded inconsistent results. Intending to support successful pattern languages, The Nature of Order states as given, that to apply the 15 properties, a shift in world-view away from a mechanistic mind-body dualism into a more holistic, integrated stance is required. In practice, this shift in view is expressed by eschewing the development of a self-contained subjective work, objectively executed as one piece. These methods instead require an integral and iterative subject-object dialog.

If as Alexander states, the insistence upon a shift in world-view is a necessity for the material application of the 15 properties –and by extension consistent success with pattern languages– it follows that otherwise identical projects that are developed in the mechanistic (drafting and computer) or integrated (modeling) modes respectively, will display measurable divergent formal properties when completed. This paper's aim is to conduct several such formal studies on a small scale to observe any objective delta between the physical outcomes of these contrasting methods of building.

Morphology; architecture, Christopher Alexander; experiment; computers;

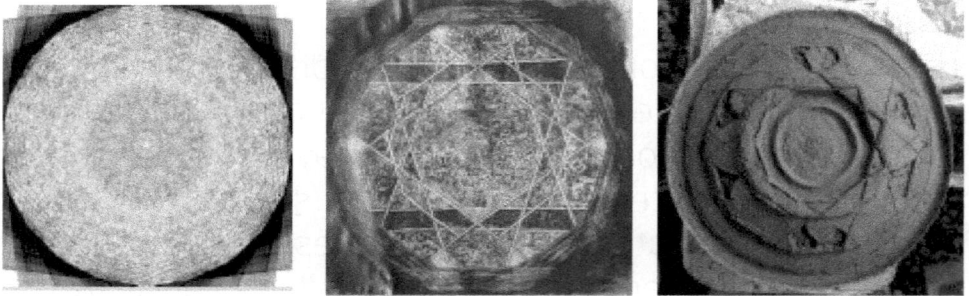

Left to right: Digital rendering, mixed media on paper, clay; Bryan Mock, 2017, prior to experiment.

1. Introduction

Our tools are never complete in of themselves. Not only do various instruments require the fuel of the users' skills, the ideas that drive them and the values fed through the context of production, but the interplay between technology, method and user creates an interlaced network of variables that profoundly impacts not just how something is made, but the form of what it is when it is finished. For a very simple example, think of how a hand-stitched jacket differs from its machine-made cousin. Immediately noticeable is the relative uniformity and consistency of the machined garment, comparing one piece to another and even among the stitches themselves. Hand-made items are more unique, usually slower to make and more expensive. Yet, despite drawbacks, strong market demand still exists for hand-sewn garments. When tailored, the fit is more precise. The strength of skilled hand stitching is adapted to the different demands of various seams. As a result, it wears better and lasts longer. Because of the time involved and the "forgiveness" of the hand-sewing process, quality control is not so much a phase at the end of a line, as a continual evaluation while the item is shaped. This simple, technological distinction in the process of making, from a needle, thimble and thread on one side, to a sewing machine on the other, has such profound consequences on the way garments are developed and the produced artifacts and the markets for them, that completely distinct categories of clothing and even businesses have grown up to express it. Drastic, recent changes in the tools and methods that architecture and design use, call for an examination and evaluation of the effects of an even more dramatic shift. Within the business of architecture, opportunities and pitfalls both have been created. Better understanding this technological and methodological delta of impact upon designed form, specifically regarding the empirical-feelings involved in Christopher Alexander's system of generative morphology, is the aim of this preliminary study. The forms of this experiment as well as this presentation of it differ significantly from scientific orthodoxy not just because the area of study is new, but because the nature of what is studied differs from the subjects of the physical, life and even social sciences. The method, as well as the mode of articulation are in a phase of growth and change, much like the technology this study deploys.

In less time than the space of one architect's career, the tools and methods of designing public space, dwellings, and everyday objects have radically changed. As happened with modes of physical expression the industrialized construction-side revolution of the 19th and early 20th centuries, from city planning to sofa pillows,[1] our current modes of informational representation have been greatly altered. The design-side methods that even during the high-modernist era, still deployed the stylus, compass, and set square –tools used from Old Kingdom Egypt past the Renaissance– have been largely replaced by keyboards, mice, and in advanced cases of disruptive innovation, touch-screens and parametric databases. And while production has changed, and the tools of creation have changed, little deliberate attention has been paid to re-examining the outlook of mind, body and feeling, the very triad at the root of the design process.

1   Ikeda, Y., & Kyōto Kokuritsu Kindai Bijutsukan. (2002). Vom Sofakissen zum Städtebau: Hermann Muthesius und der deutsche Werkbund: Modern design in Deutschland 1900-1927. Kyoto, Japan: National Museum of Modern Art.

Much attention has been rightly taken up to merely understand the impact of the facility of these new technologies, and how they are to be best deployed. However, neglecting to compare old methods to the new, failing to guide and course-correct the formation of the new practices can lead to either rudderless celebration of, or resistance against novelty, where one labors to reinvent the wheel, and calls it discovery. An instructive example for application of the kind of critical perspective that is called for, is outlined by Christopher Alexander within A Pattern Language.

Central to the critical perspective is that it is a pattern language, not the pattern language. Regarding many of the entries, Alexander urges the reader that "it would be wise for you to treat the pattern with a certain amount of disrespect – and that you seek out variants of the solution [...] not covered by what we have written"[2] Indeed, the great variability of outcome in the application of pattern languages has led to criticism of the method by Alexander and others.[3] A Pattern Language itself was very much a reply to the concerns he voiced in reaction to his earlier work, Notes on the Synthesis of Form.[4] Likewise, in response to the limits of patterns as a method, Alexander began investigating and writing what became The Nature of Order, discussing among other things how specific, successful pattern languages function as a framework for a more general generative process of objective, geometric fundamental properties. At each step, a new method was examined, criticized and contrasted to earlier approaches.

As those books are descriptive, pragmatic theory of empirical investigations, we in this study also rooted our investigation in the physical process of making. The intent is to begin a reproducible series of ongoing studies, generating falsifiable results, with the understanding that in order for the heretofore seemingly irreconcilable design problems of our era to be addressed, we must examine what and how we build while at the same time, stretching our vision beyond the limits of the world-view to which we have been accustomed.

2. Metaphysical: The need for an amended world-view

When global circumstances drastically change, and our ways of thinking and behavior do not adapt to that change, a formalized civilization is made considerably vulnerable. This is the material fact that underlies a requirement that sounds so abstracted as "we need to

2   Alexander, C., Ishikawa, S., & Silverstein, M. (2010). A Pattern Language: Towns, buildings, construction. New York: Oxford Univ. Press., xiii
3   Protzen, Jean Pierre (1980). The Poverty of the Pattern Language, Concrete: Journal of the Students in the Department of Architecture, November,1977; University of California, Berkeley; reprinted in Design Studies, vol. I, no. 5 (London, July 1980), 291-98.
4   See the remarks in the preface: "These diagrams, which, in my more recent work, I have been calling patterns, are the key to the process of creating form." Alexander, C. (2002). Notes on the Synthesis of Form. Cambridge, Mass. [u.a.: Harvard Univ. Press.

change our world-view." What our current world-view is, what it means to change it, what actions are required and what challenges we face are topics of enormous import, and require further, separate treatment. For the purposes of this study, we provide here a summary, stemming from observations asserted within The Nature of Order.

One serious challenge is to merely come to agreement on if there is such a thing as a coherent worldview, and how much of an impact it has before we decide how to react in amending it. But leaving aside those discussions for the moment, it is reasonable to put forward that there is a current, more-or-less global dominance in at least the economic sense. This hegemony of production –while sectors within it are often by necessity ruthlessly at odds with each other– has effectively eliminated cultural and economic competition from alternate (usually centuries-old and traditional) systems of production. Where international industrialized markets have not yet fully penetrated, the momentum is held back either by fatiguingly active resistance, or extreme geographic isolation.

While global capital is to a large extent, nothing new,[5] the overwhelming power that industrial markets currently wield is a relatively recent phenomenon. Before the broad maturation of industrial economies in the mid-19th-century, alternate systems of production, and consequently, alternate ethics of culture and governance were viable and even enviably competitive, from the Ottomans, to staunchly independent Ethiopia, and further from Europe, in the empires of Persia, Mughal India and Qing Dynasty China. The military, navigational and economic force behind the West's new power was (and is) to a great extent, fueled by applied science. And while science itself does not strictly constitute a world-view, the influence of certain philosophies popular at the time of modern science's 17th century formalization have worked their way into the broader culture, to the point of near-invisible pervasiveness.

This pervasive philosophy is what one may call the "mechanistic worldview." Despite how distant it may at first seem from the imperatives of architecture, Alexander writes that, he has "come to believe that architecture is so agonizingly disturbed because we –the architects of our time– are struggling with a conception of the world, a world-picture, that essentially makes it impossible to make buildings well."[6] How is this defined? "What I mean, roughly, is [...] a picture of a world made of atoms which whirl around in a mechanical fashion." Isolated physical entities interacting based on determinable physical laws is precisely the view forwarded by Descartes in the 17th century in his attempt to clearly articulate how

---

5   Markets have always sought deep interconnection over as broad an effective scope as possible. For examples of what I mean, the curious researcher may easily observe the interknit eastern Mediterranean in the Late Bronze Age, Alexander's Greek colonies in Afghan Bactria, documented Chinese embassy to Byzantine Syria, and India's consistent role as a bridge between the far east and Mesopotamia, as early as the Harappan period.
6   Alexander, C. (2004). The Nature of Order: Book One, the Phenomenon of Life. London: Taylor & Francis. 7.

we may most rigorously deal with facts.[7] Alexander, while having great admiration for Descartes, rgues that the cartesian way of looking at the world has presented us with severe limitations regarding things we consider valid as fact.[8] The cartesian view clarified physical observations, but at the eventual expense of our ability to communicate about shared facts of feeling and beauty. Descartes' heuristic, which liberated him and many other scientists to study and discover physical phenomena strictly as such, was to separate the world into the res extensa and the res cogitans. Respectively, separating that which is external and physical, from the internal world of perception which mixes sense data with ideas within the personal mind. From this viewpoint, with varying degrees of skepticism (see Hume and much later the extreme nominalism of the post-structuralists), it is granted to speak with more certainty on measured sensory observations of the res extensa than anything else except the existence of a subjective self. As a tool for chemists and physicists, this is extremely practical. (Biology would be another matter.) When stated dogmatically as how the world exists though, the mechanistic view limits many things, including our ability to come to agreement on how to practically address the way that the built environment makes us feel. Within this world-view, aspects of externally measured function or mathematically rationalized form are front and center. Hardly having confidence, within a mechanistic worldview we are today barely left with the vocabulary to assert human feeling in anything but a purely idiosyncratic manner. To make meaningful decisions in architecture, discussions of feeling need to be at least in an intersubjective agreement, that is, consistent within a given group. Yet, adherence to strict dualism dismisses this ground out of hand.

Such difficulty of communication stems from a consequence of the pervasive conceptual divide between res extensa and res cogitans. This has come to be known as strict mind-body dualism, a separation of the personal, living world inside the thinking head, from the mechanical (or as Descartes formulated it, divinely animated) world of the physical. Though it is nearly invisible without contrast, it is very distinct from the Hindu conception of the world as the manifested dream of the godhead (Tat tvam asi. "In that way, are you."),[9] or the Neo-Confucian conception of "Li" (理), involving form as self-organizing outflow of "energy" (Qi,氣).[10] Our current Western conception of mental and physical, living and dead, contains a much, much sharper binary than other systems of thought. This mental divide is the primary obstacle that must be overcome if we are to be coherent in advancing architecture beyond the constraints of industrial modernism.

Fortunately, an amendatory critique to this western worldview was formulated not long

7   Descartes, René (2017). Discourse on Method. Broadview Press.
8   Alexander, C. (2004). The Nature of Order: Book One, the Phenomenon of Life. London: Taylor & Francis. 16-17.
9   Staal, Frits. (2008) Discovering the Vedas: Origins, Mantras, Rituals, Insights. New Delhi: Penguin Books. 180.
10   Leibniz, Gottfried Wilhelm Freiherr von, Cook, Daniel J. and Rosemont, Henry (1994) Writings on China. Chicago: Open Court. 99.

after Descartes' initial publications. In 1710, Gottfried Leibniz published Théodicée, his only major philisophical work published during his lifetime. In it, the German polymath treated many topics, including the problem of evil, the question of free will, and in the incredibly profound "parable of Sextus Tarquinius," Leibniz vividly illustrates the nature of limited human perception as contrasted to infinite divine perception.[11] Fortunately, an Austrian nobleman[12] asked for an executive summary. Composed near the end of his life and only published later, this (unsent) letter would become the most influential philosophical work of Leibniz's life: "The Monadology."[13] At 90 paragraphs long, it summarizes the monist-influenced world-view asserted in Théodicée, directly addressing shortcomings of cartesian dualism along the way.

One aspect of amendatory critique is on the nature of life itself. Descartes contended that all matter not endowed with a soul was mechanical, pushed directly by the finger of God. Leibniz wondered why this distinction existed. What kind of God touches only some things? The apparent distinction must be because of human consciousness, which is merely the awareness of perception. Leibniz wrote that "the Cartesians made a great mistake, for they disregarded perceptions which are not perceived,"[14] which he lays out as a simpler and more holistic way of understanding physical reactions/responses; cause and effect. For example, a bell would express that it has the perception of being struck, by ringing. The life-nature of the bell makes it ring,[15] but is not complex enough to let the bell be aware that it rings. This view removes the strict division between life and not-life in favor of a more pragmatic understanding of life as a gradation of organized complexity. "Thus, there is nothing fallow, sterile, or dead in the universe; no chaos, no confusions, save in appearance."[16] With this monadic perspective, it becomes completely reasonable to consider how one's body has a kind of "dialog" with a living (or less-living) architectural space, an entirely pragmatic idea that currently, is almost taboo.

Having established the difference between the life of humans and mechanisms as a distinction not of kind, but of degree, Leibniz criticizes Descartes' conception of the homunculus, that odd idea of a miniature agent of "self" inside us that is so pervasive that it has made its way into the plots of Woody Allen and Disney movies. This conceptual need for the body to have a personal "driver" is a fundamental consequence of mechanistic, strict dualism. But even aside from a problem of infinite regress, (Who drives the drive that drives the driver?) the further absurdity of the homunculular consciousness is revealed. Consider how both

---

11 Leibniz, G. W., & Kirchmann, J. H. (1878). Theodicee: 1. u. 2. Leipzig: Erich Koschny.
12 Prince Eugene of Savoy, (1663-1736)
13 Leibniz, G. W., & Strickland, L. (2014). Leibniz's Monadology: A new translation and guide. Edinburgh: Edinburgh University Press.
14 Leibniz, G. W., & Loemker, L. E. (1989). Philosophical papers and letters. Dordrecht, Holland: Kluwer Academic. 644.
15 This is a strikingly Taoist formulation of what being alive means. Leibniz was in correspondence with Jesuit missionaries traveling to China. See the cited: Writings on China.
16 Ibid. 650.

the body and machines are similar. "If we pretend that there is a machine whose structure enables it to think, feel, and have perception, one could think of it as enlarged yet preserving its same proportions, so that one could enter it as one does a mill. If we did this, we should find nothing within but parts which push upon each other; we should never see anything which would explain a perception."[17] Rather than limiting souls to thinking humans, it makes far more sense to Leibniz that he generalizes the principle to all things, re-conceptualizing the soul as a "monad," an eternal irreducible atom, not of matter, but an atom of form. Additionally, at each level of organization within a given object or system, one finds many monads; mutually reinforcing recursive centers of life nested within life, forming a rich network of interplay. This anticipates the cybernetic systems-analysis that allows design to treat the occupant, building and context as a holistic system. The dualist method of imagining a conceptual machine in detail and then executing it, while excellent in some applications, is damagingly limited for sufficiently complex systems. This amended view addresses those shortcomings.

These interlaced monads were capable of only two things, perception and appetition. Each monad had driven purpose or momentum and perceived a unique image from its vantage point within universe. But this is no more problematic to questions of objectivity than that, "the same city viewed from different sides appears to be different and to be, as it were, multiplied in perspectives, so the infinite multitude of simple substances, [atoms of form] which seem to be so many different universes, are nevertheless only the perspectives of a single universe according to the different points of view of each monad."[18] Thus the internal and external worlds of the monads were united in what Leibniz called the "pre-established harmony," which he believed was metaphysically consistent with and consequent from the physical law of conservation of momentum.[19] The fact that this law was unknown in Descartes' day is why Leibniz charitably believed that Descartes was compelled to invent strict dualism to begin with. In fact, Leibniz' metaphysical work in the "Monadology" and elsewhere anticipates the physical discoveries of unified space-time and the matter/energy equivalence.[20] Group that equivalence with the laws of conservation of matter/energy, and you have an alternate way to formulate the pre-established harmony that deals with the mind/body distinction in a much more ready way than the res extensa.

These are large ideas, and amending a limited world-view is a large challenge. This section is merely a summary, and these conceptual tools of Leibniz' are just as much a heuristic lens as are Descartes' formulations. They are not statements of what the world is, but alternate

17   Ibid. 644.
18   Ibid. 648.
19   Ibid. 651.
20   Ibid. 641.

ways of understanding how the world works. Both Leibniz' and Descartes' metaphysics, risk the rigidity of dogma if they are perceived as fact. But too often, these dualistic separations, of life from not-life, self from-world are seen exactly as fact. If we wish to understand how the built environment can be a better-integrated system, to relate more successfully to human feeling, to embrace the natural environment, not as mindless matter, but as a living system upon which we depend, this shift of heuristic, and consequently of worldview is the place to begin. And Bryan and I discovered in the process of this study's investigation, understanding of these alternate principles did directly lead to a more fluent application of Alexander's morphogenetic methods. Understanding this impact of ideas and process on built form is as important as understanding the capacity and facility of changing technologies, but the pace of recent historical change has been so rapid, that emphasis on the latter has been much more visible than the former.

3. Historical Context

Our case study does not appear to as yet have many repeated or similar instances. On looking into experiments conducted by Christopher Alexander and his students, I did not discover any attempts to do a controlled study of the application of different methods across several similar and controlled cases, as most of the time and energy spent on methodological experimentation was done in the context of active projects or formal learning exercises. Publications on the impact of technology on design method and outcome have tended to focus on the unique capacity of the technology itself. This is a legitimate and important aim. The capability of new methods must be understood. But it should not be ignored that at the end of the process, and literally at the end of the day, we come home to places that have served the same basic purpose for millennia. Comparing the effect of new methods and new technologies on the outcomes of criteria that hold consistent across the shifts in modes of practice, is as important as understanding a novel practice itself. Without such controlled comparisons, we run the risk of not being even fully aware of what is being lost or eroded as methods change. This study endeavors to make just such a consistent trans-method comparison.

Studies of method and technology impacting form in the past have taken varied approaches. As recently as 1985, with the then-new "home" computers breaking into desktop publishing and already having become pervasive in other industries, George Banz wrote that "Full use of computers in architectural design is still far away from a reality."[21] However,

21 Banz, George (1985). An Iterative Approach to Computer-Aided Architectural Design. Journal of Architectural and Planning Research, 2 (3), 187.

he did suggest "an urgent need for design methodologies that accommodate computer applications." The emphasis here, seems to be on adapting the practice to the tool, rather than shaping the tool to fit the practice, a common reaction to new technology. Yet, despite such enthusiasm, and in stark contrast to today's incredible confidence in the power of algorithms, Banz argues that, "architectural design does not yield readily to algorithms and systematic treatment."[22] But he concludes the article by claiming that "The final challenge will be to move beyond the notion of fixed sets of constraints which, if not met, void a design. Instead, the ultimate aim must be combinational procedures that adapt to flexible constraint conditions."[23] He had somehow made the argument that while architecture is not amenable to algorithmic constraints, increasing the amount of test algorithms you can run is what architecture needs. This formulation is a direct expression of the mind-machine heuristic from Descartes' thought where the more easily you can run a conceptual model of something, the better it should be.

Christopher Alexander's work is mentioned several times in the piece. Banz credits Notes on the Synthesis of Form with creating the very theory behind the algorithmic approach of hierarchical composition of fluid constraints that he advocates, but calls the book's approach, "at best questionable."[24] He reacts more favorably to A Pattern Language, seeing within the book (much as computer scientists of the time did) a logical structure very similar to that of a relational database. Very importantly, he makes the distinction between functional programming and the value of object-oriented programming that won A Pattern Language renown in the computer science community and made possible the software that drives our smartphones today. "The diagrams [in pattern languages] contain no dimensions. That is because patterns are concepts, and, as such, have no [exactly quantified] physical attributes. Once these physical attributes are defined, [...] the pattern is incorporated into a 'design unit.' "[25] This distinction between language's pattern and "design unit" is the same distinction between a software framework's object and a specific instance of implemented code.

Crucially, this flexible (rather than prefab) object-oriented method of working breaks down the division between a precise, dualistic "thought machine" where the spec is called out in detail in advanced planning, and a more integral method where an existing framework of objects is contextually adapted onto a unique whole as it is being built. This article does not venture to examine the consequences of shifting to "object-oriented" from "functions-based" software or hardware building. But it does open the door to the kind of adaptive modeling that this study examines.

22 Ibid.
23 Ibid. 199.
24 Ibid. 189.
25 Ibid. 194

In 1987, Moura Quayle published further steps in envisioning a future of computer design, but as is often the case with predicting the future of technology, it was very difficult to see past the next product release. Far from an algorithmic accelerator or an AI, this vision called for the mass-2-way-communications capabilities of computers to aid in community design, allowing for rapid revision and review of 3D models.[26] While this capacity certainly exists, especially today with smartphones in every pocket, the author didn't address a shortcoming we still have not solved in widespread practice. Namely, when a dualistically narrow limitation on what can be observed as fact remains in place, the ability of a community to provide constructive input in a planning process remains severely constrained, no matter if the revision technology is photocopied handouts at a community review in a school gym, or interactive 3D animations posted on Facebook. The built applications of pattern languages have given us an opening to address this issue of structuring constructive input, but even the best pattern language, created for the most committed community, will still come up against serious obstacles if the mechanistic mainstream mode of design, planning and construction is adhered to.

An article that instead of exclusively exploring technological ability, comes somewhat closer to a consistent trans-method comparison, is George C. Skarmeas' "From HABS to BIM."[27] HABS is the Historic American Buildings Survey. The article explores the impact that computer technology will have on efforts of preservation. Tellingly, a long-term view to the project viability is taken in this case, and the crucial question of if the project documentation will remain openable in years and decades ahead. The idea of project file maintenance is raised. The advantages of laser scanning, what has become today's reality-capture, is mentioned, but it is cautioned that this new method contains a literal blind spot. Human observation of sites is maintained as continually important, as a studied preservationist will be able to know through observation combined with learning, how a building is jointed and even be able to accurately infer the condition of these joints, something the technology can't duplicate. It is a crucial reminder that in the enthusiasm for useful new methods, old practices should not be forgotten. The author is concerned that intelligible standards of method be developed that are in tune with current preservationist practice. However, the study is pro-spective and theorizes about what may come, rather than examining the impact of a given computer-assisted project and nowhere is the fundamental nature of the building process questioned or challenged. The article is a lucid examination of how new tools can enhance what is already done in the field.

26 Quayle, Moura (1987). Computer-Aided Participatory Design: Sitesee. Journal of Architectural and Planning Research, 4(4), 340.
27 Skarmeas, George. (2010). From HABS to BIM: Personal Experiences, Thoughts, and Reflections. APT Bulletin, 41(4), 47-53.

A fascinating look at how the opportunities of technology are already pushing us beyond strict dualism, while our conscious conceptions adapt to keep up is presented in, "Society in the Making: the Study of Technology as a Tool for Sociological Analysis." While the essay does not address questions of building, the non-dualist nature of an agent within a networked system is precisely described.

> *The actor network is reducible neither to an actor or a network alone nor to a network. Like networks it is composed of a series of heterogeneous elements, animate and inanimate, that have been linked to one another for a certain period of time. [...] An actor network is simultaneously an actor whose activity is networking heterogeneous elements and a network that is able to redefine and transform what it is made of.*[28]

This definition of an actor-network, where subject is co-determinately interlinked with the environment, which consists of other nodes or centers who likewise impact the network from a unique standpoint, echoes relations of the monads to the physical world and to each other. What we may struggle to describe and work with while not having a framework, can potentially be understood more clearly with the help of a clearly defined mental model. This is why such heuristics are so important in shaping the world-views that underlie our actions and decisions.

As we noted earlier, so many published articles were looking at new technology that they (correctly) expected to impact design in the future, and therefore did not have many recently past examples to compare the impacts of various methods on similar or identical projects, as our study attempts. However, technology is not the only influence on method. As we have seen even in creating this paper, ideas and theory impact practice as well. And this distinction points us to the closest replicant of our experiment that we were able to discover.

In 1927, Kasimir Malevich –accompanied by a KGB minder– visited Berlin, hoping to reach the Bauhaus. He didn't manage that connection, but did speak with architect Ludwig Hilberseimer, a great admirer of the Russian painter and sculptor, ever since the famous "Monument to the Third International" had been exhibited in Germany. Hilberseimer helped Malevich to publish The Non-Objective World, a longish pamphlet, often abridged and billed as the "Suprematist Manifesto," but it contains what documentation survives, of a fascinating experiment.

Just as rapidly changing technology affords us an opportunity to observe the impact that this

28 Callon, M. (1987). "Society in the Making: The Study of Technology as a Tool for Sociological Analysis." in The Social Construction of Technological Systems. Bijker, W.E., Hughes, T.P., and Pinch, T.J., eds. Cambridge, MA: MIT Press. 83-103.

change has on design, Malevich in the early 20th century, saw painting that began in romantic symbolism, rush through Cézanne and Cubism, to full abstraction via his countryman and sometime colleague, Wassily Kandinsky. This varied environment surely would have had an impact on what was painted and how. Malevich wrote that "The peculiar character of any new visual environment, exercising its effect upon us, constitutes that additional element [emphasis mine] which brings about a change in the normal relationship between the element of consciousness and that of the subconscious."[29] In the 1920s, furnished by the new Soviet government with fully-funded students, he would experiment with controlling the visual art-input of painters. For example, a man who painted in a pastoral style would be surrounded by nothing but cubist works.

> *I prescribed for a painter who leaned strongly toward Cézanne a large dose of the cubist combination of the curve and the straight line from various stages in the development of all four phases of Cubism. The simultaneous effects of two pictorial cultures (that of Cézanne and that of Cubism) attained in this way shook powerfully the artistic conceptions and methods of representation of the painter. An object being represented changed its proportions; under the influence of the sickle form of Cubism, certain lines dropped out of the visible object temporarily and then, however, the object reappeared, as such and in its entirety.*[30]

We lack any records of how these experiments were carried out, and any documentation of the results. We are thus unable to assess bias or levels of rigor, but it certainly appears that exposure to a specific visual environment will concretely influence what an artist or designer produces. This recent yet remote historical precedent does indicate that repeated experiments of measuring the impact of circumstance on method and output, can be successfully conducted.

Just as new ideas opened up possibilities in painting, new information technology has opened up a space where we are able, and indeed compelled, to question old assumptions and methods. But as the HABS article demonstrated, to question means neither to outright abandon, nor to blindly embrace new practices as "desirable and inevitable." Here, with this challenge of overcoming the dualist, mechanistic worldview as a pre-requisite to successful application of Christopher Alexander's morphogenetic method, we have explored the impact of tools and method on morphology in the instance of computers, drawing and modeling.

29 Malevich, K. S. (2003). *The non-objective world: The manifesto of suprematism.* Mineola, N.Y.: Dover Publications. 12.
30 Ibid. 52

4. Case study structure

The most basic objective of this study has been to create circumstances where the physical output from developing a design-object can empirically test the relative effectiveness of Christopher Alexander's morphogenetic method as carried out under distinct circumstances. The spark of the idea came in knowing how A Pattern Language represented a breakthrough in design process, but varying modes of implementation led to inconsistent results in built projects.

If this circumstance is true for the patterns, it is likely true for the methods in The Nature of Order. While the 15 fundamental properties represent another significant step forward in the maker's toolkit, it is entirely possible that a "perfect storm" of circumstances will make it likely that a designer could rely upon the 15 properties as such with strict adherence yet miss the objective of vibrantly living form entirely. And if the most fundamental pre-requisite to success is the need to reformulate how one looks at the self, life and the world, a limited outcome is almost a certainty.

And just as a pattern language itself is one tool among many, intended to bring about living form in the built environment, the methods explored in this study are not intended to stand alone. Our focus here on any given method is not an endorsement of that method, nor is it meant to favor one over any other. Instead, the relatively narrow methodological focus we employed in this study –in contrast to the wide variety of actions appropriate in a built project– isolates variables as far we were able, as is required for accurate scientific observation.

The practical use of this case-study is as a scientific report, informing strategies of built-practice. Not only does it employ rigorous control-based experimentation that would be unethical to apply in built-practice in a client's life, but it uses a live, physical project to investigate consequent effects. The fact that it is not possible to commit to scientific investigation without employing controls, and that it is not ethical to use a built-project as a control within a study, highlights the importance of engaging in experimentation such as we have attempted here. Our focus on the 15 fundamental properties in this study is an attempt to empirically describe the dynamics of their application in a way that is not possible in either professional practice or typical student work. We certainly encourage further experimentation, using this study as a landmark.

4.1. Objective and hypothesis

Our objective was to determine while testing the effectiveness of an application of Alexander's method, if the variables that lead to the output of work based on the 15 properties being more successful or less successful could be isolated and identified as consequently effective.

Our hypothesis was that since the reformulation of a post-dualist, non-mechanistic world-view was stated by Alexander as a pre-requisite to successful creation of living-form, that tools and processes which involved integration of the self with the end-product would yield better results than methods that would separate concept from implementation and from self.

While computers and drawing could certainly be used in a successfully integrated non-dualist project, the separation away from a full-scale in-person example as well as the computer's added quickness and facility of creation would open up so many paths away from the relatively few wholeness-enhancing solutions, that the more integrated approach of direct work on a full-scale sculpted implementation would present significant comparative advantages.

4.2. Givens

» Effectiveness of Alexander's methods

Our first assumption of the experiment was that Alexander's methods as described in The Nature of Order present a constructive and effective way to create more successful and more beautiful results than would be typically achieved with similar time and resources otherwise.

The best presentation of the method is of course explicated within The Nature of Order and also, in a more compact and construction-ready version in, Battle for the Life and Beauty of the Earth, (Alexander, Neis & Moore Alexander, 2013). To give an extremely brief outline here, The Nature of Order asserted that there are physical environments that are objectively more healthy and less healthy, more alive and less alive, more beautiful and less beautiful. Pattern languages are an important factor in creating such spaces. However, at a more fine-grained level than pattern languages address, are the specific geometric characteristics of objects. Ultimately when dealing with the built environment, it is the physical form of the thing that will greatly influence the degree of life and beauty. Places shaped with a high degree of life also evince these more-or-less 15 properties.

1. Levels of scale

2. Strong centers

3. Boundaries

4. Alternating repetition

5. Positive space

6. Good shape

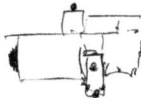

7. Local symmetries

8. Deep interlock and ambiguity

9. Contrast

10. Gradients

11. Roughness

12. Echoes

13. The void

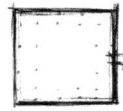

14. Simplicity and inner calm

15. Not-separateness

The 15 Properties: from, The Nature of Order, Book One (Alexander, 2004) 239-241.

These properties are not compositional elements, but epiphenomena of a process of form generation that has operated by gestational structure-preserving-transformations that develop –in the mean– starting from the large and general and ending with the small and particular. This stepwise method of form generation is known as the fundamental process. This process creates areas of concentrated form known as "centers." Much as with monads, centers are units of form that are indivisible without becoming something else. Each center possesses a degree of wholeness, gestalt-strength, beauty and life. Centers mutually reinforce each other in a recursive network (each center is itself, made of centers,) dynamically generating a field effect of a larger, interrelated whole. Biology and geology tend to create these measurable centers and properties through natural processes. The process of unfolding living form in design does not copy nature in the sense of biomimicry but seeks to achieve a similar level of beauty and well-adaptedness. Alexander's method of morphogenesis has this objective in mind as something that should be accessible to anyone with knowledge of the process.

» The objective (or at least intersubjective) nature of the beauty and wholeness

None of this effort would be meaningful if these values of beauty and life were arbitrary or purely individually determined. Many of these properties are reflected in and observed by human feeling of identifying in a positive way with the object at hand. This is known as the "mirror of the self test."[31] We used this test throughout the experiment at each point of decision.

» The inability to isolate the variable of the experimenter's or the observer's self from the active variables at hand.

When conducting this experiment, we discovered by David's failing to orient himself as an experiment-conducting observer of Bryan's work on this project, that it is impossible to remove one's involvement of feeling and personal investiture in the process and remain effectively involved in it.

This given is consequent of the means to how the objective nature of beauty is expressed and discovered. It also presents a controversial challenge for scientific observation. Prior to the early days of introspective psychology in the 19th century and later on, the efforts of phenomenology, modern science cornered itself with external phenomena that were only physically measurable. The attempts to empirically observe internal phenomena like thoughts, and sense perception met with mixed results to say the least. We are still in the early days of investigating the phenomenon of wholeness in making. The challenge of reliable metrics might prove an insurmountable obstacle, but progress in construction of built projects indicates otherwise. The dualistic restriction on what is regarded as true, or "falsifiable" is operable exactly on this point.

It may be that the physically geometric nature of the properties will aid in this respect. While

---

31 Alexander, Christopher. (2004). The Nature of Order: Book One, the Phenomenon of Life. London: Taylor & Francis. 313.

the 15 properties are an external phenomenon, the measured event is an interaction of inside and out, the feeling of belonging, or waking of personal life arising in concert with the stimulus of the definite geometric properties. While this is a challenge for a scientific investigation, it is likely that the inability to become personally distant from a process of design becomes an advantage for making things in the built environment.

» There is inherent asymmetry of resource utilization by the three distinct methods.

We used three tracks to make three sculpted objects: drawing, computer generation and direct-sculpted modeling. We set time and labor utilization (the only constantly controllable resource variables available to us) as equal as possible across the three methods.

While this kind of distinction with resources is certainly something we wanted to observe between the methods, it presented a conceptual challenge. How do we control as much as possible for consistency across three results when time and tools are used in such different ways that a similar amount of decisions will use a drastically different amount of resources?

How much time is given to planning, how much to execution? Since the direct-modeling control is all execution, is it correct to set that time equal to the others? Of course, in professional production, time and cost are closely linked. However, the physical modeling process when compared to a computer, (and less extremely so with drawing) is slower in respect to each step taken. Yet, due to the rich feedback that a full-scale object sends to a mirror of the self-test, in respect to gain towards the objective –that is, generation of living form– the model was faster in respect to –helpful– steps taken. So, depending on what is counted as progress, total steps taken vs effective steps taken, a computer method would be faster overall, but investing time in modeling and full-scale mockups may lead to a faster or better achievement of objectives.

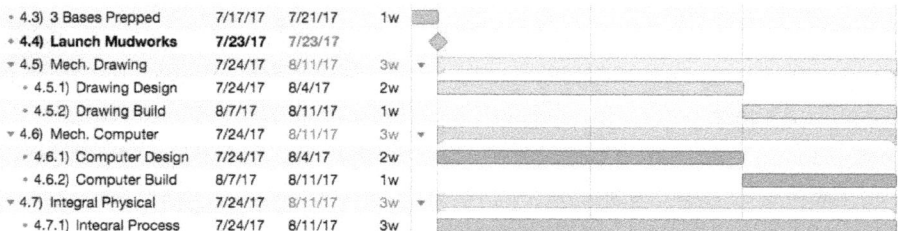

• 4.3) 3 Bases Prepped	7/17/17	7/21/17	1w	
• 4.4) Launch Mudworks	7/23/17	7/23/17		
▼ 4.5) Mech. Drawing	7/24/17	8/11/17	3w	▼
• 4.5.1) Drawing Design	7/24/17	8/4/17	2w	
• 4.5.2) Drawing Build	8/7/17	8/11/17	1w	
▼ 4.6) Mech. Computer	7/24/17	8/11/17	3w	▼
• 4.6.1) Computer Design	7/24/17	8/4/17	2w	
• 4.6.2) Computer Build	8/7/17	8/11/17	1w	
▼ 4.7) Integral Physical	7/24/17	8/11/17	3w	▼
• 4.7.1) Integral Process	7/24/17	8/11/17	3w	

The Gantt schedule of the 3-week "making" phase.

5. Bias

In addition to the pitfalls implicit in not being able to conduct and observe while isolating the observer, when only two people are doing the experiment, double-blinding is not an option. We were forced by circumstance to embrace this limitation. David realized this part-way through the experiment, (on Monday July 31, 2017, the three-week experimental phase had started one week earlier). The genuine, active engagement that resulted, stood in very positive and consequential contrast to the haltingly ineffective efforts at self-removal. These moments will be explored further along. This apparent positivity is either a striking case of confirmation bias, or evidence that involvement of the self in the process of making is crucial to achieving the objective of well-adapted form.

There was also a question as to how the three experimental tracks would cross-contaminate each other. Since one person would work on all three, would an idea conceived of during the computer time "bleed over" and favor the advantage of the other two? Since it was impossible to anticipate this, we have assumed that each track has contaminated the other, but that they did so more or less equally. A schedule rotation helped protect for this. For future experiments, it would be advisable to have a large group of people conduct the experiment and run sufficient isolation controls for each method track.

Bryan was largely unfamiliar with the fundamental process before beginning. There is an inescapable tradeoff here between the benefit of a "tabula rasa" lack of preconceived notions on one hand, and the obstacle of a learning curve this presented on the other. We advise future experiments to, when possible, use participants unfamiliar with the process, educate them in an extremely consistent way, documenting variable reception of ideas, and then consistently fast-track (for project management, meaning to extend the task duration backwards) the "making phase" schedule as far as is needed to overcome the obstacle of the learning curve.

As there were only two people in the study, Bryan was fully exposed to David's preconceptions, such as believing the integral modeling phase to present advantages for the mirror of the self-test. This may have affected results. Future experiments should see that each building track is presented in as neutral a way as possible, with the participants' preferences for and ability in the methods documented. Bryan was intrigued by the integral approach, but largely unfamiliar with it. He was certainly predisposed to a love of drawing, though he is perfectly capable in the digital realm.

6. Physical: Conducting the study

6.1. The means of making

We wanted to start with something small, yet scalable, where decisions of form and spatial arrangement –while certainly not identical to a larger project– would be similar in type. This is why we chose the creation of three 15"-square, relief tiles. Prior to the active "building" phase of the experiment, Bryan prepared the physical mud sculpture materials and worked with David to become familiar enough with the process to make this an initial attempt. As we will see further along, the results were fairly effective, with the learning curve presenting less of an obstacle than expected.

The making phase consisted of one mud-tile sculpture developed by means of computer, one by means of paper drawing, and one by generating the forms directly in the full-scale model itself, effectively erasing the commonly bivalent distinction between planning and execution, design and product. Drawing and computer work, in part because they required further subdivision into separated "design" and "build" phases, were regarded as "mechanistic tracks" where the direct-action work to be done at full-scale went for the whole three weeks in a more or less steady and consistent process of decision, examination, correction and implementation.

Tellingly, the computer phase split into two tracks as the speed at which alternatives could be explored allowed for the creation of a "mini competition." At the end of the two weeks, Bryan chose which computer track he preferred to implement.

What variables could be documented and controlled for were. Bryan's sleep schedule was as far as possible kept consistent across the three weeks. Weekends were not used for work, though it was admitted that subconscious deliberation and sudden inspiration cannot be controlled for. Along those lines, dreams –being an active expression of that sub-conscious work on a project– were recorded. It is not apparent if ideas were influenced or gleaned, but design activity certainly occurred as a plot-point of some dreams.

Communication between David and Bryan on daily work was documented, dated and time-stamped. Bryan's time use on each phase was documented using a phone-based time-clock application. Time tracking totals are as follows.

Tile	Total Duration (hours)
Drawing	19.95
Computer	22.68
Integral	22.55

Table: Total hours for each track

Despite the attempts to keep the times equal, the drawing came in shorter. This is largely due to a decision to instruct Bryan that if there was no further work felt needed within a given work-slot, that there was no need to force "busywork" decisions into the design form in order to make the hours come out even. Computer and integral stand roughly equal. Bryan was most familiar and happily fluent with the drawing process, so it is reasonable to conclude that this time differential was an expression of his skill in that area. While the computer was potentially "faster," it was so fast to draw on, that it constantly opened up enough design decisions to explore, that the track was bifurcated into two competing plans, which likely kept it at maximum schedule allotment.

Bryan was encouraged to rotate his work schedule so that no track got the benefit of staying last in the day or the disadvantage of occupying a time-slot of naturally low productivity.

6.2. Reflective Documentation

Bryan kept journals reflecting on the morning's objectives, each track's daily session and any general conclusions or reflections gathered at the end of the day. He began the experiment recording his extant impressions of the fundamental process and ended the 3-week session with a concluding statement of how he felt those impressions had changed. The learning curve certainly was a recorded obstacle at the beginning. Bryan stated that, "I seem to be able to recall only a part of the list" of the 15 properties. Additionally, at such a point of pre-internalization of the concept, it is difficult for a practitioner to not see the properties as pre-set elements to be copied in or assembled, rather than as the result of a series of dynamic transformations. Though Bryan was quite close to a certain kind of fluency without acknowledging it as such in remarking that "It's quite a lot to keep in one's head. Especially when something just feels right but you can't name it as a property or transformation." Of course, this is a sign that although the information was new, he had a good feel for how the mirror of the self-test would operate.

Throughout, the creative urge to rush ahead and make a lot of choices at once was an obstacle to making the best choices in the most optimal sequence. At the end, Bryan' first remark after acknowledging the success of the results was saying "Making only one move is still difficult for me." However, the times when Bryan slowed down the most, were when David observed the biggest breakthroughs. Bryan commented on appreciating learning about simplicity of moves, especially regarding economy of effective action as time is always at a premium on any project. The integral method helped awaken a sense of increased economy in his work.

He also wrote that understanding the theory of the Monadology had been very helpful.

"The idea of centers being made of centers all the way down seems to nestle nicely with the Monadology. It also seems that The Monadology has a similar concept to Levels of Scale in that machines and other non-living things have little [relatively less] life in them since you jump from the scale of, say, a gear, to the scale of an atom." For understanding recursion and the networked field-effect of centers, Leibniz' heuristic seemed to help remove obstacles for Bryan's work. Interestingly, regarding David's "failure" to remove the bias of self-involvement, Bryan wrote at the end of his journals that, "It takes a shocking amount of openness to be able to do this consistently, and it certainly has helped to have a guide through this process." When you are using an awareness of a sympathetic reflection of your higher self, or "true self" within the form of an object, it is necessarily a very personal journey, but also one that must be shared. This in a nutshell is ultimately one of the core objectives of both art and design, to create something profoundly beautiful that moves the maker as much as those who receive it.

6.3. Formal results

And readers of this paper, you have the opportunity here to reflect upon the core idea of this experiment. Which of the three below is the most profoundly beautiful to you, is the truest reflection of your higher self? Send your answer to experiment@buildingbeauty.net. We may continue to glean helpful reactions about this study, thank you.

We have deliberately shown you those pictures unlabeled and in the form arrived at when the allotted work-time expired so that your perception of results would be fresh as we now explore some of the details of how these were made. Each tile started from one root "site" design that was elaborated upon.

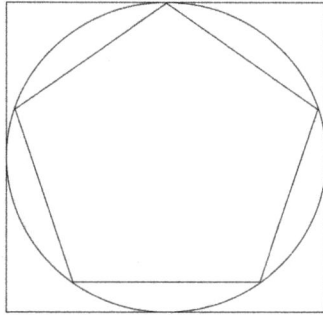

The root design

This simple pattern was the starting point for all tracks. Bryan was instructed that for each track, every design move was to be made employing structure-preserving transformations, using the mirror of the self-test. Clearly, from identical conditions, greatly divergent patterns can emerge. The question at hand is, how did each method impact the results?

The images on the previous page are from left to right, the final integral track, the final computer track and the final drawing track. Clearly, (and ironically) the computer track stands at an unfair disadvantage regarding allotted completion time. As a combined result of the distance between the physical implementation needed, and the extreme freedom and rapidity of design afforded, the computer track took on a form that was exceptionally difficult to execute. Both the drawing and computer tracks were implemented using dot-transfer. Though Bryan developed this solution on his own, it is a well-known craftsman's aid that is at least as old as Michelangelo using it to mock-up the charcoal drawings that would form the start of a mural's fresco.

We'll let you digest which one you consider to be the most successful result while we show you some of the progress of the tracks.

Early on, the integral track was providing Bryan with a lot of frustration. He had felt it was not living up to the exquisite detail that the computer, and especially drawing tracks were showing at that stage. At this same time however, he wrote that "Making a thing is the most spiritual experience I've ever had. [...] It is almost like there is another presence guiding the hands or directing the eye when making a beautiful thing." (July 26)

That same day, he wrote that, "The computer process continues to be the one with the most freedom. Must have something to do with layers." "I am also able to mirror things in ways that are not possible with drawing and in the mud. This has actually lead to a massive jump in complexity and overall interest to the piece that has yet to show up in the other modes. I'm much less cautious with the computer. At the same time, I seem to be making less mistakes." Photoshop was the main application used. A halting attempt was made to do 3D until it was discovered that for a relief, the awkward nature of the computer app made exploration of 3D surface in the digital ream more time-consuming than it was worth for a tile.

On July 31, Bryan was enjoying the physically connected nature of manual drawing. "There's just nothing like working with the motions of the body." A few days later, he said of the same track, "I'm trying to think about these lines as cuttings made by a force which ripples through to the opposite side, as if cutting into a mass of gelatin." That may or may not be an expression of structure-preserving transformations, but it is a shift in mental perspective from euclidean elements to perceiving centers and field effect. Early on, Bryan had been somewhat stuck in a distinct mode of geometric composition, focusing on connections between vertices. David encouraged him to move past this, as working with the 15 properties includes vertices to some degree, but expands formal vocabulary much farther.

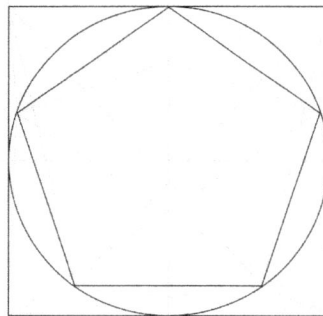

Vertices from the computer, July 24

On August 4, Bryan wrote about the split between sub-track 1 and sub-track 2 on the computer. "On the Computer Track 2 you see something that I would characterize as more simplistic, more radial, and more hand based. Track 1 used a lot of computer translations in Photoshop to separate out different areas and add texture. It also used a lot of pixel duplication and movements whereas Track 2 was done on a Samsung Galaxy 10 (from 2012) with a touch sensitive stylus. Track 1 also used a sensitive stylus, but the drawing plane was locked during production, as well as separate from the drawing surface. [A Wacom-style tablet.] I would say that Track 1 was more "automatic" but also much, much quicker in its development. It will be interesting to see how the two translate into the mud." Formal sim-plicity coincided with the use of a stylus, a tool that took the computer track closer to the realm of drawing. This adjustment to method significantly demonstrated an impact on form consistent with the delta evident between drawing and the computer's mouse-work.

On August 4 in the integral track, Bryan was not happy with the sate of things. "The work is going quite slow. And it isn't as rich and complex as I would like it to be. When I look at this one as compared to the others I'm a little disappointed." Clearly, this would change by the time that the integral track was fully "grown" and the computer track remained too difficult to complete in time.

On August 7, the start of the last week as the "design phases" stopped and the mechanistic plans get implemented, a kind of fluency in the methods began to set in. "Starting to under-stand the meaning of centers and their relation to Wholeness. Was also listening to How Life Comes from Wholeness all day so this is no surprise. Carving felt really good today. It started to feel like swimming again. [...] The drawings, especially, seem far removed now. Of course, this could have been helped with shading...but who has the time to spend "repre-senting"?"

On August 8, Bryan and David had a key moment of collaboration. This is where a decision on the integral track came to the slowest, most deliberate point, but proceeded to open up a whole new realm of development. The struggle was with this area shown below.

The slow integral point

In the earlier image on the left, Bryan had inadvertently traced out what had been two com-peting ideas that overlapped. David saw he had taken one as shown in the acanthus-like motif on the right side above. David encouraged him to explore his other idea; the vase-like line that he had traced and had felt that the vase-line was far more structure-preserving. After encouraging him to think of how line use could have many options, looking at Japanese ink painting, at the whiplash curves of Van de Velde –none of that was imitated– but as with Malevich's Cubism experiment, exposure to visual "additional elements" broke a mental log jam, and Bryan discovered the articulation that you see in the left half of the right photo, something that he was far happier with than either of the previous two solutions. David liked this as well and was quite pleasantly surprised at how Bryan's sculpting of this line used depth of surface in a harmonious way.

The other highlight of productive dialog came earlier on July 24 as the drawing track was taking some very formative steps.

Bryan had iterated to the point of this pattern:

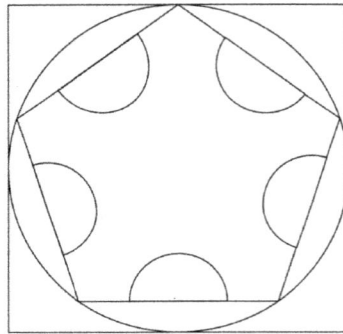

Vertices from the computer, July 24

David and Bryan were discussing what and how would be the next application of structure-preserving transformations. It was apparent that some "good shape" as well as "simplicity and inner calm" was needed. As close as one can get to a suggestion of two individuals demonstrating the objective nature of the wholeness, these photos were uploaded to each other after having been drawing them at the same time for the prior 10 min, not seeing what the other was working on

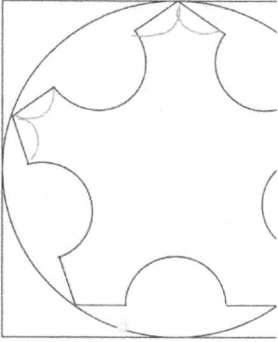

Bryan, July 24 at 8:10 PM GMT

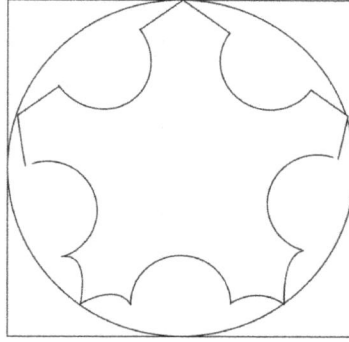

David, July 24 at 8:11 PM GMT

It was a remarkable moment of independent discovery that reinforces our confidence in the objectivity of the properties and the transformations. Though, one incidence is hardly a confirmation. An interesting prospect is that these "seed beds" of form can be tested to see what various people conclude should be the next step, or in observing it, which next step works best.

7. Chronology of forms

Drawing

Computer

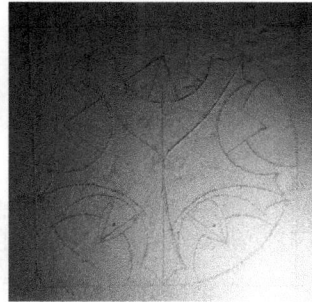

Integral

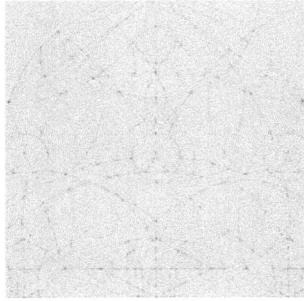
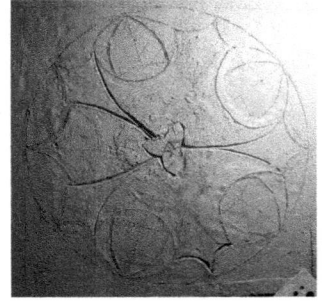

| Drawing | Computer | Integral |

August 3

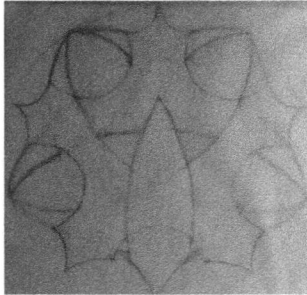

| Drawing | Computer design not chosen for execution | Integral |

August 14

8. Conclusions

Above all, the experimentation of this study demonstrated two things, that scientific exploration of Alexander's methods is not just possible but also useful, and that these explorations are obliged to challenge the current model of scientific inquiry itself.

The methods used in the investigation rely on well-established principles, but due to the requirement of measuring feeling, it is needed to firstly, take at least a Pascal's Wager and act as if the measurement of such things is possible, and second, be willing to engage with this new mixture of personal involvement and observation. Bryan had remarked on how one needs to be very open for the morphogenesis to work, and David learned that one must be either a totally distant observer, or completely commit to making in the process.

When the core of human feeling in design is being explored, it will be difficult to be halfway about anything. The resources in time and personnel for this experiment were limited, bias impacting the conclusion remains at uncertain levels, but nevertheless, both participants felt what was gained through the experience was well worth it.

Within a context of academic study, repeated investigations, improving on the precedent of this study stand to make significant and practical discoveries, not just for the understanding of the morphogenetic method, but for practical applications within architectural practice as well. Further understanding of how projects can implement modeling methods which are time-intensive, may accelerate the achievement of supremely well-adapted living form. This knowledge and method can be a valuable asset in creating beautiful spaces for clients' lives.

It is our opinion that while the detail of the drawing track was executed in some strikingly lovely patterns of overlapped tracery, the integral track shows the most wholeness, coherence and vitality of life as a mirror of the true self. This reinforces the expectation of the hypothesis that tools emphasizing connection between idea and physicality will increase wholeness while tools that do the opposite decrease wholeness. The tools explored here are not to be monolithically accepted or shunned, but to be used for the advantages they present with an eye kept to the drawbacks discovered. Of course, confirmation bias on our part is a risk, and repeated tests are needed. We encourage discussion on the matter.

None of the tracks are perfect. Bryan reported that he was "not done" at the point of closing and continued to develop the tiles after the experiment ended. But the goal was not to "finish," the goal was to document how methods impacted progress in pursuit of the objective of living form. And in that respect, this project was a success. Further explorations will be made.

9. References

Alexander, Christopher, Ishikawa, S., & Silverstein, M. (2010). A Pattern Language: Towns, buildings, construction. New York: Oxford Univ. Press.

Alexander, Christopher. (2004). The Nature of Order: Book One, the Phenomenon of Life. London: Taylor & Francis.

Alexander, Christopher (2002). Notes on the Synthesis of Form. Cambridge, Mass. [u.a.: Harvard Univ. Press.

Banz, George (1985). An Iterative Approach to Computer-Aided Architectural Design. Journal of Architectural and Planning Research, 2 (3), 187-200.

Callon, M. (1987). "Society in the Making: The Study of Technology as a Tool for Sociological Analysis." in The Social Construction of Technological Systems. Bijker, W.E., Hughes, T.P., and Pinch, T.J., eds. Cambridge, MA: MIT Press.

Descartes, René (2017). Discourse on Method. Broadview Press.

Descartes, René (2016). Principles of Philosophy. Lanham: Dancing Unicorn Books.

Ikeda, Y., & Kyōto Kokuritsu Kindai Bijutsukan. (2002). Vom Sofakissen zum Städtebau: Hermann Muthesius und der deutsche Werkbund: Modern design in Deutschland 1900-1927. Kyoto, Japan: National Museum of Modern Art.

Leibniz, G. W., Cook, Daniel J. and Rosemont, Henry (1994) Writings on China. Chicago: Open Court.

Leibniz, G. W., & Strickland, L. (2014). Leibniz's Monadology: A new translation and guide. Edinburgh: Edinburgh University Press.

Leibniz, G. W., & Loemker, L. E. (1989). Philosophical papers and letters. Dordrecht, Holland: Kluwer Academic.

Leibniz, G. W., & Kirchmann, J. H. (1878). Theodicee: 1. u. 2. Leipzig: Erich Koschny.

Protzen, Jean Pierre (1980). The Poverty of the Pattern Language, Concrete: Journal of the Students in the Department of Architecture, November,1977; University of California, Berkeley; reprinted in Design Studies, vol. I, no. 5 (London, July 1980)

Quayle, Moura (1987). Computer-Aided Participatory Design: Sitesee. Journal of Architectural and Planning Research, 4(4).

Skarmeas, George. (2010). From HABS to BIM: Personal Experiences, Thoughts, and Reflections. APT Bulletin, 41(4).

Staal, Frits. (2008) Discovering the Vedas: Origins, Mantras, Rituals, Insights. New Delhi: Penguin Books.

A Pattern Language for Designing Regenerative Refugee Camps

Crawford, Gregory
Tittle, Nick
Sulzbach-Petry, Maina
Godeau, Geoffroy
Deriemaeker, Brecht

Our contribution is towards improving the impoverished conditions that the 65 million displaced people
currently find themselves in; refugee camps, slums and
other haphazard and neglected informal settlements
around the world. Today's problem solving formula
is in critical need of fundamental reconsideration. By
utilizing systems-thinking, permaculture design and a
pattern language, we seek to offer regenerative solutions to the global refugee crisis. Effective integrated
design can leverage the embodied skills of displaced
people to empower them towards breaking the cycle
of dependency while creating settlements that contain
the quality without a name for those most in need.

Refugee, Displacement, Pattern language, Regenerative design, Human settlements

1. Context

Worldwide, upwards of 65 million people are either refugees or internally displaced; 20 people are displaced every minute, and over 10 million have been newly displaced during 2016[1].

Refugee situations are becoming increasingly protracted, with camps designed for short-term use but occupied for long-term durations. By the end of 2016, 4.1 million people are in displacement situations of over 20 years[2]. Refugee camps are often overcrowded, on marginalized land, where water and food supplies tend to be unreliable, culminating in an imbalance with human life and the ecological surroundings.

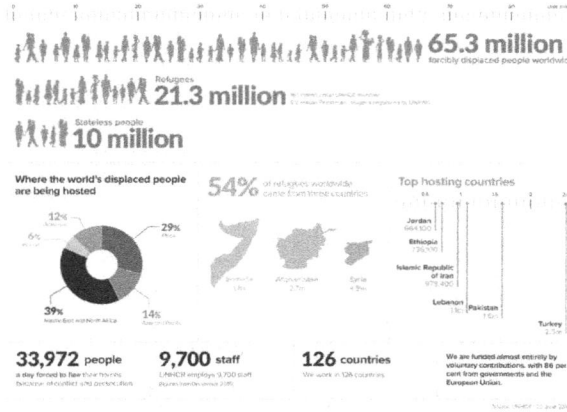

Figure 1.1 - Refugee crisis in numbers, source: UNHCR 19th June 2017

The United Nations Refugee Agency seeks the "progressive removal of restrictions on the ability of refugees to exercise their rights and seek to build linkages between the camp and host communities and anchor the camp within the local economy, infrastructure and national social protection and service delivery systems, in order to transform them into sustainable settlements"[3] However, developing regions currently host 84 per cent of the world's refugees with the least developed countries providing asylum to a growing proportion[4]. This situation creates an ever increasing pressure in those regions, where the context is already brittle; socially, economically and environmentally.

1   UNHCR, http://www.unhcr.org/globaltrends2016/
2   UNHCR, http://www.unhcr.org/globaltrends2016/
3   UNHCR, Policy on Alternative to Camps
4   UNHCR, http://www.unhcr.org/globaltrends2016/

2. Methodology

This is a collaborative research and design project between Surplus Permaculture Design, The Blueprint Alliance and Tamera, whose principal aim is to establish a pattern language and toolkit for regenerative refugee camp design, operation and maintenance that:

» fits into the current humanitarian response and development sector

» offers a new paradigm for existing best practices

» enables participatory design and collaboration for stakeholders (including displaced peoples, refugees, refugee camp designers and managers, humanitarian aid agencies, governmental and non-governmental organizations).

The global humanitarian crisis of displaced people is an incredibly complex array of social, political and environmental problems attempting to be solved by dispersed actors on a global, international and local level. Such complex and evolving problems and consequences cannot be addressed through the same paradigm that created them. The prevailing cluster approach of the humanitarian world attempts to create order within the multitude of stakeholders by segregating social needs, food, shelter and safety so that each can be tracked and coordinated independently. While this approach helps aid agencies to cooperate among themselves, it often leads to fragmented solutions which do not take into account their externalities on the other systems at play. With the pattern language portrayal of an integrated holism - in this case acknowledging all facets of settlement design (politics, ecology, built environment, economics, human rights, well-being, basic needs and meaning, etc.) - a profound growth and resilience through systemic inter-connectivity can emerge for the world's most vulnerable people. The pattern language invites integrative design, identifying acupuncture points and offering recommendations that create wholeness and the quality without a name. Effective design can lead settlements to regenerate human growth, environmental conditions and cross-cultural cohesion.

This pattern language is one component of a larger toolkit which provides context, solutions and steps towards regeneration. The combination creates a more robust and complete selection of considerations and strategies to solve these complex problems. The ethics, principles and guidelines give a foundation from which to work. The continuum allows users to see their current context on the regenerative scale and visualize succession towards regeneration by illustrating where improvements can be made and identifying potential solutions which fit the pattern recommendations. The entire toolkit has been designed to fit into the existing humanitarian framework, while simultaneously pushing it to evolve.

Regenerative Refugee Camp Design Toolkit

1. Ethics, Principles and Design Guidelines

Core ethics, principles and guidelines direct and inform design decisions and promote effective action to achieve change and regeneration

2. Regenerative Continuum

Contextualized solutions placed upon a continuum of outcomes - from degenerative towards regenerative.

3. Pattern Language

92 pattern problem/solution sets for refugee camp design and management

The regenerative toolkit will first be applied to a 200-person model site in Portugal as a proof of concept of regenerative ethical guidelines, patterns and outcomes. The model site will provide a double-feedback loop between the real-world demonstration site and the associated emerging pattern language.

3. Pattern Language Structure

This pattern language is an evolving family of problem/solution sets seeking to engage all aspects of settlement design and maintenance. Figure 3.1 shows the familial branching.

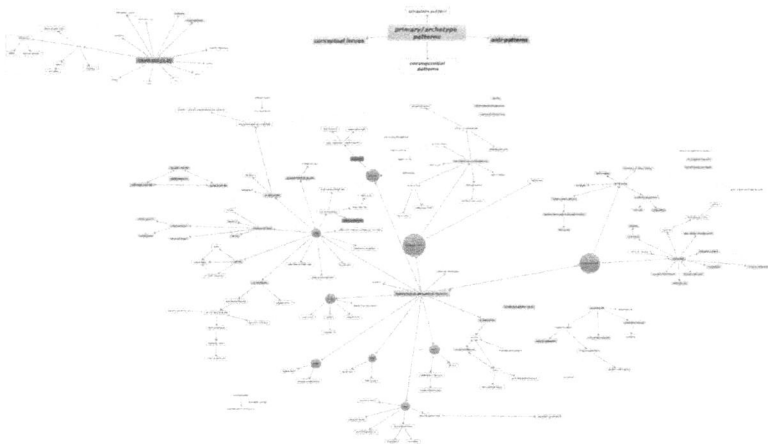

Figure 3.1 - Family tree

Our pattern language structure is differentiated into families (Figure 3.2) which correspond to the cluster approach within the realm of humanitarian aid. The structure within each family of the language starts at the broadest level and details towards household-scale problems. Each family set is a whole in and of itself, yet has ties and links to the other families so that the entire language is itself a whole. A card deck format has been chosen to allow users maximum mobility and flexibility. As each family is a set, contextualized cross-family groupings can also be made that form specific wholes for specific situations. See figure 3.3 as an example.

Figure 3.2 - Family iconography

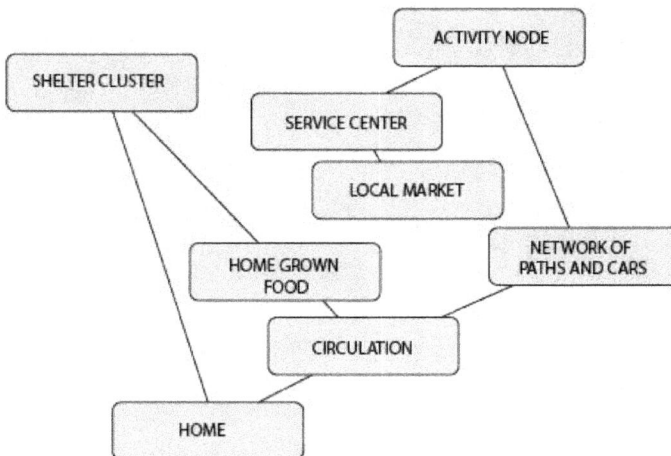

Figure 3.3 - Pattern grouping

Our pattern language has close familial relations to Christopher Alexander's original pattern language and thus builds upon and interacts with his. Many patterns Alexander laid out for a city, village or household are still relevant within the humanitarian sector and refugee camps, with simple, small tweaks. When possible we have attempted to utilize Alexander's existing patterns and have incorporated them into our language structure.

In addition to the eight families, there are two sets of additional cards: the design parameter cards and perception cards. Our pattern language is intended to be utilized by non-experts, thus the design parameter cards give guidance from various points of view such as Christopher Alexander's 15 properties, permaculture design, systems thinking, cradle to cradle design and scale of permanence. The perception cards provide assorted considerations which overlay

onto one's chosen patterns. Selection depends on the circumstance, use-case and the stake-holders involved and include 'balance', 'harmony', 'immediacy of need', 'sequence', and many others.

4. Example Patterns

Figure 4.1 - SHELTER CLUSTER, front of the pattern card

Shelters are often placed in ways that isolate individual units, undermining any opportunity for shelters to relate and communicate with one another. Shelter placement must allow for the formation of strong, collectivized and unified wholes. Arranging shelters into clusters permits interrelation, highlighting the space between units and respective orientation. Shelter arrangement affects the dynamism of personal and shared space, while creating conditions for sense of belonging, identity and safety. See Figure 4.1 and 4.2 for SHELTER CLUSTER pattern card.

⊡ PROBLEM

× The way shelters are grouped and arranged strongly influences the re-establishment of social life, ACCESS TO SERVICES, and impact on environment.

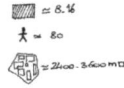

⊞ FACTORS

+ Degree of permanence
+ INTAKE PROTOCOL
+ RELATION TO SOCIAL REGION
+ Culturally appropriate
+ Climate appropriate
+ Vernacular architecture
+ Family unit size & spatial preferences
+ SERVICE CENTERS
+ Sanitation
+ Active Participation
+ Time since displacement
+ Camp residents + management relationship
+ Public Space
+ Shelter

‖ RECOMMENDATIONS

As per the layout of COMMUNITY UNITS, arrange houses to form very rough but identifiable clusters of 8-16 households, totalling about 80 people. Orient clusters around PUBLIC SPACE, gardens, and service access points (toilet, shower, refuse bins, water). A minimum cluster area of 2,400 sq m; 3,600m is preferred. The basic cluster design should correspond as closely as possible to that with which the refugees are most familiar, utilizing active participation, integrated design, and climate appropriate solutions. Relationship and unity among each SHELTER strengthens the resulting SHELTER CLUSTER.

SHELTER CLUSTER

Figure 4.2 - SHELTER CLUSTER, back of the pattern card

Figure 4.3 - ACCESS TO WATER, front of the pattern card

Ultimately, our relationship to water must become personalized, re-aligned with regional and local sources, culminating in a comprehensive and curative understanding of the water cycle - something we both depend upon and are a part of. See figure 4.3 and 4.4 for ACCESS TO WATER pattern cards.

PROBLEM

× Water is a vital building block for life and is a prerequisite for human health, safety, and fulfillment.

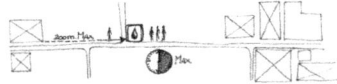

RECOMMENDATIONS

Identify settlement location within the REGIONAL WATERSHED to facilitate human connection to water source and use. Access to water must be culturally appropriate, with facilities centrally located per SHELTER CLUSTER and not too far from dwellings, with minimum waiting times. Adequate water for all needs must be provided, ensuring equitable distribution and equitable access for all stakeholders. Utilize WATER IN THE LANDSCAPE, built-in redundancy, water purification, and when possible gravity-fed systems, to ensure reliability and safety of water supply. Additionally, active participation of displaced people, surrounding host community, and other sectors should be involved in water system development and operation to ensure integrated design.

FACTORS

+ Scarcity and abundance of water
+ WATER IN THE LANDSCAPE
+ Need for ACCESS TO WATER at all times
+ BIOREGION
+ CLIMATE APPROPRIATE
+ BRITTLE ENVIRONMENT
+ Pollution
+ SANITATION
+ WASTEWATER REUSE
+ CULTURALLY APPROPRIATE
+ GENDER ROLES
+ AGE-RELATED ROLES
+ Erosive and enhancing potentials (environmental and social)
+ Politics and regional relationship to water (used and viewed)
+ Human and non-human beneficiaries of regional water sources

ACCESS TO WATER

Figure 4.4 - ACCESS TO WATER, back of the pattern card

Figure 4.5 - PUBLIC SPACE, front of the pattern card

Within the compact confines of a refugee camp, private space alone cannot provide the sense of community, camaraderie and belonging that people yearn for and deserve. Public space allows for relaxation, self-expression and accidental as well as intentional meetings. See figure 4.5 and 4.6 for PUBLIC SPACE pattern cards.

PROBLEM

PROBLEM

× Public space is where community life happens. Well designed public spaces have a huge impact on perceived and actual safety of residents creating bonds and human activity.

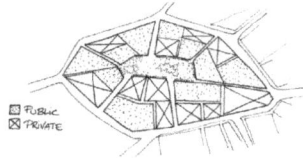

FACTORS

+ Degree of permanence
+ Cultural fracture
+ Size of camp
+ RELATION TO SOCIAL REGION
+ GREEN SPACE
+ CIRCULATION
+ SHELTER
+ NETWORK OF PATHS AND CARDS
+ COMMUNITY UNIT
+ BIOREGION
+ SAFETY
+ MALE/FEMALE DYNAMIC

RECOMMENDATIONS

Create a mosaic of private and public spaces designed around ACTIVITY NODES; the personality of a given public space is largely derived from its associated COMMUNITY UNIT. Connect public spaces to private areas with a NETWORK OF PATHS AND CARS, and ring public spaces with community activities and smaller intimate public spaces. Place public spaces within view of SHELTER CLUSTER, MARKETPLACE, and/or other SERVICE CENTER. Make the public spaces no greater than 15 sq. M/ per average person in the area, and no more than 30 M wide in the short direction. Accentuate the public space with GREEN SPACE, PUBLIC OUTDOOR ROOMS, SOMETHING ROUGHLY IN THE MIDDLE, and PLACES TO SIT.

PUBLIC SPACE

Figure 4.6 - PUBLIC SPACE, back of the pattern card

Figure 4.7 - HOMEGROWN FOOD, front of the pattern card

If the source of food production is un-tethered from where it is consumed, land degradation is likely. The closer to home food is grown, the more likely a caretaker relationship can develop, so that environmental regeneration can occur. See figure 4.7 and 4.8 for HOME GROWN FOOD pattern card.

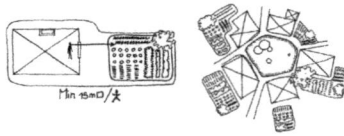

PROBLEM

× Food prodution results in cooperation or exploitation of the environment. Local food production and regional sourcing are an integral part of food security, nutrition and connection with the environment.

FACTORS

+ GREEN SPACE
+ PUBLIC SPACE
+ MARKET PLACE
+ ACCESS TO MATERIALS
+ ACCESS TO INFORMATION
+ RELATION TO SOCIAL REGION
+ Skill pool
+ Climate appropriate
+ BIOREGION
+ FOOD SECURITY
+ Culturally appropriate

HOMEGROWN FOOD

RECOMMENDATIONS

Individuals and community clusters need access to land, materials, and information to manifest FOOD SECURITY. Minimum 15 sq m per person should be allocated for food production and must be located as close to housing clusters as possible (if not possible, utilize vertical space). Kitchen gardens ideally should be located next to each shelter, while larger staple crops and fruit trees can be planted in PUBLIC SPACES. Culturally appropriate animals should be incorporated as close as healthy sanitation standards permit. Utilize integrated design INTEGRATED DESIGN to coordinate symbiotic relationships for of COMPOST, SEED SAVING, NUTRIENT CYCLING and DOMESTIC WATER USE.

Figure 4.8 - HOMEGROWN FOOD, back of the pattern card

Figure 4.9 - SERVICE CENTERS, front of the pattern card

Accessibility to various services hinges upon the physical distance from one's home to services and the ease with which one can access them. Services should be aggregated in order to allow for convenient and efficient access. See figure 4.9 and 4.10 for SERVICE CENTERS pattern card.

PROBLEM

× The distribution and interconnectivity of services offered affects the population's ability to equitably receive, offer and exchange services.

FACTORS

+ LOCAL TOWN HALL
+ NECKLACE OF COMMUNITY PROJECTS
+ SMALL SERVICES WITHOUT RED TAPE
+ CIRCULATION
+ MARKET PLACE
+ PUBLIC SPACE

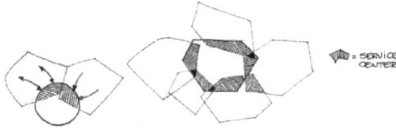

SERVICE CENTERS

RECOMMENDATION

Wherever communities overlap, there is inherent potential for human interactivity. Along the boundary of COMMUNITY UNITS (clusters, neighborhoods, blocks, sectors, settlements), foster ACTIVITY NODES and access points which hold service centers. Service centers should be grouped around a public square, have direct access to a public thoroughfare, be as autonomous as far as possible, employ members from the immediate communities, and form a combination of facilities which are mutually supportive. Service type and size corresponds to the scale of the surrounding COMMUNITY UNITS (i.e. clinic at neighborhood level, health center at block level, hospital at sector level, referral hospital at regional level).

Figure 4.10 - SERVICE CENTERS, back of the pattern card

Figure 4.11 - ACTIVITY NODES, front of the pattern card

Service centers, public spaces, markets and community facilities should be nested and balanced within a greater whole; the more diverse and relevant (culturally and climatically) the range of facilities and activities, the more successful the totality can be. See figure 4.11 and 4.12 for ACTIVITY NODES pattern card.

⊠ **PROBLEM**

× Intersection points create unique opportunities for human interaction and enrichment by collecting services, resources, information, and belonging within dynamic multi-use spaces.

∷ **FACTORS**

+ CIRCULATION
+ Access and distribution
+ ACCESS TO INFORMATION
+ SERVICE CENTERS
+ CAMP SIZE
+ COMMUNITY UNITS
+ NETWORK OF PATHS AND CARS
+ PATH SHAPE
+ SHELTER CLUSTER
+ PUBLIC SPACE
+ MARKET PLACE
+ LOCAL TOWN HALL
+ NECKLACE OF COMMUNITY PROJECTS

ACTIVITY NODES

∷ **RECOMMENDATION**

Create nodes of activity throughout the community, spread about 300 meters apart. These nodes should correspond to junctions between similar COMMUNITY UNITS (i.e. where four SHELTER CLUSTERS form a neighborhood, or four neighborhoods form a block). Then, at the center of each node, make a PUBLIC SPACE, and surround it with a combination of mutually supportive community facilities (MARKETPLACE, SERVICE CENTER, LOCAL TOWN HALL, and/or NECKLACE OF COMMUNITY PROJECTS).

Figure 4.12 - ACTIVITY NODES, back of the pattern card

Figure 4.13 - CIRCULATION, front of the pattern card

Movement within refugee camps is often heavily restricted, depriving access to services, information and facilities while also complicating effective distribution. Efficient and safe movement requires careful curation and systemic consideration. See figure 4.13 and 4.14 for CIRCULATION pattern card.

PROBLEM

x   The settlement layout and movement options determines how safely and effectively people are able to move, interact, and access good & services.

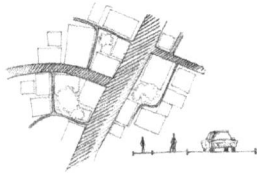

FACTORS

+   Modes of transportation
+   Degree of permanence
+   SIZE OF CAMP
+   COMMUNITY UNITS
+   SHELTER CLUSTER
+   SERVICE CENTERS
+   MARKET PLACE
+   ACTIVITY NODES
+   Active participation
+   EXCHANGE
+   SETTLEMENT ENTRANCE
+   RELATION TO SOCIAL REGION

RECOMMENDATION:

CIRCULATION

Effective circulation promotes a safe, user-friendly layout. In order for traffic design types to correlate to their respective COMMUNITY UNIT scale, various patterns apply per condition:
    Settlement & Sector: RING ROADS, PARALLEL ROADS, ACTIVITY NODES
    Block & Neighborhood: PARALLEL ROADS, NETWORK OF PATH AND CARS, BIKE PATHS, ACTIVITY NODES
    SHELTER CLUSTER: NETWORK OF PATHS AND CARS, BIKE PATHS, PATH SHAPE
Where paths and roads intersect, establish RAISED ROAD CROSSING. Where roads intersect, establish 'T-JUNCTIONS'. Local transport areas; high speed arteries / ring roads; parallel roads; activity nodes; T-junctions; networks of paths and cars; road crossing, PATH SHAPE; bike paths.

Figure 4.14 - CIRCULATION, back of the pattern card

Figure 4.15 - RELATION TO REGION, front of the pattern card

Settlements must not be isolated; in order for environmental and social regeneration to occur, settlements must regain their relative placement with their contextual region.

Symbiotic, reciprocal and harmonious exchange is required for long-term regional stability. See figure 4.15 and 4.16 for RELATION TO REGION pattern card.

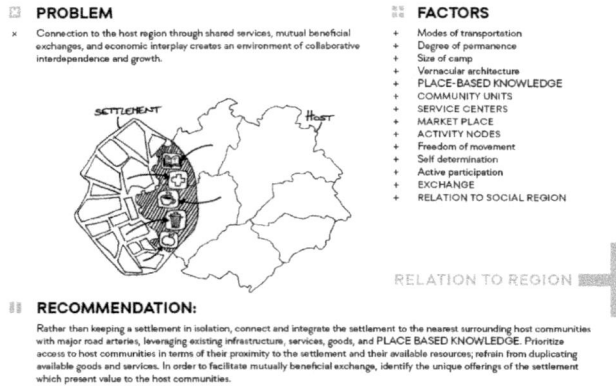

PROBLEM

x Connection to the host region through shared services, mutual beneficial exchanges, and economic interplay creates an environment of collaborative interdependence and growth.

FACTORS

+ Modes of transportation
+ Degree of permanence
+ Size of camp
+ Vernacular architecture
+ PLACE-BASED KNOWLEDGE
+ COMMUNITY UNITS
+ SERVICE CENTERS
+ MARKET PLACE
+ ACTIVITY NODES
+ Freedom of movement
+ Self determination
+ Active participation
+ EXCHANGE
+ RELATION TO SOCIAL REGION

RELATION TO REGION

RECOMMENDATION:

Rather than keeping a settlement in isolation, connect and integrate the settlement to the nearest surrounding host communities with major road arteries, leveraging existing infrastructure, services, goods, and PLACE BASED KNOWLEDGE. Prioritize access to host communities in terms of their proximity to the settlement and their available resources; refrain from duplicating available goods and services. In order to facilitate mutually beneficial exchange, identify the unique offerings of the settlement which present value to the host communities.

Figure 4.16 - RELATION TO REGION, back of the pattern card

5. Pattern Utilization

The holistic nature of pattern theory lends itself to extremely complex situations, such as the humanitarian crisis. The pattern recommendations build upon existing humanitarian standards but bring about a life-enhancing element that is not always present in refugee camps or displaced settlements. To demonstrate the potential of this pattern language and associated regenerative toolkit, it will be applied to a demonstration and education site in Portugal, acting as a proof of concept and feedback mechanism. The site will be a living example of the potentiality and will be utilized for aid advocacy, trainings, conferences and peace reconciliation talks.

To-date, two schematic designs have engaged the pattern language and are in beta trials. Project implementation will occur at Tamera, a peace research village in Odemira, Portugal. Each design attempts to reconcile a major contradiction within the humanitarian sector. Figure 5.1 addresses the difficulty of climate appropriate strategies, while Figure 5.3 seeks to portray the range of strategies available within the three distinct states of permanence.

Schematic 1: Climate Appropriate

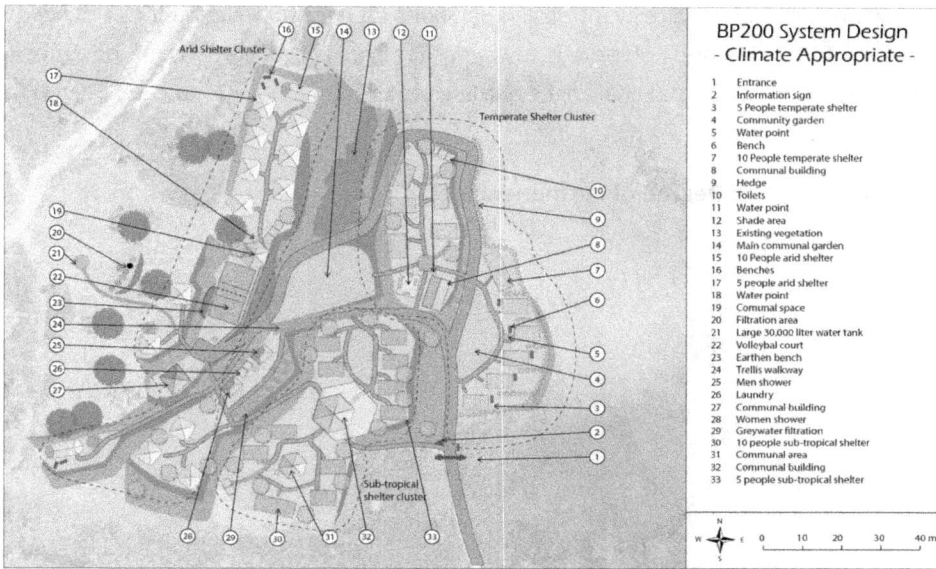

Figure 5.1 - Climate Appropriate Schematic design

In the face of the expanding global displacement crisis, one-size fits all solutions are being employed as a given assumption that a good solution always works. This ignores the complex web of interrelated factors at play on an environmental, social and political level.

Climatically appropriate design solutions must be employed to utilize local knowledge, materials and resources in order for a regenerative settlement to be realized.

Figure 5.2 - Permanence essence drawing

This design proposes creative solutions for three different climates: temperate, tropical and arid. Each climate has been paired with a particular refugee crisis around the world to draw awareness and offer relevant design solutions (Saharawi in Algeria for arid; Syrians in Lebanon for temperate; Rohingya in Myanmar for tropical). All systems are designed to reflect the unique needs and challenges of the given climate as well as to capitalize on the particular opportunities.

Schematic Design 2: Degree of Permanence

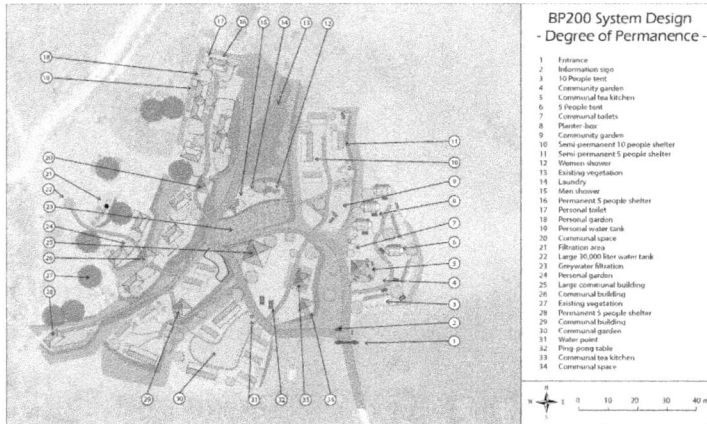

BP200 System Design
- Degree of Permanence -

1   Entrance
2   Information sign
3   10 People tent
4   Community garden
5   Communal tea kitchen
6   5 People tent
7   Communal toilets
8   Planter box
9   Community garden
10 Semi-permanent 10 people shelter
11 Semi-permanent 5 people shelter
12 Women shower
13 Existing vegetation
14 Laundry
15 Men shower
16 Permanent 5 people shelter
17 Personal toilet
18 Personal garden
19 Personal water tank
20 Communal space
21 Filtration area
22 Large 30,000 liter water tank
23 Greywater filtration
24 Personal garden
25 Large communal building
26 Communal building
27 Existing vegetation
28 Permanent 5 people shelter
29 Communal building
30 Communal garden
31 Water point
32 Ping-pong table
33 Communal tea kitchen
34 Communal space

Figure 5.3 - Degree of Permanence schematic design

Camps continue to be designed for temporary use, even as the world sees no resolution for many protracted refugee situations (a situation in which 25,000 or more refugees from the same nationality have been in exile for five or more years in a given asylum country), conditions which approximately 12 million people find themselves in. Furthermore, there is a resistance that inhibits refugees to fully settle in a new place; one that is not their own.

Figure 5.4 - Degree of Permanence drawing

When systems become permanent and large decisions are taken, they imply that the way back home is closed. As a baseline it is clear that when possible long-term solutions should be designed and enacted, but at any level of permanence human fulfillment and determination must be prioritized; and this looks different everywhere. This system design proposes a range of appropriate solutions for 3 states of permanence and the relative changes for shelters, food, water, energy and social organization.

6. Conclusion

Through the application of Christopher Alexander's pattern theory and the creation of centers and wholes that provide the quality without a name, social and environmental regeneration within refugee camps is possible. We have created a deck of pattern cards to be utilized by refugee camp managers, funders and various stakeholders as well as perception and design guideline cards which are used in combination with the regenerative continuum. All patterns are hinging and building upon existing standards and practices within the humanitarian sector. To continue development of the pattern language, it is being integrated into a demonstration model site that will act as a double feedback loop for the pattern language.

The central role of artifacts in processes of knowledge production: an empirical investigation of three projects of participatory urban design using Pattern Languages

David, Aurelio
Institute for Urban Planning and Design, University of Duisburg-Essen
aurelio.david@stud.uni-due.de

Research on participatory urban design and architecture lacks insight on how experts and laymen interact to generate knowledge. Understanding such interactions is relevant under the following assumptions. First, citizens are repositories of a distributed local knowledge (Rydin, 2007; Corburn, 2003, 2005). Second, part of such knowledge is vital to addressing a design problem (Edelenbos, van Buuren, and van Schie, 2003; Fischer, 2000; Rittel and Webber, 1973). Third, participation is the only way for experts to get exposed to local knowledge.

Building on some of the partial findings from my PhD dissertation, in this paper, I study three projects of participatory design carried out with Pattern Languages (Alexander et al., 1977), e.g. Mexicali (Alexander et al., 1985), Vellore (Davis, Week, and Moses, 1993), and Eishin (Alexander, Alexander and Neis, 2012). A qualitative investigation based on document analysis and interviews with two designers involved in the projects reveals the central role of patterns and other artifacts, e.g. mockups and marking flags, in generating and implementing design-oriented knowledge.

In particular, I argue that artifacts, and pattern languages in particular, (1) may act as containers and displayers of knowledge; and (2) can ground ideas and design principles into an intelligible form. Finally, I discuss the lessons learned from the Pattern Language, and how they can positively influence other participatory design methods. .

Pattern Language, Public Participation, Boundary Objects, Qualitative Research, Case Study Research.

1. Introduction

1.1. Public participation in urban disciplines. A democratic approach to decision-making

The debate on public participation applied to urban disciplines, e.g. urban planning, urban design, and architecture, has historically been revolving around topics of democracy, justice, and distribution of power. As a prominent example, the paper that popularized the idea of public participation, Arnstein's A Ladder of Public Participation (1969), has a strong political and transformative implications.

The emphasis on the political nature of public participation was a reflection of the failure of the managerial model of decision-making in most fields of human activity, including urban planning (Hall, 1988; Lane, 2005). Politicians and planners proved unable to cope with the complexity of social problems of the 20th Century using top-down plans grounded on a deterministic outlook. Since Arnstein's seminal paper, practitioners and scholars from various disciplines have been conceptualizing and testing alternative paradigms of participatory decision-making. In the urban sector, their effort was initially focused on urban planning because of its evident political implications. In this context, it is worth mentioning Davidoff's Advocacy Planning (Davidoff, 1965), Friedman's Transactive Planning (Friedman, 1973), and Healey's Communicative Planning (Healey, 1992). Despite their theoretical and procedural differences, these paradigms proposed frameworks for a more inclusive urban planning. To what extent their preaching permeated national legislations and professional practice, is the subject of other works.

Suffice to say that, where participation is a widely understood and shared approach in urban planning, its application in the practice of urban design and, especially, architecture is comparably small. Arguably, the "small" scale at which urban design and architecture operate encompasses a lesser degree of conflict and, therefore, of public interest. Furthermore, in the current procedures of architecture, the product of design, e.g. an office building or a condominium, is often designed for a "standardized user" because the developer has little, or no, cognition of who will buy, rent, or use it. These circumstances have discouraged the adoption of participatory approaches. For if an architect is appointed to design a high-density residential complex, which units are sold upon construction, who should be involved in the definition of its internal layout and facade?

1.2. Beyond democracy: the epistemological value of participatory design

Despite such dilemmas, since the 1970s, a handful of architects have been experimenting with participatory design, a practice that integrates citizens' input into all phases of design. Giancarlo De Carlo, Christopher Alexander, Jahn Gehl, and Alejandro Aravena[1] are only a few of the most prominent contributors to this practice.

In some of their works, these architects demonstrated that participation may enrich a design process with the knowledge held by local communities. More importantly, their work revealed the epistemological dimension of public participation: when properly engaged, citizens can contribute to a design process not only by expressing preferences, but also by co-generating relevant knowledge and properly orienting the assumptions underpinning a project.

The idea that laymen can contribute to addressing apparently complex and technical issues has emerged through the work of several philosophers and scholars, albeit with no specific reference to urban planning, design, and architecture. The most pertinent description of this situation was conceptualized by the German philosopher Horst Rittel (1984) under the notion of symmetry of ignorance. "The use of knowledge is a central element in achieving change through planning" (Rydin, 2007), but knowledge is unevenly distributed among various stakeholders outside traditional planning organization (Sandercock, 1997). The implication of this idea is that, the knowledge built up by planners and designers throughout years of practice might not be self-sufficient to address "the next project" (Friedman, 1973). Because every project is situated in a different socio-cultural, and geographical context, experts may address it adopting false assumptions, which may result in substandard design solutions (Newig, Pahl- Wostl, and Sigel, 2005). Of course, this predicament does not apply

---

1   Many more names could be added to the inventory of architects adopting participatory design. This list includes those who contributed the most to spread the principle and methods of participatory design through their writings and in virtue of their coverage in architectural journals.

to every project and, in some instances, the cost of undertaking participation might not justify its epistemological benefits (Irvin and Stansbury, 2004). However, today, planners and architects often disregard the utility of public input not because of the simplicity of a project, but because of their belief that their expertise does not require validation from the public.

Until architects and urban designers gain confidence in the epistemological value of public participation, it will continue to be relegated to its political dimension only.

1.3. The aim of this paper

Drawing from the PhD dissertation of the author, this paper attempts to bring insights into the mechanisms underlying lay-expert interaction, e.g. the system of reciprocal influences fostered by the communication between designers and citizens during instances of participatory design carried out using Pattern Languages. In particular, this paper focuses on the role of artifacts, e.g. sketches, maps, the pattern languages, and marking flags in conveying the image of a product of design and building a shared pool of knowledge.

2. Methodology

This research relies on qualitative investigation of three case studies of participatory design conducted by the Center for Environmental Structure (CES) between the 1970s and 1980s. These case studies are the projects conducted in Mexicali, Vellore, and Eishin. The design process of each project represents the unit of analysis of this research.

To address the risks of qualitative approaches, e.g. biases and lack of internal and external validity of the obtained results, the author designed this research according to the procedural framework proposed by Eisenhardt (1989) and the methodological suggestions from Yin (2011). Data have been collected from multiple sources, e.g. in-depth content analyses of relevant literature (Alexander et al., 1985; Davis, Week, and Moses, 1993; Alexander, Alexander Moore, and Neis, 2012), documents (e.g. maps, diagrams, and architects' field notes), and interviews with two of the leading designers involved in the three projects, Arch. H.N. and Arch. H.D. Data has been organized into a comparative analytical framework comprised of a set of matrices, reflecting the two analytical steps recommended by Eisenhardt (1989), namely within-case, and cross-case, analyses.

3. Results

Despite some methodological differences, the analyzed design processes followed a similar three-step procedure.

First, definition of a Pattern Language. Architects laid out a verbal action plan developed from a set of interviews (e.g. Eishin), group meetings (e.g. Mexicali), or ethnographic research (e.g. Vellore). The outcome of this first design stage was the definition of a general pattern language, i.e. a collection of guidelines to orient the design process. In all case studies, the pattern language was then used as a basis for a collective discussion aimed at improving it.

Second, implementation of patterns governing site layout. The architects relied on selected patterns to develop a layout for the site. This process was conducted on site and was influenced by members of the local communities. Flags were used to mark key spots and "materialize" the volume of the buildings and their relationship with one another. It was at this stage that the first technical drawings of the area were drafted to reflect the position of the flag on the site.

Third, implementation of patterns governing construction. Buildings were designed and built on site, consulting pertinent members of the local community. Families would design their own house at Vellore and Mexicali. At Eishin, teachers would help in the internal layout of classrooms, while students would decide on the cafeteria of the campus. The pattern language would be used as a compass to discuss on key spatial relationships and the order in which they ought to be implemented.

The analysis of the three case studies revealed some recurring mechanisms governing communication and knowledge generation processes. Such mechanisms can be traced back to three factors (1) a step-by-step design process, (2) on-site involvement, and (3) the use of the pattern language and other tools to ground discussion on a shared reality (Figure 1).

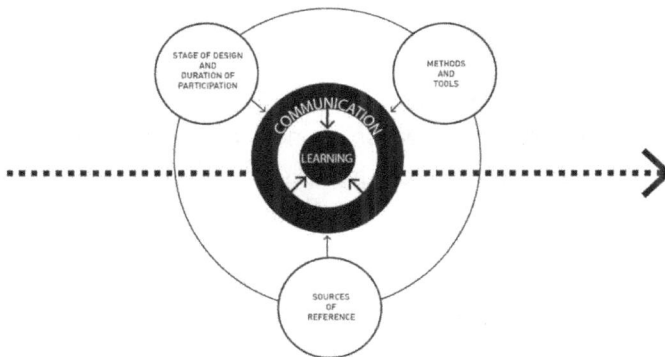

Figure 1: Conceptual diagram illustrating the key factors governing lay-expert interaction and knowledge generation processes.

The interplay of these three features explains how participation affected design in the analyzed projects. Likewise, it provides a framework to understand the process of communication and knowledge generation.

3.1. Stage and duration of participation: a multi-level, pyramidal involvement

3.1.1. The multi-level, pyramidal mode of public participation. Efficiency and pertinence.

The three case studies present similar patterns of public involvement. At the beginning of each project, architects organized large group discussions in order to establish a first contact with local community, explain the goal of the projects, and capture public aspirations. As major design decisions about the project were fixed, e.g. the program and the budget, the architects worked with smaller groups of citizens (or individuals) to determine the general site layout and, finally, to develop individual buildings.

> *"So, I think [participation] was relevant at all levels, but it was more like a pyramid: at the beginning, there were many more people, and the more and more the process developed, there were more particularly interested people involved. And that happened a lot because then we could [...] go into the business at a much more deeper way, rather than having to explain to a lot of people what we were actually doing". [Arch H.N., interview about the Eishin project]*

H.N. testimony refers to the Eishin project, but evidence from Vellore and Mexicali reveals that they were also characterized by a multi-level, pyramidal mode of engagement.

In general, a multi-level, pyramidal organization of participation responds to two principles: the "principle of efficiency" and the "principle of pertinence".

Efficiency pertains to complete a design process without unnecessary slowdown and waste of resources. As a general rule, participation is synonymous with involving large groups into a decision-making process. Yet, decisions are taken more efficiently by small groups. As a design process progresses, certain decisions at the larger scale must be fixed in order to deal with a smaller scale.

Pertinence implies that citizens ought to partake design decisions proportionally to their stake on certain parts of the masterplan. For example, the whole community has a stake in how the site is laid out. However, the internal space of a house should be determined by the family that would own it.

Large-group participation at all times would demand extra time to update everyone on the latest decisions and would increase the risk of conflicts over decisions already made. Instead, organizing participation in sessions of large and small groups (i.e. in a multi-level, or "pyramidal" way) was an effective solution to this conundrum.

At Mexicali and Vellore, a multi-level, pyramidal participation was mainly due to the "principle of pertinence". In both projects, the common land was shaped by the whole community through group meetings. The design of individual houses, however, was in control of the individual families. In both projects, special attention was paid in the definition of the boundaries between public and private space. Such decisions were crucial to move from large-group to small-group participation without conflicts.

At Eishin, the "principle of pertinence" followed another logic, since the dichotomy "public-private" could not be applied to the campus. There, the general layout was constructed and approved by the community as a whole, while individual buildings were developed together with small groups of teachers, administrators, and students, according to their use. For example, the math teachers worked on the shape of ordinary classrooms. The music teacher defined the details of the music room; the students, the cafeteria. And so on (see Chapter 12 of Alexander, Moore Alexander, and Neis, 2012). In this case, "pertinence" is associated with the proclivity of certain groups to use, and know about, certain spaces.

To implement multi-level, pyramidal participation, the architects devised a step-by-step, or piecemeal, design process. The division of a process into its sub-parts was essential to determine "when to involve who", e.g. the whole community or an individual member. By fostering participation at all stages of design, the architects elicited continuous public feedback on all aspects of a project, thus controlling its quality and adherence with the initial goals.

The following section explores the tools and strategies that supported this kind of step-by-step, multi-level participatory design process.

3.2. Tools and methods for participation: the pattern language, flags, and the contact with reality

Three kinds of artifacts were used throughout the design processes of the three case studies: (1) the pattern language, (2) marking flags, and (3) full-scale mockups. The tools described in this section enabled the piecemeal participatory design (explained in Paragraph 3.1), while fostering the emergence of local knowledge (explained in Paragraph 3.3).

3.2.1. The pattern language as an explicit repository of shared knowledge

The investigation of the Mexicali, Eishin, and Vellore projects reveals variations in the integration the pattern language in their design processes. These differences could be linked to multiple factors, e.g. the client, time and resources allocated, and the complexity of the project.

At Vellore, patterns were developed by the architects as a result of an extensive ethnographic research prior to any public meeting. The architects used the pattern structure as a framework to systematize their observations. Indeed, unlike the Mexicali and Eishin pattern languages, the Vellore language appears as a systematic collection of field notes.

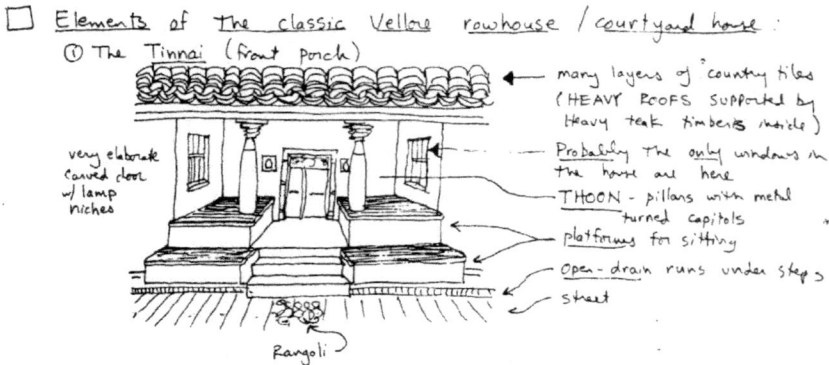

Figure 2. Excerpt from the Vellore Pattern Language. Sketch and descriptions about a traditional front porch in Vellore. Courtesy of Arch. H.D.

> "Certainly, it has "Title", it has "Sketch". It has not so much with the "Problem-Solution", but when you read it, you'll see that somehow it is in there. Not "connections with other patterns", no. That's not there. So, it's certainly more than just design guidelines, because when you will read it, you will realize the social reason for the patterns". [Arch. H.D. interview about the Vellore project]

In other words, the architects used patterns as an atlas of guidelines to understand the local environment, foreign to them, in order to prepare and discuss with the local community.

At Mexicali, the architects selected a set of patterns from previous research. Such patterns were concise and mirrored their intent for the project.

At Eishin, patterns were inspired by extensive interviews with the local community. Further meetings changed and refined the language, who was then implemented in a collective manner. Implementing a pattern language requires to follow a sequence of patterns, from the big scale to the small one. Hence, the pattern language guided the architects in defining subsequent steps. The implementation of each pattern was a moment for public consultation.

Regardless of how patterns were developed, e.g. by architects or through a collective endeavor of architects and citizens, in all three projects, patterns were explicit repositories of knowledge, accessible to all stakeholders and understandable by the local communities.

3.2.2. Marking flags and full-scale mockups

In the three projects, implementing patterns from a well-defined pattern language marked the transition from "design" to "construction". The architects from the CES conducted this phase on site, together with small groups of citizens aided by full-scale mockups of building elements and flags to mark the land.

Flags were necessary to convey the size and position of buildings on the site. With a bit of imagination, citizens could see how the physical environment would be transformed, and suggest modifications accordingly. Only when consensus was reached did the architects marked the positions of the flags on paper and prepare technical drawings. Similarly, mockups and on-site walkabouts helped to take decisions about the construction details (Figure 3).

Figure 3. Photography of the rice field of Eishin. The white flags were used to mark the land and indicate the position of corners and other spatial landmarks.
Source: http://www.livingneighborhoods.org (accessed 14 September 2017)

3.3. Sources of reference: reality, realities, and imagination.

A step-by-step approach to design, the pattern languages, marking flags, and mockups served to coordinate communication between architects and locals. To understand how these tools influenced the input and feedback provided by the public, it is necessary to delve into the sources of references used by the members of the Eishin, Vellore, and Mexicali communities in the respective design processes.

Evidence from all three case studies suggests that, in fact, reality was a common and recurring source of reference throughout the participatory process. "Reality" assumed a different meaning in each case. For example, the "reality" of Mexicali and Vellore was the everyday domestic life of people; while at Eishin, students and teachers tapped into their school experience. Reality was brought to the fore and related to the design task thanks to the aforementioned tools, e.g. the pattern language, marking flags, and – at Mexicali and Eishin – full-scale mockups. In particular, dealing with reality enabled people to participate in a meaningful way, since local knowledge could emerge at various points in time. In some instances, experts noticed an inclination of non-experts to provide useful and sophisticated insight only when reality was part of the discussion. This phenomenon occurred across case studies and across different stages of design, as the following section demonstrate.

3.3.1. The lack of a shared reality

During preliminary stages of design at Eishin and Vellore, participation was used as an exploratory tool. The goal of the architects was to understand to what extent local aspirations could be realistically fulfilled by the product of design. Thus, one-on-one interviews (Eishin) and group meetings (Vellore) took place when no decision was fixed yet. Evidence from interviews with the architects and literary sources suggests that, in the absence of inputs, non- experts communicated through images from their own experience and expectations. For example, the people of Vellore wished to have flat-roof, concrete houses, like the rich from the city. At Eishin, a common image emerging from interviews was modern-Japan high school concrete buildings (Alexander, Moore Alexander, and Neis, 2012:118-119). Such sources of reference produced unreliable ideas that had to be soon dismissed by the architects. For example, Davis mentions that, behind the powerful images of a modern, concrete architecture emerging at Vellore lied problems of insulation and budget.

"Because the budget for the houses was actually determined by how much money these people could pay each week [...] for a certain period of time. And that amount of money was not much. And what that meant was that they couldn't really have these concrete houses with flat roofs, because they would just be much too expensive" [Arch H.D., interview about the Vellore project]

Neis and Alexander make similar remark for the Eishin campus. The goal of the project was to design something different from modern architecture, and therefore they attempted to go beyond such ideas. (Alexander, Moore Alexander, and Neis, 2012:118)

Overall, the lack of a shared framework of reference during the preliminary stages of design brought about idiosyncratic, subjective "realities". In general, one must deal with these realities with caution. On the one hand, these creative impulses may suggest novel ways to approach a project. On the other hand, they tend to produce ideas that may not be realistically or successfully pursued. The narratives of Eishin and Vellore points to the latter.

> *"We tried to have these big meetings, to ask questions about this and that, but...I don't remember those being very effective. [...] What was effective was dealing with individuals and - also - dealing with reality. [Arch H.D., interview about the Vellore project].*

3.3.2. The emergence and negotiation of a shared reality

As design developed, certain general ideas had to be fixed and become the basis for further discussions. No process is ever straightforward, and iterations were common in the three projects analyzed. However, as a general rule, site layout has to be defined before any building can be designed, so that the latter would fit into the former. Likewise, to arrange a kitchen in a house, one must first place the entrance.

In the Eishin and Mexicali projects, general ideas were fixed in a pattern language in the form of general descriptions. The language (a document) provided the public with a framework of reference that was used in two ways: (1) to grasp the overall image of the project and (2) to anchor inputs and comments into a central place. Collective dialogue was then focused on improving the pattern language, which acted as a common repository of design-knowledge. As further inputs enriched the pattern language, the architects and the local community could flesh out a shared vision for the project.

The most detailed description of how the pattern language fostered a shared reality is an account from Eishin. In particular, the transition from the general "crude language" to the exhaustive "final language". Traces of inputs from the school community were integrated in some patterns (see Chapter 9 of Alexander, Moore Alexander, and Neis, 2012).

However, the pattern language in itself was not always sufficient to trigger relevant feedback from the public. The site layout for the Mexicali and Vellore housing projects, for example, was not developed as a pattern language. In fact, three data sources, e.g. an interview with Arch. H.D., Alexander et al. (1985), and Ruesjas (1997), mention that families did not react to the pattern language in the initial phase of site layout.

In both cases, layout decisions were taken on site, by a recursive process of consultation with local leaders. Questions like "Where is the entrance to the site?", or "Where is the temple?" informed the architects about spatial relationships to be fostered to cater to local traditions. As Arch. H.D. recalls:

> 🔾🔾 *"[...] we started to talk about very specific things, like where is the temple. [...] And they were [in a] position to answer the question. And they could say where the temple was. [For example, the temple] can't be facing a house specifically; it has to be in the so called "rounded" and circumambulate the temple. So, at that point, once real stuff was introduced, the discussion had to do with that real stuff, and not with more general issues of what's your vision and what's your image" [Arch H.D., interview about the Vellore project].*

Hence, the Vellore and Mexicali projects reveal that the pattern language is not the only, nor the primary, referential object for citizens. Reality is. Under this perspective, it is likely that the pattern language performs as a referential object only insofar as it succeeds in generating an intelligible verbal reality.

3.3.3. The concretization of a unique reality

The final stage of design involved the development and construction of individual buildings, e.g. single-family houses at Mexicali and Vellore, and the school facilities of the Eishin campus. In all case studies, this process was carried out collaboratively on-site, with the help of marking flags. At Eishin, the architects relied also on full-scale mockups of building elements. The adoption of such strategies was meant to project a 1:1 virtual reality on site. Thanks to these artifacts, architects and locals could have a general preview of the campus and the housing clusters. Flags were placed according to the guidelines from the pattern language and people could interact on the spot to suggest amendments. Overall, it was the contact with their new, emerging houses that fostered relevant inputs from the locals. In particular, the diversity of the Mexicali house plans reflects how individual choices, channeled through a smart system of piecemeal design, produced significantly different outcomes (Figure 4).

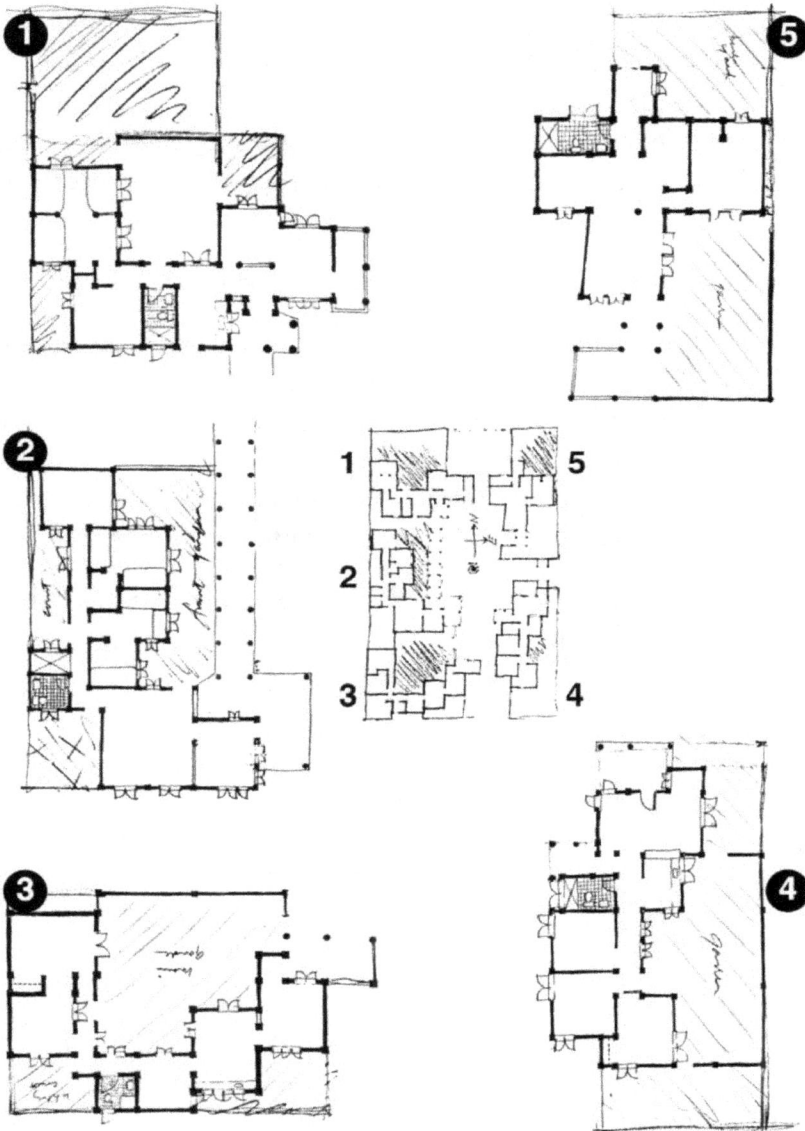

Figure 4. Collage of the Mexicali site layout (center) and the individual houses developed for the families (around). Elaborated from Alexander, et al., 1985.

3.4. Discussion

The projects at Eishin, Vellore, and Mexicali provide insight on how the pattern language can be used to promote participation and integrate local knowledge throughout all stages of a design process. Evidence obtained from the three case studies reveals how the pattern language and other artifacts (e.g. marking flags), when integrated into a piecemeal, multi-level, pyramidal mode of participation, successfully elicit local knowledge throughout multiple stages of a design process.

In fact, the structure of the pattern language mirrors and support a piecemeal mode design.

On the one hand, patterns are verbal guidelines dividing a project into its constituent parts. This allowed experts and citizens to keep the conversation focused on key issues, e.g. the COMMON and POSITIVE SPACE of the internal courtyard of Mexicali. On the other hand, patterns provide explicit instructions to develop a project. In the case of Eishin, where patterns were written and reviewed properly (Alexander, Moore Alexander, and Neis, 2012:123-127), they dictated the precise logical sequence for the construction of the campus.

Most importantly, in all projects each step of the sequence was a circumscribed arena for public consultation and negotiation (Figure 5).

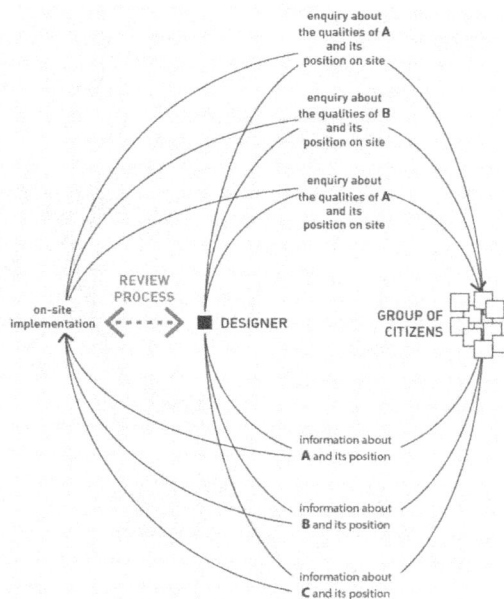

Figure 5. A diagrammatic representation of the piecemeal, one-site design process enabled by the Pattern Language. The letters A, B, and C indicate patterns. The overall diagram can be conceptualized as a series of feedback loops between architects and members of the local community.

Furthermore, the analysis revealed that non-experts need referential objects that link their experience to reality in order to sustain fruitful design-oriented conversations with experts. In the context of participatory design, referential objects are proxies for ideas and concepts about the project. They serve to convey the image of a future reality, one that includes the planned transformation of space. Different referential objects include a more or less comprehensive and detailed descriptions of a design. Hence, they pertain to different stages of design.

Overall, early stages of design require general, low-resolution descriptions, e.g. patterns and pattern languages. Patterns can emerge from citizens' ideas (Eishin), from architects' expertise (Mexicali), or from ethnographic research and observations of local environment (Vellore). Regardless, pattern language act as verbal referential objects, conveying a fragmented image of a future reality.

As a design process progresses, however, ideas need to be communicated specifically and with a higher resolution. The architects from the CES solved this problem by making decisions about buildings and building details directly on site, with the help of flags and mockups. This idea mirrors the standard protocols of design, whereby preliminary schemes are always less detailed than construction documents.

In fact, the absence of any referential object was experienced by the architects in terms of less productivity.

> *"if you ask people about: "How do you like that house?" or, you know, it was just too abstract, right. But faced with reality, I think, people could respond much more effectively". [Arch H.D., interview about the Vellore project].*

Hence, artifacts like patterns, flags, and mockups, adopted on-site, through a continuous mode of participation may create the conditions for a timely and meaningful exchange of knowledge between experts and citizens. Such artifacts seem to empower citizens with the capacity to sustain dialogue with experts, while providing an environment where local knowledge can emerge and influence design.

Finally, the case studies of Eishin, Vellore, and Mexicali provides with lessons for practitioners who are not only interested in the pattern language, but also in participatory design.

1. The pattern language can be integrated in participatory design in several ways. Its effectiveness, however, is enhanced by other principles, such as a step-by-step design-construction process, and a multi-level, "pyramidal" organization of participation.

2. Participatory design provides countless opportunities for learning from locals. To foster learning and creativity, designers need to manage the level of control they exert in a design process. By allowing citizens to be in charge of some aspect of design, unexpected and divergent insight may flow into the conversation. This may result in unconventional design that is still sensitive to the local culture.

3. When citizens are involved in design, their ideas are potentially implementable. As a consequence, the expert-citizen dichotomy tends to blur. Citizens should be treated as co-designers, i.e. their good ideas should be incorporated into the design, whereas bad ideas must be challenged.

4. To keep a good balance between broad involvement and effectiveness, experts could use the "principle of pertinence". According to this principle, locals should be involved to partake decisions about spaces in which they have a stake. For example, large groups should reach consensus over site layout and public space, while smaller interest groups should be invited to design buildings and facilities.

4. Conclusions and future outlook

This paper has explored the epistemological dimension of participatory design by exploring three projects of architecture carried out following the Pattern Language theory developed by the CES. Evidence from the case studies of Vellore, Mexicali, and Eishin suggests that three factors govern lay-expert interaction and affect knowledge generation processes. The three factors are: the stage and duration of participation,

By controlling and influencing the sources of references used by local communities, various artifacts, e.g. pattern languages and marking flags, deployed at various stages of design, e.g. preliminary or ongoing phases, elicit relevant instances of local knowledge.

Overall, the efficacy of the joint use of pattern language, flags, and mockups seems to be related to their capacity to bring reality at the center of the design process. This observation leads to two non-exclusive conclusions: (1) that non-experts are better equipped to deal with concrete, specific reality, as opposed to abstraction and (2), that non-experts need initial inputs and/or limits in order to effectively and meaningfully participate in a design process.

5. Bibliography

Alexander, C., Davis, H., Martinez, J., & Corner, D. (1985). The production of houses (Vol. 4). Oxford University Press on Demand.

Alexander, C., Ishikawa, S., Silverstein, M., i Ramió, J. R., Jacobson, M., & Fiksdahl-King, I. (1977). A pattern language (pp. 311-314). Gustavo Gili.

Alexander, C., Neis, H. J., & Alexander, M. M. (2012). The battle for the life and beauty of the earth: a struggle between two world-systems. Oxford University Press.

Arnstein, S. R. (1969). A ladder of citizen participation. Journal of the American Institute of planners, 35(4), 216-224.

Corburn, J. (2003). Bringing local knowledge into environmental decision making: Improving urban planning for communities at risk. Journal of Planning Education and Research, 22(4), 420-433.

Corburn, J. (2005). Street Science: Community Knowledge and Environmental Health Justice (Urban and Industrial Environments).

Davidoff, P. (1965). Advocacy and pluralism in planning. Journal of the American Institute of planners, 31(4), 331-338.

Davis, H., Week, D., & Moses, P. (1993). The Village Meets the City. Architecture Plus Design, 10(2), 51.

Edelenbos, J., van Buuren, A., & van Schie, N. (2011). Co-producing knowledge: joint knowledge production between experts, bureaucrats and stakeholders in Dutch water management projects. Environmental Science & Policy, 14(6), 675-684.

Eisenhardt, K. M. (1989). Building theories from case study research. Academy of management review, 14(4), 532-550.

Fischer, F. (2000). Citizens, experts, and the environment: The politics of local knowledge. Duke University Press.

Friedman, J. (1973). Retracking America: A Theory of Transactive Planning, Anchor. Garden City, TX.

Hall, P. (1988). Cities of tomorrow. Blackwell Publishers.

Healey, P. (1992). Planning through debate: the communicative turn in planning theory. Town planning review, 63(2), 143.

Irvin, R. A., & Stansbury, J. (2004). Citizen participation in decision making: Is it worth the effort?. Public administration review, 64(1), 55-65.

Lane, M. B. (2005). Public participation in planning: an intellectual history. Australian Geographer, 36(3), 283-299.

Newig, J., Pahl-Wostl, C., & Sigel, K. (2005). The role of public participation in managing uncertainty in the implementation of the Water Framework Directive. Environmental Policy and Governance, 15(6), 333-343.

Rittel, H. (1984). Second-generation design methods. Developments in design methodology, 317-327.

Rittel, H. W., & Webber, M. M. (1973). Dilemmas in a general theory of planning. Policy sciences, 4(2), 155-169.

Ruesjas, A. L. (1999). The Mexicali experimental project: An analysis of its changes.

Rydin, Y. (2007). Re-examining the role of knowledge within planning theory. Planning theory, 6(1), 52-68.

Sandercock, L. (1997). Towards cosmopolis: Planning for multicultural cities. Academy Press.
Yin, R. K. (2011). Applications of case study research. Sage.

Alexander's patterns in contemporary city and transport planning processes – A comparison of theory and practice

Frey, Harald
Institute of Transportation, Research Center of Transport Planning and Traffic Engineering, Vienna University of Technology
harald.frey@tuwien.ac.at

Krasser, Robert
Salzburg Institute for regional planning and housing (SIR)
robert.krasser@salzburg.gv.at

Alexander's essay "Nature of Order" constitutes not only a basis for architects and city planners, but also represents a central element in human-compatible transport planning due to its system-analytic character. The first part of the paper discusses the aspects of mobility which are implicitly included as Alexander focuses on human scale, public space and the density and quality of transport networks. But the gap between theory and practice does not seem to have diminished over the years. The second part describes the implementation of "A Pattern Language" in public participation, awareness building processes and in architectural competitions for community buildings. Several village and town development plans as well as architectural competitions were evaluated. A survey concerning the implementation of patterns and design rules focused on builders and municipalities showed that architects have heard about Alexander's patterns but most of them don't use them. Government and planning authorities often fail to communicate simple patterns.

Human scale, transport planning, human behavior, street design, city planning;

1. Patterns in the transport system

1.1. The effects of the transport system

Cities and villages developed and exist for thousands of years based on walking speed of pedestrians. This led to dense, efficient and well-organized settlements. The short distances allowed minimal body energy expenditure and were the cohesion of all cities: All basic needs could be satisfied in striking distance of the residence. The dense pedestrian network was a complex social network that constituted a livable settlement. Personal encounters, visual or auditory perceptions, observations and habits shaped the human being and learning processes (Knoflacher, 1996).

The (spatial) growth of cities has to be considered in interdependency with the speed of the transport system (Knoflacher, 1996). While public transport due to its efficiency and focus on lines (with clearly defined access points) was still able to integrate into the urban fabric, the car began to disperse the dense functions and structures, which were mainly divided into small sections. The effects of individually constant travel time budgets combined with the excellent accessibility of the private car and its high travel speed brought an enormous increase in travel distances (Knoflacher, 1997).

While the urban development (until about the year 1920) in the European cities resulted in structures that required a specific settlement and transport area usage about 50m² per capita and below, the car-oriented urban structures have a specific area demand of about 300-400m² per capita and much further. The traffic area in the city districts of Vienna varies between 14m² ("Gründerzeitviertel") to 50m² (outskirts) per capita (Frey, 2012).

This enormous land consumption is the result of the large specific area requirements of car traffic compared to other means of transportation promoted by a car-oriented urban development in the last decades characterized by structures with a comparatively low-density.

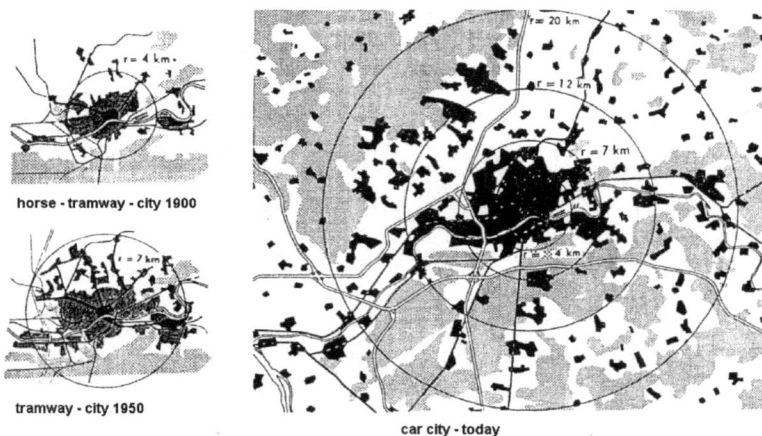

horse - tramway - city 1900

tramway - city 1950

car city - today

Figure 1: The city at 1900, 1950 and today ("car city"). The settlement structures were expanded by the first means of public transport, enlarging the zone of influence into the hinterland. Ultimately high speed public and private transport pushed the city borders even further and enabled urban sprawl. This extensive construction of infrastructure coincided with separation of functions and the triumph of the car (Wortmann, 1985; Macoun, 2010).

1.2. Changes in infrastructure, changes in behavior

Within towns and villages, the streets were conceived as public space, not intentionally separated in sidewalks and lanes. The amount of information in the manifold streets at that time went far beyond the possibilities of drivers in order to implement responsible actions at high speed levels. Transport and city planners therefore reduced the information density by removing any other road users out of the movement space of the cars. At the same time national traffic rules were passed and new control devices for the organization of the motorized individual traffic itself were required. These elements, like traffic signals, were also assigned on non-motorized road users. Under the disguise of traffic safety, barriers for pedestrians, like protective gratings, pedestrian underpasses and crossovers were built (see below), in order to prevent pedestrians from crossing the car lanes in a disturbing manner. Detours and waiting times for pedestrians reduced the number of walking people rapidly and go with sometimes high social costs. Pedestrian over- or underpasses are always affiliated with time-and energy losses; they work in very rare circumstances and only under constraints and sometimes make the other side unreachable for the disabled (Frey, 2013).

Since the mass motorization of our cities and villages starting in Europe from the 1950s, people were displaced from their original residence and communication, recreation, adventure and experiential space. The speed of the car changed public space and its perception by the residents. In addition to the direct transport-related purpose of public (living-)space it is primarily a space for social exchange.

It was further a common-, communication, recreation and adventure space, which provided social closeness and experience of neighborhood and allowed a complex set of different uses. The public space was cut by lanes and transformed into a "storage yard" for cars. If the cohesion across the street is interrupted or weakened, the settlement begins to degenerate. The crucial cross-relationships that promote small scale structures and enable social contacts are suppressed (Appleyard, 1981). The responsibility for the area in front of the house was given up, because its misuse and devaluation to a mono-functional transit area did not meet the needs of the residents. Parking cars in public space destroy and interfere with the social and economic human relations in the settlements. 10 to 20 people could stay on an area of one parking car. The design of our settlements is an expression of values of our society. Studies about the barrier properties of car-designed streets show, that children that grew up in a car-free environment, play more out-door (45% longer), have more playmates in their living environment (ratio 9:2), more contacts to their neighborhood (ratio 7:3) and a stronger social network (ratio 7:2) (Hüttenmoser, 1995).

Figure 2: Pedestrian crossings in Ankara (Turkey) (Öncü, 2007) and Vodice (Croatia) (Wurz, 2009).

1.3. Mobility and the key role of speed

By determining speed as a normative command variable in standards and guidelines, the meaning and significance of the (straight) line and - what is less clear - of right and justice was set (compare French: "la droite" – line, straight, right; "le droit" – justice, droit) (Virilio, 2001). The straight line as a planning element and the influence of speed on planning parameters (e.g. the length of the straight line) changed human behavior regarding the choice of means of transportation (Schafer, 2000; Schafer, 2005).

The right of those (motorists) who are moving along the roads with their individual speed becomes injustice - a barrier - for all other non-motorized road users who want to cross the street. Social and economic relationships often extend transversely to the direction of lanes. Transport or city planning that ignores these principles promote a form of technological fundamentalism (Virilio, 1993).

Since traditional transport planning has adjusted it's planning principles to motorized traffic, it deals with the reprimand of road users. Thereby the consequences on the attractiveness of walking and cycling and hence resulting behavioral changes and needs of road users, esp. pedestrians and cyclists, were not considered in transport planning on a strategic level. Regarding actual planning standards focusing mainly on motorized traffic from a historical point of view some more "human behavior-" and less car-oriented tools for infrastructure planning are discussed (Frey, 2013).

The findings obtained so far show us, that much of what has been planned, has to look different, if the mechanisms of human behavior, based on needs and motives of very diverse traffic participants, would be taken into account. The planning in the past has expected a certain form of behavior, for instance, that pedestrian crossings are only necessary in certain places, which resulted in the penalization of pedestrians who do not use the provided crossing infrastructure. The prejudice of the planners was therefore confirmed by practical experience and reprimanded by laws.

1.4. Resizing / Re-seizing the City

In Vienna 65% of street space are used for the moving individual motorized traffic or as parking space (Stadtentwicklung Wien, 2015). This restricts the possibilities for a multifunctional use of public space. Additionally, growth of the urban population is increasing the challenges in the transport system and the demands for the usage of public space. In order to enhance sustainable and active modes of transport, the availability and accessibility of public space is essential (Linder, 2012).

Although a consistent, effective, area-wide conceptual extension of gentrification of public space is missing to date (Frey, 2012), a decline in the degree of motorization between 2002 and 2016 by around 6 %, based on the improvement of public transport and cycling infrastructure and the implementation of a consistent parking management was achieved. This initiates a potential for the usage of public space in its original diversity and is a necessary starting point for the resizing process in the city.

Based on the knowledge of our evolutionary features as well as the socio-psychological (OECD Indicators for Quality of Life QoL aspects) we can derive two important parameters for transport planning (Knoflacher, 1995):

» "fast" is everything above 3 - 4 km / h

» "far" is everything over 200-300 m

This fundamental parameters based on the physiological "configuration" of human beings fits perfectly in the "Pattern Language" of Christopher Alexander.

1.5. Transport related patterns in Alexander's pattern language:

About 28 patterns in Alexander's pattern language are directly addressed to the transport system. Not all of them can be assumed one-to-one in contemporary transport planning, but all them indicate relevant issues of human scale transport planning. Exemplarily are mentioned the aspects of parking organization and the problems occurring through parking in public space, the arrangement of squares, bike paths or pedestrian streets. We also identified some – to our regard - missing traffic planning patterns, e.g.:

» the importance of the width of a street (this pattern deals with the correlation between speed of cars and the width of streets)

» name and psychology of streets (this pattern deals with the character of a street and its typology)

» shared Space and encounter zones

» the impact of public transport (and it's speed) on city structures (e.g. tramways as an essential part for the quality of public transport or the effects of underground lines on the other side)

» further aspects of cycling (e.g. cycling Infrastructure)

2. Patterns in contemporary planning processes

For more than 10 years the department of village and town renewal of the Land of Salzburg in Austria is trying to use and implement "A Pattern Language" in public participation, awareness building processes and in architectural competitions for community buildings. The objective of the non-profit institute is to consult communities in architectural, spatial and urban development. Several village and town development plans as well as architectural competitions were evaluated. A survey concerning the implementation of patterns and design rules focused on builders and municipalities was done.

The results as well as the acceptance were ambivalent. Architects have heard about Alexander's patterns but most of them don't use them. Government and planning authorities often fail to communicate simple patterns. Subsequently a brief overview of the acceptance of different types of planning processes will be given.

2.1. Architectural competitions, Building construction

In 4 architecture competitions from 2003-2006 the Department of Village and Town Renewal requested all participating architects to follow the patterns of Alexander in their design work. A reference of the German edition of "A Pattern Language" was given in the tender.

The results where sobering. A survey under the participating architects (in total 35) after the architectural competitions brought up that none of the architects owned a copy of the book. Only one participant heard about Alexander's patterns in university.

In following 8 awarded architecture competitions 2007-2017 the department of village and town renewal provided all participating architects with a digital copy of "A Pattern Language" and ask specifically to consider relevant patterns in their design-concept. Also, the jury of the competitions was briefed. The results where disillusioning again. After a brief survey under the participation architects (50) about 60% had a look to the added file. Some of them saw the patterns as a source of inspiration for their design. But none of them "worked" with the patterns intensely. Most of the architects believed that the patterns were old-fashion, outdated and not relevant to the 21st century architecture.

2.2. Landscaping and street design competition

The results concerning the usage of Alexander's patterns in 12 landscaping and street design competitions where slightly better. 95% of all participants used the patterns in their design process in an "isolated" way (e.g. they designed "stair seating" (Pattern 125) and highlighted them). The context to the other patterns and the relevance where mostly not explained.

2.3. Urban Planning / Public Participation Processes

Since 2012 the Department of Village and Town Renewal focuses on (so far 9) public participation processes also known under the term "Charrette". In contrast to an architectural competition the architect/urban planner was selected before the design work started. The architect/urbanist was in a team with a traffic-planner and an economy expert. Within 6-12 month a new urban masterplan was elaborated.

In such processes Alexander's patterns are very helpful to structure the work and to find a starting point in the design process. In all urban re-development and re-densification processes the following patterns where the most helpful ones. One outstanding pattern to start a process is the pattern "Activity Nodes".

Pos.	Pattern #	Pattern Name [EN]	Pattern Name [DE]
1	92	BUS STOP	Bushaltestelle
2	123	PEDESTRIAN DENSITY	Fußgängerdichte
3	165	OPENING TO THE STREET	Öffnung zur Straße
4	122	BUILDING FRONTS	Gebäudefronten
5	103	SMALL PARKING LOTS	Kleine Parkplätze

6	121	PATH SHAPE	Die Form von Wegen
7	30	ACTIVITY NODES	Knoten der Aktivität
8	101	BUILDING THOROUGHFARE	Passage durchs Gebäude
9	120	PATHS AND GOALS	Wege und Ziele
10	87	INDIVIDUALLY OWNED SHOPS	Geschäfte im Privatbesitz

Table 1: 10 helpful patterns in the processes of village and town development

3. Conclusions

The suggestion that architects should use Alexander's Patterns in design competitions failed, due to the lack of academic knowledge. In the current curriculum of architecture "A Pattern Language" is not compulsory in difference to the British, Anglo-American or African universities.

Therefore, we make the following suggestions:

» embedding Alexander's patterns philosophy ("A city is not a tree") as a compulsory subject to architectural students according to British, Anglo-American and African universities.

» make all the patterns easy accessible

» visualize the 253 patterns in short movies in TED-/Wendover Production Style

» initiate an annual "Pattern-competition" where students analyzing existing patterns, visualize them, verify them if they are still contemporary; also give the possibility to develop their own new patterns and publish them.

» start a "translation process" to strengthen and simplify the implementation of Alexander's patterns in city and town planning.

» add new patterns especially:

  › traffic planning patterns

  › urban reconstruction patterns

  › practical-planning-methodical patterns (public participation)

4. References

Appleyard, D. (1981). Livable Streets, University of California Press, Berkeley.

Frey, H. et.al (2012). Resizing / Re-seizing the City - Requirements for Diversity. In: Proceedings of the 17th International Conference on Urban Planning and Regional Development in the Information Society".

Frey, H., Chaloupka-Risser, C. (2013). Human behavior, infrastructure and transport planning. in: "Advances in Human Aspects of Road and Rail Transportation", Taylor & Francis Group, 2013, ISBN: 978-1-4398-7124-9, S. 351 - 362.

Hüttenmoser, M. (1995). Lebensräume für Kinder, Bericht des Nationalen Forschungsprogrammes NFP 25, Nr.70, Zürich.

Knoflacher, H. (1995). Fußgeher und Fahrradverkehr, Wien, Böhlau Verlag.

Knoflacher, H. (1996). Zur Harmonie von Stadt und Verkehr. Böhlau Verlag, Wien.

Knoflacher, H. (1997). Landschaft ohne Autobahnen, Böhlau Verlag, Wien.

Linder, F., Wührl, B. (2012). Nahmobilität 2.0; Arbeitsgemeinschaft fahrradfreundliche Städte, Gemeinden und Kreise in Nordrhein-Westfalen e.V. (Hrsg.); Krefeld; 1.Auflage.

Macoun, T., et.al. (2010). Reaching sustainable settlement and building structures as a problem of choosing intelligent indicators. Central Europe toward Sustainable Building 2010, CESB 2010 Prague Conference.

Schafer, A. and Victor, D.G. (2000). The future mobility of the world population. In: Transport Research Part A 34 (2000), p.171-205.

Schafer, A. (2005). Transportation, Energy, and Technology in the 21st Century. GCEP Advanced Transportation Workshop. October 2005. Stanford University.

Stadtentwicklung Wien, MA 18, (2015). – Stadtentwicklung und Stadtplanung: STEP 2025 – Fachkonzept Mobilität - miteinander mobil; Werkstattbericht 145; Wien.

Virilio, P. (2001). Fluchtgeschwindigkeit, Fischer Verlag, Frankfurt/M.

Virilio, P. (1993). Revolution der Geschwindigkeit, Merve Verlag, Berlin.

Wortmann, W. (1985). Wandel und Kontinuität der Leitvorstellungen in der Stadt und Regionalplanung; in: Berichte zur Raumforschung und Raumplanung, Heft 3-4/1985.

The Nature of Pattern Languages

Falkenthal, Michael
Institute of Architecture of Application Systems, University of Stuttgart, Germany
falkenthal@iaas.uni-stuttgart.de

Breitenbücher, Uwe
Institute of Architecture of Application Systems, University of Stuttgart, Germany
breitenbuecher@iaas.uni-stuttgart.de

Leymann, Frank
Institute of Architecture of Application Systems, University of Stuttgart, Germany
leymann@iaas.uni-stuttgart.de

Patterns and pattern languages have emerged in many disciplines to capture deep domain expertise and knowledge about solving frequently recurring problems by proven solutions. Thereby, patterns capture the essence of many implementations along with descriptions about how to apply them in combination with other patterns, which manifests in pattern languages.

Although pattern languages are a powerful means to preserve and reuse expertise, a clear definition is missing about what a pattern language actually is. Pattern languages are primarily described as being networks of patterns which does not provide a clear and unambiguous foundation to reveal their nature. This lack of rational about the structure behind pattern languages hinders reasoning about them to grasp what connections between patterns are and how the interplay of patterns from different pattern languages can be authored and managed.

Therefore, we present a formal notion of pattern languages as node-colored and edge-weighted directed multigraphs. We show how this model can be used to sharpen Alexander's idea of pattern languages. Thereby, we illustrate how pattern languages can be authored and adapted to establish living networks of patterns. We further introduce that patterns are specific renderings of such a graph depending on actual problems and use cases at hand. This manifests in the fact that our graph concept extracts relationships between patterns from the patterns themselves, which enables easily adaptable networks of patterns. This can be leveraged as the formal meta-model for developing tool support for authoring and sharing pattern languages among communities via IT-based systems.

Pattern Language; Formalization; Pattern Language Composition; Pattern Graph

1. Introduction

The comprehensive documentation and efficient reusability of knowledge has been one of the most important challenges for many decades. In 1977, Christopher Alexander and his colleagues published their pioneering idea of *pattern languages*, which are linked documents describing proven solutions for problems that frequently occur in certain contexts (Alexander, Ishikawa, & Silverstein, 1977). Originally their idea of pattern languages was born in the domain of architecture and urban design with the aim of supporting architects in creating well-designed buildings and landscapes. As a proof of the brilliant nature of this idea, we can see the many pattern languages that have emerged in the meantime: Pattern languages can be found in various domains such as, for example, education, systemic transformations, and information technology. They range from languages that capture the essence of learning and teaching (Iba & Miyake, 2010), to languages that provide compelling guidance at emergency situations such as earthquakes (Furukawazono et al., 2013). Also in technical domains such as information technology, pattern languages have been successfully authored and applied, e.g., for designing cloud applications (Fehling, Leymann, Retter, Schupeck, & Arbitter, 2014) or to integrate different systems of an enterprise (Hohpe & Woolf, 2004). Moreover, besides the documentation of proven solutions, pattern languages are also often used to foster the comprehensibility of domains by acting as a domain-specific jargon or as lingua franca.

Pattern languages consist of *patterns* that are linked with each other. A pattern is a human readable document that describes a general solution principle to solve a frequently recurring problem in a certain context. The solution a pattern describes is typically documented in an *abstract* manner in order to enable solving many *concrete* instances of the conceptual problem. For example, Christopher Alexander and his colleagues documented the general principles about how to build well-designed Farmhouse Kitchens in the form of a pattern (Alexander et al., 1977). This pattern is documented abstractly enough to be applied to many concrete buildings, but nevertheless describes all the key solution principles and best practices the authors gained during their many years of architecting houses. Thus, other architects may take such a pattern to get an idea of a proven conceptual solution, which they can refine to solve their concrete problem at hand. Therefore, patterns typically provide a certain degree of freedom for applying the solution principles to a vast amount of concrete instances of the conceptual problems (Alexander et al., 1977).

To unfold the actual generativity, patterns are typically organized as *pattern languages*, which provide a comprehensive means to connect patterns for solving different problems that often occur together. Organized as pattern language, patterns are not just isolated junks of proven solution knowledge but support the navigation through the language along relevant problems that may occur together with the original problem that needs to be solved (Zdun, 2007). For example, if a farmhouse kitchen needs to be designed, typically also the *cooking layout* must be considered. By documenting related patterns, pattern languages form a *network of patterns* that reveals generative combinability of an entire set of patterns, which are typically applied in combination (Alexander et al., 1977; Alexander, 1979; Buschmann, Henney, & Schmidt, 2007). Based on this concept, readers can navigate through the pattern language and select a pattern that solves a particular part of the problem at hand and then navigate to the next patterns along references from the formerly selected one.

Since people constantly create new knowledge, pattern languages typically evolve over time and increase in their size. Therefore, a pattern language cannot be seen as a static result of documenting all important knowledge about a certain domain, but is rather subject to constant change – it's a *living network of patterns.* Moreover, due to this ongoing process of documenting proven solutions in the form of new patterns, also interrelations between different pattern languages become more and more important: Two pattern languages, which originally had different areas of application, may converge through new related patterns that are part of the two languages. Therefore, also the *dependencies* between pattern languages constantly change and must be documented to support users in solving all related problems.

However, especially this key concept of living pattern networks is ironically in contradiction with the typical way pattern languages are documented: Many languages are published in books, papers, or journals, which are static documents that are hard to change. Thus, these forms of documentation only provide *static snapshots* of proven solutions at a certain point in time, but do not reflect the *liveliness of knowledge* in general. To tackle these issues, many authors publish their pattern languages also on webpages that allow for constant changes. Unfortunately, also these webpages often consider only one single pattern language and do not document the dependencies to other languages. Therefore, our overall vision is to support realizing Christopher Alexander's main idea of living pattern networks by information technology. Pattern authors need intuitive means to publish, adapt, and interrelate pattern languages via globally accessible media such as webpages that are linked with each other. To realize this vision, a clear definition of the concept of a pattern language is required.

However, the definition given by Alexander is a summarization of characteristics in natural language: Although he gives a clear mathematical definition of the decomposition of problems into diagrams of forces based on the mathematical rigor of set theory in *Notes on the Synthesis of Form* (Alexander, 1964), there is no such formal definition of a pattern language.

Therefore, in this paper, we translate the ideas of Christopher Alexander and his colleagues, which have been documented only in natural language, into a formal mathematical definition of pattern languages as directed node-colored and edge-weighted directed multigraphs. This reveals *the formal nature of pattern languages* and provides the basis for further mathematical considerations that are required to realize our vision of globally accessible, living pattern networks based on information technology. We further introduce that patterns are specific renderings of such formal multigraphs depending on actual problems and use cases at hand. This manifests in the fact that our multigraph concept extracts relationships between patterns from the patterns themselves, which enables easily adaptable networks of patterns. In the following, we explain in detail and step by step how the characteristics of pattern languages as described by Alexander in natural text can be translated into formal mathematical definitions. Moreover, we show how our formal definition can be used to interrelate different pattern languages by the original concepts described in *The Timeless Way of Building.*

The remainder of this paper is structured as following: In Section 2 we reveal the nature of pattern languages by developing a formal model stepwise on the basis of the fundamental theory of graphs. In Section 3 we discuss related work, which our approach is built on. We conclude this work in Section 4 by pointing out future research topics we are going to tackle.

2. Revealing the Nature of Pattern Languages

Alexander (1964) clearly describes in *Notes on the Synthesis of Form*, the preceding work of *A Pattern Language* (Alexander et al., 1977), how complex design problems can be decomposed into subproblems that are more easily to grasp and solve. Thereby, he provides a fundamental formal notion of design as the process of remedying identified misfits. He specifies his approach with mathematical rigor by means of set theory and the analysis of correlations between misfits. This is especially remarkable because he translates thoughts, concepts, and an overall method into a mathematical model, which allows to logically reason about the presented approach. Thus, the concept of *patterns* he introduced in the succeeding works goes back to this clearly described model. The main aspect about patterns is that they typically are not isolated but are organized into pattern languages that unfold generative power by the combined expressiveness of all interrelated patterns. However, the model of a pattern language as described in *A Pattern Language* (Alexander et al., 1977) and *The Timeless Way of Building* (Alexander, 1979) is pretty much a summary of qualitative statements without the preciseness used for the fundamental concepts patterns build on. In the following, we discuss the characteristics of pattern languages by descriptive quotes from both mentioned works. We incorporate additional characteristics of pattern languages that have arisen in the domain of IT, where pattern languages are widely used. These identified characteristics describe the concepts behind pattern languages, which we then translate stepwise into an emerging general formal, mathematical meta-model of pattern languages.

2.1. A Network of Patterns

The general understanding of what a pattern language is can be ascribed to the fact that patterns are not just isolated proven solutions for common non-trivial problems. Alexander refers to this by pointing out the collaborative character of patterns. In a *Timeless Way of Building* he states that *"the structure of a pattern language is created by the fact that individual patterns are not isolated"* (Alexander, 1979, p. 311). Thus, there exist inherent relations between different patterns according to the *things* they represent. Moreover, he describes this structural characteristic of a pattern language to be a network of patterns by the quotes *"[a] pattern language has the structure of a network"* (Alexander et al., 1977, p. xviii) and *"[t]he structure of the language is created by the network of connections among individual patterns [...]"* (Alexander, 1979, p. 305). Based on the idea of a network of patterns, he introduces the concept of *completeness* of patterns and, thereby, substantiates the inherent relationships between patterns even more. This is because a pattern does not provide a single finalized solution, but rather the actual solution is completed by other patterns it is related to. He underpins this by the statements *"[e]ach pattern sits at the center of a network of connections which connect it to certain other patterns that help to complete it. [...] And it is the network of these connections between patterns which creates the language"* (Alexander, 1979, p. 313). Moreover, Alexander states that *"[i]t is, indeed, the structure of the network which makes sense of individual patterns, because it anchors them, and helps make them complete."* (Alexander, 1979, p. 315). Thus, he raises the relationships between patterns to the backbone and core of a pattern language.

The relations between the patterns, i.e., the *paths* through the network of patterns restricts the combinability of patterns to only suitable and relevant ones. Hence, we can grasp the connections between patterns and so the paths through the network of patterns as necessary constraints that eliminate variations of pattern combinations that do not lead to meaningful good solutions. Although, at a first glimpse this seems to limit a pattern language exactly these restrictions increase the usability and expressiveness of a pattern language immensely to elaborate good solutions. Alexander points this out by the following statement:

"At this stage, we have defined the concept of a pattern language clearly. We know that it is a finite system of rules which a person can use to generate an infinite variety of different buildings – all members of a family – and that the use of language will allow the people of a village or a town to generate exactly that balance of uniformity and variety which brings a place to life." (Alexander, 1979, p. 191)

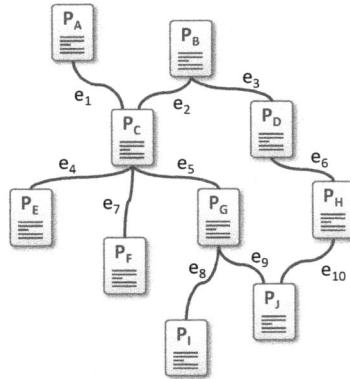

Figure 1: Network of Patterns as a Graph of Patterns consisting of Nodes and Edges

From this statement we can derive that a pattern language consists of a finite set of patterns and connections between patterns due to the fact that it is a *"finite system of rules"* (Alexander, 1979, p. 191). Thus, if we draw a figure based on the above identified characteristics we result in a mathematical structure that is called a *graph*. Such a graph is exemplarily depicted in Figure 1. Therein the patterns $P_A - P_J$ are the nodes of the graph and the connections between patterns $e_1 - e_{10}$ the edges of the graph. Therefore, we refer to a pattern language as being a *pattern graph* because a graph inherently consists of nodes and edges, which provide us key entities to form networks of patterns as described by Alexander. Based on this interpretation of a pattern language, we provide the following definition of its basic structure.

Definition 1 *(Pattern Graph):* We define that a pattern language is a pattern graph $\mathcal{G}$ specified as a tuple $\mathcal{G} = (N, E)$. The finite non-empty set N is the set of all patterns of the pattern language and the set E is the set of all edges connecting patterns to form an overall network. Sequences of patterns connected by edges form so-called paths through the graph indicating combinations of patterns that are relevant.

We define

$$\mathcal{G} = (N, E)$$

with

    (i) N is a set of patterns
    (ii) $card(N) \in \mathbb{N}$
    (iii) $E \subseteq \wp(N)$
    (iv) $\forall e \in E : card(e) = 2$

(v) $n_1, n_2, \dots, n_k \in N$ is a path from n_1 to $n_k: \Leftrightarrow \{n_1, n_2\}, \{n_2, n_3\}, \dots, \{n_{k-1}, n_k\} \in E$

(vi) A path $n_1, n_2, \dots, n_k \in N$ is a simple path $: \Leftrightarrow \forall 2 \leq i, j \leq k - 1: n_i \neq n_j$ ∎

By this definition we enable the analysis of pattern languages by mathematics and well-known algorithms operating on graphs. For example, by this definition we can explain the concept of adjacency of patterns, which plays a core role in Alexander's theory, because it is the network a pattern is centered in that helps to develop complete solutions of the pattern. For this reason, if we want to investigate how to complete a pattern, we now have a formalism that explicitly defines which patterns are adjacent to each other, namely by the edges of the graph that connect them. Referring to the abstract pattern language depicted in Figure 1 we can easily determine that the patterns P_A, P_B, P_E, P_F, P_G are required to complete pattern P_C because P_C resides in the center of the network connecting all these patterns via edges.

Further, if we want to extract parts of a pattern language which are relevant to solve a concrete problem at hand, we can determine them by searching for simple paths between patterns we are interested in. For instance, if we require the patterns P_A and P_J to be part of a solution to a problem at hand, then we can determine the path P_A, P_C, P_G, P_J that contains relevant patterns in this case. As a consequence, the selected patterns can now be used to investigate all patterns they are connected with in order to complete them. The problem of determining paths through a graph is well investigated and, thus, further motivates the understanding of pattern languages by a mathematical formalism because many mathematical approaches dealing with graphs can be used to support the application of pattern languages (Schöning, 2001).

2.2. Organizing the Network of Patterns

In the following, we further refine our meta-model of pattern languages by considering more statements by Alexander. First of all, we incorporate one important aspect which can be derived from the characteristics of patterns. According to Alexander, patterns step in to a process of creating things starting from larger structures to more and more fine-grained structures. Thus, as part of a pattern language each pattern creates so-called *morphological structures*, which are then filled in by other patterns. Thereby, when creating a solution from a pattern it is important to also consider the structure, which the pattern is contained in because it influences respectively restricts the freedom of elaborating the solution. The solution is constrained by the other patterns and their solutions with which it has to form an overall whole. Alexander emphasizes this need by the phrasings:

"[…] when you build a thing you can not merely build that thing in isolation, but must also repair the world around it, and within it, so that the larger world at that one place becomes more coherent, and more whole; and the thing which you make takes its place in the web of nature as you make it." (Alexander et al., 1977, p. xiii)

"Each pattern then, depends both on the smaller patterns it contains, and on the larger patterns within which it is contained." (Alexander, 1979, p. 313)

"And you see then what a beautiful structure a pattern language has. Each pattern is itself a part of some larger pattern [...] And each pattern itself gives birth to smaller patterns [...]" (Alexander, 1979, p. 322)

As a result, the ordering of the network of patterns is based on the fact that there exist patterns that are *larger* than other patterns and, vice versa, there are patterns that are *smaller* than other ones. However, the concept of morphological structures, which arose from the domain of architecture as discussed above can be generalized if we also consider the application of the pattern approach in other domains. For instance, in the domain of information technology many pattern languages have been successfully authored and are widely used. There are pattern languages for software architecture such as the cloud computing patterns by Fehling et al. (2014), the enterprise integration patterns by Hohpe and Woolf (2004) but also currently emerging research fields such as the internet of things (Reinfurt, Breitenbücher, Falkenthal, Leymann, & Riegg, 2016, 2017) are tackled with the pattern approach, to name just a few. Interestingly, the concept of morphological structures is not equally present in these pattern languages, though we can also discover the concept of ordering of patterns in the network. Thereby, patterns allow to create designs, software artifacts, or components that can be combined and refined with solutions provided by other patterns. Buschmann et al. (2007) call this characteristics *Sustainable Progression* and *Tight Integration* and explain it by the quotes: "*Sustainable progression. Pattern languages must connect their patterns appropriately to ensure that challenges are addressed in the right order, which is essential to creating sustainable designs incrementally and via stable intermediate steps [...]*" (Buschmann et al., 2007, p. 269) and "*Tight integration. Pattern languages must integrate their constituent patterns tightly, based on the roles each pattern introduces and the inter-relationships between them.*" (Buschmann et al., 2007, p. 270). Hence, we can deduce that the relations between patterns only have proper meaning if we give them direction, so that we can express that one pattern is larger than other patterns or that one pattern has to be applied earlier in the process of design than others. This is depicted in Figure 2 as an example of larger and smaller patterns.

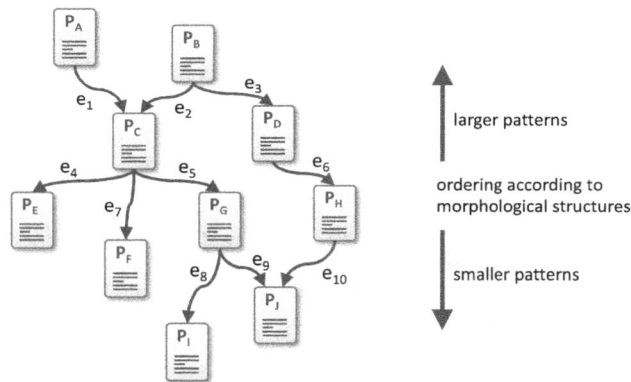

Figure 2: Pattern Language as Directed Graph

Therefore, these characteristics of patterns, be it their effect on morphological structures or on the process of creating artifacts in the domain of information technology, have explicit impact on the network of patterns and, thus, on the pattern graph. This means that the fundamental organization of patterns in a pattern language needs to be reflected by more specific relationships in the structure of the pattern graph. Thus, we refine E to be the set of ordered pairs of patterns. This refines G to be a directed graph (digraph). Consequently, we can express the semantics of a relationship between two patterns by defining that they are connected by an edge, which connects a *larger pattern* with a *smaller pattern*, i.e., the edge between two patterns directs from the larger pattern to the smaller one. Directed edges are commonly drawn as arrows, thus, a directed edge between two patterns is drawn as an arrow whose tail is connected to the larger pattern and whose head is connected to the smaller pattern. Based on this we can refine our model of a pattern graph to be an Alexandrian pattern graph capturing the expressiveness elucidated in the original pattern language theory by Alexander. Of course this differently applies to domains like information technology where the direction provides other semantics because there are no morphological structures present. Therefore, we first define the Alexandrian pattern graph covering morphological structures and afterwards relax this formalism towards a graph that contains arbitrary semantics on edges between patterns.

Definition 2 (Alexandrian Pattern Graph): We define an Alexandrian Pattern Graph as a directed acyclic graph (DAC) by refining the set of edges E to contain ordered pairs of nodes expressing the direction from larger to smaller patterns.

We define

$$\mathcal{G} = (N, E)$$

with

- (i) N is a set of patterns
- (ii) $card(N) \in \mathbb{N}$
- (iii) $E \subseteq N \times N$
- (iv) $e \in E$, then $\pi_1(e)$ is the starting point or tail of an edge, respectively, the arrow connecting two patterns and $\pi_2(e)$ the endpoint or head
- (v) $\forall e \in E : \pi_1(e) \neq \pi_2(e)$
- (vi) $n_1, n_2, \dots, n_k \in N$ is a path from n_1 to $n_k : \Leftrightarrow (n_1, n_2), (n_2, n_3), \dots, (n_{k-1}, n_k) \in E$
- (vii) A path $n_1, n_2, \dots, n_k \in N$ is a simple path $: \Leftrightarrow \forall 2 \leq i, j \leq k - 1 : n_i \neq n_j$
- (viii) $\forall\, n_i, n_{i+1}, \dots, n_k \in N$ that are simple paths holds $n_i \neq n_k$ ∎

Such a pattern graph describes the fundamental structure behind a pattern language according to Alexander because it incorporates structural order of patterns. This kind of order is the core expressiveness of a pattern language that allows to navigate purposefully from things that have to be present before other things can be created, from larger structures to the things that are contained in them. Thus, we lift the relations between the patterns to first-class elements in the understanding of a pattern language that carry implicit semantics, which is underpinned by the phrase by Alexander *"[i]n this network, the links between the patterns are almost as much a part of the language as the patterns themselves."* (Alexander, 1979, p. 314).

2.3. Semantics of Relations between Patterns

So far, we introduced in Section 2.2 the concept of directed edges to represent the implicit semantics of larger and smaller patterns and, hence, purposeful navigation structures through pattern languages. In the following, we will investigate the semantics of relations between patterns in more detail. As described above, the directed edges in an Alexandrian pattern graph do not only employ navigation structures with a direction but are means to express the semantics that one larger pattern *contains* several smaller patterns as it creates a structure, which gets filled by the smaller patterns. Thus, directed edges are the elements that add actual semantics to the model of a pattern language. This is explained by Alexander in the statement:

"However, when we use the network of a language, we always use it as a sequence, going through the patterns, moving always from the larger patterns to the smaller, always from the ones which create structures, to the ones which then embellish those structures, and then to those which embellish the embellishments." (Alexander et al., 1977, p. xviii)

However, in domains besides towns and building architecture the morphological structures are not as obvious and comprehensible. Thus, in these domains the structuring of pattern languages via different link types has emerged. For example, further introduced relationships focus on different types of references between patterns such as "*see also*" and "*consider after*", which are used in the pattern languages on cloud computing (Fehling et al., 2014). Reiners (2013) describes link types that support to express AND, OR, and XOR semantics to specify the interaction of patterns. Further, we have so-called composite patterns, which describe the interplay of different other patterns. They do not aim for describing morphological larger structures but rather describe combinations of patterns for solving strongly-related problems, i.e., they provide an aggregated solution to such composite problems (cf. Buschmann, Henney, & Schmidt, 2007; Fehling, Leymann, Retter, Schupeck, & Arbitter, 2014). These patterns can be linked with the patterns they are composed of via a link type "*composed of*" to indicate the patterns that are part of the composition. In addition to this, the pattern community has created a lot more domain-specific dependencies between patterns, however, for the sake of brevity we focus on the above mentioned as evident examples to further refine our meta-model.

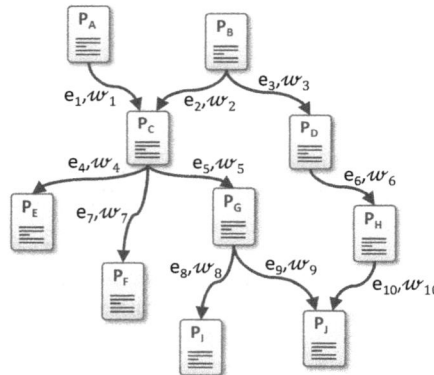

Figure 3: Directed Weighted Pattern Graph

Referring to the mentioned examples, we can generalize different link semantics to be arbitrary weights assigned to edges. Thus, we can refine our model of a pattern graph as depicted in Figure 3. Therein different weights are assigned to edges. In the following we transfer this concept to our formalism.

Definition 3 (Directed Weighted Pattern Graph): To assign weights to edges we associate the pattern graph $\mathcal{G}$ with the set of weights $\mathcal{W}$:

$$\mathcal{G} = (N, E, \mathcal{W})$$

with

    (i) N is a set of patterns
    (ii) $card(N) \in \mathbb{N}$
    (iii) $E \subseteq N \times N \times \mathcal{W}$
    (iv) $\mathcal{W} \neq \emptyset$
    (v) $e \in E$, then $\pi_1(e)$ is the starting point of the edge e, $\pi_2(e)$ is the endpoint of the edge e and $\pi_3(e)$ is the weight assigned to an edge e

(vi) $\forall e \in E : \pi_1(e) \neq \pi_2(e)$

(vii) $n_1, n_2, \dots, n_k \in N$ is a path from n_1 to $n_k : \Leftrightarrow (n_1, n_2), (n_2, n_3), \dots, (n_{k-1}, n_k) \in E$

(viii) A path $n_1, n_2, \dots, n_k \in N$ is a simple path $: \Leftrightarrow \forall 2 \leq i, j \leq k - 1 : n_i \neq n_j$

(ix) $\forall n_i, n_{i+1}, \dots, n_k \in N$ that are simple paths holds $n_i \neq n_k$

(x) $\forall e_i, e_k \in E : \pi_1(e_i) = \pi_1(e_k) \land \pi_2(e_i) = \pi_2(e_k) \Rightarrow \pi_3(e_i) \neq \pi_3(e_k)$ ∎

It is obvious that a pattern graph according to Alexander corresponds to this definition if and only if all edges represent the semantics *contains*, i.e., $\forall e \in E : \pi_3(e) = contains$. Thus, the weight of all edges in the Alexandrian pattern language is "*contains*".

Besides Alexanders pattern language that only uses a single implicit relationship, many pattern languages use arbitrary kinds of relationships between patterns to interrelate them. Most often, important details about relationships to other patterns are described directly in the pattern document in natural language. This is exemplarily depicted in Figure 4 where pattern documents are depicted that reference other patterns by means of specific labels on edges that indicate the semantics of the references and text passages the provide more information about these references However, having such additional descriptions that detail the references directly captured in pattern documents makes it really hard to extend or adapt them if new patterns join the language. Therefore, we discuss this problem in detail in the next section.

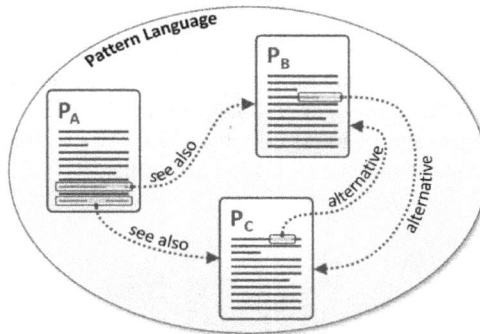

Figure 4: Different Semantics on Edges

2.4. The Combination of Patterns to Form an Overall Whole

For some pattern languages, it is important to provide a defined structure for the weights along with predefined domains of allowed values. This is for example important if programs should be used to automatically traverse pattern graphs parsing and processing the weights on the edges. For these cases, we allow the annotation of edges by *domain-specific types*. These types further enable to add arbitrary type-specific information describing the relation of two patterns in detail, while the allowed values are defined by type-specific domains. Thus, this concept enables to extract the formerly described details about references to other patterns out of the pattern document to the edges themselves, which separates concerns and eases adapting and extending the pattern language in regard to its liveliness.

An example for this concept can be studied by the sophisticated dependencies between *Remoting Patterns* as presented by Zdun, Hentrich, & Dustdar (2007), which are further extended by Zdun (2007). There, the semantics of the relations between patterns are enriched by additional descriptors that describe the effect of the application of a pattern to the quality attributes of an IT application architecture. This means that following an edge from one pattern to another pattern it is annotated to the edge that for instance quality attribute A increases but quality attribute B decreases. For instance, such quality attributes can be used, e.g., to document the negative side effect that combining two patterns decreases the overall performance of an application. However, for our investigation it is not of importance what a quality attribute exactly is or what "increases" and "decreases" specifically means in this context. Much more important is that the edges between patterns are used to not only describe how two patterns are related to each other by means of a semantic keyword but also provide more detailed description about how this relation is defined in the specific case. For example, if two patterns are interrelated with a reference having the type "*can be combined with*", additional descriptions directly on the edge provide the user all information required to actually combine the two patterns. Please note, that today this information is often contained in the pattern documents themselves, which makes it hard to maintain the pattern language as all related pattern documents must be adapted if something changes. Therefore, our formalization is not bound to certain semantics but supports the generative nature of pattern languages as arbitrary information can be annotated.

Definition 4 (Domains of Edge Types): There is a set $\mathcal{D}$ that is the set of all domains of types used to specify value ranges for type-specify descriptions on edges. The domains of types are used to define reusable structures to add type-specific descriptions to edges. ■

Definition 5 (Directed Pattern Graph with Types): The weights $\mathcal{W}$ are refined to represent types assigned to edges between patterns whereby each type specifies a reusable structure to add type-specific descriptions to edges to detail the relationship of two patterns. Thus, for all cases that require such expressiveness on edges, we refine the directed weighted pattern graph $\mathcal{G}$ to be a directed pattern graph with types as weights.

We define

$$\mathcal{G} = (N, E, \mathcal{W}, \mathcal{D}, \alpha, \beta)$$

with

   (i) N is a set of patterns
   (ii) $card(N) \in \mathbb{N}$
   (iii) $E \subseteq N \times N \times \mathcal{W}$
   (iv) $\mathcal{W} \neq \emptyset$
   (v) $e \in E$, then $\pi_1(e)$ is the starting point of the edge e, $\pi_2(e)$ is the endpoint of the edge e and $\pi_3(e)$ is the type assigned to an edge e
   (vi) $\forall e \in E: \pi_1(e) \neq \pi_2(e)$
   (vii) $n_1, n_2, \dots, n_k \in N$ is a path from n_1 to $n_k: \Leftrightarrow (n_1, n_2), (n_2, n_3), \dots, (n_{k-1}, n_k) \in E$
   (viii) A path $n_1, n_2, \dots, n_k \in N$ is a simple path $: \Leftrightarrow \forall 2 \leq i, j \leq k - 1: n_i \neq n_j$
   (ix) $\forall n_i, n_{i+1}, \dots, n_k \in N$ that are simple paths holds $n_i \neq n_k$
   (x) $\forall e_i, e_k \in E: \pi_1(e_i) = \pi_1(e_k) \wedge \pi_2(e_i) = \pi_2(e_k) \Rightarrow \pi_3(e_i) \neq \pi_3(e_k)$
   (xi) $\alpha: \mathcal{W} \rightarrow \wp(\mathcal{D})$
   (xii) $\beta: E \rightarrow \bigcup_{e \in E} \times_{D \in \mathcal{D}_{\alpha(\pi_3(e))}} D$
   (xiii) $\forall e \in E : \beta(e) \in \times_{D \in \mathcal{D}_{\alpha(\pi_3(e))}} D$

where α is a map that assigns subsets of all domains to weights and β is a map that assigns type-specific descriptions to edges. ■

This definition allows to enrich edges between patterns by arbitrary information about the dependency of the connected patterns. Thus, this formalism can be used to add descriptions about how to combine two patterns to edges that is yet part of the plain text of pattern documents. We argue that this formalism is now powerful enough to represent the real nature of pattern languages because we are capable of moving all information describing dependencies between patterns to those entities of the network of patterns which are meant to reflect them – the edges. Let's investigate this in more detail. Pattern languages are today not present as networks of patterns but the network exists implicitly because pattern documents reference each other and, thus, the edges of the pattern graph are not authored as entities. However, as a consequence of our formalism the pattern documents as authored today are just renderings of a directed pattern graph with types. This means that by rendering the graph in order to produce human readable plain text the information provided on the edges of the graph is inserted into the pattern documents. Thus, our formalism reveals the real nature of pattern languages that was pointed out by Alexander by the statement *"[i]n this network, the links between the patterns are almost as much a part of the language as the patterns themselves"* (Alexander, 1979, p. 314).

Beyond this, our formalism also supports to efficiently extend pattern languages by new patterns. This is because we conceptually overcome the problem that adding new patterns to a pattern language leads to the rephrasing of already present patterns in order to reference the newly added one, which is depicted in Figure 5. This is motivated by Alexander's statements that *"[w]e must [...] invent new patterns, whenever necessary, to fill out each pattern which is not complete"* (Alexander, 1979, p. 319) and *"[a] living language must constantly be re-created in each person's mind"* (Alexander, 1979, p. 338).

Our formalism enables that references to other patterns are no longer contained in pattern documents in the form of describing text but are part of the actual references themselves. Thereby, adding new patterns only requires to add new references between the present patterns and the new one. Then, the created edges can be annotated with the information that describes the dependency of two patterns.

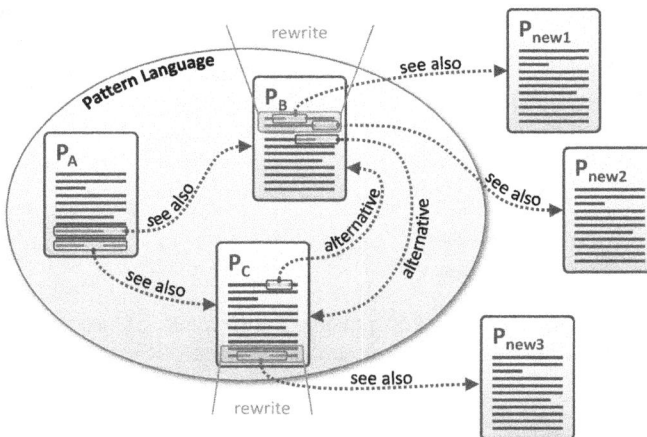

Figure 5: Problem of rephrasing patterns when new patterns are added to a language

2.5. Living Networks of Patterns

Alexander describes pattern languages as living networks of patterns. This means that they are not just static structures but are liable to change, be it because of the addition of new patterns to a pattern language or also the combination with other pattern languages. In the first case, an existing pattern graph G is extended by new nodes and edges as described in the former section. This means new patterns are added to the set of patterns N and connections to other patterns are expressed by new edges added to the set of edges E of G.

However, the second case, the combination of pattern languages requires more investigation. Often the knowledge about different aspects of a domain is spread among different pattern languages. For instance, in the domain of information technology the remoting patterns (Zdun et al., 2004), the cloud computing patterns (Fehling et al., 2014) and enterprise integration patterns (Hohpe & Woolf, 2004) are often used together to design application architectures although they were authored almost isolated from each other in the first place. This is conceptually depicted in Figure 6 where patterns from one pattern language do not reference patterns from another pattern language.

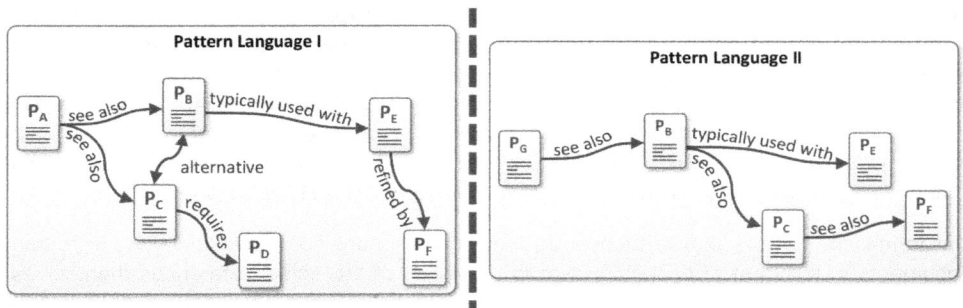

Figure 6: Isolated Pattern Languages

This leads to time consuming elaborations of solutions based on the isolated pattern languages because no guidance is provided by means of references between them, although they are used often in combination. Therefore, this scenario motivates that we need a means to combine the pattern languages somehow to support and ease their combined usage. Also Alexander motivates this by discussing that pattern languages that are shared among communities typically diverge and thus, have to be integrated again in order to create structures that inherently work together. He points this out by the quote:

"We see then, that a language which is shared within a town is a vast structure, far more complex than an individual language.

Not merely a network, but a network of networks, a structure of structures, a vast pool of changing, varying, languages which people create for themselves as they take on their different building tasks.

And once this kind of structure exists, we have a living language in a town, in just the same sense that our common speech is living" (Alexander, 1979, p. 341f).

Therefore, based on our formal notion we introduce the operator $\odot$ to support the combination of pattern languages, which combines two graphs to a single one.

Definition 6 (Pattern Language Aggregator): The set $\mathfrak{G}$ is the set of all pattern language graphs. Two pattern languages are aggregated to a single one by aggregating the underlying graphs based on a set of new edges $\mathcal{E}$:

$$\odot : \mathfrak{G} \times \mathfrak{G} \times \mathcal{E} \to \mathfrak{G}$$

is the *pattern language aggregator function* that aggregates two pattern language graphs to a single one containing new edges $\mathcal{E}$. ∎

Exemplarily, two pattern graphs $\mathcal{G}_1 = (N_1, E_1)$ and $\mathcal{G}_2 = (N_2, E_2)$ are aggregated to $\mathcal{G}_3$ based on new edges $\mathcal{E}$ connecting patterns from $\mathcal{G}_1$ with patterns from $\mathcal{G}_2$ as following:

$$\mathcal{G}_3 = \odot (\mathcal{G}_1, \mathcal{G}_2, \mathcal{E}) = (N_1 \cup N_2, E_1 \cup E_2 \cup \mathcal{E})$$

For the sake of simplicity, we write $\mathcal{G}_3 = \mathcal{G}_1 \odot_{\mathcal{E}} \mathcal{G}_2$ to indicate that $\mathcal{G}_1$ is aggregated with $\mathcal{G}_2$ via the new edges $\mathcal{E}$.

The pattern language aggregator $\odot$ is associative and commutative according to the fundamental union operation of set theory because it unions the sets of nodes and the sets of edges and new edges of two pattern graphs.

Proof: $\mathcal{G}_1 \odot_{\mathcal{E}_{1,2}} \mathcal{G}_2 = \left(N_1 \cup N_2, (E_1 \cup E_2) \cup \mathcal{E}_{1,2}\right) = \left(N_2 \cup N_1, E_1 \cup E_2 \cup \mathcal{E}_{1,2}\right) = \left(N_2 \cup N_1, E_2 \cup E_1 \cup \mathcal{E}_{1,2}\right) = \left(N_2 \cup N_1, (E_2 \cup E_1) \cup \mathcal{E}_{1,2}\right) = \mathcal{G}_2 \odot_{\mathcal{E}_{1,2}} \mathcal{G}_1$ ∎

Therefore, the aggregation of different pattern languages can be written in general as following, whereby the order of the graphs to be aggregated can be changed ad libitum:

$$\mathcal{G}_{n+1} = \mathcal{G}_1 \odot_{\mathcal{E}_{1,2}} \mathcal{G}_2 \odot_{\mathcal{E}_{2,3}} \mathcal{G}_3 \cdots \odot_{\mathcal{E}_{n-1,n}} \mathcal{G}_n$$

Based on this operator we can also explain Alexander's idea of pattern language aggregation as mentioned in *A Timeless Way of Building* (Alexander, 1979). He describes that two yet isolated pattern languages can be aggregated into an overall pattern language by authoring a larger pattern that is more general than at least two patterns from the pattern languages to be combined. Then this pattern can be used to connect both pattern languages into one larger structure because it is used to connect to at least one smaller pattern from each of the pattern languages to be combined. He summarizes this concept as following:

"And, more subtly, we find also that different patterns in different languages, have underlying similarities, which suggest that they can be reformulated to make them more general, and usable in a greater variety of cases." (Alexander, 1979, p. 330)

"Gradually it becomes clear that it is possible to construct one much larger language, which contains all the patterns from the individual languages, and unifies them by tying them together in one larger structure." (Alexander, 1979, p. 330)

As a consequence, we can apply the introduced aggregation operator to this scenario. Let's assume that two pattern languages $\mathcal{G}_1$ and $\mathcal{G}_2$ have to be combined. Further, a newly authored larger pattern can be grasped as a pattern graph $\mathcal{G}_l$ that contains just one pattern and, hence, no edges. Then $\mathcal{G}_l$ can be aggregated with $\mathcal{G}_1$ via a set of edges $\mathcal{E}_{l,1}$ connecting the larger pattern in $\mathcal{G}_l$ with patterns in $\mathcal{G}_1$. Likewise, $\mathcal{G}_l$ can be aggregated with $\mathcal{G}_2$ via a set $\mathcal{E}_{l,2}$. Therefore, we can specify the aggregation of $\mathcal{G}_1$ and $\mathcal{G}_2$ by a larger pattern into an aggregated pattern graph as $\mathcal{G}_l \odot_{\mathcal{E}_{l,1}} \mathcal{G}_1 \odot_{\mathcal{E}_{l,2}} \mathcal{G}_2 = \mathcal{G}_{aggregated}$.

3. Related Work

Alexander et al. (1977) introduce a pattern language as a web of patterns, which supports the navigation through a set of patterns by references between them. The important point is that the relations between the patterns establish so-called pattern sequences, which comprise the generative power of the whole pattern language. Such sequences unfold paths through the pattern language that are typically used to start building a solution based on one pattern, while then, the solution is refined stepwise utilizing the following patterns in the sequence. This is what they call the piecemeal growth that is inherently provided by patterns that build upon others in order to create a whole solution. In contrast pattern sequences the solution paths discussed in this paper are not just navigation structures contained in a pattern language but the actually selected patterns at the time a user chooses applicable patterns in order to solve a concrete problem at hand. Thus, if a pattern sequence allows to choose either one pattern or another at some point, the actual choice of a user is reflected in a solution path. Hence, modelling pattern languages mathematically as presented in this work allows to reflect the nature, i.e., the structure and coherence of a network of patterns appropriately.

Porter et al. (2005) have shown that selecting patterns from a pattern language is a question of temporal ordering of the selected patterns. They show that combinations and aggregations of patterns rely on the order in which the patterns have to be applied. This leads to so called pattern sequences which are partially ordered sets of patterns reflecting the temporal order of pattern application. Their approach requires clear structures and semantics that enables the navigation through a pattern language. Thus, the presented formalization in this paper lays a proper base for the navigation through a pattern language to enable the selection of patterns.

Henney (2006) show how stories can be the nucleus in order to find valuable sequences in a pattern language. Investigating the pattern *Encapsulate Context* by Allan Kelly he shows how a single pattern can be split and integrated into a brief pattern language. Starting from typically occurring problems in the form of stories that reveal a chain of problems and design considerations he shows how sequences through the authored pattern language can ease the application of the knowledge formerly contained in just one pattern more efficiently und clearly. Further, he shows practically how sequences can be related to pattern languages in order to ease their application and to bring out their generative power by piecemeal growth. Both aspects can be covered by the expressiveness of our introduced formalization for pattern languages by means of directed weighted graphs and the selection of proper subgraphs.

Building upon Henney, Zdun (2007) introduces to formalize sequences through pattern languages by means of pattern language grammars. The selection of a pattern is seen as an event in the design process of solutions. According to the temporal order of applying patterns from a pattern language one after the other based on the work of Porter et al. (2005), their formalism considers patterns to be terminal symbols in a formal language, while relationships between patterns are grasped as the production rules of the pattern language grammar. The proven sequences through a pattern language correspond to words, which can be derived by the production rules of the grammar. The effects of a pattern regarding on how it refines and changes the present solution once it is applied is annotated to the grammar in terms of effects on the quality goals of a software architecture. Thus, in contrast to the pattern language by Alexander et al. (1977) the approach by Zdun requires the capability of annotating relationships between patterns by additional semantics. This can be enabled via attaching arbitrary weights on edges. The understandability and unambiguity of attached weights can be maintained by means of ranges of allowed values, which we introduced as type-specific domains.

Mikkonen (1998) tackles the issue on how to formalize the temporal behavior of components introduced by design patterns in system design. He shows how to overcome the lack of clear semantics in the informal description of pattern solutions, especially focusing on communication aspects between system components described by a pattern. Besides formalizing single patterns also combinations and instantiations of patterns are formalized by means of temporal logic of actions. Although he focusses on formalizing the combination of patterns, i.e., their combined usage in software systems the approach lacks support for clearly specifying clear navigation structures through pattern languages, which our approach allows.

Mirnig & Tscheligi (2014) introduce a general pattern framework based on set theory. This framework provides a general theory of patterns in order to explicate knowledge in pattern structures and relate patterns into pattern languages. Their approach is general due to the definition of patterns and pattern languages by means of set theory and, therefore, provides a domain independent fundamental method to define patterns and pattern languages. Further, they introduce a conceptual mechanism by means of descriptors and targets to combine patterns from different domains and pattern languages, respectively. In contrast to our approach, they do not introduce the concept of pattern relations as first-class citizens in their meta model as we do by means of weighted edges that can carry arbitrary semantics and descriptions. Thus, while our formalization focusses on the structure and characteristics of a pattern language and reveals it as a certain kind of graph their approach unfolds from a pattern centric view. Thereby, their approach lacks concreteness about how it supports and guides to create structures that conform to what is known as a pattern language, because the introduced concepts of descriptors and targets are specified to vaguely.

Bayley & Zhu (2010) describe the composition of patterns via operators. These operators can be used to formally specify the relation between patterns and, thus, form a pattern language. The introduced operators are examples of specific weights of edges as described in this work.

Salingaros (2000) describes the structure of pattern languages. He mentions that patterns can be grasped as nodes of a graph that are connected to each other but does not give a clear formalism about that graph as we do in this work. He further describes that ordering of patterns depends on hierarchical levels, i.e., the structure that evolves by smaller and larger patterns. However, he does not clearly describe how such semantics can be expressed via the concept of a graph.

Falkenthal, Barzen, Breitenbücher, Fehling, and Leymann, (2014a), (2014b) and Falkenthal et al. (2016) have shown that specific link types can be used to establish navigation structures through pattern languages towards concrete realizations of the contained patterns. Falkenthal and Leymann (2017) further introduced the concept of solution languages to organize concrete implementations of patterns similarly to pattern languages to ease and guide their reuse. Since all of these concepts build upon the core ideas and characteristics of pattern languages also the introduced formalism in this work can be applied to them which lays a basis for the development of integrated pattern and solution repositories with sophisticated user support.

Barzen and Leymann (2015) derive a formalization of pattern languages based on the interplay of clothing in the domain of costumes in films. They present an ontological description of effects of clothing, which is used to express patterns as clothing with similar effects regarding impressions on the audience of films. Thereby, they define a set of domain-specific relations that allows to create a graph representing a costume language. An environment that supports this language is outlined by Fehling et al. (2015)

Finally, different authors (Borchers, 2000; Coplien, 1996; Porter et al., 2005; Reiners, 2012) have mentioned that a pattern language can be grasped as a directed acyclic graph. However, none of them derived the actual semantics of such a model clearly from the core ideas and thoughts by Alexander and refined them towards a sophisticated meta model as expressive as ours.

4. Conclusion and Future Work

In this paper, we derived a formal notion of pattern languages on the basis of fundamental mathematical concepts from graph theory. Thus, we provide an explanation about what pattern languages are on the basis of structural dependencies that can be interpreted, i.e., we revealed the underlying nature of pattern languages. Thereby, the general formal model of a pattern language is developed stepwise so that we believe that our formalism covers the structural backbone of most, if not even all present pattern languages. We presented different manifestations of our formalization differing in their expressiveness. Hence, readers from different domains can step into the formalization that is mostly suitable for developing pattern languages in his domain.

However, we grasp this work as the basis for our research about how to efficiently support the authoring, the maintenance, and development of pattern languages across communities by means of appropriate pattern repositories. Thus, we envision to leverage the whole expressiveness of the presented formalism in the form of collaborative pattern language repositories that inherently incorporate and support the features as shown in this work on the basis of mathematical structures. We especially plan to force investigations on enabling the application of graph algorithms that are now applicable on the basis of graph theory.

5. References

Alexander, C. (1964). *Notes on the Synthesis of Form*. London: Oxford University Press.

Alexander, C. (1979). *The Timeless Way of Building*. New York: Oxford University Press. http://doi.org/10.1080/00918360802623131

Alexander, C., Ishikawa, S., & Silverstein, M. (1977). *A pattern language: towns, buildings, construction*. New York: Oxford University Press.

Barzen, J., & Leymann, F. (2015). Costume Languages as Pattern Languages. In *Pursuit of Pattern Languages for Societal Change (PURPLSOC) - The Workshop 2014: Designing Lively Scenarios With the Pattern Approach of Christopher Alexander* (pp. 88–117).

Bayley, I., & Zhu, H. (2010). A Formal Language of Pattern Compositions. *PATTERNS 2010, The Second International Conferences on Pervasive Patterns and Applications*, (c), 1–6.

Borchers, J. O. (2000). A pattern approach to interaction design. *Proceedings of the Conference on Designing Interactive Systems Processes, Practices, Methods, and Techniques - DIS '00*, 369–378. http://doi.org/10.1145/347642.347795

Buschmann, F., Henney, K., & Schmidt, D. C. (2007). *Pattern-Oriented Software Architecture: On Patterns and Pattern Languages*. Wiley & Sons.

Coplien, J. O. (1996). *Software Patterns*. SIGS Books & Multimedia.

Falkenthal, M., Barzen, J., Breitenbücher, U., Fehling, C., & Leymann, F. (2014a). Efficient Pattern Application: Validating the Concept of Solution Implementations in Different Domains. *International Journal On Advances in Software*, 7(3&4), 710–726.

Falkenthal, M., Barzen, J., Breitenbücher, U., Fehling, C., & Leymann, F. (2014b). From Pattern Languages to Solution Implementations. In *Proceedings of the 6th International Conferences on Pervasive Patterns and Applications - PATTERNS 2014* (pp. 12–21). Xpert Publishing Services (XPS).

Falkenthal, M., Barzen, J., Breitenbücher, U., Fehling, C., Leymann, F., Hadjakos, A., … Schulze, H. (2016). Leveraging Pattern Applications via Pattern Refinement. In *Proceedings of Pursuit of Pattern Languages for Societal Change*.

Falkenthal, M., & Leymann, F. (2017). Easing Pattern Application by Means of Solution Languages. In *Proceedings of the 9th International Conferences on Pervasive Patterns and Applications - PATTERNS 2017*. Xpert Publishing Services (XPS).

Fehling, C., Barzen, J., Falkenthal, M., & Leymann, F. (2015). PatternPedia – Collaborative Pattern Identification and Authoring. In *Pursuit of Pattern Languages for Societal Change (PURPLSOC) - The Workshop 2014: Designing Lively Scenarios With the Pattern Approach of Christopher Alexander* (pp. 252–284). epubli GmbH.

Fehling, C., Leymann, F., Retter, R., Schupeck, W., & Arbitter, P. (2014). *Cloud Computing Patterns: Fundamentals to Design, Build, and Manage Cloud Applications*. Springer.

Furukawazono, T., Studies, I., Seshimo, S., Studies, I., Muramatsu, D., & Iba, T. (2013). Survival Language : A Pattern Language for Surviving Earthquakes. In *Proceedings of the 20th Conference on Pattern Languages of Programs* (p. Article No. 30). ACM.

Henney, K. (2006). Context Encapsulation: Three Stories, a Language, and Some Sequences. In *Proceedings of the 10th European Conference on Pattern Languages of Programs (EuroPlop 2005)*. Irsee.

Hohpe, G., & Woolf, B. (2004). *Enterprise Integration Patterns: Designing, Building, And Deploying Messaging Systems*. Addison-Wesley.

Iba, T., & Miyake, T. (2010). Learning patterns: a pattern language for creative learners II. In *Proceedings of the 1st Asian Conference on Pattern Languages of Programs (AsianPLoP 2010)* (p. I-41--I-58). New York, USA: ACM Press. http://doi.org/10.1145/2371736.2371742

Mikkonen, T. (1998). Formalizing Design Patterns. In *International Conference on Software Engineering* (pp. 115–124). Kyoto.

Mirnig, A. G., & Tscheligi, M. (2014). Building a General Pattern Framework via Set Theory : Towards a Universal Pattern Approach. In *Proceedings of the Sixth International Conferences on Pervasive Patterns and Applications (PATTERNS)*. (pp. 8–11). Xpert Publishing Services (XPS).

Porter, R., Coplien, J. O., & Winn, T. (2005). Sequences as a basis for pattern language composition. *Science of Computer Programming*, *56*(1–2), 231–249. http://doi.org/10.1016/j.scico.2004.11.014

Reiners, R. (2012). A Pattern Evolution Process - From Ideas to Patterns. In *Lecture Notes in Informatics - Informatiktage 2012* (pp. 115–118). Gesellschaft für Informatik (GI).

Reiners, R. (2013). *An Evolving Pattern Library for Collaborative Project Documentation*. RWTH Aachen University.

Reinfurt, L., Breitenbücher, U., Falkenthal, M., Leymann, F., & Riegg, A. (2016). Internet of Things Patterns. In *Proceedings of the 21st European Conference on Pattern Languages of Programs (EuroPLoP)*. ACM.

Reinfurt, L., Breitenbücher, U., Falkenthal, M., Leymann, F., & Riegg, A. (2017). Internet of Things Patterns for Devices. In *Proceedings of the 9th International Conferences on Pervasive Patterns and Applications - PATTERNS 2017* (pp. 117–126). Xpert Publishing Services (XPS).

Salingaros, N. a. (2000). The structure of pattern languages. *Arq: Architectural Research Quarterly*, *4*(2), 149–161. http://doi.org/10.1017/S1359135500002591

Schöning, U. (2001). *Algorithmik*. Springer.

Zdun, U. (2007). Systematic pattern selection using pattern language grammars and design space analysis. *Software: Practice and Experience*, *37*(9), 983–1016. http://doi.org/10.1002/spe.799

Zdun, U., Hentrich, C., & Dustdar, S. (2007). Modeling process-driven and service-oriented architectures using patterns and pattern primitives. *ACM Transactions on the Web*, *1*(3), 14–es. http://doi.org/10.1145/1281480.1281484

Zdun, U., Kircher, M., & Völter, M. (2004). Remoting patterns: Design reuse of distributed object middleware solutions. *IEEE Internet Computing*, *8*(6), 60–66. http://doi.org/10.1109/MIC.2004.70

Illuminating Egoless Creation with Theories of Autopoietic Systems

Iba, Takashi
Faculty of Policy Management, Keio University, Japan
iba@sfc.keio.ac.jp

Yoshikawa, Ayaka
Faculty of Environment and Information Studies, Keio University, Japan

This paper examines one of the most important but overlooked concepts in pattern language theory; creation processes without the self (ego). Christopher Alexander, the inventor of the pattern language concept and methodology, focused on a generative mechanism beyond the individual designer level and claimed that creation originated from this basis. In this paper, first, the similarities between Alexander's arguments and those of fiction writers who claim that, 'the author does not intentionally create the story; the characters in the story act on their own, and the story unfolds itself' are examined under an 'egoless creation' concept. Then, egoless creation is examined through the theories of autopoetic systems: Social Systems Theory and Creative Systems Theory. It was found that egoless creation is a state in which the chain of generated discoveries within a creative system is experienced by the psychic system, that the patterns in a pattern language work primarily as `discovery media' within the creative system, and that pattern language facilitates a structural coupling of the psychic and the social systems. Through these analyses, this paper illuminates the egoless creation concept from a systems theory perspective.

Autopoiesis; Creation; Creative Systems Theory; Egoless; Pattern Language; Social Systems Theory

1.   Introduction

Christopher Alexander argued that in any city and building design process, the designers' intentional control must be omitted, stating that 'when a place is lifeless or unreal, there is almost always a mastermind behind it. It is so filled with the will of its maker that there is no room for its own nature'. (Alexander, 1979, p.36) He claimed that creative processes must be egoless and generative, and proposed the pattern language method to enable this egoless process. The need for designers to go beyond their own ideas and develop generative designs was an important theme throughout Alexander's work, such as Notes on the Synthesis of Form (Alexander, 1964), The Timeless Way of Building (Alexander, 1979), and The Nature of Order (Alexander, 2002a, 2002b).

Despite the significance of this concept to the pattern language method, there are few who fully understand the concept, primarily because of the general understanding that design (creative act) is essentially the result of someone 'taking action'. The perpetuation of this 'general' belief tends to imply that the notion of the 'egoless creation' proposed by Alexander is only idealistic and cannot be applied in reality.

This paper develops a theoretical framework to enhance the understanding of egoless creations by elucidating the creative process elements. To do this, first, the definition for Alexander's egoless creation concept is reviewed, after which similar observations from fiction authors about the larger creation context are examined. Then, the autopoietic systems theories; social systems theory and creative systems theory; are introduced to analyze the egoless creation concept.

2. Egoless Creation and Pattern Language

Christopher Alexander, in The Timeless Way of Building, introduced the 'quality without a name', a quality that 'flows out from the process of creation of its own accord', and which cannot be made in the presence of the designers' individual intentions.

> 'the quality without a name cannot be made, but only generated by a process. It can flow from your actions; it can flow with the greatest ease; but it cannot be made. It cannot be contrived, thought out, designed. It happens when it flows out from the process of creation of its own accord'. (Alexander, 1979, p.159)

> 'When a thing is made, it has the will of the maker in it. But when it is generated, it is generated, freely, by the operation of egoless rules, acting on the reality of the situation, and giving birth, of their own accord. ...' (Alexander, 1979, p.160)

Alexander claimed that cities of great quality were not created by a single designer (or a single team) but resulted from many cycles of 'diagnosis and repair' (Alexander, Silverstein, et al., 1975). Modern cities and buildings, however, lacked this quality as they were developed solely based on the original designer's intent and control. In other words, a city, a building or a community should be shaped gradually by the people living in it and decisions should not solely be in the hands of outsiders who do not know the intricate details of the residents' lives (Alexander, Davis, et al., 1985). Therefore, Alexander believed that design must be generated from within.

> 'To make a building egoless, like this, the builder must let go of all his willful images, and start with a void. .... you must start with nothing in your mind'. (Alexander, 1979, p.538)

> You are able to do this only when you no longer fear that nothing will happen, and you can therefore afford to let go of your images'. (Alexander, 1979, p.538)

In other words, designers must ignore their own intentions before engaging in the creation process as the designer is merely the medium required for the design to take place.

> 'Your mind is a medium within which the creative spark that jumps between the pattern and the world can happen. You yourself are only the medium for this creative spark, not its originator'. (Alexander, 1979, p.397)

However, this abstraction is difficult to achieve, as many people don't understand how something can arise from a completely void state, primarily because the act of 'creation' is believed to be an intentional process. To combat this disbelief, Alexander wrote A Pattern

Language (Alexander, Ishikawa, et al., 1977), in which he documented and named the generative rules for the creation of towns and buildings. Alexander argued that the patterns in a pattern language were the rules that operated within a creative process that was free of the designer's intentions and by following these patterns, the designer could achieve egoless creation.

> *'Get rid of the ideas which come into your mind. Get rid of pictures you have seen in magazines, friends' houses ... Insist on the pattern, and nothing else. The pattern, and the real situation, together, will create the proper form, within your mind, without your trying to do it, if you will allow it to happen. This is the power of the language, and the reason why the language is creative'. (Alexander, 1979, p.397)*

> *'To do it, you must let go of your control and let the pattern do the work. You cannot do this, normally, because you are trying to make decisions without having confidence in the basis for them. But if the patterns you are using are familiar to you, if they make sense to you, if you are confident that they make sense, and that they are profound, then there is no reason to be afraid of giving up your control over the design. If the pattern makes sense, you do not need to control the design'. (Alexander, 1979, p.399)*

The patterns Alexander speaks of do not individually exist, but have a certain sequence and are interrelated; therefore, if the pattern sequence is followed, the creation proceeds autonomously similar to the growth of a living organism.

> *'the order of the language is the order which the patterns need to operate on one another to create a whole. It is a morphological order, similar to the order which must be present in an evolving embryo. And it is this very same order which also allows each pattern to develop its full intensity. When we have the order of the language right, we can pay attention to one pattern at a time, with full intensity, because the interference between patterns, and the conflicts between patterns, are reduced to almost nothing by the order of the language'. (Alexander, 1979, p.401-402)*

> *'We are ready, now, to see just how a sequence of patterns can create a building in our minds. It happens with surprising ease. The building almost "makes itself," just as a sequence seems to when we speak'. (Alexander, 1979, p.407)*

As Alexander explained, patterns enable designers to let go of their intentional control.

> *'Once you learn that the pattern language and the site together will genuinely generate from inside your mind, from nothing, you can trust yourself to let go of your images entirely'. (Alexander, 1979, p.538)*

> *'For a person who is unfree, the language seems like mere information because he feels that he must be in control, that he must inject the creative impulse, that he must supply the image which controls the design'. (Alexander, 1979, p.538-539)*

> *'It is a fearsome thing, like diving into water. And yet it is exhilarating — because you aren't controlling it. You are only the medium in which the patterns come to life, and of their own accord give birth to something new'. (Alexander, 1979, p.426)*

> *'once a person can relax, and let the forces in the situation act through him as if he were a medium, then he sees that the language, with very little help, is able to do almost all the work, and that the building shapes itself. This is the importance of the void. A person who is free and egoless starts with a void and lets the language generate the necessary forms out of this void. He overcomes the need to hold onto an image, the need to control the design, and he is comfortable with the void, and confident that the laws of nature, formulated as patterns, acting in his mind, will together create all that is required'. (Alexander, 1979, p.539)*

As explained, when people gain experience in using the patterns and engaging in egoless and generative creations, it eventually becomes unnecessary to refer to the patterns because what is essential is the egoless and generative creation itself, with the pattern language being merely the tool that steers the creation. Alexander claimed that 'it is just your pattern language which helps you become egoless' (Alexander, 1979, p.543), and that 'in this sense, the language is the instrument which brings about the state of mind, which I call egoless'. (Alexander, 1979, p.546)

> *'Gradually, by following the language, you feel free to escape from the artificial images society has imposed upon you. And, as you escape from these images, and the need to manufacture things according to these images, you are able to come more into touch with the simple reality of things, and thereby become egoless and free'. (Alexander, 1979, p.544)*

> *'... at that moment he no longer needs the language. Once a person has freed himself to such an extent that he can see the forces as they really are and make a building which is shaped by them alone and not affected or distorted by his images ——— he is then free enough to make the building without patterns at all ——— because the knowledge which the patterns contain, the knowledge of the way the forces really act is his'. (Alexander, 1979, p.543)*

The relationship between Alexander's idea of egoless creation and pattern language is the essential message in The Timeless Way of Building, but has often been overlooked or misunderstood. Although focusing on actions, Creation with pattern languages for human actions, which we call Pattern Language 3.0 (Iba, 2016), should be also egoless as same to creation with Alexander's pattern language in architecture. The idea of the egoless creation differs psychologically from the everyday definition for 'creation'; however, when considered from a wider context, many others have made the same observations. The next section introduces similar arguments from various fields and relates them to Alexander's egoless creation concept.

3. Egoless Creation in Other Creative Domains

Arguments similar to Alexander's have been made by fiction writers and movie directors who have claimed that the characters in their works 'cannot be controlled by the creator's intentions', and that 'they take on a life of their own'. There are some writers who have claimed that as stories cannot be artificially created, they do not know how they will end until they are written. Haruki Murakami, for example, made the following observation.

> *'When I start working on a book, I do not have any plan whatsoever. I simply wait, patiently, for the story to come to me. There is not a time when I intentionally make decisions about what kind of story it will be, or what will happen in it'. (Murakami, 2010, translated by the authors in this paper)*

Murakami further elaborates in detail as follows.

> *'It is of course the author who comes up with the characters. However, if the characters are truly alive, they will at some point take off and begin acting on their own. This is not just my opinion, but is an awareness shared by many fiction writers. In fact, if such a phenomenon were not to take place, writing a book would be an extremely grueling and painful process. Once a book gets on the right track, the characters begin moving on their own and the story proceeds naturally; hence, the writer takes on the pleasant role of simply transcribing the events that are occurring. In some cases, the character may even take the author by the hand and lead him/her to some surprising place the author had not expected to see'. (Murakami, 2015, p.232, translated by authors in this paper)*

Similarly, writer Stephen King also stated that he did not control the actions of the characters in his stories.

> *'I often have an idea of what the outcome may be, but I have never demanded of a set of characters that they do things my way. On the contrary, I want them to do things their way. In some instances, the outcome is what I visualized. In most, however, it's something I never expected'. (King, 2010)*

> *'For me, what happens to characters as a story progresses depends solely on what I discover about them as I go along — how they grow, in other words. Sometimes they grow a little. If they grow a lot, they begin to influence the course of the story instead of the other way around'. (King, 2010)*

Writers have also claimed that the writing process was merely a medium within which the story self develops, and their role is to simply transcribe what occurs. King claimed that 'the job of the writer is to give them a place to grow (and transcribe them, of course)'. (King, 2010) and 'if you do your job, your characters will come to life and start doing stuff on their own. I know that sounds a little creepy if you haven't actually experienced it, but it's terrific fun when it happens'. (King, 2010, p.195)

Murakami expressed a similar feeling; 'I feel like the novel has already moved on and now I'm chasing after the images'. Kawa i& Murakami, 2016, p.68). Movie director Hayao Miyazaki echoed this sentiment; 'So in effect, I myself wasn't in the lead in creating this story; I was just trying to keep up with it'. (Miyazaki, 1996, p.396).

Therefore, both writers experienced a process in which they were not actively creating the story but were overseeing the story's self-generation. As they do not know beforehand where the story is going to go, they experience these stories as they occur and then transcribe them; therefore, there are times when the authors encounter a surprising event, which they learn from and which can change the direction of the story. Murakami stated that 'I myself do not know what the storyline will be' (Murakami, 2010, translated by authors in this paper), and described his experiences as follows;

> *'The journey that the main character goes through is also the journey I go through. When I'm writing, I experience the same feelings my main characters experience and endure the same trials. In other words, after completing a book, I am a different person than I was before beginning the writing process'. (Murakami, 2010, translated by authors in this paper)*

Michael Ende, a fantasy fiction writer has also made a similar statement.

> *'What I often say is that the writing process is like a journey. Where that journey takes me and how that journey will end is unknown even to me. Therefore, for every book I have written, I have become a different person each time. In fact, my life can be broken down based on the books I have written as each writing process has changed who I am'. (Ende, 2000, translated by authors in this paper)*

These statements therefore are in contrast to the perception that 'writers write about what they come up with'. If writers only transcribed things they already knew, no new discoveries or transformations would take place. The experiences related above are not unique and have been mentioned by many writers as well as Jiro Kawakita, a cultural anthropologist;

> 'A creative act involves the creation of the object itself, but also generates change within the individual who is engaging in the creation. In other words, the subject is also being created. A creation that is done one-sidedly is not truly a creative act. The more creative an act is, the more remarkable the change in the subject is'. (Kawakita, 1993, p.86, translated by authors in this paper)

Creators in other domains have also explained that the creative processes are not controlled by the creator but are guided by a force within the object itself. Hayao Miyazaki made the following observation.

> 'When people talk about making films, they often use fancy and hip phrases like `being creative;' however, in reality, you do have creative choices until you select the topic for your film. ... Now, you may make this choice based on some deep subconscious desire, but once you have decided to make your film, you're not really making the film --- it will be making you'. (Miyazaki, 1996, p.109-110)

> 'The film tries to become a film. The filmmaker just becomes a slave to the film. The relationship is not one of me creating the film, but rather of the film forcing me to create it'. (Miyazaki, 1996, p.430)

Composer Jo Hisaishi, who often creates music for Miyazaki's films, also shared a similar experience.

> 'If you are trying to create the music inside your head, you are only at the very beginning stage. What is essential in the composing process is to dive deep into a state of unconsciousness and discover yourself within the chaos as you would have never imagined. If you have to consciously force yourself to create something, it most likely means that you are still thinking inside your head'. (Hisaishi, 2006, translated by authors in this paper)

> 'You find yourself at a point where it is difficult to find order; you undergo agony, you struggle, and you try with all your strength to create something. When you go beyond that and reach a state where you are freed from your own intentions /control; only then, can you create music powerful enough to move people'. (Hisaishi, 2006, translated by authors in this paper)

The interesting argument by these people involved in creative processes is that the stories and music they create are 'not created from within their minds' but instead 'exist in some outside place'. King stated that 'I believe that stories are found things, like fossils in the ground' and that, 'Stories are relics, part of an undiscovered pre-existing world. The writer's job is to use the tools in his or her toolbox to get as much of each one out of the ground intact as possible'. (King, 2010, p.163-164)

Hayao Miyazaki also said; 'I think my films are not inside my head, but are in a space above my head. The film already exists'. (Miyazaki, 1996, p.430), thereby indicating that his creative process was external to his own mind. He elaborated further:

> *'It sounds impressive when I say I'm being creative, but that's not what's really going on. There is only a single best solution given the combination of my present abilities and the objective conditions in which I am placed. Once I decide on a method for the production and a direction, although there are many ways of determining the direction, there is only one way to proceed each time. My work consists of nothing more than discovering how I can get as close to that direction as possible'. (Miyazaki, q1996, p.430)*

The poet, Shuntaro Tanikawa, also made a similar statement;

> *'In creating a written work that is ultimately a mere combination of different words, we decide which word follows the word that comes before it. In making this decision, we feel a sense of necessity which is unquestionable'. (Tanikawa, 2006, translated by authors in this paper)*

> *'Is it possible to make linguistic decisions in an active way at all times? Are there not times when words gravitate toward us, sometimes against our will; or better yet, when it feels as though the words themselves have chosen us?' (Tanikawa, 2006, translated by authors in this paper)*

Jo Hisaishi, a composer, also explained that; 'composition is not about using your own senses to write music; it is rather a process of figuring out whether "this works here", and continuing to search when you feel "there is something wrong", "something is off..." ' (Yoro and Hisaishi, 2009, translated by authors in this paper)

> *'It becomes a matter of whether you feel you are allowed to make changes to the music; questioning whether it feels like it is you who is making that decision. When you get far enough along the path to really pursuing something, you begin to get a sense that it is not you who is creating the music or choosing each note; that instead, there is a definite best solution somewhere that puts all of the pieces into their right places and that you must search until you find it'. (Yoro and Hisaishi, 2009, translated by authors in this paper)*

161

Thus far, the quotes from various creators regarding their experiences of egoless creation have been examined. From the observations, we understand that in a creative process, a sense of what 'should be' prevails over the creator's own will. Therefore, Alexander's egoless creation is a concept common to creators in other domains, and while it is not a concept perceived in everyday life, it is in fact the very core of the creative process.

However, the question of how egoless creation takes place remains unclear. To understand the egoless creative process and how such processes are possible, it is necessary to go beyond simply observing and analyzing the actions that take place. Therefore, in the next section, these questions are examined in reference to systems theories.

4. Understanding Egoless Creation using Systems Theories

In this section, we examine the egoless creation mechanism from a Theory of Autopoetic Systems perspective. Autopoetic systems is a theory proposed by Humberto Maturana and Francisco Valera in relation to biology (Maturana and Varela, 1972). Niklass Luhman, a sociologist who applied the autopoietic system concept to sociology (Luhmann, 1984), described the theory, as follows;

'Autopoietic systems are systems that themselves produce not only their structures but also the elements of which they consist in the network of these same elements. The elements (which from a temporal point of view are operations) that constitute autopoietic systems have no independent existence. They do not simply come together. They are not simply connected. It is only in the system that they are produced (on whatever energy and material basis) by being made use of as distinction'. (Luhmann, 1997, p.32)

The reason this paper focuses on the theory of autopoietic systems is because this theory can provide a general answer to 'what something is'. Luhmann researched the theory of autopoietic systems when seeking to deal with the questions of 'what is sociology?' and made the following remark;

'From this viewpoint, the theory of autopoiesis is a meta-theory and an approach that in its own way, once again answers "What?" questions, such as "What is life?" or "What is consciousness?" or "What is social?" (that is to say, "What is a social system independent of the specific formation in which it occurs empirically?"). The concept of autopoiesis answers such "What?" questions - this, too, is a thought of Maturana'. (Luhmann, 2002, p.81)

This paper specifically deals with the question of 'What is creation?'; therefore, to answer this question, creativity must not be considered from a psychological perspective, but instead the focus must be on the creative process itself. Therefore, creation, and in particular, egoless creation, needs to be viewed from the perspectives extolled in the theory of autopoietic systems.

First, an overview of the Psychic System and Social System concepts from Niklas Luhmann's Social System given, after which the Creative System concept from Creative Systems Theory (Iba, 2010) is introduced. Then, the 'action' and experience' concepts as defined by Luhmann are used to demonstrate what occurs in the egoless creation process.

4.1. Psychic Systems and Social Systems

In his Social Systems Theory, sociologist Niklas Luhmann conceptualized thought as a psychic system that was a theorization of society from a systems perspective. Psychic Systems are autopoietic systems that arise from the continuous generation of 'consciousness' (which are elements within the system); that is, a certain consciousness is generated from a pre-existing consciousness, and then becomes the precedent upon which the subsequent consciousness is generated. Luhmann argued that this continuous consciousness generation was the essence of thinking.

In a psychic system, consciousness (the elements) can only be born within the system; that is, a psychic system cannot input or import elements from outside the system as each psychic system is 'operationally closed'. Therefore, for people to develop good relationships with others it is necessary to communicate. Luhmann, for that reason, defined communication and social systems based on the understanding that psychic systems were autopoietic (Figure 1).

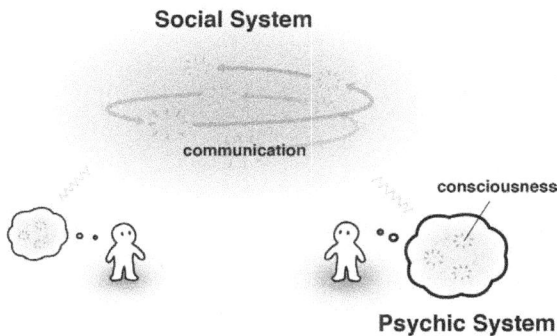

Figure 1: Psychic System and Social System

Luhmann's Social Systems Theory claims that society is a system in which 'communication' is merely an element. While communication elements make up the social system, communication is also generated from within that system. Similar to consciousness, as communication is an element that disappears as soon as it is generated, it must be continuously generated. Social systems are also systems that are 'operationally closed', as the elements can only be generated from inside the system. As such, Luhmann's Social Systems Theory places the generation of communication as the foundation of the social system.

How then is communication, as an element in a social system, generated? Luhmann, claimed that communication emerges when three components; information, utterance, and understanding (Figure 2); exist. That is, from a social systems perspective, communication is generated when certain information is uttered with a certain intention and is understood.

> 'Information is a surprising selection from among several possibilities. As a surprise, it can be neither enduring nor able to be transported; and it has to be produced within the system, since it presupposes comparison with expectations. Furthermore, information cannot be gained purely passively as a logical consequence of signals received from the environment'. (Luhmann, 1997, p.36)

> 'Through utterance the system refers to itself. Utterance actualizes the possibility of recursively relating further communication to the system. Through information, in contrast, the system typically refers to its environment'. (Luhmann, 1997, p.53)

In Luhmann's Social Systems Theory, communication is not understood as the transfer of information between the addressor and the receiver; 'We must therefore abandon the classical metaphor that communication is a "transmission" of semantic content by one psychic system that possesses it to another'. (Luhmann, 1997, p.57) Instead, his Social Systems Theory states that the elements in a social system are generated within that system and that they emerge separately from the psychic system.

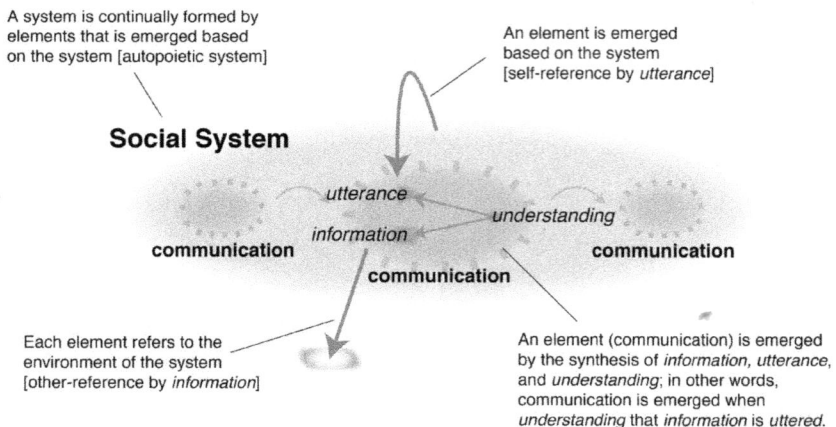

Figure 2: Emergence of Communication as a System Element through the Synthesis of Information, Utterance, and Understanding.

The three necessary communication components cannot, therefore, be viewed from the perspective of the people's actions that caused them; 'If we understand communication as an entity comprising the three components information, utterance, and understanding, which are produced only when communicating, this excludes the possibility of assigning ontological primacy to one of these components'. (Luhmann, 1997, p.36). In other words, observation must take place within the social systems as 'communication is thus a certain way of observing the world by means of the specific distinction between information and utterance'. (Luhmann, 1997, p.37).

'In this context, information is always part of a communication. It is something that functions as information only within the system and within its autopoiesis" (Luhmann, 2002, p.216)' and:

> 'Here, as in the case of the concept of information, what is meant is not an external state --- say, the psychic state of the one who understands --- but a condition that guarantees that communication can continue. In other words, understanding and non-understanding must be distinguished'. (Luhmann, 2002, p.218-219)

Only with this type of model is it possible to put the psychic system aside and focus on communication itself. Observing the mechanisms of society without a dependence on the people or other subjects is the basic principle of Luhmann's Social Systems Theory, in which the meaning of the information in the communication is not decided by the psychic system but is decided (selected) on through a chain of communication. With this understanding, it is possible to express a state in which the communicator's original intent was misunderstood due to the ongoing communication context.

This of course does not mean that people or other subjects are unnecessary for communication to take place, as they are essential communication components; however, they are only environmental components, and not essential parts of the social system.

> 'The environment is, of course, always involved, and without it nothing, absolutely nothing can happen. The term production (or simply poiesis) always refers to only part of the causes an observer can identify as required, namely, the part obtainable through the internal networking of the system's operations, the part with which the system determines its own state'. (Luhmann, 1997, p.52)

To examine the autopoietic system elements in a more abstract way, it would look like the following. An element emerges when a reference (observation) to outside the system and a reference (observation) to the system itself are combined; in other words, an element is generated through a combination of an other-reference (hetero-reference) and a self-reference. Therefore, in communication, 'information' is the other-reference and 'utterance' is a self-reference (Figure 2). Luhmann explained that the psychic system produces elements in the same way; 'psychic systems, too, work by means of the coupling of self- and hetero-references' (Luhmann, 2002, p.57)

> *'Meaningfully operating systems reproduce themselves in the ongoing implementation of the distinction between self-reference and other-reference'. (Luhmann, 1997, p.39)*
>
> *'In short, meaning is `autopoietically' constituted by systems that can only recognize their own boundaries in the process of constituting meaning by providing themselves with inward and outward references, their own distinction of a self and other-reference'. (Luhmann, 2000, p.86)*

This concept can be applied to the element generations in a creative system. In the next section, Luhmann's Social Systems Theory approach is used to re-establish an understanding of creativity.

4.2. Creative Systems

Creative Systems Theory, proposed by one of the authors of this paper, Takashi Iba, is a theory that sees creation as an autopoietic system guided by an internal context (Iba, 2010), in which the act of creation is seen as one creative system, and the elements within the creative system are 'discoveries'; that is, a creative state occurs when a chain of discoveries is generated.

In line with Luhmann, this theory sees 'discovery' as a system element that is separate from human thought. Conventionally, in the area of psychology, creativity has tended to be studied from a human consciousness viewpoint; however, here, creativity is seen as separate from the psychic system (Figure 3), thereby allowing for a focus on the creation itself, but assuming that creative thinking is when there is collaboration between the psychic system and creative system functions.

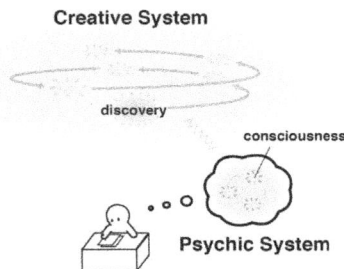

Creative System

discovery

consciousness

Psychic System

Figure 3: Psychic System and Creative System

As stated, the elements in the Creative System are discoveries, which are generated from within the system and can only emerge in relation to that particular creation; that is, the generated elements together constitute the system. As with communication, as the elements of discovery disappear the moment they are generated, they must be generated continuously for the system to exist. Therefore, it can be concluded that the creative system is an autopoetic system; the elements constitute the creative system, which in turn cause new elements to emerge, thereby enabling the system to exist.

In creative systems theory, discovery emerges from a synthesis of the following three components: ideas, associations, and findings (Figure 4). In other words, discovery occurs only when a finding is obtained as a result of an idea that is associated with the on-going creation; that is, the idea is a hetero-reference that refers to the system environment; association is a self-reference that refers to the system; and the finding combines these two reference types, the hetero-reference and the self-reference, the synthesis of which gives rise to the system element, discovery.

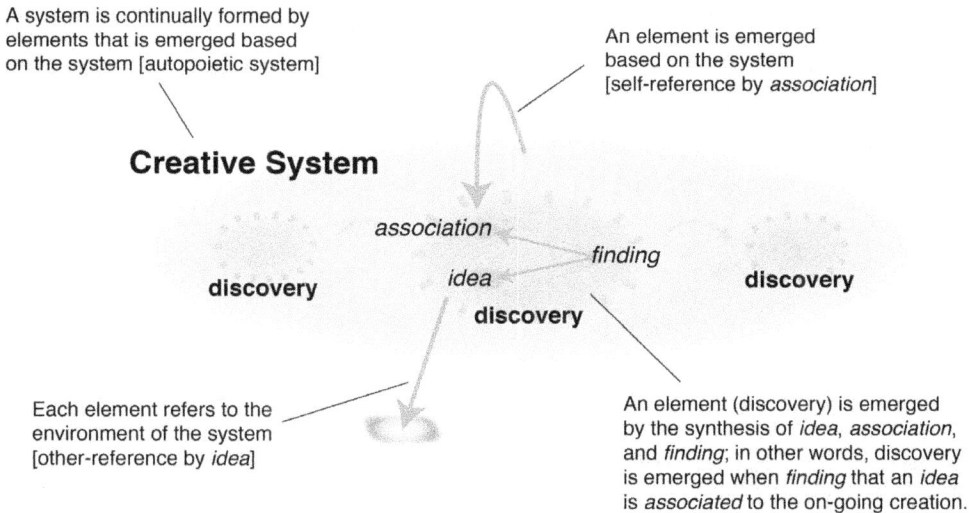

A system is continually formed by elements that is emerged based on the system [autopoietic system]

An element is emerged based on the system [self-reference by *association*]

Creative System

association

finding

discovery   *idea*   **discovery**

discovery

Each element refers to the environment of the system [other-reference by *idea*]

An element (discovery) is emerged by the synthesis of *idea*, *association*, and *finding*; in other words, discovery is emerged when *finding* that an *idea* is *associated* to the on-going creation.

Figure 4: Emergence of Discovery as a System Element by Synthesis of Idea Association, and Finding.

Here, the term 'discovery' refers to any instance that progresses the creative process. In other words, it is an element that has resulted from a previous discovery that has caused a subsequent discovery and exists independently from the psychic system. By viewing the creative process in this way, it is possible to observe the generation and succession of discoveries that occur within the creative process that are separate from human thinking.

For instance, when creating a product, it is necessary to decide on the function, shape, and color. Through the creation process, discoveries are made about the function it will perform, the shape that fits the function, what color is best, etc. As each of these 'discoveries' is made, the product begins to take shape.

Regardless of the psychic process, as ideas and decisions (discoveries) are made, the creative process proceeds through a chain of discoveries when searching for ways to meet the necessary product factors (the 'should be's'), such as what shape suits the function, what color would make it more beautiful, etc. When applied to the development of a novel, the characters, with their certain personalities and experiences, have limited possibilities in terms of how they think and act within the assigned setting of the book. By abiding by the natural flow within the set parameters, the characters' thoughts, actions, and stories unfold; therefore, the 'discoveries' do not occur within the psychic system, but occur as the creation itself, which is why the creative system and psychic system must be separately defined.

This phenomenon can be applied to any creative process whether it is done by one person or by multiple people, as what is most important is the generation and succession of discoveries. In fact, from the perspective of the creation itself, it is not important whether the creation was done by one person or by multiple people if the same chain of discovery takes place (Figure 5). To phrase this in systems theory terms; what is essential to creation is the generation/succession of discoveries, and as long as this takes place, the involvement of one or multiple psychic systems is irrelevant to the creative system.

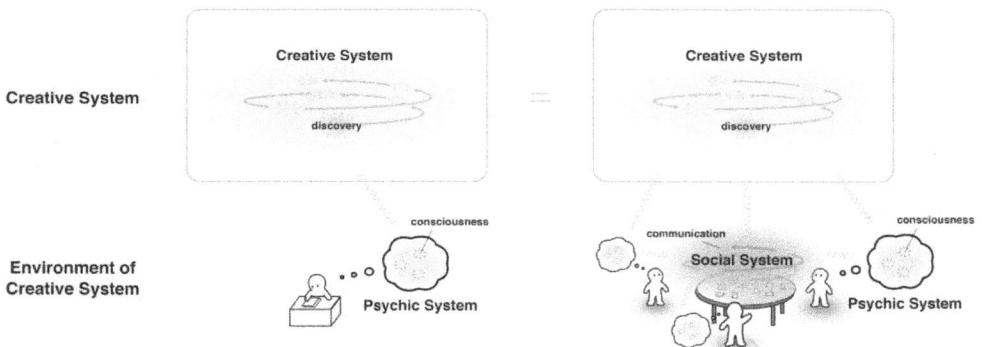

Figure 5: Psychic System and Social System are located in the Creative System Environment

4.3. Action and Experience

The remaining concepts essential to understanding egoless creation are 'action' and 'experience'. 'Action' is a term used by Luhmann for when the cause for the resulting conclusion arises from within the system, and 'experience' is when the cause for the resulting conclusion arises from the environment.

In the theory of autopoietic systems, the emergence of an element is understood as a 'selection' that has taken place in a contingent state from other possibilities; that is, from the many different existing possibilities, only one was selected and only one survived. Through selection, a reduction in complexity takes place and a certain meaning is born; that is, a discovery with a certain meaning emerges as an element.

When such selection attribution is assigned to a certain system, the selection is understood as the action of that system; however, when the selection is made by the environment (including other systems), the selection is understood as an experience of that system.

> *'According to the distinction of attribution, a meaning system distinguishes experience and action in relation to itself and in relation to other systems: if the meaning selection is attributed to the environment, then what occurs is characterized as experience, and the system turns to its environment to seek points of contact for further measures (even if the system was involved as experiencing!)'. (Luhmann, 1984, p.84)*

Using the concepts so far examined, we apply this relationship between the creative and psychic system to a creative activity, whereby the egoless creation is referred to as 'Creation Type A', and the intentional creation is referred to as 'Creation Type B' to examine the differences. Figure 6 visualizes the differences in the way the actions/experiences are assigned to each type.

For an intentional creation based on a creator's intentions (Creation Type B), the discoveries that take place are intentionally selected (Figure 6, right); that is, the psychic system takes the selection action and the creative system experiences it. Therefore, while the discovery is controlled by the person engaging in the creative activity, the chain of discovery is artificial and intentional.

On the other hand, in an egoless creation (Creation Type A), the discoveries that take place within the creative system are initiated by the system itself (Figure 6, left). In other words, the discoveries are selected based on the contexts within the creative system; that is, the psychic system experiences the discoveries selected as actions by the creative system. It should be stressed that on the systems level, even the person involved in the creative activity merely experiences the discovery in their psychic system.

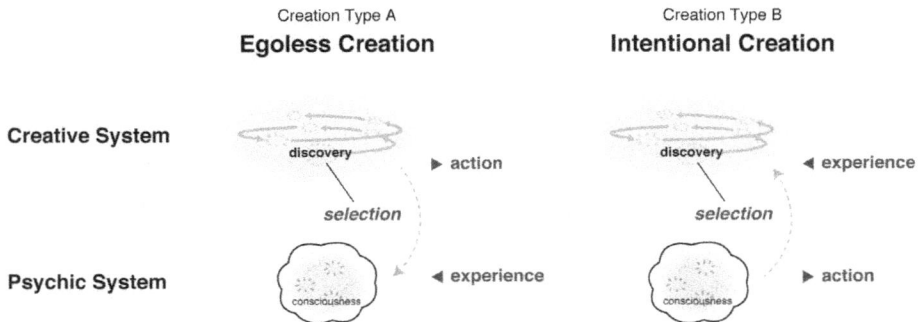

Figure 6: Differences between Egoless Creation and Intentional Creation, demonstrated using the concept of Action/Experience from autopoietic systems theory

Based on this view, it is possible for a chain of discoveries to occur in a creative system without the need for psychic system control. When writing a novel, the characters' speeches and actions are discovered as actions within the creative system based on the parameters of the personalities and the situations, with the author only experiencing them in their psychic system. Therefore, a chain of discoveries take place within the creative system that is outside the psychic system, which only observes the creative process. By observing the chain of discoveries, a writer can understand and transcribe what they have witnessed; that is, the psychic system does not actively control the creative system, but rather passively observes the workings of the creative system and collects the results.

5. Functions of Pattern Language in Egoless Creation

From the argument thus far, it can be concluded that egoless creation is possible and that the psychic system experiences the creative process as it unfolds in the creative system. In this section, the role of pattern language in supporting egoless creation is examined using Creative Systems Theory and Social Systems Theory. First, the functions of the patterns in creation are examined, after which the function of pattern language as a language of collaboration between multiple people is elucidated.

5.1. Patterns as discovery media in a Creative System

In a creative system, each individual pattern provides a discovery as to how to create something. 'Each pattern is a rule which describes what you have to do to generate the entity it defines' (Alexander, 1979, p.182).

> 'As an element of language, a pattern is an instruction, which shows how this spatial con-figuration can be used over and over again to resolve the given system of forces wherever the context makes it relevant. The pattern is, in short, at the same time a thing which happens in the world and the rule which tells us how to create that thing and when we must create it'. (Alexander, 1979, p.247)

Each pattern describes a context, a problem that is likely to occur in that context, and a solution to resolve the problem. The relationships between these components provide a new discovery for the ongoing creation. Imagine for instance, that you are involved in a creative process and have found a pattern that fits your context. In such a case, the pattern offers a solution that describes what needs to be done. With the pattern offering a solution (idea), it is possible to find an association to apply that solution to your creative process, thereby generating a discovery, as explained by Alexander;

> 'Each pattern is an operator which differentiates space: that is, it creates distinctions where there was no distinction before'. (Alexander, 1979, p.373)

This quote implies that by observing the creative system, the idea of a solution suggested by the pattern is selected from contingent possibilities. In this way, the patterns in the pattern language function as 'discovery media' which enables what was originally an improbable discovery to become probable.

Patterns as language are capable of supporting an entire chain of discoveries, which is the effect created by the pattern language structure and sequences as individual patterns are not independent but are interconnected with other patterns in a network structure.

> 'Each pattern sits at the center of a network of connections which connect it to certain other patterns that help to complete it'. (Alexander, 1979, p.313)

There is also a pattern sequence;

> 'Since the patterns are arranged in order of their morphological importance, the use of the language guarantees that a whole is successively differentiated, so that smaller and smaller wholes appear in it as a result of the distinctions which are drawn'. (Alexander, 1979, p. 373-374)

Therefore, by following the pattern sequence, it is possible to focus on one pattern at a time. As mentioned in the chapter titled 'One Pattern at a Time' in Alexander's The Timeless Way of Building, 'Within the sequence the language defines, you can focus on each pattern by itself, one at a time, certain that those patterns which come later in the sequence will fit into the design that has evolved so far'. (Alexander, 1979, p.402)

For this reason, Alexander believed that 'the sequence of patterns for a design — as generated by the language — is therefore the key to that design'. (Alexander, 1979, p.382), and he refers to the sequence as an operator that has created the aforementioned distinctions;

> *The language is a sequence of these operators, in which each one further differentiates the image which is the product of the previous differentiations'. (Alexander, 1979, p.373)*

In summary, individual patterns make it easier to find the kinds of solutions (forms) that should be associated as ideas, and ultimately makes it easier to generate discoveries. The pattern sequences also enable the chain of discoveries to take place (Figure 7). Because the patterns contain an essence that generates a certain quality, an object created from the patterns will have wholeness and quality.

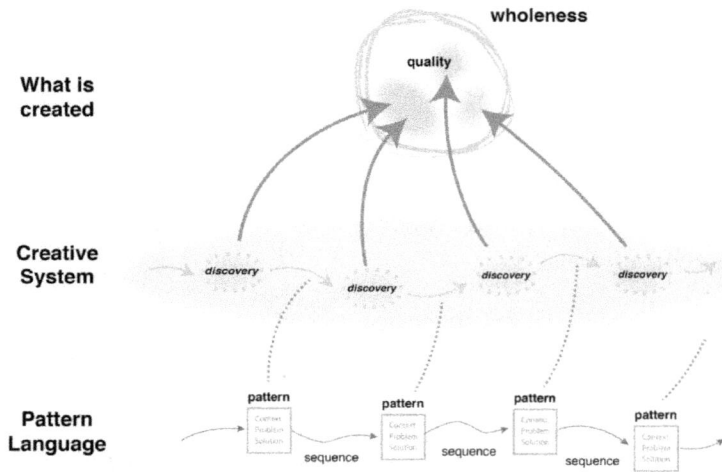

Figure 7: Pattern language supporting a chain of discoveries

What must be emphasized here is that the patterns do not dictate everything. What they do provide is a parameter for possible outcomes to proceed in an abstractly defined direction. To phrase this in terms of the theory of autopoietic systems, a pattern functions as a 'structure'. Luhmann describes the term, 'structure' as follows.

> *'Structures are conditions for restricting the area of connective operations, and are hence conditions for the autopoiesis of the system'. (Luhmann, 1997, p.261)*

> *'structures always realize themselves only in directing (restricting the possibilities for) progression from operation to operation'. (Luhmann, 1997, p.261)*

A pattern functions as the structures or conditions within the ongoing autopoietic creative system. Although the terms 'system' and 'structure' are generally used interchangeably, in the theory of autopoietic systems, they are defined as two completely different terms.

While the function of pattern language in a creative system has now been explained, how does this apply to the creative activities of the fiction writers mentioned earlier in the paper? To answer this question, we refer again to Alexander. In the Timeless Way of Building, Alexander discusses those patterns not explicitly expressed but existing inside a person's mind.

> *'In short, each one of us, no matter how humble or how elevated has a vast fabric of rules of thumb in our minds which tell us what to do when it comes time to act. At the time of any act of design, all we can hope to do is to use the rules of thumb we have collected in the best way we know how'. (Alexander, 1979, p.205)*

Therefore, the creative activities of the fiction authors can be understood as using rules of thumb or patterns in their minds to generate discoveries about the character's thinking, speech, action, communication, development, changes in human relationships, the natural flow of the story, and beyond. The patterns in the mind that propel the story also have forces behind them; as the thoughts and actions are naturally discovered with the assistance of these forces and are applied continuously, the story moves and unfolds. In this way, fiction authors entrust their creative development to these 'patterns in mind'.

These rules of thumb are heavily dependent on experience and are obtained through a long process of practice and mastery. The purpose of pattern languages is to share such rules so they can be usable by anyone.

5.2. Pattern Language for the Structural Coupling of the Psychic and Social System

What has been examined thus far are the functions pattern language has in the creative system. In this section, how pattern language functions as a collaborative tool among multiple people is further investigated.

After explaining how to use pattern language in a design process in The Timeless Way of Building, Alexander discusses how it can used as a collaborative tool involving multiple people: 'In the same way, groups of people can conceive of larger public buildings on the ground by following a common pattern language, almost as if they had a single mind'. (Alexander, 1979, p.427). A significant function of pattern language is that it not only supports discovery through what is written in the patterns (the contents) but that the individual patterns are named and can be used as vocabulary in thought and communication. Pattern languages when used as common vocabulary support collaboration.

To further this understanding, it is necessary to focus on the 'language' aspect of pattern language in relation to the psychic system and social system perspectives. As already established, both the psychic system and social system are operationally closed autopoietic systems. However, the social system is a system that exists in tandem with the psychic system, and vice versa. Luhmann explained how these systems interacted using the 'structural coupling' concept proposed by Maturana.

> *'What is the mechanism of structural coupling between psychic and social systems, between consciousness and communication? I am tempted to answer: `Language!' Language is the answer to a theoretical problem that is posed very precisely. Language is obviously double-sided. It can be used psychically as well as communicatively, ...' (Luhmann, 2002, p.202)*

> *'Plainly, the regular structural coupling of consciousness systems with communication systems is made possible by language' (Luhmann, 1997, p.60)*

As Luhmann stated 'Language is obviously double-sided' (Luhmann, 2002, p.202); that is, language functions as structure in both the psychic system and the social system. In the psychic system, language affects what is selected in people's minds. To use Luhmann's words; 'seen from the psychic standpoint, language is an attractor of attention'. (Luhmann, 2002, p.202) However, in the social system, language affects what information is selected in the communication. Therefore, as a language, pattern language functions as a structure in both systems, and these systems are also structurally coupled.

However, as discussed, structure is merely the condition that guides the generation of the elements in an autopoietic system, and therefore does not determine the system's state from the outside. Even when structurally coupled, the two autopoietic systems interact as operationally closed systems, and the condition of the system is not determined from the outside: 'Structural couplings do not determine the state of the system'. (Luhmann, 2002, p.88)

In this way, in collaboration, pattern language not only supports the discoveries in the creative system (as seen in the previous subsection) but also facilitates the structural coupling of the psychic and social systems (Figure 8), which is what occurs when using pattern language in a design process with multiple people.

Alexander recommended visiting the actual building site to gain a clearer idea when designing with multiple people. In other words, he stressed the importance of sharing not only the language but also the design place, as this is an important reference for observations in both the psychic and social systems.

> 'Of course, they no longer have the medium of a single mind as an individual person does. But instead, the group uses the site 'out there in front of them', as the medium in which the design takes its shape'. (Alexander, 1979, p.449)
>
> 'The site speaks to the people — the building forms itself — and people experience it as something received, not created'. (Alexander, 1979, p.449)

In this way, both the psychic and social systems experience the generation/succession of discoveries in the creative system, with language functioning as the coupling; however, to experience the creative system, the ideas suited to the context must be associated. For that discovery to take place, it is not only necessary to have patterns, but also to have an enabling context, which is why it is necessary to share the creation place; once this is done, it becomes possible to observe all three systems (creative, psychic, and social) and their generated elements (discovery, consciousness, and communication).

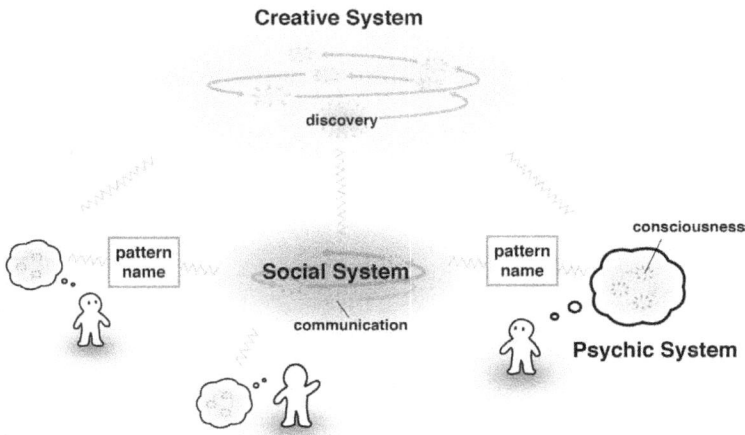

Figure 8: Pattern language enabling a structural coupling of the psychic system and social system

6. Conclusion

This paper examined the goals of pattern language by focusing on egoless creation, an important concept repeatedly mentioned by Alexander in The Timeless Way of Building. Alexander argued that 'the builder must let go of all his willful images, and start with a void'. (Alexander, 1979, p.538) and that 'you yourself are only the medium for this creative spark, not its originator', (Alexander, 1979, p.397); ideas that are not easily understood in modern thinking. However, as demonstrated in this paper, such arguments have also been made by creators in various domains.

This paper examined creativity from a theory of autopoietic systems perspective and reached the conclusion that egoless creation is a state in which the generation/succession of discoveries within the creative system are being experienced by the psychic system. It was also established that pattern language functions as the discovery media that support discovery selection in a creative system and supports collaboration through its structural coupling of the psychic and social systems.

Although Alexander did not refer to the theory of autopoietic systems, it can be surmised that this was in line with his thinking. From Notes on the Synthesis of Form to The Nature of Order, Alexander continued to emphasize the limitations of intentional design, and worked on finding a mechanism for generation that was beyond individual abilities or experiences. In Notes on the Synthesis of Form, Alexander observed a transition from an age of the 'un-selfconsciousness process' to an age of the 'self-conscious process' and sought solutions to the realization of quality by taking the self-conscious age into account.

Because a receiver's frame of thinking is heavily dependent on modern thinking, Alexander's most important arguments have been perceived as 'mystic'. This paper, therefore, opens a path to understanding Alexander's 'mystic' arguments through a systems theory perspective. We hope that this paper can act as a trigger or stimulus for future discussions on pattern language.

7. References

Alexander, C. (1964). Notes on the Synthesis of Form. Harvard University Press.

Alexander, C., Silverstein, M., Angel, S., Ishikawa, S., Abrams, D. (1975). The Oregon Experiment (Centre for Environmental Structure Series, Vol. 3). Oxford University Press.

Alexander, C., Ishikawa, S., Silverstein, M., Jacobson, M., Fiksdahl-King, I. & Angel, S. (1977) A pattern language: towns, buildings, construction. Oxford University Press.

Alexander, C. (1979) The Timeless Way of Building, Oxford University Press.

Alexander, C., Davis, H., Martinez, J., Corner, D. (1985). The Production of Houses (Centre for Environmental Structure Series, Vol. 4). Oxford University Press.

Alexander, C. (2002a), The Nature of Order: An Essay of the Art of Building and the Nature of the Universe, Book 1: The Phenomenon of Life, Centre for Environmental Structure.

Alexander, C. (2002b), The Nature of Order: An Essay of the Art of Building and the Nature of the Universe, Book 2: The Process of Creating Life, Routledge.

Alexander, C., Ishikawa, S., Silverstein, M., Jacobson, M., Fiksdahl-King, I. & Angel, S. (1977) A pattern language: towns, buildings, construction. Oxford University Press.

Ende, M. (2000) Monogatarino Yohaku: Ends ga Saigoni Hanashitakoto [The Peripheral of a Story: Ende's Last Words], in Japanese, Iwanami Shoten.

Hisaishi, J. (2006). Kandou wo Tsukuremasuka? [On Evoking Deep Emotion], Kadokawa Shoten.

Iba, T. (2010). "An autopoietic systems theory for creativity". Procedia-Social and Behavioural Sciences, 2(4): 6610-6625.

Iba, T. (2016) "Pattern Language 3.0 and Fundamental Behavioural Properties", Peter Baumgartner, Tina Gruber-Muecke, Richard Sickinger (Eds.), Pursuit of Pattern Languages for Societal Change. Designing Lively Scenarios in Various Fields. Berlin: epubli, pp.200-233.

Kawai, H. and Murakami, H,. (2016) Murakami Haruki Kawai Halo ni Aini Iku [Haruki Murakami Goes to Meet Hayao Kawai]., in Japanese, Shinchosha. English translation is published as Haruki Murakami, Hayao Kawai, Haruki Murakami Goes to Meet Hayao Kawai, Daimon Verlag, Einsiedeln, 2016

Kawakita, J. (1993) Sozo to Dento: Ningen no Shino to Minshushugi no Kongen wo Saguru [Creation and Tradition: Search for Foundation of Human and Democracy], in Japanese, Shodensha.

Luhmann, N. (1984). Soziale Systeme: Grundriß einer allgemeinen Theorie, Frankfurt: Suhrkamp. (English translation: Social Systems, John Bednarz Jr., Dirk Baecker.(translator), Stanford: Stanford University Press, 1995).

Luhmann, N. (1997) Die Gesellschaft der Gesellschaft, Suhrkamp Verlag Frankfurt, English Translation was published as Theory of Society, Translated by David Rhodes Barrett, Stanford University Press, 2012

Luhmann, N. (2000) Die Religion der Gesellschaft, Suhrkamp Verlag Frankfurt, English Translation was publiished as A Systems Theory of Religion, Translated by David A. Brenner with Adrian Hermann, Stanford University Press, 2013

Luhmann, N. (2002) Einführung in die Systemtheorie, Carl-Auer-Systeme Verlag, English Translation was published as Introduction to Systems Theory, Translated by Peter Gilgen, Polity Press, 2013

Maturana, H. R. & Varela, F. J. (1972). De Maquinas y Seres Vivos. Editorial Universitaria S.A. English Ediftion was published as Autopoiesis and Cognition: The realization of The Living, Dordrecht: D. Reidel Publishing Company, 1980

Miyazaki, H. (1996) Shuppatsutenq 1979-1996 [Stating Point 1979-1996], in Japanese, Tokuma Shoten, English translation was published as Starting Point: 1979-1996, translated by Beth Cary and Frederik L. Schodt, VIZ Media,2006.

Murakami, H. (2010) Yume Miru Tameni Maiasa Bokuha Mezameru Nodesu [Wake Up Every Morning in Order to Dream], in Japanese, Bungei Shunju.

Murakami, H. (2015) Shokugyo Toshiteno Shosetsuka [Novelist as a profession], in Japanese, Switch Publishing.

Tanikawa, S. (2006) Shi wo Kaku: Naze Wabash ha Shi wo Tsukurunoka[On Writing Poems: Why I Create Poetry], in Japanese, Shinchosha.

Yoro, T and Hisaishi, J. (2009). Mimi de Kangaeru: Nou wa Meikyoku wo Hossuru [Thinking with the Ears: The Brain Craves Masterpieces], Kadokawa Shoten.

When Thievery Isn't an Option or
An Overview of Embodied Making

Quillien, Jenny
Embodied Making Institute, Freedom Lab Campus, Amsterdam
jenny@product-foundry.com

As a nascent pattern craft, Embodied Making draws deeply and respectfully from preceding traditions (notably Alexandrian pattern languages, phenomenology, and Kaizen), but, perforce, must engage in its own pathfinding. It has chosen to abide not in the hallowed halls of academe but in the ordinary streets and workplaces of ordinary folk and embrace the messy instability of life characteristic of its generation. It's a 'start-from-scratch' approach, still imperfect but gaining in track record, still with very few practitioners but growing, and still really hard work. Part Zen and beginner's mind, part standard ethnographic field work, part participative, part solo, part tallying up forces (bone achingly boring) and part soaring like a bird to intuit wholeness: it's an art of sense-making, solutioning, and patterning. The Amsterdam headquarters for its practice and training fancies itself more of a dojo than a mass production facility.

Embodied; Patterns; Domain Knowledge

1. From Whence

The Big Big Frame. Embodied Making draws energy from the natural tension that exists between humanity's two basic and conflicting paradigms for understanding the future. On the one hand is Socrates, Wahabism, Predeterministic Fate, and any MBA curriculum. The future is knowable, constructible, controllable. It's all about bringing knowledge to the center and shaping the present in terms of the future. On the other hand is Heraclitus, Taoism, Yoga, and Sufism. The future is accepted as unknowable and, as in aikido, one does not pre-guess the next move but remains alert in the present. Sages of this tradition redistribute knowledge from the center back to the edges.

The Big Frame. Very specifically, Embodied Making takes lineage from a) phenomenology and action research, b) Zen principles applied to manufacturing by Toyota (interestingly twisted by envious Anglo-Saxon onlookers back toward fear-assauging control with inventions such as Six Sigma and Lean) and c) the pattern-language work done in the 1970's.

The Frame. In this essay, for this audience, more attention will be given to this third heritage. To briefly recall some of the history and salient features of pattern-language work, the United States Government (ah! Those were the days!) wanted to explore the relationship between human well-being and the built environment. A team in Berkeley was engaged to do the research. The upshot was a 'walkabout' where existing stable configurations which successfully framed human comfort were noticed, analyzed, documented, cataloged, and named. The investigation was Second Order Science where the observers were explicitly included in the results. For example, nobody likes to feel the precariousness of a narrow ledge but everybody's quite happy to enjoy a view and connectedness to the street from a deeper SIX FOOT BALCONY.

For another example, the Berkeley team noticed that generous overhanging roofs seemed a plus: gave shade, a place to sit next to a house, read, chat, keep an eye on children at play. A physical ease, a sort of animal sense of security prevailed and distinguished these buildings from the ones with more perfunctory caps on their heads. Such a SHELTERING ROOF, as this pattern came to be called, could be found in building traditions from California to Borneo, the variations among them reflecting the texture of local materials, tooling, and social fabric.

Here in Figure 1 is a sketch of the old style Black Forest farm with its SHELTERING ROOF and a description from Heidegger (in Building, Dwelling, Thinking) noting how the forces at play (technology, geography, culture) intersected and found resolution.

> ". . .It placed the farm on the wind-sheltered mountain slope looking south, among the meadows close to the spring. It gave it the wide overhanging shingle roof whose proper slope bears up under the burden of snow, and which, reaching deep down, shields the chambers against the storms of the long winter nights. It did not forget the altar corner behind the community table; it made room in its chamber for the hallowed places of childbed and the "tree of the dead" - for that is what they call a coffin there: the Totenbaum – and, in this way, it designed for the different generations under one roof the character of their journey through time." (Heidegger)

Figure 1. Black Forest farmhouse (Source: alamy.com)

The published compilation of the patterns, A Pattern Language, was (and remains) immensely popular. From a compact notation about a building solution, readers could take inspiration for their projects or simply increase their phenomenological appreciation, their reflective perspicacity, about their own lived experience and the built environment.

> When I was reading this pattern, I thought of my niece who has a village house in France where family sometimes gathers for long summer weekends. Once, when I was there, my niece's husband walked in the kitchen with a bag of groceries and a bottle of gin. "My wife," he chuckled, "doesn't drink a lot but she drinks steadily." The house had one of those 'perfunctory caps' but the adjacent barn had a massive overhanging roof that came close to the ground. It was always to the shade and comfort of that old barn roof that we retreated around five in the afternoon for conversation and my niece's ritual gin and tonic.

The original pattern-language efforts lie within the Western preference for knowledge at the center where the past can be exhumed, explained, and used in the present to control a future of choice—which, in the case of A Pattern Language, teeter-totters on the brink of a rather nostalgic interpretation of the past.

2. When Thievery Isn't an Option

In the 1990's people in disciplines far afield from building (software, education, adminis-tration, town planning, politics) sensed in pattern-languages a powerful tool that could be generalized. Fabulous amounts of information could be expressed in memorable units of repeatable solutions, combined, recombined in new ways, and developed.

However, to underscore a most significant point, the depth, power, intelligence, and beauty of the original pattern-language work comes, in great part, from the superiority of thievery over design from scratch. The Berkeley team wasn't inventing building techniques. They simple knew a good thing when they saw it. They were riding on the shoulders, not of giants, but ordinary people, hundreds of them, who, over hundreds of years, had experimented and honed solutions to problems, and not just any old problems, but their own problems that they knew intimately. The Washington anointed experts were documenting the peo-ple's 'un-self-conscious process,' as Christopher Alexander had come to call it.

The Berkeley team was very explicit: No poor sap of an architect drawing up a blueprint miles removed from the site and not really knowing the lives of the inhabitants will ever ever ever get a design right. It's too hard. There are too many variable, too many forces at play.

But, alas, let's face it. We are poor saps. Whatever our field (pedagogy, civic development, digital media), we must devise patterns from scratch because there is nothing to steal. Things are too new, too unstable, too changing. There are too few successful configurations to simply go cherry picking on a pleasant walkabout.

So, it is here that enters Embodied Making, which addresses the need for patterns for today's world. And it is here that Embodied Making makes a zig and a zag back to where knowledge hangs out at the edges and to where attention is on the here and now.

3. The Reader's Thanks and Forgiveness

In a short introductory overview aiming to provide only a helicopter view without overbur-dening the reader ('thanks' says the reader) we must sacrifice some subtleties, complexities, and understanding that can come only from practice.

We must also sacrifice an adequate sense of directionality. The directionality of the origi-nal pattern-language method was that of collection and curation: a) notice a configuration that supports well-being, b) analyze the forces that intersect and find resolution in that configuration, c) intuit an abstract form from multiple concrete renditions of that problem/

solution relationship, d) research for relevant psychological or sociological background e) give the pattern a short memorable name and fill in a standard format (context, problem, forces, image that captures the essential forces at play, and a 'therefore' rule-of-thumb set of instructions).

Since Embodied Making isn't about cataloging established patterns, and since there are no existing configurations as start points, Embodied Making must contend with a multi-directional flow of inquiry and solutioning. It's about grappling with the lack of patterns in the chaos and rapid technological changes of our times. It feels more like a big ball of spaghetti where the practitioner might dig in from any point than a plate of nicely combed out threads. How, for example, do we coherently digitalize city life in Amsterdam, by that we mean not only use cell phones to locate nearby bikes to rent but coordinate various smart city apps, defend the small local coffee shop against the deep-pocketed Starbuck's digital presence, intercede on traffic lights and get the ambulance through in minimum time, support a neighborhood in self-organization, protect the citizen's digital rights of privacy. However, for initial comprehensibility we'll do some combing out and therefore falsifying. ('I forgive' says the reader).

That agreed, a rather skeletal summary runs as follows.

4. A Short Overview

As a way to make sense of situations and solve problems, the practitioner of Embodied Making relies on an ability to think with analogies and metaphors, and, in the best of cases, on a general polymath background. He or she looks to the edges and ordinary folk, gathers (a bit like an ethnographer), stories (thick descriptions) of everyday life. This is done in order to understand real experiences and develop a deep-felt textured grasp of that situation. The practitioner derives forces from the stories to understand exactly why people have the experiences they do. Forces are then, to use a cooking metaphor, 'reduced' to a concentrate and 'ingested' by the practitioner. Intuiting the latent 'wholeness' from the dynamic interplay of these forces, the practitioner resolves them in elegant effective solutions.

That's it. . . But, a little unpacking can go a long way.

Embodied Making itself is formulated in procedural and decision patterns about the investigative process. Practitioners use these process patterns in different combinations depending on the project they're working on and their starting point in the big ball of spaghetti. To illustrate a few of the most frequently used patterns (NAMES IN SMALL CAPS) we can reformulate a summary in these terms:

Embodied Making grounds itself in domain knowledge, that concrete nitty gritty grasp of some piece of reality, say a craft or a business or a neighborhood or new technology or whatever is of interest. The practitioner typically doesn't possess the requisite domain knowledge so the process is, by necessity, a surrogate one. The practitioner has to locate KEY STONES, people who live, work, eat, and breathe that domain. That doesn't mean KEY STONES can give a nice clean lecture on the domain. In fact, they usually can't: their expertise tends to be tacit, i.e., more in their hands than in their vocabulary. Besides, they usually don't want to—they would rather get on with real work than entertain some Sherlock Holmes snooping around.

Typically, the practitioner has to identify KEY STONES and get to them through CHANCE CONVERSATIONS with other more accessible but less skilled people in the domain who know that, whatever the organizational chart might indicate, the place really depends on that gruff old shop floor supervisor who is the only one who can fix all the machines. Or maybe they know that the heartbeat of the neighborhood really lies with the green grocer with an ear to the ground and a mind like a steel trap. Or maybe the KEY STONE is the teacher who has been at the school for twenty years and taught the same course fifty times.

With both CHANCE CONVERSATIONS and KEY STONES, the most common job is to elicit STORIES OF REAL EXPERIENCE, narratives of day-to-day lives. A good story eschews lofty abstractions and stays close to the ground with events, facts, details, a bit like a video camera that can't film an abstraction (such as 'motivation' or 'social capital') but can film what people say and do. From collected stories the practitioner (patiently and tediously) pulls out a BODY OF FORCES, those facts or beliefs or behaviors which give shape to what is going on.

Sometimes the process demands that the practitioner reiteratively return to a storyteller to substantiate a force, its occurrence, experienced quality, consistency and result. So sometimes a story leads to a force. Sometimes a force leads to a story. Storying has its own

forces: it's a selective memory of the past; different people experience the same event differently; stories are selectively shared; some stories are public, some private; stories can be vehicles for publicizing the storyteller, and so on.

Sometimes the start point is a general malaise about a new development still in a shakedown phase. Imagine, for example, that we are exploring the general theme of how new virtual workspaces can be integrated most effectively with physical ones. [And this is true. It's one of the explorations in progress at the Embodied Making Institute.] Within that larger question, we might consider the smaller domain of video conferencing with technologies such as Skype or Zoom which are far from perfected. A sampling of some story excerpts,

ILLUSTRATIVE STORY SHORTS:

> *I don't want to drive to main campus for Faculty meetings. It's not only the three hours to drive there and back, the meetings themselves are a horrendously boring waste of time. But they're mandatory. I attend from home through Zoom and prepare by collecting things I can discreetly do at my desk while pretending to be attentive to the meeting. Paying bills and doing my nails and stuff like that.*

I got my degree on-line. I always had two computers set up. One to sign into class and the second for the video games I played during class.

My employer sometimes lets us work from home and report in on skype. It's nice but when I sign on to skype the people at the office can see into my room. It's messy and I don't want them to see it but I also don't want to clean it up.

I teach on Zoom and require students to have a camera but sometimes they tilt the camera to the ceiling and I have to stop class and tell them to readjust their camera so I can see them. If nothing happens I note them as absent.

About fifteen of us, spread out on three continents, get together on Zoom to study the work of an English philosopher, J.G. Bennett. It's great. I'm working with people in Sweden, Scotland, Australia, Holland, and the U.S. The technology is iffy. Last week was really bad. The main facilitator is in Edinburg and his voice was distorted, sometimes sounding like chipmunk chatter and sometimes really slow. This guy in Edinburg isn't very tech-savvy so another participant in Holland tries to help. So last week we experimented by turning off participant cameras and share screens and at one point we all signed out while the guy in Edinburg shut down his computer and then rebooted. With all that we didn't get much done and have fallen behind in our schedule.

I teach on-line now and the names of the students in the virtual classroom are listed on the screen but I have to constantly scroll up and down the list to scan all the names and see who has the hand icon up for wanting to ask a question. It's clunky. In a real classroom, you can see the audience, sense when to field for questions or move on to another topic or develop the one you're on with another example. And some of the best questions surface in the margins, you know, at break, or just before or after class. All that subtlety is gone.

All of our meetings are held at headquarters with people from the sites in other towns dialing in. I dial in. The talking takes place between the headquarters people while the distance people just sit passive. The video equipment is placed so that all we see is the back of heads and sometimes we have to guess at who is speaking and what they are saying. We have microphones but it's hard to interrupt and even though the headquarters people can see us on the screen at the back

of the room they usually don't look. Not that I blame them all that much. I've been at head-quarters for meetings and people on the back screens show up about as big as marbles. If an important topic comes up I usually end up sending in an e-mail after the meeting.

From such stories, we derive forces. Practitioners often collect as many as one thousand forces before they feel they are ready to 'reduce' them to FORCE CLUSTERS and ENCAPSU-LATED FORCES. There is no simple way to know how much information is enough to cover a domain. It's a gut feel but a rule of thumb is that we need a decent sampling of informants, i.e., a MOSAIC OF PARTICIPANTS, a dozen KEY STONES, and STORIES OF REAL EXPERIENCE that yield about one thousand forces. Why so many forces? Because we want solutions ca-pable of handling a rich variety of facts and situations. And what else will help is to maintain a beginner's mind. We're exploring. We don't know. We stay open to possibilities.

In a short paper, we can't do enough stories to yield a thousand forces but a taste is called for. A few of the forces implicit in the story excerpts above would include ones such as:

Video conferencing technology affords more (and different) ways to hide disinterest than physical meetings. [A force can be an index of many experiences.]

Available bandwidth can influence the transmission of sound. [An ELEMENTAL FORCE can't be broken down further.]

Video conferencing technology may have a built-in power imbalance between central and peripheral attendees. [A force may require validation by collecting additional stories.]

Voluntary and involuntary attendees may exploit the technology differently. [A force may engender an ontology. Perhaps we need a taxonomy of video conferencing uses leading to different sets of features or software.]

The quality of meetings is affected by the technological proficiencies of the users.

The quality of meetings is affected by the robustness of the technological infrastructure.

Some users may not want the video camera in their personal space. (Forces may lead to wider considerations about the domain such as changes in the qualities of ordinary distinctions between public/private intimate/shared which are brought about by the technology.)

The subtleties and richness of human interaction that prefer marginal times and spaces (before/after, body language and other non-verbal signaling) is lessened with existing video conferencing technology.

5. Intuiting Wholeness Through FORCE INTERACTION

The crux. The crucible. The real craft of the embodied making. By 'ingesting' forces, the practitioner must feel phenomenologically (not intellectualize) the pushes and pulls, the weights, and intersections of the forces at play.

Embodiment is what happens to us, for example, when we take a pottery class and attempt to center the clay on the wheel. We fail repeatedly at it until the various forces, pressure of our hands on the clay, specific inconsistencies in the clay, speed of the wheel, all fall into place in our muscular understanding of what to do. Or, take the astronomer Kepler who knew that the planetary orbits were not circular but he could not yet make sense of his measurements. He sat with them and sat some more and still sat perplexed. Through the sitting, the assimilating of the numbers into the core of his being, he suddenly realized, "it breathes." From that holistic insight, he then could work out the rhythmic slightly irregular elliptical movements. Or, consider the chemist Dimitri Mendeleev who covered his living room floor with notes written on bits of paper and for three days systematically shoved them around in different configurations. At the end of the three days he had the periodic table. Closer to home, for some of the readers anyway, Agile masters such as Kent Beck insisted on a Mendeleev-esque handling of user stories and Peter Naur spoke of building a theory of the world and how software was to support it. And so it will go with us. We 'gotta grok' the forces. Out of 'holistic' groking will come prototyping and solutions.

And we must embrace forces as the slippery dancing eels they really are. In this very partial example of video conferencing, we can already see so many interactions possible between, say, camera, desire to participate, camera control features, group size, chairing skills, privacy, infrastructure, and we haven't scratched the surface. Or we might look at the spatial arrangement of video conferencing shown below in Figure 2 and start to sense the forces it resolves and the ones that it doesn't: group size would be constrained but the arrangement might help resolve power imbalance or make faking attentiveness more difficult.

Figure 2. Spatial arrangement for small group videoconferencing (Source: sketch adapted from advertisement for brandmatrix Pakistan).

FORCE INTERACTION is a big deal. The topic commands demonstration even in a short introduction. For clarity and brevity, a simple and familiar example might serve our purposes best.

Imagine that we are in Amsterdam and we take the mundane pattern, the ordinary WINDOW that obviously resolves three forces: a need for ventilation, a need for light, and a need for a view upon the world. Add a fourth force, a HIDDEN FORCE, that was so ambient that we ignored it: the temperature range of temperate climates.

Let us, say, replace temperate climate with harsh Saharan sun and heat, and, suddenly, all bets are off. The WINDOW pattern (Figure 3) is no longer an effective resolution of the four forces. The first three forces must be de-clustered and reconfigured with other forces in the environment. Totally different patterns (which our Middle Eastern brethren have figured out) emerge as successful. Tiny LIGHT WELLS (Figure 4) are sufficient for ample light and block excessive heat and, also, they serve the cultural force of strong privacy of interior spaces. Ventilation and coolth are better served by BAGDIR (wind towers) (Figure 5). The MASHRABIYA pattern (Figure 6) resolves the forces of a view upon the world, coolth through a sort of swamp cooler, and the cultural force of privacy. ROOF TOPS become a linked pattern resolving coolth, view upon the world and privacy—except, of course, when King David managed to spy upon Bathsheba bathing atop her house and history took a different course.

Figure 3. The ordinary window resolves these forces: need for light, air, view to the outside, within temperate climates.

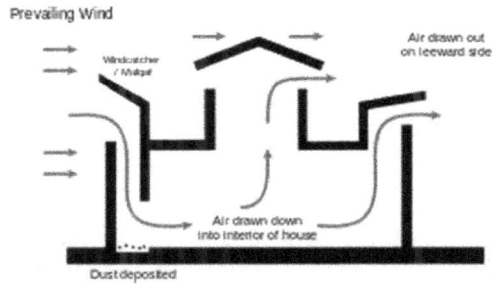

Figure 4. Light wells are small opening that let in ample light and block excessive sun and heat (Source Sketch by Australian Weaver Hawkins done in 1922 of a street in Tangiers).

Figure 5. Bagdir or wind towers optimize ventilation and coolth through air circulation (Source Wikipedia).

Figure 6. Mashrabiya. A 'window-esque' construction that allows you to see out but nobody can see in. It is heavily shaded and often accompanied by 'swamp coolers' of pottery filled with water.

Embodied Making, intensive in time and skill requirements, typically won't be used for problems that are simple (just a few variables as in WINDOW) or for questions best handled through statistics, but rather with complex problems where a handful of forces interact dynamically with each other. Examples could be a new technology, like video conferencing that changes how people work, or bringing a derelict neighborhood back to life, or a business that needs to maintain stability and simultaneously revamp their product lines. When investigating such complexity (a nod here to Jane Jacobs' comments on investigating city life) attention is paid to processes, work proceeds from the particular to the general, and the eye is on the watch-out for unaverage clues.

6. Realms of Practice

For sure, Embodied Making is a work in progress but there are already quite a few patterns currently around three main themes: civic society, digital society, and developing software products. Just like the parent methodology from the 1970's, a constant value is framing human well-being, and, just like the parent methodology, patterns are prized for their formatting which provides a convenient vocabulary so that people can converse easily about their situation. A few patterns used with clients from software product engineering:

PLACE IN SOCIETY

A product needs to find a meaningful connected place in a society, which it establishes by co-existing with the status quo, supplanting some established products, or creating a new space and redefining a part of that society.

SALIENT PURPOSE

Although a product can solve many problems, its primary identity is established around an elegantly summarized problem it solves better than any other product.

FIRST LANDING PLACE

Determine where in the market the product would find its first fertile ground for adoption.

7. Technology

Nothing in this introductory basic method requires more than paper and pencil. For larger scale projects, collaborative software helps a great deal. Practitioners of Embodied Making use a collaborative platform called CLAY. Information becomes compressible, recordable, shareable, and scalable. With a move to collaborative software, other questions such as knowledge representation and ontologies come to the fore.

8. In Short

Understanding forces is the essential intellectual capital in Embodied Making. Not an exo-skeleton or a method of step 1-2-3, it's a craft calling us to develop our natural artistry for midwifing patterns yet-to-be-born.

9. References

Alexander, Christopher, Sarah Ishikawa, Murray Silverstein, with M. Jacobson, I. Fiksdahl-King, S. Angel. (1977). A Pattern Language, New York: OUP.

Heidegger, Martin. "Building, Dwelling, Thinking." From Poetry, Language, Thought (1971) translated by Albert Hofstadter. New York: Harper Colophon Books.

Pedagogy of Wholeness: Accounting for the missing heart in educational research

Pinto, Ana
The University of Sydney, Centre for Research on Learning and Innovation, Sydney, Australia
apin8882@uni.sydney.edu.au

How we think, and what we see, is influenced by our language. This paper suggests that Alexander's theory of centers and wholeness is useful for understanding and creating inspiring and nurturing learning environments, which is important not least because cognitive and affective systems together influence how learning activity may be affected by the physical setting in which it occurs. A centers-based approach assists in revealing design elements not picked up using conventional analytic work used to identify reusable patterns. Perhaps not surprisingly, many of these elusive, yet important, design features reflect those experiences we may all have, "momentary perhaps, something we consider a haze of emotion… a feeling we recognize as deep, as vitally important… it lasts for a few seconds, perhaps even for a few minutes… and then our rude cosmology dismisses it" (Alexander, 2004, p. 21).

Educational Design; The Nature of Order; Mechanistic Science; Wholeness; Centers-based approach

1.   Introduction

"I said the name To-ku-fu-ji syllable by syllable over and over again, until the driver understood. We drove far across town... We stopped in a deserted place, outside a huge stone wall... I got out, passed through the walls, into the temple complex. Inside the atmosphere was astonishing: wild grasses, bushes, stones. It was like overgrown nature, almost completely wild, and yet I felt that it was cultivated, and in use... I found myself on a tiny path that seemed to lead away from the temple, up into the hillside. I followed this path up steps cut in the hillside, partly stone, set into the grass. The path went on and on, a shallow staircase, up into the hill, between two hedges. It was getting narrower and narrower all the time. Toward the top, it got trapped between two low rambling hedges. Suddenly it ended... There was nowhere to sit, except on the top step, and that is where I sat, looking down on the temple precinct, watching it, tired, happy to sit there, quiet, only the wind now instead of the sounds of the temple business. As I sat there, a blue dragonfly came and landed on the step beside me. It stayed. And as it stayed I was filled with the most extraordinary sensation. I was suddenly certain that the people who had built that place had done all deliberately... they had made that place, knowing the blue dragonfly would come and sit by me. However, it sounds now, at the time when it happened, ... there was no doubt in my mind at all that there was a level of skill in the people who had made this place that I had never experienced before. I remember shivering as I became aware of my own ignorance. ... [I] stayed in the temple all day long, filled, for the whole day, by my awe in the face of what these people had known, and by the beauty of the place. Most of all I was simply shocked by the certainty... that the grasses, the steps, the wind, the dragonfly, were all deliberately placed by their hands" (Alexander, 2002a, pp. 434-437).

Christopher Alexander's testimony of his visit to the Buddhist temple, Tōfuku-ji, near Kyoto in Japan, suggests a subtle, inextricable connection between the emotional and perceptual characteristics and needs of ourselves as human beings and the surrounding physical world that is in clear contradiction with prevailing dualist sciences, which insist on a separation between the 'two worlds'. In an extraordinary effort to advance Western scientific thought beyond a predominantly mechanist canon, in The Nature of Order: An essay on the Art of Building and the Nature of the Universe (2002-2005) Alexander presents a wholesome model in which human joy and health stands in an inextricable relationship with the geometrical organization of the world. This is a timely and important development. The mechanistic scientific tradition is at least in part behind an unfortunate recurrent issue I experienced during my early career as an adult literacy educator in Rio de Janeiro, when regular schooling teachers kept their classrooms locked after school hours. The decision meant that adult literacy students and teachers were restricted to the least enticing class-rooms for their night time lessons. While the major issue underlying this decision was that a few adult literacy students had in the past tampered with some children's drawings, the day time teachers seemed genuinely convinced that the choice of classrooms would make no difference for the adult learners. The teachers' typical argument was that the adult students largely came from 'the middle of nowhere, without electricity and virtually nothing, and had better concentrate on learning how to read and write'. The majority of my students did come from the largely impoverished North and Northeast regions of Brazil. Hence when I visited the school/classroom pictured in Figure 1, situated in the middle of the Amazon Forest, the issue came back to mind, as it did also when reading the testimony above.

Figure 1: A school in the Amazon Forest.

Interestingly, when we entered the classroom the children of the family travelling with me, aged between seven and twelve, started elbowing one another as each wanted to be the 'teacher'. Given that I was acutely aware that none of them was fond of my choice of the teaching profession, I was particularly impressed. All these experiences just described prompted for me, as a teacher, an important question: how does the physicality of the classroom and learning resources, physical and digital, affect one's attitude toward learning and teaching, and learning activity? When exploring this question, I found that Alexander's work, particularly the theory presented in the four volumes of The Nature of Order (TNO) collection, provides new powerful and useful insights. For example, looked at through a conventional lens for analysis of learning environments, the classroom pictured in Figure 1 is rather simple and features too-small, traditional chairs/tables, etc. This kind of evaluation however neither explains why it drew in a holidaying family and the positive response of the children nor does it shed light on the dissatisfaction felt by my 'migrant' students in Rio de Janeiro, obliged to inhabit classrooms otherwise spacious and better resourced, but facing the concrete walls of neighboring buildings. The explanation fails because it is based on a mechanistic view of order, in which parts are independent and the whole they come to form does not include humans and their feelings.

Such a position stands in stark contradiction with the understanding of order Alexander presents in TNO. He describes the everyday world in objective terms while at the same time considering the feelings it may raise in all of us. Alexander's model makes no difference between ornamental and functional order, and it identifies a subtle but pervasive structure that simultaneously has an objective reality 'out there' and a personal reality in people's hearts. Looked at through the lens of this non-mechanist theory, the learning environment pictured in Figure 1 then inherently comes to include the moving waters of the river and the dozens of colorful birds on the trees seen through the large window, their singing, and other peripheral and/or ephemeral potentially contributing 'entities' in the surrounding environment. It also includes an emergent global structure (the wholeness) created by such configuration, which necessarily relates to, and is also prompted by, the overall human activity, and therefore learning within that space.

Where once there were stand-alone classrooms, now there are hybrid learning networks; we are in the midst of ever-growing and interpenetrating digital and brick-and-mortar infrastructures for learning. My contention is that we need a more focused way of observing learning environments, one that can account for the 'missing heart' in educational research. As educational philosopher and passionate adult literacy educator Paulo Freire eloquently once said "we need to say no to neoliberal fatalism... We need [a science that permits us] to speak about love without fear of being called ascientific, if not antiscientific" (2005, p. 25-26). Both Alexander and Freire embrace a history of possibilities in which people should work together to construct a world that is more beautiful, harmonious, and just.

When it comes to educational design, it is generally the case that existing guidelines almost exclusively support decision-making in respect to matters directly related to cognition and learning. I have tried to illustrate with the opening example that little details can make a difference between whether learning resources and spaces will be loved or hated by students, which in turn will affect how or what they learn. When designing 'things' intended to support other people's learning, most teachers want to create artefacts and spaces that students will appreciate. Yet, in both my studies and practice as a school counsellor responsible for supporting adult basic education and primary school teachers with design and development of learning resources, the guidelines I have had access to have dealt with a limited range of learning environment factors: support for learners to achieve desired learning goals (effectiveness) and issues related to time and cost and other resources (efficiency). Part of the problem is that, when it comes to the evaluation of designs for learning, of the three basic criteria of effectiveness, efficiency and appeal (Reigeluth & Carr-Chellman, 2009) the latter is given little consideration, if any at all. Taking inspiration from Alexander's work, we should not allow mechanistic sciences prevent us from taking into consideration the full breadth of human experience. The general neglect of how appealing or disheartening designs for learning might feel is perpetuated by research that prioritizes effectiveness and efficiency at the expense of feelings and emotions.

My choice to start with Alexander's testimony is in part motivated by the fact that he conveys conflicting feelings and strong emotions (e.g., "I became aware of my own ignorance"; "I was filled with the most extraordinary sensation"). They are commonly experienced by many designers during the process of searching for adequate solutions to design challenges, but are rarely openly acknowledged. This omission may be due to several factors but often includes the fact that feeling is not perceived as being something of primary importance in design science, or any science for that matter, an assumption that can also be related to the problem of my students' authentic feelings about their learning environments being wrongly invalidated, year after year. The new concepts Alexander advances in TNO seem particularly important and useful in this day and age when the work of teachers increasingly involves the design of physical and digital learning artefacts and spaces, and much learning activity takes place remotely.

In what follows, I first provide an overview of core concepts discussed in TNO. Then, a case study involving an online network is presented to illustrate the value of Alexander's theory as a complementary approach to analysis and design for learning. An initial analysis of the AlphaPlus network focused on understanding the relations between its structural qualities, the practices members engaged in, the forms of knowledge they produced, and the nature of the context (see Pinto, forthcoming). A follow-up extended analysis, partially presented in this paper, then confirmed Alexander's claim that there seem to be two worlds in our minds: a scientific world involving complex systems of mechanisms and our experiential world of everyday life. As it will be demonstrated in the case study section, a centers-based approach is particularly useful in that it helps to reveal design patterns that capture subtle, yet fundamental, aspects of educational settings and situations, while bringing attention to the kind of sensitivities necessary to prevent the 'architecture of death', denounced by Alexander, taking over educational design practice. Much as learners' activity is socially situated, so too, is the activity of designers for learning, or any human activity for that matter. Design activity is naturally influenced by the social and cultural contexts in which designers live and practice. This socially situated nature of design activity requires, I argue, refined concepts because mainstream science adheres to mechanical understandings of the world.

2. A new concept of Life

In formulating a model to counterbalance what he calls a 'by and large soul-destroying modern architecture', Alexander advances in TNO a broad conception of life beyond self-reproducing organisms. What he calls life is a "general condition which exists, to some degree or other, in every part of space: brick, stone, grass, painting, daffodil, human being, forest, city" (2002a, p, 77). His basic hypothesis is that 'every part of space – every connected region of space, small or large – has some degree of life, and that degree of life is well defined, objectively existing, and measurable" (Alexander, 2002a, p. 77). Life stands for a quality that exists in all kinds of structures – be they architectonic, social, or natural. It exists and is visible in the form of a building, in the gesture negotiated by two people shaking hands, and in the structure of a wave. It is important to note that when talking about the life of waves, Alexander is not referring to the purely mechanical hydrodynamical system of moving water, as normally thought of within physics and other sciences. Rather, he understands that in addition to the mechanical order, a wave has life in itself. "We feel their life as a real thing, they move us. Of course, in the narrow mechanistic view of Biology there is no life in the wave... But it is undeniable – at least as far as our feeling is concerned – that such a moving, breaking wave feels as if it has more life as a system of water than an industrial pool stinking with chemicals. So does the ripple on a tranquil pond' (2002a, p. 32, emphasis in original). In this way, while his proposition about degrees of life challenges mainstream science, it aligns with our ordinary experience; at least intuitively, it is not an uncommon feature of our ordinary experience to appreciate life as a quality that occurs in varying degrees all around us.

The empirical method that, according to Alexander, most reliably measures 'life' in things is a test that entails asking the observer which of two objects induces the greater wholeness in herself/himself. Therefore, Alexander's way of conceiving order requires that "statements about relative degree of harmony, or life, or wholeness – basic aspects of order – are understood as potentially true or false" (2002a, p. 22). This does not mean, of course, that he is proposing that science should embrace subjective opinion. Rather, such judgments involve what I have elsewhere called 'subjective shared values' (see Pinto 2016a), based on Alexander's distinction between shared judgment and personal opinion or idiosyncrasy. "We feel that a certain tree, or a certain rock, or a certain clearing, has great power or spirit – or at least we acknowledge that we feel awe in that place, or we feel an intensity or life. Furthermore, this experience is shared and common. It is not idiosyncratic. Many people feel the same way about … this garden gate, this room, this bridge, this stream, this beach" (2002a, p. 72, emphasis in original). Alexander states that the idea that all judgment is always subjective is a misconception originated in the dry positivistic and mechanistic ways of thinking in 20th century science. He insists that as subjective as it may sound to 'mechanist ears', the kind of measurement that engages the feelings of observers is nonetheless objective, and it can render shareable, repeatable results just like those experiments and observations permitted by the Cartesian method. In this way the matters addressed in TNO bridge the gulf existent in the Cartesian worldview where the objective structure of the world is completely separate from the human.

Alexander is convinced that the feeling that there is more life in one system than the other correlates to a structural difference in the things themselves, and such difference can be made precise. Although measured through the subjective experience of the observer, the structure of the wholeness and the system's behavior have an objective standing in physical reality. This is to say that rather than merely a cognitive impression the quality that most of us perceive is an objectively real physical phenomenon that occurs in space. Lying behind these ideas is not only a new conception of order but an entirely different understanding about the nature of order. Alexander's basic premise that every part of space has a certain degree of life that can be formulated precisely in structural terms relies on two interrelated concepts: centers and the wholeness, which build on the notion of wholeness.

3. Wholeness, Centers and the Wholeness

At the core of the theory formulated by Alexander in TNO is the concept of wholeness, which is central to his approach to design. Accordingly, he does not consider a building an isolated entity but rather a part of an extended continuum, which includes a system of centers that involves inhabitants' activities, gardens, street, other buildings, and so forth. Wholeness is a global, overall field-like structure that is completely distinct from the parts which appear in the wholeness in question. A classic example that helps to make the concept clear appears in an essay on portraiture by Henry Matisse (Figure 2). In all four drawings, Matisse manages to catch the overall character of his face despite using different shaped nose, chin, eyes, mouth, moustache, glasses, shirt collar, eyebrows, etc.

Figure 2: Matisse's essay on portraiture (Alexander, 2002a, p. 97)

Alexander calls the coherent entities from which wholeness originates, 'centers'. A center, as he defines it, refers to "a physical set, a distinct physical system, which occupies a certain volume in space, and has a special marked coherence" (2002a, p. 84). A center is thus not a point, but a field of organized force in an object or part of an object, which makes that object, or a part of it, exhibit centrality. This field-like centrality is at the core of Alexander's other central concept, the wholeness: "in any given region of space, some subregions have higher intensity as centers, other have less. Many subregions have weak intensity or none at all. The overall configuration of the nested centers, together with their relative intensities, comprise a single structure... the wholeness of that region" (2002a, p. 96). Where centers are more dense and cooperate with one another more intensely in a given region of space, that region of space become more connected with the human self. Therefore, even though the structure of the wholeness exists in the world out there, it forms a unity 'in here', inside a person's heart (2002a, p. 308). In this sense, this way of looking at reality necessarily requires evaluative statements where human observers can reach shared agreement about wholeness.

Alexander is convinced that all reality is dominated by the existence of this structure he calls the wholeness. However, he argues that prevailing mechanistic views of the world often interfere with our ability to see, or look at, this kind of structure in the world around us. Take for example the image shown in Figure 3. Alexander asserts that if asked to identify the coherent entities or centers in this scene, virtually all of us will merely name the obvious parts for which we have easy names: a person, a bicycle, a tree, and a road.

Figure 3: An everyday scene of ordinary life (Alexander, 2002a, p. 93)

Yet, if one learns to pay attention to the structure of wholeness, numerous other funda-mental centers can be identified. For example, a major center is the great swath of space, wider than the road, which extends to the distance and includes the flat land on either side of the road. Another main center is the tree's cotton-wool top and its beehive shape. Looking attentively, one sees an obvious 'place' between the road and the tree, and the spot where the man is leaning is yet another prominent center. In addition, one should see a flat, ring-shaped swath of space under the tree, almost like a flat cylindrical donut, caused by the fact that the tree's foliage has been trimmed to just above head height all around. Alexander states that it is important to note that all these subtle centers are induced struc-turally by the overall configuration; centers, like wholeness, are real physical structures that are induced in the geometry of space. Most importantly, it is the configuration formed by those less obvious centers that most likely invited the biker to stop there. Implicit here is that centers create a field effect that actually "control the real behavior of the thing, the life that develops there, the real events which happen, and the feelings people have about the living thing" (2002a, p. 95). Most significantly, according to Alexander, the wholeness of the scene is created by all the centers together, which "are really there, actually existing centers in space" (2002a, p.92). This proposition entails a new way of looking at reality that stands in stark contradiction to prevailing mechanistic conceptions of order.

3.1. The Subtlety of the Structure of Wholeness

Alexander illustrates the subtlety of the structure of wholeness by drawing a dot on a blank sheet of paper. By itself, the blank sheet has a particular kind of wholeness. This wholeness dramatically changes with the addition of the tiny dot (Figure 4). Following the plotting of the tiny dot, about twenty entities become coherent, or differentiated, where before they were not.

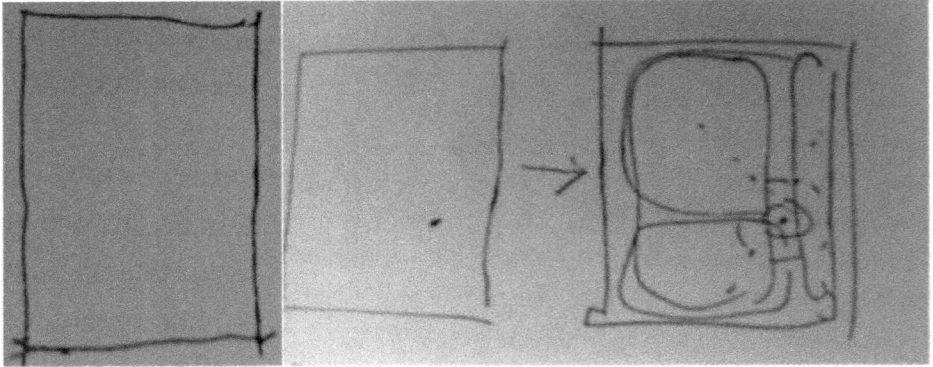

Figure 4: A diagram of the wholeness (Alexander, 2002a, p. 82)

The entities or zones of space that become visible include the sheet itself, the dot and the halo around it, the four largest latent rectangles, which create four others in the corners by their overlap, a system of four diagonal rays 'pointing' in different directions, etc. These zones or entities, together, define the structure that we recognize as the wholeness of the sheet of paper with the dot. "The wholeness in any part of space is the structure defined by all the various coherent entities that exist in that part of space, and the ways these entities are nested and overlap each other" (2002a, p. 81). The wholeness is a structure which results from the mathematics of the space itself, depending on the density and intensity of centers that form in it.

4. Living Structures

Alexander calls the quality of life, in its geometrical aspect, living structure. Centers appear in both living structures and non-living structures. But in the living structures, there is higher density and degree of cooperation between centers. How life occurs because of wholeness results from aspects inherent in the structure of centers, including that centers themselves have life, and that the life of one can intensify the life of another. It follows that all systems in the world acquire their lives to the extent to which the centers in it cohere and help each other. This helping is not automatic, though. Alexander suggests a simple test to tell which of two centers may be helping the other. Supposing that there is a center A and a center B in a certain region of space, with the introduction of the 'I' into the process, one can look at

A-B together and then A without B. Always using the criterion of the 'felt' degree of life, one can tell whether A together with B, or A without B, has more life. B is helping A if the pattern A-B exhibits more life than the other option. As an example, looking at the image shown in Figure 5, the reader may agree that the life of the low wall is increased by the existence of the flower box, which appears placed on top of it.

Figure 5: The flower box helps the low wall, and vice versa (Alexander, 2002a, p. 114)

Conversely, if the reader covers the flower box with the hand (or takes it away mentally), you will 'see the life of the low wall drop down, diminish' (Alexander, 2002a, p. 114). Implied in this test is the fact that the character of being a center with more, or less, life is not a local phenomenon. Rather, it is determined by the way one specific center sits in the system of other centers. "Various zones in the pattern become centers because of their position and character within the pattern. This in turn depends on the relative position and intensity of other centers that spring up all around" (2002a, p. 126). Living structures only come about when centers unfold from the whole, binding everything together.

The process in which parts or sub-wholes are induced within the wholeness, and come from the wholeness, is of course the general rule in nature, "where parts are adapted and modified, in shape and size, by their position within the whole" (2002a, p. 87). Similarly, to natural processes, a living structure originates as a result of an unfolding process, which draws structure from the whole, by progressive differentiation. The nature of a living whole depends on the way any one part of that whole plays its role within the larger whole. Understanding the mutual helping among centers may give designers the secret to create living structures. The secret to creating a living center is gradually introduce other centers to intensify the field effect. Alexander has identified and formulated fifteen properties which, according to him, help with the task of creating living centers.

4.1. The properties of Life

After the publication of A Pattern Language (Alexander et al., 1977), Alexander began to notice that each invariant spatial pattern concerned with balancing a system of conflicting forces contained, in itself, a deeper structure. Following systematic comparison of thousands of pairs of 'objects' and subsequent analyses of common structural features in those exhibiting more life, Alexander eventually isolated fifteen recurrent geometric properties. Together, the properties form a kind of deeper structure that recurs in both man-made structures and nature, and despite taking different forms each time it occurs, it is "yet, nevertheless always the same" (2004, p. 2). "Each of the properties describes one of the possible ways in which centers can intensify each other" (2002a, p. 241). They are: Strong center, Levels of Scale, Boundaries, Alternating Repetition, Positive Space, Good Shape, Local Symmetries, Deep Interlock and Ambiguity, Contrast, Gradients, Roughness, Echoes, The Void, Simplicity and Inner calm, and Not-Separateness.

Eventually, Alexander noticed that despite seeming distinct these properties are in fact intertwined and interwoven. Such interdependence appears marked with an asterisk in the matrix shown in Figure 6. It was this pattern of interdependence among the properties that indicated to Alexander the existence of the field of centers, where 'centers create wholeness and wholeness intensifies centres' (2002a, p. 238).

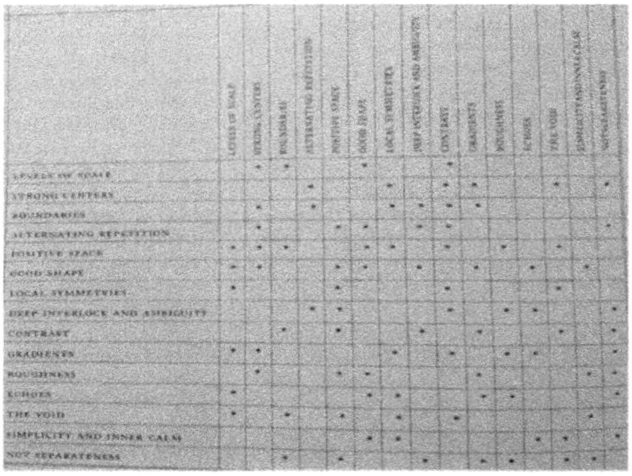

Figure 6: The interactions of the fifteen properties (Alexander, 2002a, p. 238)

Alexander notes that it is significant that the properties are equally visible and recur in natural physical phenomena and play a significant role in the stability of the systems. Since they appear in and are responsible for naturally occurring phenomena, purely cognitive explanations cannot stand. Herein lies the evidence base for his conclusion that they are part of a real field, the field of centers, which exists in space. This in turn provides evidence that space itself, matter itself, has life in varying degrees, and the existence of these degrees of life throughout space is a fact of the world. From this understanding follows "a new view of space based on the wholeness, in which these properties appear naturally and inevitably from the nature of wholeness, and in which it becomes clear how and why life occurs in space, not as an attribute of living organisms, but as an attribute of space itself" (2002a, p. 238, emphasis in original). Based on this understanding, Alexander insists that the field of centers and the properties actually describe how the world works and "must be viewed as fundamental to the existence of wholeness in the world" (2002a, p. 244).

From a design perspective, what is most significant about the formulation of the properties is that, if they really work as Alexander suggests, they provide designers a grasp on the actual physical and geometrical character which living systems have. That is, the idea that there can only be a limited number of transformations governed by the fifteen properties as the driving force of all emergences that leads to geometric coherence is significant in that, at least in principle, it is possible to understand objectively how designs that imbue life may be created. This scheme contradicts the inherent arbitrariness of the mechanistic worldview since "both those parts of the world which are still natural... and those which are clearly man-created... may either go towards greater value and greater wholeness, or to-wards greater ugliness and confusion" (2002a, p. 295). Talks about harmony must then not be seen as an individual position and something outside science.

In what follows, I illustrate how these propositions have illuminated a broader analytical work involving a large online learning network. It will be argued that while aesthetic value is commonly dismissed as idiosyncratic opinion, thus unimportant for design science, a cen-ters-based approach importantly reveals design features that reflect those experiences we may all have, 'momentary perhaps, something we consider a haze of emotion... a feeling we recognize as deep, as vitally important... it lasts for a few seconds, perhaps even for a few minutes... and then our rude cosmology dismisses it' (Alexander, 2004, p. 21, my emphasis).

5. Case Study: The AlphaPlus Learning Network

AlphaPlus is a not-for-profit Canadian organization that has been supporting adult literacy education since 1998. Funded by the province of Ontario, its main mandate is to provide free professional development for local adult literacy educators. Professional development with AlphaPlus varies along a continuum between informal and formal learning, depending on whether the participant chooses to engage in open online networking and/ or training in Moodle. In the AlphaPlus main website one finds a range of potentially valuable tools and resources, research publications and reports, and current news related to the field of adult literacy education; training in Moodle involves a formal program that takes place within password protected environments. An initial analysis was informed by a networked learning framework that considered the set, epistemic, and social elements designed in advance, while paying close attention to the ways and extent to which participant activity is shaped by and influences such configuration (Goodyear & Carvalho, 2014). This initial analytic work revealed a plethora of patterns worth sharing (Alexander et al., 1977; Alexander, 1979), particularly in respect to the Moodle training, which takes place in three interconnected Moodle based learning environments (Figure 7: a, b, c): the Moodle training site, the Virtual Classroom for Adult Educators (VCAE), and the Virtual Classroom for Adult Learners (VCAL), respectively. This rich set design allows for design knowledge to be collectively produced, shared and refined in a way that resembles a design studio approach (Schön, 1984), but in a 'virtual' version (see Pinto, forthcoming).

Figure 7: (a) Moodle training site; (b) VCAE; (c) VCAL

While in the Moodle Training for Adult Educators site participants take part in formal training to learn to develop content in Moodle, within the two virtual classroom sites trainees participate in or create and deliver courses. The VCAE houses courses created by participating educators for their colleagues. The VCAL site is for courses where the audience are learners. The training program allows for participating educators to create, control and distribute knowledge, while benefiting from and contributing to a productive community of practice. Despite its highly flexible character, the program incorporates aspects of educational design practice that are essential for creation of designs driven by pedagogy, rather than technology. AlphaPlus has also enlisted a number of additional tools and services to support, promote and extend activities hosted in both the open and closed digital environments. The representation shown in Figure 8, drawn on a large writeable design studio wall during initial analyses, captures some of the ways in which the primary learning spaces (main website and Moodle learning environments) and secondary digital spaces (e.g., conference tools and social media) relate to one another, and to parts of the physical world. This representation is obviously a simplification, and the combination of these diverse learning spaces implies that there are a number of elements and interactions that are not necessarily visible within any one single learning environment but would nevertheless influence the practitioners' learning processes and activities.

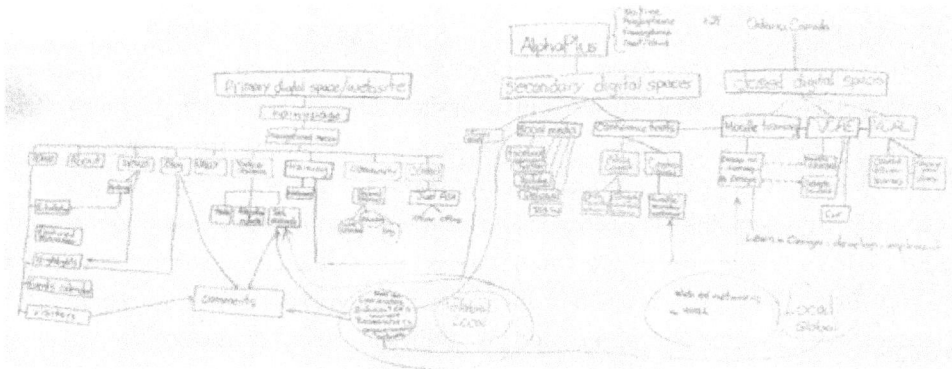

Figure 8: Architecture of the AlphaPlus learning network

However, following my studies of Alexander's theory, I found the need to complement this type of mapping. One of the resulting representations is shown in Figure 9. It contrasts to the one above in that it includes some small details such as: a slide from a Moodle webinar and an unusual highly philosophical posting (top row); the image of a bird that features in the first module of the Introduction to Moodle training course (central portion), recognizing the human reaction to learning and assessment by seeking to reassure; and the Tech Tuesdays webinar slide comprising a beautiful landscape (bottom right) draws the physical environment into the learning space.

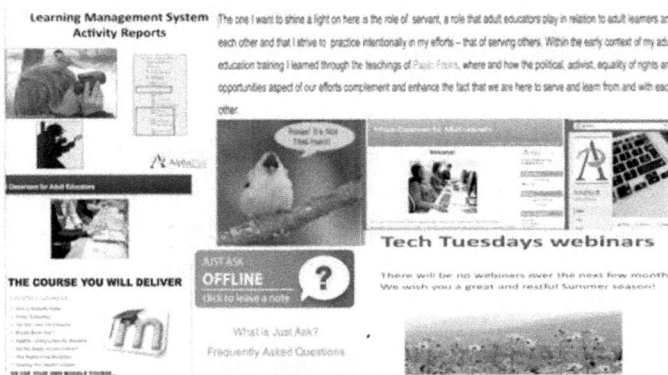

Figure 9: Collage of digital resources comprising the learning network's design

Applying a Centers-based approach, all these artefacts are important in that they are each centers that form the wholeness of the learning environment. Given that centers are recursive, these are naturally comprised of many further centers. For example, looking at the three artefacts located in a diagonal line starting from the top left of Figure 9, a few of these further centers include: (1) in the Moodle webinar slide: the boy, his head and the bird; (2) in the Moodle module page: the encouragement message where the bird features again; and (3) in the Tech-Tuesday webinar slide: the mountains, hills and flowers. Of particular interest to me is that consideration of these selected artefacts does seem to suggest that the idea that objects have life, and that the degree of life that these systems have is important in connecting them to their users, is not totally foreign to the Alphaplus designers. To ground this argument, the Moodle webinar slide mentioned above is shown to the left of Figure 10. The artefact to the right of the figure has been created by myself for the purpose of comparison. It is suggested here, and the reader is invited to make their own comparison and assessment, that the 'life' represented in the original artefact created by the AlphaPlus designers decreases substantially if its (more encompassing) image is replaced with the one I used in the composition of the artefact on the right-hand side.

Learning Management System   **Learning Management System**

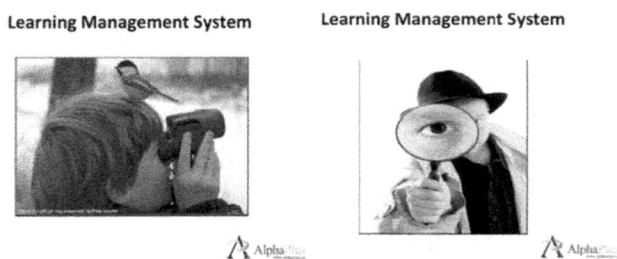

Figure 10: Artefacts with different degrees of life

The assessment that one artefact has more life than the other can actually be explained using the theory of centers, specifically the hierarchy of centers present in the configuration to the left. In that configuration, 'life' is present in the structure formed by the boy's head and hair, his active features including his ears, hand, and fingers, as well of course by the bird which in its way is interacting with the boy via a dynamic story of evading the boy's prying eyes, through the binoculars. Other items contributing life are those created by the setting: the trunk of the tree for the bird's habitat, the snow and plants giving and 'breathing' a season into the overall picture. Further, and most importantly, these centers reinforce one another. Many of TNO's fifteen properties are at work linking them and as a result creating a living structure or geometry. By contrast, the artefact I have created (on the right in Figure 10) not only has fewer centers but also these do not help one another. That is to say, it lacks many of the fifteen properties. For example, the property non-separateness and connectedness is present through the background in the artefact to the left but is missing in the other. The center represented by the boy's hat (on the right) does not present a strong center compared with the bird on the top of the other boy's head (on the left). Considered together and with the proposition that where centers intensify one another the region of space those centers 'inhabit' exerts life, it follows that the greater life in the Moodle slide (left) exists objectively.

Another nuanced aspect that only came to light in the extended analysis concerns the screenshot of one weekly Moodle module shown in Figure 11. Originally analyzed in terms of the epistemic design (e.g., type of task) and social design (e.g., synchronous meetings in the form of webinar), the life constituted by centers such as the bird and its message was overlooked in identified design patterns. As with the case discussed earlier, involving the low wall and the flower box (see inset image), if one pictures this artefact without these subtle centers, the wholeness of the learning environment would be different, its life decreased. Once one accepts Alexander's proposition that the structure of wholeness resonates with the human self, consideration of all centers that may contribute to the life of a learning environment is important.

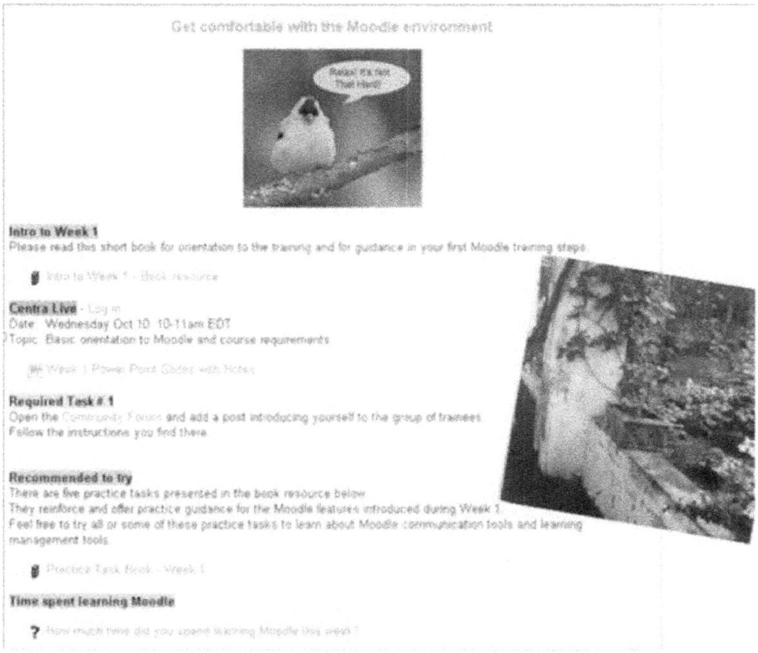

Figure 11: AlphaPlus Moodle Training Module

There is a great deal more that could be said about the life of these artefacts but instead I want to bring the focus to an apparent misalignment in the AlphaPlus design. Based on the above description of selected artefacts, it could be argued that the AlphaPlus designers do seem to have a certain intuition about life in artefacts. Yet, the subject of 'living structure' is not part of the network's professional development program, and, most notably, is missing in the educators' training in Moodle course design. I argue that this misalignment between the AlphaPlus practice of design and what it addresses in design education is rooted in the prevailing rude cosmology mentioned above. There is a definite and ultimately limiting 'disjuncture'. The prevailing mechanistic picture of the world does not accept the idea that felt emotive connection to artefacts has value or even legitimacy. Nevertheless, designers operating within that mechanistic paradigm do, in any case, seem to believe that it is not only possible but important to create artefacts that are likely to resonate positively with educators' engagement with the topic, even though these may not be particularly exciting (e.g., the mechanics of a LMS). Such belief is, of course, not part of the science of educational design, and hence the subject itself does not feature in the Moodle training program. Alexander's theory can make a contribution to bridge what appear to be the two separate complex mechanisms and the everyday experience. My own early-on observations and experiments with adult literacy learners suggest that the geometry of learning spaces and resources plays a more fundamental role in effective learning than convention would have it (see Pinto 2016a,b).

Since we learn through our embodied existence (Kiefer & Trumpp, 2012), always immersed in the environment, educational designers need to ensure learning environments and resources trigger emotions that will affect us positively instead of interfering with how and what we learn. A holistic approach to analysis and design helps reveal how 'secondary' design elements – those less prominent designed features that only occasionally and/or ephemerally 'materialize' around a main network – nevertheless, show intricate connections among the core activities taking place. I argue that unless such relations are unveiled and understood, the essential core of a learning network cannot be entirely grasped.

6. Conclusion

Giving proper attention to the functional basis of a learning network (e.g., to what people need and want to learn in order to achieve their goals) is paramount. But according to Alexander, "the question of what a building does, and how well it does it, can be understood properly only in the context of the geometry" (2002b, p. 342). Drawing on Alexander's design sensibility, I have suggested that educational designers should strive to design not only effective but also nurturing learning resources and spaces that may potentially lead to heightened harmony between people and the environment. Once one accepts Alexander's proposition that the structure of wholeness resonates with the human self, consideration of all centers that may contribute to the life of a learning environment is fundamental. A center-based approach to analysis and design for learning helps us understand why some places make us feel more inspired than others, which is not unimportant in the context of contemporary educational design.

I am not suggesting that educational design research is insensitive to the fact that affective systems influence cognitive processes. This is, indeed the case. Neither am I saying that the concept of affordance, which is based on human perception, is not useful for educational design. I am, furthermore, aware that there is already widespread recognition that cognitive and affective systems together influence how humans may perceive affordances and interpret their surrounding environment. Cognitive neuroscience, in particular, has been instrumental in shedding light on how neurochemical signals are activated in the brain and cognitive and emotional experiences are interdependent and affect learning activity (Immordino-Yang & Damasio, 2007).

What I am arguing is that analysis concerned with abstracting design patterns needs to strive "to make sense of the digital as well as the material and their hybrids, and to trace links between world, mind, brain, and body" (Carvalho et al., 2016, p. 4, my emphasis) while ensuring the human heart gains an explicit place in this equation, and in educational research more generally. While in a conventional analysis the analyst may consider all subtle elements, when thinking in terms of centers he or she must, or will naturally, do so. This is important also because the message of the designer conveyed by the elements together is very different in each particular case (Krippendorff, 2005). Moreover, if Alexander is right that the life we experience in any moment of our existence is deeply correlated with, and cannot be separated from, the geometry of the systems in which we find ourselves, careful attention to spatial considerations is essential. "In any case, the [digital] world can become beautiful, as a result of this new understanding" (Alexander, 2006, p. 10).

7. References

Alexander, C. (2002a). The nature of order: an essay on the art of building and the nature of the universe, Book One: The Phenomenon of Life. New York: Oxford University Press.

Alexander, C. (2002b). The nature of order: an essay on the art of building and the nature of the universe, Book Two: The Process of Creating Life. New York: Oxford University Press.

Alexander, C. (2005). The nature of order: an essay on the art of building and the nature of the universe, Book Three: A Vision of a Living World. New York: Oxford University Press.

Alexander, C. (2004). The nature of order: an essay on the art of building and the nature of the universe, Book Four: The Luminous Ground. New York: Oxford University Press.

Alexander, C. (2006). Empirical findings from the nature of order. Environmental and architectural phenomenology newsletter, 18(1).

Alexander, C., Ishikawa, S. & Silverstein, M., et. al. (1977). A Pattern Language. New York, NY: Oxford University Press.

Alexander, C. (1979). The timeless way of building (Vol. 1). New York: Oxford University Press.

Carvalho, L., Goodyear, P., & de Laat, M. (2016). Place, Space, and Networked Learning. In Place-Based Spaces for Networked Learning (pp. 1-10). Routledge.

Freire, P. (2005). Pedagogy of the oppressed 30th anniversary. edition translated by Myra Bergman Ramos.

Gibson, J. J. (1977). The theory of affordances. Perceiving, acting, and knowing: Toward an ecological psychology, 67-82.

Goodyear, P. & Carvalho, L., (2014). Framing the analysis of learning networks architectures. In: Carvalho, L. and Goodyear, P., eds. The architecture of productive learning networks, New York, NY: Routledge.

Immordino Yang, M. H., & Damasio, A. (2007). We feel, therefore we learn: The relevance of affective and social neuroscience to education. Mind, brain, and education, 1(1), 3-10.

Kiefer, M., & Trumpp, N. M. (2012). Embodiment theory and education: The foundations of cognition in perception and action. Trends in Neuroscience and Education, 1(1), 15-20.

Krippendorff, K. (2005). The semantic turn: A new foundation for design. crc Press.

Pinto, A. (2016a). Educational design and Birds on Trees. In Carvalho, L., Goodyear, P., de Laat, M. (2016). Place-based spaces for networked learning. New York: Routledge.

Pinto, A. (2016b). Pedagogy of Wholeness: the poetic whole of our existence. PUARL Conference 2016. https://blogs.uoregon.edu/puarl2016/papers/

Pinto, A. (2018). Pedagogy of wholeness. Unpublished PhD thesis. The University of Sydney, Australia.

Reigeluth, C. M., & Carr-Chellman, A. A. (2009). Understanding instructional theory. Instructional-design theories and models: Building a common knowledge base, 3, 3-26.

Schön, D. A. (1984). The reflective practitioner: How professionals think in action (Vol. 5126). Basic books.

Active Learning Patterns for Teachers

Iba, Takashi
Faculty of Policy Management, Keio University, Japan
iba@sfc.keio.ac.jp

Utsunomiya, Yoshihiro
Benesse Corporation
y_utsunomiya@mail.benesse.co.jp

This paper presents 'Active Learning Patterns for teachers', a pattern language which describes good practices for teachers to support students in becoming active learners. This pattern language consists of 45 patterns, which are classified into three different categories: (A) Identify the seeds of curiosity, help them grow, (B) Lift them up to the next level and (C) Enhance each other and keep changing. It was created based on the interviews conducted with several teachers in Japan who have their own teaching styles, devices and tips to enable active learning in students. Recently, we have been holding workshops for teachers in Japan to promote the introduction and application of these patterns in schools. In this paper, we describe the process of creating this pattern language and present the 45 patterns created.

Education; Pedagogy; Pattern Language; Pedagogical Patterns; Educational Patterns

1. Introduction

Our society has been dramatically changing because of informatization and globalization. We are, therefore, asked to have enough creativity and ability to solve various problems so as to enable the coexistence of different values and restructure the society. In this fast-changing and increasingly complex society, what should children know and which abilities do they need to develop for their future? Although there are many important things to learn, it would be most essential for them to have the ability to figure out what is necessary in any situation and develop their abilities to achieve a particular goal; in other words, the need to develop the ability to keep learning by themselves.

In Japan, the Curriculum guidelines were recently revised by the Ministry of Education, Culture, Sports, Science and Technology (MEXT) to develop active and interactive ways of learning in school. Because of this educational innovation, the idea of active learning is common nowadays, and many schools have been trying to practice this. According to the 'survey on the influence of the change in educational systems and university entrance qualification 2017', around 40% of high schools in Japan have already started trying to improve their styles of education, to develop students' active learning skills and abilities to think, judge and express their own ideas. Over 70% of schools answered that they wanted to improve their classes from the perspective of active learning.

However, many schools are still struggling with the introduction of active learning into the actual class activities. Many teachers expressed concerns, such as 'It would be difficult for students to learn something essential from the interactive activities and discussions'; 'We don't have enough time for extra activities in class'; 'Even though we know the great examples of active learning, this style would not suit our students'.

Based on this background that we created, 'Active Learning Patterns for Teachers', by compiling many good practices of teachers for the active learning of students. This pattern of language comprises 45 patterns for teachers to support their students to be active learners and continue to develop themselves.

It is especially useful for the following types of teachers (1) those who are not sure as to how to apply the idea of active learning in a class (2) those who have difficulty in describing how they have been approaching active learning and (3) those who want to systematically introduce this concept to the entire school. Using these patterns, it will be easier for teachers to self-reflect and share their experiences with other colleagues. These 'vocabularies' were created based on the actual experiences of some teachers who have been trying to design their classes in terms of active learning.

In this paper, we will describe the process of creating active learning patterns for teachers, present the 45 patterns created and three different ways of expressing this pattern language and introduce some examples of its application.

2. Creation Process

Active Learning Patterns for Teachers was created using our standard process of creating a pattern language (Figure 1). It contains three different phases (Iba and Isaku, 2016); Pattern Mining, Pattern Writing and Pattern Symbolizing, as is summarized below.

Figure 1: The Process of Creating a Pattern Language

2.1. Pattern Mining

In the phase of Pattern Mining, we first conducted 'Mining Dialogue' to extract practical knowledge from some teachers through a dialogue, 'Clustering' for finding out some common patterns from the collected data and 'Seed Making' for organizing them by writing down the ideas in a specific format as 'Seed of Pattern'.

In Mining Dialogue, we extracted good practices (rules of thumbs and tips) from 12 teachers who daily design their classes in the active learning style. They all had different teaching backgrounds with different subjects and different types of schools; both public and private elementary schools, junior high school, high school and university in different geographical areas. Every Mining session was conducted with 2 to 4 teachers within four hours (Figure 2). In the end, 430 elements which, according to the teachers, are important for active learning, were collected and written down onto sticky notes.

Figure 2: Mining Dialogue in the phase of Pattern Mining

In Clustering, we classified the collected data into groups, based on the KJ method (Kawakita, 1967). Twelve people collaborated together to figure out the essence of the contents written on the individual sticky notes, and arrange their positions according to their meanings. In this way, after 8 hours, groups of notes with similar meanings gradually appeared, and 430 fragments of data were classified into 131 groups. Because we had too many cards, it was better to work on the clustering on the floor although it is usually conducted on a big table (Figure 3). After 8 more hours of organizing the sticky notes, 45 groups remained in the end (Figure 4).

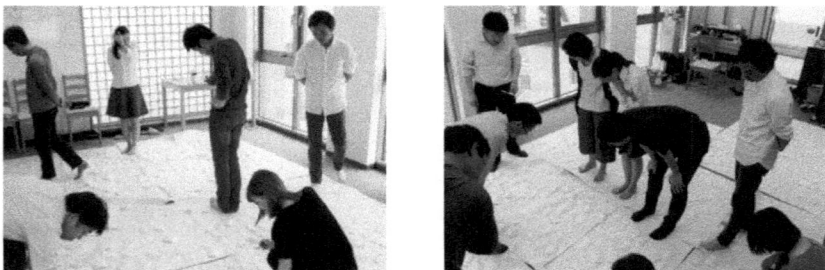

Figure 3: Clustering (First Half) in the phase of Pattern Mining

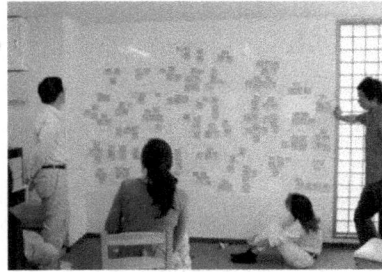

Figure 4: Clustering (Second Half) in the phase of Pattern Mining

In Seed Making, every single group generated in the clustering was written down into a specific format of 'seed of pattern' to summarize the context, problem and solution of each idea. Writing them down in a simple form, helped us avoid the duplication of ideas and leakage of important elements and also made the step of Structure Building much easier and faster. Structure building is a process of figuring out the whole picture of 'good practices of teachers for active learning' from the similarities and relations among the 46 patterns (Figure 5). It starts with a bottom-up approach; however, it is also important to consider the readers' perspectives, such as readability and the heuristic level of each pattern. In the end, three main categories—A, B and C — were generated.

Figure 5: Structure building in the phase of pattern mining

2.2. Pattern Writing

Pattern writing is the next phase of creating a pattern language, where we wrote the full description of seed of pattern; context, problem, force, solution, action and consequence. In this phase, it is necessary to consider the positions of every single pattern in the whole picture, as well as what was discussed in the Mining Dialogue.

In pattern review, we brushed up the patterns written by individual writers in a group discussion (Figure 6). All the patterns should be looked at from different perspectives to eliminate any misunderstanding and improve the quality of the description. Sometimes it is necessary to reconsider the relationships and positions of patterns and re-structure them. In fact, this phase of revising and correcting were repeated over and over again, to make our patterns reach the expected level of quality.

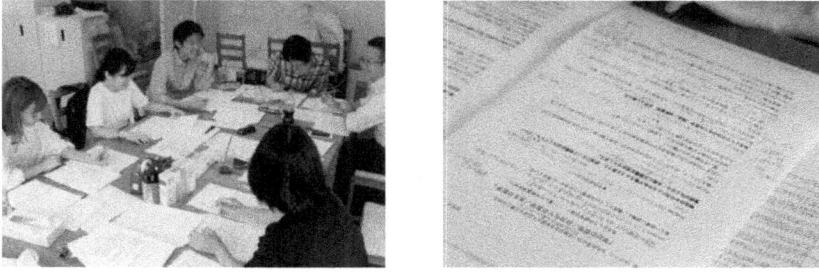

Figure 6: Pattern review in the phase of pattern writing

2.3. Pattern Symbolizing

Pattern symbolizing is the last phase of creating a pattern language and it includes pattern naming and pattern illustration to symbolically express the patterns (Figure 7). This process is still explorative and some contents of the patterns could be further improved in this phase since the essence of patterns has to be reconsidered to draw symbolic illustrations. Active learning patterns for teachers were finally completed with the designed booklet and cards.

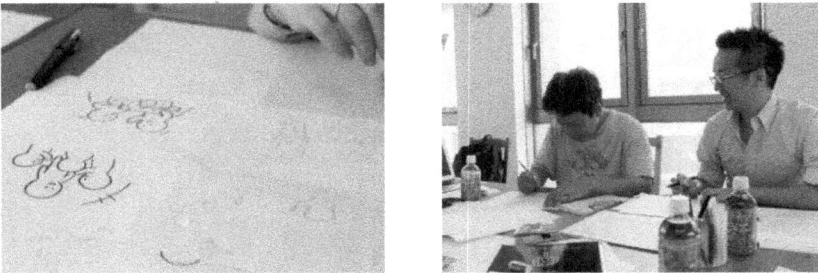

Figure 7: Pattern Illustrating in the phase of pattern symbolizing

3. Patterns

Active Learning Patterns for Teachers consists of three different categories: (A) Identify the seeds of curiosity, help them grow, (B) Lift them up to the next level, and (C) Enhance each other, keep changing. In this section, we introduce the patterns in these three categories.

3.1. (A) Identify the Seeds of Curiosity, Help Them Grow

The first category consists of the following pattern groups; 'Make the learner-centered class' 'Open one's heart' 'Find out the seeds of curiosity' 'Feel the fun of broadening' and 'Make a connection between learning and oneself'. These categories summarize the basic ideas for the education with active learning and each of them consists of three patterns for the better practices of teachers. For example, in order to 'make the learner-centered class', the following patterns are necessary; 'Active learner', 'Standing on the same side' and 'Growth in the long run'. Table 1 shows all the 15 patterns in the category (A) Identify the seeds of curiosity, help them grow.

A. IDENTIFY THE SEEDS OF CURIOSITY, HELP THEM GROW			
No.	Pattern Name	Pattern Illustration	Context, Problem and Solution
A1	**Active learner**		You want your students to learn things more actively. In this context, students will however keep expecting teachers to tell them what to do, as long as you believe that you are at the center of the class, organizing everything for them. Therefore, create an environment which encourages students to recognize important things to learn and try to take action by themselves.
A2	**Standing on the same side**		You expect your students to learn things more actively. In this context, students are likely to expect their teachers to tell them a correct answer, without trying to work out a solution by themselves. Therefore, you have to stand on the same side as your students and design a class in such a way as if you're trying to figure out the answers together.
A3	**Growth in the long run**		You want your students to acquire essential skills to live well in the future society. In this context, it might not be easy for teachers to focus on the training for long-term results, especially when they have to show some visible results of their teaching in the coming exams and so on. Therefore, find out an ability which would be very important for students' future, share its significance with their parents and incorporate it into the class activities and the assessments.
A4	**Everyday talk**		You want to know more about your students. In this context, however, talking about the class during the break time may not help you so much to understand your students. Therefore, enjoy the conversation with your students, in the way you usually talk with the people who you are personally interested in.

A5	Friendly neighbors		You want to design a class in which students influence each other to improve themselves. In this context, it might be difficult for some students to express themselves in class when they worry too much about what other people would think. Therefore, create opportunities for students to gradually build good relationships with each other to be able to feel relaxed to talk about themselves.
A6	Natural Response		You expect your students to concentrate on the class and learn things more deeply. In this context, students could easily lose their concentration, especially when they are supposed to sit still in the chair, keep quiet and just listen to the teachers. Therefore, create some activities for students to talk and move actively in class and let them feel free to express their physical and psychological reactions.
A7	Signs of Interest		You want to figure out what actually interests the students. In this context,, you may simply ask your students about their current interests, but it is sometimes difficult even for them to understand their preference and express it in their own words. Therefore, give attention to the emotional changes in your students during the class and ask them later on why they reacted strongly on a specific topic or activity.
A8	Curiosity Digging		You want students to enjoy learning. In this context, students may get a negative impression about learning, if they are always asked to study different subjects thoroughly and get rid of all the weak points by studying harder. Therefore, create opportunities for them to learn about things which they are truly interested in, in order to let them experience the real fun of learning.
A9	Visualizing Ideas		You want to support your students to deepen their own ideas. In this context, however, as long as students keep their ideas in their own mind, it would be difficult to deepen and develop these ideas because teachers cannot easily support this process. Therefore, create opportunities for students to output their ideas in various ways.
A10	Good and Better		You are going to make some comments on what students have done. In this context, students may get demotivated if you simply praise them with lenient criteria or you just strictly point out the weaknesses. Therefore, make sure that you first point out some good parts of what they have done and then tell them the points which could be improved.
A11	Upgraded Perspectives		Students have something they are curious about or some challenges they have in their lives. In this context, however, in their processes of exploring what they are interested in, they might get stuck on some problems or easily lose their enthusiasm about it. Therefore, show them other possibilities to develop what they are currently interested in, or find some connection with something else from different perspectives.

A12	Links for Discovery		You expect your students to experience the real fun of learning. In this context, it might be difficult for students to keep motivated if learning means only obtaining knowledge and becoming able to solve problems on the exams. Therefore, create opportunities for students to understand the phenomenon in the society using the knowledge they just gained from the class and let them experience how the networks of different knowledge could bring them new discoveries.
A13	Position Mapping		You want your students to learn something more deeply. In this context, they tend to be passive learners who just keep studying what is provided in class, if they do not know the significance and the goal of what they are currently studying about. Therefore, show them the position of what they are currently learning about, in the wide range of studies.
A14	Underlying Intentions		You expect your students to maximize their opportunities of learning. In this context, however, they cannot effectively conduct any activities or tasks unless they get the point of doing them. Therefore, tell the students about the point of your class and the purpose of every assignments.
A15	Future Reflection		You expect your students to think about what to learn and how to learn, for their own future. In this context, things would not be effectively learned if students did not know why they are important to them. Therefore, talk with the students about their future, encourage them to think what skills they need and how they should acquire them.

Table 1: Patterns in the category (A) Identify the Seeds of Curiosity, Help Them Grow

3.2. (B) Lift Them up to the Next Level

The next category consists of the following pattern groups; 'Get the power to change' 'Create opportunities to go forward' 'Broaden the current world' 'Challenge yourself to go beyond' and 'Keep improving'. These are for teachers who support students to keep being active learners. Table 2 shows the patterns in the category of (B) Lift Them up to the Next Level.

B. LIFT THEM UP TO THE NEXT LEVEL			
No.	Pattern Name	Pattern Illustration	Context, Problem and Solution
B1	Learning How to Learn		You expect your students to become life-long learners. In this context, however, it is not possible for you to support the students to learn something outside of school or after their graduation. Therefore, keep in mind that school is the place for students to learn 'how to learn', and try to improve the students' skills for active learning.

B2	Questioning Skills		You want your students to think for themselves to solve a problem. In this context, however, students cannot develop their ability to think about something deeply and their opinions may be easily swayed, if they just keep trusting the information provided. Therefore, encourage students to raise a lot of questions about various phenomena and motivate them to want to know about the things in the world.
B3	Persistent Efforts		There is specific knowledge and certain skills that students need to acquire. In this context, however, students will not develop their abilities to learn from a failure if they keep being evaluated by a single exam. Therefore, provide assignments which allow students to start all over again, by asking their friends for advice and improving the way to tackle the problem.
B4	Attractive Entrance		Some students are not willing to study. In this context, they tend to get more de-motivated if you try to teach them enthusiastically or talk about the significance of learning. Therefore, set a clear goal to achieve, start the class with something fun for students and lead them to get them into the mood for learning.
B5	Easier Steps		You want every student to try to complete the assignment. In this context, however, some students easily give up trying, especially when there are too many things to memorize and when the tasks seem too hard for them. Therefore, keep the goal of the assignment as it is, but try to make the questions sound easier for students to keep motivated.
B6	Several Ways to Join		You want your students to make use of the opportunities, such as class activities and school events, to improve themselves. In this context, some students are willing to participate in school events and class activities, whereas others miss on such opportunities to grow. Therefore, set different ways to participate in an event, so that it is easier for more students to join it.
B7	Tools for Exploration		Students are about to start explorative activities. In this context, if you let students decide everything by themselves, they may not be able to go beyond what they can already do. Therefore, make it clear what students should learn from the activities and provide them any means, method or information if necessary.
B8	Experience of Ideas		You are teaching students a new idea. In this context, ideas taught in class will never become a useful knowledge for students, if they keep trying to memorize them for exams. Therefore, create an opportunity for them to actually experience the idea you have taught in class.

B9	Positive Confusion		You expect your students to learn things in more active way. In this context, students would not get motivated to study more, if the class is too strictly organized, or if they feel they could understand everything in the class. Therefore, ask students a question at the end of the class, which would make them keep thinking about what they learned.
B10	Ignition to Challenge		You want your students to go beyond what they are today. In this context, if you let your students set up their own goals and problems, they tend to stay in what they can already do today and, therefore, it would be difficult for them to make a rapid progress. Therefore, draw out the motivation of students, by setting a problem which would be solved with a fair amount of effort, and keep reminding them of the value of challenging themselves.
B11	Chance to Show Off		Students are conducting a project or another activity. In this context, they would not get motivated to strive for better quality of the output if they were only presenting it in class. Therefore, make an opportunity for students to present their project in front of external audiences and get them motivated to polish up the outputs.
B12	Quality Borderline		Students are conducting their own projects. In this context, it is difficult for them to imagine which level of quality is required to achieve their own goals. Therefore, show them the expected level of the output quality by using examples.
B13	Decision-Making Experience		You expect your students to open the way to their own future. In this context, they will not learn to make important decisions themselves if they keep following somebody else's decisions. Therefore, give them a lot of opportunities to make their own decisions and learn from the results.
B14	Food for Change		You expect your students to be positive about receiving comments or opinions from others and to try to learn things from them and improve themselves. In this context, they tend to take the comments from others as criticisms and be afraid of expressing themselves. Therefore, support the students and provide positive experiences of having different opinions or points of view and let them understand how these differences could bring them new discoveries or opportunities to improve themselves.

B15			You expect your students to learn things from their own activities or experiences and develop their practices by themselves. In this context, independent reflection of activities may not bring them any deep insight about the points to improve and possibilities to develop. Therefore, let them have a dialogue with others to look back on their projects from more extensive points of view, so that they can learn more from their own experiences.
	Reflective Dialogue		

Table 2: Patterns in the category (B) Lift Them up to the Next Level

3.3. (C) Enhance Each Other, Keep Changing

The last category of patterns are for teachers to 'Think about the authentic roles of teachers', 'Change the focus', 'Collaborate with students', 'Make the learning active and attractive' and 'Enhance each other with other teachers'. These patterns explain how teachers can keep improving their practices. Table 3 shows the patterns in the category of (C) Enhance Each Other, Keep Changing.

C. ENHANCE EACH OTHER, KEEP CHANGING			
No.	Pattern Name	Pattern Illustration	Context, Problem and Solution
C1	**Learning Teacher**		You want to provide students with a better education. In this context, however, because your daily tasks take first priority, there is not enough time for yourself to gain new knowledge or learn new ways of teaching. Therefore, keep in mind that it is important to get opportunities to learn new stuff and keep challenging yourself, in order to improve the quality of your teaching.
C2	**Connection to the World**		You want your students to get enough skills to live actively in the future society. In this context, the goal of learning in the traditional system is for students is to receive good evaluation on the performance at school. Therefore, talk about the wider world beyond the classroom, pose a question and let students learn things in the connection with the actual society.
C3	**Teaching Principles**		You want to provide students with a better education. In this context, the traditional educational system is not always flexible enough to adapt to the fast-changing society. Therefore, figure out the abilities or skills which will be required in the future society and share your educational principles with your students, their parents and your colleagues.

C4	Room for Trials		You want to develop a new way of teaching for the active learning of students. In this context, there are already too many things to teach and there is not enough time to teach additional things in class. Therefore, capture the whole picture of the teaching curriculum provided, order your teaching priorities and focus on what you really have to teach in class, so that you can spare time for additional challenges.
C5	Passionate Topics		You want to make your class more exciting and attractive. In this context, if you keep teaching the same subject in the same way every year, your class might be boring both for you and your students. Therefore, get excited about the material yourself first, by exploring some topics which you are currently curious about.
C6	Try First		You want to try a new way of teaching. In this context, you may be afraid of making a mistake, hesitate to hesitate to use new tools and just repeat the same way of teaching. Therefore, if you think it is necessary for students, try first and later think about how to improve it.
C7	Spontaneous Adjustments		You want to design a class which draws out the students' active learning. In this context, however, when some students are not interested in what you have prepared, or when they unexpected challenges, the class does not go as you planned, Therefore, make a solid plan for the core part of teaching, leave the other parts flexible, so that you can organize the lessons in response to the actual reactions of the students.
C8	Stock of Techniques		You want to design a class more flexibly in response to the students' reactions. In this context, the class may end up being unorganized. Therefore, have ready as many different means, tips or techniques of teaching as possible, to be able to choose the most appropriate of them depending on the class goal and the actual reactions of students.
C9	Collaborative Improvement		Students seem to be not very interested in the lesson. In this context, they might not be satisfied with how the class is going on and therefore do not actively participate in the class. Therefore, tell the students honestly about your intention and struggles in the class, ask their opinions and improve the class together through continuous dialogue.
C10	Change of Scenery		You are about to trying a new way of teaching. In this context, even if you have new contents or means to teach, students would not learn a lot from the class if their attitude towards learning remains the same. Therefore, choose another place which will be more appropriate for its contents and means, without being too strict about following the customs in school.

C11	Unexpected Contents		Unexpected things happened during a class. In this context, you may get irritated if the class does not go as well as you planned and it makes students uncomfortable as well. Therefore, take the unexpected event in a positive way, by welcoming it as a great opportunity to make the class unforgettable for students.
C12	Editor for Learning		Your class has some individual or group projects for students. In this context, students may not be able to learn things deeply enough from the independent work, although it is effective in the way of motivating them to learn. Therefore, take a time in the class to visualize the ideas generated in the individual or group works, 'edit' them to show what they actually mean and bring the students a deeper understanding of the subject.
C13	Case-Study Cafe		Every teacher in your school has different styles of teaching. In this context, it may be difficult for you to keep finding new ways of teaching, because you sometimes feel the limitation of generating new ideas and analyzing them for a better education and lose confidence in your style of teaching. Therefore, make a time to talk with other teachers about the different ways of teaching, the roles of teachers and so on.
C14	Inter-Subject Collaboration		You want your students to have fun while learning the subject you are teaching about. In this context, although you want to teach about your subject in the connection with other subjects, you don't have enough time to prepare for teaching something beyond your specialty. Therefore, ask other teachers for a help and show the connection between what you teach and material from the other subjects.
C15	Diversity of Strengths		You want to make your school more attractive. In this context, it is hard for teachers to work independently to manage the tasks they have in school, as they all have their own strengths and weaknesses. Therefore, emphasize the importance of different personalities and specialties of individual teachers and create a big team various teachers have different strengths.

Table 3: Patterns in the category (C) Enhance Each Other, Keep Changing

4. Tools for Utilizing Patterns

In order to make the introduction and application of active learning patterns to the actual teaching environments easier, we outputted it in three different ways; 'ALP Assessment' for teachers to self-assess how many tips they have already put into practice, 'ALP cards' for them to share their experiences with others in the workshops and 'ALP booklet' which describes every single pattern with some examples.

4.1. ALP Assessment

ALP assessment is a tool for teachers to check how many patterns for Active Learning they have already put into practice and evaluate themselves. The radar chart visualizes the whole picture of one's teaching experiences in terms of patterns (Figure 8). It clearly tells you the aspects that you have already achieved as well as some weaknesses to improve, and therefore, helps you to set a clear goal for a better education with the Active Learning approach. Furthermore, it is also effective as an organizational self-assessment tool for a school to improve its teaching environment as a whole community.

The results of the ALP assessment totally depend on how individuals evaluate themselves (Figure 9), and cannot simply be compared with others. However, it helps them visualize the balance of their own teaching style or some features of each school, and encourages the teachers to reflect on themselves and think about how they could improve their ways of teaching.

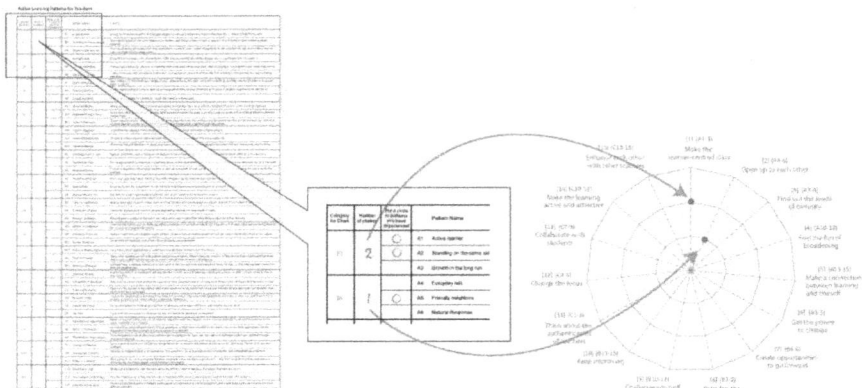

Figure 8: ALP Assessment

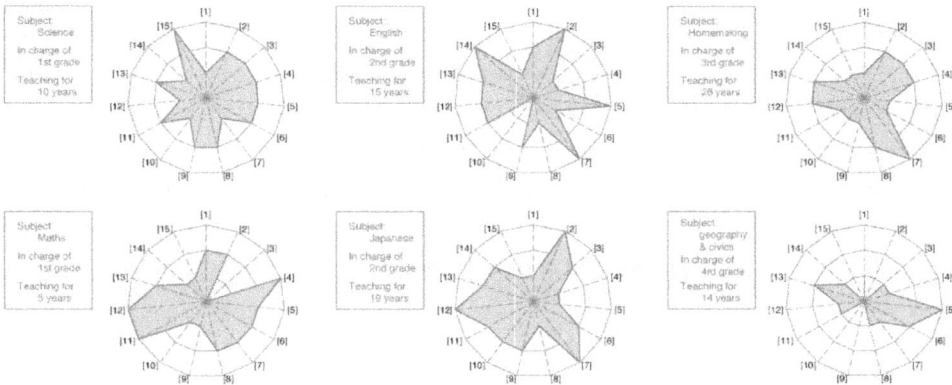

Figure 9: Diversity in ALP Assessment

4.2. ALP Cards

Every single ALP Card shows a Pattern Name and its symbolic Illustration, and states the key sentence of Context, Problem and Solution (Figure 10). This set of cards can be most effectively used in the Dialogue Workshop, where teachers share their own experiences with others, and learn from each other. Although it is usually difficult for teachers to make a comment on the other classes, this pattern language does not refer to any specific subject, and, therefore, ALP Cards can help them share opinions beyond one's specialities. They can also help you ask someone else to tell you the experiences with Active Learning. It helps teachers to talk about things that they already know about but find it difficult to explain.

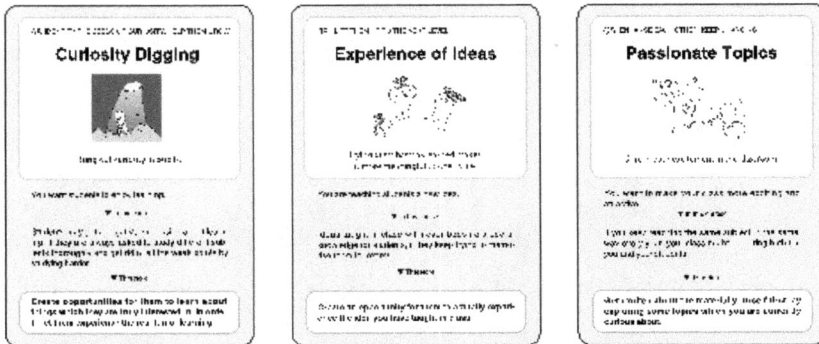

Figure 10: ALP Cards

4.3. ALP Booklet

ALP Booklet has a full description of all the patterns (Figure 11), whereas ALP Assessment and ALP Cards show only the quick overview of each pattern. Therefore, ALP Booklet is useful especially when you want to know more details about the patterns. In addition, this booklet introduces some experiences of teachers from the Mining Dialogue. These actual experiences would make the abstract patterns sound more fresh and real. In a nutshell, this booklet works as a dictionary for teachers to look up some patterns, and also as a reference book to think about their own ways of applying them.

5. Process of Utilizing Patterns

For the most effective application of Active Learning Patterns, ALP Assessment, ALP Cards and ALP Booklet should be used according to their intended purpose (Figure 12). For example, teachers could use the ALP Assessment to evaluate their current teaching style, and share their experiences with others to learn from each other in the workshop, with the help of ALP Cards. In this way, they would be able to imagine how to apply the patterns in their own classrooms. Even if there are some patterns which have never been experienced by anyone in the workshop, teachers can at least read the ALP Booklet to discuss how to introduce these patterns to their own school environment.

Collaborative Improvement

**It is not just teachers,
who can design the class**

Students seem to be not very interested in the lesson.

▼ In this context

They might be not satisfied with the way the class is organized, and therefore do not actively participate in the class activities. Teachers who sensed such atmosphere in class tend to be distracted and become unable to concentrate on the lecture. The situation gets even worse if you try to solve it in a strange way, such as scolding.

▼ Therefore

Tell your students honestly about your feelings and struggles in the class, ask for their opinions, and discuss with them to improve the class. You should first state that you want to improve the situation at the moment, ask students what they think about the problem, and then make time to discuss it with students. For example, if you are not sure whether your teaching plan is appropriate for your students or not, you should directly ask for their opinions to find the best way to proceed.

▼ As a result

Participating in the discussion to improve their own learning environment will not only improve the quality of class itself, but will also become a good experience for students. In addition, the fact that teachers and students know each other well, will enable both of them to be more relaxed and concentrate on the lectures. This attitude of teachers who are trying to improve the class with students, is very important to earn their trust and create a collaborative relationship with them.

Figure 11: Pattern Description of the ALP Booklet

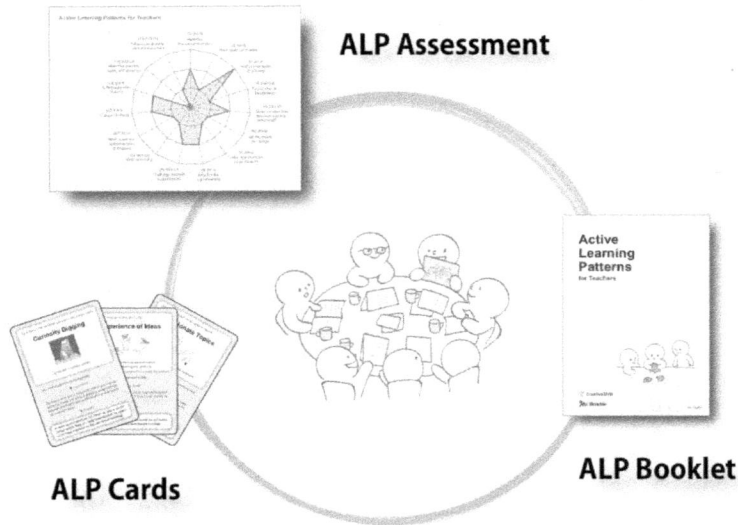

Figure 12:Utilising Process with ALP Assessment, Booklet and Cards

Figure 13 and 14 show actual applications of Active Learning Patterns for Teachers in the training session of teachers in a Japanese high school. Figure 15 shows the workshop carried out in an educational conference in Japan. Upper photos are from the workshop in which the participants walked around the room to talk with someone else to share their own experiences, and lower photos are from the Dialogue Workshop with ALP Cards.

We got the following feedback from the ALP users. These responses were obtained in Japanese, summarized, and translated into English for this paper.

» It became much easier to have a dialogue with others because all the important tips are clearly stated.

» Patterns are very effective to evaluate my own way of teaching and learn from others through a dialogue.

» I could think, talk, and ask about things I was not aware of.

» I became confident with my way of teaching, as I could get some positive feedback from others.

» The dialogue with others brought me some new discoveries and opened ways to challenge myself.

» I learned some tips in the ALP training, and could apply them to the actual teaching plan.

» The feedback I got from other teachers on my teaching style showed me some new aspects of the ALP.

» We used ALP Cards in the meeting and were able to identify some problems in our school.

Figure 13: Training session for Teachers in Yaeyama Highschool (Okinawa, Japan)

Figure 14: Training session for Teachers in Seigakuin Junior & Senior Highschool (Tokyo, Japan)

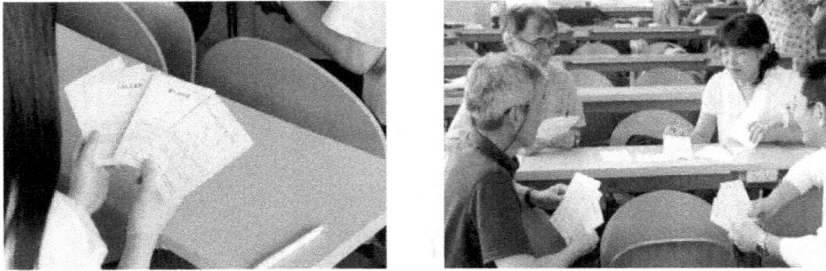

Figure 15: Dialogue workshop in an educational conference (Kanagawa, Japan)

6. Conclusion

In this paper, we have presented the Active Learning Patterns for Teachers, which describe the best practices of teachers who support the students to become active learners. The pattern language was created from scratch based on the Mining Dialogue with teachers in Japan. There are, however, many patterns proposed as Pedagogical Patterns or Educational Patterns in the pattern conferences, for example, Bergin, et al. (2015), Köppe & Schalken-Pinkster (2013), Köppe & Portier (2014), Köppe, C., et al. (2015a, 2015b, 2015c), Pedagogical Patterns Editorial Board (2012). We need to compare and clarify the similarities and differences between them in our future work.

Furthermore, we created many patterns for learners, in addition to the pattern language for teachers presented in this paper: specifically, Learning Patterns (Iba & Iba Lab, 2014a), Presentation Patterns (Iba & Iba Lab, 2014b) and Collaboration Patterns (Iba & Iba Lab, 2014c). There should be many connections between patterns for learners and patterns for teachers, which will also be the focus of our future work.

Finally, although the introduction and application of this pattern language to the actual teaching environments is still in the first stage, we have started distributing it to teachers for free. We are also planning some events for teachers to experience different ways of utilizing this pattern language. Through these activities, we expect teachers to make effective use of this pattern language in their daily practice in the classroom and for better communication with their colleagues, in order to enable the bigger improvements in the current educational systems.

7. Acknowledgement

We would like to thank the project members from CreativeShift Inc. and Benesse Corporation. We would also like to thank our interviewees. We would like to express our gratitude to Konomi Munakata for translating patterns into English and supporting to write this paper.

8. References

Bergin, J., Kohls, C., Köppe, C., Mor, Y., Portier, M., Schümmer, T., & Warburton, S. (2015). Assessment-driven course design foundational patterns. In Proceedings of the 20th European Conference on Pattern Languages of Programs. ACM, New York, NY, USA,, Article 31, 13 pages.

Iba, T. and Iba Laboratory (2014a) Learning Patterns: A Pattern Language for Creative Learning, CreativeShift.

Iba, T. and Iba Laboratory (2014b) Presentation Patterns: A Pattern Language for Creative Presentations, CreativeShift.

Iba, T. and Iba Laboratory (2014c) Collaboration Patterns: A Pattern Language for Creative Collaborations, CreativeShift.

Iba, T. and Isaku, T. (2016) 'A pattern language for creating pattern languages: 364 patterns for pattern mining, writing and symbolizing', In Proceedings of the 2016 Conference on Pattern Languages of Programs.

Kawakita, J. (1967) HassouHou [The Abduction Method: For Creativity Development], in

Japanese, Chuo-Koron.

Köppe, C., & Schalken-Pinkster, J. (2013). Lecture design patterns: improving interactivity. In Proceedings of the 20th Conference on Pattern Languages of Programs (PLoP '13). The Hillside Group,, USA,, Article 23, 15 pages.

Köppe, C., & Portier, M. (2014). Lecture design patterns: improving the beginning of a lecture. In Proceedings of the 19th European Conference on Pattern Languages of Programs (EuroPLoP '14). ACM, New York, NY, USA,, Article 16, 12 pages.

Köppe, C., Eekelen, M.v., & Hoppenbrouwers, S. (2015a). Improving student group work with collaboration patterns: a case study. In Proceedings of the 37th International Conference on

Software Engineering - Volume 2 (ICSE '15), Vol. 2. IEEE Press, Piscataway, NJ, USA, 303–306.

Köppe, C. & Schalken-Pinkster, J. (2015b). Lecture design patterns: laying the foundation. In Proceedings of the 18th European Conference on Pattern Languages of Program (EuroPLoP '13). ACM, New York, NY, USA,, Article 4, 27 pages.

Köppe, C., Niels, R., Holwerda, R., Tijsma, L., Diepen, N.V., Turnhout, K.,V., & Bakker, R. (2015). Flipped classroom patterns: designing valuable in-class meetings. In Proceedings–of the 20th European Conference on Pattern Languages of Programs (EuroPLoP '15). ACM, New York, NY, USA,, Article 26, 17 pages.

Köppe, C., Portier, M., Bakker, R., & Hoppenbrouwers, S. (2015c). Lecture design patterns: more interactivity improvement patterns. In Proceedings of the 22nd Conference on Pattern Languages of Programs (PLoP '15). The Hillside Group, USA, Article 24, 13 pages.

Pedagogical Patterns Editorial Board (2012) Pedagogical Patterns: Advice For Educators, Createspace.

THE SEARCH FOR
CHRISTOPHER
ALEXANDER

PURPLSOC

Designing hybrid spaces for creative work

Kohls, Christian

Department for Computer Science, TH Köln, Gummersbach, Germany

christian.kohls@th-koeln.de

Münster, Guido

Department for Computer Science, TH Köln, Gummersbach, Germany

guido.muenster@th-koeln.de

This article deals with the planning and design of hybrid spaces for innovation and learning processes using a design pattern language. Firstly, strategic and operational goals for the design of innovation spaces at universities are presented. Based on existing frameworks for the design of innovation spaces as well as an inductive-empirical analysis of existing good practices and technologies, we derived about 80 patterns. This paper provides an overview of the language and presents three example patterns: hybrid learning space, physical to digital, and digital to real. The design patterns made an important contribution in the concrete planning of three innovation rooms at TH Köln (Campus Gummersbach). Using the patterns we made design decisions consciously and justified unconventional solutions by discussing the forces behind the patterns. The patterns can provide important design guidelines for similar projects at other universities.

Design patterns; socio-technical systems; study rooms; innovation tools; design thinking

1. Introduction

The term hybrid space (or blended space) refers to an interplay of different spaces, such as the physical, digital, informational, conceptual and social space (Benyon, 2014). Blending such spaces is more than just adding the functions of each (not just "best of both worlds"). We believe that entirely new scenarios for creative and collaborative work emerge (that is we enter "new worlds"). We planned and designed the interior design of three rooms for the computer science and engineering campus of TH Köln (the University of Applied Sciences in Cologne). In particular, the rooms should encourage students to run through the different phases of design thinking.

The rooms should create space for innovation, encouraging the various activities during a design project with both analogue and digital tools. It is important for us to achieve a seamless fusion of both worlds, for example by digital artefacts being mapped onto tangible physical objects, and analogous work results can be digitized directly and without fractions. Thus, they can be further manipulated within digital environments. There are already various approaches and frameworks for the planning of such work and learning environments. These frameworks help in decision-making for certain technologies and design options. In our view, however, these frameworks are often on too abstract levels. While they indeed define important criteria, they do not always provide action-oriented (and empirically verifiable) recommendations. As an alternative, we propose the development of a design pattern language that captures the good practices in the design of hybrid learning spaces. The design pattern approach is widely applied in the computer sciences, in particular in the field of software development (Gamma et al., 1995), but is also found in many other areas (Kohls, 2014), including interaction design (Borchers, 2001) and the design of socio-technical systems (Schümmer & Lukosch, 2007). The approach is originally grounded in architectural theory (Alexander et al., 1977) and therefore seems particularly suitable for the design of rooms. This article presents an overview of the language and three selected design patterns. It reflects on the planning process for three innovation rooms using this pattern language. First, however, the goals are outlined and existing frameworks are presented. From there we derive design patterns using a mix of methods for pattern mining. The conclusion is based on our experience in the use of the design pattern language for concrete spatial planning and implementation.

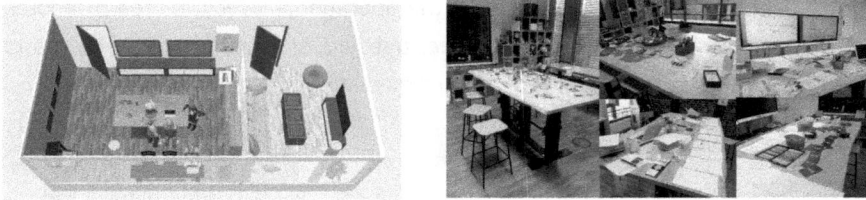

Figure 1. Left: conceptual rendering. Right: Actual innovation room in action.

2. Objectives in the design of hybrid innovation spaces

The innovation rooms are linked to certain strategic and operational objectives, which relate both to the university context and to social development - for example, to enable social innovation or social entrepreneurship.

2.1. Strategic objectives

At the strategic level, the main goal is to increase the creativity and the innovative potential of student projects. A hybrid innovation space should facilitate methodological skills, enable interdisciplinary encounter and support design thinking. Another goal is to intensify the student's identification with one's own university as a place of innovation. Nowadays collaborative learning formats are the main reason for the encounter on-campus because learning materials are available digitally and can be used from home or on the road off-campus. The rooms should therefore be extraordinary places that offer opportunities not available at home.

A further strategic goal from the computer science perspective is the development of new devices and applications. In the context of Bachelor, Master and PhD theses, the room is to provide a "playground" for developing and testing new apps, widgets and gadgets for creative and collaborative work. The third strategic objective is the empirical testing of space constellations and digital tools. The research questions are, for example: How do different interactive technologies influence collaboration compared to traditional tools and artefacts? How must a creativity app be designed so that it can be used effectively in as many scenarios as possible?

2.2. Operational objectives

On the operational level, the issue is how the rooms influence learning scenarios and how the space has to be set up so that it can be used as an experimental "playground" and at the same time as an everyday working space. At the operational level, the area promotes project-based and skill-driven learning. It establishes a results-oriented "maker culture" and supports playful approaches to the development or mediation of serious content.

2.3. Impact for university development

The importance of interior design in academic teaching contexts has been highlighted recently (DINI, 2013; Kohlert & Cooper, 2017). Skerlak, Kaufmann & Bachmann (2014) note about learning environments at the university that there is an increase of learning spaces for self-directed learning, that they are used for informal learning and that open spaces for developing innovative teaching and learning occur. The Horizon Report (Adams Becker et al., 2017) has picked up this topic in recent years, again and again under the themes "Maker Space", "Bring your own device", "Flipped Classroom", "Internet of Things", "Wearables" and "Redesigning learning spaces". An approach to these concepts should be of strategic importance. A commission of experts of the "Hochschulforum Digitalisierung" (Panel for digitization in higher education) concludes in "The Digital Turn" (HFD, 2017) that "maker spaces and creative spaces" and "digital collaboration tools" are among the key technologies of a digital university.

2.4. Enable Design Thinking

A central goal of the innovation rooms is to support the processes of design thinking, in particular the phases of ideation (generate new ideas) and rapid prototyping. Design Thinking is a conceptual framework developed at the Stanford School of Engineering for design processes (Lindberg, Noweski &, Meinel, 2009). The aim of design thinking is enabling innovation systematically (Meinel & von Thienen, 2016). It is an iterative process of "delivering results to solve complex problems" using a user- and customer-centric approach (Uebernickel et al., 2015). The design thinking process consists of both analytical phases (collecting, organizing, evaluating) as well as from synthetic phases (developing, testing, enhancing) (Plattner, Meinel & Weinberg, 2009). A key element of design thinking is early prototyping. It is assumed that on the concrete model - even if this is only rudimentarily implemented - weak points and further development potentials are better recognized. Sketches, drawings and simple models enable designers the exploration of problem and solution space simultaneously (Cross, 2001). Therefore, in the planning of the spaces it was very important that a large variety of tools and building material is available, allowing users to develop and tests new forms as early prototypes.

3. Hybrid innovation rooms

A hybrid space or a blended space emerges when, for example, digital and physical areas are closely linked and overlap (Benyon, 2014). The result of this mixing is a new area that has its very own, new emergent properties and thus is more than the sum of its parts.

3.1. Blended Spaces

The blended space approach can be found in various environments and applications, such as interactive tourist guide (Benyon, 2014), "Living History" areas in museums or Interactive Collaborative Environments (Benyon & Mival, 2016). Its origin can be linked to the blending theory of Fauconnier & Turner (2008), which is applied and further developed for blended spaces by Benyon (Benyon, 2014). Benyon & Mival (2015) show different spaces or areas of importance for the blended space approach. These include the physical space, the digital space, the information space, the conceptual space, the navigation space, and finally the social space. The task of a designer in the blending of the aforementioned spaces into a blended space is to create new environments as natural and intuitive as possible.

3.2. Frameworks for interior design

The blended space approach already provides a good theoretical framework for deriving design principles. In addition, there are several frameworks that deal with the design of innovative spaces or blended spaces. For example the TACIT framework is derived directly from the blended space approach (Benyon & Mival, 2015) by identifying key elements. These include the territoriality, awareness, control and interaction. Moultrie et al. (2007) develop a framework that does not discuss specific design elements but rather the related goals. They distinguish between strategic and symbolic goals, innovation efficiency and effectivity, enhanced teamwork, stronger involvement of stakeholders and expanding entrepreneurial skills on a general level. The framework operationalizes these objectives and differentiates between factors for the planning of the space as well as factors for the evaluation of the degree of attainment.

Bustamante et al. (2015) compare the criteria of different frameworks for the design of innovation spaces. All of these frameworks have in common that they name important principles, criteria and directives for planning and even testing. However, when it comes to the concrete design of a new space, they remain very general and often too abstract. Therefore, in our view, the design pattern approach of Christopher Alexander (Alexander et al., 1977; Alexander, 1979) seems to be a better alternative. It keeps the general reasoning but provides tangible and holistic advice to implement solutions.

4. Design patterns for design

Design patterns capture proven solutions in generic form and convey tested design knowledge. They are at a more specific level than frameworks, as they propose concrete solution forms and their consequences for certain contexts and situations. At the same time they are general enough to be adapted to the specific needs of a room setup. The design pattern approach therefore seems promising to raise the design options to a more concrete and better informed level.

4.1. Empirical Basis: Pattern Mining

Identifying and documenting design patterns is called pattern mining. There are different approaches for pattern mining (Kohls & Panke, 2009). The approach taken here is a typical mix of methods of inductive and deductive research:

» Deriving requirements and factors from the frameworks

» Analysis of existing good practices for interior design

» Visits to tradeshows and exhibitions, browsing product brochures, explore existing rooms

» Testing of classic and digital tools

» Participatory design sessions with later users of the space (students, docents)

» Evaluation of different design options with mockups

In the process of identifying the general forms of the patterns, the findings from the general frameworks mentioned before can be considered as driving factors. Moreover, we found recurring structures in case studies of existing facilities: i-Land (Streitz et al., 1999), ICE (Benyon & Mival, 2012), Maker Spaces (Forest et al, 2014) and iRoom (Johanson, Fox & Winograd, 2002). Furthermore, numerous analog tools (e.g. methods cards, innovation games) and digital tools (e.g. iPads with pen, touch screens, table tops) were tested in the laboratory or at exhibitions. Various design options for the room were played with, for example using mock-ups to explore the optimal size for a center table that should be used as a "stage" for the creative process.

Various pattern candidates have emerged from the analysis. Pattern candidates that we can support empirically by several examples and that can be explained plausibly using establishes theories, have been selected to plan the rooms. These patterns can be characterized and clustered into categories of different problem groups: work materials and tools, atmosphere, session management, navigation and blended interaction.

4.2. An abundance of analog and digital materials

The first category is about the materials and tools that should be available in innovation spaces. Since we cannot always predict which materials will be needed in a creative session, an abundance of materials should be available. Thus, giving users freedom of choice, allowing them to select the right materials and tools depending on the situation. Moreover, we reasoned that extraordinary materials may inspire extraordinary ideas. Boxes with work materials are frequently found for design thinking (Uebernickel et al., 2015) and the design agency IDEO has cabinets with work materials (Kelley & Littman, 2001). These examples lead to the pattern ABUNDANCE OF MATERIAL which is further refined. BUILDING MATERIAL relates to building materials, for example Lego bricks for prototyping, metaphor construction and Serious Play (Kristiansen & Rasmussen, 2014), and other materials for tinkering. The room should provide several THOUGHT TRIGGERS that provide impulses for ideas. Examples are random images, story cubes, and stimulus words both in analog and in digital form. For visualization we provide A BUNCH OF PENS AND PAPERS and in addition digital tablets and interactive whiteboards. CURIOUS THINGS are unusual objects to stimulate lateral thinking. Such objects can be spread around or hidden as a surprise element in containers (SURPRISE). Furthermore, various project templates (WORK TEMPLATES, e.g. Business Model Canvas) should be provided for analytical processes. The filled out templates can be digitized automatically and possibly trigger other actions (TEMPLATE TO ACTION), e.g. automatic sorting into various digital lists (such as pros and cons), or using drawings within other programs (games, living mockups). Here is a summary of the patterns:

ABUNDANCE OF MATERIALS: Provide many different types of materials, let users chose the right material depending on the situation.

BUILDING MATERIALS: Provide materials that users can use for rapid prototyping: boxes, bricks, glue.

THOUGHT TRIGGERS: Provide materials that trigger thoughts, e.g. photos, questions, random words.

CURIOUS THINGS: Place some unexpected surprise elements in the room to make people think into very different directions. Examples: a bottle of butter beer, small toys.

A BUNCH OF PENS AND PAPERS: Make it as easy as possible to write down an idea.

WORK TEMPLATES: Provide templates (such as business model canvas, SWOT analysis) to work with.

TEMPLATES TO ACTION: Provide automatic analysis / digitalization of templates (for example scan all items from a SWOT matrix, and put each item into the correct category automatically).

SURPRISE: Provide unexpected opportunities.

LIVING MOCK-UPS: Enable users to create mock-ups that work.

4.3. Atmosphere

The atmosphere of the room also plays a special role in creative work. For this reason, we have identified many patterns in the physical space, such as the general ambience, plants, high-quality furniture, bar stools and workbenches, sofas, pictures and sound. However, the equipment with digital tools brings new problems and requires additional solutions. These include patterns such as NO CABLE (there should be no visible cables), control of sound and illumination (e.g. illuminating certain areas of work, atmospheric lighting). In the category "Food & Convenience" we also found patterns in the interest of general well-being, such as the provision of (healthy) snacks and explicit permission for students to bring drinks and snacks into the room. Such explicit permissions are important because many other rooms, especially computer rooms, do not permit any food. In creative areas, FOOD IS NO HAZARD. Furthermore, we need a ROOM CONCIERGE who will make sure that all the tools are ready for the next meeting. Here is a summary of the patterns:

AMBIENCE / FURNITURE: Use high quality furniture that sets the right design spirit

Moods: Support different moods with illumination and sound

PLACE OF RETREAT: Have some space to relax, let the mind wander (phase of incubation)

PLANTS: Add organic and natural elements to the room

SOUND: Provide fast access to sound backgrounds (e.g. coffee shop noise, Zen relaxing sounds)

ILLUMINATION: Use light to set moods and direct attention

SOUNDPROOF BY CHOICE: Make sure no one is distracted by noises from neighboring rooms.

NO CABLES: Hide all cables.

NOBLE ENVIRONMENTS: Use high quality furniture and equipment to let users feel valuable.

4.4. Session Management

Session management requires solution patterns to safe sessions, restore them and take them into other (physical) rooms without seams. A backup functionality must be available for data security. To retrieve lost data back, restore functionality must be given. The roll-back enables the applications and systems to return to a prior state (BACKUP - RECOVERY - ROLLBACK). This is often a standard feature in online tools such as Google Docs or Wiki-pedia. Nevertheless, we consider the explicit documentation to be important as a model for the design of new tools.

ROOM RESET refers to a quick way to reset all systems and return them to their original state. This solution is very important to avoid unauthorized access to work results, i.e. if the next work group enters the room all prior writings should disappear. Room reset features are often found in software systems for interactive whiteboards (such as SMART Boards, Microsoft Surface Hub).

If a group of users returns to the room a week or a month later, they should continue to work where they had stopped. Hence, it must be possible to access a history to prior re-sults. All devices in the room are restored to this state and provide the same set-up of the last event (ACCESS TO OLD SESSIONS). Since there are several independent innovation rooms, we need a way to take the complete session to another room. This is also relevant for break-out sessions. This leads to the pattern CROSS-ROOM INTERACTION. Here is a summary of the patterns:

BACKUP – RECOVERY – ROLLBACK: Enable different configurations for the room, especially when experimental setups are run.

ROOM RESET: Self-clean all digital devices by resetting their configuration and delete confi-dential work results.

ACCESS TO OLD SESSIONS: Save a session and restore all files and screen set ups in the next session.

CROSS-ROOM INTERACTION: Take the work results from one room to the next. Collect re-sults from break-out sessions in one room.

PHYSICAL TURN OFF OF RECORDING DEVICES (Big Brother goes blind): Add physical shut-ters to cameras and enable users to disconnect mics to have privacy by design.

4.5. Navigation

The navigation space must also be considered in a hybrid room concept. There are different solutions that help users to find their way around the room - for example, certain analogue and digital tools can be explained ad-hoc. In a space that offers many possibilities, not everything can be draped at first sight or be intuitively usable. For orientation and guidance we can use TANGIBLE INSTRUCTIONS such as menu cards with brief instructions, overview maps or "cookbooks" that provide step-by-step guidance and highlight which building blocks are useful. Using QR codes, these physical elements can in turn call up video instructions for smartphones or wall displays.

Icons of the digital user interfaces should be fully self-explanatory. Users should see at first glance which action is trigged if a button is pressed. Objects in the room need to be placed in such a way that users are encouraged to use them. For example, Lego bricks and sticky notes should not be hidden in a cabinet. They should be accessible right away and offer a high affordance. The pattern is INVITE ACTION.

The patterns DEFAULT APPS and FAST ACCESS deal with the fact that quick access to key features and tools must be provided. Standard applications should be accessible directly in such a way that they do not have to be searched for long. Tablets, for example, have no long boot times. Systems should be switched on before the work session starts or they have to start very quickly. Here is a summary of the patterns:

TANGIBLE INSTRUCTIONS: Provide instructions that are fun and tangible (such as a menu card with design methods).

(INTERACTIVE) VIDEO INSTRUCTIONS: Integrate on-the-fly video instructions to the room

ILLUMINATE: Use light (Projectors, LED, etc.) to point to specific tools.

INVITE ACTION: Equipment should have a high affordance to interact with.

CHOOSE YOUR TOOL: Let users freely choose from a large set of different tools.

DEFAULT APPS: Provide important software tools on interactive whiteboards, screens and tablets.

FAST ACCESS: Start the most important apps and templates quickly. Do not lock sticky-notes into a cabinet but place them on the table.

4.6. Blended Interaction

Perhaps the most interesting category is Blended Interaction, as it is concerned with solutions that enable a seamless integration of the analogue and digital world.

The pattern PHYSICAL TO DIGITAL regards physical actions and artefacts that can be digitized immediately. When a user sketches with a pencil on a digital surface or a sheet of paper, it is to be digitized immediately by a touch-sensitive surface or a camera. The complementary pattern is DIGITAL TO REAL. Objects created in the digital space should not remain only digital but are brought in to the real world. Examples are projections onto physical objects, walls or on the floor, the printing with photo or 3D printers, as well as the controlling of robots or Raspberry Pi modules.

Moreover, physical objects are used as simple triggers for interaction between the digital and analogue world (PHYSICAL OBJECTS TRIGGER ACTIONS). An example is digitizing a sketch by pressing a physical button.

Rooms that contain several digital devices need some means to connect them and share data (DEVICE ORCHESTRATION). Examples are: sending brainstorming items from smart phones to interactive walls, sketch characters or labyrinths on tablets and use them on game arcades, or selecting the content for large displays using small interactive tablets.

One step further, we can orchestrate the connected devices to one large unit (COUPLED DEVICES). This way several independent devices can be connected to form a larger contiguous workspace. Examples are: dual projections of interactive whiteboards controlled by one computer, small info screens that connect to a large info screen, interconnected wall screens, tablets on a coffee table forming a temporary interactive tabletop.

Integrating personal devices of users is another design pattern, BRING YOUR OWN DEVICE. Students or employees use their personal devices to enter data and send it to shared workspaces, or for voting (e.g. audience response systems). As we want to avoid a lot of cable in the room (NO CABLE), we need to provide CHARGING STATIONS, for example small boxes to recharge smart phones or tablets.

To control devices input possibilities should be further thought, too. In addition to the handwritten input and the control by tangible objects, voice control is an option. It opens up completely new ways of interaction when the systems listen and pick up what is said to perform particular actions. Instead of searching a template for a SWOT analysis somewhere on the computer, one can speak direct commands to the room, such as "idea space, open SWOT Template". The orientation and position of furniture can also serve as input for the digital world (FURNITURE AS INPUT). For example, one can count how many times objects have been used or which chairs have been moved together. Here is a summary of the patterns.

PHYSICAL TO DIGITAL is about bringing physical artefacts instantly into the digital world.

DIGITAL TO REAL is about making digital information visible or touchable in the real world.

HANDWRITTEN INPUT is about using our "natural" way of sketching and writing on digital devices.

CHARGING STATION is about providing energy to individual mobile devices.

SPEECH CONTROL is about using voice recognition to trigger actions in the digital world.

DEVICE ORCHESTRATION is about the seamless interplay of several digital device within one space.

BYOD is about integrating the individual device of participants.

COUPLED DEVICES is about connecting several devices to one larger unit

INSTANT CONNECTION is about simple and fast connection individual device

5. Example patterns

In this section we will present three example patterns.

5.1. Hybrid Learning Space

The dichotomy of digital and non-digital artefacts is resolved in a hybrid learning space by seamlessly bridging different types of artifacts, making digital data touchable and graspable, enhancing physical objects with digital information and digitizing physical objects.

We live in the real physical world, digital and connected devices are ubiquitous. Very often both worlds exist in their own space, and are only superficially interrelated. Things we can sense (feel, touch, see, hear…) are more meaningful to us. We like to tinker with real things. Very often we either work in the physical world only or in the digital world only.

Working in the physical world limits the way of sharing and manipulating objects – the digital has much more to offer. However, the digital world limits the richness of interactions to a predefined set. Moreover, the digital world lacks the embodiment of actions, such as playing and tinkering with objects physically with your hands (or

other body parts) and arranging them spatially in a natural way.

Ease of use. Interaction with objects is easier when they are real and tangible. Digital objects can be easily manipulated, edited, shared and distributed.

Representations. Objects of the real world often can be represented as virtual objects (for example a sticky-note can be a real piece of paper or a virtual object). Physical object of our world can be augmented with additional information and functions using digital tools. The mode of optimal representation depends on what you want to do with the object. Do you want to touch it? Move it in real physical space? Or do you want to share it across remote locations and work on it with remote participants? Very often both is needed.

Therefore, merge both physical and virtual space into one hybrid space where real world objects can be digitized and represented in virtual space, and the digital space can be brought into the real world using tangible objects and devices.

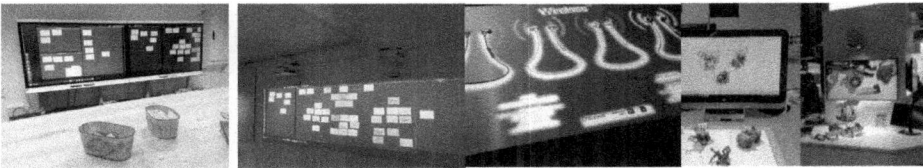

Figure 2. Blending physical and digital worlds.

Both the physical and digital worlds have their own strengths and weaknesses. To empower the best of both we need to enrich both worlds with each other seamlessly. Every smartphone is capable of digitizing physical objects by simply making a photo. Special apps can support the extraction of meaningful information: identifying single sticky notes, mapping whiteboards to images, recognizing objects and gestures. Document cameras can quickly scan 2D-documents and 3D objects and send them to digital work spaces. Objects of the real world can also trigger the display of meaningful digital information. For example, a QR code or a specific layout on book pages or playing cards can start-up programs or blend in additional information. This additional information can appear on the smartphone screen (augmented reality) or on additional screens. On the other hand, the information of the digital world can be projected into the real world. Each smartphone becomes a window to the digital world. Projectors can display information on walls and even on objects. Physical objects can be enriched with small displays or other outputs (audio, motion) based on digital processes. Objects in the real world are always at hand (you don't have to turn on a computer), and many actions are more natural in the real world. For example, feeling the surface and weight of objects gives you direct clues how to hand and work with them. Setting up new arrangements is fast, straight-forward and requires no training. Writing and drawing on paper still provides a richer experience than most digital tools offer. The interaction of surface properties, pen type, layers of color etc. is still a richer experience.

Examples:

» Document cameras to scan objects and show them on an interactive whiteboard.

» Apps to photograph sticky notes and bring them to the digital world.

» 3D printers to make virtual objects tangible.

» Digital twins are computerized companions of physical assets.

» Put cards on a scanner and map the content to virtual objects.

You may expect: The real and digital worlds merge. Benefits of the digital world are mapped to real world objects. Real world objects can be represented seamlessly in the digital world, thus making sharing and manipulation easier. Information can be mapped to real world objects, allowing rich learning experiences. Tinkering with objects – real and digital – is encouraged and creative learning is more likely to happen.

However: To make the transfer between both worlds seamless, a lot of hardware and software is needed. Thus, the experience is often bound to special rooms. It requires a lot of knowledge about methods and technology to unleash the full potential. While playing with things is a good and encouraging experience, it can also lead to using the technology for the sake of using technology.

5.2. PHYSICAL TO DIGITAL

Bringing physical artefacts instantly into the digital world

You are working in an innovation space, with many physical materials. You have created good clusters of ideas, or even some prototypes. But now you want to test something new, or move on to the next project.

Cleaning the physical work space may destroy work results for ever. Storing work results permanently and re-storing them later to continue the work is very difficult and in many cases impossible. Good work gets lost.

Perception. We perceive our environment with all our senses. In particular, when you are in a process of innovation you need an abundance of different stimuli in order to develop new ideas. These opportunities are ubiquitous in the physical world we live and interact in.

Volatile. The paths and steps we follow in the process of ideation and prototyping are hard to capture in the physical world. Each state of differentiation is volatile. Also, undoing decisions and alterations of physical artefacts up to a certain point is usually not possible.

Capture. One needs an option to capture the development process without seams between different media to avoid loss of information. Capturing interesting results should happen immediate and not interrupt the flow of works.

Simplicity. A technology that offers such opportunities should be low-threshold and self-explanatory because casual users should be able to use it as well. Executed actions (such as capturing) need to give feedback about the status because users need to know whether the action was successful or not.

Invite exploration. People are more likely to try out new things if they know that they can restore prior achievements and have saved their good work results. However, if this requires a lot of effort, people are unlike to take these actions.

Therefore, provide an instant technology to digitize objects and process results of the real world with one action step.

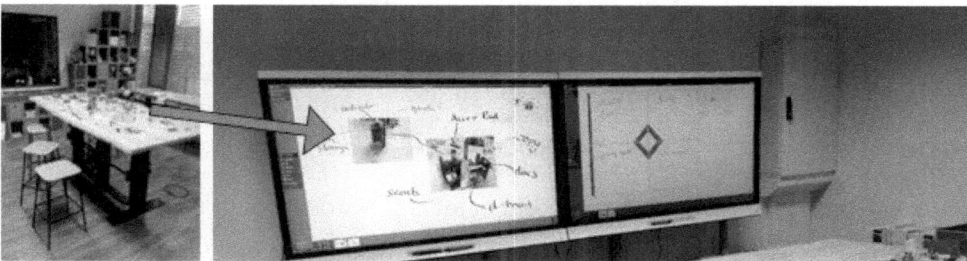

Figure 3. Instant capturing and digital annotations.

Such a service needs to run continuously or should be triggered with one-click to capture data directly without any delays.

Examples

» Smartphones to capture sketches or prototypes

» HP Sprout for 2D and 3D capturing

» Visualizer

» Digital Camera

» Touchscreen with Pencil

» Interactive Whiteboard

» Sensors for temperature, humidity, air quality, ...

You may expect: By representing physical objects in the digital world we will lose their haptic properties. On the other hand we gain new properties that are not given in the physical world. Results can be saved and edited independent of time and location. Objects can be duplicated with one click, annotated with additional information, and edited with simple actions. In the physical world you can do whatever the physical world allows you to do – but not more. The limitations in digital space on the other hand are set by the software environment. Editing capabilities may exceed the capabilities of the physical world but they are limited by whatever the software offers.

However: Some people may feel uncomfortable in a space equipped with many cameras (or other capturing devices) because they feel observed or spied on. Hence, they will no longer act freely in the space and this may have negative impact on the creativity. In general a space with a lot of technology inside might cause irritating feelings when users are overwhelmed or feel threatened by the technology.

5.3. DIGITAL TO REAL

Making digital information visible or touchable in the real world.

You are designing a prototype or a concept in the digital world. You can work on a single workstation or share a collaborative digital space.

Digital artefacts are like thought experiments. They are great to explore and tinker with alternatives. But they are not the real thing. They tend to hide limitations, opportunities and side effects of the real world.

Rich editing. Digital tools provide rich options for editing artefacts digitally, such as 3D models, sketches, mind maps, plans or plain texts. Very often setting up or defining properties is a complex task that needs rich editing tools, e.g. modelling 3D objects or program robots or small devices.

Flexible and rich interfaces. Sometimes we need a richer interface to setup an entity than the entity itself can provide (for example, programming an industrial robot can be a very complex task and digital tools can support the development process visually).

Theory and practice. Exploring concepts or models that have impact in the real world on a theoretical level only will not show all effects of their practical realization. It's hard to imagine how the objects feel and operate in the real world. Very often there are hidden side effects that can only be seen if the real artefact is tested. At some point you need to test your ideas and concepts.

Conversation with artefacts. Design thinking suggests that creators should have a "conversation" with physical prototypes to test their real properties. However, sometimes creating and manipulating objects in the real world is very difficult or expensive. Hence, it is not always possible to work with real materials right away.

Space. Objects in the real world consume physical space (which may be limited). Physical objects are often bound to specific locations whereas digital artefacts can be manipulated everywhere. On the other hand, the presence of artefacts makes them more important because putting something into physical space (which is a scarce resources) implies their priority over other things. People put more focus on things that are present permanently.

So, at the one hand side we want to benefit from all the tools and manipulation features of the digital world. At the other hand we want to explore, test and tinker with objects in the real world.

Therefore, bring digital artefacts into the world either by automatically creating new real world versions (e.g. 3D prints, photo prints, regular prints) or controlling existing

real world artefacts (e.g. control robots or lights).

Figure 4. Maker space with 3D printers and graphic tablets.

If you use digital devices such as interactive whiteboards or mobile devices, and you want to trigger printouts seamlessly, you need to define interfaces and enable DEVICE ORCHESTRATION.

Examples:

» Put 3D printers into a maker space in order to explore object properties.

» Print out texts to spread them out on the table, mark with a pen or cut out pieces and rearrange them.

» Program robots or Raspberry Pies using a computer or interactive whiteboard: Users can drag&drop program bricks (visual programming) on an interactive whiteboard. A group can discuss alternative algorithms. The programming is done in the digital world. But the execution is not only on the computer screen. Rather, the robot moves or the Raspberry Pie blinks (or does some other action).

You may expect: You can touch and feel the physical objects. Physical objects allow fast and natural interaction and exploration, digital objects allow fast and rich manipulations. Paradoxically, very often the work space in the physical world is larger than in the digital world (for example a table top or a wall is larger than a computer screen) but the available physical space is limited (you can have millions of 3D objects on a hard drive but only a few printouts in the room).

However: Orchestration between devices from different vendors often is a hazard. Users need more know-how about connecting devices, they are often not aware of all the options. Using production devices requires additional skills from users, especially if the production is expensive, difficult or dangerous (for example super glues for infiltration of 3D objects). Production devices for high quality results (3D prints, photo prints) are often very expensive. Production devices often require a high maintenance and consume a lot of resources (printing materials). Creating physical objects often creates a mess and somebody has to take care of the work environment (for example, a ROOM CONCIERGE).

6. Conclusion

The identified design patterns have implemented to a large extend for the innovative rooms we have designed. They have proved to be a very good planning tool. The design pattern are based on the observation, analysis and experimentation with existing solutions. They do not replace the mentioned frameworks, but make them a step more concrete and thus empirically verifiable. The frameworks also provided a theoretical foundation for the establishment of the solutions.

During the planning process, the patterns helped us to check concrete technologies with regard to the properties we had required. The lower abstraction layer created by patterns helps to make concrete implementation decisions and to justify them. By discussing the consequences of a design pattern, not only the positive effects but also possible limitations become transparent. For example, there are some patterns that may have a negative impact on users' sense of privacy, such as automatic speech analysis and the numerous cameras in the room. Through the explicit naming of subsequent problems it is possible to search for further solutions.

Patterns also help to convey the elements of the space better to address other stakeholders. The forces provide solid justifications for design decisions – even for unconventional elements. For example, the use of Lego bricks and innovation card games may confuse some people. The patterns, however, explain what has driven us to use these elements: their combinatory qualities to explore, the playfulness to challenge assumptions, and their inspiring potential.

Furthermore, the patterns have helped break up a complex spatial composition into individual components that can be considered nearly independent while still fitting into the overall concept. The harmonious interaction is ensured by cross-references between the patterns.

To some extent design patterns also reveal technological deficits. The design pattern DE-VICE ORCHESTRATION is indeed not a utopia but derived empirically from concrete examples of linking devices. Yet the interplay of all digital devices in the room is currently not fully implemented due to missing protocols and technical interfaces. Nevertheless, DEVICE ORCHESTRATION remains a valid solution. It is just that the implementation is more complex and cannot be implemented for all devices in the short term. For many devices and systems it is a missing solution. Similar constraints as well as unexpected potentials have been uncovered by identifying the patterns.

Patterns that are not sufficiently empirically confirmed yet are considered as proto-patterns, that is proposals for a better future. However, most of the identified patterns are based on existing space solutions and usage concepts. Nevertheless, only future will show whether the rooms are accepted and used as we intended. The actual use of space will thus lead to a confirmation or falsification of the patterns inductively determined. These experiences will reveal where our patterns need to be modified, for example, whether a context needs to be wider or needs to be made more restrictive. Also, the hypothetical formulated forces, which establish a fit between the solution and the problem described, can be empirically verified. Based on these findings, the patterns are to be expanded and described in more detail. Our next goal is to put all our patterns into an action-oriented booklet and a deck of cards.

Through the experience gained, further research and development, and closing the gap of missing system components, it will be easier in the future to transform other rooms respectively. The patterns help not only in the concrete design process but provide arguments why certain interventions for a more creative work environment of the students are conducive.

7. References

Adams Becker, S., Cummins, M., Davis, A., Freeman, A., Hall Giesinger, C., & Ananthanarayanan, V. (2017). NMC Horizon Report: 2017 Higher Education Edition. Austing, Texas: The New Media Consortium, Austin, Texas, 2017.

Alexander, C., Ishikawa, S., Silverstein, M., Jacobson, M., Fiksdahl-King, I., Angel, S. (1977). A pattern language: towns, buildings, construction. New York: Oxford University Press.

Alexander, C. (1979). The timeless way of building. New York: Oxford University Press.

Benyon, D. (2014). Spaces of interaction, places for experience. Synthesis Lectures on Human-Centered Information. 7(2), S. 1-129, 2014.

Benyon, D., & Mival, O. (2012). Blended spaces for collaborative creativity. In Proceedings of Workshop on Designing Collaborative Interactive Spaces AVI2012.

Benyon, D., & Mival, O. (2015). Blended Spaces for Collaboration. Computer Supported Cooperative Work (CSCW). 24 (2-3), S. 223-249, 2015.

Benyon, D., & Mival, O. (2016). Designing Blended Spaces for Collaboration. Human Computer Confluence Transforming Human Experience Through Symbiotic Technologies. 18, 2016.

Borchers, J. (2001). A pattern approach to interaction design. Hoboken: John Wiley & Sons.

Bustamante, F. O., Reyes, J. I. P., Camargo, M., & DuPont, L. (2015). Spaces to foster and sustain innovation: Towards a conceptual framework. In Engineering, Technology and Innovation/International Technology Management Conference (ICE/ITMC). p. 1-7. IEEE.

Cross, N. (2011). Design thinking: understanding how designers think and work. London: Bloomsbury Academic.

DINI (2013). Die Hochschule zum Lernraum entwickeln. Empfehlungen der Arbeitsgruppe "Lernräume". Kassel: University Press.

Fauconnier, G., & Turner, M. (2008). The way we think: Conceptual blending and the mind's hidden complexities. New York: Basic Books.

Forest, C. R., Moore, R. A., Jariwala, A. S., Fasse, B. B., Linsey, J., Newstetter, W., & Quintero, C. (2014). The invention studio: A university maker space and culture. Advances in Engineering Education. 4(2), S. 1-32, 2014.

Gamma, E., Helm, R., Johnson, R., & Vlissides, J. (1995). Design Patterns: Elements of Reusable Object-Oriented Software. Reading: Addison-Wesley.

Johanson, B., Fox, A., & Winograd, T. (2002). The interactive workspaces project: Experiences with ubiquitous computing rooms. IEEE pervasive computing. 1(2), S. 67-74.

Kelley, T., & Littman, J. (2001). The art of innovation: lessons in creativity from IDEO, America's leading design firm. New York: Currency.

Kohlert, C., & Cooper, S. (2017). Space for creative thinking: Design principles for work and learning environments. Munich: Callwey.

Kohls, C., & Panke, S. (2009). Is that true...? Thoughts on the epistemology of patterns. In Proceedings of the 16th Conference on Pattern Languages of Programs. New York: ACM.

Kohls, C. (2014). The theories of design patterns and their practical implications exemplified for e-learning patterns. https://opus4.kobv.de/opus4-ku-eichstaett/frontdoor/index/index/docId/158. Retrieved: 28.03.2014.

Kristiansen, P., & Rasmussen, R. (2014). Building a better business using the Lego serious play method. Hoboken, New Jersey : Wiley

Lindberg, T., Noweski, C.,& Meinel, C. (2009), Design Thinking: Zur Entwicklung eines explorativen Forschungsansatzes zu einem überprofessionellen Modell. Neuwerk Zeitschrift für Designwissenschaft 1, S. 47-54.

Meinel, C.,& von Thienen, J. (2016). Design Thinking. Informatik-Spektrum. 39(4), S. 310-314.

Moultrie, J., Nilsson, M., Dissel, M., Haner, U. E., Janssen, S., & van der Lugt, R. (2007). Innovation spaces: Towards a framework for understanding the role of the physical environment in innovation. Creativity and Innovation Management. 16(1), S. 53-65.

Plattner, H., Meinel, C., & Weinberg, U. (2009). Design thinking: Innovation lernen - Ideenwelten öffnen. München: Mi-Wirtschaftsbuch.

Schümmer, T., & Lukosch, S. (2007). Patterns for computer-mediated interaction. Chichester: John Wiley & Sons.

Skerlak, T., Kaufmann, H., & Bachmann, G. (2014). Lernumgebungen an der Hochschule. Auf dem Weg zum Campus von morgen. Münster: Waxmann.

Streitz, N. A., Geißler, J., Holmer, T., Konomi, S. I., Müller-Tomfelde, C., Reischl, W., & Steinmetz, R. (1999) i-LAND: an interactive landscape for creativity and innovation. In Proceedings of the SIGCHI conference on Human Factors in Computing Systems. p. 120-127. ACM.

Hochschulforum Digitalisierung (2016). The Digital Turn – Hochschulbildung im digitalen Zeitalter. Arbeitspapier Nr. 27. Berlin: Hochschulforum Digitalisierung.

Uebernickel, F., Brenner, W., Pukall, B., Naef, T., & Schindlholzer, B. (2015). Design Thinking: Das Handbuch. Frankfurt am Main: Frankfurter Allgemeine Buch.

Patterns for Hybrid Pedagogy

Kohls, Christian

Department for Computer Science, TH Köln, Gummersbach, Germany

christian.kohls@th-koeln.de

Köppe, Christian

Academy of Communication and Information Technology (ICA), HAN University of Applied Sciences, Arnhem, Netherlands

christian.koppe@han.nl

Nørgård, Rikke Toft

Rikke Toft, Centre for Teaching Development and Digital Media, Aarhus University, Aarhus, Denmark

rtoft@tdm.au.dk

This paper discusses patterns for hybrid pedagogy. Hybrid pedagogy aims at dissolving the dichotomies within education such as physical-digital, academic-nonacademic, online-offline, formal-informal, learning-teaching and individual-collective. It takes a more holistic view and takes the diversity of students and teachers into account. About 85 patterns have been mined at a 4-day workshop (EduPLoP 2016) by a group of researchers. The patterns have been clustered into different categories: Hybrid Learning Space, Student Agency, Hybrid Production, Collaboration, Hybrid Assessment, Outside In, Inside Out, Sharing is Caring, Performance. This paper presents one pattern of each category and reflects about the process of finding and applying these patterns.

Hybridity, e-learning, blended theory, collaboration, value-driven design

1. Introduction

Hybridity refers to the interplay and mix-up of concepts that are traditionally separated. Hybrid pedagogy refers to a mixture of different learning forms. For example, a mixture of formal and informal learning, or a mixture of digital and non-digital artefacts. Mixing different forms of learning, such as online and offline, has been termed "blended learning" frequently in other contexts. However, "blended learning" often does not denominate real blends. Rather than truly blending concepts, and thereby give birth to new forms, the blends in learning are often just mechanical combinations. For examples, a "blended learning scenario" may differentiate into online and offline phases, synchronous and asynchronous work, individual and group work. On the other hand, hybridity takes into account that in today's digital world these lines no longer are clear. Students can join on-site meetings remotely via conference systems. Then, groups are no longer online or offline, they are both at the same time. Online becomes part of the offline activities. Likewise, offline activities can merge with online events. For example, online lectures, webinars or online group work are often seen as formats where each student sits home alone. Such scenarios have strongly emphasized the benefits of remote connections but ignored that students want to meet in real space as well. So why not have both at the same time? Rather than sitting alone at home, students locally meet up to watch and discuss while attending an online lecture. Such hybrid scenarios combine benefits of distance learning (bringing together students, teachers, and experts from remote places), and social interaction on-site. The online event interplays with offline activities. Learning cafés, public libraries and other intellectual spaces may pop up to connect people both locally and over long distances.

2. Patterns

"Blended learning" scenarios often regard online and offline as dichotomies – learning takes place either online OR offline (it's an exclusive OR). Hybridity means that both forms take place at the same time. There is an ambiguity that opens new potentials and mind sets. To some people, all this mix-up may sound like awful chaos. While ambiguity opens doors and spans a wide space, one could also argue that the scenarios are somewhat arbitrary. Moreover, strong evidence for successful hybrid learning scenarios is often missing. Indeed, most hybrid scenarios are rather experimental and by far not all of them are successful. Failure, however, is not necessarily a bad thing because we can learn from it. Hybrid pedagogy embraces experiments and allows some failures. It is, however, important to recover and learn from misleading paths. In order to judge about different forms and test them empirically, we need to share a common understanding of the relations between contexts, problems and potential solutions in hybrid scenarios. We have to describe their structures and give them names. We need to reflect about their values and describe the forces that led to the solutions. Moreover, we need to build on the ideas and experiences from practitioners and give them a language to express their needs and describe what they are doing. That is why we believe that patterns can help us to capture and communicate emerging ideas in the field of hybrid pedagogy.

2.1. Hybrid pedagogy patterns

A conscious choice for good design leads to improvements of our environments. In Christopher Alexander's view when a place becomes more alive, more whole and has a "quality without a name" its goodness cannot be reduced to single properties – it has at the same time freedom, life, wholeness, comfort, and harmony (Alexander, 1979). This quality is found in designs that have an inner balance and that do not contradict their environmental needs. Such improvements occur if we replace a bad design by a better form. They also occur when a new system is implemented based on good designs, rather than problematic or untested solutions.

Hybrid pedagogy patterns capture solutions forms that have been carefully designed to address pedagogical values. They also include patterns that emerged accidently or as the result of a series of piecemeal changes to existing pedagogical scenarios. For example, by introducing new technology and testing different activities, tweaking instructions and tinkering with materials.

2.2. Pedagogical patterns

In general pedagogical patterns suggest interventions that have shown to have positive effects. It does not matter whether the original design emerged naturally or by planning. The important fact is that we can create new instances of the good design based on observations what has worked in the past. Those new instances are created by deliberate intervention. Existing educational patterns cover areas such as learning with technology (Goodyear & Retalis 2010, Mor et al. 2014), MOOC-design (Warburton & Mor 2015), assessments (Bergin et al. 2015), flipped classrooms (Köppe et al. 2015), lecture design (Köppe 2013), seminars (Fricke & Völter 2000), or general pedagogical practices (Bergin et al. 2012).

2.3. Holistic design thinking

It is important to note that we do not see the pattern approach just as a neat vehicle that provides helpful templates for writing down solutions. Rather, the pattern approach provides a holistic mindset fostering design thinking. A form only becomes a solution when it is applied in the appropriate context. It is meaningless to speak of solutions or good designs without considering the context. Explicitly discussing the context to which a form fits allows the adequate usage of methods, tools and technologies. Such literacy in selecting the right tools for the task at hand is very well understood by every craftsman. The hammer cannot be used to saw (wrong context of use) but that does not lower its value to hit a nail (correct context of use). This works the other way around as well. Hitting a nail into the wall can be supported by a hammer rather than a saw or a newly invented tool altogether. Moreover, to successfully hit a nail one has to use the hammer in the right way, i.e. not using the wrong side and not hitting the fingers accidently. Hence, knowledge of the right use and training are necessary.

2.4. Patterns or design patterns?

While there are infinite patterns in the world not every pattern counts as a pattern of good design and not every good design is captured in the literary form of design patterns. We can use the following ontology to clarify the term "patterns" (Kohls, 2014):

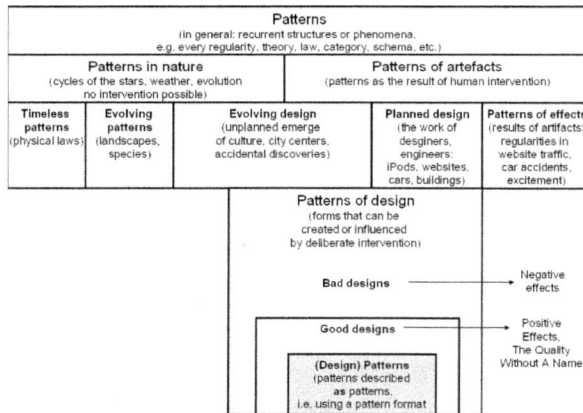

Figure 1. A pattern ontology

2.5. The process of pattern mining

The patterns presented in this paper have been mined at EduPLoP 2016. At this 4-day workshop we mined about 85 patterns of hybrid pedagogy. Hybrid education is firmly based within the field of critical pedagogy (Stommel, 2012; Roraboaugh & Stommel, 2012) and is focused on designing for educational experiences and interactions. Hence, the group took a human-centered and empathic (Gagnon, 2014; Köppen & Meinel, 2015) approach to (designing for) hybrid education. In doing so, EduPLoP16 was structured in a way that bears some resemblance with the concept of value-based vision-driven educational design thinking (Aaen & Nørgård, 2016; Mor, Warburton, Nørgård & Ullmo, 2016) where design patterns are formed on the ground of specific virtues and values and driven by value-based visions. Thus, we started with a value-based workshop where each hybrid participant expressed individual core values of their teaching. This was followed by a vision-driven workshop to identify the collective values that should be supported by the design patterns. This workshop helped to clarify the shared intent of the design patterns we were looking for. Once this stage was set, the group started a brainstorming session collecting known examples of hybrid education on post-its. The post-its were clustered into higher level categories using the KJ-method. These categories have been the foundation for pattern writing. In small groups we generalized the solutions and wrote a synopsis for each pattern collaboratively using Google Docs. Based on this synopsis we developed full pattern descriptions based on a template. Other participants of the group monitored the writing and gave comments. At the end of the workshop, we defined categories with closely related patterns and assigned lead authors to the patterns – that is care takers who further develop the patterns into publishable versions. Since we wanted to get a holistic map of the hybrid patterns we know so far, many of the pattern descriptions were in a rudimentary state at the end of the workshop.

The whole EduPLoP workshop, which took place in Sandbjerg Estate (supported by Aarhus University, DK, and University of Surrey, UK), was a hybrid experience as we had participants on-site and others joining remotely, and we switched continuously from digital to analogue media.

3. Pattern clusters and examples

The result of the EduPLoP16 was approximately 85 unique pattern candidates distributed between 9 categories. Köppe, Nørgård, & Pedersen (2017) have created a map that shows the different categories and their relations.

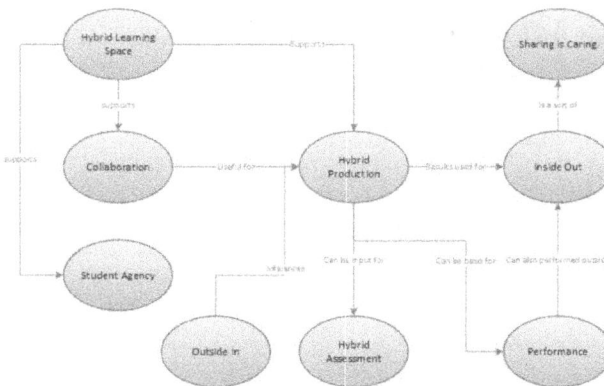

Figure 2. Map of hybrid education pattern categories.

HYBRID LEARNING SPACE is a configuration that enables students to work, interact, collaborate, and to learn in a manner suitable to their needs: online/offline, on campus/off campus. The structure of a HYBRID LEARNING SPACE has been described as a pattern itself. It supports student agency, collaboration, and hybrid production. Patterns for student agency utilize the knowledge students bring to the classroom and benefit from the different interests and perspectives in a productive way. As an example we will present the pattern MULTIPLE LEARNING PATHS. An example pattern for collaboration is STUDENT SHARED RESOURCE SPACE. BUILD YOUR OWN METAPHOR is an example for HYBRID PRODUCTION, the production of artefacts using both digital and non-digital tools and artefacts, integrating different places, times, or ways of collaboration. HYBRID ASSESSMENT blends different forms of formative and summative assessment, peer-to-peer, supervision and feedback. We will present SNAPCHAT ASSESSMENT as an example pattern. OUTSIDE IN covers solutions to bring the public – experts and regular citizens – as resources and collaborators into the classroom. Taking learning to the public space is proposed by INSIDE OUT patterns. The two examples present in this paper are INTEGRATING PRACTITIONERS and RUNAWAY CLASSROOM. SHARING IS CARING patterns describe opportunities to share learning resources, knowledge and new ideas to promote a culture of sharing. In this paper we present SHOW THE PROCESS. PERFORMANCE patterns are about public performance whereby students are sharing and presenting their work to a wider and more heterogeneous audience. One example is STUDENT BOOKLETS.

In the next section we will provide one example pattern for each category.

3.1. Interactive Tangible Objects (Hybrid Learning Space)

Make tangible objects connect to the virtual world. A tangible object can trigger digital actions, e.g. opening a web site or digital worksheet.

There needs to be control over the content of the digital world.

Standard input devices (mice, keyboards, cameras) do not bridge the dichotomy between the real world and digital world artefacts.

Standard devices provide very narrow interfaces for specialized tasks, such as typing, moving a mouse pointer or adding pictures.

Real world objects are more real than virtual objects. People like to play with things. Touch is important. Haptic feedback is rich.

Therefore, use tangible objects as input and output devices.

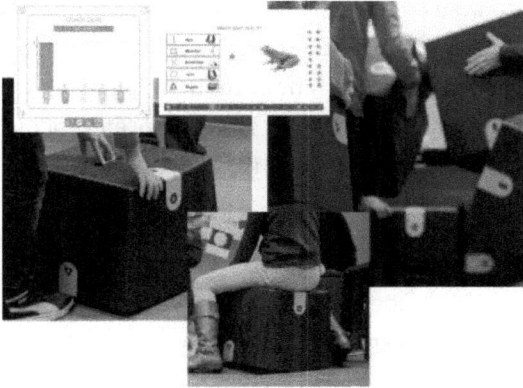

Figure 3. Interactive chairs can be used to submit quiz answers.

All objects of the real world can be input and output devices. They can be equipped with sensors or cameras can capture their orientation and appearance. The orientation of tangible objects, such as cards, paper sheets, cubes or even furniture, can be interpreted as input.

Likewise, tangible objects can be output devices, showing different images, numbers, or colors. They can make different noises, move to different positions, or display images. Digital images can be projected to physical objects. The content of physical objects can be scanned and interpreted as input parameters.

Examples: QR codes on 3D objects or method cards, furniture location to provide quiz answers, clickers, buzzers

You may expect: Tangible objects offer a more natural interaction. They have a higher affordance and invite for action. They offer other ways of combinations than digital objects do. Software tools only allow the types of manipulation provided by the tool developers. Real objects offer options and limitations of the real world.

However: Physical objects are more expensive, require storage space and only a limited number of objects is available. Working with the objects can be messy, which is great in a design process but requires clean up and setup time.

3.2. Multiple learning paths (Category: Student Agency)

Design your course to allow alternative paths, combining hybrid interactions in different ways, for reaching the learning objectives to account for diverse learner circumstances and preferences.

You defined the LEARNING OBJECTIVES for a course or project and want to start with assembling or creating the materials and defining the overall structure.

Allowing only one predefined learning path (including predefined tools, methods and materials) towards the learning objectives can be problematic for some students. It might be that personal circumstances hinder them in following this path sufficiently or that the path does not match with their learning preferences. Both cases might increase resistance to learning and even be frustrating.

Most learners have personal preferences of how they learn, based on personality and previous learning experiences. Sometimes it's good to challenge these, sometimes it's good to respect these. However, some students like to work in a way they haven't worked before, they want to take control of their learning and meta-cognitive skills.

On the other hand, some teachers tend to think that their students' only identity is that of being a learner and that everything else is subsidiary.

Therefore, design your course so that alternative paths towards the learning objectives via different combinations of hybrid interactions are possible.

Let students choose their own paths, either because they prefer it or because circumstances force them to use it. Also provide a standard learning path as option for those who need more guidance.

You may expect: Allowing different paths towards the learning objectives likely increases the number of learners that will reach them. As students can choose a path that fits their preferences in a better way than a predefined one, the student satisfaction will improve and in consequence their motivation.

However: Offering multiple ways without giving sufficient guidance on how to choose or follow one of them might be difficult for some students. It therefore should be checked regularly that all learners have found a good path and can follow it without blocking problems. Learners having difficulties with finding a path should be offered a standard one.

3.3. Build your own metaphor (Category: Hybrid Production)

Making new ideas and thought tangible by explaining them with well-known concepts.

In a creative session, you have a spark of insight. If the idea is very new it is hard to explain your thoughts because you can hardly reference to anything that exists. Metaphors are a known use-case for explaining unknown or new structures with well-known concepts.

However, metaphors do not always fit to the actual structure. Particularly for a new idea there is often a lack of analogous structures. If wrong metaphorical structures

are employed, people will build wrong mental models, and may work with miscon-
ceptions and wrong schemas.

Metaphors can be used for construction of models of new concepts because they blend
and mix existing things. Metaphors use a source domain, typically a known concept and a
target domain (typically a new, an abstract or a non-well-structured concept) and a vehicle
that contains the function of representation and correspondences. Very often these structures do not 100% fit to the target domain.

When new ideas are generated in an innovation process, the new concepts do not exist yet
– that is the target domain is unknown.

Sometimes, a fitting source domain is missing as well. For many abstract or unknown target
domains it is hard or impossible to find an adequate metaphor. If there is an analogous
structure that is only partially correct, the risk of building wrong mental models is huge.

The best metaphors have full structural isomorphism. That means that there is a strong fit
between the source and target domain. However very often such perfect analogies do not
exist or it takes very long to find them.

A metaphor should offer correctness, consistency and avoid wrong interpretations. Moreover it should not introduce any unnecessary structures because this could lead to confusion and makes communication harder (noise). Missing elements in a metaphor lead to
wrong mental models. On the other hand too much elements can be overwhelming and it
is easy to lose the focus.

**Therefore, build your own metaphor by constructing a source domain with simple
haptic building materials or interactive digital tools.**

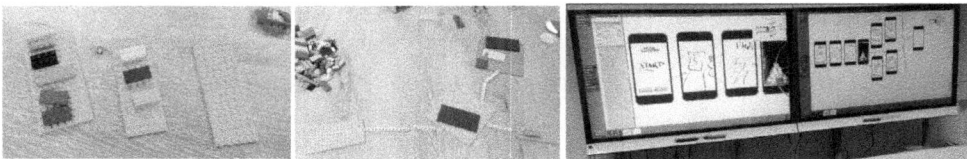

Figure 4. Use Lego bricks to build or interactive whiteboards to mash-up metaphors.

The construction with haptic buildings materials creates a customized source domain. At
the same time we use that source domain for a new explanation (vehicle) to construct or
reconstruct a target domain. This allows you to construct new ideas, and even invent new
things. The materials should be robust and/or cheap, so that persons are not afraid to break
it. The building materials should be very flexible to represent many different concepts.

Digital tools allow to mash-up existing concepts, alter them and combine them with different media. Reconstruct existing concepts helps to explain them in another (more simple) way.

Your own metaphors should be self - explanatory, easy to change and diverse. It should implicitly be an invitation to do something (play, build, take it). Build things that everybody can realize, touch, see etc., so that one uses the most sensory channels.

You may expect: Full control of the things you build. Abstract concepts are made tangible. Invisible processes may become visible. The interpretation of physical materials is intuitive and natural. The structure of the source domain can be constructed in a way to fit exactly to the target domain.

However: While the metaphorical concept may fit very well, sometimes the tangible objects are abstractions or placeholders for other concepts. For example, you can use Lego bricks to explain the concept of programming a stack. The concept of the stack is well covered by putting one brick on other (showing the order of in and out correctly), however, each Lego brick symbolizes a variable value. So, the metaphorical structure is correct but the used elements need further interpretation.

Building the full concepts for the source domain takes time. It needs a huge amount of diverse materials. Materials are not very mobile, so you are bound to specific places unless you limit yourself to digital metaphors only.

3.4. Student shared resource space (Category: Collaboration)

In order to promote ownership of resources and have students make experience with looking for resources, provide a space where they can share resources and have experience of doing non-textual literature searches that are meaningful.

You are teaching a subject with difficult concepts or theories, and this subject is presented and discussed in various contexts online - for instance in videos and discussion forums.

Students do not take ownership of the concepts, if they are presented with a fixed list of texts and resources.

This pattern is placed in the initial phase for students to enter the difficult concepts and theories. Students do not understand the provided concepts and theories as presented in texts and in class. A challenge is to balance between giving students resources and encouraging them to find relevant resources themselves.

Therefore, provide an online space, where students are encouraged to share resources with their peers and articulate why these resources were helpful. Peers are encouraged to give feedback about how the resources helped deepen understanding and how the concept becomes relevant/real.

What is important is the process of finding and exploring resources. The aim is not to have a collection of resources in the end. It is an opportunity for students to find their own way into the difficult subject matter, and where the concepts should become relevant to them and their own practices.

The online space should be easy to access and be in line with students' daily social media routines. Students should take part in deciding which tools to use. Examples of online spaces/tools are: Google documents, Wikis, Facebook group.

The space should be presented as an offer, but not as a compulsory task. As the teacher you can frame a space for sharing by initially sharing resources that demonstrate the use or presentation of the subject matter in other forms than texts. The teacher is responsible for checking that the resources are relevant and applicable and give guidance if they are not.

If there are many available resources and there is a high chance that students get overwhelmed   by the amount. To further scaffold students' search, you could limit the search space using a custom search engine (CSE). The teacher then makes it possible for the students to access the resources that s/he has in mind, by foregrounding a list of websites and make them more likely to appear in the result list. The students still have the whole web at disposal. Eventually, the students are engaged in further developing/refining the CSE.

You may expect: Students create ownership of concept and theories. They broaden the discussion on the subject matter. Students get practice in research methods and finding literature resources.

However: There might be an explosion of resources. There is also a risk of finding misleading and poorly documented resources. That is why it is important for teachers to participate with a moderating function. Some students will just want the list so they can read the literature and get a good grade. If the students do not use the shared space this may be because they understand the literature and do not have the need to find extra resources

3.5. Snapchat Assessment - Nobody is Perfect (Category: Hybrid Assessment)

Snapchat is ephemeral and for sharing imperfection. Unlike Instragram, Snapchat is an invitation into the 'backstage areas' of life, where you allow yourself to look sleepy, ugly, hung-over as a

contrast to the filtered and aestheticized performances of Instagram. This happens because you know the snap will vanish and similarly we should think how we can invite the backstage into our learning, development and assessment practices through e.g. ephemerality.

You are teaching a course where collaboration and reflection is a central working method. You are experiencing learners struggling with sharing their thoughts in the open due to fear of failure or to appear as incompetent to the teacher and other students.

Student's creative potential can be limited by fear of harsh criticism that sticks to them for a long time.

Even raising your voice during class or posting in shared forum in a class can be experienced as a moment of assessment for learners. Moments of assessments are usually critical for students and arenas where they have to perform and present themselves as 'excellent' students who are in command. Many strive for perfection. Products for assessment need to be finely polished reports or products that leave no questions unanswered and glosses over doubts, questions and the messy thinking that went into ordering the product. This leaves little ground to collaboratively reflect on insecurities, questions and doubts, which are in fact great stepping stones for learning and formative assessment. Thus, a problem is that students and teachers seldom explore these more messy arenas of learning together. These conditions can be further aggravated in online learning where there is a persistent record of the student's activity e.g. a forum post or the like. Getting away with stickiness and persistence could perhaps enhance student willingness to share unfinished thoughts.

Therefore, you should try to establish trust by allowing learners to be messy and imperfect together with the teacher as opportunities for learning and development.

This could take different forms and work at different levels of scale (e.g. small learning task to longer term collaborative reviews of draft texts). And also vary between intimate (between learner and teacher) and semi-public spaces (involving peer-review, peer-discussion and peer-assessment). Metaphorically we should see assessment similar - we should look as assessment as formative and where the teachers is invited into the messy machine room of learning and allowed to see students insecurities, doubts, anxieties, mistakes and so forth rather than only being presented with the final polished work of the student. Somehow this assessment should also - as snapchat - be ephemeral and the ugly snaps that the teacher gets to see, should disappear.

You may expect: Liberated students who take more risks and try out new things. You reduce insecurities and fear and you create an open atmosphere for inspiration. Failures are seen as learning moments rather than embarrassing encounters.

However: Make sure that you do provide constructive feedback rather than praise everything. Students do welcome suggestions for improvement. As you have created an environment for more openness, you will encounter new ideas and solutions. It takes more time and intellectual effort to evaluate and comments such artefacts.

3.6. Integrating practitioners (Category: Outside In)

Connecting a course to real-world practices by bringing into the classroom people, activities, problems and tools. They can take on the form of cases.

The subject matter in a course calls for a connection with society and practices.

However, the course tends to close around itself. Assignments can seem artificial for students, because they are simulations of practice.

Learning should be authentic and meaningful. Learners have to understand why the need to learn certain topics and how they can be used in real life. Companies expect students to be prepared for doing business. Most theories have practical relevance but very often it is not clear to students how the skills can be applied on the job.

Therefore, bring empathetic practitioners in from outside who demonstrate the relevance of knowledge and skills in practice early on in the process. Allow dialogues to develop throughout the process.

Prepare both practitioners and students to meet each other. Set up a joint project space with practitioners. Let the practitioners frame problems. Let the practitioners respond to preliminary ideas, arguments, products, etc. of students. Let the practitioners evaluate and discuss student solutions/end products.

You may expect: Valuable classroom experiences by developing dialogues and relationships between students and practitioners (different from academic experts). Theory is made relevant through practice.

However: Working with practitioners may take more time and it is harder to plan. The schedule of practitioners varies often and sometimes they might not be able to provide input or feedback on time. Too complex projects can also be confusing, since content is not optimized as it is in textbooks.

3.7. Runaway Classroom (Category: Inside Out)

The classroom doesn't like its static walls anymore. It escapes the walls of the institute. It runs to the city, to mountains, to the sea, wherever it wants to be. This pattern can bring the classroom to the city. It is complementary to bringing the city to the classroom.

Students are equipped with mobile devices that can be used for learning anytime and anywhere. They often learn while they commute to school. Students are nomadic and learn at many different places, yet teaching still takes place in the walls in classroom.

Many of the real world problems can be discussed in a classroom only on a theoretical level while the action is outside of the classroom. Classroom walls are static and isolate learners from the real world.

Outside of a classroom there is an abundance of different environments adequate for learning, inquiring, inventing, evaluating and many other high level academic activities. Students should learn to engage with real experts, and travel to authentic sites. Many phenomena are best experienced or observed in the field. That is why field trips are organized. However, thus trips are exceptional and they do not integrate in to the daily learning life. Yet a classroom can be anywhere, and nomadic students can form a classroom everywhere.

Therefore, run lessons and other events at the place at interest rather than in the classroom.

Runaway classrooms can be supported or organized by a teacher that takes the entire classroom 'in the backpack' and into the world. In this way the runaway classroom has left the campus to go somewhere else.

You may expect: Consequently, the classroom can be everywhere creating a hybrid in the form of a digital un-classroom or a physical re-localized classroom camping somewhere else whether it is the city, the sea, the sky or underground. In this way teaching is taken to the streets. Making education something that takes place in the public domain.

However: While digital media support many learning activities you may miss some of the standard equipment of classrooms, such as (digital) whiteboards, power plugs for large groups, adequate tables and work materials. Taking classrooms out of the "isolated" environment can also be distracting – sometimes isolation has the benefit of focusing and concentrating on what matters most.

3.8. Show the process (Category: Performance)

Instead of just showing the final results, the whole process is captured. The lessons learnt are shared as well.

People often present the proud results of their work. The path to success (with all its detours and failures) is rarely shown.

Learning requires you to understand the story behind products.

A product does not reveal its story: where does it come from? Which alternatives were considered? Which lessons have been learnt in creating the product? Creative learning requires students to understand the production process as well as the products. Reflecting about the process of creating something leads to new insights and may inspired others.

Therefore, show the process of making a product.

The product can be any learning outcome (e.g. an essay, a website or a game). Make pictures or snapshots of each development step and share it with others. This can be done in a poster session or in a blog.

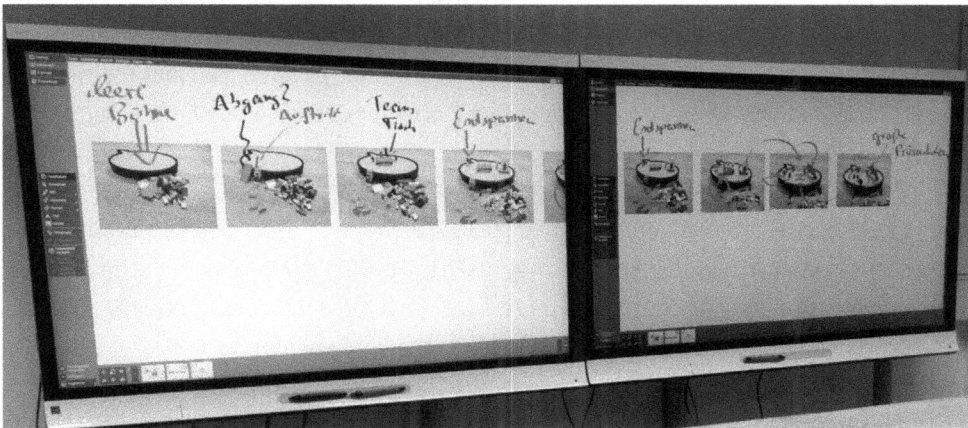

Figure 5.

This pattern is related to Open Development / Open Research. This pattern, however, presents (steps of) the process when the product is done (it is some kind of SHARING PRODUCTS). While this is less risky than sharing a work in progress, reflecting and showing the process afterwards is less authentic as it represents a polished story. But this telling the storing can help others understand how a product was created. Moreover, the creators have to reflect on the creation process if they show it to the public as well.

You may expect: Deeper reflection, as single process steps are documented. Students get feedback earlier. The learnings of the process are shared as well. The process documentation is another artefact that can contribute to the student's performance (for example improve the grade).

However: Documenting the process is extra work. Negative feedback can also be destructive. Ensure that people are aware that you share half-baked products rather than the final product. Ensure commenters to provide constructive feedback and suggestions.

4. Conclusions and Learnings

This section summarizes the learnings in our collaborative pattern mining process. Our goal is to search for patterns that make a place or a design more whole, more alive. "The specific patterns out of which a building or a town is made may be alive or dead. To the extent they are alive, they let our inner forces loose, and set us free; but when they are dead they keep us locked in inner conflict" (Alexander, 1979, p. 101). Good solutions are liberating because they harmonize with human needs. A place or object that does not reflect your needs – that requires you to adapt – cannot be whole. A building that is in conflict with human needs cannot be a good design. We have to ask whether the patterns of hybrid pedagogy reach this quality we are looking for. Speaking of quality we refer to both, the patterns we have actually observed and we want to see re-created, and our descriptions of these patterns.

4.1. Quality without a name

Do the pedagogical interventions and their structures we have described as patterns really possess the quality without a name? Do they make the lives of students and teachers better, do they make these stakeholders feel more alive? In some cases there certainly is doubt. Not all sorts of hybrid pedagogy is as successful in the implementation as we hope. For example, when we connect several participants throughout the world via video conferencing it is not the same as meeting face to face. Indeed, these meetings are sometimes uncomfortable and awkward. But collaborating with people from other continents has its own quality, and it is very inclusive. That we still have disharmony in such meetings does not disqualify the concept in itself – it just shows that our technology, our environment, and our social protocols are not there yet. Thus, the patterns we have described are sometimes rather future oriented. They all bring in some quality and benefits but they also point out drawbacks and liabilities. Some of the patterns, however, truly have already the quality without a name. These are the patterns that let students go beyond their old limits and grow. They set them into a flow experience that makes learning meaningful, and they start contributing to the society in stronger ways. These feelings, these magic moments, show the quality.

4.2. Quality of Writing

About the quality of the written patterns, we can also argue that they need to evolve over time. Writing collaboratively is a great experience but we also find that the many different styles of writings sometimes lead to incoherent texts. The pattern format itself helps to standardize what is discussed but there are still many differences. Whether it is the length of the pattern description, the scope of the pattern, the level of abstraction or the maturity of empirical support – the pattern descriptions have a wide range of variation. The patterns presented in this paper show this lack of uniformity. We improve the pattern documents by running them through iterative feedback loops, getting feedback from peers in a shepherding process and get feedback in Writer's Workshop. But even if some of the patterns are rather sketches at the moment, we think they can already be inspiring. Rather than holding back the ideas and polish everything until it is outdated, we like to share them. Thus, the patterns can be commented and revised. In the end, designers should not follow the advice of patterns without reflection. Patterns only come to life through the designers.

4.3. Empirical Evidence

It is also true that many of the patterns lack empirical evidence. Some might even be just wishful thinking. There are some pattern folks who might think that this is outrageous. In the software pattern community, there is a strong requirement to apply the rule of three. That is, one should find at least three known uses before one identifies a pattern. However, this is a limited view of the pattern approach. While there are a lot of benefits in identifying solutions that have shown to work, the pattern approach is also a very good way to design new solutions. It considers wicked problems and tries to find a fitting solution by balancing all the different forces. This holistic and iterative design process can help to find new innovative ways of teaching and learning. Even if a solution has not been established several times, the pattern descriptions can work as thought triggers.

4.4. Embrace practitioners

What we have seen is that participants new to the pattern approach quickly understood the concept and appreciated the ways of reflection. It is a very useful tool to access implicit knowledge and expectations of stakeholders in a holistic way. It is important to note that we do not see the description format as the driving force. It has often been criticized that Christopher Alexander's design philosophy has been reduced to use templates and methods mechanically. However, using these tools fruitfully does not neglect the higher goal of striving for good design that is more alive and show the quality without a name.

To achieve this, we actually started with values and not with solutions. The values helped us to understand which interventions make sense and have the opportunity to create that quality. What we have not developed yet, however, is a set of fundamental properties for hybrid education. It has been shown that Alexander's fifteen fundamental properties can be transferred to other fields than architecture, including software design and education (Kohls & Köppe, 2015). Moreover, Iba et al. (2015) have shown that it is a promising path to identify fundamental properties for other fields, such as behavior and collaboration. But for the hybrid pedagogical patterns it seems too early to derive such generalized properties, let alone to identify the processes that strengthen these properties.

4.5. Keeping pace

While we mined patterns very quickly at the on-site workshop and continue to write and improve the patterns, we also lost somewhat of a momentum after the workshop. During the workshop we kept writing patterns and discussed the patterns right there. But after the workshop, the patterns did not really evolve – except the ones that were compiled into a paper for one of the PLoP conferences. If we look into the online repository right now we find a lot of inspiring ideas that are not accessible to the public yet. The next steps should be, then, to follow up and continue writing the patterns. Given the number of patterns, this will take some more time. Meanwhile, we will work on a set of pattern cards. They do not reflect as deeply as the full pattern descriptions, but they can already be useful as building blocks for teachers who want to open the education process through hybrid scenarios. A design cards holds one brief version of a pattern. Takashi Iba (2012) and his colleagues use very brief and abstract pattern descriptions that stimulate discussions and the sharing of experience about patterns. In these cases the full meaning is not provided in the description of the patterns briefs but constructed in personal communication. It requires prior knowledge from the participants to unfold the pattern. Cards allow for fast and effortless recombination, thus allowing to blend each of the solutions with others.

4.6. Future orientation

Hybrid pedagogy pattern do not only propose solutions. They discuss problems of today's learning environments. It is often overseen that the power of patterns is not only to provide a solution but helps us to understand the problem space. Very often we are not even aware of the problems that cause our sometimes miserable feelings about the world. A lecturer who tortures his students with overcrowded PowerPoint slides is certainly not aware that the amount of information should reflect the human capabilities of information processing. A conference without well planned coffee breaks ignores that attendees not only need a rest between the presentations and workshops but also need time to reflect and chat about the sessions in a comfortable environment.

Without the awareness of problems it is impossible to do something about them. To understand the problem in depth is the key to find an appropriate solution. Experts very often do not only know good solutions but are more aware of common problems. Thus, we tried to capture what needs to be changed and which values we want to support with the patterns.

5. References

Aaen, J. H., & Nørgård, R. T. (2016). Participatory academic communities: a transdisciplinary perspective on participation in education beyond the institution. Conjunctions. Transdisciplinary journal of cultural participation, 2(2), 67-98.

Alexander, C. (1979). The timeless way of building. New York: Oxford University Press.

Bergin, J., Eckstein, J., Völter, M., Sipos, M., Wallingford, E., Marquardt, K., Manns, M. L. (Eds.). (2012). Pedagogical Patterns: Advice for Educators. New York, NY, USA: Joseph Bergin Software Tools.

Bergin, J., Kohls, C., Köppe, C., Mor, Y., Portier, M., Schümmer, T., & Warburton, S. (2015). Assessment-Driven Course Design - Foundational Patterns. In Proceedings of the 20th European Conference on Pattern Languages of Programs, EuroPLoP'15. Irsee, Germany: ACM.

Fricke, A., & Völter, M. (2000). Seminars - A Pedagogical Pattern Language about teaching seminars effectively. In Proceedings of the 5th European Conference on Pattern Languages of Programs, EuroPLoP 2000 . Irsee, Germany.

Gagnon, C., Ct, V. (2014). Learning from others: a five years experience on teaching empathic design. In: Lim, Y.K., Niedderer, K., Redstrm, J., Stolterman, E., Valtonen, A. (eds.) Proceedings of Design Research Society Biennial International Conference DRS 2014: Designs Big Debates, pp. 16–19. Ume Institute of Design, Ume University, Ume, Sweden, June 2014

Goodyear, P., & Retalis, S. (Eds.). (2010). Technology-Enhanced Learning: Design Patterns and Pattern Languages. Sense Publishers.

Iba, T. (2012). A Pattern Language for Designing Workshop to Introduce a Pattern Language. 18th European Pattern Languages of Programs conference. Irsee, Germany: ACM.

Iba, T., Kamada, A., Akado, Y., Honda, T., Sasabe, A. & Kogure, S. (2015). Fundamental behavioral properties, part I: extending the theory of centers for pattern language 3.0. In Proceedings of the 20th European Conference on Pattern Languages of Programs (EuroPLoP ,15). New York: ACM. DOI: http://dx.doi.org/10.1145/2855321.2855333

Kohls, C. (2014). The theories of design patterns and their practical implications exemplified for e-learning patterns. https://opus4.kobv.de/opus4-ku-eichstaett/frontdoor/index/index/docId/158. Retrieved: 28.03.2014.

Kohls, C., Köppe, C. (2015). Evaluating the Applicability of Alexander's Fundamental Properties to Non-Architecture Domains. In P. Baumgartner, R. Sickinger (Hrsg.) PURPLSOC: Pursuit of Pattern Languages for Societal Change / PURPLSOC: The Workshop 2014: Designing Lively Scenarios With the Pattern Approach of Christopher Alexander. Berlin: epubli.

Köppe, C. (2013). Towards a Pattern Language for Lecture Design: An inventory and categorization of existing lecture-relevant patterns. In Proceedings of the 18th European Conference on Pattern Languages of Programs, EuroPLoP'13. Irsee, Germany: ACM.

Köppe, C., Nørgård, R.T., & Pedersen, A. Y. (2017). Towards a Pattern Language for Hybrid Education. Proceedings of VikingPLoP 2017. New York: ACM.

Köppe, C., Niels, R., Holwerda, R., Tijsma, L., Van Diepen, N., Van Turnhout, K., & Bakker, R. (2015). Flipped Classroom Patterns - Designing Valuable In-Class Meetings. In Proceedings of the 20th European Conference on Pattern Languages of Programs, EuroPLoP'15. Irsee, Germany. http://doi.org/http://dx.doi.org/10.1145/2855321.2855348

Köppen, E., Meinel, C.: Empathy via design thinking: creation of sense and knowledge. In: Plattner, H., Meinel, C., Leifer, L. (eds.) Design Thinking Research. Understanding Innovation, pp. 15–28. Springer, Switzerland (2015)

Mor, Y., Mellar, H., Warburton, S., & Winters, N. (Eds.). (2014). Practical design patterns for teaching and learning with technology. Rotterdam/Boston/Taipei: Sense Publishers.

Mor Y., Warburton S., Nørgård R.T., Ullmo PA. (2016) MOOC Design Workshop: Educational Innovation with Empathy and Intent. In: Verbert K., Sharples M., Klobučar T. (eds) Adaptive and Adaptable Learning. EC-TEL 2016. Lecture Notes in Computer Science, vol 9891. Springer, Cham

Rorabaugh, P., & Stommel, H. (2012). Hybridity, part 3: what does hybrid pedagogy do. http://www.digitalpedagogylab.com/hybridped/hybridity-pt-3-what-does-hybrid-pedagogy-do/

Stommel, J. (2012). Hybridity, part 2: what is hybrid pedagogy. http://www.digitalpedagogylab.com/hybridped/hybridity-pt-2-what-is-hybrid-pedagogy/

Warburton, S., & Mor, Y. (2015). A set of patterns for the structured design of MOOCs. Open Learning: The Journal of Open, Distance and E-Learning, 30(3), 206–220.http://doi.org/10.1080/02680513.2015.1100070

A Pattern Language Remix for ATS2020

Using Existing Pedagogical Patterns to Create a New Language for Formative Assessment within the ATS2020 Learning Model

Grundschober, Isabell
Danube University Krems, Austria
Isabell.Grundschober@donau-uni.ac.at

Ghoneim, Andrea
Danube University Krems, Austria
Andrea.Ghoneim@donau-uni.ac.at

Baumgartner, Peter
Danube University Krems, Austria
Isabell.Grundschober@donau-uni.ac.at

Gruber-Muecke, Tina
IMC University of Applied Sciences Krems, Austria
Tina.Gruber-Muecke@fh-krems.ac.at

Within the EU project "ATS2020 – Assessment of Transversal Skills" about 10 000 students between 10 and 15 years participated in piloting the ATS2020 learning model, which aims to support the development of transversal skills. The learning model requires significant changes of traditional teaching as it means moving from a teacher- to a learner-centered way of education. Furthermore, digital tools are central within the ATS2020 learning approach. Not all teachers have expertise in using digital tools in class and in knowing how to use them in order to support transversal skills. A pattern language for feedback and assessment supports teachers in applying the ATS2020 learning model, as it builds on good practice experiences in the past. In the last decades, pedagogues all over the world have mined many patterns as well as pattern languages and communities of practices emerged, like the pedagogical patterns project.

We would like to make use of existing pedagogical patterns and to adapt them for teachers in specific learning and teaching settings. Through the example of ATS2020, we want to show how existing pattern languages could be remixed and how new configurations could be found between patterns from different languages. A new pattern language can be tailored to the needs for teachers, who want to use the ATS2020 learning model in school.

Pedagogical patterns, pattern selection, pattern application, feedback patterns, assessment patterns

1. Introduction

The project "ATS2020 – Assessment of Transversal Skills" aims at the development and assessment of transversal skills in K12-schools in 10 European countries. An ePortfolio-based learning model was developed, which is shaped by assessment for learning as well as student-centered teaching and learning. All in all, almost 250 schools in Belgium, Cyprus, Estonia, Greece, Finland, Ireland, Lithuania, Slovenia and Spain took part in the classroom pilot during the school year 2016-2017. Around 1000 teachers and more than 10 000 students participated in piloting the ATS2020 learning-model. Traditionally, learning environments in school are influenced by teacher-centered teaching and learning styles (Elen, Clarebout, Léonard, & Lowyck, 2007, p. 106). Therefore, before the start of the pilot, the teachers were trained to implement the ATS2020 learning model, which implies a shift to student-centered teaching and learning (ATS2020, 2017b). These teachers successfully applied the model in their teaching and learning environments, but how can the teaching and learning with the ATS2020 learning model be shared with teachers, who have not been part of the project? This is especially relevant also for teachers, who are not experienced in assessment for learning, the ePortfolio-approach and student-centered learning.

We believe that pedagogical patterns and pattern languages could be a practicable way to guide teachers and learners towards a teaching and learning style, which supports transversal skills. In this paper, we show how existing pedagogical patterns from different pattern languages could be connected and used to support teachers in designing new teaching and learning applications using a learner-centered, ePortfolio-based learning model in class.

2. Why patterns?

In the late 1970s, a research group lead by Christopher Alexander developed an approach to communicate architectural notions between laymen and architectural experts. They tried to find a way how people without professional training as designers could express their ideas about the configurations and relationships of the different elements of their envisaged living space.

The main idea was to describe a situation ("pattern") as a three-part rule. They used the limited ability of language to express configurations by focusing on the relation between (1) a certain context, (2) a formulated problem and (3) a proposed solution:

Each pattern describes a problem which occurs over and over again in our environment, and then describes the core of the solution to that problem, in such a way that you can use this solution a million times over, without ever doing it the same way twice (Alexander, Ishikawa, & Silverstein, 1977).

Therefore, a pattern is a description and an instruction at the same time. Through patterns, tacit knowledge from experience can be documented and is accessible for others (Bauer, 2014, p. 15).

It turned out that the method they developed was also suitable for experts to communicate their architectural knowledge to novices. This is also relevant for pedagogy: Experiences can be efficiently communicated in a structured way, not only to other experienced colleagues, but even to novices in teaching practice (Bauer, 2014, p. 244). Pedagogical patterns can help to design new teaching and learning applications as well as improve existing ones (Fioravanti & Barbosa, 2016, p. 1).

The power of patterns is even stronger, when they are related to other patterns, e.g. as part of a pattern collection, or even better, as part of a fully grown pattern language (Köppe, Inventado, Scupelli, & Van Heesch, 2016, p. 11). The relations between patterns are the basis for the creation of a pattern language (Köppe, 2015, p. 2).

In 1994 the first Pattern Language of Programs (PLoP) conference was held and since then many patterns have been written, not only in the area of programming and IT, but also in many other fields. The aim of pattern conferences is to promote, improve and publish patterns (Köppe et al., 2016, p. 2). Design patterns were especially useful during the shift to the new programming paradigm of object-oriented technology. Software developers who were used to other paradigms found it difficult to get adapted to object-oriented programming. A consequence of the paradigm shift was the need for teaching and learning the new technology. Therefore, the Pedagogical Patterns Project was started in 1996 (Eckstein, Manns, & Voelter, 2001, p. 9 and Magnusson, 2006, p. 1) Originally, pedagogical patters were designed for teaching object-oriented technology and teachers of software engineering have been experimenting with pedagogical patterns since then. Over time it became obvious that the problems described in these patterns had much in common with other disciplines. Most patterns are written in a general way and are applicable in various educational settings, not only for teaching and learning programming (Magnusson, 2006, p. 2).

Since the start of the Pedagogical Patterns Project, manifold patterns for teaching and learning were mined, covering didactical aspects like active learning, handling different learning styles, focussing on areas like educational technology as well as patterns for feedback and assessment (Köppe, 2015, p. 2). In this paper, we want to make use of existing patterns for the ATS2020 project and benefit from good practice examples of teaching and learning using feedback and formative assessment.

3. The ATS2020 Learning Model: Learning through Feedback and Assessment

Our aim is to collect pedagogical patterns, which are useful for feedback and assessment within the ATS2020 learning model. As a next step, we want to find connections between the selected patterns to start an attempt of forming a new pattern language. For this reason, it first needs to be clarified, which main aspects of learning and teaching are inherent part of the learning model.

The ATS2020 learning model is based on a learner-centered ePortfolio-approach, supporting the development of skills and competences in five areas:

» Information literacy

» Autonomous Learning

» Collaboration and Communication

» Creativity and Innovation

» Digital Literacy (ATS2020, 2017a)

Students actively participate in developing these skills and competences, whereas teachers are taking the role of the coach and assessor. ATS2020 learning model is based on a learning cycle-model, containing 6 phases:

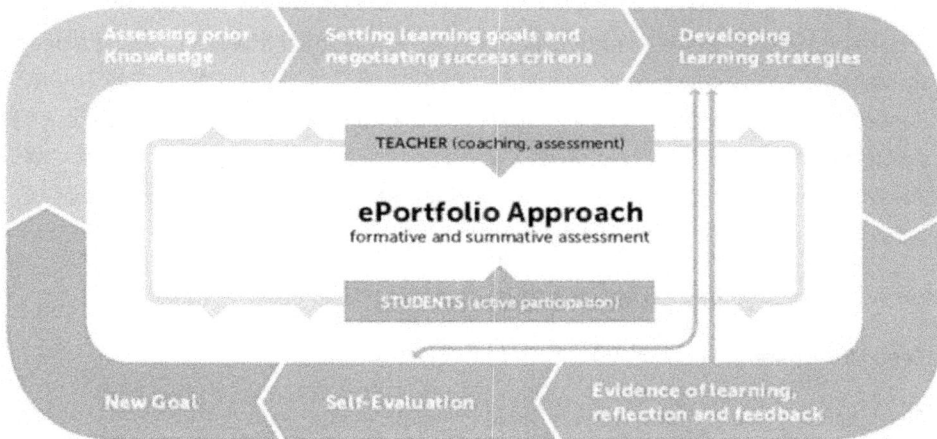

Figure 1: The ATS2020 learning cycle - an ePortfolio approach (ATS2020, 2017b)

Not only assessment of learning as in summative assessment focusing on the learning product, but also assessment for learning in the sense of formative assessment is a basis for the ATS2020 learning model. Students can redesign and improve their learning artefacts throughout the learning cycles they are going through. Figure 1 shows the learning cycle, which is starting with the student checking his or her prior learning and setting goals and ending with self-evaluation and setting new goals for the next learning cycle. Students ask themselves the following questions during the six phases:

1. Assessing prior knowledge: What do I already know on the subject? What kind of skills do I already have?

2. Setting goals: What are my goals? How will I know that I reached my goal?

3. Strategies: What can I do to reach my goals?

4. Evidence: What kind of evidence do I need to prove my learning achievements?

5. Self-evaluation: Did I achieve my goals? What could I do better?

6. Setting new goals: What are my new goals based on my learning experiences? Where do I want to succeed? (cf. ATS2020, 2017b)

Especially feedback and assessment have an important role in this learning model. Feedback is understood as information given by an agent, like a teacher, peer, parent or the learner's own experience, regarding aspects of a learner's performance (Hattie & Timperley, 2007, p. 102). Within the ATS2020 learning model, peers, self-evaluation and the teacher as learning coach are agents for feedback.

In each phase, the teacher acts as a learning coach, using formative assessment and feedback to help students on their learning pathway, improving their artefacts, getting a deeper understanding and to reach their learning goals (Rupnik Vec et al., 2015, p. 21). Feedback influences learning processes, but its impact could always positive. There are various factors determining, if feedback reinforces a learning process. For example, feedback has a positive influence, when it is combined with setting clear goals, like mentioned in phase 2 of the ATS2020 learning model (Hattie & Timperley, 2007, p. 93).

Hattie & Timperley (2007, p. 87) define three questions for effective feedback:

» Feed Up: Where am I going? Which goals should be attained?

» Feed Back: How am I going? How is the learning process going?

» Feed Forward: Where to next? What are the next steps, next goals?

Feedback that is considering these three questions can support students' learning pathways in a positive way. The answers to these questions reinforce learning when there is a gap between what is understood and what is aimed to be understood during a learning process (Hattie & Timperley, 2007, p. 102) Also, the ATS2020 learning model reflects these questions – "Feed Up" is given in phase 2, "Feed Back" is given in phase 3, 4 and 5 and "Feed Forward" is provided in phase 6.

Hattie & Timperley furthermore differentiate between four types of feedback, which work for all three questions above:

» Task level: Corrective feedback on how well the task was performed.

» Process level: Feedback on the learning process/learning strategy used to perform the task.

» Self-regulatory level: Feedback on self-monitoring as well as self-regulation of actions.

» Self-level: Personal evaluations and affects about the learner, usually in a positive way (Hattie & Timperley, 2007, p. 87).

Not all teachers are experienced in student-centered teaching and learning or the ePortfolio approach and know how to support students in developing the necessary skills for studying with the learning model. Most feedback in class, around 90% is corrective feedback on the task level, which is very often mixed with feedback on the self-level, which is diminishing the power of the task feedback (Hattie & Timperley, 2007, p. 91). Supporting transversal skills through a student-centered approach means not only giving feedback on task level, but also on the process level and self-regulatory level. Using student ePortfolios with not only showcase-functions but also developmental aspects supports especially feedback on the process level, as the learning process is documented, can be shared and students can collect feedback or reflect on it themselves. Reflections can be added to artefacts and used for feedback on self-regulatory level, too.

Patterns, a collection of connected patterns or in the future even a pattern language, could help teachers and students to use feedback and assessment for applying the ATS2020 learning model at school.

4. Pattern Search and Selection

Various helpful pedagogical patterns already exist, but only few address the problems we are facing when designing pedagogical scenarios using the ATS2020 learning model, which is following a student-centered ePortfolio-approach. Therefore, we searched the internet for pedagogical patterns in general and more specific patterns for feedback/ and or assessment. To bring structure into the variety of pedagogical patterns and to make the search less complex, we decided to use categories for providing a better overview and to support usability. Usually, a pattern can be placed in multiple categories (Köppe, 2015, p. 2), so we considered this aspect when defining the criteria for the pattern selection. The six phases of the ATS2020 learning model were chosen as categories. Following selection criteria were used for choosing pedagogical patterns:

» They have to fit into one or more of our pre-defined categories.

» They have to address formative feedback/assessment.

Categories are practicable when selecting individual patterns, related to the context of the pattern, its problem or its solution. The selected patterns reflect how feedback can be given in a "good" way, implying that it is enhancing the learning process and supporting transversal skills. More in detail, the patterns show which methods can be used and how the educational environment could be designed so "good" feedback and assessment can emerge.

After agreeing on criteria to select patterns we also had to think how to present the outcomes of our search and selection. Pattern authors often have their own preferences in how to write and structure patterns (Köppe et al., 2016, p. 3). Some patterns in our ATS2020 feedback and assessment patterns collection are very detailed and include many more sections than just problem, context and solution (see "Schaufenster des Lernens" by Bauer & Baumgartner, 2012); others are very short and to the point (see "A Pattern Language for Active Learners" by Iba, Miyake, Naruse, & Yotsumoto, 2009). Furthermore, we wanted to avoid copyright issues when presenting the pattern collection. Köppe, Salvador Inventado, Scupelli and van Heesch (2016, p. 3) suggested using pattern abstracts or pattern summaries including links to the original pattern. We found this approach practicable and applied it in organizing the ATS2020 feedback and assessment patterns collection. Not only can copyright issues be avoided, but also the diversity of pattern formats can be respected this way. The summary conveys the most important aspects of the pattern through referring to problem-solution pair.

The ATS2020 feedback and assessment patterns collection therefore consists of pattern references. Each reference is constituted by the following format:

» Category

» Active Role (either teacher or student)

» Pattern Name and reference where it was published

» Pattern Language

» Pattern Summary

» Example for technological support

"Category" shows, which phase or phases of the ATS2020 learning model the pattern is referring to. "Active Role" informs the reader who can apply the pattern (either teachers and/ or students in this case). Furthermore, the pattern name and a reference to the publication where the pattern was published are provided as well as the pattern language or name of the pattern collection. The pattern summary indicates the problem-solution pair and helps teachers to quickly understand if they could make use of the pattern. The example for technological support gives a deeper insight how the pattern could be realized in a learning environment, which is supported by digital tools.

4.1. Selected Patterns

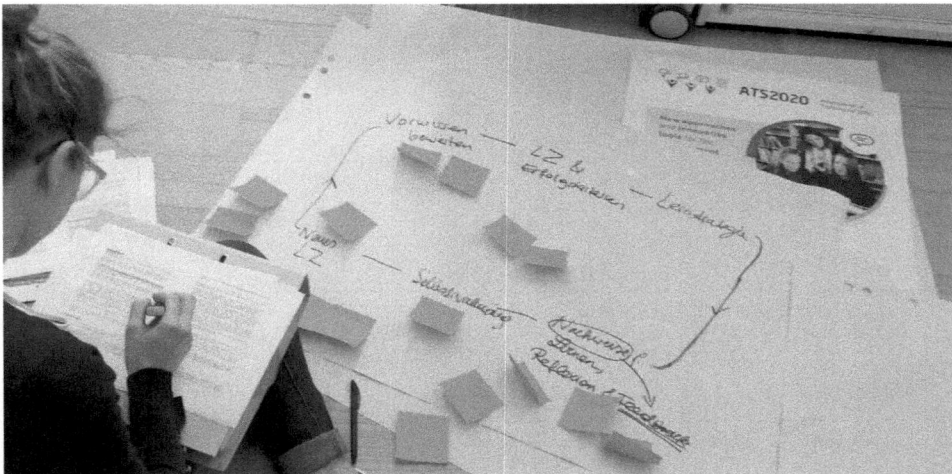

Figure 2: Categorization - matching existing pattern to pre-defined categories.

Figure 2 shows how we approached the patterns selection process. After reading through patterns, we decided if it fulfilled our pattern selection criteria. Additional categories emerged during the process of pattern selection/ pattern matching:

» **Meta-Patterns**: Patterns in the category "Meta-Patterns" do not fit in the six phases, but they are important for establishing a feedback- and assessment culture for supporting transversal skills.

» **All Phases**: Patterns which are in the category "All Phases" could be applied in each phase of the ATS2020 learning model. These patterns describe how feedback could be given or how feedback could be received.

All other categories are directly referring to feedback/assessment patters matching the phases of the ATS2020 learning model. A few patterns fit in several categories and therefore occur more than one time in the pattern overview below.

4.1.1. Overview of ATS2020 Feedback and Assessment Patterns

Meta-Patterns	ACTIVE STUDENT INVISIBLE TEACHER TRUSTED SPACE ASSESSMENT-DRIVEN COURSE DESIGN CONSTRUCTIVE ALIGNMENT TRANSPARENT ASSESSMENT/OPEN INSTRUMENTS OF ASSESSMENT/ VISIBLE ASSESSMENT TRUSTED SPACE LOOK, BUT DO NOT TOUCH
All Phases	FEEDBACK (Bergin et al.) FEEDBACK (Bauer, Baumgartner) PEER FEEDBACK FEEDBACK SANDWICH THREE STARS AND A WISH DIFFERENTIATED FEEDBACK STUDENT ONLINE PORTFOLIOS THIS IS FEEDBACK
1) Assessing Prior Knowledge	TELL ME ABOUT IT ACT ON FEEDBACK SELF-EVALUATION REFLECTING BLENDED EVALUATION
2) Setting Learning Goals and Negotiating Criteria	LEARNING OUTCOMES ASSESSMENT CRITERIA LIST/ ASSESSMENT CONTRACT CRITERIA REFINEMENT/ CRITERIA DETAILS REVISING LEARNING CONTRACT
3) Developing Learning Strategies	LEARNING CONTRACT RELEASE YOUR THOUGHT DELVE THE DEPTHS OPEN THE PROJECT
4) Evidence of Learning, Reflection and Feedback	REFLECTING BLENDED EVALUATION RELEASE YOUR THOUGHT DELVE THE DEPTHS OPEN THE PROJECT SHOWCASE PEER REVIEW PRESENT MY MIRROR ADOPT-AN-ARTIFACT REFLECTION
5) Self-Evaluation	REFLECTING REVISING BLENDED EVALUATION TELL ME ABOUT IT ACT ON FEEDBACK PERFORMANCE SHEET/ ASSESSMENT CONTRACT/ RUBRIC/ SCORE SHEET ASSESSMENT DIVERSITY PRESENT MY MIRROR SELF-EVALUATION

6) New Goals	LEARNING OUTCOMES ASSESSMENT CRITERIA LIST/ ASSESSMENT CONTRACT CRITERIA REFINEMENT/ CRITERIA DETAILS LEARNING CONTRACT REVISING ACT ON FEEDBACK

Table 1: Pattern categories and matching patterns

4.1.2. Full List of ATS2020 Feedback and Assessment Patterns

The following list contains 36 patterns from 11 pattern languages. The selected patterns are ordered according to categories, starting with meta patterns, followed by patterns matching all phases in the ATS2020 learning model and the phase of the learning model. Each pattern is listed once, even if it fits more than one category.

It became obvious that several patterns from phase 5 fit also to phase 1 and patterns from phase 6 fit phase 2. This is due to the nature of the learning model. It is designed as a template for starting with the ATS2020 learning model. Once gone through the first four phases, phase five and six are closely connected to phase one and two – where the next learning cycle starts. Regarding the addressed role of the pattern, many patterns were written for teachers and just a few for students, nevertheless many patterns written for teachers (marked as "T") are also suitable for students if adapted accordingly (marked as "S"). These patterns are marked as "T*/S". If a pattern was written for students and teachers alike, the pattern is marked as "T/S".

Cat.	Active Role	Pattern Name	Pattern Language	Summary	Example for Technological Support
META	T*/S	ACTIVE STUDENT (Eckstein, Bergin, Sharp, & Manns, 2002b, p. 1)	Patterns for Active Learning	As learning is an individual construction process, passive students do not learn as much as active students. Teachers want to maximize student learning and therefore keep students active in class (Eckstein et al., 2002b, p. 1).	The ePortfolio-approach supports students to be active as it is student-centered and belongs to the student, not the teacher.

META	T	INVISIBLE TEACHER (Eckstein, Bergin, Sharp, & Manns, 2002b, p. 9)	Patterns for Active Learning	Traditional learning environments usually have the teacher in the center and students only trust the teacher to be competent enough to give feedback or to provide help when struggling during the learning process. In everyday life, the teacher will not be around to help. Therefore, the teacher supports peer mentoring in class (Eckstein, Bergin, Sharp, & Manns, 2002b, p. 9).	The teacher is invisible but still supportive, if he or she provides necessary information online, e.g. in a Wiki or as FAQs. This way, the teacher helps students to help themselves and to be independent learners. A further support of peer mentoring can be opening up online spaces for the mentee and the mentor, maybe offering a structure (workflow, bullet points, questions, ...), as well.
META	T	ASSESS-MENT-DRIVEN COURSE DE-SIGN (Bergin et al., 2015b, p. 3)	Assessment-Driven Course Design Foundational Patterns	A teacher designs a new course and wants to prevent a mismatch between what/how is taught and the assessment of the pre-defined learning outcomes. Therefore, the teacher uses assessment as driver to develop the course and its content (Bergin et al., 2015b, p. 3).	ATS2020 provides a macro-design template for developing assessment-driven course designs. Examples how it is used can be accessed at the ATS2020 Resource Portal.
META	T	CONSTRUCTIVE ALIGNMENT (Bergin et al., 2015b, p. 3)	Assessment-Driven Course Design Foundational Patterns	To match the learning and assessment objectives of a course and therefore providing authentic assessment activities, teachers use learning outcomes as a basis for developing assessment processes and assessment criteria (Bergin et al., 2015b, p. 3).	ATS2020 provides a macro-design template which supports constructive alignment. Examples how it is used can be found at the ATS2020 Resource Portal.

META	T	TRANSPARENT ASSESSMENT/ OPEN INST-RUMENTS OF ASSESSMENT/ VISIBLE ASSESS-MENT (Bergin et al., 2015a, p. 3)	Assessment-Dri-ven Course Design – Fair Play Patterns	To prevent miscon-ceptions of what is required from students to pass a course, teachers share the ASSESSMENT CRITERIA LIST and ASSESSMENT INSTRU-MENTS with students and encourage self- and peer-assessment of students' artefacts/ performances (Bergin et al., 2015a, p. 3ff.).	The teacher could create a teaching ePortfolio to transpa-rently communicate assessment criteria and assessment in-struments. Students and parents could benefit from this online service.
META	T	TRUSTED SPA-CE (Warburton, Bergin, Kohls, Köppe, & Mor, 2016, p. 3)	Dialogical Assess-ment Patterns for Learning from Others	Sometimes learners hesitate to share their work with peers. Therefore, teachers create an encouraging learning environment in which students feel safe to share their le-arning artefacts and to receive feedback on it (Bergin, Kohls, Köppe, & Mor, 2016, p. 3f.).	Next to ice-brea-ker activities, also activities to support the understanding of privacy and sharing settings in a student ePortfolio support autonomy and developing a trusted space. Furthermo-re, establishing a netiquette and FAQs for giving and recei-ving feedback help to develop a shared understanding.
META	T	LOOK, BUT DO NOT TOUCH (Larson, Trees, & Weaver, 2008, p. 23)	Continuous Feed-back Pedagogical Patterns	When students are facing difficulties on their learning pathway, teachers give advice and offer guidance instead of solving the problem for the student (Larson et al., 2008, p. 23).	FAQs could help here, as well. Further automatized guiding tools (like chat-bots) could be helpful, but such an infrastructure goes beyond the scope of ATS2020. Learning Analytics can be another scaffolding tool for guidance on the learning path.
ALL	T/S	FEEDBACK (Bauer & Baum-gartner, 2012, p. 291)	Schaufenster des Lernens. Eine Sammlung von Mustern für das Arbeiten mit E-Portfolios	To support the learning process and/ or finding a solution to a problem, peers and teachers can give detailed feedback to learning artefacts (Bauer & Baumgart-ner, 2012, p. 291f.).	Feedback could be given either through comments or in an online forum (in text, audio or video).

ALL	T*/S	FEEDBACK (Eckstein, Bergin, Sharp, & Manns, 2002a, p. 2)	Feedback Patterns	Teachers want students to challenge their understanding and help them to know what level of understanding they have achieved. Therefore, they give feedback to the student's performance (Eckstein, Bergin, Sharp, & Manns, 2002a, p. 2).	Feedback could be given either through comments or in an online forum (in text, audio or video).
ALL	T*/S	PEER FEED-BACK (Eckstein, Bergin, Sharp, & Manns, 2002a, p. 9)	Feedback Patterns	Teachers want students not only to learn how to act on feedback but also how to give feedback. Therefore, they invite students to evaluate their peers' artefacts (Eckstein, Bergin, Sharp, & Manns, 2002a, p. 9).	In many learning environments and ePortfolio spaces, like Mahara, it is possible to establish groups so students can work with their peers in groups (Ghoneim, n.d.). In their discussion group they can easily share their artefacts and discuss them.
ALL	T*/S	FEEDBACK SANDWICH (Eckstein, Bergin, Sharp, & Manns, 2002a, p. 4)	Feedback Patterns	The teacher wants to give feedback to students in a way, that misunderstandings are corrected but still the students' confidence is not undermined. Therefore, the teacher gives feedback in a way that he/she starts and ends with a positive comment and places a suggestion for improvement in between (Eckstein, Bergin, Sharp, & Manns, 2002a, p. 4).	This feedback strategy is not only suitable for teachers but also for peer feedback. It could be provided in an online FAQ section by the teacher to help students in giving feedback to each other's artefacts. Furthermore, assessment rubrics can be offered as templates for the students.
ALL	T	DIFFERENTIA-TED FEEDBACK (Eckstein, Bergin, Sharp, & Manns, 2002a, p. 4)	Feedback Patterns	To respect students as individuals, the teacher tailors the feedback to the needs of each student (Eckstein, Bergin, Sharp, & Manns, 2002a, p.	Technological support allows multi-media feedback, e.g. in a video & thus the chance to meet the media preferences of the student as well as to document the feedback.

ALL	T*/S	THREE STARS AND A WISH (Larson et al., 2008, p. 21)	Continuous Feedback Pedagogical Patterns	Teachers want to give feedback to a student's performance in a sensitive way. Therefore, three positive aspects of the students work (three stars) as well as a suggestion for improvement (the wish) are mentioned in the feedback (Larson et al., 2008, p. 21).	This feedback strategy is not only suitable for teachers but also for peer feedback. It could be provided in an online FAQ section by the teacher to help students in giving feedback to each other's artefacts.
ALL	T*/S	STUDENT ON-LINE PORTFO-LIOS (Eckstein, Bergin, Sharp, & Manns, 2002a, p. 11)	Feedback Patterns	Teachers want to give students the possibility to receive feedback to their artefacts/performance from a wider audience (peers, relatives, etc.). Therefore, teachers provide the means for students to publish their best work in an ePortfolio (Eckstein, Bergin, Sharp, & Manns, 2002a, p. 11).	There are many online platforms for student ePortfolios. In ATS2020, the ePortfolio-platform Mahara (Mahara, n.d.) as well as One-Note Class Notebook (Microsoft, 2017) are/were used in class (Ghoneim, 2017).
ALL	T*/S	STUDENT ON-LINE PORTFO-LIOS (Eckstein, Bergin, Sharp, & Manns, 2002a, p. 11)	Dialogical Assessment Patterns for Learning from Others	Students might not always recognize when feedback is given to them, therefore feedback processes are signposted (Warburton et al., 2016, p. 8f.).	Feedback could be signposted with (animated) gifs to make them stand out. Furthermore, students can be asked to keep an e-collection of feedbacks and of their reaction on them to create awareness.
1, 5	T*/S	TELL ME ABOUT IT (Larson et al., 2008, p. 27)	Continuous Feedback Pedagogical Patterns	To make connections between new learning and prior learning, students periodically reflect upon what they have learned and how they might apply new learning in their lives (Larson et al., 2008, p. 27).	Within the student ePortfolio, created artefacts can be reflected through writing a text, recording an audio-comment or taking a video.
1, 5, 6	T*/S	ACT ON FEED-BACK (Warburton et al., 2016, p. 10)	Dialogical Assessment Patterns for Learning from Others	The teacher has given feedback and wants to ensure that students act on it. Therefore, a learning environment is created, which actively gives room for reflection of the given feedback and the next steps to face within the learning process (Warburton et al., 2016, p. 10f.).	In an ePortfolio, collected feedback (either in text, questionnaire, audio or video) can be saved online and linked to the artefact. Students can compare their self-perception and the received feedback and reflect on it.

1, 5	S	SELF-EVALUA-TION (Bauer & Baumgartner, 2012, p. 240)	Schaufenster des Lernens. Eine Sammlung von Mustern für das Arbeiten mit E-Portfolios	Students develop autonomous learning skills through regularly evaluating learning artefacts and learning processes (Bauer & Baumgartner, 2012, p. 240f).	ATS2020 provides a self-assessment tool for students which supports criteria-led self-assessment.
1, 4, 5	S	REFLECTING (Bauer & Baumgartner, 2012, p. 253)	Schaufenster des Lernens. Eine Sammlung von Mustern für das Arbeiten mit E-Portfolios	Students want to get a better idea of their strengths and weaknesses, therefore they reflect their learning processes and artefacts through creating an ePortfolio (Bauer & Baumgartner, 2012, p. 253f).	Within the ATS2020 the ePortfolio-Platform Mahara (Mahara, n.d.) as well as One-Note Class Notebook (Microsoft, 2017) were used (Ghoneim, 2017).
1, 4,5	T*/S	BLENDED EVALUATION (Comber, 2014, p. 293)	Practical Design Patterns for Teaching and Learning with Technology	Classical grading only provides feedback by a single person, usually the teacher, and typically the quality of information conveyed is rather low. Therefore, a blended evaluation approach can be followed, combining the view of different agents (self, peers, teacher) and using various assessment methods (Comber, 2014, p. 293).	A learning environment, preferably an ePortfolio space, is the ideal place to collect the formative assessment of various assessors – together with the learning artefacts and reflections which are assessed/ evaluated.
2	T	LEARNING OUTCOMES (Bergin et al., 2015b, p. 6)	Assessment-Driven Course Design Foundational Patterns	If teachers set clear and measurable learning outcomes, students have a better idea towards where to work to and can organize their studies accordingly (Bergin et al., 2015b, p. 7).	Teachers can use the Learning Outcome Generator provided by the University of Indiana to write transparent learning outcomes (Indiana University Bloomington, n.d.). The scaffolding tool/template "My Learning" can be used for documentation of the Learning Outcomes.
2	T	ASSESSMENT CRITERIA LIST/ ASSESSMENT CONTRACT (Bergin et al., 2015b, p. 7)	Assessment-Driven Course Design Foundational Patterns	An ASSESSMENT CRITERIA LIST indicating minimum requirements, deriving from LEARNING OUTCOMES, should be clearly communicated so prevent students from running in the wrong direction/ perform poorly (Bergin et al., 2015b, p. 7).	Google forms is an online survey tool and a practicable way to provide an assessment criteria list. Furthermore, Assessment Criteria can be documented in "My Learning" (in the section "Criteria for Success").

2	T	CRITERIA REFI-NEMENT/ CRITERIA DETAILS (Bergin et al., 2015b, p. 9)	Assessment-Driven Course Design Foundational Patterns	Criteria from the ASSESSMENT CRITERIA LIST are refined and it is specified how they are measured (Bergin et al., 2015b, p. 9).	ATS2020 provides a formative assessment scaffolding tools for teachers, which refines the ATS2020 assessment criteria.
2, 5, 6	T/S	REVISING (Bauer & Baumgartner, 2012, p. 200)	Schaufenster des Lernens. Eine Sammlung von Mustern für das Arbeiten mit E-Portfolios	Students want to revise their ePortfolios and improve them. Therefore, students and teachers together develop a criteria list for (self-) evaluation of their ePortfolios' to understand potential for improvement (Bauer & Baumgartner, 2012, p. 200).	ATS2020 provides a self-assessment tool for students which supports criteria-led self-assessment.
2/ 3	T*/S	LEARNING CONTRACT (Larson et al., 2008, p. 5)	Continuous Feedback Pedagogical Patterns	Through agreeing on a learning contract between students and teachers, clear goals and learning strategies are set and students take responsibility for their own learning (Larson et al., 2008, p.	The learning contract could be added to the student's ePortfolio so it is can be linked to learning artefacts. This could happen either in an ePortfolio-Platform like Mahara (Mahara, n.d.) or also in One-Note Class Notebook (Microsoft, 2017).
3, 4	S	RELEASE YOUR THOUGHT (Iba, Miyake, Naruse, & Yotsumoto, 2009, p. 18)	A Pattern Languages for Active Learners	If learners are stuck in the learning process, they look for others (peers, teachers, parents,..) to talk to and explain their ideas/problems. Learners use the reactions to their ideas/problems for the next steps in their learning process (Iba et al., 2009, p. 22).	Opening a new thread in a forum can help to explain an idea and to share what students are working on to collect feedback. Additionally, students can be encouraged to share their ePortfolios with peers to stimulate discussion and ideas.
3, 4	T*/S	DELVE THE DEPTHS (Larson et al., 2008, p. 25)	Continuous Feedback Pedagogical Patterns	A teacher didn't expect a certain solution presented by a student and does not know how to react. Therefore, teacher and students together compare several students' solutions and evaluate them (Larson et al., 2008, p. 25).	In class, several digital artefacts could be compared through projection on a wall or using a smart board. Students can also present their solutions through a video presentation.

3,4	T*/S	OPEN THE PRO-JECT (Harashi-ma, Kubota, & Iba, 2014, p. 7)	Creative Education Patterns: Designing for Learning by Creating	It is difficult to assess a project if one was involved in the project's progress. Therefore, to receive objective feedback, one to three persons who were not involved in the project can be asked to assess it (Harashima et al., 2014, p. 7).	Feedback could be given either through comments or in an online forum (in text, audio or video).
4	T*/S	SHOWCASE (Warburton et al., 2016, p. 5)	Dialogical Assessment Patterns for Learning from Others	For some more complex artefacts it is difficult to completely define assessment criteria. Therefore, the teacher makes the presentation of these artefacts and receiving feedback on it a part of the learning and teaching process (Warburton et al., 2016, p. 5f.).	In an ePortfolio, like provided by Mahara, it is possible to share pages, artefacts and page collections with a selected audience. In other VLEs, like OneNote Class Note-book, an additional discussion space, like Yammer, helps to share and discuss artefacts and to provide feedback.
4	T*/S	PEER REVIEW (Warburton et al., 2016, p. 7)	Dialogical Assessment Patterns for Learning from Others	Teachers often do not have time to give feedback to all learning artefacts that students produce but they still want them to benefit from feedback to improve their work. Therefore, the teacher develops assessment processes which are including peer review and support students' autonomous learning skills (Warburton et al., 2016, p. 7).	Google forms is an online survey tool and a practicable way to provide a guideline how to review other students' artefacts. Templates like a rubric (created like a table in a text program or as a sheet) can be another solution. The templates can be offered alongside with the teacher's portfolio.
4	T*/S	ADOPT-AN-AR-TIFACT (Eckstein, Bergin, Sharp, & Manns, 2002b, p. 14)	Patterns for Active Learning	Students need to understand different perspectives how to solve a problem. Therefore, students improve and extend artefacts from peers instead of their own (Eckstein, Bergin, Sharp, & Manns, 2002b, p. 14).	Digital artefacts can be easily copied, remixed, changed, improved and shared – provided the owner of the artefacts allows it.

4	T*/S	REFLECTION (Bergin, Eckstein, Manns, & Wallingford, 2001, p. 8)	Patterns For Gaining Different Perspectives	The knowledge, skills and competence of the teacher are limited. Student need to gain trust into their own competence in solving problems. Therefore, students discover the problem and find answers for themselves. Teachers support reflection through asking students how they could apply in everyday life what they have learned (Bergin et al., 2001, p. 8).	Students can compare self-perception and received feedback and reflect on it. Teachers could support this process through commenting on student's artefacts. In other VLEs, online presentation/collection tools like SWAY or PADLET can take up this function.
4,5	S	PRESENT (Bauer & Baumgartner, 2012, p. 229)	Schaufenster des Lernens. Eine Sammlung von Mustern für das Arbeiten mit E-Portfolios	Students want to make their learnings visible to themselves, peers, relatives and/ or the teacher to show what they have achieved and to collect feedback. Therefore, they present selected artefacts in a showcase-ePortfolio (Bauer & Baumgartner, 2012, p. 229f.)	In an ePortfolio, like provided by Mahara, it is possible to share pages, artefacts and page collections with a selected audience.
4,5	S	MY MIRROR (Bauer & Baumgartner, 2012, p. 235)	Schaufenster des Lernens. Eine Sammlung von Mustern für das Arbeiten mit E-Portfolios	Students want to make their learning process visible to themselves and to others. Therefore, they document their learnings in learning journals/ developmental ePortfolios (Bauer & Baumgartner, 2012, p. 235-239).	In an ePortfolio, like provided by Mahara, students can create pages to collect digital artefacts documenting the learning process.
5	T/S*	PERFORMANCE SHEET/ ASSESSMENT CONTRACT/ RUBRIC/ SCORE SHEET (Bergin et al., 2015b, p. 3)	Assessment-Driven Course Design Foundational Patterns	The teacher created an ASSESSMENT CRITERIA LIST, found CRITERIA REFINEMENT and wants to assess a complex artefact/ performance. Therefore, the teacher prepares a sheet that includes all refined criteria and is easy to fill out (Bergin et al., 2015b, p. 3).	ATS2020 provides a formative assessment scaffolding tool for teachers as well as a self-assessment tool for students.

| 5 | T*/S | ASSESSMENT DIVERSITY (Bergin et al., 2015a, p. 10) | Assessment-Driven Course Design – Fair Play Patterns | To consider various learning modalities and the fact that student react differently to assessment instruments, a variety of assessment instruments should be used (Bergin et al., 2015a, p. 10f.). | In ATS2020, instruments like reflective sentence starters (https://prezi.com/sn57iolth9rt/using-eportfo-lios-to-foster-trans-versal-skills/?utm_campaign=sha-re&utm_medium=-copy, Slide 14), Rubrics, Online questionnaires etc. are used. |

Table 2: Full list of selected patterns for the ATS2020 feedback and assessment patterns collection

5. Pattern Connecting and Structuring

There is a limitation when organizing the selected patterns in categories: the relations between the patterns in terms are predecessors-, successor, support- and alternative patterns (see chapter 6.1) are not captured, which explain how to implement them in a broader context. This is especially difficult, as we are working with patterns from different pattern languages. The patterns themselves do not indicate which patterns are preceding or following in our new ATS2020 pattern collection to support formative assessment within the ATS2020 learning model. These relations between patterns potentially also form a pattern language, tailored to the implementation of the ATS2020 learning model.

Furthermore, as another limitation of organizing patterns in categories, placing patterns in the same category doesn't necessarily mean that they are related to each other (Köppe, 2015, p. 3).

Therefore, once we have found matching patterns, which are fulfilling our two criteria for selection, the question arose how these patterns are related to each other, how these relations could be communicated and visualized. We chose concept maps to visualize the relations between patterns, as they allow representing tacit expert's knowledge (Novak & Cañas, 2008). We used Cmaps for creating the concept map, a collaborative online tool, provided by the Florida Institute for Human and Machine Cognition, IHMC (IHMC, 2014). As connecting 36 patterns is a complex task, we started with paper-prototyping before creating the digital representation. Paper-prototyping allowed us to get a first overview and to try out different pattern connections. We worked with pieces of paper, which were indicating the pattern name, the pattern language and the pattern summary. This was a practicable way of working with the selected patterns, as the pattern name alone would not have been enough to remember and connect all 36 patterns. Figure 3 below shows the pieces of paper indicating the patterns with their summaries. In this first stage of finding connections pattern structures are developed, reassembled and improved in an iterative manner.

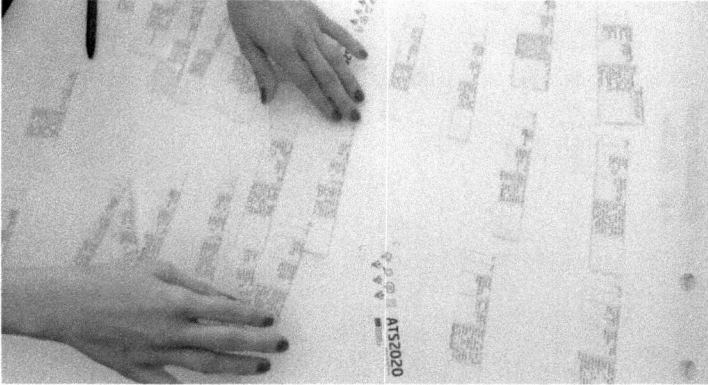

Figure 3: Connecting selected patterns in a paper-prototype.

We structured the pattern collection in several stages and documented each stage. This way, it was easier to compare different collection structures, to rethink and to improve them. Figure 4 below shows an example of a pattern collection structure documentation from a rather early stage of the process.

Figure 3: Connecting selected patterns in a paper-prototype.

Figure 4 shows that at this early stage of connecting the selected patterns, diffuse pattern clustering was dominant, but a first sequence has emerged already. In figure 5 you can see an advanced stage in the pattern connection and structuring process, already containing more explicit sequences of patterns and less clustering. This pattern structure in figure 5 was the last prototype before working with Cmap and visualizing the pattern collection and its relations digitally.

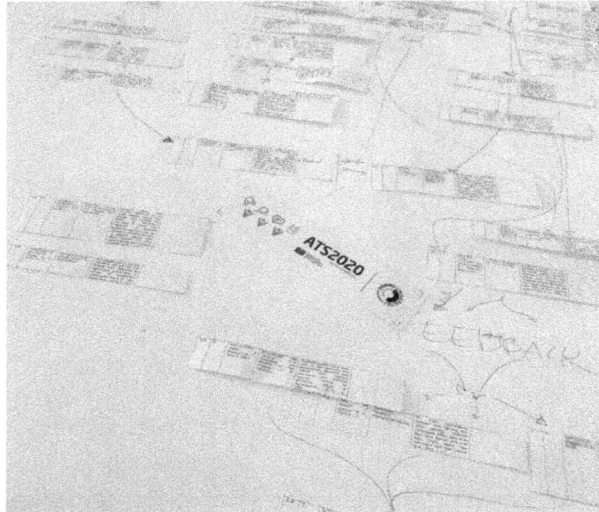

Figure 5: Reassembling connected patterns – final stage of paper-prototyping.

Through paper-prototyping a first idea of the pattern relations emerged, it was facilitated by the pattern summary and the fact that patterns could be reassembled any time. It was a rough draft for starting the digital concept map, but necessary as a starting point. It reduced complexity and working with this draft structure made it easier to handle the patterns digitally, where only the pattern name and the pattern language were displayed. The key patterns emerged during paper-prototyping and served as an important basis for creating the concept map online.

6. The ATS2020 Feedback and Assessment Patterns Collection as Concept Map

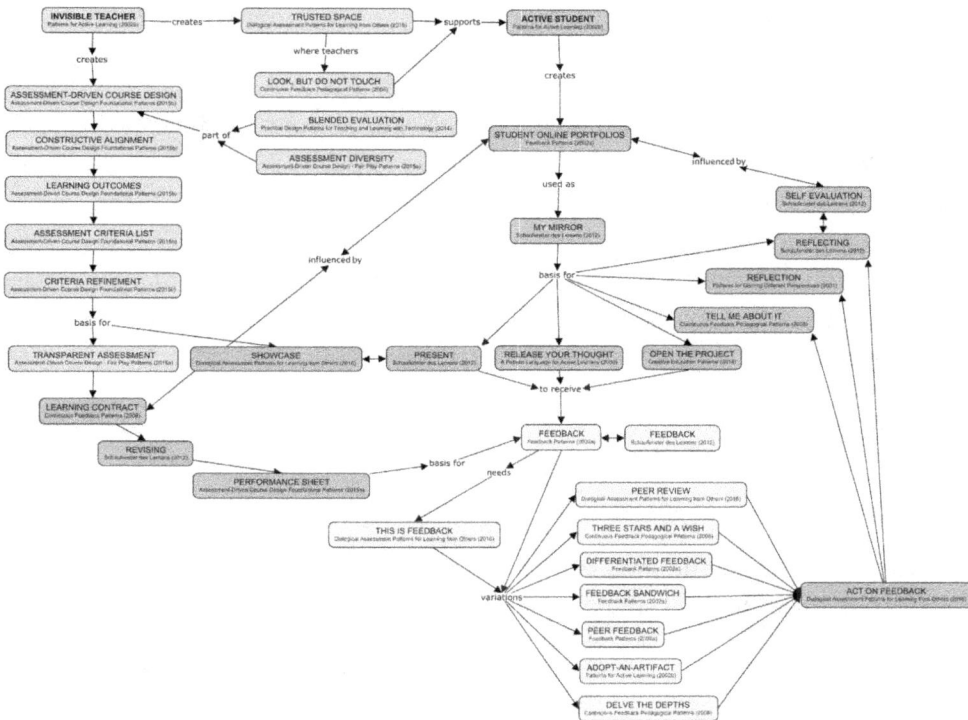

Figure 6: Final concept map – visualizing connections between the selected feedback and assessment patterns.

During paper prototyping two central patterns have emerged, INVISIBLE TEACHER and AC-TIVE STUDENT. They are both key actors within the ATS2020 learning model. The INVISIBLE TEACHER designs the course/ lessons based on ASSESSMENT DRIVEN COURSE DESIGN, which is further detailed with CONSTRUCTIVE ALIGNMENT, LEARNING OUTCOMES, an AS-SESSMENT CRITERIA LIST, CRITERIA REFINEMENT and TRANSPARENT ASSESSMENT. The teacher is active in creating a learning environment, which supports the development of transversal skills. It is the meta-framework, which is the foundation for student-centered activities in class. Furthermore, the INVISIBLE TEACHER creates a TRUSTED SPACE to support the ACTIVE STUDENT in class. These patterns, where teachers have an active role, are colored orange in the concept map to support visual differentiation. Patterns, in which students get active, are colored pink. They create and own the STUDENT ONLINE PORTFO-LIO and use it to share, present and discuss their learning process and artefacts. It is an important basis to collect feedback given by the teacher, peers and for reflection (which has a self-evaluation function), as well. Patterns, in which both the teacher and the student get active, are colored in an orange-pink mix. Within the LEARNING CONTRACT, pre-defined learning outcomes from the curriculum, which are communicated by the teacher and self-defined learning outcomes from students, are negotiated. Assessment criteria are discussed and agreed on and a PERFORMANCE SHEET helps student in self-assessment, peer feedback and reflection. Yellow-colored patterns are feedback and assessment patterns, which could be used by the teacher and/or students to give feedback. Most of the yellow patterns were originally written for the teacher, but when it comes to peer feedback, they could be helpful for students, too. It would make sense to rephrase these patterns so they are suitable for the students' age and teachers could provide them in a Wiki or in a FAQ list, where the pattern problem is formulated as a question.

6.1. Types of Pattern Relations

In the ATS2020 concept map, relations are symbolized through arrows between patterns. Following relation types can be identified:

» **Pattern predecessor or successor**: The pattern needs another pattern to define its context or the pattern defines the context of the following pattern (Voelter, 2000, p. 3). Therefore, the arrow is pointing into the direction of the pattern it is defining the context of. The following part of the ATS2020 concept map shows this kind of relation:

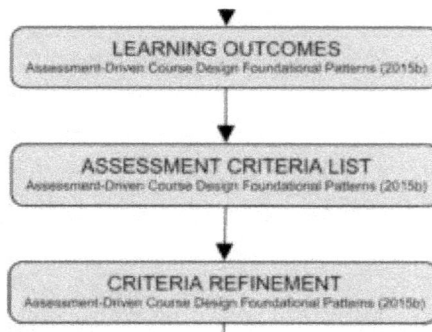

Figure 7: Example of pattern successor.

» **Pattern support**: A pattern can be used to help implementing the current pattern. The following section of the ATS2020 concept map is an example of pattern support, the linking phrase emphasizes the pattern relation type:

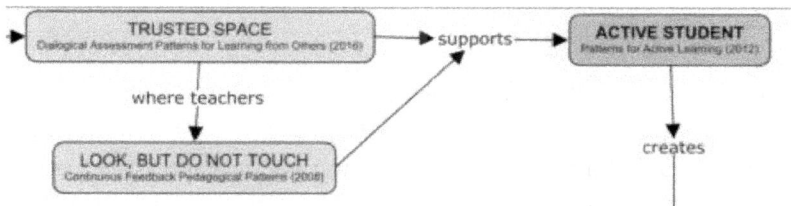

Figure 8: Example of pattern support.

» **Pattern alternative**: The pattern could be alternatively used for another pattern, figure 9 below is an example for this pattern relation, showing an arrow pointing in both directions:

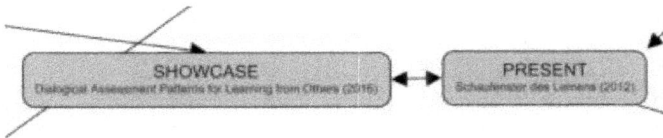

Figure 9: Example for alternative patterns.

Linking phrases like "where teachers", "supports" or "creates" in figure 8 above have the role of facilitating the communication of relations between patterns and to make the pattern collection better understandable. We used one cross reference between STUDENT ONLINE PORTFOLIO and LEARNING CONTRACT, where arrows point in both directions, where not an alternative is symbolized but rather that both patterns are influenced by each other. This understanding is supported by the linking phrase "influenced by" (see figure 6).

7. Making it Handy for Teachers

All in all, we developed following resources to visualize and make accessible patterns matching feedback and assessment within the ATS2020 learning model:

Category overview and matching patterns: The overview helps teachers to find patterns for a specific phase in the ATS2020 learning model. If the teacher wants to know more about the pattern, he/she can search in the full pattern list for it.

Full pattern list: The full list provides pattern references, containing summaries, hyperlinks to the original pattern language and examples how technology could support the activities described in the pattern.

Concept map: The concept map offers an approach different from the category overview. The concept map illustrates relations between patterns and shows how they could be applied in a sequence to facilitate the emergence of good feedback and assessment within the framework of the ATS2020 learning model.

In the full pattern list as well as in the concept map, we provide hyperlinks to the original pattern languages, we are referring to. This way we hope to make it easier for teachers to access relevant literature to apply patterns. We established a WordPress-Website, where the concept map as well as all pattern references and categories are shown: http://imb. donau-uni.ac.at/ats2020patterns/

8. Conclusion and Outlook

Many pedagogical patterns were developed in the last two decades and there is a lot of potential to make use of these patterns for current, complex pedagogical problems. Through a selection process with the help of categories, 36 patterns were chosen to be suitable for supporting feedback and assessment within the ATS2020 learning model. Especially pattern relations are important, as they take full effect of a pattern's meaning. Therefore, through concept-mapping, we created a new structure how these patterns could be understood and used for feedback and assessment in student-centered teaching. Of course, this collection is not finite, but rather a start to build a pattern language, which could be extended by freshly mined patterns as well as other patterns, we have not discovered yet during our pattern search. Cmaps is an online tool for concept maps, which could also be used to work collaboratively. Therefore, there is a great potential to invite others to improve and expand the pattern collection in a meaningful way and with a focus on pattern relations so it can develop into a more sound and coherent pattern language.

Many patterns were written for teachers, but they could be highly useful for students, too. Rewriting existing patterns, so they fit to the vocabulary of students, and providing them in an online school/class Wiki or an online FAQ section could be a handy resource for students in a student-centered teaching and learning environment. Providing this kind of resource could help students to help themselves and therefore in developing autonomous learning skills.

9. References

Alexander, C., Ishikawa, S., & Silverstein, M. (1977). A Pattern Language: Towns, Buildings, Construction. New York: Oxford University Press.

ATS2020. (2017a). ATS2020. Retrieved May 11, 2017, from http://www.ats2020.eu/transversal-skills

ATS2020. (2017b). Classroom Pilot. Retrieved July 26, 2017, from http://ats2020.eu/classroom-pilot

Bauer, R., & Baumgartner, P. (2012). Schaufenster des Lernens. Eine Sammlung von Mustern zur Arbeit mit E-Portfolios. Münster: Waxmann Verlag.

Bergin, J., Eckstein, J., Manns, M. L., & Wallingford, E. (2001). Patterns for Gaining Different Perspectives. In Proceedings of PLoP 2001 (Vol. 2001). Allerton Park, Illinois. Retrieved from http://pedagogicalpatterns.org/current/gaindiffperspective.pdf

Bergin, J., Kohls, C., Köppe, C., Mor, Y., Portier, M., Schümmer, T., & Warburton, S. (2015a). Assessment-Driven Course Design - Fair Play Patterns. In Proceedings of the 22nd Conference on Pattern Languages of Programs (p. 25). The Hillside Group. Retrieved from http://www.hillside.net/plop/2015/papers/panthers/4.pdf

Bergin, J., Kohls, C., Köppe, C., Mor, Y., Portier, M., Schümmer, T., & Warburton, S. (2015b). Assessment-driven Course Design Foundational Patterns. In Proceedings of the 20th European Conference on Pattern Languages of Programs. New York, NY, USA: ACM. https://doi.org/10.1145/2855321.2855353

Comber, O. (2014). Blended Evaluation. In Y. Mor, H. Mellar, S. War, & N. Winters (Eds.), Practical Design Patterns for Teaching and Learning with Technology (pp. 293–300). Rotterdam: Sense Publishers. Retrieved from https://www.sensepublishers.com/media/1937-practical-design-patterns-for-teaching-and-learning-with-technology.pdf

Eckstein, J., Bergin, J., Sharp, H., & Manns, M. L. (2002a). Feedback Patterns. In Proceedings of EuroPLoP 2002. Konstanz: Universitätsverlag Konstanz. Retrieved from http://ai2-s2-pdfs.s3.amazonaws.com/4703/32f0945d95dec9530ee0fbfde36fea51c620.pdf

Eckstein, J., Bergin, J., Sharp, H., & Manns, M. L. (2002b). Patterns for Active Learning. In Proceedings of PloP 2002 (Vol. 2002). Allerton Park, Illinois. Retrieved from http://www.cs.unca.edu/~manns/ActiveLearningV4.doc

Eckstein, J., Manns, M. L., & Voelter, M. (2001). Pedagogical Patterns: Capturing Best Practices in Teaching Object Technology. Software Focus, 2(1), 9–12. https://doi.org/10.1002/swf.19

Elen, J., Clarebout, G., Léonard, R., & Lowyck, J. (2007). Student-Centred and Teacher-Centred Learning Environments: What Students Think. Teaching in Higher Education, 12(1), 105–117. https://doi.org/10.1080/13562510601102339

Ghoneim, A. (n.d.). ATS2020 User Support - Guides for Tools (D. 2.4) - ATS2020. Retrieved February 10, 2017, from http://mahara.ats2020.eu/view/view.php?id=468

Harashima, Y., Kubota, T., & Iba, T. (2014). Creative Education Patterns: Designing for Learning by Creating. In Proceedings of the 19th European Conference on Pattern Languages of Programs. New York, NY, USA: ACM. https://doi.org/10.1145/2721956.2721989

Hattie, J., & Timperley, H. (2007). The Power of Feedback. Review of Educational Research, 77(1), 81–112. https://doi.org/10.3102/003465430298487

Iba, T., Miyake, T., Naruse, M., & Yotsumoto, N. (2009). Learning Patterns: A Pattern Language for Active Learners. In Conference on Pattern Languages of Programs (PLoP). Retrieved from https://hillside.net/plop/2009/papers/People/Learning%20Patterns%20A%20Pattern%20Language%20for%20Active%20Learners.pdf

Iba, T., & Sakamoto, M. (2011). Learning Patterns III: A Pattern Language for Creative Learning. In Proceedings of the 18th Conference on Pattern Languages of Programs (p. 29:1–29:8). New York, NY, USA: ACM. https://doi.org/10.1145/2578903.2579166

IHMC. (2014). Cmap. Retrieved September 5, 2017, from https://cmap.ihmc.us/

Indiana University Bloomington. (n.d.). Learning Outcome Generator. Retrieved September 1, 2017, from https://www.indiana.edu/~oidd/tos/gen2/

Köppe, C. (2015). Towards a Pattern Language for Lecture Design: An Inventory and Categorization of Existing Lecture-Relevant Patterns. In EuroPLoP'13 Proceedings of the 18th European Conference on Pattern Languages of Program. New York, NY, USA: ACM. Retrieved from http://dl.acm.org/citation.cfm?id=2739014

Köppe, C., Inventado, P. S., Scupelli, P., & Van Heesch, U. (2016). Towards Extending Online Pattern Repositories: Supporting the Design Pattern Lifecycle. In Conference Proceedings of the Pattern Languages of Programs (PLoP). New York, USA: ACM. Retrieved from https://hillside.net/plop/2016/papers/four/14.3.pdf

Larson, K. A., Trees, F. P., & Weaver, D. S. (2008). Continuous Feedback Pedagogical Patterns. In PLoP'08 Proceedings of the 15th Conference on Pattern Languages of Programs. New York, NY, USA: ACM. Retrieved from http://hillside.net/plop/2008/papers/PLoP2008_26_Larson+Trees+Weaver.pdf

Magnusson, E. (2006). Pedagogical Patterns – A Method to Capture Best Practices in Teaching and Learning. In 4: e pedagogiska inspirationskonferensen, 2006. Lund: Lunds Tekniska Högskola. Retrieved from http://www.lth.se/fileadmin/lth/genombrottet/konferens2006/PedPatterns.pdf

Mahara. (n.d.). Home - Mahara ePortfolio System. Retrieved September 1, 2017, from https://mahara.org/

Microsoft. (2017). OneNote-Class Notebook. Retrieved September 1, 2017, from https://www.onenote.com/classnotebook

Novak, J., & Cañas, A. (2008). The Theory Underlying Concept Maps and How to Construct Them (No. Technical Report IHMC CmapTools 2006-01 Rev 01-2008). Pensacola, FL: Florida Institute for Human and Machine Cognition. Retrieved from http://cmap.ihmc.us/docs/theory-of-concept-maps#[1]

Rupnik Vec, T., Novak, L., Gros, V., Mikeln, P., Kodric, V., Breznikar, B., … Turk, M. (2015). Eportfolio of a Student. Experiences and Ideas of Slovenian Teachers in International Project European ePortfolio Classrooms (EUfolio). Ljubljana: The National Education Institute Slovenia. Retrieved from http://www.zrss.si/pdf/eportfolio-of-student.pdf

Voelter, M. (2000). OOPSLA 2000 Workshop: Mining Pedagogical Patterns. Minneapolis: ACM Conference on Object-Oriented Programming, Systems, Languages, and Applications 2000. Retrieved from http://voelter.de/data/pub/pppworkshop.pdf

Warburton, S., Bergin, J., Kohls, C., Köppe, C., & Mor, Y. (2016). Dialogical Assessment Patterns for Learning from Others. Presented at the Proceedings of VikingPLoP - 10th Northern Conference on Pattern Languages of Programmes. Retrieved from http://koeppe.nl/publications/Warburton_VikingPLoP16_AssessmentPatterns.pdf

Patterns for Utilizing Patterns towards Dementia-Friendly Communities

Kaneko, Tomoki
Faculty of Environment and Information Studies, Keio University, Japan
tkaneko@sfc.keio.ac.jp

Iba, Takashi
Faculty of Policy Management, Keio University, Japan
iba@sfc.keio.ac.jp

This paper presents a collection of patterns on how to utilize patterns, particularly focusing on people who want to utilize 'Words for a Journey', a pattern language for living well with dementia, towards forming Dementia-Friendly Communities (DFCs). This collection of 12 patterns, called 'Patterns for Utilizing Patterns', was created based on our own practical experiences and experiences collected from 127 people from 42 different prefectures in Japan. These patterns have already been applied in several workshops for people who want to make use of 'Words for a Journey' in their own circumstances. This paper provides an overview of Patterns for Utilizing Patterns and presents the creating process and examples in which these patterns were actually used to support practitioners.

Pattern Language; Pattern Language 3.0; dementia; Words for a Journey, Dementia-Friendly Communities

1. Introduction

Dementia is a worldwide and rapidly increasing syndrome. Approximately 50 million people are currently diagnosed, and there are 10 million new cases every year (World Health Organization, 2017). In Japan, the number of elderly people living with dementia, aged ≥65 years and with mild cognitive impairment is estimated to be 8.46 million, and it is an emerging social issue (Ministry of Health, Labour and Welfare, 2015). In this context, the concept of 'dementia friendly', the collaboration of people for a better life with dementia has been a topic of growing interest in the welfare domain (Alzheimer's Disease International, 2016).

Recently, 'Words for a Journey', a pattern language for living well with dementia, has been used as a tool to promote conversations and actions to realize *Dementia-Friendly Communities (DFCs)* without any specific knowledge or experience related to dementia (Iba et al., 2015a). It is the first time that a pattern language has been applied in the welfare domain. This pattern was formed by interviewing people who are living well with dementia and describes the knowledge of practices to achieve a better quality of life (Iba *et al.*, 2016). The pattern language comprises patterns to be utilized not only by people living with dementia but also by their families and by the society. It also provides media for communication involving NPO staff, volunteers, researchers, caregivers, people working for municipalities and governmental agencies, companies creating new products and services, and even people who do not yet have first-hand experience with dementia (Iba et al., 2015b). By utilizing it, we can generate 'dementia-friendly' ideas. In fact, various *DFCs* are emerging through the use of 'Words for a Journey' in Japan (Kaneko et al., 2016; Iba *et al.*, 2017).

For realizing more *DFCs*, we foresee that it will become necessary to support and increase the number of people who can utilize 'Words for a Journey'. Under this idea, we think that the use of a pattern language (Alexander et al., 1977; Iba, 2016), which aims to share the knowledge of good practice, can support practitioners to make effective use of 'Words for a Journey'. That is why we created 'Patterns for Utilizing Patterns', a collection of patterns on how to utilize patterns, particularly focusing on people who want to utilize 'Words for a Journey' towards forming *DFCs*.

In this paper, we provide an overview of Patterns for Utilizing Patterns and present the creating process and examples of using Patterns for Utilizing Patterns for practitioners.

2. The Motivation for Creating Patterns for Utilizing Patterns

Although in Japan there are many *DFCs*, taking care of people living with dementia is still understood as an 'extra activity for social contribution', such as volunteering. In order to realize true *DFCs*, everyone in society should take the initiative to understand and support the daily lives of people living with dementia and their families (Hayashi, 2017).

In this situation, 'Words for a Journey', a pattern language for living well with dementia, is becoming a topic of growing interest, particularly among those who have medical and welfare backgrounds (Figure 1). By using it, we can focus on how to live well with dementia in everyday life, not on medical aspects or techniques of caregiving. It enables us to imagine actions for living well and stimulates discussion towards DFCs. It has already been proved effective in some cases in Japan, for example at a day-care center for the elderly, at a cafe gathering, in the education of undergraduate nursing students, and in training courses for care staff and hospital staff (Iba *et al.*, 2017; Kaneko *et al.*, 2017).

Figure 1: Book and Cards of 'Words for a Journey'

In order to increase the number of *DFCs*, we need more people who can utilize 'Words for a Journey'. So, far, in many cases, creators of pattern languages or people specialized in facilitation have held workshops to instruct participants in the usage of patterns. Although many people who have never engaged in pattern languages are interested in holding their own workshops and activities using patterns, it has been difficult for them to make effective use of those patterns. A similar thing is happening with 'Words for a Journey'. Therefore, we created Patterns for Utilizing Patterns to clarify how to utilize patterns effectively. This set of patterns contains 12 patterns which were created based on our practical experiences and experiences collected from 127 people in 42 different prefectures in Japan (Figure 2).

Figure 2: 127 Collaborators of Our Research

3. Patterns for Utilizing Patterns

Patterns for Utilizing Patterns contains 12 patterns and comprises four categories: (A) Learn, (B) Mind, (C) Action and (D) Creation. In this section, we introduce the patterns in these four categories.

The first category *(A) Learn comprises Utilization Field Trip, Pioneer Reliance, and Practitioner Role Model* (Table 1). The next category *(B) Mind comprises Lighter Mindset, Dialogue Seeds, and Ongoing Progress* (Table 2). The third category (C) *Action comprises Favorite Start, Nearby Experiment, and Daily Use* (Table 3). The last category *(D) Creation comprises Individual Context, Just a Trigger, and Expanded Plan (Table 4).*

(A) LEARN			
No.	*Pattern Name*	*Pattern Illustration*	**Context, Problem and Solution**
A1	*Utilization Field Trip*		**You want to utilize pattern language. In this context, even if you want to adopt it in your own activity, you are unable to carry out the plan since there are no images of how to put it into practice. Therefore, grasp the image of using pattern language by participating in activities in which it is effectively utilized.**

| A2 | Pioneer Reliance | | *You want to apply pattern language in your own circumstances. In this context, as you start to utilize it, you are not quite able to make the most of it as you imagined.* **Therefore, ask practitioners how they use it and think of how you can adopt it in your own activity.** |
| A3 | Practitioner Role Model | | *You are trying to apply pattern language in your workplace. In this context, you may struggle with using it because you have not yet grasped your most suitable way of utilizing it.* **Therefore, copy some practitioners' utilizing method to grasp a rough sketch of its application.** |

Table 1: Patterns in Category (A) LEARN

(B) MIND			
No.	Pattern Name	Pattern Illustration	**Context, Problem and Solution**
B1	Lighter Mindset		**You want to utilize pattern language. In this context, you think there is a 'right way' to follow, so it becomes difficult to start utilizing it. Therefore, see pattern language as a tool to help resolve your worries and problems.**
B2	Dialogue Seeds		You want to introduce pattern language in your project or activities. In this context, it is difficult to imagine how you can make effective use of patterns and have not utilized the patterns yet. **Therefore, take it easy and try to use the patterns as a communication tool to do something with people living with dementia and their families.**
B3	Ongoing Progress		You want to introduce pattern language in your workplace. In this context, it is difficult to explain the actual effects of patterns to others. **Therefore, it is important to understand that having a dialogue itself is a part of a big change.**

Table 2: Patterns in Category (B) MIND

(C) ACTION			
No.	Pattern Name	Pattern Illustration	**Context, Problem and Solution**
C1	Favorite Start		**You want to make use of pattern language in your own circumstances. In this context, you do not know which pattern to start with. Therefore, start by using patterns, which you are emotionally influenced by.**
C2	Nearby Experiment		You want to introduce pattern language in your project or activities. In this context, you put pressure on yourself by expecting a big change after introducing patterns. Therefore, try to use patterns little by little.
C3	Daily Use		You want to introduce pattern language in your workplace. In this context, it is difficult to make enough time for holding workshops. Therefore, apply the pattern language in the current, daily activities, rather than starting something new.

Table 3: Patterns in Category (C) ACTION

(D) CREATION			
No.	Pattern Name	Pattern Illustration	**Context, Problem and Solution**
D1	Individual Context		**You want to make use of pattern language in your own circumstances. In this context, it is difficult to make effective use of patterns by following a concrete method. Therefore, keep in mind that you can develop a new way of application in your practices.**
D2	Just a Trigger		You want to introduce pattern language in your community. In this context, it is difficult to make a concrete plan for utilizing pattern language. Therefore, plan an opportunity to talk about the application of pattern language in the community, share the ideas with others and start putting them into practice.

D3	Expanded Plan		You want to introduce pattern language in your workplace. In this context, you know how to utilize patterns, but there is no opportunity to utilize them. Therefore, link your project and pattern language so that you can plan something bigger and make the opportunities more influential.

Table 4: Patterns in Category (D) CREATION

4. Creating Process of Patterns for Utilizing Patterns

Patterns for Utilizing Patterns is based on the results of two investigations: interviews for mining patterns for utilizing 'Words for a Journey' and trials for utilizing 'Words for a Journey'. After these two investigations, we started creating a pattern language, organizing the collected data, writing the description of the pattern, and drawing symbolic illustrations (Iba & Isaku, 2016; Shibata *et al.*, 2016). In this section, we introduce the activities and the process of creating Patterns for Utilizing Patterns.

4.1. Two Investigations for Mining Patterns for Utilizing Patterns

First, we conducted interviews. The participants had a variety of occupations, such as caregivers, nurses, doctors, social workers, city official staff, long-term care support specialists, facility managers of nursing homes, facility managers of health and welfare services for the elderly, etc. In these interviews we asked the following questions: 'What was your intended purpose of utilization?', 'How did you use the pattern language?' and 'How do you want to use it in the future?'. Some of the participants had already been successfully utilizing 'Words for a Journey', while others were planning to utilize the language in the near future (Figure 3).

Figure 3: Interviews for Mining Patterns for Utilizing 'Words for a Journey'

Next, we held various workshops and events to explore ways to better utilize 'Words for a Journey'. At the same time, we investigated what kind of problems could occur in utilizing the patterns in various places, such as local cafés, workshops for local residents, workshops in lecture meetings, workshops for university students, etc. (Figure 4).

Figure 4: Trials for utilizing 'Words for a Journey'

From these two investigations, we collected data from our practical experiences and the experiences of 127 people from 42 different prefectures in Japan. In the process, we noticed various needs, such as the want to know a specific way of use, the want to know the correct way of use, the want to know how to use the patterns in dialogues, the want to know how to incorporate the patterns into their own activities, etc.

4.2. Creating Patterns for Utilizing Patterns

After these two investigations, we started organizing the collected data based on the *Jiro Kawakita (KJ) method and classified the clusters into categories* (Kawakita, 1967). From this process, we found that there are four approaches to utilizing 'Words for a Journey': (1) 'How to learn to utilize 'Words for a Journey'', (2) 'How to think about utilizing 'Words for a Journey'', (3) 'How to start utilizing 'Words for a Journey'' and (4) 'How to create a practical place for utilizing 'Words for a Journey''.

Then, we wrote down the pattern description in the following format: *Pattern Name, Context, Problem, and Solution*. We created four categories to correspond to the four approaches and described each pattern. We revised the drafts of the patterns repeatedly, until each pattern reached the expected level of quality. Finally, we polished up the pattern names and illustrations by considering how they would be introduced and how they would be utilized in actual and practical situations (Figure 5).

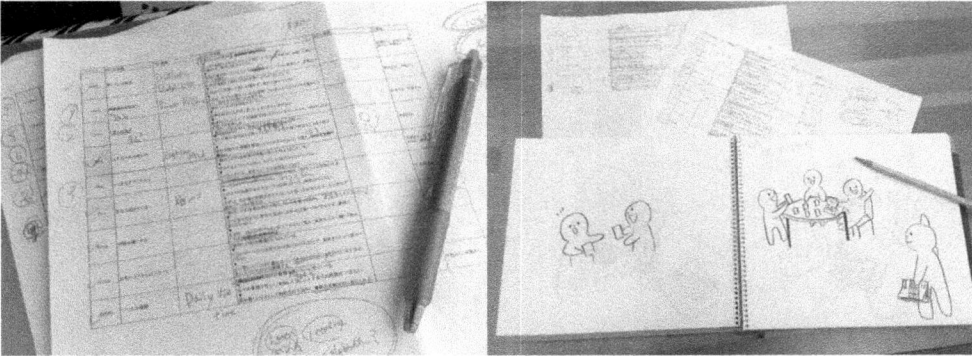

Figure 5: The Writing and Illustrating Process of Creating Patterns for Utilizing Patterns

5. Support by 'Pattern Concierge'

While creating the patterns, we conducted 'Pattern Concierges' for people who wanted to make use of patterns and for those who wanted to maximize the effects of Patterns for Utilizing Patterns. Through this supporting process, we found new patterns and points for correction. In this section, we introduce 'Pattern Concierge' and three cases which we conducted using Patterns for Utilizing Patterns.

'Pattern Concierge' is a consultation activity to help identify a person's needs, introduce appropriate patterns, and promote the application of patterns to realize a better future for that person (Mori *et al.*, 2016). By adopting 'Pattern Concierge', pattern language takes a participatory, bottom-up approach. The dialogue will encourage the participants to think and design their actions proactively with the concierge, rather than passively taking in suggestions in the form of a top-down proposal. The three cases were all conducted with the following three steps.

The first step is *Needs Mining*. The concierge starts by talking about the participants' activities. The concierge then asks the participants what they expect of 'Words for a Journey.' This step helps the concierge to grasp the participants' goals and circumstances. At this point, the concierge does not introduce Patterns for Utilizing Patterns yet, in order to focus on the dialogue about the participants' goals.

The second step is *Pattern Suggestion*. From *Needs Mining*, the concierge suggests Patterns for Utilizing Patterns that may be helpful in the participants' situations. In order to expand the participants' concrete image of 'dementia-friendly' activities, the concierge introduces multiple suitable patterns and examples of their utilizations in other areas.

The third step is *Idea Generation*. Based on *Pattern Suggestion*, the concierge and participants decide what kind of action should be taken and at what kind of place it could be realized. At this point, it is important for the concierge to play the role of a generator, someone who leads and iterates the process of a collaborative inquiry that is motivated by his or her own creative desires, and along the way, involves the people around him or her into the process by enhancing their creative desires (Nagai *et al.*, 2016).

5.1. Case 1: Workshops for Thinking about Caring for People Living with Dementia

In this case, we conducted 'Pattern Concierge' for those who want to utilize patterns for the first time.

We started with *Needs Mining*. Participants told us that they have a *Care Lab Regalo*, a place where care-related people learn from each other. They knew of 'Words for a Journey' and thought to try utilizing it at the *Care Lab Regalo*, but they had no idea how to conduct a conversation with others outside their community using 'Words for a Journey'.

Therefore, at *Pattern Suggestion*, we introduced *Dialogue Seeds*, i.e. to try to use the patterns as a communication tool to participants who are interested in the dialogue. We also presented examples of its utilization in a *Dialogue Workshop*. The workshop provides an opportunity for participants to reflect on their experiences, talk about their experiences with others and make a plan for future actions using the pattern language (Iba, 2015).

Then, at the *Idea Generation* step, participants decided to hold a *Dialogue Workshop* on caring for persons with dementia. However, since there are 40 cards in total in 'Words for a Journey', the participants were unsure which pattern they should start the dialogue with. Therefore, we introduced *Favorite Start*, i.e. to start the dialogue by using patterns which they are emotionally influenced by, in order to think about what kind of workshops we should conduct.

Finally, participants decided to hold a Dialogue Workshop focusing on two memorable patterns from 'Words for a Journey'. One was *Personal Connections*, i.e. to create a connection with an actual person living with dementia and learn necessary information by spending time with them. The other was *Delivering the Voice*, i.e. to help deliver the voice of the people living with dementia and their families to as many other people as possible. Later, a study group was held to gather people who wanted to learn about living well with dementia (Figure 6).

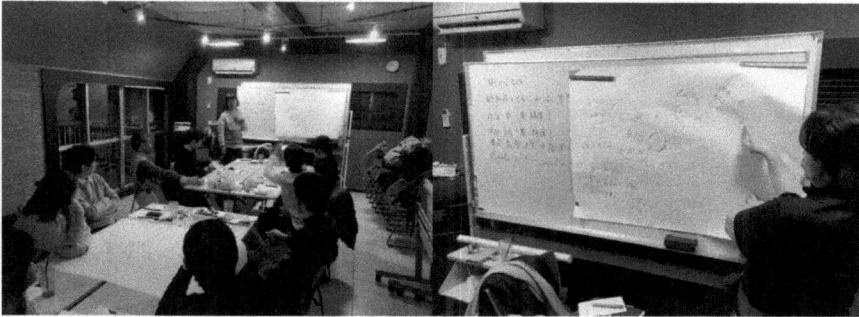

Figure 6: Workshop at Care Lab Regalo

5.2. Case 2: Practice of Individual Patterns–*Can Do List*

This case supports the development of new practices for someone who is already using 'Words for a Journey'.

We started with *Needs Mining*. The participant, who had held workshops in various places, was a great practitioner of 'Words for a Journey'. However, the workshops were difficult to prepare and took place in unusual locations, so this participant wanted to make use of the pattern language in daily-life situations, for example, at their local day-care center for the elderly.

At *Pattern Suggestion*, we introduced *Daily Use*, i.e. to apply the patterns in current, daily activities, rather than starting something new. We introduced cases of Daily Use, which were implemented in other day-care centrescenters for the elderly, where everyone sits in a circle and reads 'Words for a Journey' patterns together.

At the *Idea Generation* step, we talked about *Daily Use*. The participant said, 'I think it would be great to read with everyone. It is nice to speak in the end, but it would also be nice to read something out loud once you pick it up'. Therefore, we decided to hold a workshop to pick patterns form 'Words for a Journey' and talk about them with others. Then, we discussed what would be the appropriate time to practice, and we decided that the morning communication time is best.

In the morning, during communication time, a woman from this day-care center picked *Can do List*, i.e. to make a list of things you can still do now, from the patterns in 'Words for a Journey'. Reading her *Can do list*, she mentioned, 'I forgot to write Kanji! I can't write well', but even then, she felt empowered, realizing that she was holding a pencil after a long time of not writing any letters at all (Figure 7).

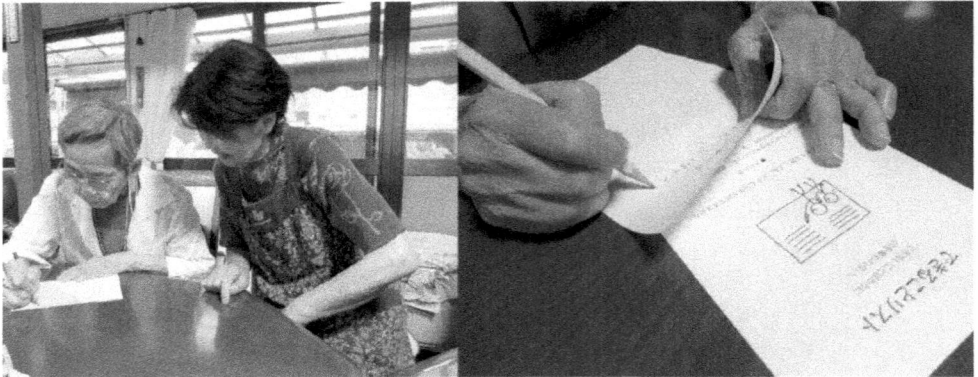

Figure 7: PractisingPracticing Can Do List at a Day-Care Centre for the Elderly

5.3. Case 3: Collaboration with Events–Run Tomo

The third case was an event collaboration with *'Run Tomo*, a long-distance relay event in which people living with dementia hand over a sash one by one across communities in Japan' (Ide, 2016).

We started with *Needs Mining*. The participant was the chairman of *'Run Tomo 2016 Niigata Prefecture'*, and he told us that he wanted to make the event become a trigger for people living with dementia, their families and supporters to think more about life with dementia. The participant wanted to collaborate with us using 'Words for a Journey.'

Therefore, at *Pattern Suggestion*, we introduced *Lighter Mindset*, i.e. to see pattern language as a tool to help resolve your worries and problems and Expanded Plan, i.e. to link your project and 'Words for a Journey'. We also introduced our cases, and after the workshops, we provided 'Words for a Journey' Cards to the participants as souvenirs.

At the *Idea Generation* step, participants planned on using *'Words for a Journey' Cards* to serve as a trigger to think more about life with dementia. As a result, participants decided to present *'Words for a Journey' Cards* to the event runners as a memorial item in *'Run Tomo 2016 Niigata Prefecture'*.

On the day of the event, the *Words for a Journey' Cards* were distributed as a gift to the participants who finished their relay running. Right after the run, dialogues were born among participants. After the event, we also heard that the *Words for a Journey' Card* was placed where the participant could see it every day on his desk (Figure 8).

Figure 8: Collaboration with Events–'Run Tomo 2016 Niigata Prefecture'

6. Conclusion

As dementia becomes a social issue, we foresee that it will become necessary to support and increase the number of people who can utilize 'Words for a Journey', a pattern language for living well with dementia, and realize more *DFCs*. Therefore, we created Patterns for Utilizing Patterns, a collection of patterns on how to utilize patterns. These patterns have already been applied and tested to support those who want to make use of 'Words for a Journey' in their own circumstances. In our research with pattern languages, we have consistently worked in the domain of dementia. However, in the creation process of Patterns for Utilizing Patterns, we noticed that these patterns could support other pattern languages as well. Therefore, the descriptions of the patterns were written in a format that was not exclusively dedicated to 'Words for a Journey'. In the future, we would like to examine how the use of other patterns and pattern languages can be supported, while we continue to improve Patterns for Utilizing Patterns.

7. References

Alexander, C., Ishikawa, S., Silverstein, M., Jacobson, M., Fiksdahl-King, I. & Angel, S. (1977) A pattern language: towns, buildings, construction. Oxford University Press.

Alzheimer's Disease International. (2016), Retrieved December 4, 2017, from Dementia friendly communities: Key principles. https://www.alz.co.uk/adi/pdf/dfc-principles.pdf.

Hayashi, M. (2017). The Dementia Friends initiative–supporting people with dementia and their careers: reflections from Japan. International Journal of Care and Caring, 1(2), 281-287.

Iba, T. (2015) "Pattern Languages as Media for Creative Dialogue: Functional Analysis of Dialogue Workshops," Peter Baumgartner, Richard Sickinger (eds), PURPLSOC: The Workshop 2014, pp.212-231.

Iba, T. (2016) "Pattern Language 3.0 and Fundamental Behavioral Properties", Peter Baumgartner, Tina Gruber-Muecke, Richard Sickinger (eds.), Pursuit of Pattern Languages for Societal Change. Designing Lively Scenarios in Various Fields. Berlin: epubli, pp.200-233.

Iba, T. & Isaku, T. (2016). A pattern language for creating pattern languages: 364 patterns for pattern mining, writing, and symbolizing. 23rd Conference on Pattern Languages of Programs (PLoP2016).

Iba, T., Okada, M., & Dementia Friendly Japan Initiative. (2015a). Words for a Journey: The Art of Being with Dementia. CreativeShift.

Iba, T., Kaneko, T., Kamada, A., Tamaki, N., & Okada, M. (2015b). Words for a Journey: A Pattern Language for Living well with Dementia," in the World Conference on Pursuit of Pattern Languages for Societal Change (PURPLSOC2015).

Iba, T., Matsumoto, A., Kamada, A., Tamaki, N., Kaneko, T., & Okada, M. (2016). A pattern language for living well with dementia: words for a journey. International Journal of Organisational Design and Engineering, 4(1-2), 85-112.

Iba, T., Okada, M., & Kaneko, T. (2017). Words for a Journey: Collaboration Toward Dementia Friendly Society, 32nd International Conference of Alzheimer's Disease International (ADI2017)

Ide, Satoshi. (2016). 'Run Tomorrow' as a Social Activity Got Searching Dementia Friendly Community, 31st International Conference of Alzheimer's Disease International (ADI2016).

Kaneko, T., Yoshikawa, A., & Iba, T. (2016). Dementia Friendly Communities with a Pattern Language for Living Well with Dementia, 2016 International PUARL Conference (PUARL2016)

Kaneko, T., Iba, T., & Okada M. (2017). Realizing Dementia Friendly Communities with "Words for a Journey", poster abstract, 32nd International Conference of Alzheimer's Disease International (ADI2017)

Kawakita, J. (1967). HassouHou [The Abduction Method: For Creativity Development], in Japanese, Chuo-Koron.

Ministry of Health, Labour, & Welfare. (2015). A Comprehensive Strategy for the Promotion of Dementia Measures: Towards a Community Friendly to the Elderly with Dementia (A New Orange Plan). In Japanese

Mori, H., Kimura, N., Ando, S., & Iba, T. (2016). Pattern Concierge: Using Push and Pull Patterns to Help Clients Design Their Future. 23th Pattern Languages of Programs (PLoP2016).

Nagai, M., Isaku, T., Akado, Y., & Iba, T. (2016). Generator Patterns: A Pattern Language for Collaborative Inquiry. 21st European Conference on Pattern Languages of Programs (EuroPLoP2016).

Shibata, S., Sakurako, K., Hitomi, S., & Iba, T. (2016). Pattern Naming Patterns: Symbolizing the content and value by expressions to facilitate intuitive comprehension. 23th Pattern Languages of Programs (PLoP2016).

World Health Organization. (2017). Retrieved December 4, 2017, from Dementia fact sheet N. 362. http://www.who.int/mediacentre/factsheets/fs362/en/. Accessed 2017-11-27

8. Acknowledgements

First, we would like to thank the project members Makoto Okada, Masai Miho and Abe Yuuri. We would also like to express our gratitude to the members of Iba Laboratory Konomi Munakata, Hitomi Shimizu, Marino Kinoshita, Aimi Burgoyne and Ayaka Yoshikawa for their support in drafting this manuscript and "Patterns for Utilizing 'Words for a Journey'" in English as well as Kazuki Toba, Namino Sakama, Ogo Iroha and Wataru Murakami for their great feedback.

Six Investigations for Clarifying Alexander's Properties of Life

Kulikauskas, Andrius Jonas
Self Learners Network
ms@ms.lt

Christopher Alexander's "The Nature of Order" (2002) describes 15 properties of life. How might a scientific community definitively establish them? 1) The Mandelbrot set might serve as a testbed for mathematically defining them. 2) 12 of the properties can be derived from 4 "mind games" as 12 conceptual circumstances. Another 3 properties - Strong Centers, Boundaries and Levels of Scale - can be identified with a learning cycle of taking a stand, following through and reflecting. 3) 12 of the properties can be thought as rules How to create which serve the 12 reasons Why artists create. 4) 24 fundamental behavioral properties of human activity described by Iba, Kimura, Akado & Honda (2016) can be identified with 12 rules How and 12 reasons Why. 5) The 12 circumstances express personal growth as 12 questions for engaging independent thinkers. 6) The 12 circumstances are building blocks in transformations of our self-identity.

The Nature of Order; Christopher Alexander; properties of life; behavioral properties; metaphysics

1. Introduction

Christopher Alexander's four volume "The Nature of Order" (2002a) presents a metaphysical vision by which all of life, in the broadest sense, is brought forth by relentless application of a single fundamental transformation which manifests itself through 15 properties of life. He argues for the reality of these properties by providing evocative examples, especially in architecture, and by discussing how the properties function together. I personally like his vision and value his intuition. I therefore am curious how to define the properties so that they would be metaphysically sound and scientifically usable. What is a property of life? In what sense are there distinct properties of life? How many are there? What is the structure of the complete set of properties? I seek answers which would yield something like a table of physical particles or chemical elements.

For twenty years, Alexander spent two or three hours a day looking at pairs of things and asking himself: Which one has more life? He asked himself further, about the examples which had the most life: What are their common structural, geometric features? He came up with fifteen structural features which are ways that centers help each other in space to come to life. (Alexander, 2002a, 144-145) As centers grow stronger, space grows coherent. The properties are the glue through which space is able to be unified. (Alexander, 2002a, 241) He describes them roughly in the order that he came to notice them: 1. Levels of Scale, 2. Strong Centers, 3. Boundaries, 4.Alternating Repetition, 5.Positive Space, 6.Good Shape, 7.Local Symmetries, 8.Deep Interlock and Ambiguity, 9.Contrast, 10.Gradients, 11.Roughness, 12.Echoes, 13.The Void, 14.Simplicity and Inner Calm, 15. Not-Separateness. Among these, Strong Centers has a kind of logical priority over the others, and Not-Separateness, which is to say, oneness with the world, is perhaps the most significant.

> The number fifteen is only rough. At various stages in the evolution of this theory, I have had a catalog of twelve, fourteen, thirteen, fifteen, sixteen. The precise number is not significant. But I do believe that the order of magnitude of the number is significant. Throughout my efforts to define these properties, it was always clear that there were not five, and not a hundred, but about fifteen of these properties. (Alexander, 2002a, 241-242)

Alexander's vagueness is honest. However, I think the lack of a program for ascertaining a system of definitive properties has kept a scientific community from transcending Alexander's personal intuition.

I propose six investigations to lay a basis for scientific agreement with a rigor characteristic of mathematics, physics and other exact sciences. First, I think that we could show the properties to be mathematically real by exploring an illustrious fractal, the incredibly intricate

Mandelbrot set, as an abstract testbed for defining each property. Second, we could show the properties to be metaphysically sound by collecting evidence for cognitive frameworks from which we might derive the properties as basic to the human mind. Third, we could link how Alexander's properties transform creations with the purposes why creators create. Fourth, we could further appreciate the link between creation and creator by relating Alexander's properties with the properties of lively human behavior that Takashi Iba and his colleagues have been identifying in pattern languages for human activity. (Iba, Kimura, Akado & Honda, 2016) Fifth, we could understand Alexander's properties in terms of personal growth by identifying them with the questions that independent thinkers engage as they grow to become pattern language creators. Sixth, we may consider our own experience of self transformation and identify the properties with the various circumstances which transform our self-identities. These six and other such investigations would allow us to agree as scientists on what we mean by Alexander's properties and in what sense they constitute a complete set. I will sketch out these six investigations and offer some preliminary results.

2. Literature

Alexander believed that the properties of life are more fundamental than the patterns and pattern languages which he is best known for. The software developers in Silicon Valley who embraced his ethos were very sympathetic to his new ideas. But from Amazon Best Sellers Rank (Amazon.com, Inc., 2017) it is clear that "A Pattern Language" (Nr.14,000) and "The Timeless Way of Building" (Nr.49,000) are vastly more popular than "The Nature of Order" Vol.1 (Nr.450,000) and Vol.2, 3 and 4 (Nr.700,000). Only 10% of Helmut Leitner's (2016) recent overview of pattern research is devoted to the properties of life.

Leitner (2016) points out:

> *Every now and then I meet researchers who feel that the list of properties is incomplete or that the descriptions are not perfect. I therefore also suggest the completeness of the set of the 15 properties as an open research question.*

For example, Markus Petz (2017) has remarked about the property of Simplicity and Inner Calm:

> *I struggle with this property, it seems to refer to a minimalist aesthetic and one that is decluttered, yet it does not seem to offer anything that is not already covered with other properties. I wonder if it is also a subjective cultural aspect.*

He is skeptical that we can be assured of the properties, and in any event, believes that we are prone to think of them as disparate elements, whereas they only apply in a spirit of wholeness.

There is a tension in Leitner's (2016) understanding of the fifteen properties. On the one hand, he believes that because they are constitutive of living systems, they are intrinsically positive features which can't be criticized for being what they are. On the other hand, he sees that the properties are not simultaneously present because they partially contradict each other. He argues that each property can function as either a poison or a medicine, depending on the dose. Their positivity depends on their interaction and how the field of centers resolves their contradictions. Leitner proposes a sixteenth property, changeability, which means being continuously in transformation, and which he reads between the lines of Alexander's books.

In general, there is a tension throughout Alexander's work between the ever flawless beauty of nature, glimpses of an even more exuberant life in humans, and the inevitably flawed reality of the typical human environment. Alexander (1979, 290) points out convincingly that if we just listen to our feelings, then we will know the simple truth that a parking garage could never make us feel whole. The same could be said of cars and roads, but then I think also of the timeless squalor of the Lithuanian countryside, where a two room cottage was not charming when it served a dysfunctional family of ten, who tended to spend as little time in it as possible. And how could we ever feel "the quality without a name" on Mars, where we may soon live underground, given Elon Musk's endeavors with rockets, solar power, electric vehicles and tunnel boring equipment. But there is something supremely human in our ability to impose ourselves and improvise a shared world even if it clashes with the existing one. It is curious that Alexander's work has had its greatest impact in areas such as software development where it seems strange to think that "the quality without a name" could ever be truly realized. The expansion of pattern languages to bolster classroom learning, in particular, and institutional learning, in general, seems to me similarly questionable. Is a pattern simply a "best practice"? Does it not have to bring a sense of peace? Alexander (1979, 283) cites the "madhouse balcony" as a "bad" pattern, a contrived idea. Moreover, how can a pattern make us whole, if it entrenches mainstream society, which itself is not whole? But yet there is something authentic about the pattern language community and at least some of its patterns are borne out by experience.

Metaphysically, I think Alexander's most profound insight is the duality of structure and recurring activity which is the basis for patterns: Recurring activity evokes structure, and structure channels activity. (1979, 69) Yet he ended up focusing on structure rather than activity, which is understandable, given that he is an architect. In the first volume of The Nature of Order, he devotes 150 pages to describe his properties structurally (2002a, 143-296) and in the second volume he adds a few pages to describe them dynamically, as the unfolding of wholeness (2002b, 65-79). But he has yet to develop a theory of the properties of recurring activity. Just as zoologists document ethograms for animals, so might anthropologists systematically describe the many thousands of recurring activities in our lives. As Iba (2016) points out with his notion "Pattern Language 3.0", much of the current interest in the pattern language community is focused on human activity.

Kohls and Köppe (2015) considered Alexander's properties of life to be fundamental and investigated how they might appear in various domains either directly or through a domain specific interpretation. Such interpretations may involve rethinking physical space as conceptual space. In particular, they thought through the eight properties of a good lecture: Domain coverage, Effectiveness, Motivation, Inspiration, Excitement, Flow, Economy and Engagement. But none of these translated into a property of life. Instead, each property of life expressed itself in two, three, four or more of these. The exploration helped them identify more properties of a good lecture: Diversity, Contextualization, Social Interaction, Orientation/Big Picture and Curiosity. They felt they came to a better understanding of Alexander's properties, yet their approach does not seem to have made his properties more definitive.

Iba and his colleagues at Keio University have taken a more radical approach by deriving their own set of 24 fundamental behavioral properties based on their experience authoring pattern languages for human activity in a variety of domains. (Iba, Kimura, Akado & Honda, 2016) They distinguish four groups metaphysically:

» Centers intensify themselves with their own energy: 1. BOOTSTRAP, 2. SOURCE, 3. SPREADING, 4.ATTRACTION, 5. INVOLVING, 6. TOGETHERNESS;

» Centers grow by the influence of other centers: 7. BUILDING UP, 8. ORGANIC GROWTH, 9. REFLECTING, 10. ACCOMPANY, 11. ENHANCEMENT, 12. EMPATHY;

» Properties become strengthened when centers are in a complex situation: 13. SELECTION, 14. SIMPLIFICATION, 15. CONSISTENCY, 16. LOOSENESS, 17. FLEXIBILITY, 18. ABUNDANCE;

» Centers intensify with the differences or commonality that centers have: 19. ENDEAVOR, 20. CONNECTING, 21.POSITIONING, 22.DIFFERENTIATING, 23.OVERLAPPING, and 24.CONTINUOUS RELATION.

They seem to me to have considered properties that objectively made the whole more lively whereas Alexander drew subjectively from a personal sense of peace or wholeness. In both cases we are dealing with a wealth of intuition.

However, sometimes intuition takes us only so far. Christopher Alexander (2002a, 238) made a table of the interactions of his fifteen properties, how one property depended on another. His table makes evident that, at least as far as his intuition can lead us, the properties are interdependent, and in particular, none of them are atomic or fundamental, as such. Iba and Sakai (2015) explored his table's interdependencies with various diagrams of their own but didn't draw any definitive conclusions. Alexander himself concluded that his fifteen properties were simply indicators of a deeper spatial structure, a "field of centers". I think his latter concept, if not mystical, is yet prescientific.

Zhyrova, Rychtáriková, Náhlík & Štys (2015) looked for Alexander's properties in the chemical waves of perhaps the simplest lifelike experiment, the Belousov-Zhabotinsky reaction. They showed that many of the properties arise naturally as a consequence of the ageing of a system. They found that in such chemically self-organizing systems, local symmetry, deep interlock, gradients and roughness occured but were mutually exclusive phenomena, with the possible exception that deep interlock and roughness can possibly coexist. The complexity exhibited depends on fortuitous initial conditions, that is, the mixing at the start. Biological systems differ in that they continuously restart themselves. The authors, who appeal to physical phenomena, are critical as to what Alexander means by life.

Can intuition guide us to a metaphysics for a science? In the case of Alexander's properties, Leitner (2016) believes so.

> In addition, I believe the fifteen properties have something to do with our cognitive system. We probably can't describe systems without referring to differences, boundaries, and most of the other properties. So I suggest another favorable interpretation of the 15 properties as categories of form. If this interpretation of his work is accepted by philosophers, then Alexander belongs with Aristotle and Kant to a small group of thinkers who enumerated fundamental categories.

I will present an account of Alexander's fifteen properties similar to what I thought through when I first studied The Nature of Order. (Kulikauskas, 2003) I set apart three of his patterns (Strong Centers, Boundaries, Levels of Scale) from the other twelve. I will relate the latter to twelve pairs of Iba, Kimura, Akado & Honda's (2016) behavioral properties. This will all develop as preliminary results from the six investigations which I now describe.

3. The Mandelbrot Set

The Mandelbrot set is a stupendously intricate subset of the two dimensional plane. (Mandelbrot set, 2017) See Figure 1. Visually, it appears to illustrate all of Alexander's properties of life. This means that scientists can discuss their understanding of the properties in terms of this single abstract mathematical object rather than refer to photographs of examples that may carry layers of personal and cultural connotations. This offers hope that we can be precise as to what we are talking about. Ultimately, we may succeed in formulating mathematically what we mean by each property. This all depends on a shared appreciation of the Mandelbrot set as an undeniably beautiful creation.

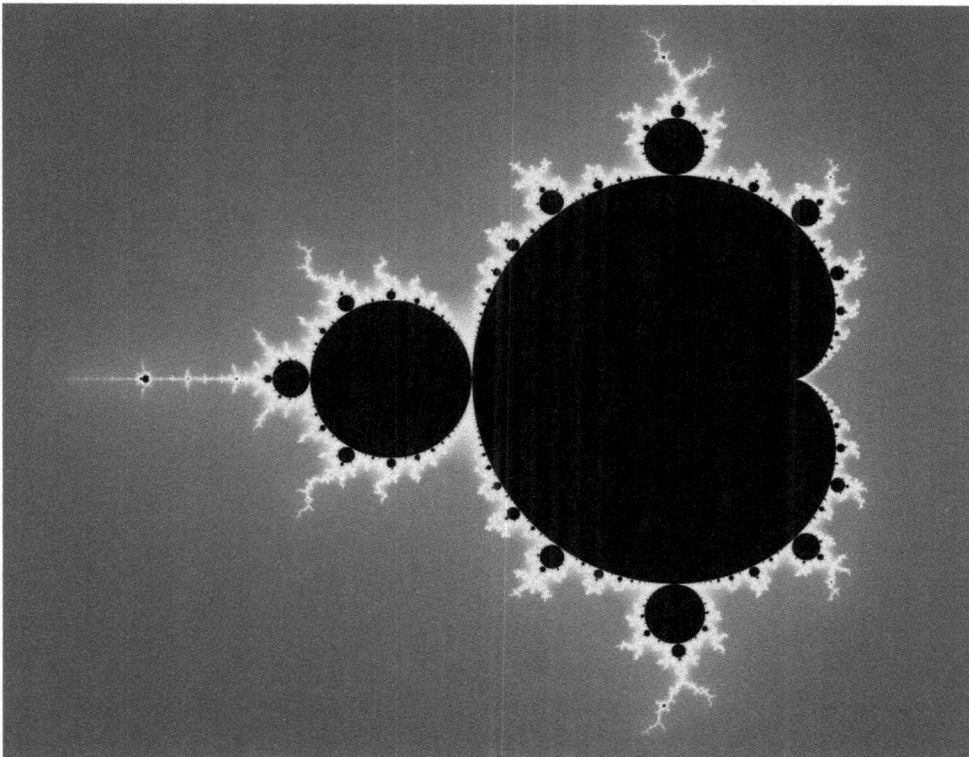

Figure 1: The Mandelbrot Set. (BenardH, Public Domain)

Whether or not a point *(x,y)* belongs to the Mandelbrot set depends on the outcome of a delicate but rather straightforward infinite procedure. This procedure elaborates the distinction between inside and outside which is arguably the most important in all of architecture. Let $c = x+iy$ be the complex number associated with *(x,y)*. Define the function $f(z) = z^2 +$

c. And then consider what happens to the sequence which first applies *f* to *0* and then to each subsequent output: *0, f(0), f(f(0)), f(f(f(0)))*... This yields a sequence of polynomials in c, namely: $0, c, c + c^2, c + c^2 + 2c^3 + c^4$, ... The lowest terms of these polynomials settle down to become the initial terms of the generating function for the Catalan numbers. For a particular c, if this sequence stays within some radius, however large, then *(x,y)* is included within the Mandelbrot set. Otherwise, if there is no such radius, then the sequence wanders off into oblivion and *(x,y)* is not included within the Mandelbrot set. (Flajolet & Sedgewick, 2009)

The sensitivity of this procedure gives rise to a wealth of complex, ever unfolding structures that define the rim of the Mandelbrot set, what is inside and what is outside. Intuitively, repeated squaring z^2 of a complex number z yields an outward spiral when $|z|>1$ and an inward spiral when $|z|<1$. However, the interspersed addition of c keeps "restarting" the system so that a point that was outside may find itself inside, and vice versa. The edge of the Mandelbrot set is that zone where the outcome is very sensitive to minute changes in c.

If we zoom ever deeper into this world, then at different levels of scale we see old and new combinations of Alexander's properties: centers, boundaries, shapes, gradients, echoes, interlock, ambiguity, repetitions, symmetries and voids. A web search for "Mandelbrot set zoom" yields videos that delve more than 100 orders of magnitude, which is to say, manifest the sensitivity of the Mandelbrot set at scales beyond 1 / 1 googol. A scientific discussion needs images and videos in the Public Domain, such as those created by David Madore. (Madore, 2017) It is also important to consider how to handle color, which can be garishly distracting.

A conceptual search for the foundations of Alexander's properties within the Mandelbrot set might explore combinatorial interpretations of the above mentioned polynomials in c. In particular, the kth polynomial counts the number of full binary trees of height less than or equal to k. See sequence A137560 in Sloane (2017). But there are many other interpretations as well, as these polynomials count the same objects, albeit in a different order, as those counted by the Catalan numbers, which are ubiquitous in the combinatorics of trees, parentheses, lattice paths, and other noncommutative structures which ever distinguish a "first" substructure which is placed "inside" parentheses, and the "remaining" structure that is kept "outside" those parentheses. (Catalan number, 2017) These are structures that reflect the duality between vertical embedding and horizontal concatenation, which again develops the theme of inside vs. outside. Such structures may reveal a sense in which Alexander's properties are mathematically real.

4. Conceptual Circumstances

I will next walk through a cognitive investigation which for me serves to define Alexander's properties metaphysically. I will describe four abstract mental activities which I call "mind games" and which we can all undertake for ourselves to arrive at shared definitions of elemental concepts. Each mind game is triggered by one concept and yields three conceptual circumstances that we can imagine. I think of each of Alexander's properties as a circumstance for stillness.

4.1. Mind games

The mind game of constancy goes as follows. Search for constancy. Either you find one example of constancy, or you constantly don't find one, in which case *all* is constantly inconstant. And each time we select and inspect something, we suppose they stay the same, and so they are *multiply* constant. Thus we define "one", "all" and "many" as circumstances. I intuit that, in this sense, Alexander's "good shape" brings out the stillness of a singluar "one", "local symmetry" manifests the stillness we attribute to the expanse of "all", and "positive space" is the stillness inherent in the regularity of "many" in parallel. In the next section, I will describe an investigation that provides more empirical evidence for these claims. But for now I want to note that this mind game offers a definition of what exactly we mean by "one", "all" and "many".

The mind game of directness goes as follows. Our attention can be directed to something else, an *object*, but then can become directed to itself, yielding a process. And a subject is the one whose attention is directed. Thus we define "object", "process" and "subject". I intuit that Alexander's "contrast" brings out the stillness of an object, "echoes" capture the stillness in a process, and "deep interlock and ambiguity" is the stillness inherent in the sensitivity of a subject.

At this point, I will more exactly define the four triggers: significant, constant, direct, true. I take them to negate four levels of knowledge - Why, How, What and Whether - which I can illustrate with a cup. Our senses, and in particular, our sight, tell us What a cup is, the image that it presents to us. A different kind of knowledge is our mental blueprint of How a cup functions, How it is created, utilized and manipulated, and How it changes. We experience What and How directly in our every day life, whereas we likewise conceive of Whether and Why but do not experience them directly. If the cup is in the cupboard, and nobody sees it, we may yet think Whether it is there. And in order to know Why there is a cup in my hand, I would have to know about everything that relates to it, including my hand, myself, and the universe.

We can identify Why with knowledge of everything, How with knowledge of anything, What with knowledge of something, and Whether with knowledge of nothing. Thus they refer to different scopes of knowledge. I define *constant* as the negation of How in that there is no change. I define *direct* as the negation of What in that there is no mediation. I define *significant* as the negation of Why, for Why is the perspective of all encompassing knowledge, but what is significant cannot be encompassed. I define *true* as the negation of Whether, for by Whether we conceive that which can be hidden, but truth is that which is obvious and cannot be hidden. Significant, constant, direct and true express what stillness means in different scopes.

The mind game of *significance* goes as follows. In the spirit of Descartes' "I think, therefore I am": If thinking is significant, then being is significant. Or more precisely, if thinking cannot be encompassed, then likewise the thinker cannot be encompassed, which is to say, being cannot be encompassed. Likewise, if being is significant, then doing is significant. For if being cannot be encompassed, then neither can the actions which characterize it be encompassed. Finally, if doing is significant, then thinking is significant. For if the actions cannot be encompassed, then neither can the thoughts that might potentially reveal them. Thus we define "being", "doing" and "thinking" as circumstances by which we step-into life. I intuit that Alexander's "roughness" manifests being, "gradients" manifest doing and "not separateness" manifests thinking.

The mind game of *truth* goes as follows. We consider the content of a statement and the form which reveals that it is true. They may be one and the same, in which case the statement is necessarily true. This is the case with proofs by contradiction. Or the form which reveals the truth may be distinct from the content which it reveals. This is the case of a statement which is actually true, as when there are grounds for consequences. Finally, what may be true or obvious may be the link between the form and the content, in which case the statement is consistent and thus possibly true. Thus we define "necessary", "actual" and "possible" as circumstances by which we step-out into a rational, logical, peaceful perspective. I intuit that Alexander's "inner calm" reflects necessity, "the void" reflects actuality and "alternating repetition" reflects possibility.

I claim that the four mind games above are understandable and reproducible. If so, then we can appeal to them scientifically to rigorously define twelve metaphysical circumstances: being, doing, thinking; one, all, many; object, process, subject; necessary, actual, possible. These are quite similar to Immanuel Kant's twelve categories from his A Critique of Pure Reason. A key difference is that he thought he could derive his categories from the different ways in which we think about logical form. However, his categories never caught on, presumably because nobody was able to validate his intuition. Whereas I believe that the four mind games are fundamental and reproducible mental activities that are available to us all. In section 5, I will show how we can appeal to them to express Alexander's properties definitively.

4.2. Divisions of everything

I still need to describe how I understand Alexander's three remaining properties: Strong Centers, Boundaries and Levels of Scale. This will also be an opportunity to present my understanding of the wider metaphysical context.

In my own quest to know everything and apply that knowledge usefully, I have looked for a foundation for absolute truth. (Kulikauskas, 2017d) Pragmatically, I mean the knowledge that I can be most certain about. Thus I seek to identify the simplest concepts from which we define all others. Such concepts must define themselves or each other. I have found most fundamental to be the concept of everything, as given by the following four properties:

» Everything has no external context. If you put it in a box, then it includes the box. If you think it, it includes you.

» Everything is the simplest possible algorithm, the one which has no filter but accepts all things, whatever we think of. This means that we all have the same Everything, although we may call it by different names, such as Being, Love, Meaning and so on.

» Everything has no internal structure. It can be chaotic or orderly. Thus, all statements are true about everything, for there is no structure to hold onto: Everything is hot, everything is cold, everything is good, everything is bad.

» Everything is a required concept. We all have it, and appeal to it, for example, when we take a stand, which we do with regard to everything. We could not have learned of Everything, because all that we know is bounded, but Everything is unbounded. We cannot rid ourselves of it as a concept. It must have always been with us.

In considering the limits of my imagination, I have further observed cognitive frameworks which characterize my thinking on various issues. For example, in thinking about existence, I always need two points of view. I need to be able to ask, Does this chair exist? In which case opposites coexist: maybe it does and maybe not. But I also need to allow for an answer, If it does, then it does. And if not, then not. Thus issues of existence give rise to a division of everything into two points of view: "opposites coexist" and "it is all the same".

It is possible to collect examples where there are these two perspectives. Note that in each case the mind slides easily from "opposites coexist" to "it is all the same" but not the other way around.

» Free will and fate. Such classic, intractable debates are important evidence for the reality of cognitive frameworks. The point is that our mind needs both perspectives.

» Outside and inside. If there is an outside of a cup, then there is also an inside. But if I fall inside the cup - if it becomes my universe - then there is only an inside.

» Theory and practice. In theory, I am detached from what I am studying, as if it were a machine that is turned off. But in practice, the machine is turned on, I am one with my experience, like a carrot going through a mill. We complement each other and are one.

» Same and different. If two cups are the same, then they must also be different. But if they are different, then they are just different. Here it is remarkable that the concept of same-ness actually involves opposites coexisting, whereas the concept of difference means that it is all the same. This illustrates the pitfalls of introspection because adding a layer of reflection typically reverses the direction in which our minds move.

In my experience, these four examples are canonical. I think they accord with the four vantage points Why, How, What and Whether.

There is another cognitive framework for issues of participation. It is a learning cycle of three perspectives: taking a stand, following through, and reflecting, ready to take a stand once again. This cycle is familiar as the scientific method of asserting a hypothesis, conducting an experiment, and reviewing the results. I think these same three perspectives distinguish Alexander's three properties Strong Centers, Boundaries and Levels of Scale.

Recurring activity is essential for Alexander's theory. The learning cycle is our activity that we live and experience, the cycle that propels our soul. Within that cycle, and perfected by it, we exhibit a perfect stillness which may be deep within us or may be far beyond us. I believe that this stillness is what defines a center as such. For example, the center of the earth is the point to which it gravitates, but alternatively, the axis along which it rotates. Stillness is an invariant, and thus a sign of a metalevel higher than our own.

As invariants, centers stand out from the activity around them. And that activity distinguish-es the centers from each other. The conflicting activity inevitably is separated by a boundary of stillness, like the line which separates traffic on the right and left sides of a road, or the riv-er bank which separates the river from the land. There is likewise a stillness, albeit as thin as possible, which keeps level and metalevel distinct. Thus, from these three perspectives, we can imagine that centers are strengthened by taking a stand, boundaries reveal the extent of following through, and levels of scale arise by reflecting upon a level from a metalevel.

I thus associate Alexander's three properties Strong Centers, Boundaries and Levels of Scale with the division of everything into three perspectives of taking a stand, following through and reflecting. His other twelve properties arise from four representations of this threesome, which is to say, the four mind games.

The four levels of knowledge - Why, How, What, Whether - may likewise be thought of as a division of everything into four perspectives for the sake of addressing issues of knowledge. This foursome has two representations. Idealists prefer to consider them as questions from the perspective of the observer: Why? How? What? Whether? and they often ignore Whether? as unimportant. Materialists prefer to think in terms of answers from the perspective of the observed: Why! How! What! Whether! and they often ignore Why! as unreal.

I think Alexander's patterns work on all four levels as recurring activity, structural solutions, competing forces and optimized preferences.

» There are eddies of stillness within recurring activity. No matter how immersed we are in life, we have a speck of stillness from our metalevel. Significance is this narrowest form of stillness, the stillness of nothing.

» A structure has a core of stillness. Constancy is this stillness of something.

» A rule of thumb resolves forces in a web of stillness. Directness is this stillness of anything.

» We apply a pattern exactly by stepping out, gauging our sense of peace, and optimizing our preferences. Truth is the stillness of everything in the decree of a creator.

Without going too far into speculative metaphysics, I conclude this foray with my main point, which is that Alexander's three properties Strong Centers, Boundaries and Levels of Scale should be considered more fundamental than his other twelve, which I argue are derivative. Also, the cognitive frameworks strongly suggest that Alexander's fifteen properties are systematic and form a complete set.

WHERE IS THE CENTER? STILLNESS? PURPOSE?
WHAT IS THE RULE WE SHOULD FOLLOW?

	Take a Stand CENTERS Indicate the metalevel	Follow Through BOUNDARIES Partition the level	Reflect LEVELS OF SCALE Separate level & metalevel
Significant	Being Be who you truly are Create roughly	Doing Live as a tool of art Vary continuously GRADIENTS	Thinking Master a conceptual language Respect relationships NOT SEPARATENESS
Constant	One Immortalize in a work of art Make a good shape	All Transform the world Tile symetrically LOCAL SYMMETRIES	Many Inspire creativity Divide space positively
Direct	Object Bring out what is unnoticed Contrast	Process Lose yourself in the joy of creating Echo	Subject Foster sensitivity to feelings Interweave ambiguity DEEP INTERLOCK AND AMBIGUITY
True	Necessity Get into your role Simplify - Settle down INNER CALM	Actuality Present reality Free a path THE VOID	Possibility Open up possibilities Alternate ALTERNATING REPETITION

Figure 2: 12 Conceptual Circumstances, 12 Reasons Why to Create Art, 12 Rules How to Create Art (Alexander's properties)

5. Purposes of Creative Activity

An empirical study of artistic purpose can clarify the link between the twelve circumstances and Alexander's properties. Robert Genn (2014) collected roughly 100 quotes about the purpose of art. In sorting these quotes, I came up with 12 groups, each of which seems to locate the purpose of art in one of the 12 circumstances. (Kulikauskas, 2014b) In each case, one of Alexander's properties suggests itself as a rule How to create art, given that purpose Why. I will give a sense of how such quotes can be used as empirical data by quoting liberally from Genn's collection. They are not simply opinions, but summarize various artists' profound personal experience, which might likewise be studied.

5.1. Stepped in

The artist may be immersed in life. They may find their purpose in being - being who they truly are, doing - living as a tool of art, and thinking - mastering a conceptual language.

Be: Be who you truly are. Alexander's *roughness* suggests that we create *roughly* in paying attention to what matters more, focusing on what is essential, thus being free to allow details to vary as needed. As McNiff says, being uncensored.

» Erich Fromm: Man's main task in life is to give birth to himself, to become what he potentially is. The most important product of his effort is his own personality.

» Shaun McNiff: Art is an articulator of the soul's uncensored purpose and deepest will

Do: Live as a tool of art. *Gradients* have us vary *continuosly* as we stay true to ourselves under changing conditions.

» Carl Gustav Jung: The artist is not a person endowed with free will who seeks his own ends, but one who allows art to realize its purpose within him.

» Andrew Wyeth: My aim is not to exhibit craft, but rather to submerge it, and make it rightfully the handmaiden of beauty, power and emotional content.

» Pablo Picasso: I go for a walk in the forest of Fontainebleau. I get ‚green' indigestion. I must get rid of this sensation into a picture. Green rules it. A painter paints to unload himself of feelings and visions.

Think: Master a conceptual language. *Not-separateness has us respect relationships.* But this requires that we master a language that makes sense of existing relationships and can contribute to them. Thinking connects the metalevel with the level.

» François Delsarte: The object of art is to crystalize emotion into thought, and then fix it in form.

» Robert McBryde: The painter's function, generally speaking, is to explore and demonstrate in his work the interdependency of forms.

5.2. Looking out

The artist may look out for an ideal causality that immortalizes one, transforms all and inspires many.

One: Immortalize in a work of art. Alexander teaches us to *make a good shape*. Such a shape is self-sufficient, distinct and complete, characterized by internal symmetries. This serves us when we seek to create a masterpiece or write the Great American Novel.

» Henry Miller: The purpose of life is to remember.

All: Transform the world. The alternative is to create empty space, which is to say, *create local symmetries, typically by tiling symmetrically.* Artists who seek to transform the world are often critical of it.

» Anish Kapoor: We live in a fractured world. I've always seen it as my role as an artist to attempt to make wholeness.

» Ron Gang: The aim behind critical art is to improve life, by pointing out that which is in need of repair or renovation. By the same criteria, landscape and other ‚beautiful' art is legitimate, as it also comes to improve the world... by elevating the spirits of those who behold it.

» Roger Scruton: Through the pursuit of beauty we shape the world as a home, and in doing so we both amplify our joys and find consolation for our sorrows.

Many: Inspire creativity. The creation of works within space requires a respect that has us *divide space positively*. Our creativity fosters a culture where we coexist as creators and inspire others to create as well.

» Mark Twain: My job is to comfort the afflicted and afflict the comfortable.

» Bob Dylan: Art is the perpetual motion of illusion. The highest purpose of art is to inspire. What else can you do? What else can you do for any one but inspire them?

5.3. Looking in

The artist may look down upon the existing world as a canvas in which they absorb themselves. Their purpose may be in bringing out an object, in losing themselves in the process, or in themselves growing sensitive as a subject.

Object: Bring out what is unnoticed. This is done through *contrast*. As Alexander notes, it must not be accidental, but must serve to bring out a center, for example, by framing it. The artist chooses what to frame.

» Tom Robbins: It is the function of the artist to call attention to what life does not.

» Norman Rockwell: Without thinking too much about it in specific terms, I was showing the America I knew and observed to others who might not have noticed. My fundamental purpose is to interpret the typical American. I am a story teller.

Process: Lose yourself in the joy of creating. If the artist is doing what they like, then their work will naturally *echo* with the angles, motifs and forms of that activity.

» Harley Brown: If art takes up much of the artist's time, then it makes sense that she/he be ‚lost' in the euphoria of creating. Isn't that one of our ultimate purposes in life?

Subject: Foster sensitivity to feelings. If our purpose is to grow sensitive, then we will *interweave ambiguity, creating deep interlock and ambiguity*. As a subject, we will engage and disengage, alternatively, linking level and metalevel.

» Max Stern: The artist has still an important task in depicting a landscape and rendering it for us with his much more sensitive eye which can concentrate on essentials and give the atmosphere of a city much better than a mechanical camera could ever do.

5.4. Stepped out

Ultimately and regularly, the artist who creates healthy art must discover a sense of peace from which they can rationally, logically, freely choose, not swayed by the biases of their self and their emotions. Then they perceive a perfect duality between life and the love that supports it, what is and what is not but makes room for it, what they unconsciously know and what they consciously don't know. Their purpose may be in the necessity of their role, the actuality of reality, or the possibility of something entirely new.

Necessity: Get into your role. The quote by Flowers suggests that it is an acceptance of one's function that lets us *simplify - settle down*, and thereby yield *simplicity and inner calm*.

» Walter Lippmann: Only the consciousness of a purpose that is mightier than any man and worthy of all men can fortify and inspirit and compose the souls of men.

» Betty Sue Flowers: When you see what you're here for, the world begins to mirror your purpose in a magical way. It's almost as if you suddenly find yourself on a stage in a play that was written expressly for you.

Actuality: Present reality. Alexander writes of *the* void as the infinite depth that is at the heart of perfect wholeness. But a study of the artist quotes suggests that the void arises when we *free a path* for the sake of presenting reality. We can't present reality without an open view.

» Henri Bergson: Art has no other purpose than to brush aside... the conventional and accepted generalities, in short everything that veils reality from us, in order to bring us face to face with reality itself.

» Max Scheler: The purpose of art is... to press forward into the whole of the external world and the soul, to see and communicate those objective realities within it which rule and convention have hitherto concealed.

Possibility: Open up possibilities. When the purpose of art is in possibility, then it must be free to exist or not, alternatingly. Thus the *alternating repetition* of being and not being is truly free, propelling itself forward, like an oscillating light wave or sound wave. Whereas mechanical repetition simply imposes the interchanging of one piece with another. The rule which opens up possibility is to *alternate the extremes of being and nonbeing*.

» Peter Schmidt: One of the functions of art is to offer a more desirable reality - a model, as it were, of another style of existence with its own pace and its own cultural reference.

» Yaacov Agam: My aim is to show the visible as possibility in a state of perpetual becoming.

5.5. Reasons Why and Rules How

Artists evidently locate their purpose in absolutely every one of the twelve circumstances which the four mind games define. Their reasons Why to create pair nicely with Alexander's properties in that the latter serve as rules How to create. I have shown that we can investigate this connection by analyzing human experience as empirical data. We can validate, clarify or challenge Alexander's intuition, for example, discovering that *the void* might be better understood as *open access*, for the latter is what is needed to present reality, which is the purpose in actuality.

We can also think about the overall creative process as relating our reason Why - the cause outside a system, and our rule How - the cause within a system. Imagine an artist who is immersed in the world - being, doing, thinking - but then, perhaps moved by emotional discord - goes beyond herself. From her world, she looks out beyond it for an ideal rule or shape. Then, beyond her world, she looks back upon it as a canvas for her to frame. Ultimately, she is beyond the world, free of herself, her feelings and her prejudices, in a sense of peace, able to identify her reason Why with wholeness in its broadest sense. She can then create healthy art, apply patterns from a sense of peace, and go back into the world to implement them with Alexander's properties as rules to guide her how.

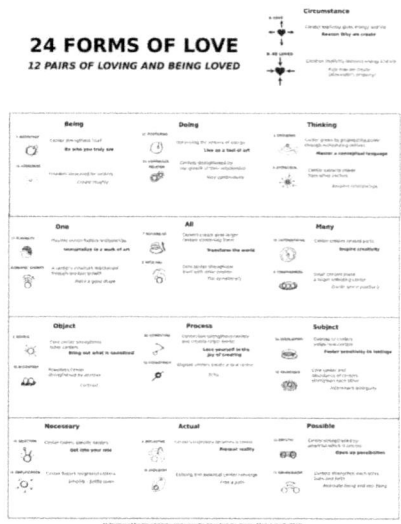

Figure 3: 12 Circumstances, 12 Pairs of Fundamental Behavioral Properties, 12 Reasons Why to Create Art, 12 Rules How to Create Art (Alexander's properties)

6. Fundamental Behavioral Properties

Alexander's theory unites activity and structure. His idea that "structure channels activity" explains How life is created by applying the properties of life as structural rules. His idea that "recurring activity evokes structure" suggests Why life is created. But this latter idea is left undeveloped. Alexander's theory seems half complete. He speaks concretely about creations, but rather mystically about us as creators.

Takashi Iba addresses this in applying Alexander's theory to human activity. Most notably, Iba, Kimura, Akado and Honda (2016) document 24 fundamental behavioral properties of wholeness in "lively" human activity. It might seem doubtful whether others could understand, validate and confirm their properties as stated. But if our imagination is as limited as I believe, then we may have a chance. Furthermore, the centers of human activity are taken to be individuals and groups, and so we can identify with them more personally than with Alexander's centers, and intuit them with more confidence, both subjectively as creators and objectively as creations.

The pairing of reasons Why and rules How developed in the preceding section seems very fruitful here. In Figure 3, I show how I have paired the 24 fundamental behavioral properties. I use numbered pictures of the properties from Iba et al's paper and add my own brief descriptions based on their summary explanations.

Some pairs are very straightforward. A center may give energy to create related parts (22. Differentiating) or it may receive energy from smaller centers it unfolds (6. Togetherness). A center may grow stronger by propagating its power through surrounding centers (3. Spreading) or by extracting power from other centers (4. Attraction). A center can be created by centers it contains (7. Building up) and as the core center it may strengthen itself with other centers (8. Involving). A core center may strengthen other centers (2. Source) and a powerless center may be strengthened by another (10. Accompany).

Such pairs reveal a trend whereby a center may grow stronger by giving energy for life, but may also by taking energy for life. These two perspectives are loving and being loved. By love I mean the support of life. Thus the 24 properties may be thought of as forms of love - of loving oneself, others or all. In Figure 3, I have interpreted 12 of them as forms of explicitly, purposefully, actively loving and 12 of them as forms of implicitly, passively being loved, and taking it for granted. I identify the latter with Alexander's structural properties, which do not have us go beyond ourselves, but rather have us identify with the whole, and may be thought of as 12 forms of peace.

More pairs suggest themselves. A center can strengthen itself (1. Bootstrap) and the resulting freedom can let centers do so likewise. (16. Looseness). This pair brings to mind the reason Why of "being who you truly are" and the rule How of "create roughly". A flexible center fosters relationships (17. Flexibility) and gradual growth maintains a center's structure (8. Organic Growth). The latter brings to mind Alexander's "good shape". A center can receive energy and explicitly give it back (12. Empathy) or it can simply participate in such exchanges as a matter of course (11. Enhancement). This brings to mind "alternating repetition".

I have worked out Figure 3 to satisfy myself that this type of investigation is fruitful. Surely I may not understand these fundamental behavioral properties as intended. My preliminary points are that it makes sense for them to come in pairs, and for those pairs to relate to the reasons Why and rules How discussed earlier.

7. Questions for Independent Thinkers

Another investigation which may yield worthwhile ideas considers 12 questions for engaging independent thinkers. (Kulikauskas, 2017b) From 1998 to 2010, I led Minciu Sodas, an online laboratory to serve and organize independent thinkers around the world. In 2010, Wael al Saad encouraged me to document a pattern language for our remarkable culture. I realized that the best way to get it across was through the questions that I found myself asking participants. These questions reflect our growth as independent thinkers and also what we need to know about each other in order to work together. Thus they may also help us characterize ideal human activity, but especially that which we can pursue by ourselves, and by which we create ourselves.

In conversing with thousands of independent thinkers, I would often first ask them what they cared about, and whether they cared about thinking. Everybody thinks, but independent thinking starts when people collect their thoughts which they'd like to return to. A few such thoughts per day leads to thousands of ideas. Thinkers develop values as they decide what's most important. They learn how to integrate clashing values. Ultimately, they are able to answer, What is their deepest value in life, which includes all of their other values? I collected answers from about 700 people and they were all different! Once people know themselves, they become interested in questions that they don't know the answer to, but wish to answer. Growing as investigators, they wish others to grow likewise, and foster a community and shared culture. But challenging others can be selfish, and so it becomes relevant to contemplate a higher point of view, such as God's, from which we can check ourselves. (Kulikauskas, 2014a)

The 12 questions helped participants to define themselves in terms of their values, investigations and endeavors, which meant that we could understand and support each other. They also helped to interact on a "first things first" basis. It's rather questionable to learn from each other or try to help each other if we don't know or care about each other's values.

I suppose that the 12 questions may express what we care about in terms of the 12 circumstances, organized as follows:

» Caring about Being: What is your deepest value, which includes all of your other values?

» Caring about Doing: What do you care about?

» Caring about Thinking: Do you care about thinking?

» Caring about One: What is a question that you don't know the answer to, but wish to answer?

» Caring about All: Where and how do you think best?

» Caring about Many: Would you think out loud?

» Caring about Object: What would you like to achieve?

» Caring about Process: How can we help each other?

» Caring about Subject: What is your dream in life?

» Caring about Necessity: What do you know?

» Caring about Actuality: What would you teach God?

» Caring about Possibility: What lessons would you teach?

All of these 12 questions were an important part of Minciu Sodas's culture, but I formulated a list of such questions only at the very end. Also, I have recently realized that my original question, What do you know of God? should rather be, What would you teach God? which is to say, what kind of testimony would you give? It's interesting that the final question could be phrased as What pattern language would you write? Perhaps what these 12 questions reveal is our own personal reasons Why - what we ourselves care about - rather than, say, God's reasons Why, or other reasons Why, that we might perceive. They also seem to link our own personal growth with our fostering of a shared culture.

8. Transformations of Self-Identity

Alexander ultimately concludes that there is a single fundamental transformation underlying all of life. I think that our own personal growth may offer the most intuition as to how such a transformation proceeds. In particular, we may study episodes in life where our own self-identity changed.

I led such a workshop and preliminary results suggest that there are 12 building blocks for transformations of our self-identity. (Kulikauskas et al., 2017)(Kulikauskas, 2017a)(Kulikauskas, 2017c) We shared 24 examples of how our self-identity had changed. The complexity of the examples grew quite overwhelming. For example: "From the behavior of others it became clear what I did not want to be like." "I faced my inability to get myself to behave as I thought I should." "In another land I realized that my own life seems strange to others."

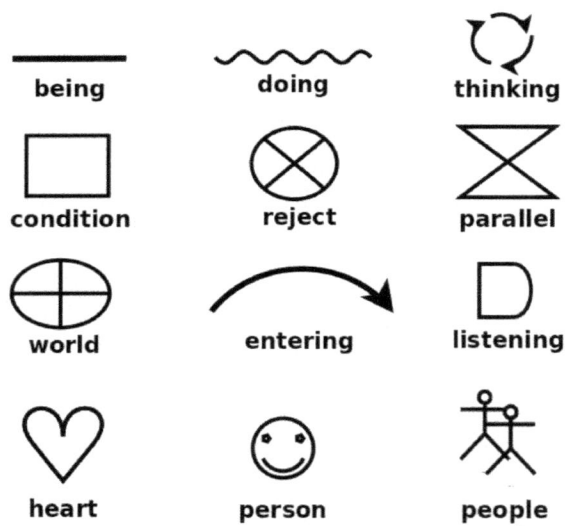

being	doing	thinking
condition	reject	parallel
world	entering	listening
heart	person	people

Figure 4: 12 Elemental Transformations of Self-Identity

But then we tried to express the examples with improvised hieroglyphics. This yielded the following graphic alphabet of 12 building blocks, as illustrated in Figure 4. I now interpret them as follows:

» A sense of being (as in another land)

» A sense of doing (as with peers)

» A sense of thinking (say, learning about myself)

» A sense of one - accepting conditionally.

» A sense of all - rejecting entirely.

» A sense of many - allowing for parallel possibilities.

» A sense of object - accepting one's own world as objective.

» A sense of process - entering a new world.

» A sense of subject - listening.

» A sense of necessity - the testimony of one's own heart.

» A sense of actuality - the testimony of a single person.

» A sense of possibility - the testimony of "people".

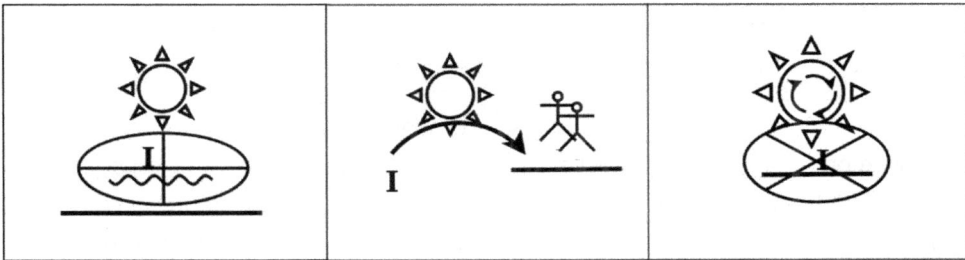

Figure 5: 3 Example "Sentences" from a Grammar of Self-Identity

Thus we may variously identify with the 12 circumstances. It is interesting by what grammar they may yield transformations of our self-identity. See Figure 5 for some sample expressions. This type of investigation of transformative episodes in our lives seems easy to do, fruitful and meaningful. It may turn out that similar transformations integrate Alexander's properties of life to yield patterns and pattern languages.

9. Discussion

The major problem with Alexander's properties is What do we mean? What exactly is a "center" and in what sense is it "strong"? What about a "boundary" is a boundary or do we actually mean something else? In general, how do we define the most primitive concepts? And then how do we refer to them? And relate them to empirical findings?

The six investigations proposed are tentative but preliminary results suggest they would be fruitful and already there is a lot to think about. Christopher Alexander has shared intuition acquired over a lifetime. How can that intuition be the basis for a scientific community? With "The Nature of Order" he has dramatically extended the implications of the ideas he presented in "The Timeless Way of Building". But still there needs to be a shared understanding as to what we mean. Alexander's properties need to be operative if they are to foster collaboration.

On the one hand, for such a science of spirit, there needs to be metaphysical research into what are the concepts that we can define as primitives and are thus available to us for expressing other concepts? Such concepts must not be words or depend on words but rather must be grounded in preverbal mental activity. Such activity includes the exploration of the conceptual limits of our imagination, the cognitive frameworks which our mind avails us, which I take to be the most pragmatic ground for absolute truths. On the other hand, we need lots of different kinds of real life experience that we want to make sense of. The most central experiences, which we might most subtly interpret, are our own experiences of personal growth and self transformation. The six investigations seek to clarify Alexander's properties conceptually and also validate them empirically.

A major theme which arises is the distinction of Why vs. How. We can think of Why as the reason or cause from outside of a system, and How as the reason or cause within a system. This distinction between outside and inside is fundamental for architecture. The combinatorial objects which are counted by the Catalan numbers, and which define the Mandelbrot set, distinguish syntactically between embedding systems vertically, within each other, as with a hierarchy, and concatenating systems horizontally, one after another, as in a sequence. This is the difference between everything's properties of having no external context, hierarchically, and its accepting all things, sequentially. It is the difference between creator and creation; between actively, explicitly loving and passively, implicitly being loved; between God beyond a system and good within a system; between God beyond conditions and a godling like us within them.

It is also the distinction between metalevel and level. What relates them is stillness that we can infer but never sense, for we only sense perturbations. Stillness is never of this world, but must be from beyond it, and we likewise, in that we can recognize it.

I think that stillness or blankness or blackness or emptiness or defaultness may be thought of as Alexander's rather mystical "field of centers". Metaphysically, or rather, cognitively, in my account, we conceive of stillness in a scope: nothing, something, anything or everything.

» Significance is the stillness of nothing. It negates the knowledge of everything, which is Why.

» Constancy is the stillness of something. It negates the knowledge of anything, which is How.

» Directness is the stillness of anything. It negates the knowledge of something, which is What.

» Truth is the stillness of everything. It negates the knowledge of nothing, which is Whether.

What this means for me is that stillness transcends the various divisions which are needed for knowledge.

The different scopes make it possible to think about the relative strength of centers. Imagine two points on a page. If you consider the page a closed system, then the center between the points will be in the plane of the page. But if you consider yourself part of the system, if you admit of an outer vantage point, then the system shifts so that now the center is out of the page. And the more it pops out of the page, the broader its scope, and the more life it has. We have to think of how to connect the system with that which is beyond it. In art, ideas like major color, minor color and accent assume that there is a viewer, that the art is not onto itself.

In my exploration of our mental activities and our cognitive limitations, I have found that Alexander's 15 properties are not accidental. His intuition and his ability to communicate it are truly remarkable. There is no room for a sixteenth property. Indeed, it can be said that there are actually 12 properties. They accord with the twelve circumstances that arise from the four mind games triggered by significant, constant, direct and true.

The remaining three of Alexander's properties are more basic - Strong Centers, Boundaries, and Levels of Scale. Like stillness itself, they have no scope. They are not within the world but beyond it. We conceive of them through the other 12 properties. But what exactly do they mean? There is a cognitive framework with three perspectives for issues of participation: We take a stand, follow through, and reflect. Four representations of this threesome account for Alexander's other twelve properties. It would make sense that the strength of centers is the stillness of taking a stand, boundaries are the stillness of following through, and levels of scales are the stillness of reflecting. It remains to interpret what exactly that could mean. In particular, what is the stillness in the boundary? Is it the periodicity of recurring activity?

The circularity of taking a stand, following through, and reflecting may very well be what Alexander is looking for when he explains the essence of centers: "Centers are always made of other centers."

> So there is a fundamental circularity which we cannot escape. This circularity is not a mistake, or an indication of something logically vicious in the argument. On the contrary, it is the essential feature of the situation. Our understanding of both wholeness and life will come into focus just at that moment when we thoroughly grasp this circularity and what it means. (Alexander, 2002a, 118)

An investigation of the purposes Why artists create yields lots of insight on how Alexander's other 12 properties function as rules How to create. Each rule manifests a purpose. This prompts us to define Alexander's properties actively. Most consequentially, it seems that given the purpose of presenting reality, the property of The Void can be understood as clearing a view onto that reality. Local symmetries are I think better understood as the elucidation of empty space by tiling symmetrically. Gradients have us vary continuously by being ourselves in changing conditions. Positive Space has us divide space positively. Not-separateness is about respecting relationships. Deep Interlock and Ambiguity have us interweave ambiguity. Alternating repetition means that we should alternate the extremes of being and not being, so that they flow out of each other freely.

All of these investigations, like Alexander's own work, are quite tenuous. Investigating from different points of view helps to clarify how things are. I first tried to identify Alexander's properties with the 12 circumstances in 2003. But in 2014, when I studied the purposes of art, I realized that I should reassign 4 of the circumstances for I had mistakenly related being with Not-Separateness, thinking with Roughness, actuality with Alternating Repetition, and possibility with The Void.

I was very doubtful that Iba, Kimura, Akado & Honda's fundamental behavioral properties could be too meaningful. I know now that I was very wrong. It's truly remarkable that their 24 properties of lively human activity, taken in pairs, could express the 12 purposes for creating art and also 12 of Alexander's properties. For me, it is a validation of the decade of experience they have working with pattern languages, but even more so, of their focus on human activity.

This illustrates the distinction between spirit and structure, Why and How, love and peace, imperfection and wholeness. Alexander tunes us into a structure's Quality Without a Name, its perfect wholeness, which we sense as peace. Whereas Iba and his colleagues focus on human activity, our liveliness, inevitably imperfect, yet which love allows for. Alexander documents forms of peace, but I think Iba et al testify to forms of love.

We can investigate a creator's love as the natural viewpoint for Alexander's fundamental structure preserving transformation of wholeness. I question his account of the fundamental differentiating process, by which we pay attention to wholeness, and sense that part of the structure which is most deeply lacking in feeling. I think it's not about our creation, but about our own growth as creators. In real life, our unconscious challenges us with powerful emotions. They prod us to step out and find peace that we may reflect. The 12 questions by which I engage independent thinkers, such as What is your deepest value? are deeply provoking. Our own deepest value is that stillness inside of us which defines who we are. If we are to understand human behavior, then it makes sense to focus minimalistically on the activities of an independent thinker, how do they grow and what brings them to interact. The 12 questions express through the 12 circumstances what we deeply care about.

The 12 questions are difficult to pin down as a system. However, each particular question generates a wealth of answers, which helps make sense of the vitality of the associated property. And ultimately, the questions, as a set, may indeed serve as 12 fundamental principles for a pattern language which enlightens humanity with a culture of independent thinkers.

It becomes interesting to study particular examples of personal growth and transformation of self-identity. Thousands of examples can yield a well defined grammar and clarify what it means for us to personally identify with each of the 12 circumstances. Such a grammar may teach us how to think of that single wholeness enhancing, structure preserving transformation by which centers yield and strengthen centers. Who knows, that may be the very same transformation which converts the two dimensional plane into the Mandelbrot set.

Ultimately, to make sense of this all, we need to take up God's point of view. Alexander (1979) dedicates "The Timeless Way of Building": "To you, mind of no mind, in whom the timeless way was born." Surely in this one sentence is the fundamental circularity we are looking for. God is that stillness which goes beyond itself into activity, which evokes structure, which channels activity, and so forth. God is the spirit of everything, and everything is the structure of God.

Imagine a God who asks, Am I necessary? Would I be if I was not? Such a Center steps aside to create a Boundary. And when a center therein arises, how do they know that they are the same Center? Because the Levels of Scale are what they both know.

A Center which wishes for nothing is self-sufficient, but we have bodies with needs. A Center which wishes for something is certain, but we have minds with doubts. A Center which wishes for anything is calm, at peace, but we have hearts with expectations. A Center which wishes for everything is loving, but we have wills with values.

The issue here is the nature of love and peace. The will loves the perfect, but God's will loves the imperfect. God's love of everything takes more seriously than we do all of our nonsensical aspirations. At least, that explains why we are ever sent forward into an imperfect world. Within that world, we are riled by what is wrong, and we seek the truth of peace. We need to step out of our selves, our feelings, our biases, our cycle of being, doing, and thinking, and from a rational, logical, peaceful vantage point consider the merits of what is and what envelops, what we unconsciously know and what we consciously don't know.

There is a dialectic by which the narrow purpose, the How, should serve the broad purpose, the Why, and not the other way around. This is so that we rise from the level to the metalevel, that we align ourselves with God beyond us, that we find peace. For example, roughness may serve me in clearing the void to free a path to present reality, but I should not free a path for the sake of roughness. Indeed, whenever I favor the narrow stillness over the broad stillness, my unconscious riles me. Only when I flip around the How and the Why do I find peace.

A science will bring us to that peace. Surely that science will need to model God. And God will send us forth into the world to love.

10.Conclusion

The six investigations presented have yielded only tentative results. However, taken together, they strongly suggest that Alexander's fifteen properties of life are not haphazard. In fact, 3 of them are basic perspectives - Strong Centers, Boundaries and Levels of Scale - which accord with a learning cycle of taking a stand, following through, and reflecting. The other 12 properties arise from 4 representations of this threesome as 12 conceptual circumstances. These cognitive derivations accord well with empirical data from a survey of artists reasons Why they create. Alexander's properties can then be understood as 12 rules How to create. Paired together, the 12 reasons Why and the 12 rules How seem to match the 24 human behavioral properties described by Iba, Kimura, Akado & Honda. We can imagine a creator's point of view from which 12 of Alexander's properties are forms of peace and the 24 human behavioral properties are forms of love, which supports life, the perturbance of peace. Furthermore, the creator's point of view can be investigated as 12 questions for engaging independent thinkers, and as 12 building blocks for transforming self-identity. Thus a scientific community can definitively clarify Alexander's properties of life by developing theoretical cognitive frameworks and conducting empirical studies of human experience.

11.References

Alexander, C. (1979). The timeless way of building. New York: Oxford University Press.

Alexander, C. (2002a). The nature of order: an essay on the art of building and the nature of the universe. Book 1, The phenomenon of life. Center for Environmental Structure.

Alexander, C. (2002b). The nature of order: an essay on the art of building and the nature of the universe. Book 2, The process of creating life. Center for Environmental Structure.

Amazon.com, Inc. (2017) Amazon.com: Online Shopping for Electronics, Apparel, Computers, Books, DVDs & more. Retrieved from: https://www.amazon.com on October 19, 2017.

Catalan number. (2017). In Wikipedia. Retrieved from: https://en.wikipedia.org/wiki/Catalan_number

Flajolet, P. & Sedgewick, R. (2009). Analytic Combinatorics. Cambridge University Press. Retrieved from: http://algo.inria.fr/flajolet/Publications/book.pdf

Genn, R. (2014). Quotes about Purpose. Retrieved from: http://www.art-quotes.com/getquotes.php?catid=249

Iba, T. (2016). Pattern Language 3.0 and Fundamental Behavioral Properties. Proceedings of PURPLSOC: Pursuit of Pattern Languages for Societal Change. pp.200-233.

Iba, T., Kimura, N., Akado, Y., & Honda, T. (2016). The Fundamental Behavioral Properties. Proceedings of PURPLSOC: Pursuit of Pattern Languages for Societal Change. pp.178-198.

Iba, T., & Sakai, S. (2015). Understanding Christopher Alexander's Fifteen Properties via Visualization and Analysis. Proceedings of PURPLSOC: Pursuit of Pattern Languages for Societal Change., pp. 434-449.

Kant, I. (2013). Grynojo proto kritika. (R.Plečkaitis, trans.) Vilnius: Margi raštai.

Kohls, C, Köppe, C. (2015). Evaluating the Applicability of Alexander's Fundamental Properties to Non-Architecture Domains. Proceedings of PURPLSOC: Pursuit of Pattern Languages for Societal Change., pp. 188-210.

Kulikauskas, A. (2003). Living by Truth. Re: The Nature of Order. September 4, 2003. Retrieved from: https://groups.yahoo.com/neo/groups/livingbytruth/conversations/topics/363

Kulikauskas, A. (2014a). The Truth: From Relative to Absolute. Retrieved from: http://www.ms.lt/sodas/Book/TheTruth

Kulikauskas, A. (2014b). Kūrybos prasmė ir meno taisyklės. Vilnius. March 22, 2014. Retrieved from: http://www.ms.lt/sodas/Mintys/K%c5%abrybosPrasm%c4%97IrMenoTaisykl%c4%97s

Kulikauskas, A. (2017a). Moral Imagination: What Do We Wish to See? Soviet Sports Palace vs. European Convention Center vs. Historic Jewish Cemetery. Vilnius. April 21, 2017. Retrieved from: http://www.ms.lt/sodas/Book/MoralImagination

Kulikauskas, A. (2017b). The Orchard of Thoughts: An Alternative Culture of Growing in Not Knowing. Tartu. May 11, 2017. Retrieved from:

http://www.ms.lt/sodas/Book/20170506PostTruth

Kulikauskas, A. (2017c). How Do Things Come to Matter? Evolution of Self-Identity in the Intercultural Debate on Whether to Restore Vilnius's Oldest Jewish Cemetery. Lublin. September 14, 2017. Retrieved from:

http://www.ms.lt/sodas/Book/20170914CultureCognitionCommunication

Kulikauskas, A. (2017d). Time and Space as Representations of Decision-Making. Vilnius. September 30, 2017. Retrieved from:

http://www.ms.lt/sodas/Book/20170929TimeSpaceDecisionMaking

Kulikauskas, A., Balčiūnas, A., Gajdosik, T., Gajdosikienė, I., Nugaras, J., Kačerauskas, T., (2017). Workshop: How Does My Self-Identity Change? Vilnius. April 10, 2017.

Leitner, H. (2016). A Bird's-Eye View on Pattern Research. Proceedings of PURPLSOC: Pursuit of Pattern Languages for Societal Change., pp. 16-37.

Madore, D. (2017). Mandelbrot Set Images and Videos. Retrieved from: http://www.madore.org/~david/math/mandelbrot.html

Mandelbrot set. (2017). In Wikipedia. Retrieved from: https://en.wikipedia.org/wiki/Mandelbrot_set

Petz, M. (2017). Learning in Indigenous Mountain Forest Communities. Case Studies in Northern Thailand: White Hmong (Miao), Sheleh Ladhulsi (Lahu), and Pgak'nyau (Karen) Peoples. (Master's Thesis) Retrieved from: http://zidapps.boku.ac.at/abstracts/

Sloane, N.J. (2017). The On-Line Encyclopedia of Integer Sequences. Retrieved from: https://www.oeis.org

Zhyrova, A., Rychtáriková, R., Náhlík, T., Štys, D. (2015). The path of ageing: Self-organisation in the Nature and the 15 properties. Proceedings of PURPLSOC: Pursuit of Pattern Languages for Societal Change., p.p. 386-411.

A Pattern Language Shaping a Desirable Environment for the Elderly

Yonesu, Masaaki
Benesse Style Care Co., Ltd., Japan
myonesu@benesse-style-care.co.jp

Kato, Io
Benesse Style Care Co., Ltd., Japan
katou-io@benesse-style-care.co.jp

Although BSC has over 20 years of experience and practice in senior living and nursing care, the practical knowledge of care is possessed by individual staff members and not necessarily shared as an effective means for creating a good environment for elderly people.

In order to make use of our past experience and knowledge, we attempted to generate common language that conveys how a good living environment for seniors is created and share it with the company.

The research method for this work is mainly based on interviews with the care workers in each facility. We used both qualitative analysis of cases and text mining. Throughout the research we read through each case to extract the key themes that are linked to the attractive and comfortable space. We categorized and formed themed groups based on the frequency of the words in all questionnaires.

We discovered 66 patterns and classified them into 12 groups. We created a book that clearly describes each pattern.

We can share this pattern language that we have obtained through conversations with the staff to aid them in shaping a more desirable environment for their elderly residents. Finally, we suggest that care service may be viewed as a creative work through the use and discussion of pattern language.

Nursing care, environment, patterns, comfort

1. Background of this work

1.1. Introduction of Benesse Style Care Co., Ltd.

» 20 years of nursing care service in Japan

> Benesse Style Care Co., Ltd. has been in the nursing care business for 20 years in Japan and operates nursing homes for seniors including fee-based homes and elderly houses with care services.

» 308 facilities providing services to 15,000 elderly people

> As of May 31, 2017, it operates 308 such facilities mainly in urban residential areas and provides care services for more than 15,000 elderly people.

1.2. What is happening in our facilities

Although we design each facility based on our own specifications, sometimes the use of the space is different than intended. Sometimes a comfortable and relaxing environment is created by the spontaneous act of the residents and care staffs.

» (Example 1) Ladies are chatting over a cup of tea at the entrance lounge which is designed as the place to welcome visitors. The Ladies choose the entrance lounge over the tea room.

» (Example 2) A gentleman reads newspaper every morning at a quiet seat by the window in the dining area. It is not a private space, but he prefers a place where other people gather.

Figure 1: Gentleman

Each space in a facility has its own functional use. We expect the residents to use those spaces following their functional needs. However, the residents do not care about such pre-determined functions and actively change the use of the spaces.

At times these spaces fail to provide any value to the residents despite their efforts to use or reinterpret the space. Other spaces thrive and become integral parts of the home providing great comfort and improving the residents' quality of life. Based on these outcomes, with this question in mind, we started our research to find the key themes that shape a desirable environment for the elderly.

The procedure of our research was as follows; first, we collected as many cases from the care staff that were available. Second, we made a list of those cases and classified them into identified groups. We paid a lot of attention to common component shared among cases. Finally, we identified key themes in each group and gave a pattern name.

2. The intention of our pattern language

Find a method that helps us to shape a desirable environment for the elderly people based on our 20 years of experience and practice

» Share pattern language among staff

» Make it possible to provide care staff the opportunity to design the space.

» Suggest that care service could be a creative work

» Support professional architects and planners to explain designs to public

3. Research method and findings

3.1. Research method

The research method of this work is mainly based on interviews with the care workers in each facility. We asked, "what are the attractive spaces in your facility?" and "are there any popular places among the residents?" We collected 603 successful cases as a result of these interviews.

3.1.1. Process A: Qualitative analysis of cases

We listed all successful cases in a table and described the details of those cases. The structure of the list is as below. Each description details a specific physical environment and the special acts done there are noted. The key themes produced by the combination of the space and acts are described.

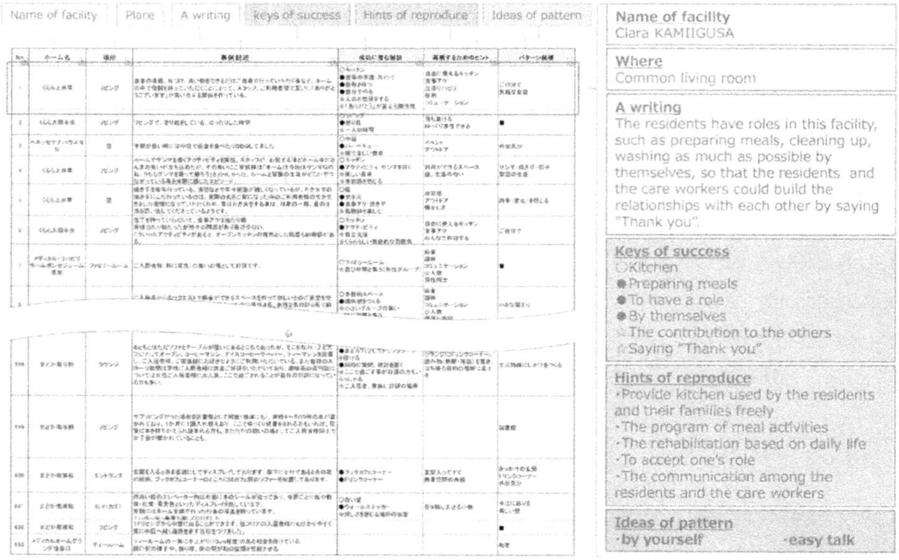

Figure 2: Analysis

» From the far-left column to the right, numbers, the name of facilities, and places where the cases happen are described.

» In the fourth column, the details of the successful cases are written. A variety of things happen at various places in a facility. We listed the original answers given from care staff. They provide us vivid scenes of the residents' daily lives.

» Next to the detailed descriptions, individual circumstances that led each case to succeed are noted. Each description details a specific physical environment and the special acts are noted. The key themes produced by the combination of the space and acts are described.

» Before the last column, tips for recreating success stories are shown and in the last column, elements to reproduce success in other facilities are briefly noted.

» Finally, we have candidate patterns.

» From each interview, we identify key themes linked to the creation of attractive and comfortable spaces.

3.1.2. Process B; Text mining

Utilizing software[1], we picked up frequently occurring words from all questionnaires including nouns, verbs, and adjectives, displaying their frequency of appearance in a simplistic image.

Figure 2: Textmining

1 User Local Text Mining, USER LOCAL Co., Ltd.

3.2. Finding 66 patterns and 12 categories

3.2.1. Patterns and Categories

a: the awareness on the part of the persons concerned

b: remove anxieties

h: a sense of distance

c: enjoy location

i: primitive space

d: the degree of open to surrounding

j: switch

e: inside and outside

k: warp

f: set a comfortable

l: chance

g: the abundance of every day

m: the timeless idea

Figure 3: Patterns and Categories

a: Understanding resident

000 Character

b: Removing anxieties

01. Being with family like in old days

02. Pride of home's external appearance

03. The entrance

04. Sense of good living

05. Spaces divided by glass

06. Lifestyle recomendations

07. Handmade media

c: Enjoying the location

08. 1st, Mt Fuji. 2nd, Fireworks. 3rd, Sakura

09. Use of the surrounding natural scenery

010. Identity of the site

011. Relishing the scenery

012. The grass is always greener

013. A room on the ground level

d: Open to surroundings

014. Communication between generations

015. Generating a friendship with the community

016. Being friendly in the neighborhood

017. A variety of boundary markers

e: Inside and outside

018. A big window

019. A keyless window

020. Passage for roaming

021. A view before us

022. A courtyard

023. Roaming outside

f: Comfortable design features

024. Providing shade

025. Top light／high-side light

026. Sitting windowside

027. Effective lighting

g: A full and rich day

028. Like going out

029. Various ceiling heights

030. Library space

031. A roof top floor with character

032. Space as a gallery

033. Artistic walls

034. Furniture placement

035. Decorating flowers

h: Space and distance

036. Easy for conversation

037. Feeling cared for

038. A salon

039. A corridor

040. Getting together with friends

041. Surrounded and protected

042. Deep consideration of space

i: Unexpected space

043. A chair generates micro-cosmos

044. Alcove

045. A pocket space

046. A big table

j: Switching activities

047. Transitions

048. Chair at the hallway's end

049. A short rest

050. Scenery transitions

051. First and second impression of the space

k: Present and surprise

052. A Japanese-style room

053. Fresh juice anytime

054. Like an open-air bath

055. Living with pets

056. Grilled fish, sweet potato, and gyoza

l: Chances to creates

057. Encouraging spontaneous efforts

058. Making picture frame

059. Potage garden

060. Live with vigor

061. We are all artist

m: Timeless but evolving

062. Storage as a showcase

063. Recreating old memories

064. Proud of my tree

065. Evolving spaces

4. The format of pattern language

4.1. The format

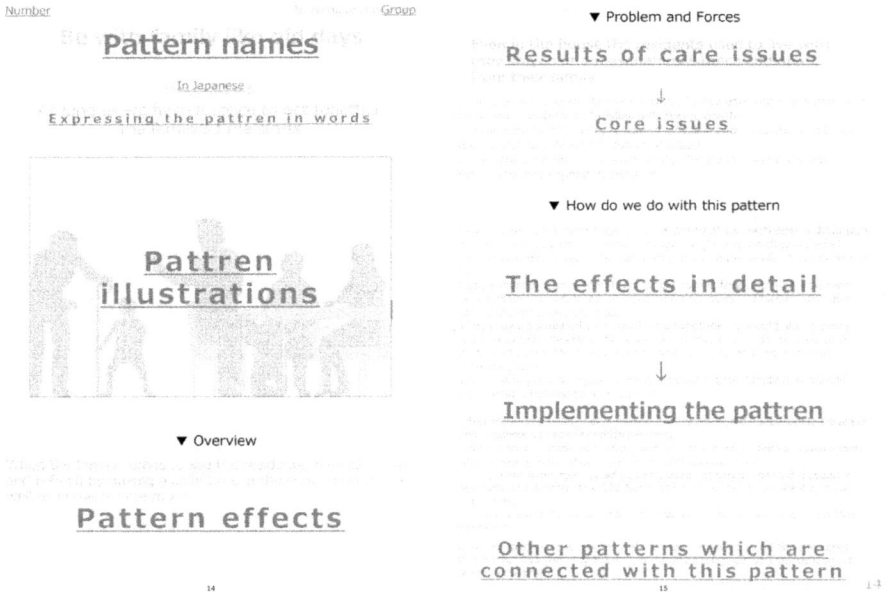

Figure 5: Format

» Pattern names

» Patterns in words

» Pattern illustrations

» Pattern effects

» Background issues

» Core issues

» The effects in detail

» Implementing patterns

» Connected patterns

4.2. Pattern characteristics

» It is important to find patterns by considering cultural, regional, and geographic factors.

» Despite the fact that some patterns are abstract, they have concrete application.

» Certain patterns are more important for certain residents and it is true that some patterns come from limited cases, however these patterns can be applied to a variety of situations.

» Although each resident has his or her own unique needs, they all respond to certain common patterns.

» Identifying patterns can be time consuming. Nonetheless, once we have identified a pattern, the process of implementing it is very quick and easy.

» What we can conclude from our research is that while residents of each home type have unique needs, they all respond to some common and fundamental patterns.

5. Implementing the pattern language in a practical way

5.1. Cards of the pattern language

Creating 66 cards each showing a unique pattern is a method to effectively implement patterns to provide good care services. These cards identify the key patterns and help staff members to implement the patterns. Thus, improving the comfort of the home for residents.

5.2. Discussion with cards

The first step to implementing the pattern language is for staff to describe the facility's strengths, for example quiet spaces, nice lighting, and other features. We only focus on the facility's positive aspects and possibilities. During this step, the staff keep residents' needs and requests in mind, because each resident has reasons for choosing the facility. Second, the staff connect these needs to the 66 pattern cards. Finally, by connecting these cards and patterns, we can see what specific services and environment is desired. Staff describe their feelings on the services and environment and then create an action plan to implement changes. From this process, you see that these cards enable staff to improve the comfort of the home and residents' happiness.

» **Step 1: Identify an issue**

> Describe the points in clear terms

> Ex.: quiet spaces, good lighting, room design

» **Step 2: Replace with card**

> Replace point with relevant pattern language cards and discuss the followings

> Ex.: quiet spaces – surrounded and protected (pattern 41)

>> » Existing services or features connected to relevant patterns

>> » Suitable patterns to implement in connection with issue

» **Step 3: Find, Identify, Develop**

> Based on Step 1 and 2, find and identify possible patterns to develop as facilities aids.

5.3. Implement to design a new facility

Opening staff of the new facility is consists of new recruitment and transfer members. In order to connect the service and the environment to the residents, it is necessary to understand the environment designed by planners. Because usually we don't have enough time in training before opening, we would utilize pattern language as a search light to discover and understand the space and environment intended by the planner and designer. Also, I would like to expect proposals for new services that make use of the environment. Probably, this utilization is effective not only for new but also for reinterpreting existing home.

» **Step 1**: Having a tour of facility with planners and designers, and the staffs discover patterns by themselves

> Planners and designers should not tell which pattern is intended

> Focusing on the environment as it is. Don't think about "if".

» **Step 2**: The staffs explain what is superior regarding the environment using the patterns found by them

» **Step 3**: Planners and designers try to tell the intention of the plan and draw future visions while discussing the future use of environmental and proposal of service.

5.4. Use of pattern language for planning and designing a new home

Considering site conditions, budget, design requirements, and the elements of the surrounding environment, chose and adopt appropriate patterns, and shape a desirable environment. Every participant may act appointed work well.

» **Step 1**: Arrangement of pattern language

> Try to arrange cards of all patterns and chose the following three types while discussing.

> Patterns provided for the characteristics of the plan like No.008 "1st, Mt Fuji. 2nd, Fireworks. 3rd, Sakura" and No.039 "corridor".

> Patterns necessary to supplement expected needs and weak points of the plan

> Patterns utilized by residents and staffs in the daily lives

» **Step 2**: Try to establish a vision through discussion on environment and service proposals

6. References

Christopher Alexander. (1977). A Pattern Language.

Christopher Alexander. (1979). The Timeless Way of Building.

Christopher Alexander. (1985). The Production of Houses.

Ingrid F. King. (1993, August). Christopher Alexander and Contemporary Architecture A+U.

Iba Takashi., Hiroshi Nakano., Heizo Takenaka., Koichiro Edo., Yasuto Nakanishi., & Eichi Hanyuda. (2013). Pattern Languages.

Kumiko Inui., & Tokyo University of the Arts Inui Lab. (2014) Little Spaces.

User Local, Inc. Textminig Tool. Retrieved 2017, from http://texitmining.userlocal.jp

Patterns of Statistical Analysis – Guiding students using Christopher Alexander`s pattern language principles

Larsen, Valerie
Department of Mathematics and Technology, Koblenz University of Applied Science, Remagen, Germany
maxjacobson@yahoo.com

Eube, Cornelia
Institute of Educational and Media Research, FernUniversität in Hagen, Hagen, Germany
cornelia.eube@fernuni-hagen.de

Vogt, Sebastian
Media Production and Media Technology, Technische Hochschule Mittelhessen - University of Applied Sciences,
Friedberg, Germany, sebastian.vogt@iem.thm.de

Statistics as a subject is becoming increasingly important for academic and professional capacity and can be termed a key competency for research in general. Despite its vital role in different academic fields, students of non-mathematical subjects confront statistics with great reservations. Fear of statistics is related to their mathematical background at school, the self-assessment of the learners, and evaluation of the practical benefits for their professional future.

The 15 properties of living structures that Alexander identified as the nuclei of his pattern language show great similarity with the core elements of statistical methods. Living systems are familiar to the learners and are anchored as spontaneous concepts in their knowledge. In this paper the proximity of statistical structures to living structures is taken up to develop a constructivist didactic concept that evades frequently negative attitudes to statistics by offering an approach to statistical models via known, non-mathematical patterns.

Pattern language; Statistics anxiety; Statistics training; Constructivist didactics

1. Introduction

Statistics as a subject is becoming increasingly important for academic and professional capacity and can be termed a key competence for research in general (Ruggeri, Dempster & Hanna, 2011). In daily routine, a basic knowledge of statistics allows us to appraise findings and information offered critically. This is an important prerequisite for reaching reflective and independent attitudes, opinions and decisions. Despite the key role played by statistics in a range of academic fields, students of non-mathematical subjects face the subject of statistics with substantial reservations (Onwuegbuzie & Wilson, 2000). Fear of statistics is connected, for instance, with their mathematical background at school, the self-assessment of the learners and an evaluation of the practical benefit of the subject for their professional and academic future (Baharun & Porter, 2009; Onwuegbuzie, 2004). Accordingly, one task of statistics education at universities is to provide an introduction to the basics of statistics that can be grasped well and that breaks down such reservations, even in cases of subject-related negative self-assessment and fears. This paper outlines an approach that can be used to achieve these goals against the background of constructivist didactics, focusing on the pattern language of Christopher Alexander (2002) as an anchor element. With his pattern language, Christopher Alexander shows basic endeavors and properties of all living structures. As an observer (in other words an empiricist), he examined systems in nature, architecture and society for recurrent structures and hierarchies (Leitner, 2007) and ordered this experience in simple, concise descriptions and patterns. The 15 properties of living structures that Alexander derived as core elements of his pattern language display a high level of similarity with the core elements of statistical methods. This leads to the guiding question of this paper, „What potential does Christopher Alexander's pattern language offer for facilitating access to statistics in university teaching?" To tackle this question, first of all different causes and dimensions of the fear of statistics are addressed (Chapter 2). This is followed by a presentation of the constructivist learning theory that opens up perspectives on non-mathematical learning causes in statistics teaching (Chapter 3). Chapter 4 presents Alexander's pattern language and the principles of living systems that he identified. The relationship between pattern language and statistical concepts then leads to the synthesis of these theoretical backgrounds and culminates in basic considerations regarding a didactic concept for introducing the theory of statistics (Chapter 5). The paper ends with a reflection and a look ahead at the prospects (Chapter 6).

2. Problem – Statistics Anxiety

As a part of methodology training, statistics is a compulsory subject in various university courses. It is felt to be demanding, precise, and for a large share (Onwuegbuzie & Wilson,

2003) of the students as particularly formidable (Perepiczka, Chandler & Beccera, 2011; Macher, Paechter, Papousek & Ruggeri, 2015; Zeidner, 1991). These reservations prevent students from assuming an open, learning-conducive attitude to statistical concepts. In order to develop didactic concepts that counteract this behavior, it is first necessary to analyze the causes, dimensions and interconnections of this statistics anxiety.

Statistics anxiety is described as an independent phenomenon and defined to varying extents by a number of different authors. The breadth of the definitions ranges from a feeling of fear during statistics courses, statistical analyses or interpretations (Cruise, Cash & Bolton, 1985), through to fear in connection with statistics of all kinds (Onwuegbuzie & Wilson, 2003). Given the complex causes, symptoms and interconnections, statistics anxiety is understood as a multidimensional construct (Kesici, Baloglu & Deniz, 2011; Onwuegbuzie & Wilson, 2003).

The experience of pronounced statistics anxiety can have significant consequences for the academic career of students. Situative behavior influences the ability to grasp and understand in the learning situation and can thus lead to poor examination results (Onwuegbuzie & Wilson 2003). Statistics anxiety is particularly widespread among students whose school and academic background has so far included little reference to and practice in mathematics or statistics (Onwuegbuzie & Wilson, 2003; Pan & Tang, 2004). Macher et al. (2015) established that a particularly large number of students of social science subjects are affected by statistics anxiety because they have less interest in mathematical-scientific issues and assess their own capabilities in this field as poor. Women express more negative attitudes to statistics (Erben, 1983) and suffer more frequently from statistics anxiety than men, although the performance achieved does not differ significantly on a gender basis (Onwuegbuzie & Wilson, 2003). Students aged above 20 and those who do not start their studies directly after schooling (Bell, 2003) report negative self-assessments and fears in connection with statistics more frequently than younger students (Onwuegbuzie & Wilson, 2003).

Many of those affected derive their negative self-assessment concerning the ability to learn statistics from bad experience and poor performance in mathematics at school (Gal & Ginsburg, 1994; Perney & Ravid 1991; Zeidner, 1991). Baloglu established that it is frequently wrongly assumed that fear of statistics and fear of mathematics are synonyms of the same construct, even though there are considerable differences in the cognitive processes of the two subjects (2004).

Two main streams are evident in the research into the phenomenon of statistics. Cognitive or non-cognitive factors can be seen as the cause and point of approach for didactic interventions (Wilensky, 1997; Zielinsky, 1980). Schooling background in mathematics and competence in dealing with structured learning strategies can be named as examples of cognitive factors. Considerations regarding preferred mental problem solutions and level of thought (concrete–visual versus formal-logical) can be placed on the same level (Birkhan & Schulmeister, 1983; Daley & Onwuegbuzie, 1997).

In addition to these cognitive causes, attitudes to the subject of statistics are to be taken into account as essential non-cognitive causes of fear of statistics. Students' attitude to the subject of statistics is shown, for example, in the way in which they talk about it. The language reflects the attitude and the framework in which an object is perceived. Rosenthal (1992, p. 281) remarks that it is customary for English-speaking students to change the name of the subject from „statistics" to „sadistics". Perney und Ravid (1991) describe the view of the compulsory subject statistics as an obstacle on the way to the desired academic qualification. Matching this, Simon and Bruce (1991, p. 22) establish that „students consider the statistic course a painful rite of a passage". All these expressions imply pain and hindrance or interference. Statistics is perceived as a foreign body that does not possess any content-related justification or relevance for one's own career (Erben, 1983). Wilensky (1997) suspects that both the standardized and rigorous appearance as well as the relationship to mathematical concepts suggest a complete disparateness and oppositeness with regard to other concepts and spheres of knowledge. However, the examples mentioned illustrate not only simple alienation, but above all aversion. As a strong, reactive and rather brief sensation, aversion can be classified as an affect (manifestation of a subjectively experienced emotion) (Macher et. al, 2015). Such reactions are triggered for example by first problems of understanding in the statistics course, which then activate negative experiences from the past (Gal & Ginsburg, 1994).

It is expedient to structure the different relevant attitudes in order to define the impact spectra and thus clearly highlight points of approach for improving these attitudes as well.

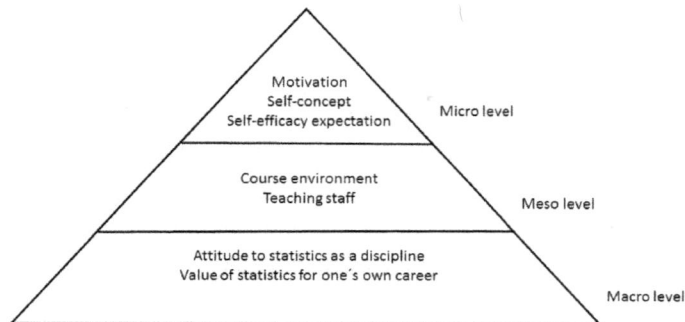

Figure 1: Levels of attitudes to statistics (own diagram)

The factors motivation and expectation of self-efficacy can be positioned at the micro level, as they cover the reach of the learners. The self-concept in relation to the mathematical-analytical character of statistics also concerns the learners' own estimation of their skills.

Teachers and the learning environment are to be positioned at the meso level, as these learning conditions have a direct influence on the learner. The transfer of educational content via media and teachers influences the grasp of the material, while the attitudes and positions of the course participants and the teachers interact with each other.

The macro level comprises generalized attitudes to statistics as a discipline and its specific value for the student's own academic and professional future. Each individual level consists of highly subjective assessments that need not bear any relation to the objective capacity of the learners (Onwuegbuzie & Wilson, 2003; Williams, 2013) or the actual personal benefit of statistics (Gal & Ginsburg, 1994).

Proposals for improving attitudes to statistics are made at all the levels mentioned. At the micro level the concept of self-efficacy after Albert Bandura (1986) is a well-researched approach. Bandura (1986) describes expectation of self-efficacy as the assessment of one's own ability to develop and deliver a certain performance. Self-efficacy expectations as situative cognition are differentiated here from the more fundamental convictions about one's own self, the self-concept (Wirtz, 2014). Finney and Schraw (2003) examined the self-efficacy theory with regard to statistics anxiety and confirmed a high positive correlation with the performance level achieved. Accordingly, students' motivation to participate in a difficult course and invest work in it depend significantly on whether they do in fact believe that they will be able to succeed (Perepiczka, Chandler & Beccera, 2011; Onwuegbuzie, 2003; Williams, 2013).

The micro level can be influenced positively by the meso level if the climate in the course is fundamentally pleasant and creates a feeling of security, making it possible to disclose and withstand one's own uncertainties and thus make clarification possible (Perepiczka, Chandler & Beccera, 2011; Gal & Ginsburg, 1994; Wilensky, 1997). A lively and learner-centered learning environment that stimulates social activities should be targeted here (Eube & Vogt, 2016).

The macro level and micro level influence each other mutually as the assessment of individual usefulness can bring about strongly integrated motivation if statistics training, knowledge and skills are assessed as expedient, beneficial and worthwhile (Gal & Ginsburg, 1994; Williams, 2003). If the course succeeds in making it clear that good statistics training is important for the desired career path, students integrate statistics into their value system as something desirable and positive (Deci & Ryan, 1993). Perepiczka, Chandler & Beccera (2011) describe this new assessment of statistics in a positive context as a reframing process. However, if statistics as a discipline is considered to be alien or contrary to one's own inclinations and values, there is at most extrinsic motivation (Deci & Ryan, 1993) that results from fear of failure and can trigger an aversive statistics anxiety (Onwuegbuzie, 2004).

3. Constructivist learning theory as a perspective on other ways of approaching statistics

The purpose of this paper is to develop a didactic concept that evades these frequently negative attitudes to statistics by offering an approach to statistical models via known, non-mathematical patterns. Here known concepts are to be associated with unknown (statistical) concepts in a manner conducive to learning and be integrated into a new understanding, into new cognitive structures. Such learning follows the constructivist learning theory, „Experience is the cause, the world is the consequence" (von Foerster, 1993, p. 46). This thesis of the cyberneticist Heinz von Foerster can be considered as a unifying basic postulate of all constructivist trends (Haan & Rülcker, 2009). It states that the consideration of all things and the subjective evaluation of this consideration determine one's own reality. The consequences of this assumption vary in the different streams of constructivism. Accordingly, perception is an activity of the subject (Fosnot & Perry, 1996) that undertakes unconscious selection. On the basis of one's own experience one only assumes what can be integrated conclusively into one's own reality. In the spirit of constructivism, learners learn through interaction with the respective environment (social and physical). From their experience in the interactions, learners individually develop a cognitive structure covering this specific environment. Learning in the spirit of constructivism is understood as a learner-centered, self-steered and above all interactive process.

Constructivism focuses on the subject as the active and individual builder of knowledge, and distances itself from the assumption that reality can be grasped objectively. Lev Vygotsky (1964) understood learning as a field of tension between development and construction. By analogy with Piaget's work (1970, 1977), he differentiated between two different conceptual forms of knowledge genesis. The spontaneous concepts evolve from everyday experience, while the more abstract scientific concepts have to be taught in structured fashion in teaching and instruction. Vygotsky (1964) assumes that scientific concepts can only evolve on the basis of spontaneous concepts. He is of the opinion that in the organized system of communicating scientific concepts, teaching has to rely on the existing spontaneous concepts (Vygotsky, 1964). This means that no higher level knowledge can be understood out of the blue. It requires a naive basis, stemming from practical experience of the learner, that can serve as an approach to the scientific concept. Furthermore, a scientific concept or a specific term requires a more general environment in which it can be embedded, one which gives the new knowledge support and places it in relation. Here we once again clearly see constructivism at work – assuming the creation of reality and knowledge from the building modules of one's own experience. Knowledge cannot be handed over or transferred to learners in a finished, objective form. Learners can only put it together themselves from their own subjective material.

The connections between the experiences of learners and their derivations from expectations, fears and attitudes have been mentioned above. Bad experiences in connection with mathematics form the material from which negative expectation attitudes of one's own learning skills in statistics are constructed (Gal & Ginsburg, 1994; Perney & Ravid 1991; Zeidner, 1991). By contrast, in the new concept to be developed, learners are not to link up with negative experiences and self-concepts, but instead with true-to-life concepts experienced in everyday life, thus paving the way for constructing an initial approach to and understanding of statistical models by analogy with previous non-mathematical experiences. For example Zielinski (1980) ascertained that cognitive strategies already learned have a positive effect on the learning and thinking performance of students. Cognitive strategies can be understood as thinking methods or recognition of regularities in a new field. The opening up of new knowledge through construction in the environment of existing structures and experiences is an assumption of the constructivist learning theory. The consequence of this idea is that teaching in organized systems has the task of drawing attention to points of connection and more than just one approach to a scientific concept. This facilitates the building and embedding of knowledge in already existing cognitive structures for learners. In this sense the patterns of liveliness and life-kindliness observed and formulated by Christopher Alexander are to serve as (unconsciously) known regularities in the concept to be developed for entering the world of statistics. These patterns may be presumed to be positive, so that they thus bypass learning obstacles based on negative attitudes and form points of connection for new cognitive structures.

4. Pattern in living systems – Alexander's pattern language

With his pattern language, the architect Christopher Alexander points out basic efforts and properties of all living structures. As an observer and hence a traditional empiricist, he examined systems of nature, architecture and society for recurrent structures and hierarchies and classified this experience in simple, concise descriptions and patterns. On the basis of these patterns that he found, he developed a system for generating positive systems and provided a medium, as it were, to describe them.

Alexander (2002) highlights efforts for liveliness or life-kindliness of processes and living spaces as the topmost goal of all structuring. Everything that is created for humans should fit in with them and their needs as far as possible and keep the big picture of an overall environment in view. This requirement applies in an aesthetic, functional and ethical sense. The architecture of objects, buildings and towns represents the starting point of Christopher Alexander's work, but in his objectives, he goes well beyond spatial construction. Alexander wants pattern language to be a basic principle of activities through its sustainability and respectful attitude to mankind and nature. This ethical dimension in Alexander's work is closely connected with an aesthetic dimension. Accordingly, alongside order and liveliness, beauty is a central concept in Alexander's terminology. In order to back up his theory of quality through liveliness, Alexander collected examples of successful - in other words living – structures from nature and various different fields of life. He systematically asked people about their spontaneous feelings concerning these examples and examined preferred examples for regularities. He discovered an amazingly high level of agreement in assessments by different test persons and concluded from this that it is possible to objectify beauty and liveliness on the basis of certain criteria. On the basis of these criteria he condensed his findings into the 15 properties of living structures (PoLs), see Table 1.

PoL No.	Icon	PoL Title
1		Levels of scale
2		Strong centres
3		Boundaries
4		Alternating repetition
5		Positive space
6		Good shape
7		Local symmetries
8		Deep interlock and ambiguity
9		Contrast
10		Gradients
11		Roughness
12		Echoes
13		The Void
14		Simplicity and inner calm
15		Non-Separateness

Table 1: 15 Properties of living structures (PoLs) after Christopher Alexander

These 15 properties describe basic principles that can be seen in a wide range of variations as the building blocks of positive, life-kindly systems. A selection of these principles should always be taken into account when creating new living structures, such as building a house, planning a town or organizing cooperation. By way of example, four of the 15 principles are set out below and visualized with symbols. In order to explain the principles appropriately and as seen by Alexander (2002), a certain depth is necessary. Four of the fifteen principles are introduced below by way of example in order not to exceed the scope of this paper.

PoL 1   Levels of scale

Good proportions induce a feeling of balance and coherence in the observer. In an overall structure, the participating individual objects should be arranged in different size relationships and be harmoniously coordinated with each other.

PoL 2   Strong centers

A strong center provides orientation and at the same time allows a view of the whole. The center as an element of a structure should not be understood in absolute terms here. This is not one center that overlies the rest of the structure, but instead the interplay between strong (in other words present) centers and smaller centers that support each other in their respective effect. The center could be understood as the justified center point that respects its surroundings and is respected by them. The positive strong center exists as a natural authority by contrast with a totality.

PoL 3   Boundaries

Boundaries are a possible element for supporting centers. The task of boundaries lies both in strengthening and protecting the structure they enclose and connecting the interior with the exterior. Here too the fine tuning and commensurability will depend clearly on the success of the principles. A good boundary moves in the field of tension between demarcation and transition.

PoL 7   Local Symmetries

Bilateral or multilateral symmetries are a key feature of ornaments and mosaics that Alexander shows particularly frequently as examples of living structures. Here too it becomes clear again that the dimension decides whether a principle has a positive effect. For instance symmetry, like repetition, can lose its positive character through exaggeration, stringency and exactness. For Alexander, successful symmetry has something organic or natural and always displays a certain variance. To put it simply, one could say that the perfection of symmetry and repetition derives from its minimal imperfection.

The pattern language briefly outlined here is frequently used in a figurative sense to communicate knowledge. If the form of samples is isolated to a certain regularity in representation, this leads to a flexible method of formulating and collecting instructions for action in standard cases and problem solutions. With these properties, which Kohls (2005, p. 65) describes as „structure regularities", knowledge can be communicated and applied particularly effectively (widely disseminated e.g. in software development). Alexander (1996) always responds a little skeptically when use of his pattern language is reduced to this format. For him the value of pattern language lies not in its property as a user-friendly format, but in its capacity to generate and strengthen life-supporting structures (Alexander, 1996). And it is precisely this true-to-life and life-kindly property of the pattern he found that is to be used in the following section to introduce statistics as a subject too. Learners are familiar with living systems and these are anchored in their knowledge as spontaneous concepts on the basis of a wide range of experience. Statistical procedures represent scientific concepts and need compatible spontaneous concepts that allow the more complex structures to be accepted. The basic procedures of statistics can be integrated into the field of spontaneous concepts by means of this coupling of everyday experiences. A remark by Fosnot & Perry explains the advantage of this transfer as follows: „scientific concepts work their way „down" imposing their logic on the child, spontaneous concepts work their way „up", meeting the scientific concept and allowing the learner to accept its logic" (1996, p. 20).

The clarity and authenticity of pattern language make it possible to show the liveliness in the scientific concept of statistics and thus initiate a development in learners bringing the two concepts closer together. The corresponding analogies and approaches to developing appropriate didactic material are explained in the following section.

5. Application of pattern language for statistics courses

The evaluation of data in statistics means creating order in the mass and diversity of raw data which will enable the reader to read and understand the statements made by a dataset. Alexander also undertook this search for the structure of living systems. Making information from a dataset useful for people means carrying out a meaningful and purposive reduction. Here the selection of operation and the statistical characteristic value are initially oriented to the message of the data that is to be emphasized and not falsified. Accordingly, alongside the technical requirement arising from the quality criteria of quantitative research, this is also about maintaining values for the benefit of social systems. On the other hand, ideally the selection is oriented to the reader for whom the evaluation is intended. Accordingly this involves authentic hierarchical arrangement of the data geared to the needs of understanding and possibilities of perception.

This is where the requirements made of statistics and the structuring of life spaces according to Christopher Alexander overlap. For Alexander (1996), the strength of pattern language lies in its ability to generate and strengthen life-supporting structures. Statistics is structure, reduction and arrangement for the benefit of readability and informative power. It is tied to quality criteria that in summary convey that the selected method can reliably map the subject of research, namely the living structure, appropriately and repeatedly. Accordingly, quality is also measured by the context of the research. Alexander too shares this claim of appropriateness: „Context is that part of the world which puts demands on this form […]

Fitness is a mutual relation of acceptability between these two" (1964, p.19). Consequently, the benefit of Alexander's research for applications in statistics lies in its value orientation. This value orientation can contribute to more open-mindedness and appreciation among students, especially where attitudes to statistics are concerned.

5.1. Dimensions of pattern language for didactic applications

In order to be able to use the potential of pattern language in targeted form and thus facilitate the introduction to the subject of statistics for students, this potential must first be considered in structured form. What aspects of pattern language could other scientific disciplines use profitably, and what aspects are suitable for didactic use and can be related to statistics? In order to find and justify the specific benefit of pattern language, it helps to conduct a semantic analysis of the term pattern (Kromrey, 2009).

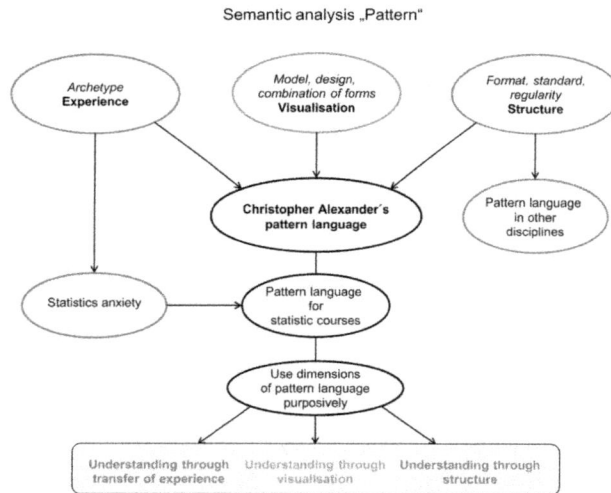

Semantic analysis „Pattern"

Archetype
Experience

Model, design,
combination of forms
Visualisation

Format, standard,
regularity
Structure

**Christopher Alexander´s
pattern language**

Pattern language
in other
disciplines

Statistics anxiety

Pattern language
for
statistic courses

Use dimensions
of pattern language
purposively

Understanding through
transfer of experience

Understanding through
visualisation

Understanding through
structure

Figure 2: Aspects and dimensions of pattern language (own diagram)

The different meanings and synonyms of the term pattern were analyzed. The matching significances for the pattern language have been ordered according to categories. Figure 2 shows the category Experience with the representative synonym archetype, the category Visualization with creative-figurative meanings, and the category Structure with formally organizing meanings. All three categories are represented in Alexander's pattern language.

Using the pattern language for an introduction to statistics entails three crucial dimensions (see Figure 2, bottom):

Understanding through transfer of experience

Understanding through transfer of experience means that the pattern language shows fundamental principles with which every human being is familiar. As these principles are represented in nature and many spheres of life, it should be possible to show all students, irrespective of their talents and preferences, fields in which they are familiar with these principles. The intention is to open up a positive space in which the sense of basic statistical procedures can be encountered and in which it is possible to link the underlying principle with positive personal experiences. In the sense of reframing, a different reference framework is to be offered and linked to personal, internalized empirical knowledge (Baumgartner & Bergner, 2014). This intention is supported by Wilensky (1997), who formulates the advantage of subjective connections as follows: „connections to the learners' knowledge that make the transition to new knowledge both safer and meaningful" (Wilensky, 1997, p.187).

Understanding through visualization

This is an approach to understanding by visualizing specific illustrative examples and possible solutions. A number of authors recommend visual-spatial methods so as not to address solely students with a formal-logical orientation (Birkhan & Schulmeister, 1983; Daley & Onwuegbuzie, 1997; Gal & Ginsburg, 1994).

The understanding through visualization approach can be considered as established, particularly for the field of statistics. Edward Tufte is Professor Emeritus of Political Science Statistics and Computer Science at Yale University and an expert in data visualization. In his work he emphasizes the informative power of clear and aesthetic presentation. He coined the term „thinking eye" (Tufte, 2015) and recommends making use of the analytical capacity and speed of the eye and the brain for understanding processes. Tufte is a statistician and creative artist, while Alexander is a mathematician and architect – both work with the interplay between aesthetics, structure and evidence (Tufte, 2006). In the field of statistics theory, digital learning materials that combine experiential learning and visualization are used successfully. For instance Daniel Kunin of Brown University has developed a software that he describes as a visual introduction to probabilities and statistics (2017).

Understanding through structure

The understanding through structure approach has been tried out through its successful implementation in the field of software development. In this work the structure of the pattern language is used as an organizing element and, following the principle of scaffolding, as a scaffold for learners (Paas, Renkl & Sweller, 2003). The reference to recurrent structures in various statistical models as well as in the structures of pattern language offers a possibility of creating links between different statistical operations and thus strengthening processes of understanding.

The dimensions outlined can be put to use for a basic didactic concept in theory of statistics. The considerations start at an early stage, at the point where students have not yet decided to become involved in statistics and where a positive foundation stone for grappling with the subject needs to be laid in order to bypass defense mechanisms and fears. Consequently the goal is not to achieve a fully comprehensive learning process in terms of content.

Students are shown the intention and significance of statistical parameters through patterns in the didactic basic concept. The description remains at a relatively superficial level, which is made possible by an open approach and willingness of students to grapple with the material. This makes use of the "understanding through transfer of experience" dimension by emphasizing the archetypal character of a few principles, such as strong centers, levels of scale or boundaries (see Figure 3). The dimension of understanding through visualisation is equally important at this superficial observation and description level, given the support it supplies for concrete-visual thinking processes.

For a somewhat more detailed, mathematical description of the specific process, it is then possible to match patterns and computing operations. Such an application is worthwhile for students who appreciate the structuring properties of pattern language and would like to use it as a method themselves. Here, above all things, the application stresses the dimension of understanding through structure and the property of pattern language as a language for specific formulation of processes.

5.2. Didactic concept and implementation approaches

In order to be able to use the advantages of pattern language, students should first be familiarized with the basic traits of pattern theory. Following Tufte's recommendations (2015), this introduction should involve the thinking eye.

Pictures from a wide range of different areas of life embody the principle to be shown and stimulate the observer's association skills. In this way students should first acquire a feeling for what is meant by the principles of living systems and how they can be observed (see Figure 3).

Figure 3: Picture representing PoL 2 Strong center of a blossom (Larsen, 2012)

A concise, simple and representative illustration is first introduced for each principle, with which the respective principle can then easily be associated and memorized. This draws on the method of iconic characters for simple and fast coding of meaning contents. According to Umberto Eco (2002), successful iconic characters activate recognition processes by condensing essential perceived properties into graphic form.

The icon as a specific medium for remembering the respective principle is not only brief and simple, but also implies the mode to be used for remembering. Following on from McLuhan (1967), the medium is not a meaningless messenger, but instead through its properties it also supplies the way of reading the message that it carries. Think in pictures! This message reaches the observer not as a formulated imperative, but instead is contained already in the icon itself as an image that guides the observer to the visual level. Accordingly, the medium itself points to the content which students have assimilated and connected (putting them "in the picture"). The design of the individual icons was inspired by Leitner (2016), who also devised a graphic overall view.

The icons stand for a certain principle, in other words a pattern, in a statistical parameter. As signposts they lead students to groups of parameters that, for instance, work with centers, display levels of scale, or draw boundaries. When presenting specific methods and parameters it is thus additionally possible to show hotspots that display the principles in optical form and lead to explanations as required by the learners (see Figure 4).

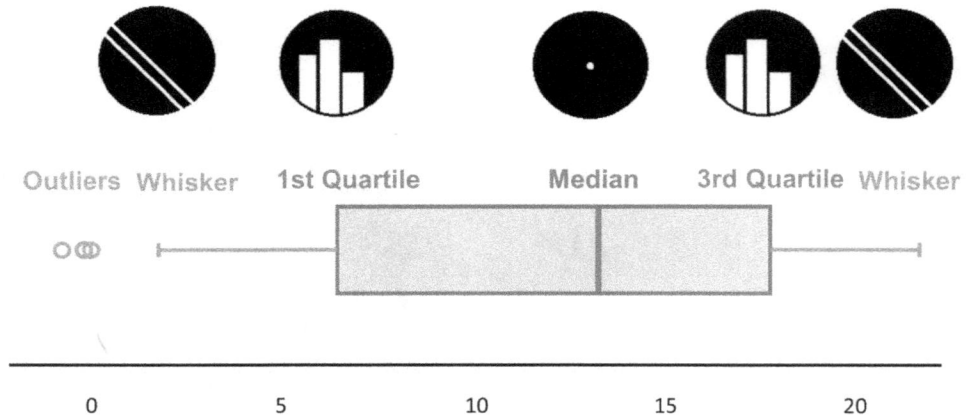

Figure 4: Effective principles in boxplots (PoL1, PoL2, PoL3) (own diagram)

In various interactive offerings students can work out the sense and intentions of statistical parameters for themselves in a playful manner by finding the underlying principles or being guided by images to analogies. One possible implementation becomes clear in the example shown in Figure 4 referring to the statistical concept boxplot. In the interactive online offering, students come to a presentation with Figure 4 as an interactive slide. The icons have been replaced by „hotspots" that students

Figure 5: Pictures representing PoL 3 Boundaries: left: Freezing course of a stream (Larsen, 2017) right: Bud (Larsen, 2012)

Figure 6: Pictures representing PoL 1 Levels of scale: left: Matryoshkas – Russian doll (source: https://pixabay.com/photo-1861410/, 2017), right: Tomato harvest (Larsen, 2012)

select with the cursor and via which they reach associated images, e.g. for PoL 3 Boundaries to the images in Figure 5, and correspondingly for PoL 1 Levels of Scale to Figure 6. They then discover formal explanations (Quartile, Median, Whisker) regarding the boxplot through links that can be found in the boxplot itself. This can be realized simply with the open-source software H5P (2017). Diverse further interactive offerings (e.g. shifting image juxtaposition, Figure 7, referring to the statistical concepts regression and residuals) can be realized. These different offerings can be integrated into a learning environment together with the introduction into pattern theory (see above) and further formal explanations and exercises in statistics – for example in a Moodle environment or on a corresponding website. Accordingly, the approach presented here benefits the ease of a visual introduction, while at the same time stimulating students to understand the concept behind statistical methods of their own accord.

Figure 7: Shifting image juxtaposition representing PoL 7 Local Symmetries (Larsen, 2017; modified version of: Jake, 2014, source: http://pgfplots.net/tikz/examples/regression-residuals/)

Conceptual understanding is the highest level of statistical knowledge (Huberty, Dresden & Bak, 1993), as it means not only knowledge of isolated concepts and facts, but also knowing when and how they can be applied expediently to solve problems – statistics is understood as a model of reality (Eube, Vogt & Hohlfeld, 2016). Lovett and Greenhouse write that it is helpful when developing well-grounded knowledge if knowledge from another context with a similar structure can be transferred to the new knowledge context (2000). This is precisely the intention of linking the principles of pattern language with the principles of statistics.

This simple, positive introduction does not discuss communicating statistical knowledge in depth, but with willingness to engage in statistical thinking (Gal & Ginsburg, 1994) it lays the foundation for conceptual understanding as the highest form of statistical knowledge.

6. Conclusion

The paper shows the potential of Alexander's pattern language to simplify access to statistics in university teaching and outlines how this can be realized in a basic didactic concept. Pattern language works with visual and spatial principles and therefore accommodates students who prefer thinking in concrete-visual mode (understanding through visualizing). As the core principles of pattern language can be observed and reconstructed in various areas (of life), this enables statistics methods to be connected with personal experiences along the lines of constructivist learning theory (understanding through transfer of experience). In place of negative and restrictive connections, positive points of approach can be offered that allow individual coding of the material. In this way the principles of pattern language refer to fundamental intentions of statistical methods and promote deeper understanding. The structured procedure of pattern language familiarizes learners effortlessly with thinking in an orderly and process-oriented manner – as is necessary in statistics. For practiced learners, the identification of patterns opens up a new approach to mathematical formulae (understanding through structure). Attitudes to statistics can be influenced positively by this approach of introducing statistics via an analogy with life-conducive patterns according to Alexander, both at the micro level (expectation of self-efficacy) and at the meso level (stimulating, true-to-life learning environment). Furthermore, the attitude to statistics as a discipline can be improved via this analogy with true-to-life structures (macro level).

A number of authors stress that there is still great demand for research into the causes of statistics anxiety and negative attitudes. Hypotheses formulated to date have for instance addressed formal-logical versus concrete-visual thinking types for the field of statistics teaching, but these have not yet been documented by studies. Nor are there as yet any targeted studies on the precise impact connections between experiences and the resulting expectation of self-efficacy.

It would be of great interest to research the backgrounds to the development of statistics anxiety within the context of qualitative surveys. With the help of subjective descriptions, it would be possible to reconstruct mechanisms of attitudes and fears in the specific learning biography and thus contribute to further improving offerings that are conducive to learning.

Within the framework of this paper the potentials of pattern language identified for statistics teaching have been integrated into a basic didactic concept, and individual approaches of implementing this concept in an online format have been presented. Consequently, alongside a study of the causes and development of statistics anxiety, the next step is to flesh out the concept presented here in practical application and to review it with regard to learning effectiveness. Students, for instance of social sciences, should be given an introduction with the help of pattern language alongside their regular courses in statistics. With the help of qualitative surveys and standardized questionnaires, a formative and summative evaluation of the suitability and usefulness of the concept developed could be conducted and, in this way, the specific proposal could be developed further along the lines of a design-based research approach. Here students could also be stimulated to supplement the online proposal themselves through collaboratively developed materials along the lines of pattern language.

To summarize, the guiding idea of the suggested concept can be outlined with a quotation from Alexander: „So from the very beginning [..] we concentrated on that fact, and concentrated on that part of human experience and feeling where our feeling is the same. And that is what the pattern language is – a record of that stuff in us, which belongs to the ninety percent of our feeling, where our feeling is all the same" (2002, p.4).

7. References

Alexander, C. (1964). Notes on the Synthesis of Form. Cambridge, Mass.: Harvard University Press.

Alexander, C. (1996, October). Patterns in Architecture. Conference on Object-Oriented Programs, Systems, Languages and Applications (OOPSLA), San Jose, California. Retrieved from https://www.youtube.com/watch?v=98LdFA-_zfA

Alexander, C. (2002). The nature of order: The phenomenon of life. Center for Environmental Structure series: Vol. 9. Berkeley, Calif.: Center for Environmental Structure.

Baharun, N & Porter, A, (2009) Removing the Angst From Statistics, in Mohd Tahir Ismail & Adli Mustafa (eds), Proceedings of the 5th Asian Mathematical Conference, Vol. III, June 2009, pp. 250-255. Penang, University Sains Malaysia

Baloglu, M. (2004). Statistics anxiety and mathematics anxiety: Some interesting differences I. Educational Research Quarterly, 27(3), 38–48.

Bandura, A. (1986). Social foundations of thought and action: A social cognitive perspective. (1st ed.). Englewood Cliffs, N.J: Prentice-Hall Series in Social.

Baumgartner, P., & Bergner, I. (2014). Lebendiges Lernen: 15 strukturelle Empfehlungen für didaktische Entwurfsmuster gestalten in Anlehnung an die Lebenseigenschaften nach Christopher Alexander. In K. Rummler (Ed.), Medien in der Wissenschaft: Vol. 67. Lebendiges Lernen gestalten. (pp. 163-173) Münster: Waxmann.

Bell, J. A. (2003), Statistics Anxiety: The Nontraditional Student. Education, 124, 157-162.

Birkhan, G., & Schulmeister, R. (1983). Untersuchung kognitiver Probleme beim Lernen der Statistik: Kognitive Operationen und Denkstile. In R. Schulmeister (Ed.), Hochschuldidaktische Materialien: Vol. 87. Angst vor Statistik. Empirische Untersuchungen zum Problem des Statistik-Lehrens und -Lernens (pp. 44–84). Hamburg: Arbeitsgemeinschaft für Hochschuldidaktik.

Cruise, R. J., Cash, R. W., & Bolton, D. L. (1985). Development and validation of an instrument to measure statistical anxiety. In American Statistical Association Proceedings of the Section on Statistics Education (Vol. 4, pp. 92-97).

Daley, C. E., & Onwuegbuzie, A. J. (1997). The Role of Multiple Intelligences in Statistics Anxiety. Retrieved from http://files.eric.ed.gov/fulltext/ED415272.pdf

Deci, E. L., & Ryan, R. M. (1993). Die Selbstbestimmungstheorie der Motivation und ihre Bedeutung für die Pädagogik. Zeitschrift für Pädagogik, 39(2), 223–238.

Eco, U. (2002): Einführung in die Semiotik. München (J. Trabant, Trans.) (9th ed.). München: Wilhelm Fink.

Erben, C. M. (1983). Einstellungen von Psychologiestudenten zu Statistik und Statistikkursen vor und nach Beginn des Reformprojektes. In R. Schulmeister (Ed.), Hochschuldidaktische Materialien: Vol. 87. Angst vor Statistik. Empirische Untersuchungen zum Problem des Statistik-Lehrens und -Lernens (pp. 207–213). Hamburg: Arbeitsgemeinschaft für Hochschuldidaktik.

Eube, C., & Vogt, S. (2016). Walk this way!?- Konzepte der Stadtplanung für die (Aus-) Gestaltung von Seamless-Learning-Räumen. Zeitschrift für Hochschulentwicklung / Seamless Learning – Lernen überall und jederzeit, 11(4), 109–121.

Eube, C., Vogt, S., & Hohlfeld, G. (2016). Sustainable and Adaptive Integration of MOOC Videos in Distance Higher Education. In Conference Proceedings The Online, Open and Flexible Higher Education Conference (p. 558–569). Rom. Retrieved from http://conference. eadtu.eu/images/Proceedings/Conference_proceedings_2016_defcompressed2.pdf

Finney, S. J., & Schraw, G. (2003). Self-efficacy beliefs in college statistics courses. Contemporary Educational Psychology, 28(2), 161–186.

Foerster, H. v. (1993). KybernEthik. Internationaler Merve-Diskurs & Perspektiven der Technokultur: Vol. 180. Berlin: Merve-Verl.

Fosnot, C. T., & Perry, R. S. (1996). Constructivism: A psychological theory of learning. Constructivism: Theory, perspectives, and practice, 2, 8–33.

Gal, I., & Ginsburg, L. (1994). The role of beliefs and attitudes in learning statistics: Towards an assessment framework. Journal of Statistics Education, 2(2), 1–15. Retrieved from https:// ww2.amstat.org/publications/jse/v2n2/gal.html

H5P (2017). Retrieved August 10, 2017, from https://h5p.org/

Haan, G. d., & Rülcker, T. (2009). Der Konstruktivismus als Grundlage für die Pädagogik. Berliner Beiträge zur Pädagogik: Vol. 7. Frankfurt am Main: Lang.

Hanna, D., Shevlin, M., & Dempster, M. (2008). The structure of the statistics anxiety rating scale: A confirmatory factor analysis using UK psychology students. Personality and Individual Differences, 45(1), 68–74.

Huberty, C. J., Dresden, J., & Bak, B. G. (1993). Relations among dimensions of statistical knowledge. Educational and Psychological Measurement, 53(2), 523-532.

Kesici, Ş., Baloğlu, M., & Deniz, M. E. (2011). Self-regulated learning strategies in relation with statistics anxiety. Learning and Individual Differences, 21(4), 472–477.

Kohls, C. (2013). The Theories of Design Patterns and their Practical Implications exemplified for E-Learning Patterns: Dissertation. Catholic University of Eichstätt-Ingolstadt, Germany.

Kromrey, H. (2009). Empirische Sozialforschung Modelle und Methoden der standardisierten Datenerhebung und Datenauswertung. (12th ed.) Stuttgart: Lucius & Lucius.

Kunin, D.(2017) Seeing Theory: Brown University. Retrieved August 10, 2017, from http://students.brown.edu/seeing-theory/

Leitner, H. (2007). Mustertheorie: Einführung und Perspektiven auf den Spuren von Christopher Alexander (1st ed.). FastBook: Vol. 5. Graz: Nausner & Nausner.

Leitner, H. (2016). Mustertheorie: Einführung und Perspektiven auf den Spuren von Christopher Alexander (2nd ed.). Graz: Helmut Leitner.

Lovett, M. C., & Greenhouse, J. B. (2000). Applying cognitive theory to statistics instruction. The American Statistician, 54(3), 196–206.

Macher, D., Paechter, M., Ruggeri, K. & Papousek, I. (2015). STARS-D: PSYNDEX Test Review. Retrieved from https://www.zpid.de/retrieval/PSYNDEXTests.php?id=9006906

McLuhan, M., & Fiore, Q. (1967). The medium is the message. New York, 123, 126–128.

Onwuegbuzie, A. J. (2003). Modeling statistics achievement among graduate students. Educational and Psychological measurement, 63(6), 1020–1038.

Onwuegbuzie, A. J. (2004). Academic procrastination and statistics anxiety.

Assessment & Evaluation in Higher Education, 29(1), 3–19. https://doi.org/10.1080/0260293042000160384

Onwuegbuzie, A. J., & Wilson, V. A. (2003). Statistics Anxiety: Nature, etiology, antecedents, effects, and treatments--a comprehensive review of the literature. Teaching in Higher Education, 8(2), 195-209.

Paas, F., Renkl, A., & Sweller, J. (2003). Cognitive load theory and instructional design: Recent developments. Educational psychologist, 38(1), 1–4.

Pan, W., & Tang, M. (2004). Examining the Effectiveness of Innovative Instructional Methods on Reading Statistics Anxiety for Graduate Students in the Social Sciences. Journal of Instructional Psychology, 31(2), 149.

Perepiczka, M., Chandler, N., & Becerra, M. (2011). Relationship between Graduate Students' Statistics Self-Efficacy, Statistics Anxiety, Attitude toward Statistics, and Social Support. Professional Counselor, 1(2), 99–108.

Perney, J., & Ravid, R. (1991). The relationship between attitudes towards statistics, math self-efficacy concept, test anxiety and graduate students' achievement in an introductory statistics course. Unpublished manuscript, National College of Education, Evanston, IL.

Piaget, J. (1970). Structuralism, Chaninah Maschler. New York: Basic.

Piaget, J. (1977) Problems of Equilibaration. In: Appel M.H., Goldberg L.S. (eds) Topics in Cognitive Development. Springer, Boston, MA (pp. 3–13).

Rosenthal, B. (1992). No more sadistics, no more sadists, no more victims. UMAP Journal,13, 281–290.

Ruggeri, K., Dempster, M.,& Hanna, D. (2011). The Impact of Misunderstanding the Nature of Statistics. Psychology Teaching Review, 17(1), 35–40.

Schulmeister, R. (Ed.). (1983). Hochschuldidaktische Materialien: Vol. 87.

Angst vor Statistik: Empirische Untersuchungen zum Problem des StatistikLehrens und -Lernens. Hamburg: Arbeitsgemeinschaft für Hochschuldidaktik.

Simon, J. L., & Bruce, P. (1991). Resampling: A tool for everyday statistical work. Chance, 4(1), 22–32.

Tufte, E. R. (2015). The thinking eye. 9th MIT Sloan Sports Analytics Conference, Boston, Massachusetts. Retrieved from https://www.youtube.com/watch?v=mvrNemNoQ5M

Vygotsky, L.S. (1964). Denken und Sprechen. Berlin: Akademie Verlag

Wilensky, U. (1997). What is normal anyway? Therapy for epistemological anxiety. Educational Studies in Mathematics, 33(2), 171–202.

Williams, A. S. (2013). Worry, intolerance of uncertainty, and statistics anxiety. Statistics Education Research Journal, 12(1), 48–59. Retrieved from http://iase-web.org/documents/SERJ/SERJ12(1)_Williams.pdf

Wirtz, M. A. (Ed.). (2014). Lexikon der Psychologie (18.th ed.). Bern: Hogrefe Verlag.

Zeidner, M. (1991). Statistics and Mathematics Anxiety in Social Science Students: Some interesting Parallels. British Journal of Educational Psychology, 61(3), 319–328. https://doi.org/10.1111/j.2044-8279.1991.tb00989.x

Zielinski, W. (1980). Lernschwierigkeiten. Verursachungsmomente, Diagnose, Behandlungsansätze: Stuttgart: Kohlhammer.

Resonating Patterns and Resonating Spaces

Potential steps for dynamic pattern technology
and digital pattern practice

Stark, Wolfgang
University of Duisburg-Essen, Germany
wolfgang.stark@stw.de

Tewes, Stefan
FOM University of Applied Sciences, Germany
stefan.tewes@realyze.de

Weber, Christian
Strascheg Center for Entrepreneurship, Germany
christina.weber@sce.de

Pattern languages and pattern science have been developing a wide array of patterns in different disciplines and multiple uses and creative tools of a ‚quality without a name' in many diverse and practical fields. Doing this, the pattern approach could show the power of implicit and tacit knowing in many fields and complement and recharge ‚rational' knowing with experiential wisdom. Nevertheless, there still are open questions to be solved in order to understand and use pattern languages as dynamic systems.

Based on our practice of using patterns, pattern languages and patterns cards with teams and groups (GroupWorks), innovative teaching in universities (Service Learning, Social Entrepreneurship Education) and disaster management, this paper tries to link an extended pattern approach (performative pattern language) with the procedures based on the Actor Network Theory (ANT).

Based on this we adress some challenges we face when we
» try to identify and validate patterns and improve interindividual and intergroup validity for pattern and
» attempt to create a dynamic pattern language with a dynamic relationship system between related patterns which will be able to learn from connections and links between patterns.

1.   Introduction

Pattern languages and pattern science have developed successfully a wide array of patterns in different disciplines (architecture and urban design, software development, agile orga-nizational development, learning in higher education) for multiple uses and creative tools of a ‚quality without a name' in many diverse and practical fields. Doing this, the pattern approach could show the power of 'implicit and tacit knowing' in many fields and comple-ment and recharge ‚rational knowing' with experiential wisdom. Nevertheless, there still are open questions to be solved in order to understand and use pattern languages as dynamic systems.

One of the major challenges for pattern science is to link the approach on patterns and pat-tern languages with other theoretical approaches in social science. Although there have been frequent references of pattern language being a systemic approach, there still is no elabora-ted relationship to other scientific theories. In respect to the ‚language' notion of Alexander´s pattern language approach, Noam Chomsky´s ‚theory of universal grammar' (1965) and Hein-rich Lausberg's ‚Ars Rhetorica' (1963) have been probed by Aspalter & Bauer (2014).

In this paper, the authors suggest linking the space-oriented concept of ‚A Pattern Langua-ge' by Christopher Alexander (Alexander et al 1977, Alexander 1979, Leitner 2007) with La-tour´s time-oriented ‚Actor-Network-Theory' (Latour 2005) to develop a space and time-ori-ented concept (SToC). We do this in order to address some challenges we face when we

» try to identify and validate patterns and improve interindividual and intergroup validity for pattern and

» attempt to create a dynamic pattern language with a dynamic relationship system bet-ween related patterns which will be able to learn from connections and links between patterns.

Based on our practice of using patterns, pattern languages and patterns cards with teams and groups (GroupWorks), innovative teaching in universities (Service Learning, Social Entre-preneurship Education)[1] and disaster management (Weber 2016), we would like to discuss

» how to generate and validate systematically patterns in social systems using digital tech-nology;

» how to develop a digital dynamic learning system resonating how people use and connect patterns and

---

1   A series of Pattern Languages, which have been developed in various areas like ‚working with groups and teams', enhance ‚collaboration' between groups, or develop ‚social entrepreneurship education', can be found on www.facebook.com/weareheyst/karten

» how to create holographic ‚dynamic resonating pattern spaces' to enhance the usability, complexity and visual and experiential quality of pattern languages.

2. Performative Patterns: Some Basic Questions for Next Steps of a Pattern Science

Contemporary organizations and social systems have to deal with accelerated complexity and growing uncertainties and ambiguities. Recent papers (Gong et al, 2008; Stark, 2015) highlight the contradictive, yet productive tension between rational process thinking and the improvisational field in entrepreneurial processes. A path to develop tools for dealing with complexity and using the strength and the art of improvisation has been offered by developing a 'Performative Pattern Language (PPL)' (Stark 2015). A PPL is based on improvisation theory and aims to allow people to use tacit knowledge in social systems to increase their flexibility, creativity and performance in settings of uncertainty and ambiguity. These kinds of settings provide a culture in which innovative approaches emerge.

2.1. Beyond Bounded Rationality

People in organizations and social systems can act and create new solutions either by (1) analysis and planning, (2) by intuition or by (3) improvisation. The vast majority of organizational learning and innovation accepted today still seems to follow the first type of procedure: rational planning based upon analysis. For most of last century, organizational theory and innovation management is rooted in 'rational cognitive mode'. Management and engineering both are focused upon numbers, influenced by rational industrial thinking, and characterized by measurement and focus on accountability. In the last 20 years, this rather one-sided approach has also been adopted by society at large and professional communities alike. It has infected our everyday way of thinking.

Rational thinking is based on the assumption that technical and social challenges can be solved by an objective, step-by-step, rational approach. Although many social scientists, as well as many practitioners, know that this approach captures only a small part of the processes and dynamics existing in both social systems and organizations, it seems to work well for traditional organizations that are based on the hierarchical model of top-down decision-making and planning. In contrast, modern network-type social systems must encourage soft factors like community-building and organizational culture in order to survive in their complex and constantly changing organizational environment. Even organizational systems which rely heavily on 'rational' key performance indicators (KPI) based on numbers end up discovering the value of 'soft' cultural organizational processes when they are confronted with unexpected dynamics or find that they must use creativity to build corporate cultures of trust and innovation.

The concept of Bounded Rationality (Gigerenzer & Selten, 2002) already challenged rationality in decision making based on experimental models. The concept proofed that rational choice is only one part of human choice; non-rational factors are highly influential in everyday decisions. Nevertheless, the majority of decision makers pretend to make rational choices although they are relying heavily on 'managerial intuition'. Therefore, complex social systems like modern companies, non-profits, political and informal communities are very often not (only) determined by clearly defined goals and strategies. Even more, the majority of business and social innovations and most web-based social networks (including Facebook, vimeo, cool ideas society, seats2meet, intrinsify.me and many others)[2] as well as many web-oriented companies are successful on the base of the idea of serendipity[3] – that is, they use opportunities that emerge from non-planned networking.

Gradually, society (re)discovers that many settings in which we live and work in are governed by unknown situations and ill-defined factors. The ability to be creative, to design innovative environments and to improvise in an ostensibly rational and structured situation may be a key factor for survival in a global world that is – in reality – unpredictable and subject to serendipity. Although non-linear and non-deterministic factors pertain to a world of constant change (Looss, 2002), they usually are not addressed by a rational approach, and thus are also neglected in engineering and the (social) sciences. Indeed, the dynamic process of organizing (Weick,1989) still is bound to a culture of numbers, planned results and rationality. The complex socio-technical network of relations is neither seen nor tackled, since practice and perception are both oriented toward attaining goals, maintaining control, and setting strategies. More problematically, entrepreneurs, decision makers, and managers – both in traditional and sustainability-driven organizations – typically lack a language to describe both their individual 'implicit knowing' (often called 'intuition') and their commonly shared and collective 'tacit knowing' (Polanyi, 1966) (including both: restrictions, fears and opportunities, wisdom) in this land of uncertainty.

2.2. Tacit Knowing and the Improvisational Field

The economy of production and organizational technology unfolds in a texture of collaboration of diverse models of partnership – from (a) the small cooperative cell (the team) within an organization or company, (b) to the organizational design of a company or non-profit-organization as an entity in itself with explicit structures and implicit knowledge, to (c) the

---

2   Although facebook and vimeo seem to be well known and linked, smaller and more specialized social networks need links to be seen: http://coolideassociety.com, https://www.seats2meet.com, http://intrinsify.me.
3   See http://en.wikipedia.org/wiki/Serendipity

strategic alliance between different types of organizations and stakeholders. These different relations share a common challenge: they all are driven inherently by implicit and 'tacit' knowing, and, quite often, emotionally-based ('intuitive') decision-making and processes. In contrast, especially in organizational settings, most processes are determined by 'rational planning' which does not grasp the hidden power and potentials of tacit knowing, which has been shown in analyzing complex and uncertain situations in organizations (Weick & Westley, 1996).

As shown in previous papers (Schümmer, Haake & Stark 2014, 2015), in our 'rational world' of buildings, business-statistics and computer/machine-based processes, complexity has not led to the use of emergent and creative operations based on the tacit knowledge of the many. Instead, decision-making still pretends to be built on planned structures that are explicit and too often planned solely using rationality, which try to reduce complexity to a level that is manageable using rational thinking. This limits our ability to cope with the ambiguity and uncertainty that is inherent to modern organizational dynamics.

Complexity may lead to the use of emergent and creative processes based on the tacit knowledge of the many. Coping with unpredictable processes is an everyday challenge in organizations and communities. In addition to codified rational operations, members of social systems usually will develop a set of tacit procedures which just prove to be viable (Glasersfeld, 1992). Similar to improvisation in jazz music, where musicians 'act-in-an-instant' (Dell 2012) on the basis of well-known explicit and implicit 'jazz patterns' (Coker et al., 1970), this kind of process can be viewed as continuously re-designing and re-arranging implicit and explicit procedural patterns based on experiential (implicit) knowledge. Social interaction here evolves from already known patterns, citing and following other patterns. Re-designing and re-arranging patterns (here: harmonies, chords, and riffs) will create a constant flow of new patterns which will be added to the body of experiential knowing (Barrett, 1998).

To develop the idea of a ‚pattern language', which is able to cope with complexity, ambiguity and uncertainty, the conventional form of design patterns therefore has to be challenged (Gabriel, 2002 & 2012; West, 2010). We need to discuss the perspective of a 'Performative Pattern Language (APPL)' which aims to open up the idea of patterns and a pattern language (APL) toward creativity and serendipity. APPL will expand possible ways to act (to learn) instead of limiting the possibilities in order to be effective (to organize). By doing this, APPL uses background from improvisation and artistic research and social philosophy.

2.3. Expanding Space-Oriented Concepts in Design Patterns

While the idea of ‚performative patterns' already expands the traditional ‚Alexandrian' concept of design patterns from ‚bounded rationality' to a more creative, tentatively artistic approach, ‚performativity' (Butler, 2010; Healy, 2015) requires dealing with the other side of the coin of a real-time context. Patterns and Pattern Languages by and large are a space-oriented concepts (SoC) (Leitner 2012).

Social (and natural) systems always display a relationship between space and time. Social complexity is felt by actors as change over time, or as temporary need of parallel ad hoc activities, or as need of subsequent action in various directions. The mobilization of social interaction spans space and time. The dynamic aspects of social interaction have long time been neglected by static theories and also pattern concepts, and therefore we suggest that it could profit from an actor-network perspective to integrate the role of time into models of real-world and local knowledge production (SToC).

This is why we propose to link pattern science with the Actor Network Theory (ANT).

The following paragraph briefly describes the time oriented evolutionary approach of ANT.

3. Actor-network theory and pattern approach

Actor-network theory (ANT) retraces empirical network operations. Thus, it enables the exploration of past collaboration and innovation processes. ANT - based on the 'science and technology studies' (STS) by Callon, Latour, Akrich and Law (see, f.ex., Akrich, Callon, & Latour, 2002; Latour, 1991; Law & Hassard, 1999) – scholars who aimed to investigate the interplay of technology, knowledge and innovation (Scacchi, 2005). But instead of observing homogeneous nodes and ties, as classical social network analysis (SNA) does, here, macro-actors become the unit of analysis, and ANT points to analyses of volatile nets between heterogeneous entities. In parallel to the pattern approach by Alexander (1979), human and non-human actors are included (Avgerou, Ciborra, & Land, 2004) into network patterns. To give an example: investigating a school class would entail interviews with pupils and teachers, but also the investigation of school computers, laboratories, buildings, software used and the recent education policy and dominant teaching practices. Or, in the field of disaster management, interviews with aid organizations, affected people and donors, but also the examination of affected livelihoods, destroyed infrastructures, governmental disaster acts, fiber glass boats and collaboration practices between all these actors. The aim for a holistic perspective forms the basis of both theories. And there are strikingly more features that link the concepts.

The ANT pioneers rejected dualism (nature-culture, subject-object, et cetera) and focused on practices. Therefore, networks and actors are seen as socio-technical ‚hybrids' (Callon,

1986; Latour, 1999; Law & Rip, 1986; Tatnall, 2011). An actor role is assigned to objects and subjects that influence others, in physical or symbolic ways (see, e.g., van Mierlo, Leeuwis, Smits, & Woolthuis, 2010). Thus, in contrast to positivist SNA frames, ANT allows no external, 'as-from-above' perspective. Analysts have to ‚follow the actor' to retrace the network practices (Dant, 2005) from several different sides. The notion of ‚actors' is close to Alexander's notion ‚centres'; both are refusing to be understood as ‚elements' that could stand or exist ‚alone' (Leitner, 2007).

Furthermore, actor-networks are assumed to be instable. Without continuous mobilization they fall apart. ANT scholars therefore tried to find out why some interactions "more or less succeed in stabilizing and reproducing themselves" (Law, 1992, p. 380). They found that to exist as an actor-network, a translation process between heterogeneous interests occurs

(Callon, 1986). The term translation makes all the difference to the above theory traditions: SNA (Mueller-Prothmann & Finke, 2004), system dynamics (cf. Besiou, Stapleton, & van Wassenhove, 2011) and innovation diffusion (Rogers, 2010) all speak of transfer. In contrast, ANT scholars hold that there is no transfer and input is always modified by other actors' interests. The enrolled actors alter the translated interests (see, e.g., Pollack, Costello, & Sankaran, 2013). Collaboration and network emergence therefore are "somewhat uncertain processes of overcoming resistance – rather than a fait accompli or a noun" (Law, 1992, p. 380). Finally, actor-networks are effects of social practices, not their causes.

Holding that "an actor is also, always a network" (Latour, 2012; Law, 1992, p. 384), a network analysis starts with the choice of perspective and enables to zoom in and zoom out specific processes. Successful network emergence leads to punctualisation (see, e.g., Austrin & Farnsworth, 2005): the making of the heterogeneous actor-network becomes invisible behind a successful network. It is punctualisation that makes networks and macro-actors real-time effective and powerful.

In sum, ANT crosses boundaries of traditional management and organization theory using a dynamic network perspective. In this, it promises to complement the pattern approach by theoretic foundation in how dynamic network pattern evolve. Just like the pattern approach, it merges managerial and evolutionary components and micro- and macro perspectives. Its translation concept helps to understand collaboration dynamics (Pollack et al., 2013). This concept is explained further in the definition and table.

Translation is the process of network evolution and consists of four basic moments: (1) Problematization, (2) Interessement, (3) Enrolment and (4) Mobilization. (Tatnall, 2011)

Table 1 contains the four operations of network emergence (left column) and management activities that relate to the network formation moments (next column). Compared with the laments of the pattern approach, it shows how (a) strategic management elements (interests) and (b) more evolutionary, systemic-driven dynamics melt in the approach.

ANT operations	Related management activities and network practices	Integral Parts of a Pattern	Pattern Approach
Problematization	Identification of specific problems; identification of actors involved in a problem in real-time (socio-technological hybrids).	Describe the problem area and the specific challenge triggering the solution	Problems and Challenges
Interessement	Practices to identify and attract interest, define and create linkages between actors' interests, translate different interests; heterogeneous actors' interests have to be channeled through an "obligatory point of passage" (OPP) to become a network.	Dynamics and interests crucial for the problem/challenge. Has a major influence on both problem and solution.	Forces
Enrollment	Negotiation of interests; practices to encourage heterogeneous actors' commitment to 'enroll' in common network activities, use of boundary objects.	Improvisational fields of application for the pattern and the specific solution.	Context
Mobilisation	Activating old and new allies for the aligned interests; continued practices to stabilize a reversible and dynamic network.	Action or design principle, which helps to solve a problem. can be used in different situations and settings.	Solution

Table 1: Actor-network evolution and management activities

A final moment in interessement is crucial for a translation process: to become a network, the interests of heterogeneous actors have to be channeled through an OPP, an ‚obligatory point of passage' (Callon, 1986; Stanforth, 2006). If an OPP (a contractual event, informal meeting or factual agreement) fails in some respect, it becomes unlikely that the actors will enroll in common network activities. The OPP designates a moment that has to happen in order to align interests and to establish a dynamic innovation network. To define the OPP makes network-actors become focal actors.

Heterogeneous networks need objects that are "able to mediate diverse actor worlds" (Briers & Chua, 2001, p. 240), called 'boundary objects'. Such artefacts can be anything from technological devices to consumer goods and symbolic artefacts such as words, claims, events, or pictures.

Ongoing network 'mobilization' remains necessary to continue the contingent and always reversible collaboration. To stabilize actor-networks over time, the inscription of practices in materials and institutional routines has to follow (Stanforth, 2006).

3.1. Collaboration in innovation processes – the need for dynamic pattern knowledge

In real-time innovation processes, as exemplified in the case of disaster management in global relief and reconstruction processes (Karan & Subbiah, 2011), recent research shows the importance of initial collaboration periods for sustainable ends (Weber, 2016; Weber, Sailer, Holzmann, & Katzy, 2014). We suggest that here is a conceptual need for combining pattern knowledge and innovation theory (ANT) to profit from implicit and explicit knowledge approaches.

In a real-time foresight concept (Weber, Sailer, & Katzy, 2015) five dynamic principles are identified that span initial, continuous and end activities of heterogeneous actors in sustainable innovation processes:

1. To become aware of a networked situation, to signal one's own position and to identify central other heterogeneous actors that are crucial to this collaboration.

2. To seek the early development of a shared vision. It should align the heterogeneous interests of focal actors which is the most important managerial element. As a continuous governance instrument, it decides long-term success.

3. 'Boundary objects' need to be identified or created for strict use to mobilize commitment, communication and network mutuality. The more heterogeneous the DINs are, the better the use of boundary objects must be.

4. To prepare for time-outs of particular network-actors. In dynamic long-term proces-ses, partial non-visibility and temporal passivity of actors must be tolerable. Intermedi-ary actors can be included to release DINs and to deliver network support.

5. Coherent collaborative leadership is crucial. Leadership has to switch from traditional strategic management to a process orientation and adequate implementation accor-ding to the focal actors' profiles. Thus, in one and the same network, focal actor roles may change over time.

We argue that an organization's capacity to engage rapidly and visibly in interaction, high-lighting the principles (2) and (3), will be enhanced by its existing, available and deployable pattern knowledge of this organization.

3.2. Critical Incident Technique

To identify network dynamics and patterns instead of just individual network actors that facilitate collaborative innovation processes, we need to assess the changes in network evolution and its governance. Critical incident technique (CIT, see, e.g., Butterfield, Borgen, Amundson, & Maglio, 2005; Flanagan, 1954), is a timeline method for gathering in-depth information on sequential changes. It enables the detection of 'tipping points' in a process. Mapping concrete CIs complements more abstract network operations of ANT and pattern approach with (1) concrete time stamps and (2) details on empirical issues and empirical problem solving. This makes visible sequential, but non-linear collaboration.

In retrospect, CIT's advantage in assessing management of ad hoc collaboration and its fit to pattern approaches is that it focuses on behavior and action (Flanagan, 1954, p. 13) instead of mapping perceptions: "The critical incident technique, rather than collecting opinions, hunches, and estimates, obtains a record of specific behaviors from those in the best po-sition to make the necessary observations and evaluations. The collection and tabulation of these observations make it possible to formulate the critical requirements of an activity" (Flanagan, 1954, p. 30). Note that, in comparison with the disruptive management proces-ses of different actors, CIT methodology allows for pattern reconstruction. Thus, CIs can be compared within and across actors and networks.

The CIT approach requires primary data collection from participants as experts of the pro-cess. Still, the collection of secondary data remains indispensable (1) for better contextual understanding and (2) for a verification of the recalled CIs. To avoid a retrospective bias

(Middleton, Middleton, & Modafferi, 2014; Sword-Daniels, Twigg, & Loughlin, 2015), all nar-rative statements need data confirmation. The more an investigated pattern or process dates back in time (Flanagan, 1954, p. 4) the more important the check becomes.

3.3. The empirical approach of pattern reconstruction using CIT and ANT

Social interaction follows well-defined and well-understood patterns. The study in disaster management cited in its resulting dynamic innovation pattern (Weber et al., 2015) above aimed to achieve a reconstruction (in ANT terminology ‚reconstruction' is a time-oriented concept) of dynamic network patterns (that have occurred in real-time), using a systematic empirical approach. Based on multiple primary and secondary data, it elaborates upon three networks as case studies and then uses CIT to obtain CI-charts. These matrices systematically display points and periods of change in a real-world collaborative management guiding the non-linear process.

Traditionally, ANT studies and pattern studies are based on ethnographic research, on rich textual and visual data and on its presentation. In the chosen new combination with CIT for systematic comparison of processes and patterns, the traditional basis can no longer be used. The coding procedure in ATLAS.ti, as well as the extended period of data collection however delivered much more explicit and rich narrative data than could be shown in the frame of this study. The unexpected richness in fact is a disadvantage compared to typical in-depth ANT studies (Bijker, 1997) that has been accepted in order to achieve something new: instead of exploring the historical emergence of actor-networks, ANT analysis here leads to exploring CIs in innovation processes in a systematic way, to gain managerial insights.

To detect patterns between and around these incidents that changed the planned course of action, it is necessary to analyze in parallel rich secondary data that was collected in a longitudinal study. Annual reports, project documents, and newspaper clippings build the background for the empirical research leading to the identification of repeating network patterns around reoccurring CIs.

4. Resonating Patterns

In physics, **resonance** is a phenomenon in which a vibrating system or external force drives another system to oscillate with greater amplitude at specific frequencies. Frequencies at which the response amplitude is a relative maximum are known as the system's **resonant frequencies** or **resonance frequencies**. At resonant frequencies, small periodic driving forces have the ability to produce large amplitude oscillations, due to the storage of vibrational energy.

The combination of dynamic patterns and the ANT-approach bear the potential – in a metaphoric sense – to resonate between the challenges/problems identified in a social system and the potential solutions. That is, learning and change in social systems can be both represented and inspired by using an extended understanding of a dynamic 'performative' pattern approach integrating ANT procedures.

'Resonating Patterns' also helps to detect the 'improvisational field' (Stark et al., 2017):

In social systems such as like organizations or communities, the 'improvisational field' is the layer beneath planning and acting. It is built upon tacit knowing and experiential wisdom and is the resonating body of organizations and social systems. Dorothy Leonard (Leonard & Swap, 2005) calls this phenomenon 'deep smarts'. According to her research deep smarts (i.e. tacit knowing) and the rational field of structures and numbers cannot be separated; instead, they need to rely on each other. Therefore, improvisation and its performative patterns do not replace the rational, cognitive mode: just as the muscle system in the body is needed for the skeleton to move, to balance and to be alert, the improvisational field and performative patterns are needed to balance structures and rules, as well as ambiguities in each situation new to routine and to be alert to innovations and creative opportunities.

To detect the language of tacit knowing we must experiment with new sensorial channels: for instance, if we could 'hear' the dynamic processes of organizations, the communicative sensorium in the workplace could be expanded to a new and deeper level which would allow us access both aesthetic and emotional dimensions of processes. Music, as a performing art[4], can be one key to the "...deep level of organizing and innovative processes" which can be used as a reflective tool for both managers and employees but also for people in communities to start a dynamic and creative process of learning for social systems and individuals. To "...imagine community processes as a piece of music..." (Stark & Dell 2013, p. 53) opens up social and organizational systems which are often stuck in strategic plans and work-flows, and helps them to creatively re-design the system.

To detect the dynamics of this hidden (implicit and tacit) system inside the visible system, a special form of musical production is necessary in order to foster learning processes in complex and constantly changing settings, which call for the ability for continuous sense-making and serendipity (Weick & Westley, 1996): the technology of improvisation has already inspired organizational theory as a metaphor (Weick, 1995; Hatch, 1999; Barrett, 1998); improvisational patterns will be even more important for organizational processes and social systems, if we look at music not only as something that can be received or interpreted, but also as a tool for sense-making. Improvisation then will open up the ability

---

4   Of course, also other types of performance such as art, dance and theater, as well as modern, performative ways of painting, could be helpful in detecting the potentials of tacit knowledge beyond rational planning (Forsythe 2003). Based on our research at www.micc-project. org, we focus in this paper on music not only as a metaphor, but also as an analytical tool.

not only to cope with unknown potentials and uncertain processes, but also to redesign patterns and minimal structures in a creative way (Dell, 2012; Stark, 2014).

This is true not only for music using arts of improvisation such as Jazz but has also been admired in many pieces of Johann Sebastian Bach (Ruiter-Feenstra, 2011), or in the base-lines of Indian music (Kurt & Näumann, 2008). It also is common ground for many forms of performative contemporary art such as theatre, dance or performing art itself (Johnstone, 1987; Forsythe, 2003; Fischer-Lichte, 2012). In everyday-life, we discover the art of improvisation in many sports activities like modern soccer, sailing, and skiing. One can therefore assume that whenever human creativity and playfulness are triggered, the art of improvisation is one of the keys to joy and self-awareness and furthermore develops skills to cope with ambiguity and uncertainty. Thus, the inventive production of improvisation becomes a norm in itself: challenge and possibility.

The ANT perspective reveals and describes similar dynamics, but rather highlights the uncertainty of successful network evolution, and the constant energy consumption it affords from all interested actors. Network-actors need to constantly signal to others and to be interested in others in order to realize their network vision and intentions. The patterns of problematization, interessement, enrolement and mobilization are enacted again and again, in various figurations, and the network itself is a temporary achievement.

5. Resonating Patterns in Resonating Spaces: The Vision of a Digital Platform

When looking at the core findings of the presented pattern approaches, five main challenges for the further development of patterns emerge.

1. How to identify patterns (pattern mining);

2. How to create and evaluate intersubjective and intergroup validity of patterns;

3. How to construct a dynamic relationship system between patterns and pattern groups;

4. How to integrate human and non-human actors into the system;

5. How will patterns be able to learn from connections and links between patterns.

Having these challenges in mind, a dynamic and resonating learning system has to be developed. The first requirement for this system is the access to the patterns at any time and in any place – a clear hint for digital transformation. Based on the real-world transformation gaining and possessing information is the success key for business and social institutions

(Kollmann, 2016). The accessibility of information in real time is ensured by cloud solutions. Therefore, the research question is: How to develop a viable digital learning system to enhance the usability, complexity and quality of pattern languages?

5.1. Platform business as key model

According to the challenges described before, a network approach for various contents in the context of patterns has to be developed. Equivalent to the variety of content challenges for organizations and companies – demographic change, health, strategic alignment to an ever-changing environment in an increasingly complex world – the digital learning system has to be able to link different contents of patterns (e.g GroupWorks, Service Learning, Social Entrepreneurship Education). Therefore, a systemic framework of the digital learning system must be determined. The basic of the framework is a digital network. Looking at organizations and companies the network approach is also known as the term online platform.

> *"'Online platform' refers to an undertaking operating in two (or multi)-sided markets, which uses the Internet to enable interactions between two or more distinct but interdependent groups of users so as to generate value for at least one of the groups. Certain platforms also qualify as Intermediary service providers" (BMWi, 2016, p. 26 combined with EC, 2016).*

Digital platforms such as search engines, social networks and trading platforms are becoming increasingly important in business and society. Digitized information on networked devices simplifies searches and reduces cost of comparison – information is always and everywhere accessible (BMWi, 2016). Google, Facebook, Apple, Amazon are best practice examples for the new business models, called platform business (van Alstyne & Parker, 2017).

5.2. From theory to the 'gut feeling' of the digital world

Creating a digital platform for pattern languages, the implicit intuition must be linked with cognitive-rational knowledge. Accordingly, the platform has to create and to resonate multi-dimensional levels of knowledge. In contrast to today's blogs, wikis etc. (documentation platforms which connect complex issues by linking only), a digital system beyond the semantic link is required.

The content bases of the platform are pattern cards. Inspired by the work on pattern languages by Christopher Alexander (both architecture, urban planning and software development), there are successful and proven patterns of action in all disciplines and fields of work. The first fundamental questions for the digital platform is how to identify patterns of implicit and tacit knowing (see no. 1). Therefore, the following questions must be digitally implemented:

» Does the idea describe something that occurs repeatedly in successful group processes?

» Does this also happen in different application fields?

» Can the pattern take different shapes?

» Does it occur in different sizes and on different levels?

» Do I recognize this pattern intuitively based on my experiences?

The construction of the system based on the identified patterns is the next challenge for the digital learning system (see no. 2). At this point the first analogous connections will be build. As shown in figure 1, action patterns identified and validated (numbered as 1–5) in the respective content areas (A–C) can be represented by these analogous connections.

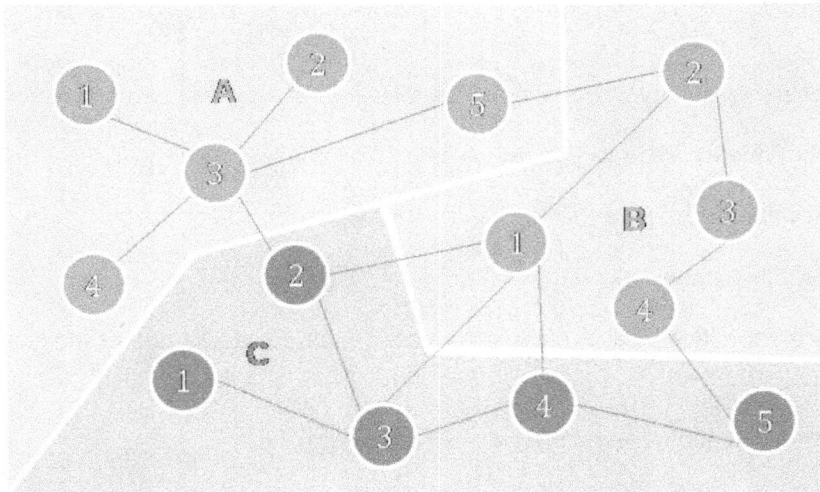

Figure 1: Logic of system based patterns

But this network of causality is insufficient for the digital learning system. The success criteria are linked to the integration of intersubjective and intergroup validity (see no. 3). Critical mass is the success factor for community networks. An increasing number of users will increase the validation of knowledge. For this reason, the validation of patterns and connections between patterns will be intersubjective constructed as well as intergroup approved. This leads from common sense to community sense. Due to the fact of nearly infinite content connection by computing power, an empirical and theoretical saturation or a criteria of saturation has to be defined. The necessary inclusion of human and non-human actors (no. 4) means to combine subjective, human thinking with cloud based digital technology. Hence the digital learning system has to be retrievable from any mobile or stationary device.

A further key of the digital platform is the ability to learn from connections and links between patterns (see no. 5). To increase the learning and using, the simplicity of the collection of knowledge is significant. Equivalent to web design, the usability of the platform and the user experience increase the dissemination to reach the critical mass. The success of learning depends further on the types of dynamics, filtering and semantic linking. Easiness and velocity of usage is one success factor. At least the of discovery of pattern space is relevant. Move and experience through the pattern card universe are the main ingredients for the use of the digital platform. The success factors of a digital platform in the context of patterns can be described as (Kohlmann, 2016; DeLeone/McLean 2003; Garton/Haythornwaite/Wellmann 1999; Lin/Lee 2006):

» **System Quality**: realization of desirable features such as accessibility and easiness of use

» **Membership quality**: importance and competence of the members as indicators

» **Content quality**: accuracy and usefulness of the information

» **Service quality**: trust mechanisms and willingness to help participants

» **Scope**: achieving the critical mass

» **Participation level**: activity of the participants – up-to-dateness, quality and quantity of the content

» **Relationship quality**: exchange between the participants

» **Community level**: identification with the community and the other participants

» **User integration**: involvement of the participants in the further development of the community

The process of the full penetration of a digital platform in the pattern community, a four-phase process is recommended (Kollmann, 2016). This admission phase is initially laid with the eRegistration and eProfile processes. If the visitor decides to join the digital platform, he must first register and provide the required minimum information about his person for profiling. In the production phase the members generate new content. These contents correspond to the already described logic of identifying system-based patterns. Content production is carried out as part of a differentiated approach directly via the eUpload or eBlogging process or indirectly via the eTagging process. The third phase is the evaluation phase. Classifying and evaluating of the patterns is key topic. In this phase, however, not only the individual contents within the scope of the user-generated content are evaluated via the eVoting process, but also related to other content and activities in the contact network via the eRanking process (see figure 1). Further a possibility can be given to pass on ratings or recommendations to other participants, which takes place through the so-called eRecommendation process. The last step is the dissemination phase. In this phase the content will be disseminated as efficient and efficient as possible for other users within and outside the digital platform. In the context of a differentiated consideration, the distribution of content takes place via the eSyndication and ePodcasting process.

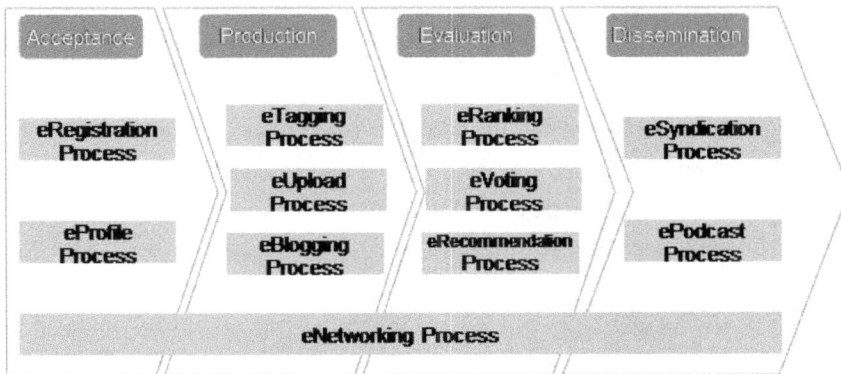

Figure 2: The process of digital connection | (Kollmann, 2016, 446)

5.3. Practical application of 'resonating' patterns in resonating digital space

To understand digital patterns a well-known example can be used: Spotify. The (pattern) algorithm meets the individualized musical taste. The weekly playlist is based on the personnel preferences of the listener. By collaborative filtering the user behavior can be predicted. Based on a similarity matrix the relation between songs is determined. So, the liking of songs will be increased. Through this approach combined with natural language processing, we hear new songs that seem familiar to one.

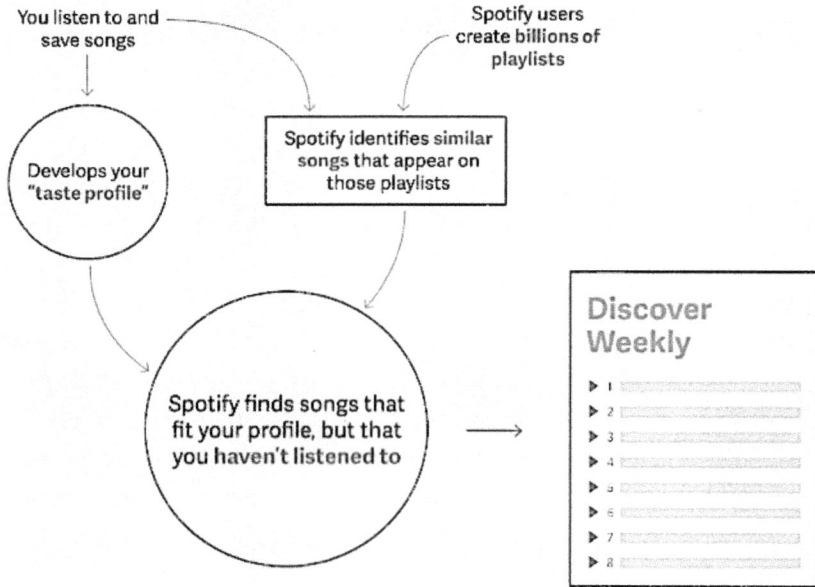

You listen to and save songs

Spotify users create billions of playlists

Develops your "taste profile"

Spotify identifies similar songs that appear on those playlists

Spotify finds songs that fit your profile, but that you haven't listened to

Discover Weekly

▶ 1
▶ 2
▶ 3
▶ 4
▶ 5
▶ 6
▶ 7
▶ 8

Figure 3: The process of digital connection | (Pasick, 2015)

Deep learning, human behavior filtering and the increasing validation of patterns are main factors for a resonating digital pattern platform. The better the system works, the more reliable patterns will be found. The described potentials will lead to diverse application areas of patterns in practice, such as: Patterns

» in business process adaptions in different locations

» for sustainable development in Third World countries

» of cooperation between nation states

» of innovative product design

» in disaster management

The success of the presented digital learning system depends on the quality of content, the competencies of the members and the frequency of use. Or in other words: "Something works if it does what it is supposed to do" (von Glasersfeld, 1997, p. 52).

6. References

Akrich, M., Callon, M., & Latour, B. (2002). The key to success in innovation part I: the art of interessement. International Journal of Innovation Management, 6, 187-206.

Alexander, C. (1977), A Pattern Language: Towns, Buildings, Construction. New York: Oxford University Press

Alexander, C (1979). The Timeless Way of Building. Oxford University Press, New York

Alexander, C. (2004), The Nature of Order, Vol. 1-4, Berkeley, CA, Center for Environmental Structure

Alexander, C. & Neis, H., Alexander Moore, M. (2013), The Battle for the Life and Beauty of the Earth. Oxford University Press

Allan, R (1998), Patterns of Preaching. Christian Board of Pubn, 1998.

van Alstyne, M./Parker, G. (2017). Plattformwirtschaft: Wo Beziehungen wertvoller sind als Vermögen. GfK MIR: Digitale Transformation, Vol. 9, No. 1, 25-30.

Austrin, T., & Farnsworth, J. (2005). Hybrid genres: Fieldwork, detection and the method of Bruno Latour. Qualitative Research, 5(147), 18.

Avgerou, C., Ciborra, C., & Land, F. (2004). The social study of ICT: Innovation, actors and contexts: Oxford University Press.

Barrett, F J (2012), Yes to the Mess: Surprising Leadership Lessons from Jazz, Harvard Business School, Boston

Besiou, M., Stapleton, O., & van Wassenhove, L. (2011). System dynamics for humanitarian operations. Journal of Humanitarian Logistics and Supply Chain Management, 1(1), 78-103.

Bijker, W. (1997). Of bicycles, bakelites and bulbs: Toward a theory of Sociotechnical Change. Cambridge: MIT Press.

BMWi (2016). Grünbuch Digitale Plattformen, Berlin.

Briers, M., & Chua, W. F. (2001). The role of actor-networks and boundary objects in management accounting change: a field study of an implementation of activity-based costing. Accounting organizations and society, 26(3), 237-269.

Brockman, J. (1995), The Third Culture. Beyond the Scientific Revolution. New York

Butler, J., 2010. ‚Performative Agency', in Journal of Cultural Economy 3:2, 147-161.

Butterfield, L. D., Borgen, W. A., Amundson, N. E., & Maglio, A.-S. T. (2005). Fifty years of the critical incident technique: 1954-2004 and beyond. Qualitative Research, 5(4), 475-497.

Buttrick, D, (1987), Homiletic Moves and Structures, Augsburg Fortress Publishers

Callon, M. (1986). Some elements of a sociology of translation: domestication of the scallops and the fishermen of St Brieuc Bay. Power, action and belief: A new sociology of knowledge, 32, 196-233.

Chomsky, N., 1965. Aspects of the Theory of Syntax. MIT Press: Boston.

Coker, J, Casale, J & Campbell, G (1990), Patterns for Jazz -- A Theory Text for Jazz Composition and Improvisation. Los Angeles, Warner Bros. Publ.

Cunha, M. P. (2005), Serendipity. Why some organizations are luckier than others, Lissabon

Dant, T. (2005). The Driver-Car. In M. Featherstone, N. Thrift, & J. Urry (Eds.), Automobilities (pp. 1-32). London: Sage.

Deleuze, G, Guattari, F (2009), Anti-Oedipus. Capitalism and Schizophrenia, Penguin

Dell, C (2002), Prinzip Improvisation (Principles of Improvisation). Walther König: Köln

Dell, C (2012), Die improvisierende Organisation. Management nach dem Ende der Planbarkeit. Transcript: Bielefeld

European Commission (2016): Public consultation on the regulatory environment for platforms, online intermediaries, data and cloud computing and the collaborative economy, https://ec.europa.eu/digital-single-market/news/public-consultation-regulatory-environment-platforms-online-intermediaries-data-and-cloud.Fischer-Lichte, E (2012), Performativität. Eine Einführung. Transcript: Bielefeld

Flanagan, J. C. (1954). The critical incident technique. Psychological bulletin, 51(4), 327

Forsythe, W (2003), Improvisation Technologies. A Tool for the Analytical Dance Eye. ZKM Karlsruhe (Germany)

Glasersfeld, E. v (1997). Wege des Wissens – Konstruktivistische Erkundungen durch unser Denken. Heidelberg: Carl-Auer.

Glasersfeld, E. v (2002), Radical Constructivism. A Way of Knowing and Learning. London: Routledge

Graebner, M., (2004), Momentum and serendipity: How acquired leaders create value in the integration of technology firms. Strategic Management Journal 25: 751-777.

Gigerenzer, G. & Selten, R. (2002), Bounded Rationality. Cambridge, MIT Press.

Gong, Y.; Baker, T.; Eesley, D. & Milner, A. (2008). Responses to Organizational Surprises in Startups: The Impact of Improvisation and Memory on Response Outcomes. Harvard University 2008

Hatch, M.J. (1999), Exploring the empty spaces of organizing: How improvisational jazz helps redescribe organizational structure. Organization Studies, 20: 75-100.

Healy, K., (2015). ,The Performativity of Networks' (PDF). European Journal of Sociology. Retrieved 2015-11-19.

Johnson, S. (2011): Where Good Ideas Come From. The Natural History of Innovation. New York: Penguin

Johnstone, K. (1987): Impro: Improvisation and Theatre. New York: Routledge

Kant, I. (1987): Critique of Judgement, Indianapolis

Karan, P., & Subbiah, S. (Eds.). (2011). The Indian Ocean Tsunami-the global response to a natural disaster. Kentucky: University Press of Kentucky.

Keidel, R. W. (1995) Seeing Organizational Patterns. San Francisco: Berrett-Koehler Publ.

Kollmann, T. (2016). E-Entrepreneurship, Grundlagen der Unternehmensgründung in der Digitalen Wirtschaft. Wiesbaden: Springer Gabler.

Kurt, R & Näumann, K (2008), Menschliches Handeln als Improvisation. Transcript: Bielefeld

Latour, B. (1991). Technology is society made durable. In J. Law (Ed.), A sociology of monsters. Essays on power, technology and domination (pp. 103-131). London: Routledge.

Latour, B. (1999). On recalling ANT. Actor network theory and after, 15-25.

Latour, B. (2012). We have never been modern: Harvard University Press.

Latour, B., (2005), Reassembling the Social: An Introduction to Actor-Network-Theory. Oxford University Press

Lausberg, H., 1963. Aspekte der literarischen Rethorik. Hueber: München.

Law, J. (1992). Notes on the Theory of the Actor-Network: Ordering, Strategy and Heterogeneity. Systems Practice, 5, 379-393.

Law, J., & Hassard, J. (1999). Actor network theory and after: Wiley-Blackwell.

Law, J. C., M.; Rip, A. (1986). Mapping the dynamics of science and technology (1 ed.). Houndmills: The Macmillan PressLTD.

Leitner, H. (2007). Mustertheorie (Vol. 5). Graz: Nausner & Nausner.

Leonard, D. & Swap, W. (2005), Deep Smarts. How to Cultivate and Transfer Enduring Business Wisdom. Cambridge, Mass., Harvard Business School Press

Looss, W. (2002), Der blinde Tanz zur lautlosen Musik (Dancing Blind to Silent Music). In: Lenz, A. & Stark, W. (eds): Empowerment Technologies. Tübingen

Manns, M L & Rising, L (2005), Fearless Change. Patterns for Introducing New Ideas. Addison Wesley 2005

Middleton, S. E., Middleton, L., & Modafferi, S. (2014). Real-time crisis mapping of natural disasters using social media. Intelligent Systems, IEEE, 29(2), 9-17.

Mintzberg, Martin & Westley, Francis: Decision making: It's not what you think. Sloan Management Review 2001; 42(3): 89-93.

Mueller-Prothmann, T., & Finke, I. (2004). SELaKT-Social Network Analysis as a Method for Expert Localisation and Sustainable Knowledge Transfer. J. UCS, 10(6), 691-701.

Pasick, A. (2015): The magic that makes Spotify's Discover Weekly playlists so damn good, https://qz.com/571007/the-magic-that-makes-spotifys-discover-weekly-playlists-so-damn-good/.

Polanyi, M. (1966), The Tacit Dimension. London: University of Chicago Press

Pollack, J., Costello, K., & Sankaran, S. (2013). Applying Actor–Network Theory as a sensemaking framework for complex organisational change programs. International Journal of Project Management, 31(8), 1118-1128. doi:http://dx.doi.org/10.1016/j.ijproman.2012.12.007.

Rogers, E. M. (2010). Diffusion of innovations: Simon and Schuster.

Ruiter, Feenstra, P. (2011), Bach and the Art of Improvisation. Ann Arbor: CHI Press

Scacchi, W. (2005). Socio-technical interaction networks in free/open source software development processes Software Process Modeling (pp. 1-27): Springer.

Scharmer, O. (2009), Theory U – Learning from the Future as it Emerges. San Francisco: Berett-Koehler Publ.

Schön, D. (1983), The Reflective Practitioner: How Professionals Think in Action, New York

Schümmer, T., Haake, J., Stark., W. (2014): Beyond rational design patterns. In Proceedings of the 19th European Conference on Pattern Languages of Programs (EuroPLoP ,14). ACM, New York, NY, USA

Schuler, D. (2008), Liberating Voices: A Pattern Language for Communication Revolution. Boston: MIT Press

Stanforth, C. (2006). Using Actor-Network Theory to analyze E-Government implementation in developing Countries. Information Technologies and International Development, 3(Number 3), 35-60.

Stark, W. & Dell, C., (2013), Tuning into the Improvisational Field. In: Grossmann, R; Mayer, K.; Lenglacher, M. & Scala, K. (2012): Learning for the Future in Management and Organizations, Information Age Publishing, Charlotte, NC, USA

Stark, W. (2014), Implizites Wissen der Improvisation für innovative Organisationskulturen verstehen und nutzen. Praeview – Zeitschrift für innovative Arbeitsgestaltung und Prävention, 1, 2014, 12 ff.

Stark, W., Vossebrecher, D., Dell, C. & Schmidhuber, H. (Hg) (2017): Improvisation und Organisation. Muster zur Innovation sozialer Systeme. Bielefeld: Transcript

Sword-Daniels, V., Twigg, J., & Loughlin, S. (2015). Time for change? Applying an inductive timeline tool for a retrospective study of disaster recovery in Monserrat, West Indies. International Journal of disaster risk reduction, 12, 125-133.

Tatnall, A. (2011). Actor-network theory and technology innovation: advancements and new concepts. Hershey: IGI Global.

van Mierlo, B., Leeuwis, C., Smits, R., & Woolthuis, R. K. (2010). Learning towards system innovation: Evaluating a systemic instrument. Technological Forecasting and Social Change, 77(2), 318-334.

Weber, C. (2016). Real-time foresight - preparedness for dynamic innovation networks. Birkach: CPI.

Weber, C., Sailer, K., Holzmann, T., & Katzy, B. (2014). Co-evolution of goals and partnerships in collaborative innovation processes. Paper presented at the ISPIM XXV, Dublin.

Weber, C., Sailer, K., & Katzy, B. (2015). Real-time foresight—Preparedness for dynamic networks. Technological Forecasting and Social Change. Weick, K. (1995), Organizational Redesign as Improvisation. In: Huber, G.P. & Glick, W.H. (Eds.): Organizational Change and Redesign. Oxford University Press

Weick, K. E., Westley, F. (1996), Organizational Learning: Affirming an Oxymoron. In S. R. Clegg; C. Hardy; W. R. Nord (Eds.), Handbook of Organization Studies (440-458). London: Sage

Arrival City: Refugees In Three + One German Cities

Neis, Hajo
hajoneis@uoregon.edu

Meier, Briana
meier@uoregon.edu

Furukawazono, Tomoki
tomokif@uoregon.edu

Portland Urban Architecture Research Laboratory (PUARL), 70 NW Couch Street, Portland, OR, USA

Since late 2015, the authors have studied the refugee crisis in Europe and the Middle East (refugee.uoregon.edu). The intent of the project is to not only study the refugee crisis in various spatial and architectural settings and aspects but also actively try to help refugees with their problems that they experience in the events from starting an escape to settling in a given host country, city, town, or neighborhood. The authors present three case studies in three different cities in Germany. Refugees are everywhere in Germany, even in smaller towns and villages. The case study cities are at different scales with Borken (15,000 people), Kassel, a midsize city (200,000), and Essen a larger city (600,000) as part of the still larger Ruhr Area Megacity. In these cities we try to understand the life of refugees from their original escape country/city to their arrival in their new cities and new countries. Our work focuses on the social-spatial aspects of refugee experiences, and their impact on urban morphology and building typology.

We also try to understand how refugees manage their new life in partial safety of place, shelter, food and financial support, but also in uncertainty and insecurity until officially accepted as refugees. Beyond crisis, we are looking at how refugees can and will assimilate or even try to integrate into their host countries, cities and neighborhoods and start a new life. Social activities and physical projects including urban architecture projects for housing and work opportunities, that help the process of integration, are part of this presentation. In this paper we include the city of Bautzen as a new case study because conditions in the East of Germany are very different from the three previous case studies, all in the West of Germany, as a journalist from the newspaper Frankfurter Allgemeine Zeitung observed.

Arrival City, Refugee Acclimatization, German Transformation, Urban Morphology, Building Projects

1. The Willkommen Kultur (welcome culture) and its implied promises

The United Nations estimates that there are about 250 million migrants in the world, of which more than 65 million people are refugees (United Nations, 2015). This means that one in every 113 people alive today are now displaced by war, violence, and persecution (UNHCR, 2017). Refugee arrivals in Europe continue at crisis levels, particularly in Germany, where more than 435,000 asylum seekers arrived in the first half of 2016 alone (UNHCR, 2016). These forced migrants joined the nearly one million earlier arrivals to Germany in 2015, most still in limbo awaiting asylum approval or appeals. In Europe and in the United States, migration issues are divisive and at the fore of public debate and protest. How the world responds to this global crisis will arguably impact the trajectory of peace and well-being on this planet for generations to come.

In 2015, in response to the ongoing conflict and humanitarian crisis in Syria, German Chancellor Angela Merkel welcomed refugees into Germany with a wide open door to help them in a direct and humanistic way. At the time she calmed down the concerns of the German people with the now famous expression 'Wir schaffen das schon" ("We will manage that") (Sommerpressekonferenz von Bundeskanzlerin Merkel, 2015).

Merkel's "Wilkommen" (welcome) policy has generated a large number of positive reactions and activities in Germany at all administrative levels of federal, state, county, and municipality, as well as an overall positive response by civil society with its social, religious, and private associations and organizations, and individual citizens. Initially, a Wilkommen Kultur (welcome culture) emerged in communities throughout Germany. German communities took on the role of "arrival city" (Saunders, 2012), and collectively generated an atmosphere of "making Heimat" ("Heimat" is a German term that means to create a place for one's own life, feeling, wellbeing, and belonging, embedded in the history and community to which one belongs) (Schmal, Elser, Scheuermann, 2016). Help and support continues today in a pragmatic fashion after two years of up and down experiences.

The Portland Urban Architecture Research Lab (PUARL) has begun initial, preliminary research by developing a set of focal areas situated within the broader context of this international crisis. These focal topics are also referred to as building blocks within this larger study of refugee escape, assimilation, integration, and return to original home country. Current building blocks that are being studied include: urban morphology studies, building and typological studies, refugee legal frameworks, patterns and pattern languages for assimilation and integration of refugees, project languages for particular design and building projects, and lastly, case studies of cities towns and neighborhoods, the first of which are presented here. Initial versions of this research were presented at the International PUARL Conference in San Francisco in October 2016. (PUARL International Conference, 2016)

In this paper we investigate the reality of this positive Wilkommen Kultur and the high expectations and implied promises that were set in 2015 by Angela Merkel and German society. Our discussion and findings are drawn from research conducted by the authors in Germany in August 2016, as well as preliminary visits undertaken by Dr. Hajo Neis in December 2015 and March 2016, and a follow-up visit in December 2016. Our research focuses on the ways in which the invitation for refugees to come to Germany is playing out in these three communities in regard to primary immediate needs for refugees, and in regard to the initial impacts on the German citizens and social-spatial aspects of German communities. In this paper, we analyze how the Wilkommen Kultur is actually working on the ground in states, cities, towns, and villages. To this end, we selected three German cities that serve as case studies with which to address our main question: the small town of Borken in the state of Hessen, the larger city and county of Kassel, and the much larger city of Essen, a part of the Ruhr Area Megacity of five million people.

Our initial research included informal interviews with German officials at various levels. Given Dr. Neis's German citizenship and wide network of contacts in Germany, we were also able to interview a number of German citizens working in the private and volunteer sectors, as well as university faculty. Professor Alexander Schmidt and doctoral candidates at the University of Duisburg Essen provided numerous interviews and tours of refugee facilities in Essen, and they also shared the final report from a masters' degree planning seminar (Wehling, Schmidt, Pozo, Casanova, Pahlen, and Kürzdörfer, 2015). We also spoke informally with numerous refugees at various camps and group housing facilities, and we met with a few Syrian refugees for detailed interviews. However, we note that this first round of case study research was an initial investigation, and our evaluations are suggestive, rather than exhaustive.

In the following sections, we provide a series of short vignettes and brief discussions that illustrate how these three communities are working to address the more immediate, basic needs of refugees. Specifically, we examine the following: a. overall support structure, b. housing, c. communication and acclimatization, d. work, and e. the formal, legal asylum application process. We end the paper with a series of initial findings and evaluations of the current situation, and a brief discussion on the outlook for the near term future of refugee integration in Germany.

2. Detailed topics of investigation in the Arrival City

2.1. Help and support structure in cities, towns and villages, counties, states, and the country

The most amazing reality for people who come from outside the country and visit Germany to observe the refugee situation is the fact that refugees are present everywhere, including in very small villages and towns, such as the interim housing in a former hotel near Dr. Hajo Neis' house in the small town of Borken. Germany has adopted a policy of distributing refugees to communities throughout the country according to the so-called "Königstein Key," which sets quotas for each state according to economic capacity (BAMF Glossary, 2017). Distribution is roughly organized in three to four levels of helping and administering refugees. At the federal level refugees are first registered, and then they are distributed to the different states. The state government then continues to distribute refugees to counties, cities, towns, and villages. After their initial placements by the government, refugees' daily life becomes a purely local event in which refugees and citizens of the towns, villages, and neighborhoods have to exist together.

It is worthwhile to emphasize that the administrative structure could not handle all these refugees through the government alone. In Germany, a well-functioning social structure has been very helpful. In addition to the city administration, religious organizations, and a number of volunteers and partially paid helpers, there is a very strong structure of 'Vereine,' which are associations for all kinds of purposes from sports clubs to historical associations, garden associations, and even rabbit clubs. In Germany one can find anything under the sun for which people might create associations. These associations tend to be extremely helpful in supporting refugees in various ways. For example, sports clubs fulfill a key role in helping young male refugees to engage their energy.

2.2. Refugee housing in Essen, Kassel, and Borken

As in much of Germany, the number of refugee arrivals in Essen in 2015 and 2016 surpassed the amount of available built spaces in which to house refugees even temporarily. During the height of refugee arrivals from 2015 to end of 2016, the City of Essen operated thirty-two temporary facilities throughout the city (Illustration 1). Due to the large number of arrivals in 2015, Essen, like other places in Germany, moved to a system of modern tent camps in order to provide basic shelter for new arrivals. Other permanent structures, such as hostels, hotels, and empty buildings, were retrofitted for temporary refugee housing. In contrast to Landkreis Kassel, where the Landkreis (county) oversees and manages all aspects of refugee support, in Essen, management of the tent camps has been contracted out to a private firm, European Home Care (EHC). EHC managed all aspects of the temporary housing, including distribution, operations, meals, and security.

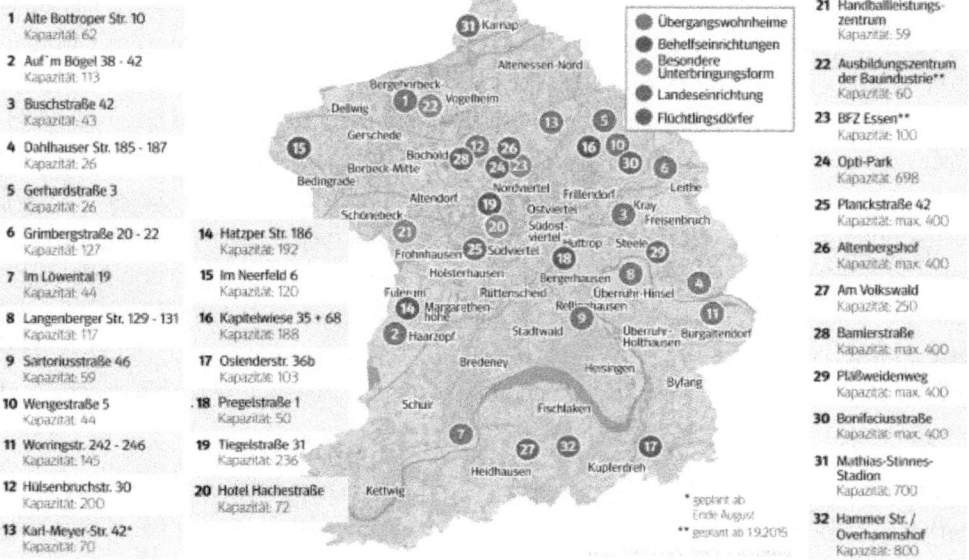

Figure 1: Map with different kinds of shelters and camps for refugees in use in the city of Essen in 2015-2016 (Source: Der Westen, 2015).

By the end of 2016, most of these temporary camps had been closed and refugees had moved to other temporary accommodations, but this time in permanent structures. During a visit in December 2016, Dr. Neis was indeed surprised that some of the camps we had visited in August 2016 were non-existent after a year of use. In December 2016, Dr. Neis visited two of these camps – Altenbergshof and Bamlerstrasse - and only found the paved floor plan remnants formerly occupied by tents and paths, with gravel still in place (Illustration 2). The question of course is where the refugees were moved to, in what kind of housing, and what kind of building structures, old and run down or remodeled and new. We were told by university researchers that refugees from one camp were partially moved to the city's edge with poor transport connections.

Figure 2 a. Temporary tent camp structure in Altenbergshof, Essen, in use in 2015, and b. after removal one year later in 2016. With researcher Aurelio David from University Duisburg-Essen.

Essen is now working with a challenging situation of accommodating these thousands of new arrivals in their own housing stock in a city with very low vacancy rates for apartments (only 3% according to the City) (Essen City Website, 2017a). The City places refugees whose asylum has been approved in their own apartments, but asylum approval can take months or even longer than a year. In addition, the City advertises for volunteer landlords to rent to refugees. Refugees are also eligible to find their own apartments after achieving refugee status, but in the meantime, they most often live in dormitory style housing with others from around the world.

During the past three years, the City of Essen, like any other city in Germany, has had to work with constantly changing forecasts for the number of refugees who will arrive. Recently, arrival rates have slowed substantially and plans to build additional dormitory style facilities or to retrofit existing buildings have been canceled. In the meantime, the City is still working to find apartment placements and to manage the facilities and needs of thousands still housed in dormitory style facilities.

In the town of Borken with about 13,500 inhabitants and about 200 refugees (number changes all the time because of new arrivals), refugees are located in the core town but also in neighboring villages that are part of the municipality. Most of the young male population lives in the core town in a former restaurant with hotel, called Bayernkeller (Illustration 3). In the village of Kleinenenglis, a number of families are housed in a four story apartment building, and in the village of Gombeth, a former community building now serves as a shelter for unaccompanied minors. Distributed in some former prefabricated 'Plattenbauten,' a few refugee families live in individual apartments rented by the City.

Figure 3 a. The restaurant and hotel 'Bayernkeller' used for refugee housing in the town of Borken, and b. conversation with refugees inside the hotel in 2016. Dr. Neis with Tahir from Pakistan.

3. Acclimatization, assimilation, communication, and living in a new local culture

After going through the federal arrival camps in a new country, then passing through the state arrival camps, refugees finally reach the local city, town or village arrival places, where they will live for quite a while and get used to local life and culture to reach their main objective of getting safe asylum status.

In practical terms, all refugees are taken care of by the government according to European Union regulations and the German Constitution. Upon arrival in Germany, all refugees are provided shelter in some form. They each receive Euro 359 for their personal use and expenses, and they are taken care of by a number of institutions, as well as private helpers and volunteers (Reddit, 2017). They have arrived in a place where some fundamental life necessities are provided for them, at least for a while.

Refugees also face a number of challenges that will take time and real effort to live up to. They are first faced with communication issues, the problem of learning a new language, the problem of learning new customs, getting used to living in a European culture, getting around in a new place and neighborhood, needing help with all kinds of paper work, and dealing with trauma from experiences in conflict zones and serious problems on their escape route from their original home to a new arrival city in a different country, language, and culture.

There are also events of coming together and just enjoying a moment of relief and understanding each other. On Christmas in December of 2015, the Protestant Church in Borken organized a live music event with modern music within the church as part of its ecumenical ongoing efforts, and all refugees were invited. Dr. Neis attended and experienced local residents and Islamic women, children, and some young men coming together to participate, clap, and sing to modern mixed music in a Protestant church. In particular, small children running around with happy red faces made one think quite positively about the future of living together.

Language skills are critically important to support even the most basic interactions between refugees and locals in host communities, and these skills are also key to opening possibilities for employment in the host country. In 2015 and 2016, during the height of refugee arrivals, government emphasis understandably focused first on meeting basic needs of safety, housing, food, clothing, etc. Work placement efforts and language training then developed in various forms according to the capacities and motivations of various government institutions, but with language training in particular, much of the municipalities efforts are well supported by the private sector through charities and informal volunteer programs.

For instance, in the town of Wolfhagen, part of the county of Kassel, retired people, particularly former school teachers, were eager to put their skills to work and so started up a variety of German language classes for the refugees at the Pommernanlage facility near the town, formerly used as a military camp. As a way of further encouraging everyday interactions, municipal buses service the Pommernanlage with regular stops between the camp and the town. Language classes are typically offered in town to encourage people to mix outside of the camp and to become part of the community. Ms. Elena Beck, a social worker at the camp, explained to Briana Meier the importance of these informal programs in helping refugees and Germans interact and connect:

> *"It is important not to make a parallel world here in the camp. It is important for people to have structure and purpose, and to feel that they have some involvement. That is why there are no groceries here (at the camp), and why the German course is offered in town." (Figures 4 and 5)*

Figure 4: Map of county of Kassel with various individual municipalities and locations, including the city of Wolfhagen with the Pommernanlage, the old airport buildings in the municipality of Calden as a federal refugee camp, and the main Social Department Headquarters location in Kassel.

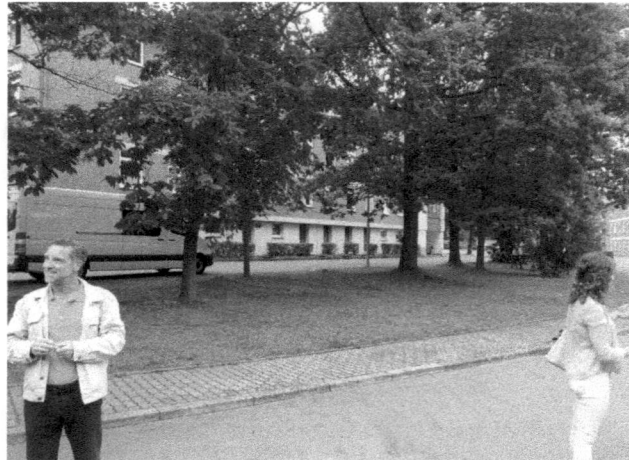

Figure 5: Pommernanlage - Social workers Mr. Zeuch and Ms. Beck at a former military barracks for a tank battalion in the town of Wolfhagen, now used as a peaceful camp for refugee

In Essen, language classes are also provided by various charities and volunteer groups, such as the Diakonisches Hilfswerk. Classes offered in various parts of the city provide refugees a chance to get out of the camps or refugee-only facilities. During a conversation with Briana Meier and Tomo Furukawazono in the private flat he had recently rented, Assaad, a refugee from Syria, explained that although the German lessons were critical for him in learning the basics of the language, the way he really learned to converse was through actual informal conversations with Germans, such as those he had while volunteering at a clothing donation center:

> *"The most important thing is to help people get better integrated. For example, to learn a language, people need to speak it, not just have lessons then go back to the camp. We got so much contact with German people through working together at the Kleider Kammer. We succeed in language without going to any school by practicing the language with our friends."*

4. Work and work-learning related activities

If there are any two major issues for refugees of importance it is housing and work, Mr. Rossberg, head of the County of Kassel refugee organization and department of social affairs, easily assured us. While housing is part of the refugee package according to German laws, work is less easily available and sanctioned (more in Finding 5 about the legal structure of work). Still, there are kinds of work that refugees can and will do if offered. These include short term help, practical, internships, apprenticeships, and other kinds of support and learning operations that also help refugees to assimilate, learn technical terms, and get to know the work culture in a particular society or particular trade or craft.

Our experience in the town of Borken shows that the young men there appreciate work of any kind, even if the additional amount of money is minor. Being needed, doing something useful, and learning a trade are in themselves of value; work experience is also considered to help in attaining asylum status. In the Bayernkeller Restaurant and Hotel in Borken where twenty or so young men are living, having work or a job is considered very important, and if one of them can attend the university in a close by city, that already counts as great success. For regular work, the City of Borken takes a number of young refugees to work in their 'builder's yard and repair facility,' with outside park, garden, and streets work and repair operations. Some refugees also work in the private sector. One young man works in a painting shop, he proudly explained to us, and another works in a car repair shop, a job he had occupied in his home country. Another works as a kitchen helper in the Italian restaurant

'Dal Circulo.' More work needs to be done to create legally sanctioned work opportunities for refugees who do not have official asylum status.

5. Asylum application, approval, or denial by authorities

At the same time that refugees and Germans are addressing housing, work, and overall acclimatization issues, refugees must also apply for legal asylum if they wish to stay in Germany. Germany is not an immigration country; there are only two mechanisms through which migrants may apply for legal residency in the country. First, Article 16a of Germany's 1949 Constitution includes provisions for asylum seekers (Basic Law for the Federal Republic of Germany, 2017). Second, federal law includes an "exception" policy, which states that the country does not allow immigration, except as appealed on a case by case basis (for example, for people who have married German citizens, for those with special work in Germany, etc.) (Federal Ministry of the Interior, 2017 and Scherer, 2016). Refugees apply for legal status through the asylum law. Asylum application processing can take from a few months to over a year. During the interim period between their arrival and the asylum decisions, refugees' are very limited in their abilities to find self-rented permanent housing and paid employment.

Asylum denials may be appealed, but the appeals process again can go on for many months to a few years. Asylum has recently primarily been approved for people from Syria, Iran, Iraq, and Eritrea, while the many others from places like Afghanistan, Pakistan, and Ethiopia and other African countries are denied. Asylum denials are increasing now that a few years have passed since the first large waves of refugees arrived, and growing numbers of people are now in precarious positions as migrants without legal status in Germany and Europe, but who are also not able to return to their home countries. This poses a serious dilemma for many of the refugees after so many days, weeks and even years of hardship.

6. Findings and evaluation: The Willkommen Kultur and its reality on the ground

Our initial research into these three towns and five major topics for refugees focused on mapping the general situation facing these communities as a precursor to more targeted and extensive research. These first visits allowed us to collect material for our initial field study cases that helped us to find research supported answers to our questions and enough data to actually accomplish some evaluations with regard to our main question of how the implied promise of the is working on the ground.

6.1. Finding 1: Help and support structure are seemingly working well, but are also becoming overwhelmed by ever increasing refugee numbers in 2015-2016.

The support structure in the three German communities we investigated seemed to be quite well organized at the administrative, public, religious, and institutional levels, at the private business level, and also at the level of private initiatives. Overall, at all levels and in each community, we encountered a generous attitude and desire to help. The overall helping attitude can be seen as a positive sign of the refugee Wilkommen Kultur. For example, when refugees began to arrive in Borken, the Free Protestant Church there soon established a place and time for refugees and locals to meet every Monday for coffee and cake to just see each other, talk about issues and problems, but also just enjoy. They call this event and space Cafe Hope. Tomo Furukawazono participated in the Cafe Hope events on various occasions. In the City of Essen, Pastor Achim Gerhard-Kemper represents one of numerous neighborhood 'Round Tables' (Essen City Website, 2017b), public stakeholder meetings where refugee issues and how to live together with refugees could be discussed in an open and constructive manner.

However, in 2016, as more and more refugees reached even the smallest villages in Germany, city officials and residents started to wonder how they could actually handle and help more and more incoming refugees. Mr. Rolf Waldeck, the head of the City of Borken ad-hoc committee on refugees, was quite confident that with a number of about 100 refugees in the town he and volunteers could handle this crisis. But when the number became more than 200 refugees for a town of 13,500 inhabitants, Mr. Waldeck reported that he started to wonder how they could continue to successfully support the refugees.

Mr. Waldeck's worried sentiment also reflected the national opinion at the time, that the ever increasing magnitude of the refugee situation started to be seen as more and more difficult. As time goes on and the numbers of refugees grow, the Wilkommen Kultur is facing its first major tests locally, as well as nationally.

6.2. Finding 2: Refugee housing is a test of Wilkommen Kultur.

A. Housing is obviously a key element in the care for refugees. And while Germany was remarkably well prepared for taking care of refugee housing, the large number of refugees more often than not created serious accommodation challenges at the local level. While refugees are first housed in large federal arrival camps, it is really the local level where refugees are housed more long term and in a more open and connected way to the local community.

B. While the general tendency in Germany is to provide housing for refugees in existing building stock structures, there are also a limited number of new building structures provided for refugee housing. The unwritten policy is to provide the same kind of low cost housing for refugees and local citizens alike so that there is no indication of special, preferential treatment of refugees. In order to test more options, one of our architectural design studios took up a live-work design exercise at the edge of the central city in Essen and the University of Duisburg-Essen to explore socio-economic integration. Professor Howard Davis carried out a successful live-work design studio for Syrian refugees in the winter quarter of 2017 at the University of Oregon, Department of Architecture in Eugene (CIU, 2017) (Illustration 6). This project raises the progressive question of next steps through which housing and work can help together with socio-economic integration.

Figure 6: ,Refugee Live-Work Design Studio in the cities of Essen (Germany) and Portland (USA)' by Prof. Howard Davis, University of Oregon, Architecture Department, Winter 2017.

6.3. Finding 3: Acclimatization requires communication; the mobile phone is key.

Daily life for refugees and how they become accustomed to their new surroundings includes a large area of practical matters, from learning a language, health issues, to connecting with the local community and keeping connections to family and friends in their home countries and cities.

A. Starting with the last first, almost every refugee has a cell phone, first for the purpose for staying in touch at home, and also for staying in touch with fellow refugees locally and in other cities in Germany or other EU countries. Smart phones and internet connection are critical tools for refugees to navigate new communities, to learn the language, and to keep up to date on their paperwork and asylum application process.

B. One of the key challenges concerning communication among refugees and citizens is that it can be difficult to commit to the level of investment required for teaching and learning a new language while it is still uncertain if refugees will be able or wish to stay in the country. Another challenge is that refugees are often coping with high amounts of stress, so it may be difficult to encourage social interaction with the pressure of learning a new language.

6.4. Finding 4: Work experience is critical for assimilation and integration, but it is difficult to get during asylum processing.

Next to housing, work is the biggest issue for refugees in terms of a regular daily life and in terms of security and outlook for a good economic future. One could say that refugees are taken care of quite well in terms of housing, health care, monetary support and other needs for daily life. In terms of work there are also a number of measures that are taken in cities and towns, such as internships, practica, and job learning, in the public as well as in the private sector. However, these activities or small jobs are not regular jobs with standard pay, insurance, and other benefits, the most important being retirement. Even for refugees with recognized asylum status there is no definite right on work with benefits. Here the promise that Chancellor Merkel made is incomplete in its results.

The welcoming invitation for refugees needs to include provision of regular jobs and support for private start-up enterprises by refugees. Socio-economic assimilation and especially integration depend largely on working opportunities in all kinds of forms, including self-help, start-ups (i.e., food related jobs), and regular paid jobs. In this area, a lot of work needs to be done to successfully help refugees become part of German society.

6.5. Finding 5: The asylum law and the German residence law are not sufficient to deal with the refugee crisis in an effective way.

One of the main reasons for a number of the difficulties and complications with refugees being fully welcome in Germany is the current legal structure regarding foreigners from outside the European Union. The two laws dealing with foreigners are the asylum law and the residence law. The asylum law gives one the right to apply for asylum and be provided for until a decision has been determined about refugee status. The residence law essentially states that non-citizens cannot live in Germany unless there are strong reasons for doing so. In a way, the United States is better able to receive refugees quickly due to the existence of immigration laws there that allow for quicker processing of applications.

Special laws need to be introduced in Germany to solve some of the problems for refugees including the right for more work opportunities or, even better, a solid comprehensive immigration law should be established by the parliament in order to provide more options for refugees to participate and become part of the host society in a faster, less troublesome, and productive way.

7. Final comments: Outlook - One cycle complete

With regard to our main question of direct or implied promises of the arrival city, best expressed by chancellor Merkel's invitation to all refugees to come to Germany, we can say that German society was surprisingly well prepared for taking on the challenge, especially on the local level of towns, cities, and villages. In the city of Borken, county of Kassel, and city of Essen, the administrations, as well as public and private organizations, and private citizens alike were managing various challenges quite well, such as housing, connections to refugees, providing work related opportunities, as well as helping with asylum matters, helping refugees to learn the language and so on. Refugees we were in contact with were well taken care of and reacted quite positively, on the one hand. On the other hand, when the numbers of refugees started to become larger and larger up to one million arrivals in 2015 alone, the general mood in the German population did swing with negative tendencies.

The choice of the three German cities was determined by specific criteria including size and scale differences, as well as availability and our own connections to universities and municipalities. However, in a discussion with Mr. Claus Muller from the renowned newspaper Frankfurter Allgemeine, Mr. Muller correctly pointed out that all our case study cities are located in western Germany, and none is in eastern Germany, where conditions are dramatically different. Consequently, and on the suggestion of Professor Ralf Weber from the Technical University of Dresden, we have decided to look at the city of Bautzen, close to the Polish border and the city of Dresden, to get a more complete picture in a more difficult context. We intend to tackle this task in the summer and fall of 2017.

The fact that our case study cities can be evaluated quite positively with regard to our main question of fulfilling the promises of the arrival city and Wilkommen Kultur on the ground is of course in itself remarkable as a positive result, and one can applaud the participating actors and organizations. However, people from other countries and around the world may also ask questions about all the negative news of hate crimes, attacks on refugee shelters with fire bombs and other nasty events that have taken place. For instance, one disturbing event occurred inside the county of Kassel at a former airport, where a large number of refugees from different ethnic backgrounds had a huge fight among themselves in the dining hall, which was reported all over the world (Deutsche Welle, 2015). We must note that this large camp is a national federal camp, not part of the responsibility of the county.

Finally, since early 2017, we hear and read more and more about young refugees who were not accepted with refugee status, but were rejected and in fact deported by police cordoned airplanes to their home countries such as Pakistan, Afghanistan, and African countries (Al Jazeera English, 2017). For example, during Dr. Neis' December 2016 visit to Borken he found out that Tahir, one of the Pakistan refugees with whom he had met the previous summer, had received notice that his asylum application had been rejected and had fled to another part of Europe to avoid deportation. This latest development in the refugee saga reminds us of the incomplete attempt for a better world. One refugee cycle has been completed with forced return to where these young men had started their difficult journey, but now they have nothing to show at home that was worth the effort (Süddeutsche Zeitung, 2017). For others who were accepted as asylants, a major step forward was achieved that continues to promise more success and start of a new life in the arrival city.

In this paper we discussed the results of initial research in three German communities, conducted primarily during August 2016. While much remains to be investigated, our visits and interviews provided insights into the five major topics summarized above and for preliminary findings. In our next step we would like to continue to explore and also confirm our findings and extend the scope of our field study work to other cities and challenging topics.

8. References

Al Jazeera English (2017), ‚Rejected from Germany: One Afghan's story' (http://www.aljazeera.com/indepth/features/2017/05/rejected-germany-afghan-story-170524152713481.html) accessed 8 June 2017.

Basic Law for the Federal Republic of Germany (2017), Bundesministerium der Justiz und für Verbraucherschutz (https://www.gesetze-im-internet.de/englisch_gg/englisch_gg.html) accessed 8 June 2017.

Borken City Website (2017), Borken, (http://www.borken-hessen.de/cms/Home/) accessed 19 May 2017

Bundesamt für Migration und Flüchtlinge (BAMF) Glossary (2017), Glossary - E - EASY, (http://www.bamf.de/EN/Service/Left/Glossary/_function/glossar.html?nn=1449076&lv2=5 832426&lv3=1504234) accessed 2 May 2017.

Collaborative for Inclusive Urbanism(CIU) (2017), (http://www.inclusiveurbanism.org/) accessed 8 June 2017.

Der Westen (2015), ‚Übersicht aller Asyl-Unterkünfte in Essen' (https://www.derwesten.de/staedte/essen/uebersicht-aller-asyl-unterkuenfte-in-essen-id11076960.html) accessed 8 June 2017.

Deutsche Welle (2015), ‚Clashes at Kassel-Calden migrant center in northern Germany leave several injured', (http://www.dw.com/en/clashes-at-kassel-calden-migrant-center-in-northern-germany-leave-several-injured/a-18745007) accessed 7 June 2017.

Essen City Website (2017a), Flüchtlinge in Essen, (https://www.essen.de/leben/fluechtlinge_1/fluechtlinge_in_essen.de.jsp) accessed 19 May 2017.

Essen City Website (2017b), Runde Tisch, (https://www.essen.de/leben/fluechtlinge_1/runde_tische.de.html) accessed 8 June 2017.

Federal Ministry of the Interior (2017), Ayslum and Refugee Policy in Germany, (http://www.bmi.bund.de/EN/Topics/Migration-Integration/Asylum-Refugee-Protection/Asylum-Refugee-Protection_Germany/asylum-refugee-policy-germany_node.html) accessed 8 June 2017.

Kassel County Website (2017), Flüchtlingshilfe im Landkreis, (http://www.landkreiskassel.de/cms09/bildung/fluechtlingshilfeLKKS/) accessed 19 May 2017

PUARL International Conference (2016), (https://blogs.uoregon.edu/puarl2016/) accessed 9 June 2017.

PUARL Refugee Research Websites (2017), Portland Urban Architecture Research Laboratory (PUARL), Refugee Integration in Europe: Pattern Language, Design and Buildings, (https://refugee.uoregon.edu/) accessed 25 May 2017.

Reddit (2017), How much money do refugees get in germany?, (https://www.reddit.com/r/europe/comments/3jcrmx/on_the_topichow_much_money_do_refugees_get_in/) accessed 8 June 2017.

Saunders, D. (2012) Arrival city: how the largest migration in history is reshaping our world (Vintage Books, New York).

Scherer, S. (Head of Youth Health and Education of Kassel County) (2016). Lecture about German asylum policy on 1 August, 2016.

Schmal, P. C., Elser, O., and Scheuermann, A. (ed.) (2016) Making Heimat (Hatje Cantz, Berlin)

United Nations, Department of Economic and Social Affairs, Population Division (2015). Trends in International Migrant Stock: The 2015 Revision. (United Nations database, POP/DB/MIG/Stock/Rev.2015).

UN High Commissioner for Refugees (UNHCR) (2016), Overview on UNHCR's operations Regional update - Europe, 28 September 2016, (http://www.refworld.org/docid/57f25a734.html) accessed 8 June 2017.

UN High Commissioner for Refugees (UNHCR) (2017). Figures at a Glance (http://www.un-hcr.org/en-us/figures-at-a-glance.html) accessed 8 June 2017.

Sommerpressekonferenz von Bundeskanzlerin Merkel (2015, August 31), Thema: Aktuelle Themen der Innen- und Außenpolitik, (https://www.bundesregierung.de/Content/DE/Mitschrift/Pressekonferenzen/2015/08/2015-08-31-pk-merkel.html) accessed 7 June 2017.

Süddeutsche Zeitung (2017), 'Abgeschoben nach Afghanistan' (http://gfx.sueddeutsche.de/apps/e359324/www/) accessed 22 May 2017.

Wehling, H., Schmidt, A., Pozo, R., Casanova, M., Pahlen, B., and Kürzdörfer, C. (2015). 'Inclusive neighbourhoods: Refugees in Essen, new challenges for community building, Cases studies: Altenbergshof (Nordviertel), Mathias-Stinnes Stadion (Karnap), Planckstrasse 42 (Holsterhausen), Hülsenbruchstraße (Altenessen) and Bamlerstrasse (Erbslöhstrasse)', Duisburg-Essen University ARUS doctoral program, Winter Semester 2015/2016, Seminar.

A Refugee Pattern Language Cluster One - The Refugee Family

Neis, Hajo
hajoneis@uoregon.edu

Meier, Briana
meier@uoregon.edu

Furukawazono, Tomoki
tomokif@uoregon.edu

*Portland Urban Architecture Research Laboratory (PUARL), 70 NW Couch Street, Port-
land, OR, USA*

The Portland Urban Architecture Research Lab at the University of Oregon is developing A Refugee Pattern Language (RPL) for refugees in Europe. The pattern method approaches social and spatial aspects in a uniquely combinatory way and is used by numerous social disciplines, as well as environmental disciplines and architecture. Originally written by Alexander, Ishikawa, Silverstein, and others, A Pattern Language (APL) comprises a collection of 253 patterns, which range in scale and mode from large regions, to cities and towns, to construction details (Alexander, Ishikawa et al, 1977). In APL, the traditional use and idea of patterns has been transformed into a modern format and system that can be used by designers, users, and builders alike.

Qualitatively, a pattern can be defined as a generic solution to an environmental context problem, derived from functional arguments. A pattern language can be defined as a coherent set of generic solutions to a complex problem. Patterns can also be considered archetypal solutions to environmental problems, and examples of good environments, which can be applied repeatedly for similar contexts or used and adapted to local conditions and specific communities. The original book, A Pattern Language, provides a general reference and point of departure for creating pattern languages for various types of socio-spatial projects in different locations that can help make sense out of otherwise complex situations such as planning, design, and decision-making processes, as well as trying to understand the refugee situation.

This paper shares a draft pattern language for refugee integration, beginning with the larger refugee family domain. This pattern language later will also include the following domains and sub-domains, with about five to seven patterns each: 1. The Refugee Family; 2. Housing and Living; 3. Economic Integration: Working and Work-learning; 4. Learning and Schooling; 5. New Integration Law: Support and Challenge; 5. Physical and Mental Health; 6. Recreation and Clubs; 7. Multi-Culture and Religion; 8. Sustainable Transportation and Communication. 9. Taking Care and Personal Help.

In summer 2016, the PUARL team completed initial field research in the German communities of Borken, Kassel, Essen, Frankfurt, and Berlin. Interviews and site observations during this research trip and from four more trips by Hajo Neis in 2015-2017 have informed this draft pattern language. The formation of a 'Refugee Pattern Language' (RPL) is one of the key building

blocks of PUARL's Initiative Refugee Integration in Europe.

Arrival City, Refugee Acclimatization, Pattern Language, Urban Socio-Spatial Patterns

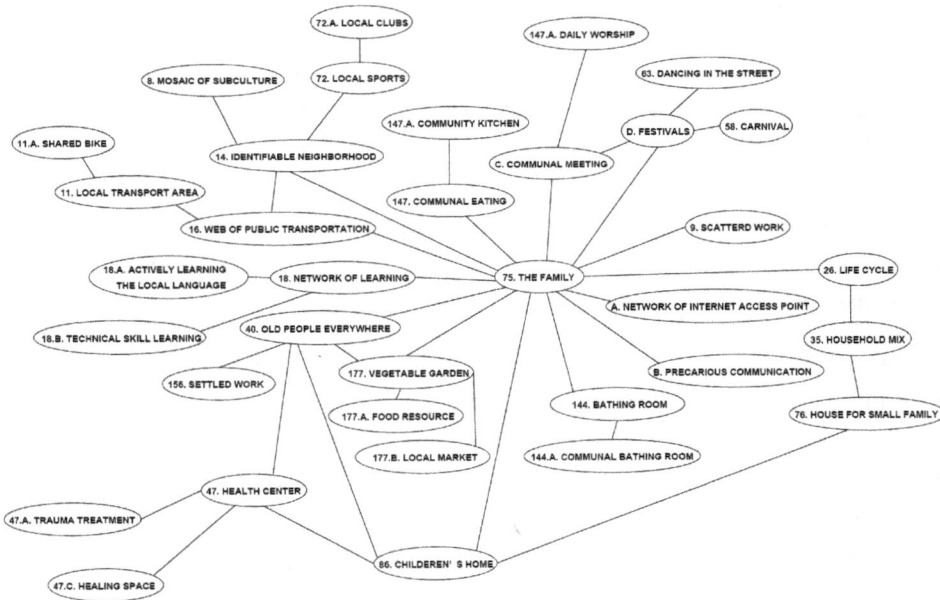

Diagram 1: Initial brainstorming version of a sketch diagram for a possible Refugee Pattern Language

1. Introduction

Much has been written about refugees and the dire refugee situation. Newspapers, governmental reports, weekly journals, and scholarly studies cover large and dramatic events, particular human problems, and specific points of support in order to understand and deal with such a huge problem in today's Middle East, Africa, Europe, and in our case, particularly Germany. Recently, work is emerging from voices who consider most of what has been written and practically accomplished as a wonderful achievement, but who find a more fundamental way of thinking about such a large problem missing. New efforts help contribute to a body of work that would guide us to fundamentally understand and address such a dramatic problem in a more deliberate and thoughtful way (First International Conference of InZentIM, Essen June 21-23, 2017).

Our own attitude to this basic critique and challenge for thinking about and approaching the refugee problem in a fundamental way, which can better comprehend and prepare for such a large crisis, is to apply and develop the methodology of patterns and a pattern language as a framework for understanding, as well as guiding action and activities for practical purposes in this large and complex body of activities and thoughts. At the same time, with the pattern language approach, we open the door to a specific humanistic outlook and method that can help to lead into more detailed studies and work to capture the essence of human exertions in this large problem.

The theory and practice of working with patterns and pattern languages is by now very well known, used, and adapted in many scholarly and also practical disciplines, so that we would like to only explain a few particular points necessary for understanding patterns and pattern languages (Neis, H. & Brown, G., eds., 2010; Neis, H. J., Brown, G., Gurr, J. M., & Schmidt, J. A.eds, 2012; PUARL International Conference ,2016; Baumgartner, P. / Sickinger, R. eds., 2015; Baumgartner, P. / Gruber-Muecke, T. / Sickinger, R. eds., 2016).

First, it is import to understand what a pattern is and how it is constructed and formed. While there might be different ways how patterns are adapted in different fields and academic disciplines, for the purpose of this article, we stay with its original format, albeit in a shortened version. In order to get an understanding of how this works, let us first look at the build-up of a pattern in its full original formulation. We will use pattern 75, 'The Family', from the original book, which can be read in full in APL pages 376-380. We are using this pattern as an example partially because we will start the pattern language for refugees with a related pattern, 'The Refugee Family.'

> » **Composition of a Pattern from the Original Text of A Pattern Language (APL)**
>
> » **Pattern Title** (in bold): **The Family*** (75)
>
> » **An Illustration** that shows the pattern in an example
>
> » **Hyperlinks I,** which connect the patterns to higher scale patterns (26 Life Cycle, 35 Household Mix, etc).
>
> » **Definition of the Problem** (in bold): "**The nuclear family is not by itself a viable social form.**"
>
> » **Main Text and Discussion of Pattern**: Here the empirical or analytical facts are discussed to demonstrate the validity of the pattern, and a number of possible solutions are being discussed. Here is the first paragraph of The Family (75) text in APL:
>
> > › "Until a few years ago, human society was based on the extended family: a family of at least three generations with parents, children, grandparents, uncles, aunts, and cousins, all living together in a single or loosely knit multiple household. But today people move hundreds of miles to marry, to find education, and to work. Under those circumstances the only family units that are left are those units called nuclear families: father, mother, and children. And many of these are broken down even further by divorce and separation..."
>
> » **Solution Proposals**: Text in bold, presenting the solution of the problem, or the social and physical connections necessary to solve them. The solution is written in form of an instruction so that one knows what to do or how to proceed: "**Set up processes which encourage groups of 8 to 12 people to come together and establish communal households...**"
>
> » **Solution Sketch/Diagram**, that shows the solution in form of a diagram.
>
> » **Hyperlinks II,** which connect to lower-scale specific patterns, and which help to complete this pattern for particular contexts (79 Your Own Home, 76 House For A Small Family, etc.).

While a full pattern is made up at least of eight to nine particular points, we will focus here on three specific points that are essential to the meaning and formulation of a pattern. These three points are:

» Definition of the problem: a recurring problem that needs a solution

» Main text and discussion of pattern: a discussion that investigates the problem

» Solution proposals: a solution/suggestion that can be applied for the problem in its different kinds of real world situations and contexts

In addition, we will work with a title, possibly also the asterisk as a qualitative expression, and also one illustration as an example of the pattern discussed. At the same time, we will suggest a sort of overarching pattern that somehow covers the cluster of the refugee family pattern in a larger perspective. We can also call this kind of pattern a cluster pattern because it pretty much defines the problem for a domain or a cluster of problems. Here is the example:

» **Modified Composition of a Pattern for A Refugee Pattern Language (in its current format) RPL**

» **Pattern Title: The Refugee Family**

» **An Illustration** that shows the pattern in an example

» **Definition of the Problem**: "The refugee family is a disrupted and fragmented family.....it lost connection to its larger family and familiar spatial context...."

» **Short Discussion of Pattern**: Here, empirical or analytical facts are discussed to demonstrate the validity of the pattern, and a number of possible solutions are being discussed.

» **Solution Proposals:** Text that shows the solution/proposal of the problem. This also includes the physical and social connections that are needed to solve the problem. The solution/proposal is given in form of an instruction, so that you know what to do or how to proceed:

  › "Do everything that helps to make the larger refugee family whole again. Set a process into motion in which these fragmented families and family members can start to become connected and whole again a) within the new country to which they fled and, b) within the remaining family in the home country.... and even as part of new family groups including host country members."

» **Connections** to other patterns (APL, RPL)

» **References** in text and at the end of paper

This highly simple example format, with its threefold division of **problem – discussion – solution**, covers the basic understanding of a pattern. There are also certain criteria that can tell you if you have found and defined a pattern or if you just express your own opinion and claims. One of these criteria is to have a universal solution to a recurring problem that can be applied to many particular situations (from universal to specific). You may have a good discussion and investigation, but if you do not have a believable solution, you do not have a pattern. Empirically speaking, if you cannot get a significant response from 20-25 people who concur with the proposed solution, statistically you do not have a pattern. (We will continue to talk about methods later in the paper.)

The second larger point then is the question: what is a pattern language? Many patterns together create a pattern language through connections and relationships. These kinds of connections are most easily understood in a particular domain under investigation. In our case, our domain is the refugee situation in general and more specifically in Europe/Germany, and we want to develop a pattern language for this domain that may be made up of more detailed domains or clusters that need to be defined for each case. In our particular case, we have loosely hypothesized a larger pattern language as a starting point (see diagram of larger pattern language). Now we are in the process of starting to discover patterns in particular clusters, following the previously defined problem-discussion-solution format. (Diagram 1: Initial brainstorming version of a sketch diagram of possible Refugee Pattern Language)

2. Refugee Pattern Language Cluster One: The Refugee Family Cluster

PATTERN 1: The Extended Refugee Family

PATTERN 2: The Small Refugee Family

PATTERN 3: Young Single Male Refugee

PATTERN 4: Single Female Refugee

PATTERN 5: Refugee Mother with Children

PATTERN 6: Unaccompanied Minors

PATTERN 7: Aged Refugee

PATTERN 8: The Precarious Migrant

PATTERN 9: The Family in the War Zone

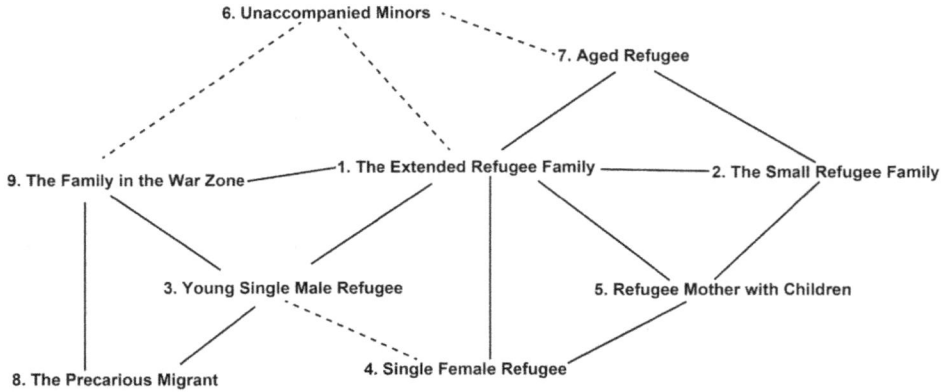

Diagram 2: Initial sketch diagram of Refugee Pattern Language RFP Cluster One: The Refugee Family

PATTERN 1: The Extended Refugee Family (connected to APL 75: The Family)

Diagram 2: Initial sketch diagram of Refugee Pattern Language RFP Cluster One: The Refugee Family © UNHCR/Gordon Welters

Problem:

The extended refugee family consists of the family and family members at home and members of the family who had to escape war and disaster and find new places to live.

The refugee family has lost connection to its larger family and familiar spatial context. It is therefore a fragmented family that needs some form of healing and coming together.

Short Discussion:

The extended refugee family is a fragmented family. It consists of several parts that are no longer in normal healthy family life. It consists first of the family at home in a war zone or other region of conflict, disaster, or struggle. Sometimes, in particularly difficult cases, some or all of the family at home may only live in memory as victims of the war. The extended refugee family also consists of other members who decided to flee and look for a new life in a different world.

When we look more closely from the perspective of the fragmented refugee family, we will recognize that almost all of individual refugees who arrive to Europe are actually part of larger families in one way or another. Refugee families are made of: single men, many who had to leave their own spouses and children behind; single women with or without children who have families left behind; young teenagers who have lost their families, and older people who have also lost their families. While the notion of a nuclear family with a mother and father with one or two children has, in recent generations, been the dominant family structure in the west, family understanding has been extended to same-sex parent families, single parent families, and other family structures. All of these people are fragments of families because they have lost close connection to their larger families.

The refugee families have also lost familiarity with their spatial context in their home towns and neighborhoods, where the larger family was distributed within a neighborhood or city, could be visited for family occasions, birthdays, marriages, even funerals, and every day events of eating and drinking tea and having a conversation.

According to the United Nations, "The family is the natural and fundamental group unit of society and is entitled to protection by society and the State" (UN General Assembly, Universal Declaration of Human Rights, 1948). For the extended refugee family, this means that it needs all the protection and help it can get to become more complete again in all its parts as an extended family.

At the same time that the refugee family has been fragmented, at least part of this fragmented family has arrived to Europe with the hope to build something new in a new community. In this way, the refugee family can grow by connecting with the host community, while the host country family can also grow by including newcomers.

Solution/Suggestion:

Do everything that helps to make the larger refugee family whole again.

Set a process into motion in which these fragmented families and family members can start to become connected and whole again in the following was: a) within the new country to which they fled, b) within the remaining family in the home country, and c) as part of new family groups, including host country members.

Connections to other patterns:

APL: The Family (75), Life Cycle (26), Household Mix (35), Communal Eating (147)

RPL: The Small Refugee Family (RPL 2), The Family in the War Zone (9)

References:

Bundesamt für Migration und Flüchtlinge (BAMF), Aktuelle Zahlen zu Asyl (12/2016), (http://www.bamf.de/SharedDocs/Anlagen/DE/Downloads/Infothek/Statistik/Asyl/aktuelle-zahlen-zu-asyl-dezember-2016.pdf?__blob=publicationFile).

Bundesamt für Migration und Flüchtlinge (BAMF), Aktuelle Zahlen zu Asyl (07/2017), (http://www.bamf.de/SharedDocs/Anlagen/DE/Downloads/Infothek/Statistik/Asyl/aktuelle-zahlen-zu-asyl-juli-2017.pdf?__blob=publicationFile).

UN General Assembly, Universal Declaration of Human Rights (1948), 10 December 1948, 217 A (III), (http://www.refworld.org/docid/3ae6b3712c.html)

Pattern 2: The Small Refugee Family

Illustration 2: A Syrian family: a father (32), a mother (26), a daughter (6), and a son (4).
© UNHCR/Gordon Welters

Problem:

The small refugee family is a part of a larger fragmented family partially still living in the home country. In a new host country and alien location and environment, the small refugee family is separated from its usual connections and may need help and close association with other refugee and local families. While an extended family or new kind of community is very helpful for starting life in a new country or city for a small family, the small family also needs its own privacy, individual space, and personal life.

Short Discussion:

The small refugee family is a fragmented family. It has lost its main connection to its larger family and its familiar social and spatial context, and it is therefore not a quite complete family in its new country of arrival and new existence. In some sense, because of this fragmentation we need to understand the family in this new social and spatial context. When we look at the statistics in European countries that are hosting refugees, we are usually confronted with roughly something like 65% single men, 15% single women with and without children, and about 12% small families similar to the Western nuclear families. There are also about 3% elderly people and unaccompanied minors (BAMF, July 2017, p. 7).

While the small refugee family (parents and children) needs its own private time and space, it also needs extensive communication and connections with other nuclear families and with the extended larger family or some other form of closely knit community. The extended family includes much more than mother, father, and child. It includes grandparents,

461

even great-grand parents, uncles, aunts, nieces, nephews, cousins, and family connections with other families through members who have married. The extended family can be seen as a small community of people who belong together by blood connections. In older times, the extended family existed mostly in the same village or region, quite often indicated by particular family names in a particular town or region.

The extended family can be considered still today a very good social model, because any member of such a larger family has so many more options to communicate with other family members than is possible in the now more typical small family. This is what the refugee small family has lost, and the task is to find an advanced, new kind of extended social group that can substitute for the older extended family. An extended, family-like community in the new country, including other refugee small families and individual people, and even some new members from the host society, may be an alternative for the lost extended family.

Within this new community, it is important that each member has their own privacy and small family social life with father, mother and children each provided with some form of private activities and spaces.

Solution/Suggestion:

Make the small refugee family more whole and complete with a new kind of community. Create an environment in which small refugee families have their own privacy, but also, at the same time, have opportunities for meeting other refugee nuclear families and aged people. This should include close connections to a number of local families, small and extended, so that they can start to create a community and have a chance for a decent and rich social life and for bringing up their children in a new environment.

Connections to other patterns:

APL: The Family (75), the Small Family (76)

RPL: The Extended Refuge Family (RPL 1), The Small Refugee Family (RPL 2)

References:

Bundesamt für Migration und Flüchtlinge (BAMF), Aktuelle Zahlen zu Asyl (12/2016), (http://www.bamf.de/SharedDocs/Anlagen/DE/Downloads/Infothek/Statistik/Asyl/aktuelle-zahlen-zu-asyl-dezember-2016.pdf?__blob=publicationFile).

Bundesamt für Migration und Flüchtlinge (BAMF), Aktuelle Zahlen zu Asyl (07/2017), (http://www.bamf.de/SharedDocs/Anlagen/DE/Downloads/Infothek/Statistik/Asyl/aktuelle-zahlen-zu-asyl-juli-2017.pdf?__blob=publicationFile).

UN General Assembly, Universal Declaration of Human Rights (1948), 10 December 1948, 217 A (III), (http://www.refworld.org/docid/3ae6b3712c.html)

Pattern 3: Young Single Male Refugee

Illustration 3: Syrian refugee Mohammad (27 who has learned how to swim and speak German since arriving in Germany. © UNHCR/Gordon Welters

Problem:

The young male refugee accounts for the largest statistic of refugees and is in an age group of refugees full of energy looking for new activities, opportunities, and work.

Short Discussion:

Young males (ages 18 to 39) comprise the largest group of refugees, at about 40% of total refugees (BAMF, December 2016, p. 7). They are the most visible refugees in the media and in public, and they form a memorable picture of refugees. Young male refugees need and desire to create a new future through meaningful work. Many are also supporting their larger families in their home countries. For many young, married males there is also strong natural desire to bring their own families to their new country.

Young males are also the populace that presents a challenging presence to European culture. Young males need friends, which they mostly find with other refugees and occasionally with local young people. They also need something to do during the arduous process of asylum application. Mostly, they need housing and work as all other refugees. While housing is mostly provided by the government during the asylum process, work as a full job is usually not provided if asylum has not been granted. This may be changing in Germany, where a new law was recently passed regarding refugees and their abilities to hold employment. However, in many towns and cities, local town halls provide internships and professional practice for learning a profession or working within an already learned profession.

Young male refugees also need cultural and social activities, including language learning, praying and going to a mosque, or participating in a local club. For example, sports clubs ("Sportverein" in German) fulfill a key role in helping young male refugees to engage their energy.

Solution/Suggestion:

Provide a variety of activities and encouragements, such as work and learning, for young male refugees for making progress with life and concretely grasping the future. Create connections to all kinds of social and cultural activities in clubs and other social institutions. In particular, sports activities are very popular for single young male refugees. Make use of the new refugee law in places like Germany to encourage work opportunities, mentorship programs, and apprenticeships.

Connected to other patterns:

  APL: The Family (75), Children's Realm (137)

  RPL: The Extended Refuge Family (RPL 1), The Precarious Migrant (RPL 8) The Family in the War Zone (RPL 9)

References:

Bundesamt für Migration und Flüchtlinge (BAMF), Aktuelle Zahlen zu Asyl (12/2016), (http://www.bamf.de/SharedDocs/Anlagen/DE/Downloads/Infothek/Statistik/Asyl/aktuelle-zahlen-zu-asyl-dezember-2016.pdf?__blob=publicationFile).

Bundesamt für Migration und Flüchtlinge (BAMF), Aktuelle Zahlen zu Asyl (07/2017), (http://www.bamf.de/SharedDocs/Anlagen/DE/Downloads/Infothek/Statistik/Asyl/aktuelle-zahlen-zu-asyl-juli-2017.pdf?__blob=publicationFile).

Pattern 4: Single Female Refugee

Illustration 5: A Syrian mother and her son in Germany; her husband and her daughter are still in Greece. © UNHCR/Daniel Morgan

Problem:

Women refugees who arrive pregnant or with children face the same sets of problems as other women who arrive to Europe as refugees, but they must navigate these issues while also addressing their children's needs.

Short Discussion:

Mothers who arrive to a host country pregnant and/or with their children, but without the support network of the spouse, the extended family, and the home society, are particularly challenged with carrying out basic tasks of applying for asylum and becoming established in the new country.

Further, most women refugees arriving in Europe come from cultures in which they had limited autonomy in comparison to women in Europe. In Europe, refugee mothers are expected to interact with agency representatives and in everyday public situations, to learn the new language, to work outside the home, and also to navigate asylum and integration processes for their children.

While many, if not most, women refugees are escaping situations of violence and trauma, mothers are also helping their children to recover from violence and other trauma and to integrate in the host country society. It is common for refugees to be escaping fear of military conscription for young boys or marital conscription for young girls, as well as fear for safety for the mothers, so attention to safety and psychological well-being is important.

According to a recent UN report, refugee programs and facilities are not typically established or managed with specific attention to the needs of mothers and children.

Temporary and long-term housing arrangements often serve to further isolate refugee mothers and their children. Efforts that connect single mothers and their children with other families with children, and special efforts to re-unite separated family members, can help to address some of the issues of safety and isolation facing these fragmented families.

Solution/Suggestion:

At all stages of refugee arrival and integration, give special support to help this kind of most vulnerable family with children through legal, financial, and practical help.

Connection to other patterns:

APL: The Family (75), Children's Realm (137)

RPL: The Extended Refuge Family (RPL 1), The Small Family (RPL 2),

References:

Bundesamt für Migration und Flüchtlinge (BAMF), Aktuelle Zahlen zu Asyl (12/2016), (http://www.bamf.de/SharedDocs/Anlagen/DE/Downloads/Infothek/Statistik/Asyl/aktuelle-zahlen-zu-asyl-dezember-2016.pdf?__blob=publicationFile).

Bundesamt für Migration und Flüchtlinge (BAMF), Aktuelle Zahlen zu Asyl (07/2017), (http://www.bamf.de/SharedDocs/Anlagen/DE/Downloads/Infothek/Statistik/Asyl/aktuelle-zahlen-zu-asyl-juli-2017.pdf?__blob=publicationFile).

UN High Commissioner for Refugees (UNHCR) (2016), Initial Assessment Report: Protection Risks for Women and Girls in the European Refugee and Migrant Crisis - Greece and the former Yugoslav Republic of Macedonia, 20 January 2016, (http://www.refworld.org/docid/56a078cf4.html)

Pattern 6: Unaccompanied Minors

Illustration 6: Mahmoud, age 13, an asylum-seeker and unaccompanied minor from Syria, who fled his home in Damascus with his older brother. © UNHCR/Giles Duley

Problem:

Children who arrive in Europe as refugees without adult guardians face a double challenge of learning to integrate into a new country and culture while learning to live without their immediate families to care for them. But there is also tremendous potential for positive development.

Short Discussion:

The laws of several European countries ensure that all minors, citizens and refugees alike, are provided with housing, food, education, medical care, and legal guardianship by the government if a family member is not able to provide care (BAMF, Unaccompanied Minors, October 2016). In this way, refugee children who are unaccompanied by an adult guardian are ensured basic care until they reach eighteen years of age.

Refugee children must make an adjustment from living with their families to living in care facilities with other refugees. At least temporarily, the government, rather than these young peoples' families, will care for their basic needs and oversee decisions about their lives. In their flight to new countries, all unaccompanied minors have been separated from their families, caretakers, and the lives and security they knew before. They must cope with the loss of their families and homes while learning to integrate in a new culture with new languages, laws, education systems, and expectations for minors. In addition to adjusting to life in a new country, young people are coping with the psychological issues of separation from their families. They also need special help to apply for asylum.

In spite of all these negative experiences and nightmares for children, there is also tremendous hope for these children if taken care of well. They are the ones who will be most affected by their upbringing in a host country. Especially the very young ones. between three to eight years old, need great investment and care because they will have a great future in their host country with a solid education and special care. The nine to twelve year old children still have a chance to get a good education and will possibly be able to get places in the well-established three year apprenticeship system in German education that starts with fourteen year olds. Older children still have solid chances to find their place in society, although they may have a number of difficulties blending in to a new society (Fennel, 2017).

Solution/Suggestion:

Make sure that children who arrive as refugees are given special opportunities to connect with other refugees from their own cultures, and to begin to integrate with the host society by connecting refugee children with both host country and refugee 'foster' families, with whom refugee minors may live, and/or experience support through ongoing interaction. Take particular care of the very young children, who will have tremendous opportunities within a new host society.

Connections to other patterns:

APL: Network of Learning (18), The Family (75), Old People Everywhere (40), Children's Home (86), Common Areas at the Heart (129)

RPL: The Extended Refuge Family (RPL 1), Refugee Mother with Children (5), Aged Refugee (RPL 7),

References:

Bundesamt für Migration und Flüchtlinge (BAMF), Unaccompanied minors, (http://www.bamf.de/EN/Fluechtlingsschutz/UnbegleiteteMinderjaehrige/unbegleitete-minderjaehrige-node.html).

Fennel, H. (2017). Personal interview.

Pattern 7: Aged Refugee

Illustration 7: A Syrian father, Mohammed (right), 51, who now works with his son Yousef (left) at the Kiel © UNHCR/Gerhard Westrich

Problem:

In 2016, less than three percent of asylum applicants (male and female) in Germany were older than 60 years. Compared with the world average of twelve percent of the population older than 60 years, there are fewer aged refugees, as one would expect (BAMF, December 2016, p. 7). This situation shows the fragmented and imbalanced nature of the refugee community, and this imbalance can also cause instability and less calm within younger refugees. While older people have their own needs for help, aged people still can contribute a lot to their family and new community.

Short Discussion:

Older people have their own needs for help in medical matters and getting help in their households. Often, they just need some care for feeling part of the community. This need of care and help is probably even more critical with older refugees, who have been through trauma and inhuman experiences. And older people of course need to be taken care in their own right and needs.

In traditional societies old people were very respected, needed, and asked for help and advice in everyday and also difficult situations:

> *"Some degree of prestige for the aged seems to have been practically universal in all known societies. This is so general, in fact, that it cuts across many cultural factors that have appeared to determine trends in other topics related to age" (Simmons, 1945, p. 69).*

Nevertheless, there are a number of older refugees who are strong enough to take leading roles in helping the community. Aged refugees in host counties can take care of younger refugees, and they can play a role in providing wisdom and practical help in a number of functions. They can help to make the fragmented families and the community work better, mostly in helping the very young and advising young families, female and male adults, and playing a leading role in guiding the refugee community. This role can lead to respect for older people by refugees and hosts alike, and it also can lead to more stability and calmness within the refugee community. This potentially critical role should also be recognized and accommodated by the local host authorities.

Solution/ Suggestion:

Therefore, encourage older refugees in their tendency to help others and also to play important and guiding roles in the refugee community as respected elders.

Connections to other patterns:

APL: The Family (75), Old people everywhere (40), Life Cycle (26), Household Mix (35), Settled Work (156), Vegetable Garden (177)

RPL: The Extended Refuge Family (RPL 1), Young Single Male Refugee (RPL 3), Unaccompanied Minors (RPL 6), Single Mother with Children (RPL 5)

References:

Simmons, L. W. (1945). The Role of Aged in Primitive Societies. New Haven: Yale University Press.

United Nations, Department of Economic and Social Affairs, Population Division (2015). World Population Prospects: The 2015 Revision, Key Findings and Advance Tables. Working Paper No. ESA/P/WP.241. (https://esa.un.org/unpd/wpp/publications/files/key_findings_wpp_2015.pdf)

Pattern 8: Precarious Migrant

Illustration 8: Hajo Neis talking with Tahir from Afghanistan, who became a precarious migrant in December 2016.

Problem:

A precarious migrant might be understood as a migrant who has not been granted asylum in the host country, but who cannot safely return home.

Short Discussion:

A precarious migrant is different from a regular migrant inasmuch as he or she is not an officially recognized refugee. Although the migrant applied for asylum, he or she was denied asylum. The reasons for a denial may be complex, but mostly fall within two broad categories of denials. First, migrants who do not come from an officially recognized country for refugee eligibility may be denied asylum. In Germany, recognized countries for the past few years are Syria, Iraq, Iran, and Eritrea.

The second general reason for denial is that, although some migrants from other countries are granted asylum, asylum is often denied if the migrant could not convince the officials that he or she deserves asylum because she or he would face a life threatening situation if she or he returned to one's home country:

> *"While people that flee brutal regimes or conflict are naturally entitled to asylum, some EU states closely scrutinize whether asylum seekers from other countries are actually entitled to safe refuge, based on whether their homeland is considered a "safe country of origin" or not. The German asylum law defines a safe country as a country wherein "neither political persecution nor inhuman or degrading punishment or treatment takes place". If an*

asylum seeker's homeland is on such a list then asylum is normally not granted, although
individual assessment and burden of proof inevitably come into play" (Weber 2016).

Precarious migrants are persons in need, who for most of their escape and stay in a host country assume that they are refugees. Precarious migrants are those initially taken care of by the host country, but who suddenly find themselves in a situation in which they have to fight for their refugee status in order to even stay in the country, otherwise, they are in danger of being deported. These people suddenly need to get the help of lawyers, and they must also pay for legal services.

Many of these migrants, mostly young men, cannot bear the pressure and start to secretly depart, thereby becoming double refugees. First, they flee from their home country, and now they also flee from their host country, possibly into another EU country. Rejecting asylum applications quite often results in the criminalization of these refugees. In the worst cases, they are being deported back to their home countries into dangerous situations, sometimes suddenly, without money or means to support themselves. In Germany, since January of 2017, precarious migrants with a criminal record are being sent home by plane to countries like Pakistan and Afghanistan, where they are left with an uncertain future (Süddeutsche Zeitung 2017).

Solution/Suggestion:

Do everything to help a precarious migrant continue to live as a regular migrant or refugee without asylum within a particular host country, possibly exploiting the 'Duldungsparagraph' in German law that permits further stay if there are some problematic issues with early departing. Even when the precarious migrant has returned to his dangerous home country because he or she had no other option, try to help her or him to come back for a second time, if she or he really wants to stay in the new host country.

Connections to other patterns:

APL: The Family (75),

RPL: The Extended Refuge Family (RPL 1), Young Single Male Refugee (RPL 3), Single Female Refugee (RPL 4), Aged Refugee (RPL 7), The Family in the War Zone (RPL9)

References:

Al Jazeera English (2017), "Rejected from Germany: One Afghan's story" (http://www.alja-zeera.com/indepth/features/2017/05/rejected-germany-afghan-story-170524152713481. html).

Bundesamt für Migration und Flüchtlinge (BAMF), Aktuelle Zahlen zu Asyl (12/2016), (http://www.bamf.de/SharedDocs/Anlagen/DE/Downloads/Infothek/Statistik/Asyl/aktuelle-zahlen-zu-asyl-dezember-2016.pdf?__blob=publicationFile).

Bundesamt für Migration und Flüchtlinge (BAMF), Aktuelle Zahlen zu Asyl (07/2017), (http://www.bamf.de/SharedDocs/Anlagen/DE/Downloads/Infothek/Statistik/Asyl/aktuelle-zahlen-zu-asyl-juli-2017.pdf?__blob=publicationFile).

Süddeutsche Zeitung (2017), "Abgeschoben nach Afghanistan" (http://gfx.sueddeutsche.de/apps/e359324/www/).

Weber, G. (2016) "Refugee country 'safe lists' complicated by European disunity," April 14, 2016, (http://www.euractiv.com/section/global-europe/news/thursday-refugee-country-safe-lists-complicated-by-european-disunity/)

Pattern 9: The Family in the War Zone

Ilustration 9: 58 year old Mohammed lost contact with his elderly parents, his two brothers, his sister, and her family of three, including two children in Al-Hosn. © UNHCR/Qusai Alazroni

Problem:

Families in home countries quite often quickly lose touch with their refugee relatives, partially because of the problems and perils of the escape itself and the lack of communication technologies available to the refugee, or worse, because the family situation at home has become intolerable through more terror, bombing, and acts of war or other disasters.

Short Discussion:

One word comes up a lot when you meet refugees: family. The destruction of family life is everywhere in the refugee crisis in Europe and the Middle East. Families have lost loved ones because of the violence, and refugees who have survived to flee have been divided from their families across borders and continents.

Refugees who have made it to safe countries don't always have ways to communicate with their family at home. They live in constant fear for their loved ones, having witnessed their family homes destroyed. The lack of communication between the refugee and his or her family back home create serious psychological issues for both parts. Every refugee aspires to get reunited with her or his family, but there are many restrictions that make the situation very complicated, if not impossible.

For refugees who have made it to Europe, the Dublin Regulation, sometimes referred to as Dublin III, provides some family reunion rights. But this regulation is not applied fairly or proactively across the European Union, and it is restrictive. Currently a refugee can be joined by their spouse and under-18 children, but anyone else would need to be granted a visa exception. Thus, facilitating communication options, even for those who cannot be together in the same location, would tremendously help refugees keep in touch with their families.

Solution/Suggestion:

Do everything to help keep refugees connected with their families at home. This can include simple means of keeping up communication by phone, internet chat, video, etc., up to the other end of the spectrum of reunification of the refugee with his or her family -especially the family members in threatening situations - by finding legal ways to bring them to the host country or reunifying at home when safe.

Connections to other patterns:

  APL: The Family (75),

  RPL: The Extended Refuge Family (RPL 1), Young Single Male Refugee (RPL 3), Single Female Refugee (RPL 4), Aged Refugee (RPL 7), The Precarious Refugee (RPL 8)

References:

3. Conclusion

With the previous nine patterns, we have covered the first cluster or domain of the 'Refugee Pattern Language' (RPL). In this first cluster, we have developed nine patterns for the refugee family in order to understand the people who are forced to migrate to Europe from other countries, including the essential reoccurring problems refugees have, and solutions/proposals to solve these problems. We have not covered all the problems, but we have addressed essential problems at the domain level of scale we are working on. Other scholars may select other domains or topics and scales; in fact, one could take each of the patterns we worked on and create a number of new patterns with each of them. The system of a pattern language can go much into depth and breadth with any pattern topic. In this work, and the level and mode we are working on, which is the socio-spatial mode for refugees, we will continue to develop new clusters appropriate for a Refugee Pattern Language.

Based on earlier work on a rough overall pattern language for refugees (see illustration of first RPL), we have initiated a range of clusters that include the following domains and sub-domains with about five to eight patterns each: 1. The Refugee Family; 2. Housing and Living; 3. Economic Integration: Working and Work-learning; 4. Learning and Schooling; 5. New Integration Law: Support and Challenge; 5. Physical and Mental Health; 6. Recreation and Clubs; 7. Multi-Culture and Religion; 8. Sustainable Transportation and Communication. 9. Taking Care and Personal Help. This rough outline will obviously be refined with work on each of these domains. There are also additional domains that may be considered more closely, such as economic integration, detailed help for refugees, and a very fascinating cluster of 'refugees on the move,' that may deserve a special kind of pattern cluster in sequence. We imagine to have a book of 160-180 pages or a few more that covers a full range of refugee issues to be solved in a practical but also qualitatively human way.

4. References

Al Jazeera English (2017), "Rejected from Germany: One Afghan's story" (http://www.aljazeera.com/indepth/features/2017/05/rejected-germany-afghan-story-170524152713481.html).

Alexander, C. (1979). The Timeless Way of Building. New York: Oxford University Press.

Alexander, C., Ishikawa, S. & Silverstein, M., et. al. (1977). A Pattern Language. New York: Oxford University Press.

Amnesty International (2016), "Female refugees face physical assault, exploitation and sexual harassment on their journey through Europe," January 18, 2016, (https://www.amnesty.org/en/latest/news/2016/01/female-refugees-face-physical-assault-exploitation-and-sexual-harassment-on-their-journey-through-europe/)

Baumgartner, P. / Sickinger, R. eds.. (2015). PURPLSOC. The Workshop 2014. Designing Lively Scenarios With the Pattern Approach of Christopher Alexander. Berlin: epubli.

Baumgartner, P. / Gruber-Muecke, T. / Sickinger, R. eds.. (2016). Pursuit of Pattern Languages for Societal Change. Designing Lively Scenarios in Various Fields. Berlin: epubli.

Bundesamt für Migration und Flüchtlinge (BAMF), Unaccompanied minors, (http://www.bamf.de/EN/Fluechtlingsschutz/UnbegleiteteMinderjaehrige/unbegleitete-minderjaehrige-node.html).

Bundesamt für Migration und Flüchtlinge (BAMF), Aktuelle Zahlen zu Asyl (12/2016), (http://www.bamf.de/SharedDocs/Anlagen/DE/Downloads/Infothek/Statistik/Asyl/aktuelle-zahlen-zu-asyl-dezember-2016.pdf?__blob=publicationFile).

Bundesamt für Migration und Flüchtlinge (BAMF), Aktuelle Zahlen zu Asyl (07/2017), (http://www.bamf.de/SharedDocs/Anlagen/DE/Downloads/Infothek/Statistik/Asyl/aktuelle-zahlen-zu-asyl-juli-2017.pdf?__blob=publicationFile).

Dedman, H. (2016) "A Woman Alone - As an English-speaking Syrian, Zeina Al-Shamaly has more opportunities than many refugees. Her future is still bleak." November 28, 2016, (http://www.slate.com/articles/double_x/gender_and_migration/2016/11/a_single_childless_woman_among_the_refugees_trapped_in_greece.html).

Fennel, H. (2017). Personal interview.

Interdisziplinäres Zentrum für Integrations- und Migrationsforschung (InZentIM), First International Conference of InZentIM, "Key elements of model communities for refugees and immigrants – an interdisciplinary perspective," Essen, Germany, June 21-23, 2017, (http://www.inzentim.de/inzentim-kongress-2017/).

Neis, H. & Brown, G., eds. (2010). Current Challenges for Patterns, Pattern Languages, and Sustainability. Portland, OR: PUARL Press.

Neis, H. J., Brown, G., Gurr, J. M., & Schmidt, J. A.eds. (2012). Generative Process, Patterns, and the Urban Challenge. Portland, OR: PUARL Press.

PUARL International Conference (2016), (https://blogs.uoregon.edu/puarl2016/).

Saunders, D. (2012) Arrival city: how the largest migration in history is reshaping our world. New York: Vintage Books.

Schmal, P. C., Elser, O., and Scheuermann, A. (ed.) (2016) Making Heimat. Berlin: Hatje Cantz.

Simmons, L. W. (1945). The Role of Aged in Primitive Societies. New Haven: Yale University Press.

Süddeutsche Zeitung (2017), "Abgeschoben nach Afghanistan" (http://gfx.sueddeutsche.de/apps/e359324/www/).

UN General Assembly, Universal Declaration of Human Rights (1948), 10 December 1948, 217 A (III), (http://www.refworld.org/docid/3ae6b3712c.html)

United Nations, Department of Economic and Social Affairs, Population Division (2015). World Population Prospects: The 2015 Revision, Key Findings and Advance Tables. Working Paper No. ESA/P/WP.241. (https://esa.un.org/unpd/wpp/publications/files/key_findings_wpp_2015.pdf)

UN High Commissioner for Refugees (UNHCR) (2016), Initial Assessment Report: Protection Risks for Women and Girls in the European Refugee and Migrant Crisis - Greece and the former Yugoslav Republic of Macedonia, 20 January 2016, (http://www.refworld.org/docid/56a078cf4.html)

Weber, G. (2016) "Refugee country 'safe lists' complicated by European disunity," April 14, 2016, (http://www.euractiv.com/section/global-europe/news/thursday-refugee-country-safe-lists-complicated-by-european-disunity/)

Wehling, H., Schmidt, A., Pozo, R., Casanova, M., Pahlen, B., and Kürzdörfer, C. (2015). "Inclusive neighbourhoods: Refugees in Essen, new challenges for community building, Cases studies: Altenbergshof (Nordviertel), Mathias-Stinnes Stadion (Karnap), Planckstrasse 42 (Holsterhausen), Hülsenbruchstraße (Altenessen) and Bamlerstrasse (Erbslöhstrasse)", Duisburg-Essen University ARUS doctoral program, Winter Semester 2015/2016, Seminar.

Patterns for Community Innovation by Empowering Indifferent People: Practice of Sabae City Office JK-section

Kimura, Norihiko
nkimura@sfc.keio.ac.jp

Wakashin, Yujun
wakashin@sfc.keio.ac.jp

Iba, Takashi
iba@sfc.keio.ac.jp

Keio University, Japan

In this paper, a pattern language for community innovation by empowering indifferent citizens is proposed. In civic collaboration activities, it is important to involve people who are indifferent to such activities so that local government can take diverse values into consideration. One of the authors developed a project called Sabae City Office JK-section; the project includes local high school girls who are indifferent to community design. This project has succeeded in getting indifferent people to participate and has achieved civic collaboration from its outset in 2014. In this paper, the project is introduced and its factors of success, which we call "loose communication", were analyzed. From interviews with JK-section and Sabae city officers, we created a pattern language for community innovation by empowering indifferent citizens. The pattern language has 12 patterns; a summary of each is presented.

Local revitalization; Community Innovation, Civic Collaboration; Loose Communication

1. Introduction

In Japan, local communities experience a number of problems, such as a declining population, which is the consequence of declining birth rates and an aging local population because of the youth migrating to cities; the latter is the cause of the Tokyo centralization and the weakened local economy. Accordingly, in 2014, a government committee reported the possibility of 896 local communities disappearing by 2040; that is, 50% of all the communities (Masuda, 2014). Consequently, in Japan, local revitalization, which is the notion of designing sustainable local communities, is an urgent task. The Japanese Government established the Ministry of Overcoming Population Decline and Vitalizing Local Economy, and has developed policies and supported local governments.

What is important to realize is that local revitalization does not only comprise money, temporary staffing and/or information dissemination, which are supported by government, but also spontaneous activities of communities. In his career, Christopher Alexander emphasized the importance of participation. According to him, it is ordinary people who are best able to manage the organic growth of the community because they are most familiar with what they want or need in their community (Alexander, 1975). Therefore, it is of paramount importance to design sustainable local communities in which residents who live in the communities can participate.

Despite its importance, it is difficult to involve people who are indifferent to such community design. People who currently participate in community design are local government workers and those who already have an interest in such activities. However, because of the diverse and complicated demands of communities, the participation of these people alone has limitations; the majority who are indifferent to such activities do not get involved. In order to realize innovative community design, it is necessary to involve indifferent people, empower them and use their power; many local governments are deliberating about such a method.

Accordingly, in this paper, our project to design communities by empowering indifferent people and a pattern language for this undertaking is presented.

2. JK-section Project and Loose Communication

One of the authors, Wakashin, proposed an experimental community design project in which ordinary local high school girls who have been indifferent to such activities can participate. The project, referred to as JK-section project, is in Sabae city office (Wakashin, 2015).

In this section, the project and the style of loose communication, which we consider to be a key concept to achieve such a project, are presented.

2.1. Sabae City Office JK-section

Sabae is a small city in the northern part of Fukui prefecture with a population of approximately 70,000. In Sabae, there have been many policies or cases about civic collaboration during the past 15 years. However, usually the people who participate in such local activities are earnest residents who are interested in such activities or problems; and gradually, in Sabae, participants become standardized. These participations are important, but it is also necessary to involve people who are indifferent to such activities, so as to discover diverse values. Accordingly, Sabae city office explored and searched for open activities so as to involve more diverse residents.

Accordingly, in 2014, one of the authors, Wakashin, proposed and developed "Sabae City Office JK-section" with the Sabae city office; a project to involve local high school girls who have been indifferent to local activities (Figure 1). JK is a slang term for high school girls (Joshi-Kousei, in Japanese). JK usually appears to be the furthest from local governance or public works; in fact, most of them have no interest in such activities. Despite that or for that reason, city office considered that JK could devise and plan innovative ideas building on a unique sense that adults like city officers or earnest people don't have.

JK-section is composed only of Sabae high school girls; it started with 13 members in 2014. In its second, third and fourth years, it had 16, 21 and 39 members, respectively. In JK-section, the girls brainstorm ideas by themselves based on their problems and/or needs that they experience in their daily lives. Furthermore, they design projects and plan to solve or achieve them. Subsequently, they execute those plans in collaboration with Sabae city office and other Sabae communities.

For example, by collaborating with local IT engineers, they developed a smartphone application that allows one to check the availability of seats for the personal study desk in Sabae library. This idea was derived from their needs: they wanted to make convenient use the local library. This led to the improvement of the original seating reservation system, which was inconvenient even though adults had not noticed it. The system proposed by JK-section was achieved by using sensors; the data thereof is published as open data by the local government and can be checked by means of the smartphone application.

Another example involved the improvement of the bus schedule: JK experienced the problem of almost arriving late at school because local busses arrived at school a mere two minutes before school started. Accordingly, they proposed improving the bus timetable to the mayor.

They have also achieved various other projects such as planning camping events, meeting with high school girls from other cities, designing spectacles, baking cakes and performing public relations activities for the fire department in conjunction with the local fire department.

Figure 1: JK-section in Sabae city office

2.2. Loose Communication

In the JK-section project, they value a type of communication style called loose communication (yurui-communication, in Japanese). Loose communication generates a laidback and relaxed atmosphere where there are no given purposes or goals; involves people without compulsion and power structures; and makes a loose, but strong relationship by collaborating with each other.

In loose communication, there are no given purposes or goals such as strict debates or meetings. There are agendas and proceedings in ordinary meetings so as to facilitate the meetings. This is to ensure that the meetings proceed as planned and that they are not disrupted by those who want to pursue their own agendas and cause disruptions. However, if personal ideas and agendas are not taken into account, innovative ideas might not be generated. Furthermore, rigid formal meetings may lead to boredom and exclude those who have no interest.

On the other hand, because of the loose communication of JK-section, there are no goals or formal rules in their meetings. They chat away completely freely without any restrictions; it resembles break time at a school and they are not concerned or affected about who is at the meeting, including the mayor. According to one of the members, approximately 70% of meetings are devoted to chatting about unrelated topics such as school life, club activities and boyfriends. In JK-section activities, such unrelated chatting is allowed and through such chatting, they explore the daily problems of their own community and gradually, chatting evolves into brainstorming ideas so as to solve the problems. Such aspects of loose communication in JK-section results in them thinking that their daily life and city public works are contiguous; this ensures that participation in activities is easy and fun.

Members of JK-section experience the activities as fun and thus, they participate and act spontaneously without any compulsion; this is another aspect of loose communication. Usually, in local activities in which there is civic collaboration, city officers teach citizens how to think about local development because of their greater knowledge thereof. This relationship in which the officers have more power than the citizens may make the latter feel that participation is being forced.

However, in JK-section, city officer or other adults do not teach or give advice about the activities; rather, JK members think and chat about them by themselves. City officers do not do anything until JK members ask for help. Instead of teaching or advising, they also chat with JK members. By building such relationships, JK-members come to Sabae city office after school casually and on their own accord; it is much like going to McDonalds. Fostering spontaneous participation through chatting rather than teaching and/or forcing participation characteristic of a typical power structure is one of the important features of loose communication. In JK-section, through such loose communication, they collaborate with each other and generate many projects; loose but strong relationships result.

Through this JK-section project in Sabae, we developed a hypothesis, namely, loose communication is fundamental to involving and empowering people who are indifferent to local activities. Furthermore, it ensures more diverse participation and helps achieve community innovations. As a result of the success of this project, we have now started a new project for designing civic collaborative activities like JK-section in other local communities. Furthermore, we have developed a pattern language from the JK-section project for designing civic collaborative projects by empowering indifferent citizens.

3. Patterns for Community Innovation by Empowering Indifferent People

We developed the pattern language for community innovation by empowering indifferent people. We created this pattern language from the JK-section project. This pattern language expresses how to design a system of loose communication that involves indifferent people in developing civic collaboration projects.

We conducted mining interviews with JK-section members and Sabae city officers who are in charge of them so as to discover the practical knowledge to achieve such a loose and innovative project. The mining interview is a method to find the seeds of the patterns from one's best experiences. We employed the Mining Interview Patterns that are utilized in mining interviews (Iba and Yoder, 2014; Sasabe et al., 2016). In order to obtain the seeds of the patterns, we conducted two mining interviews; one was with Sabae city officers who were in charge of JK-section and the other with 11 JK-section members (Figure 2).

Figure 2: Mining Interview
(Top: with Sabae city officers; Bottom: with JK-section members)

Through the mining interviews, we created a pattern language for local innovation by empowering indifferent people. The main target of this pattern language is the local government who wanted to design a project in which indifferent people can participate. At present, there are 12 patterns, which are categorized in three groups.

The first group of patterns concerns developing chatting places and contains four patterns: Pastured Chatting, Daily Atmosphere, Curious Zone, and Relieved Place (Table 1). The second group of patterns deals with chaotic discussions and contains four patterns: Divergent Emotions, Wait Thoroughly, Casual Sense and Pieces of Ideas (Table 2). The third group of patterns involves managing a project and contains four patterns: Consider Together, Trust and Leave, Connection with Communities, and Unity with Differences (Table 3).

No.	Pattern Name	Pattern Illustration	Summary
1	**Pastured Chatting**		You want to involve indifferent people in your project or activity. Too much preparation or control in meetings will make your project rigid and boring for them. Therefore, develop your project in a relaxed mood and let them chat as they would at break. Free and loose chatting generates new ideas.
2	**Daily Atmosphere**		You want your project to be conducted in a relaxed atmosphere. If the place you hold meetings at generates rigidity like the conference room of city office, participants will get nervous. Therefore, ensure the atmosphere is like daily life for participants. For example, put out snacks or sweets, and/or play music.
3	**Curious Zone**		If participants think that the activity has a correct answer, they will try to find or to be taught the answer and become passive. Therefore, tell participants that the activity does not have any correct answer and you welcome novel ideas. Then, they will become more active and think they can think and speak freely.
4	**Relieved Place**		Participants are in various positions in their other communities like schools or workplaces. If you evaluate or rate them, they will worry about their positions or evaluations at the other places and will not be able to think or speak freely. Therefore, associate with them as people who are gathered for your activity, which means that will not mind positions or evaluations.

Table 1: Patterns in Making Chatting Places category

No.	Pattern Name	Pattern Illustration	Summary
5	**Divergent Emotions**		If you try to make agreements at the beginning of a discussion, the meeting will end up without any questions or a sense of incongruity of participants. Therefore, ensure participants share their personal emotions with each other.

6	Wait Thoroughly		In the meetings, sometimes the discussion may become heated and confused. If you intervene in such chaotic situations, their identities will be impaired. Therefore, wait patiently for them to improve their feelings of satisfaction.
7	Casual Sense		You want participants to come up with unique ideas that are unexpected for city officers like you. Therefore, welcome ideas from the casual sense that they experience in their daily life. Since those feelings are personal, the ideas may be inconceivable.
8	Pieces of Ideas		In the meeting, participants cannot propose a detailed plan because they are amateurs at town planning. However, they can chat and speak from their unique casual sense. Therefore, recapture their chats as pieces of ideas and combine them. Many a little make a mickle.

Table 2: Patterns in Dealing with Chaotic Discussions category

No.	Pattern Name	Pattern Illustration	Summary
9	Same Worry		If participants have problems and you give some answers to them, they may think you know everything and become passive. Therefore, as a person who has the same problems, be worried with participants and consider solutions together.
10	Trust and Leave		If you control your project or teach participants how to act, they become passive and get bored. Therefore, trust participants and leave activities to them. Your reliance makes them active and builds relationships of trust.
11	Connection with Communities		Even though participants are active, they have limitations of realizing their plan by themselves because they are amateurs. Therefore, connect them with other teams who also live in the same communities and can help your project, within your connections.

12			If diverse people are involved in your project, participants do not always have the same feeling and share the same direction. Therefore, allow difference of opinions and build unity.
	Unity with Differences		

Table 3: Patterns in Managing a Project category

4. Conclusion

In this paper, the JK-section project in Sabae was introduced. It is a project involving indifferent people so as to achieve local innovations. Subsequently, from the project, we proposed a pattern language for local innovation by empowering indifferent people; in this paper 12 patterns were presented.

We have just started a new community design project in which indifferent people participate at Nogata in Fukuoka prefecture. In this project, we intend to apply our pattern language and support them so as to achieve community innovation like the JK-section project. We will also update our patterns through this process.

Our other aim is to develop the pattern language to pursue the style of loose communication, proposed in this paper. In recent years, several studies have been conducted on new dialogue methods or communication styles such as Open Dialogue in the psychotherapy domain (Seikkula and Olson, 2003); one of the authors proposed a pattern language for it (Iba et al., 2017). There are many similar points between open dialogue and loose communication. It is our intention to study these new styles of communication or dialogue in the future.

5. References

Alexander, C. (1975). Oregon Experiment. Oxford University Press.

Iba, T., and, Yoder, J. (2014). "Mining Interview Patterns: Patterns for Obtaining Seeds of Patterns." 10th Latin American Conference on Pattern Languages of Programs 2014.

Iba, T., Nagai, M., Asano, R., Isihida, T., and, Matsumiya, A. (2017). "Open Dialogue Patterns: A Pattern Language for Collaborative Problem Dissolving." the travelling pattern conference (Viking PLOP 2017).

Masuda, H. (2014). Disappearing of Local Communities: A rapid decreasing of population due to Tokyo centralization (in Japanese). Chuko Shinsho Press.

Sasabe, A., Kaneko, T., Takahashi, K., and, Iba, T. (2016). "Pattern Mining Patterns: A Search for the Seeds of Patterns." 23rd Conference on Pattern Languages of Programs 2016.

Seikkula, J., Olson, M. E. (2003). "The Open Dialogue Approach to Acute Psychosis: Its Poetics and Micropolitics." Family Process, Volume 42, issue 3, pp.461-475.

Wakashin, Y. (2015). Creative Listlessness: Loose Communication that changes tight and rigid society (in Japanese). Kobunsha Shinsho Press.

Ways of Everyday World-Making: Living well with Working and Parenting

Ogo, Iroha
Faculty of Policy Management, Keio University, 5322 Endo, Fujisawa, Kanagawa, Japan
iro8ogo@gmail.com

Iba, Takashi
Faculty of Policy Management, Keio University, 5322 Endo, Fujisawa, Kanagawa, Japan
iba@sfc.keio.ac.jp

Ito, Kimie
Lifestyle Research Center, Kao Corporation, 2-1-3, Bunka, Sumida-ku, Tokyo, Japan
itou.kimie@kao.co.jp

Miyakawa, Seiko
Lifestyle Research Center, Kao Corporation, 2-1-3, Bunka, Sumida-ku, Tokyo, Japan
miyakawa.seiko@kao.co.jp

This paper presents a pattern language for living well in combination with working and parenting, which we named 'Ways of Everyday World-Making', and shows some examples of its application. The pattern language comprises 34 patterns that suggest ways to live well while working and parenting. Today, many young people in Japan feel insecure about having and raising children while working. Therefore, these patterns were created to help young people reduce their anxiety over becoming a working parent. In this paper, we introduce the concept of Everyday World-Making, theme categories and pattern names, and describe select points in the making process. This paper also goes into detail on some of the workshops we held with students, people working in companies and working parents. We discuss the future possibilities for generating communication in regard to living well while being a working parent.

Pattern Language; Pattern Language 3.0; Working and Parenting; Quality of Life; Dialogue

1. Introduction

Although raising children while continuing one's job is an enjoyable experience, support from people who are close to working parents is an absolute necessity. The enactment of the Act on Promotion of Women's Participation and Advancement in the Workplace in 2015 and an overall increase in public support has caused a decrease in early retirements due to childbirth and an increase in continued employment after giving birth. However, after more than 30 years since the Equal Employment Opportunity Law was enacted in 1986, only around 50%o of the total number of working women continue to work through pregnancy and childbirth (National Institute of Population and Social Security Research, 2015). In addition, only a small proportion (3.2%) of men take childcare leaves from work (Ministry of Health, Labor and Welfare, 2016). In reality, there are not enough practical systems in place for balancing child-rearing and work. As a result of the research conducted through the cooperation of Iba Laboratory and Kao Corporation, it has been revealed that most young people nowadays feel insecure about having and raising a baby while continuing to work.

A simple question comes up to mind: What is necessary, not only in relation to work, for working women to achieve the lifestyle balance that they really want? Many young women want to be successful both in raising their children and in their careers. However, the perceived difficulty in following both the paths means that some women give up on either having a baby or pursuing their career. To address this situation, we conducted interviews with women who have succeeded in maintaining both work and family. We aimed to find the key for keeping a good balance between work and family. Using the results of these interviews, we created a pattern language of 'Everyday World-Making'. Because the language, like a seed, is the genetic system which give our millions of small acts the power to from a whole (Alexander, 1977).

Through the process of creating the leaflet 'Ways of Everyday World-Making', we realized that by doing daily chores, raising children, working and interacting with our social network, we personally build the daily life that we live in.

The 34 tips we provide here were created with the purpose of encouraging people to cherish their lives. These patterns are intended to help the youth recognize the value of both working and raising a family, and to feel proud of oneself while doing it. Below, we demonstrate the process we used to create the patterns, explain the purpose of 'Everyday World-Making', and introduce the 34 patterns.

2. Ways of Everyday World-Making

This chapter describes the concept and structure of 'Ways of Everyday World-Making'. We will also introduce the 'Ways of Everyday World-Making' pattern names and their summaries.

2.1. Concept and target audience

'Ways of Everyday World-Making' is the concept that we, ourselves, 'make the everyday world we live in, including how we 'raise our children, work and spend our own time (Figure 1). Thirty-four different patterns were designed to support this concept.

At first, 'Ways of Everyday World-Making' was targeted towards working women aged in their twenties. Its original goal was to deal with the insecurities these working parents face in terms of balancing work and family. As the method was polished, it came to be what we know as the 'Ways of Everyday World-Making' concept which invites anyone to make use of it, regardless of age or sex.

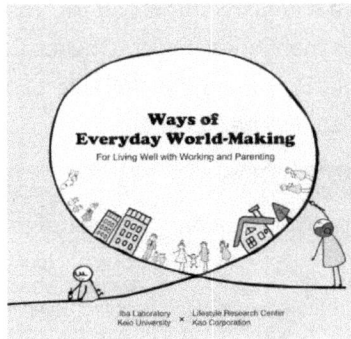

Figure 1: Cover Image of the Ways of Everyday World-Making Patterns

2.2. Categories and patterns in 'Ways of Everyday World-Making'

'Ways of Everyday World-Making' consists of a core "Own World-Making" and seven categories which are shown in Table 1.

Category	Summary
Original Color	There is no correct answer on how to be a working parent or how to live. Discover your own life style.
Smart Juggling	It is difficult to keep a good balance between work and family, but there are some tips to help manage this.
Helping Hands	With the busy day-to-day life of a working parent, there will be times that you try to take it all on by yourself. However, there are many people around you, such as your family or co-workers, who would like to help.
Turning Point	As a working parent, there will be crossroads in which you must choose to keep working or to quit your job. There are patterns for both cases.
Growing with the Child	You may be thinking solely of the growth of your child, but you are growing as a parent as well.
Thoughtful Gift	Although it is important to take time for yourself and your family, as a working parent there will be times that you are too busy to care for both yourself and your family.
Dear Future	Being a busy working parent, it is sometimes difficult to think about the future. This category provides three ideas for the future of your family.

Table 1: Seven categories of Ways of 'Everyday World-Making'

In this section, we will introduce all 34 patterns from the 'Ways of Everyday World-Making'. Number Zero, Everyday World, is the core pattern and explains the concept of 'Everyday World-Making'. Table 2 shows a summary of this pattern. The remaining patterns are categorized into the seven groups mentioned earlier: Original Color (Table 3), Smart Juggling (Table 4), Helping Hands (Table 5), Turning Point (Table 6), Growing with Child (Table7), Thoughtful Gift (Table 8) and Dear Future (Table 9).

CORE: Own World-Making			
No.	Pattern Name	Pattern Illustration	Context, Problem and Solution
0	Everyday World		You want to live a lively everyday life in your own way while working and parenting. In this context, even if you are putting in 100% effort, there are times where things are not manageable, and you are torn between parenting and working. This leads you to worry and think, 'What am I even doing?' Therefore, with the mentality that through housework, parenting and working, you are making the 'world' you live in, you, along with your family and colleagues, will continue to make your own unique 'world'.

Table 2: A pattern in a core category

Original Color			
No.	Pattern Name	Pattern Illustration	Context, Problem and Solution
1	Natural Balance		There are a number of things you should and want to do: family related, work related and personal matters. In this context, if you try to put the same time and effort into everything, it will become too much to handle and none of it will go well. Therefore, make time to confront your feelings, and think of how to allot the parts of your lifestyle in a way that suits you.
2	Pallet Mixing		You want to keep a good balance between working and parenting. In this context, if you try to separate parenting and working completely, because each responsibility is so great, balancing these two things will end up seeming more difficult. Therefore, mutually make use of the information and realizations gained from parenting and working.
3	Search for Style		You want to be a superior parent. In this context, because parenting is a new thing, there will be a lot of cases in which you will not be sure what to do. Therefore, take into consideration your family member's personalities and current situation, and explore the perfect parenting style that suits your family.

Table 3: Patterns in Original Color

Smart Juggling			
No.	Pattern Name	Pattern Illustration	Context, Problem and Solution
4	Plenty Simple		In your daily life, small things end up taking up a lot of your time. In this context, if you focus on all the small things and try to tackle them all, you may become preoccupied and end up failing necessary things. Therefore, re-examine for unnecessary things and be sure to make your actions, plans and environment as simple as possible.
5	Compose the Day		You have a lot that you need to do, and it seems as though you will not have enough time. In this context, if you try to tackle everything in a random order, there's a chance you will not be able to complete all that you need to in a day. Therefore, lay out all the things you must do on that day and make a plan on how to complete everything.

6	Good Stopping Point		There may be times when your child is hurt or not feeling well, and you will need to suddenly take a break from work. In this context, if you suddenly have to take time off work, not only will you be hindering your co-workers, but you may also build an obstacle in your own work. Therefore, always keep in mind that you may have to miss work the next day and make sure to end each workday at a good stopping point.
7	Quality Chore Time		You are overwhelmed with chores and feel that you are not able to spend enough time with your child, even though you are home. In this context, if there's a chore that needs to be done today, it is easy to postpone the time spent with your children. Therefore, try to work on chores with your child.
8	Favor for Future		How busy you are depends on the state of your work and family. In this context, when busy times at home and work overlap, you end up not being able to achieve the things you can usually do. Therefore, if you have even a little spare time, use that time to finish things in advance.
9	Focus and Simplify		You want to do well in both working and parenting. In this context, when you have limited time and are unable to do your work or housework with the quality you hoped for, you end up stressed and wishing you had done things better. Therefore, if you are able to properly finish the important things, it is okay to postpone other things.

Table 4: Patterns in Smart Juggling

Smart Juggling			
No.	Pattern Name	Pattern Illustration	Context, Problem and Solution
10	Empathetic Friends		You have worries about your children or work that you want to consult with others about. In this context, you may take everything upon yourself and not rely on anyone else, because it is your family's matter. Therefore, find someone who is in a similar situation or has a similar thinking style and consult with them.

11	Ask for a Gift		You may have to suddenly change plans due to your work. In this context, if you try to handle everything yourself, things may go badly and create a huge problem. Therefore, express your situation and confide in those around you, and ask for help with the things that are unmanageable.
12	Family News		We do not know what may happen in our life as working parents. In this context, suddenly asking for co-worker's support when you have trouble is something that makes you uncomfortable. Therefore, actively talk about your family to your close co-workers so they can get to know them.
13	Dinner Table Meeting		You perform your role in your family every day. In this context, although things started well, you and your family's feelings become out of sync. Therefore, keep in mind that a household is made by every individual member of the family. Meet and thoroughly talk with everyone about the allotment of chores, everyone's situations and everything else that has to do with the household.
14	Tight-Knit Team		Housework is your responsibility, so you strain yourself to make sure you do it. In this context, when only one member of the family is in charge of everything, if they end up getting sick, the family will not be able to function well. Therefore, make it a habit for everyone in the family to cooperate and share tips on housework.
15	Parent Ally		As they grow older, your child starts to spend more time away from home. In this context, there's no way to know what your children are doing away from home. Therefore, along with the people involved in your child's various communities, watch over your child from multiple perspectives.

Table 5: Patterns in Helping Hands

Turning Point			
No.	Pattern Name	Pattern Illustration	Context, Problem and Solution
16	Job with Joy		It is difficult to make time to spend with your child while balancing your family and work. In this context, by constantly pondering whether you should quit your job for your children's sake or to continue as is, your feelings end up growing darker. Therefore, think of the various experiences you gained through work as precious and joyous things.
17	A Part of Me		You are worried about whether you should quit your job in order to give priority to raising your children. In this context, if you quit your job, you may end up feeling like there's a huge hole in your heart. Therefore, regard it as a way to express your work and yourself and explore ways to continue your work.
18	Invent the Workplace		You think it is possible for you to work more while still raising your children. In this context, if you work according to your company's system and choices, you cannot fully demonstrate your abilities. Therefore, consult with and make suggestions to people from your company about work styles, and operate in such a way to make a more comfortable workplace.
19	Growing Strength		You are thinking of quitting your job to change your work style. In this context, if you feel uneasy about stopping your current career and losing your connection with people, it will be difficult to take that step. Therefore, to create new strong points, try to work with a new level of effort, and think of the strong points you already have and work them into your current job.
20	Follow the Gut		It may be necessary to make a judgement or choose an option in regard to your job and family. In this context, if you make decisions on the basis of surrounding information and advice, you will eventually become out of sync with your feelings and regret your decisions. Therefore, cherish the feeling of 'What do I really want to do' and become honest to your true feelings.
21	Brand New Start		You feel it is difficult to continue working with your current work style. In this context, if you look for a new job with the same kind of work as before, you may feel unsatisfied by the amount and content of work. Therefore, move to a completely different job and think of it as an opportunity to meet a new you.

Table 6: Patterns in Turning Point

Growing with the Child			
No.	Pattern Name	Pattern Illustration	Context, Problem and Solution
22	Share the View		You are getting busier with work and the time you are away from your children is increasing. In this context, if you do not properly talk to your child about your circumstances, the time spent apart will create a distance between you both. Therefore, make sure to talk to your children about your job and current situation.
23	Child in Charge		You want to make your child more accustomed to doing things alone. In this context, if you worry too much about time and efficiency, you might end up unintentionally doing things for your child that they can do themselves. Therefore, devise ways to give your children opportunities to do things that they can do by themselves.
24	Take-Off Chance		You need to ask the people around you to watch your children because of work or other important plans you have. In this context, you feel apologetic towards your children or the people watching them and begin to constantly feel sorry. Therefore, think of your children having connections with people other than their parents as an opportunity to grow, and be brave enough to let your children be away from your side.
25	Journey of Parenting		There is limited time and effort that you can spare for work while raising children. In this context, there are times that you feel you missed experiences or skills that should have been gained through work. Therefore, consider the period of time that you are simultaneously parenting and working as a period of time that you can learn various things.
26	Test for Fit		You want to improve your family lifestyle. In this context, if you avoid new things because you do not know if it will fit your family's lifestyle or if it will have a superior outcome, nothing will change. Therefore, think of yourself as a test subject and try things out, and then decide whether to continue according to the results.
27	Ready for Chance		An opportunity that may lead to your growth has appeared. In this context, by worrying whether you can manage everything, you may miss important opportunities before being able to make a decision. Therefore, think about whether this is an opportunity you do not want to miss, and, if so, prepare yourself to grab it.

Table 7: Patterns in Growing with the Child

Thoughtful Gift			
No.	Pattern Name	Pattern Illustration	Context, Problem and Solution
28	Reflection Check		You are working hard on balancing both work and family. In this context, even though there are a lot of things that you succeeded at, you tend to focus on the failures or mediocre efforts, leading you to feel as though you are unsuccessful overall. Therefore, recognize that you did well, even in things that you think of as the norm.
29	Time for Favorites		You are getting overwhelmed with balancing work and parenting. In this context, by holding back on what you want to do and using parenting or work as a reason, your stress will build up. Therefore, be sure to make time for the things that are indispensable to your lively lifestyle.
30	Gesture of Love		The time you have to spend with family is limited. In this context, if you do not spend enough time with each individual family member, you may gradually drift apart. Therefore, make sure to actively express to each family member that family is the most important thing.

Table 8: Patterns in Thoughtful Gift

Dear Future			
No.	Pattern Name	Pattern Illustration	Context, Problem and Solution
31	Sketch of Future		You are putting 100% of your effort into what you should be doing now. In this context, if the same lifestyle continues on and on, every day begins to feel meaningless and life's value begins to fade. Therefore, thinking about fun plans for the near future will color in your life and make it possible to feel the expanse and possibilities from here on out.

32	Warm-up for the Hike		You have a wish you want to come true or something you want to try someday. In this context, you tend to give up on things you want to do because you think it is difficult to manage alongside parenting and work. Therefore, share your wishes and what you want to do with your family and, where possible, incorporate them into your daily life together.
33	Precious Memories		You make the everyday world you live in. In this context, if you follow only what is right in front of you, the days may pass with you unable to savor the rare moments of your child's growth. Therefore, savor and value the irreplaceable time you spend with your family.

Table 9: Patterns in Dear Future

3. Creation Process

'Ways of Everyday World-Making' was created with the process that Iba Laboratory has cultivated for over 10 years (Iba and Isaku, 2016). The first stage was to conduct a 'Mining Dialogue' to extract knowledge of practice through dialogue. We interviewed 15 women who raise children while working.

The next stage was 'Clustering'. We clustered tips and advice that were mined from interviews using the visual clustering method (Iba and Isaku, 2012, 2016; Sasabe et al., 2016). After clustering, we made 107 CPS (Context, Problem, and Solution) cards.

Next, we merged CPS cards that had a similar essence. Then, we divided the CPS cards into three groups and made 34 patterns. Finally, we wrote patterns on the basis of the seeds of patterns. As we wrote these patterns, we drew 'Pattern Illustrations' for each one (Iba and Iba Lab, 2015; Miyazaki et al., 2015). In what follows, we introduce the main points that were carefully considered throughout the study process.

3.1. Mining Dialogue

To hear first-hand experiences and gather useful tips on keeping a good balance between work and family, we interviewed 15 working mothers who have experienced various working styles (Figure 2). We were especially careful to pick women who work either full- or part-time and choose their own working style, such as a researcher or promoter.

We interviewed these women and asked for advice and a description of what problems would occur if the advice was not followed. We then wrote these tips down on sticky notes. In addition to the advice we received from the working mothers, we had the chance to get the opinions of working fathers through feedback from our research publications in the summer of 2016. It became clear through reflecting on these comments that patterns can be used regardless of age or gender.

Figure 2: Mining Dialogue

3.2. Clustering

After interviewing 15 women, we ended up with 920 sticky notes: 256 blue sticky notes that contained problems and 668 yellow sticky notes that contained tips. We divided all of them into 11 topics, including jobs and household chores, and then clustered them into groups. Even with clustering, some elements extended over several topics, so we kept the sticky notes placed so that we could see all of them (Figure 3).

In addition, we prepared Environment for Focusing and did One to One Comparison again. Afterwards, we did Discovering the Islands from all sticky notes (Sasabe et al., 2016).

Figure 3: Clustering

3.3. Writing and Structuring

Once the initial patterns were completed, we repeatedly revised the patterns in order to raise the quality (Figure 4). In doing so, we kept two points in mind. First, we made sure to use words that do not give an unpleasant impression, even for people who do not correspond to our target audience. Second, we aimed to create this pattern language to encourage young women and to resolve their worries about balancing work life and private life. Therefore, when we were writing patterns, we tried to choose positive or catchy expressions. While improving the quality of the content, we inserted a structuring process twice (Figure 4). The contexts of patterns were lined up along the time-series of life events, and the level of abstraction was organized. We also kept in mind that readers should be able to understand the patterns without difficulty, whether they read them in order or not.

Figure 4: Writing and Structuring Process

3.4. Symbolizing

When we were doing 'Pattern Illustrations', we wanted to make sure that no one would feel 'excluded or isolated when looking at our drawings. For example, in Number 33 Precious Time, the coffee cup symbolizes the bonds between parents and children as a circle holding the family together. In the version on the left, the father is not present in the cup, which may make him feel excluded. Thus, we decided to use the version on the right, where he is present (Figure 5).

We used some patterns from the text 'Pattern Symbolizing Patterns' as a reference tool (Iba and Isaku, 2016). For instance, we remembered Centre Words when deciding the age of the children in our drawing, in order to make it appropriate to the pattern we are talking about. In addition, we used Emotional Actions when drawing character expressions, in order to convey the subtlest emotions possible. Finally, a pattern language for living well with working and parenting was conveyed through a booklet and cards as 'Ways of Everyday World-Making'.

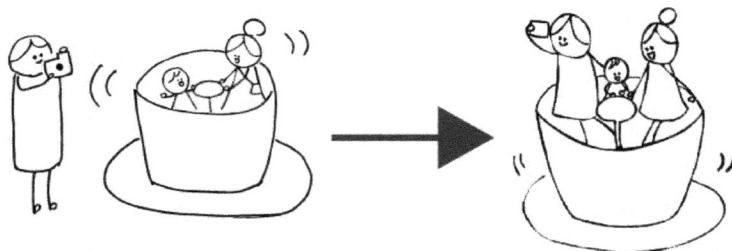

Figure 5: Improvement of Pattern Illustration

4. How to Use 'Ways of Everyday World-Making'

By promoting the use of 'Ways of Everyday World-Making', we hope to encourage as many people as possible to work positively while raising children. To do this, we need not only to distribute the 'Ways of Everyday World-Making' but also to teach people how to use it. Therefore, in this section we describe how to use 'Ways of Everyday World-Making' and its practical applications. First, we introduce practical examples from four workshops held at the SFC Open Research Forum (ORF). Next, we present practical examples from the dialogue workshop for university students. Then, on the basis of the reactions obtained at these workshops, we will consider the possibility of utilizing 'Ways of Everyday World-Making'.

4.1. Four kinds of workshops

At ORF, held on 18 and 19 November 2016, the results of this project were presented to the public. We also conducted workshops using 'Ways of Everyday World-Making' to verify the possibility of using patterns. There were four kinds of workshops: A dialogue workshop (Iba, 2012), a workshop to think about a better life in apartments, a workshop to think about life with an ideal family, and a workshop to think about our own parenting and work in the future (Figure 6). In each workshop, we used pattern cards that summarized the content of patterns (Figure 7). We also used Emotional Actions when drawing character expressions, in order to convey the subtlest emotions possible.

Figure 6: Four kinds of workshops

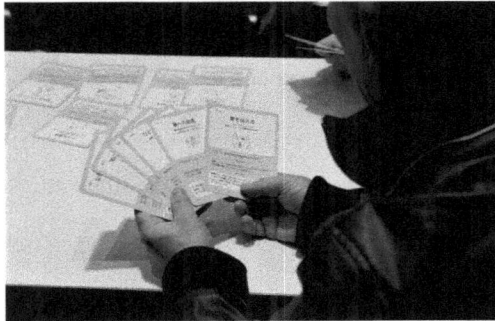

Figure 7: Ways of Everyday World-Making Cards

All workshops were held for about 30 minutes. These workshops elicited a great variety of views from participants, and the patterns of 'Ways of Everyday World-Making' triggered dialogues and ideas. Furthermore, some participants gained opinions or solutions that had never occurred to them. With this feedback, we can verify that the patterns have the potential to cause personal change. Additionally, by holding various kinds of workshops, we found that the patterns have various types of utilization. In contrast, some participants, while they understood the message conveyed, did not quite believe the practicality of the patterns. So, our next agenda was to create more concrete descriptions and enhance the reality of the content.

4.2. Workshop for university students

The main target audience of this pattern language is young people who will simultaneously work and raise children in the future. As such, it was necessary to verify how both working adults and students react to the patterns. Therefore, we held the workshop for university students using 'Ways of Everyday World-Making' (Figure 8). The workshop was held on December 21, 2016, with seven female participants. Firstly, participants read the pattern cards of 'Ways of Everyday World-Making'. Next, participants chose a pattern they want to adopt in the future and talked about it. If there was a pattern that a participant was currently practicing, she conversed about the experience. Finally, on the basis of what we talked about in the workshop, we asked participants to write letters to the future.

Figure 8: Workshop for university students

As a result of the above practice and questionnaire, three impressions were obtained. The first was 'Changes in the image of keeping a balance between work and family'. By using positive content patterns, it was possible to dispel the negative image of managing both child-rearing and work. The second was 'Learning new ideas from the pattern'. Many participants could ease their mind because they learned new solutions and ideas. The third was 'To be able to imagine a future vision'. Thinking about the pattern that they want to adopt, participants could create a concrete image of when they become mothers in the future. It became clear that, even within one hour, 'Ways of Everyday World-Making' could generate changes in recognition and ways of thinking.

5. Conclusion

In this study, we tried to describe 'Working Well with Parenting' through creating 'Ways of Everyday World-Making'. We distributed this to the public as leaflets at the ORF and held dialogue workshops with pattern cards. In addition, we create a Pattern Song "Everyday World-Making" based on this pattern language (Iba, et al., 2017). Moreover, the patterns are shared on the Kao Corporation website, with a current download count of approximately 2,000. The patterns are also reported in Nikkei DUAL which is the information site for working parents. We have received positive feedback from readers, such as 'The patterns show much consideration for my feelings' and 'I'd like to recommend this leaflet to people around me'. Through these practices, the patterns may help dissolve anxieties for young people who will enter the workforce after graduation. In addition, it may provide a new perspective for people who already work while raising children.

We believe that the 'Everyday World' patterns will bring about a transformation that goes beyond a personal level. Therefore, for the future of our work, we plan to continue to investigate changes in households, workplaces, regions and society as a whole. Through the power of encouraging participants to talk about their experiences, a pattern language can function in any community that balances working with parenting. However, people rarely talk about their experiences in daily life (Iba, 2012). By using pattern languages in each respective community, we hope to promote the understanding of others and the personal creation of suitable systems that balance parenting and work. Because these patterns were mined from only Japanese participants, they might be specific to Japanese culture. Thus, we are interested in feedback from foreigners. By conducting an international comparison, we will be able to see any cultural differences (Hong et al., 2015).

6. Acknowledgement

We would like to thank the project members from Kao Corporation: Chie Akita, Nobuko Yoshida and Yumiko Imazu. We would also like to thank our interviewees: Yumiko Mori, Miyuki Mizutani, staff of Kao Corporation, and product testers of Kao Corporation. We would also like to express our gratitude to Ayaka Yoshikawa and Aimi Burgoyne for their support to write this paper in English and other members from Iba Laboratory for their helpful feedback on the patterns.

7. References

Alexander, C., Ishikawa, S., and Silverstein, M., Jacobson, M., Fiksdahi-King, I. and Angel, S. (1977). A Pattern Language: Towns, Buildings, Construction, Oxford University Press.

Hong, J., Akado, Y., Kogure, S., Sasabe, A., Saruwatari, K., Iba, T. (2015) "Exploring Cultures through Pattern Mining: Practices from Generative Beauty Workshops," 5th International Conference on Collaborative Innovation Networks.

Iba, T. (2012) "Dialogue Workshop Patterns: A Pattern Language for Designing Workshop to Introduce a Pattern Language", in the 17th European Conference on Pattern Languages of Programs (EuroPLoP2012).

Iba, T. and Isaku, T. (2012) "Holistic Pattern-Mining Patterns: A Pattern Language for Pattern Mining on a Holistic Approach," PLoP'12 Proceedings of the 19th Conference on Pattern Languages of Programs.

Iba, T. and Iba Lab (2015) Pattern Illustrating Patterns: A Pattern Language for Pattern Illustrating, CreativeShift.

Iba, T. and Isaku, T. (2016) "Creating a Pattern Language for Creating Pattern Languages: 364 Patterns for Pattern Mining, Writing, and Symbolizing," in the 23rd Conference on Pattern Languages of Programs.

Iba, T., Ueno, M., Yoshikawa, A. (2017) "Pattern Song: Taking Patterns from Visual Media to Auditory Media," 2nd World Conference on PURPLSOC (Pursuit of Pattern Languages for Societal Change).

National Institute of Population and Social Security Research. (2015) "Marriage and Childbirth in Japan Today: The Fifteenth Japanese National Fertility Survey, 2015 (Results of Singles and Married Couples Survey)", in Japanese.

Miyazaki, N., Sakuraba, R., Harasawa, K., and Iba, T. (2015) "Pattern Illustrating Patterns: A Pattern Language for Pattern Illustrating," in the 22nd Conference on Pattern Languages of Programs (PLoP2015)

Ministry of Health, Labor, and Welfare. (2016) "Basic Survey of Gender Equality in Employment Management", in Japanese.

Sasabe, A., Kaneko, T., Takahashi, K., and Iba, T. (2016) "Pattern Mining Patterns: A Search for the Seeds of Patterns", in 23rd Conference on Pattern Languages of Programs.

Cooking Fun Language: Sharing the Hidden Fun of Cooking

Shimizu, Hitomi
Faculty of Policy Management, Keio University, Japan
s15417hs@sfc.keio.ac.jp

Yoshikawa, Ayaka
Faculty of Environment and Information Studies Organization, Keio University, Japan
t14595ay@sfc.keio.ac.jp

Iba, Takashi
Faculty of Policy Management, Keio University, Japan
iba@sfc.keio.ac.jp

This paper proposes Cooking Fun Language, a Fun Language that verbalizes the hidden fun of cooking. The Cooking Fun Language was created to encourage young people to cook, in response to the declining cooking population especially among young people in Japan. Fun language is a collection of Fun Words, each showing a way of enjoying a certain cooking-activity that are unknown to those with little experience in cooking (Iba et al. 2017). It is similar to pattern language 3.0, but it differs in that while pattern language 3.0 shares how to do something better, Fun Language strictly focuses on how to have fun with something. Cooking Fun Language, presented in this paper, contains twenty-five Fun Words, or ways to make cooking more enjoyable. This paper contains the creation process, a list of the Fun Words, the function of the Cooking Fun Language, and future work.

Fun language; cooking, pattern language; enjoyment; motivation

1. Introduction

In this paper, we will introduce Cooking Fun Language, which shares the hidden enjoyment of cooking using a new concept called Fun Language. Ready-made foods have become widely available in Japan, and many people, especially the younger generations who live alone, tend to rely on these foods, instead of cooking on their own. Through interviews, it became apparent that cooking is thought of as a heavy load or a too difficult thing to handle in their busy lifestyles. However, there can be a big gap in how cooking is perceived from the outside and the inside. For example, the purpose of cooking may be seen as solely to prepare food in order to get nutrition, a troublesome chore to feed oneself. But with a shift of frame, the purpose may be to enjoy the act of cooking in itself. Each person has a reason to cook, and it is natural that the purpose or the meaning of cooking differs depending on how one is doing it and who is doing it. For those who enjoy the act of cooking as a hobby, cooking means much more than a process of nurturing the body. It also gives the person joy and comfort. For example, take Alice Waters; chef, author, food activist, and the founder and owner of Chez Panisse Restaurant in Berkeley, California; she finds enjoyment in many aspects. Her list of the underlying principles of good cooking displays much joy and delight, showing us her love and enjoyment of cooking.

"Eat Seasonally.

Choose food in season. Even where the growing season is short, organic gardening and farming can be grown in cold frames and greenhouses, and there are always local foods that can be stored, dried, and canned for the winter months. Eating seasonally inspires your menus, gives you a sense of time and place, and rewards you with the most flavorful food."

"Conserve, compost, and recycle.

Take your own basket and to the market. Reuse whatever packaging you can. Keep a compost bucket nearby when you cook to recycle kitchen scraps. The more you conserve, the less you waste, the better you feel."

"Cook simply, engaging all your senses.

Plan uncomplicated meals. Let things taste of what they are. Enjoy cooking as a sensory pleasure: touch, listen, watch, smell, and, above all, taste. Taste as you go. Keep tasting and keep practicing and discovering" (Waters 2007).

As understood from this list, there can be many ways and many kinds of enjoyments in cooking. Fun exists everywhere. But for people who are completely unfamiliar with the enjoyment of cooking, the idea that cooking is fun is extremely surprising and new. They of course do not know how to enjoy it.

If the enjoyment of cooking is better expressed, more people will know how to enjoy cooking, and become positive about the cooking process. This can lead to the increase in the cooking population. To spread this philosophy, we created a tool to share the enjoyments of cooking for anyone to understand what cooking means for people who have fun at it. We aim to inspire this way of thinking, giving them a trigger for changing their mindset towards cooking.

2. Background

The background of creating the Cooking Fun Language came from creating the Cooking Patterns (Akado et al. 2016), which are patterns about the cooking process, and the Cooking Life Patterns, which deal with how to incorporate cooking into everyday life (Yoshikawa et al. 2016). These pattern languages were created to organize and share the good practices of cooking, but were more a kind of pattern language to lead readers in the "right direction", towards improvement (Iba et al. 2017).

From creating the patterns above, we found out that pattern language can serve as effective tools for offering small tips to those who seek improvement in technical skills but are limited in speaking to the hearts of those who are new to cooking. Therefore, to reach out to those out of the original range, we created Cooking Fun Language: a fun language for cooking, to encourage people to feel that they too, might like to enjoy cooking.

3. Fun Language

Fun Language is a collection of perspectives and actions that allows one to "enjoy" a certain activity. The term Fun Language, like pattern language, points to both the methodology and the languages themselves (Iba et al. 2017). As Fun Language consists of ways to enjoy a certain activity, we call these small units, "Fun". Each "Fun" unit contains information about when and how to enjoy that particular activity, and is named with a "Fun Word" (Iba et al. 2017).

The function of Fun Language is specialized in sharing the tips of how to enjoy a certain subject, aiming to switch people's mindset in a positive direction. The purpose of this language is to make an action on a specific subject more enjoyable. Unlike pattern language, which Alexander created in order to generate quality in an object that is produced through a process of constructing/creating: "quality without a name" (Alexander 1979), the intention of Fun Language is to enhance the "quality of experience" of the person who is working on a certain subject. Since the focus of this language is on mindset, the ultimate goal is to enhance the "quality of experience" of the people. Therefore, since Fun Language speaks directly to people's hearts, it is effective in raising people's motivation to become engaged in a certain activity. When one discovers an element of "fun" in an activity, it gradually leads to "enjoyment", which then develops into a more long-term feeling of "joy" (Iba et al. 2017).

4. Adaptation of the Pattern Language Format

The format of the Fun Language is adapted from that of a pattern language (Alexander et al. 1977). A pattern in a pattern language consists of a Context, Problem, Solution, and a Consequence, which help solve or prevent an undesirable situation. While this format is suitable in providing practical knowledge, a somewhat different format should be used for a language that deals more closely with the emotional side of an activity. In a Fun Language, the ideas presented do not arise from a "problem" to be solved. In other words, a Fun Language deals with actions that are not necessarily essential, but help to upgrade the quality of the experience itself. Therefore, the "problem" statement is omitted from the format; Fun Language simply describes a Context in which a Solution is enacted, which leads to a certain Consequence (Iba et al. 2017).

5. Cooking Fun Language

Cooking Fun Language shares ways to enjoy cooking, which were created in order to invite people who do not usually cook to see the fun side of cooking and make them want to cook.

The language is made up of 25 Fun Words, each containing ways to make cooking more enjoyable (Figure 1).

COOKING FUN LANGUAGE

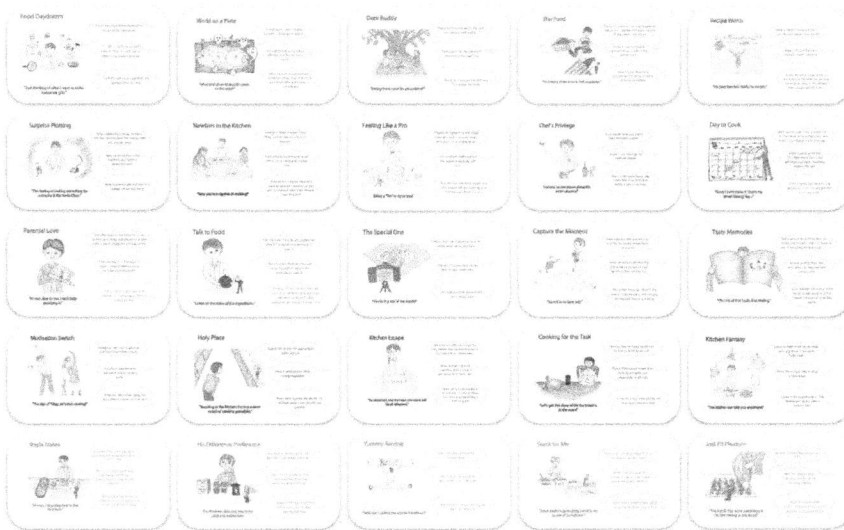

Figure 1: The overview of Cooking Fun Language

5.1. Creating Process

The creating process of Fun Language is very much the same with that of pattern language: Pattern Mining, Pattern Writing and Pattern Symbolizing (Iba 2016; Iba & Isaku 2016).

The creating process of Cooking Fun Language begins with mining (Iba & Yoder 2014; Sasabe et al. 2016) the fun experiences from university students who cook more than once a month. During the "Mining Dialogue" (Iba & Isaku 2016), we focused on getting the interviewees to relax and enjoy the conversation in order to extract the Fun seeds from them through a natural dialogue. By creating a relaxed and comfortable dialogue setting, we were able to get the interviewees to describe their core happy feelings using spoken language as well as onomatopoeia.

After extracting what they do to enjoy cooking and where they feel the most enjoyment, we wrote down the Fun seeds on sticky notes and conducted "Clustering" to find out some common patterns from the collected data (Sasabe et al. 2016) using the KJ method (Kawakita 1967). Lastly we wrote down the Fun contents of each group.

Then, in the writing process, we extracted three specific examples for each Fun, and wrote out the thoughts behind the enjoyment in a monologue tone, summarizing it in a simple phrase (Iba et al. 2017).

Lastly, for each Fun Word, we assigned a name and illustration. When naming each Fun, we focused on expressing the essential idea. As this follows a similar process as when naming a pattern, we referred to Pattern Symbolizing Patterns (Shibata et al. 2016), which provide insight on how to capture its essential ideas. For the illustrations, we picked a scene from the most representative action example, and drew illustrations using the Pattern Illustration Patterns (Iba & Iba Lab. 2015; Harasawa et al. 2015) as reference. The illustrations were added to better enable the readers to imagine/grasp the contents and joy of the fun.

Cooking Fun Language was then put together in a booklet, which contains the 25 Fun Words in a card format (Figure 2).

Figure 2: The Cooking Fun Language booklet (Japanese)

5.2. Categories within the Fun Language

We divided the 25 Fun Words into 5 categories based on the kinds of enjoyment, in other words, the different emotions one experiences when enjoying the Fun Word as below (Figure 3).

» Daydream: enjoyment of using your imagination in cooking.

» Trick: enjoyment of becoming a little childish and plotting small tricks for pleasure.

» Love: enjoyment of becoming motherly and showing love in things.

» Shift: enjoyment of switching your feelings into a better state.

» Victory: enjoyment of becoming proud and feeling great about yourself.

Daydream	Trick	Love	Shift	Victory
Food Daydreaming	Surprise Plotting	Parental Love	Motivation Switch	Best Dishes
World on a Plate	Newbies in the Kitchen	Talk to Food	Holy Place	No Difference Preference
Date Buddy	Chef's Priviledge	The Special One	Kitchen Escape	Yummy Serving
Star Food	Feeling Like a Pro	Capture the Moment	Cooking for the Task	Stock for Me
Recipe Worm	Day to Cook	Tasty Memories	Kitchen Fantasy	Just Fit Pleasure

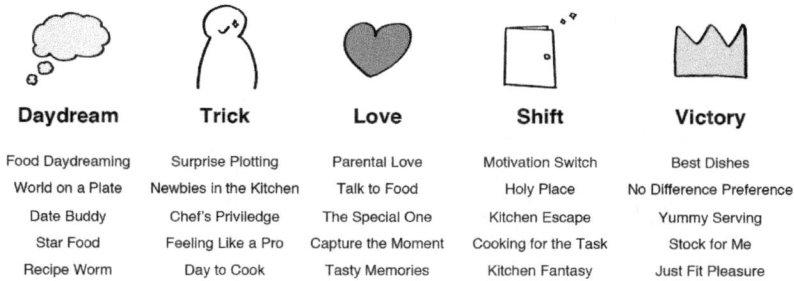

Figure 3: The 5 categories and Fun Words of Cooking Fun Language

5.3. Format of a Fun Word

The Cooking Fun Language is introduced in the card format, and each card has 5 elements. We used the card format in order for people to easily share and talk about them (Figure 4).

(1) Name of the fun

(2) Introduction

(3) Three example actions

(4) An illustration of one of the actions

(5) The thoughts behind the enjoyment

Here we introduce 5 Fun Words from each category as examples. First, we present one from the "Daydream" category, called "Star Food". In general, we all have something we admire, and this enjoyment is to dream about a certain rare or expensive ingredient that you admire like a superstar, longing for it to someday come into your hands. The examples are, daydream how an "admirable ingredient" that is difficult to get would taste like through recipes and articles, or hope for an "admirable ingredient" to go on sale for you to buy. This superstar lights up the day by just appearing into your eyes. When you catch a glimpse of it, there is no choice but to jump at it.

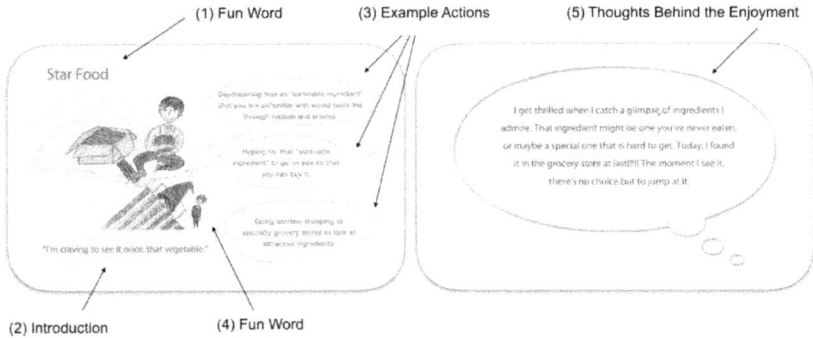

Figure 4: "Star Food" from the "Daydream" category

The second is from the "Trick" category, called "Day to Cook". This is the enjoyment of letting yourself put cooking into the priority list no matter how busy you are. The examples are, make Cooking a part of your schedule and book the day no matter how busy you are, and have it as your highest priority of the day, or to set a family event like "This Saturday is Taco Day!" and have your family members reserve that day. Everyone has the right to enjoy what they like, and cooking is no exception either. Feel free to get absorbed in the process without any interruptions.

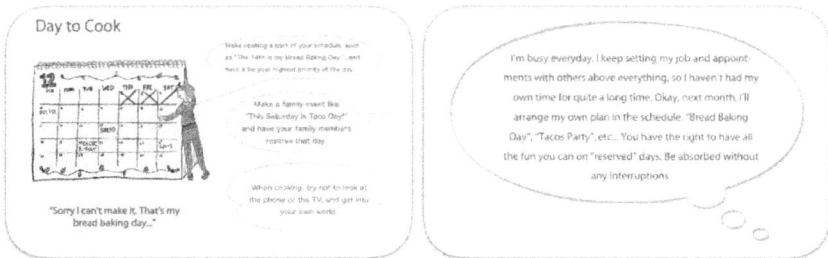

Figure 5: "Day to Cook" from the "Trick" category

The third Fun Word is from the "Love" category, called "The Special One". This Fun is to enjoy the good ones and not intended ones in shapes and such, and take especially good care of your favorites. The examples are, feature the best-shaped cookie in the center when taking a picture, or give the most beautifully served plate to loved ones. Since every finish is unique, there is no such thing as failure in cooking. Admire the favorites of course, but do not forget that the favorites shine thanks to the out of shaped ones.

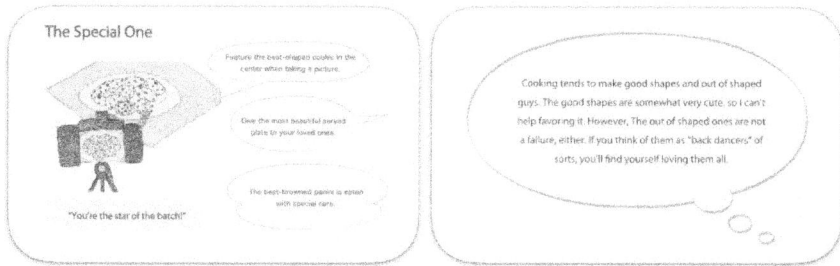

Figure 6: "The Special One" from the "Love" category

Next, we present "Kitchen Fantasy", from the "Shift" category. This is the enjoyment of leading yourself into a different world with the trigger of music, or clothing that fits the mood of the cooking process. The examples are, don't hesitate to turn Indian music on and dance to it, stirring the curry rhythmically with the smell of curry in the lead, or to start from the style of the world by wearing a china dress when making Chinese food. After having jumped into the world without hesitation, it is twice the fun to come to your senses and laugh out loud (Iba et al. 2017).

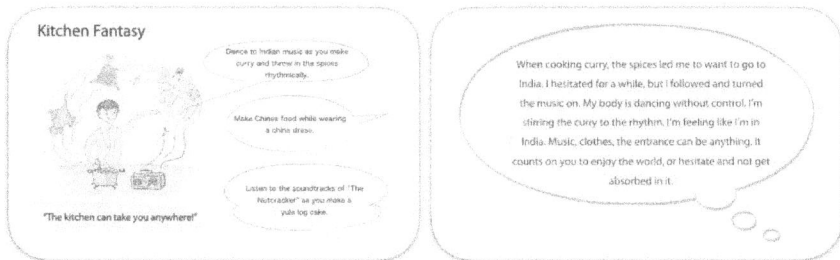

Figure 7: "Kitchen Fantasy" from the "Shift" category

Last but not least, the Fun Word for the "Victory" category is "Just Fit Pleasure". This enjoyment is about the accomplishment of something becoming "just right". The examples are, when the meringue perfectly fits the oven, or when there is just the same number of shrimp in the pasta to divide for everyone. "Just right" might happen intentionally, or maybe not, but the process of working hard to make it fit is somewhat thrilling, and when it went out "just right", the beauty is breathtaking, excited and exhilarated with fulfillment.

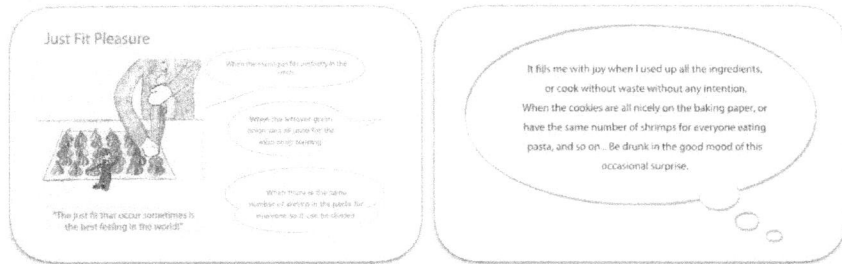

Figure 8: "Just Fit Pleasure" from the "Victory" category

5.4. Overview of the 25 Fun Words

Table 1- 5 contains the contents of the 25 Fun Words in 5 categories in the Fun Language for Cooking.

Category	No.	Fun Word	Introduction	Action Examples	Thoughts
Day-dream	1	Food Day-dream	"Just thinking of what I want to make makes me grin."	» Daydream what dishes to make for the upcoming special day. » When too busy to cook, make a "Want to cook" list to satisfy your cooking desires. » Look through recipe websites and imagine what to make.	I often spend time thinking about what to make. What should I make this weekend? I go on searching for the best recipes. I want to make pretty much everything, but really, I don't have the time! Hey! Maybe I can imagine that I'm making them! Problem solved!
	2	World on a Plate	"What kind of world should I create on the table?"	» On Halloween, think of adding pumpkin or ghost motifs to your dishes. » Think about how to recreate a dish from your favorite movie scene. » When planning special meals like a Christmas dinner, make a sketch of your dinner table and scribble on until satisfied.	When I'm in charge of the meal, I first set the theme. The table is where I can freely create a little world. Then, I sketch that world's image roughly. I can adjust it to a season's event, or reproduce a meal from a scene of a film. When I'm making that world, I'm a creator.

	3	Date Buddy	"Eating there must be exceptional!"	» Taking a homemade pie to the park and eating it with friends. » Eating your favorite sandwich barefoot by the seashore. » Going on a railroad trip with your homemade lunchbox.	Sometimes, I eat food in other places. By eating at your favorite spot, or where you simply admire, the atmosphere somehow becomes the spice of your meal. I'm planning to go to "my place" this weekend. And I'll probably bring along my favorite dish.
Day-dream	4	Star Food	"I'm craving to see it once, that vegetable."	» Daydreaming how an "admirable ingredient" that you are unfamiliar with would taste like through recipes and articles. » Hoping for that "admirable ingredient" to go on sale so that you can buy it. » Going window-shopping to specialty grocery stores to look at attractive ingredients.	I get thrilled when I catch a glimpse of ingredients I admire. That ingredient might be one you've never eaten, or maybe a special one that is hard to get. Today, I found it in the grocery store at last!!!!! The moment I see it, there's no choice but to jump at it.
	5	Recipe Worm	"He goes that far!? Really, he is a pro."	» Make a "Recipe Bookworm Day" and take time reading your favorite chef's cookbook. » Enjoy reading difficult and authentic books of patsies. » Imitate the tips and ingredients of the author of the cookbook, and feel the authors' taste, or the detailed touch designed by the author.	My pleasures in the weekend these days are to read my favorite cook looks. Like imitate writing in your favorite style, when I my favorite chefs' recipe, I want to imitate it. As I feel the authors' detailed sense, I get absorbed in the authors' greatness. As I turn the pages, I can help but smile at how much thought goes into the recipes.

Table 1. Fun Words in Daydream Category

Category	No.	Fun Word	Introduction	Action Examples	Thoughts
Trick	6	Surprise Plotting	"The feeling of making something for someone is like Santa Claus."	» When celebrating a family members' birthday, secretly bake the cake at night and surprise them. » Wake up earlier than usual and treat your family a weekend brunch. » Make homemade jam and send it to faraway friends and family.	I usually can't express gratitude toward my loved one's. For those people, delight them with a surprise. When everyone is fast asleep, sneak into the kitchen with a secret plan. Making things for someone can't help you smile with the surprised face in your mind.
	7	Newbies in the Kitchen	"Now you're a captive of cooking!"	» Arrange a "Make Yourself Pizza Party" with everybody's favorite toppings. » Have a friend experience a recipe with a fun or interesting cooking step » Invite an anti-cooking friend and make an easy dish together to gain self-confidence, have them thinking, "I can do it too!"	Cooking is fun. Therefore, it is natural to want to have fun cooking with others. However, I don't want to force them to cook. Then, all I have to do is to plan a party that's fun to cook for everyone. If this party can be a start to someone's' love in cooking, that's a big success.
	8	Chef's Privilege	"Hahaha, no one knows about this secret pleasure!"	» On weekends, drink wine from a glass while making pasta. » Sneak in one lucky egg roll filled with cheese. » When cooking with friends, take sneak-peak bites of the food before it gets to the table.	When cooking for everyone, I, a "chef" could appreciate having a little treat. Tricks and privileges that I have because I am in the kitchen fill me with giggles, making me want to be in the kitchen and make food for people. Now, which plate should I put the "bingo" /prize in today?
	9	Feeling Like a Pro	Being a "Pro" is up to you!	» Prepare all ingredients and weigh them, and cook in a good tempo as if you're in a cooking show. » Use a sashimi knife, and cut the sashimi beautifully with care. » Put your favorite black pepper in a cool pepper mill and finish up your with the movement of a pro.	I sometimes become a professional in cooking. Sometimes, is because being a "Pro" is up to how you feel. Try to excite yourself even more by some ideas, and cook as if you are a really good cook. Dishes made from the "good cook" seem much more delicious than always, and trust me, it's not just in your imagination.

| | 10 | Day to Cook | "Sorry I can't make it. That's my bread baking day…" | » Make cooking a part of your schedule, such as "The 14th is my Bread Baking Day.", and have it be your highest priority of the day.
» Make a family event like "This Saturday is Taco Day!" and have your family members reserve that day.
» When cooking, try not to look at the phone or the TV, and get into your own world. | I'm busy every day. I keep setting my job and appointments with others above everything, so I haven't had my own time for quite a long time. Okay, next month, I'll arrange my own plan in the schedule. "Bread Baking Day", "Tacos Party", etc… You have the right to have all the fun you can on "reserved" days. Be absorbed without any interruptions. |
| Trick | | | | | |

Table 2. Fun Words in Trick Category

Category	No.	Fun Word	Introduction	Action Examples	Thoughts
	11	Parental Love	"It's too dear to me, I can't help polishing it."	» Treat your favorite cookware like a pet, polish it preciously, and talk about it with pride to other people like a loving parent. » When dealing with chestnuts, or hard to peel ingredients, work on it like a caring parent. » Name your dish and make it an original, reconfirming your feelings toward the dish.	The other day, I treated myself a blender. It's my No.1 favorite, so when I use or clean it, I get happy and treat it too neatly. That reminds me, I feel the love of parenting in my heart these days when I'm cooking these days. Even if it's a hard preparation, I end up having fun thinking, "Oh, you're such trouble!". And, I'm starting to name all of my cooking utensils… Is this too crazy?
Love	12	Talk to Food	Listen to the voice of the ingredients.	» Ask a tomato "How do you want to be cooked?" to decide the best way to cook it. » Saying "It's finally your turn buddy!" to the too hard to eat avocado that was on the waiting list, and cook when it's edible. » Feeling "I'm the only one that can save you!" when meeting eyes with clearance goods or crooked vegetables and putting it in the cart.	Before starting the cooking, I put the ingredients on my hand and ask it "How do you want to be cooked?" Then, it tells you how their condition is that day; too ripe, or hard, and so on. I listen to their voices, and help them shine in the best way. That is how you get along with those carefree ingredients.

	13	The Special One	"You're the star of the batch!"	» Feature the best-shaped cookie in the center when taking a picture. » Give the most beautiful served plate to your loved ones. » The best-browned panini is eaten with special care.	Cooking tends to make good shapes and out of shaped guys. The good shapes are somewhat very cute, so I can't help favoring it. However, The out of shaped ones are not a failure, either. If you think of them as "back dancers" of sorts, you'll find yourself loving them all.
Love ♥	14	Capture the Moment	Save it in its best suit.	» Take a picture with a small prop that fits the foods' atmosphere or season » Wake up early in the morning just to take a picture of your sweets in the morning sun. » Don't miss the action shot of the dishes' highlight scene, for example, the moment cheese is melting.	Foods cooked with much effort are a little "mottainai" to eat! To visually keep the dish as it is, the only way is to take a picture. I start being more particular about taking pictures, and then become particular of dishing up, or ingredient choosing. To preserve it in its best look, I find myself trying this and that.
	15	Tasty Memories	"Oh, I recall that taste, that feeling."	» Take pictures of the scenes of foods you cooked, and sometimes recall your memories, like "Yeah I ate this with that person...". » Keep a cooking diary, and write what you made and your memory of it. » When having a taco party, don't forget to take pictures of the cooking process and everyone eating.	Turning pages of the album, I found the meal I cooked that time. "I used to do play basketball, and do other things..." A lot of memories are swimming in my head. Cooking can be a symbol of a daily scene. Foods made or foods eaten link to memories or how you felt that time, more than you imagine.

Table 3. Fun Words in Love Category

Category	No.	Fun Word	Introduction	Action Examples	Thoughts
Shift	16	Motivation Switch	"The sign of "Okay, let's start cooking!""	» Actually do warm ups to pump up your blood flow before cooking. » Put on your favorite apron and switch to your "cooking mode". » Wash your face before going into the kitchen to freshen up your mind.	Even if you want to cook, you tend to become lazy without a trigger. In situations like that, I use my little spell to turn me into cooking mode. If I can get my mind ready before I stand in the kitchen, I know I'll have a good time in the kitchen.
	17	Holy Place	"Standing in the kitchen, I'm in a solemn mood of cooking gracefully."	» Bow to the kitchen for appreciation when going in. » Keep a good posture when cutting vegetables. » Even when washing the dishes, try to keep every action smooth and graceful.	I have times when I lose self-confidence. In times like that, I go to the kitchen and cook. By making sure my movements are proper and graceful, I become positive minded. Thinking that there is a "Kitchen Spirit" watching over you in the kitchen will naturally get you good postured. You will feel better about by the time you finish making a dish.
	18	Kitchen Escape	Be absorbed, and the heart and mind will be all refreshed.	» After having an argument with a friend or a family member, make dumplings from scratch and concentrate on wrapping them. » When business becomes frustrating, make a stock of side dishes for a heads' rest. » Make jam and concentrate on cutting tons of fruits to refresh your mind when something is bothering you.	When you devote yourself to a cooking process with much effort and trouble, it can actually be soothing. While concentrating on simple work, quiet and peaceful time passes by. There are times when you're down, or have something that bothers you. In times like this, shut yourself in the kitchen and cook foods that take time and effort. After the cooking process, you will find your heart and mind refreshed.

| | 19 | Cooking for the Task | "Let's get this done while the bread is in the oven!" | » Resting time for bread dough can be time to finish homework.
» Check bothersome emails after cooking and while your productivity is still high.
» Study for a test while stirring the stew every now and then. | When loaded with tasks, you become lousy without any motivation. That is when I need some kind of a timekeeper. For example, bake bread from scratch. Proofing time is the most productive work time, so I hurry to my PC. After I set the bread in the oven, I might as well clean the room! It's so funny that bread is my timekeeper. |
| Shift | 20 | Kitchen Fantasy | "The kitchen can take you anywhere!" | » Dance to Indian music as you make curry and throw in the spices rhythmically.
» Make Chines food while wearing a china dress.
» Listen to the soundtracks of "The Nutcracker" as you make a yule log cake. | When cooking curry, the spices led me to want to go to India. I hesitated for a while, but I followed and turned the music on. My body is dancing without control. I'm stirring the curry to the rhythm. I'm feeling like I'm in India. Music, clothes, the entrance can be anything. It counts on you to enjoy the world, or hesitate and not get absorbed in it. |

Table 4. Fun Words in Shift Category

Category	No.	Fun Word	Introduction	Action Examples	Thoughts
Victory	21	Staple Dishes	"Hmmm, I'm getting close to that ideal taste."	» Keep making fresh homemade pasta in many ways to reproduce the taste you had in Italy. » Pick a theme of the month, and keep making dishes in that theme until you're satisfied with the result. » Collect tips on how to make a certain dish better by reading books go eating what the pro makes.	Cooking has the joy of trial and error, just like a science experiment. There are dishes that are difficult to master, but you just can't help but smile when you made the "perfect taste". It's a pleasure to keep changing the ways, seeking for the best. Beside, when you have tons of knowledge on a particular menu, you can't help sharing them with people like a cooking geek.

Victory ♕	22	No Difference Preference	The fondness that only you know produces satisfaction.	» Have a salt collection and use the best fitting salt for each purpose. » Buy kitchen utensils, or small tools that you don't really need, but desperately want. » Use as much ingredients from the area as you can when cooking local food.	I have small preferences that other people don't realize. The detailed the preferences, the less possibility that other people will notice. Small preferences like that are the ones you become fond and proud of, and makes you think you're the best cook in the world. The deeper in detail I go, the more I want to master it.
	23	Yummy Serving	"How can I perfect the outward tastiness?	» Pair a hot stew with a warm wooden bowl. » Use a place mat that adds spice to the color of the dish. » Refresh leftovers by changing the plate it is served on.	Food can become tastier just by the way it looks to the eyes. "How should I serve the food to make it most delicious?" I choose the table settings and plates that will fit the food the most. Even if you mess-up the food or it's a leftover, you turn it into a delicious dish by the way you serve it.
	24	Stock for Me	"Stock made in an exciting mood is my power of confidence."	» Keep a stock of pre-cooked food for lunch boxes and for dinner. » Stock cookie dough in the freezer so you can bake it and give it as a present any time. » After making pepperoncino, freeze the unused garlic for another dish.	Sometimes I get a "Cooking high" that makes me want to cook a lot. When I have the time and will, I make many side dishes or pre-cooked things to use later on. By stocking up, I gain self-confidence and a sense of accomplishment. Using the stock later on, I become proud of myself, praising "Well done, me!" and start grinning.

| | 25 | Just Fit Pleasure | "The just fit that occur sometimes is the best feeling in the world!" | » When the meringue fits perfectly in the oven.
» When the leftover green onion was all used for the miso soup topping.
» When there is the same number of shrimp in the pasta for everyone so it can be divided. | It fills me with joy when I used up all the ingredients, or cook without waste without any intention. When the cookies are all nicely on the baking paper, or have the same number of shrimps for everyone eating pasta, and so on... Be drunk in the good mood of this oc-casional surprise. |
| Victory | | | | | |

Table 5. Fun Words in Victory Category

6. The Implication of Cooking Fun Language

The Cooking Fun Language has mainly 3 implications, as outlined below.

6.1. Shares the Hidden Know-How to Enjoy Cooking

First, Fun Language opens the hidden ways to enjoy cooking. We usually focus more on improvement in cooking skills, but Cooking Fun Language allows one to concentrate more on the emotional side of cooking, that is; how to better upgrade the experience of cooking. By making explicit the hidden enjoyment behind cooking processes, people can approach the activity through not only the technique-aspect, but also see how cooking can be an enjoyable experience that can enhance the quality of daily life.

6.2. Present Cooking in a Positive Light

Second, for those who are inexperienced in cooking, Cooking Fun Language can present a new realization towards cooking-the cooking process can be enjoyable. One of the main reasons why people do not cook is because they have a negative image towards the cooking process. For example, that it is very difficult or that it takes too much time. However, once a person grasps how to enjoy cooking, it can become a hobby, rather than a dull chore. In this way, Cooking Fun Language can invite people to see the enjoyable side of cooking.

6.3. Allows Individuals to Define their "Meaning of Cooking"

Cooking Fun Language allows people to discuss and deepen their understanding of the enjoyment of cooking. By having the Fun Words as a starting point to discuss how each individual finds enjoyment/satisfaction in the cooking process, it enables different people to gain insight/inspiration from each other, as well as to realize what role cooking plays in enhancing their daily lives. Through redefining the meaning of cooking, cooking will naturally become something of a higher priority.

7. Conclusion

In this paper, we proposed Cooking Fun Language, a Fun Language that shares 25 Fun Words that encompass the ways of enjoying cooking. These were created in the hope that readers will understand the fascinating enjoyments of cooking and shift mindsets to wanting to cook for fun in their daily lives. As future work, we may look into more detail in regard to the function Fun Words can play in fostering conversation/ a deeper understanding of the enjoyment of cooking for beginners by holding dialogue workshops. Furthermore, we would like to explore possible implementations of the Fun Words on recipe websites run by our research collaborator, Cookpad Inc., as a new way to help website users expand their cooking repertoire and enjoyment habits.

Note: this was conducted as a joint project with Cookpad Inc, the largest recipe site and cooking community in Japan, as research into ways to make cooking enjoyable and accessible for beginners.

8. Acknowledgement

First, we would like to express our appreciation to our research partners from Cookpad, inc.: Takuji Ikeda and Ryo Katsuma, as well as Akimitsu Sano for giving us the opportunity to create Cooking Fun Language through joint research. We also thank all interviewees for sharing their unique and wonderful Fun seeds in cooking, as well as Marino Kinoshita, Tomoki Kaneko among other members from Iba Laboratory for their great feedback for this paper.

9. References

Akado, Y., Shibata, S., Yoshikawa, A., Sano, A., and Iba, T. (2016) "Cooking Patterns: A Pattern Language for Everyday Cooking," 5th Asian Conference on Pattern Languages of Programs (AsianPLoP2016).

Alexander, C. (1979) The Timeless Way of Building, Oxford University Press.

Alexander, C., Ishikawa, S., Silverstein, M., Jacobson, M., Fiksdahl-King, I. and Angel, S. (1977) A Pattern Language: Towns, Buildings, Construction, Oxford University Press.

Iba, T. and Iba Laboratory (2015), Pattern Illustrating Patterns: A Pattern Language for Pattern Illustrating, CreativeShift Lab.

Iba, T., Yoshikawa, A., and Shimizu, H. (2017) Fun Language: Sharing the "Fun" to Motivate People to Do Daily Activities," will be presented in the 24th Conference on Pattern Languages of Programs (PLoP2017).

Kawakita, J. (1967) HassouHou [The Abduction Method: For Creativity Development], in Japanese, Chuo-Koron.

Harasawa, K., Miyazaki, N., Sakuraba, R., and Iba, T. (2015) A Tale of Pattern Illustrating, CreativeShift Lab.

Sasabe, A., Kaneko,T., Takahashi,K., Iba, T. "Pattern Mining Patterns: A Search for the Seeds of Patterns", the 23th Pattern Languages of Programs, 2016.

Shibata, S., Kogure, S., Shimizu, H., Iba, T., "Pattern Symbolizing Patterns: Showing the content and value by expressions to encourage intuitive comprehension," 23rd Conference on Pattern Languages of Programs (PLoP2016), USA, Oct., 2016

Waters, A. (2010). The Art of Simple Food: Notes, lessons, and recipes from a delicious revolution. Clarkson Potter.

Yoshikawa, A., Akado, Y., Shibata, S., and Iba, T. (2016) "Cooking Life Patterns: A Pattern Language for Enjoying: Cooking in Everyday Life," 21st European Conference on Pattern Languages of Programs (EuroPLoP2016).

A Cooking Language: A Pattern-Based Tool for Discovering and applying History-Based Cooking Ideas

Isaku, Taichi
CoCooking co., Ltd, Japan
tisaku@sfc.keio.ac.jp

Iba, Takashi
Faculty of Policy Management, Keio University, Japan
iba@sfc.keio.ac.jp

This paper proposes the cooking language method, along with its first sample created from the Japanese cuisine: the Washoku Language. Cooking language is a method/tool, derived from pattern language that captures recurrent structures among meals of a cuisine that bring good cooking/eating experiences. Similar to the purpose of the original patterns by Alexander, a cooking language allows for active participation in the kitchen. The paper will briefly cover philosophical aspects of the method, describe its creation method, introduce the first instance of a cooking language (the Washoku Language), and show results and analyses from two test cases of cooking using a cooking language. This paper concludes that the tool has the following purposes: 1) providing frameworks for thinking of menus, 2) suggesting topics to trigger conversations, 3) opening up the train of thought to allow for collaborative design, and 4) providing an opportunity to discover, experience and create the cuisine.

Cooking; Creativity; Culture; Collaboration; Design

1. Introduction

Imbued with inspirations from Alexander, the cooking language is a method based on pattern language that captures recurrent structures within a cuisine that brings good taste, gives it a name, and then structures the words into a coherent whole. The new set of vocabularies helps people recognize, understand, explain, share, and discover ideas about cooking, thus allowing its users to create a connection with their food. The tool aims to enhance understanding, communication, and ideas in the kitchen.

This paper will cover the necessity for such a tool and method, describe the creation process of a cooking language, introduce a first example of a cooking language describing qualities of the Japanese cuisine, the Washoku Language, and show example operations of the cooking language in actual use.

2. Background

2.1. Our Paradoxical Disconnection from and Aspiration for Food

Over the past few decades, there rose an increasing group of people called the foodies. Johnston and Baumann [2009] described them as someone who is always on the lookout for the next big thing in eating. Food and cooking has gradually earned its seat in the world of entertainment [Kamp, 2006: xiii], with books, magazines, TV shows, and online media about food and cooking has becoming a huge industry. Many people, well beyond the foodies read about the cooking techniques and philosophies of celebrity chefs.

However, this movement didn't necessarily mean that more people were cooking for themselves. The annual Eating Patterns in America report [2015] by the NPD Group concluded that though people in the US are eating out less recently, over half of those meals eaten at home were not cooked there. Though many media from the foodie movement provide us with specific information on recipes we can make, shops and producers we can buy from, and small actions we can start today, we rarely pursue these actions, catching ourselves reaching out for the easier option.

And hence, we have the paradoxical situation where, though there is an increased amount of interest for food and cooking, less and less people are actually cooking for themselves [Guptill et al., 2013].

The increased disconnection between us and the food we eat is slowly but surely becoming an issue. With so many players intervening in the farm-to-table pathway, cause-effect relationships and responsibilities become blurred. By the time the food is consumed, many personal and environmental problems have become bleached, resulting in many social issues such as the issue of food loss.

My provision with the cooking language is simple: if there was a way we could recreate and enforce the connection between people and the food we eat, it would become first steps to resolving many of these issues.

2.2. Pattern Language as a Tool for Personalization and Participation

One of the things Christopher Alexander, father of pattern languages, criticized was the mass-production houses that all looked alike. His claim was that being forced to live in one of the "hundreds of houses produced by one form or another of semi-automatic processes" was the cause of the "alienation and despair which many people feel" [Alexander et al., 1985:22]. He attributed this problem to the separation between the families—the architect—and the people who actually build it— the builders. He believed that homes should fit the delicate and distinct needs of the families that are going to live in it, and therefore this separation would create misfit homes.

For Alexander, the simplest solution to achieving a process that generated a home that met the distinct needs of its inhabitants, was the participation of the inhabitants themselves into the building process [Grabow, 1983]. Not only would such a process create connections between the people and their environment, the citizens themselves are the experts on their own needs after all.

For this kind of a process to happen, he needed a tool that would give citizens, all complete novices, the knowledge on how to build homes. This is exactly what Alexander's pattern language did: with vocabulary about architectural knowledge provided, the citizens can discover, discuss, communicate, and materialize their needs. The Mexicali Project introduced in detail in The Production of Houses [Alexander et al., 1985] was one of Alexander's most considered experiments where he actually gathered a group of families to have them build their own homes using a pattern language. Here, this personalization effect is illustrated in detail.

From these points, I believe pattern language is not only a tool for sharing knowledge, but also a tool that allows for the participation of people into the creation process, which in turn contributes to them getting a personal sense of the process. I believe we can find hints here for recreating the human-food connection.

2.3. Pattern Languages and Cooking

Though the cooking language is a derivative of the pattern language method, its fundamental philosophies are shared with the original method. As we already saw above, cooking and architecture share many similarities that hints the possibility of the method to be transposed.

To better understand the relationship, I will use Hesse's [1970] model of analogies to compare the two fields. Hesse introduces three types of analogies that are made: positive analogies, where the connections between the two systems are clear and are known to exist, negative analogies, where it is known that one system has a quality but the other system lacks it, and finally neutral analogies which are possible connections that are still uncertain if they exist. Where there exists both positive and negative analogies, there is the possibility for the system to extend its applicability. The neutral analogies each become a hypothesis for how it can be extended.

No.	Architecture	Analogy Type	Cooking
1	Towns and homes are an essential staff of life that everybody needs.	positive	Food is an essential staff of life that everybody needs.
2	Architecture requires both an aesthetic and functional quality.	positive	Food requires both an aesthetic quality and functional quality (good taste, nutrition, etc.).
3	Towns and homes are physical entities that must be formed.	positive	A dish is made of physical entities that are formed.
4	There is usually a separation of between the architect and the residents.	positive	There is usually a separation between the chef and the guest.
5	There are well-regarded architects who are very skilled at design.	positive	There are chefs who are highly skilled at cooking.
6	Architectural projects take days ~ months to complete.	negative	A session of cooking takes a couple of hours max.
7	When one architectural project is complete, it takes a while for another to begin.	negative	Cooking has frequent iterations that can occur several times a day.
8	Architecture today is considered a professional skill, and not everybody is required to have architectural skills.	negative	Cooking is an activity that many of us can and actually do at home on a daily basis: many people wish they had the skills to cook (compared to gaining architectural skills).

9	There is a certain quality of an atmosphere that many of us can feel comfortable and alive in (the quality without a name).	neutral	There are certain quality of dishes and meals that make a person fulfilled when they eat it.
10	The existence of a pattern langu-age would allow for a generative process of architecture without a masterplan to happen.	neutral	The existence of a cooking langu-age would allow for a generative process of cooking without a recipe to happen.
11	Alexander's pattern language hel-ped participants understand and communicate about their homes.	neutral	A cooking language will help a chef understand and communi-cate about their dishes that they made.

Table 1: Analogical comparison of architecture and cooking

I believe the positive analogies that can be made (no.1-5 in the table) are sufficient to hint the potentials that pattern language would have in its application to cooking. The negative analogies (no.6-8) are also worth some consideration. For example, if we look at analogy no.6, we realize that architecture is on the far-right side of the spectrum of design when it comes to the length of time that a project takes, while cooking is on the opposite side. Similar observations can be made for analogy no. 7 and 8, where cooking and architecture fall on opposite ends of the axis when plotted using the provided criteria.

Now let's take a moment here to consider the field of software design, one of the areas where pattern languages spread quickly and are the most prominent today [Eto, 2009]. If we consider the analogical relationships between architecture and software, we notice sim-ilar negative analogies to those we saw between architecture and cooking: faster projects, quicker iterations, higher demand for the skill. With the similar structure and the prosperity of patterns in software we see today, I think cooking has a good chance.

2.4. Past Work on Pattern Language and Cooking

Cooking has been a hot topic for pattern researchers these recent years. To introduce a few by myself: The Generative Cooking Patterns [Isaku and Iba, 2014 a system of pattern-driven cooking, where a perception from one of the five senses will trigger a pattern, and the solu-tion of the pattern would take the cooking dish to a different phase, eventually generating a dish. Another, the Ingredient Language [Isaku et al., 2015] is another collective set of indi-vidual languages that each focus on a specific ingredient, showing how the item contributes to the taste/quality of a dish. Ideally, this language would answer the question "I have some eggs in the fridge, what can I cook from it?" (The dish language, when presented in the previ-ous paper, was originally named the cooking language. However, after some considerations in naming the language in this paper, we decided to give the name to the language discussed in this paper, while renaming the original cooking language to ingredient language.)

The list continues: The Creative CoCooking Patterns [Isaku and Iba 2015, 2016a], Cooking Life Patterns [Yoshikawa et al., 2016], Cooking Patterns [Akado et al., 2016], etc. These pattern languages, including the cooking language introduced in this paper, all attack a different problem in the vast field of cooking, and in no way are they mutually exclusive from the above introduced patterns. Any of these cooking-related pattern languages can be mixed and matched for a fun, social, improvised, and/or creative meal.

3. Defining the Cooking Language

To begin the discussion, I would like to make the following correspondence of terms:

original concept	corresponds to	one instance
pattern language	cooking language	Washoku Language
pattern	cooking word	washoku word

Table 2: Correspondence of terms

Cooking language is the cooking equivalent of pattern language, and cooking words correspond to patterns. One other thing to note is that, as I will introduce the first example of a cooking language, it is given the name Washoku Language (washoku is the Japanese word referring to its own cuisine), consisting of washoku words. Alexander took an entire book [1979] to describe what a pattern is, what a pattern language is, and how it can be used to create towns and buildings. I could consider each of his concepts and claims to consider if it applied to cooking or not, but to make things simple, we assume that any idea that applies to patterns and pattern languages will, unless otherwise defined, respectively apply to cooking words and cooking languages to some extent. Through such an analogical thinking, we will be able to generate several hypotheses about a new process of cooking.

3.4.1. Defining a Cooking Word

We start by looking at Alexander's description of a pattern:

> *"...a unitary pattern of activity and space, which repeats itself over and over again, in any given place, always appearing each time in a slightly different manifestation." [Alexander, 1979:181]*

Notice the last portion of the description. Alexander challenged himself by asking why it was possible that what he is trying to define as patterns can take a different structure every time. His solution was that it was not the physical entities themselves that are repeating, but the relationships between elements that are repeating. These relationships themselves do not have a physical structure, and therefore can appear in different forms every time the pattern is applied. Therefore, a more precise description:

> *"a morphological law, which establishes a set of relationships in space"* [1979:90]

Thus, each pattern is talking about a transformation. A pattern usually describes this transformation process through the following four sections: the context, problem, solution, and consequence. This format is highly inspired by how Alexander thought of design: the process of finding problems, and using form to resolve it. [Alexander, 1964]

Bringing this view of patterns into the kitchen, there is no doubt cooking, design in the kitchen, has a lot to do with resolving a conflict (between ingredients, heat, moisture, etc.) with some kind of a physical transformation. And therefore, patterns have high affinity with cooking.

However, not all aspects of food and cooking are understood in a mere problem-solution relationship. There are many things we do to our food just because "it is better that way." Though it would be completely fine without the entity, adding the extra aspect would enhance our feelings, joy, and affection towards the food. Hence, both approaches are needed: while some cooking patterns [Isaku and Iba, 2014] [Akado et al., 2016] aim to capture the mere problem-solution relationship of cooking, the cooking language is my effort to capture the other half of entities that enhance our experience with food (but does not solve any problems).

With these discussions made, I below provide a definition of a cooking word:

» A cooking word is a morphological law that establishes an abstract pattern of relationships in a dish and/or its surrounding atmosphere.

» This relationship forms a physical entity that appeals either to 1) one of our five senses, 2) our intellectual curiosity), or 3) our emotional satisfaction. (In other words, the body, brain, or heart.)

» These are entities that are recurrent across several ages within a specific cuisine, always appearing each time in a slightly different manifestation.

3.4.2. A Word on Culture: What does a Cooking Language do? What does it not do?

The fact that many of the cooking words are culture dependent brings up rather hard but inevitable questions: *Do we have to define the precise borders of a cuisine/culture in order to create a cooking language? Or, does the creation of a cooking language in turn define a culture/cuisine?*

Fortunately (or not), answers to both questions I believe are no. First of all, defining a culture and setting its borders is a meticulous and controversial process that anthropologists would do a much better job than I would. Second, the goal of a cooking language is not to define or argue the borders of a culture, nor to map out its entirety. Instead, the goal lays in inspiring people with ideas that are rooted in a culture's history to enhance their everyday cooking experiences. To achieve this goal, a clear-cut definition of the cuisine/culture need not be necessary.

To summarize, A cooking language will:

» help spot characteristic attributes rooted in the history of a cuisine in dishes.

» provide one coherent framework (though not necessary complete) in understanding the culture.

» help gain a deep understanding of a dish (either cooked by oneself of by others) in terms of the cuisine's historical contexts.

» provide ideas that would help make the dish have qualities inherited from the cuisine in topic, when cooking a dish/designing a meal occasion.

» help a chef describe the dish they created and its intent in detail in terms of the cuisine's characteristic features and its historical background.

» enhance communication when cooking with multiple people.

» enhance a person's experience cooking with a recipe by providing deeper understandings and connections between recipe (thus enhance the learning process)

A cooking language will not:

» define the culture/cuisine of the topic.

» specify attributes that are exclusively present in that cuisine.

» guarantee that a dish designed with the language will have qualities of the cuisine in topic (though in most cases it will to some extent).

» guarantee that a dish cooked will have good taste (though it may provide a good guidance)

» become a replacement for a recipe.

3.1. The Format of a Cooking Word

Synthesizing our discussions up to this point, a cooking word can be thought of as a piece of idea for transforming the state of a dish/atmosphere that is inspired by historical contexts of the cuisine.

Like how a pattern's format allowed it to describe its process of transformation, a cooking word also describes its transformation process through four distinct but continuously flowing sections (roughly corresponding to the sections of a pattern). However, due to the nature of the cooking language where 1) good cooking/eating experiences are not always explained in a mere problem-solution relationship, and 2) a cooking word captures entities that are recurrent across several ages of a specific culture (and therefore needs to provide information rooted in its historical contexts), some modifications to the format becomes necessary.

The sections of a cooking word format are described in the list below.

» **Context** - Some information on conditions which the cooking word can be applied, most likely when it can be used. Roughly the same idea as a context of a pattern

» **History** - Historical information, events, and patterns about the cuisine that would provide the cook with some insights on actions she can take in the context.

» **Idea** - The idea, action, or quality derived from the history that can be applied to the dish the user is cooking.

» **Application** - Specific examples that are seen/is possible to do in the present day. This section also functions as the cooking word equivalent of a consequence, since it provides a future vision or a resulting context after the idea has been applied.

This written format is accompanied by a visual representation (a photograph), a name for the cooking word, and a sometimes a list of related cooking words.

3.2. From Cooking Words to a Cooking Language

Though a cooking language will not define the entirety of a cuisine, the set of cooking words found from the certain cuisine should provide one coherent structure that expresses qualities of the topic cuisine.

The reason behind this can be found in Alexander's view of pattern languages. Alexander clearly states for several patterns to be combined when using it [Alexander, 1979]. Each pattern may provide some insightful knowledge to its reader, but a just a collection of patterns would be no different from, say, a mere list of life-hack tips we can find on online media. The method shows its power most when relationships between the patterns are defined. Here, interconnected patterns enforce one another, creating an emergent quality that Alexander called quality without a name.

The same applies for cooking words. The application of a single cooking word would only enhance a dish to a certain extent. Nor would just one cooking word alone create the sense of a culture by itself. However, when multiple washoku words from the Language are applied, the words would start to enforce one another, eventually creating an emergent feeling of Japanese-ness in the dish. This Japanese-ness is the Washoku Language equivalent of the quality without a name.

4. Creating a Cooking Language

This section will – briefly- introduce one method of creating a cooking language. The creation process follows a similar process of that of creating a so-called "3.0-style" [Iba, 2013, 2015] pattern language [for example: Iba and Isaku, 2013, 2014; Isaku and Iba, 2015, 2016a; Iba and Kajiwara, 2016; Sasabe et al., 2016a]. This kind of a creation method differs much from that of Alexander's original pattern language, but it is a method that has been revised and optimized for patterns language in the creative age over the course of seven years.

There is a "Pattern Language for Creating Pattern Languages" [Iba and Isaku, 2016] [Sasabe et al., 2016b] [Shibata et al., 2016] that provides a set of meta-patterns for what the title suggests. Though it is not patterns that we are creating, since patterns and cooking words mostly share the same qualities, mostly the same process can be followed.

The only (and important) structural difference between the two ideas is in its format, and therefore some alterations will occur in the process when looking for the right information during the mining phase, and when writing the cooking words in its format. Below I will briefly introduce the creation process of the Washoku Language, highlighting important aspects to consider exclusive to the cooking language.

4.1. Element Mining

In the element mining phase, relevant literatures are searched for insights that can potentially be included in a cooking word. If we were to give any categorical structure to the kind of literature to search through, roughly they fall in two categories: A) references that look at the particular cuisine in terms of its historical development, and B) references that explain the status quo of the cuisine today (this includes cookbooks and how-to texts). For the Washoku Language, I referenced the following resources on the Japanese cuisine: [Ako, 2015] [Ehara,2012] [Morikawa, 2013] [Hata, 2009] [Takanashi, 2013] [BKG, 2008] [Nozaki and Okumura, 2015] [JECHI, 2011, 2015] [Takahashi, 2015] [Miyazaki, 2009] [Kumakura, 2009].

When reading through information, both practical and conceptual information that meet the following criteria are extracted: 1) Specific styles and methods of eating/cooking that are (were) done, 2) Cultural customs/traditions that are (were) performed around food, 3) Reasoning behind the actions/customs 4) Pattern of similar thoughts/actions present across regions/ages. Each point of information is written down on a slip of paper and are collected on a large sheet of craft paper (figure below). More elaborate description of the process is given in [Sasabe et al., 2016b] and [Iba and Isaku, 2012].

Figure: Each piece of information found from the resources are written down on a note and pooled onto the craft paper.

4.2. Clustering

In the element clustering phase, relationships between the notes found in the pattern mining phase are considered to generate groups of related notes. This process is based on a process known as the KJ method [Kawakita, 1967]. This is a method similar to the Grounded

Theory that forms bottom-up categories of elements through observations of local similarities. An elaborate explanation on performing the KJ method in the context of pattern mining (hence altered a bit from the original Kawakita version) is provided in [Sasabe et al., 2016b], and the same process was followed for creating the Washoku Language.

When this process is continued, eventually small to medium groups of elements will start to form. Each of these groups will become a seed for a cooking word. Once the groups are distinct, the potential cooking words go through another round of the KJ method to get a structure of the cooking language.

4.3. Writing and Visualizing

Once the "seeds" for the cooking words are found, the information in each of the groups are synthesized into the cooking word (context-history-idea-example) format. Though the section formats are different from patterns, the process described in the Pattern Writing Patterns were followed.

For the visual representation of cooking words, we used photographs that capture their culinary qualities. We had a Japanese chef look through the list of cooking words, and collaboratively brainstormed on how each cooking word should be expressed as a photo. In the process, the pattern symbolizing patterns [Shibata et al., 2016], which provides ideas on how to visualize patterns in a memorable way was referenced.

5. A Cooking Language: The Washoku Language

he Washoku Language is a cooking language describing qualities of the Japanese cuisine. This section will first give brief background on the Japanese cuisine to show the need for a cooking language. Afterwards, the 42 "washoku words" will be introduced: ten of them will be given in full text, and the rest will be shown as abstracts.

5.1. Some Context on the Japanese Cuisine

The Japanese cuisine, washoku, is unique in several ways. The small country, with its unique geography and climate, has long developed a particular cuisine that is appreciated by people both in and out of the country.

 As an island country with complex coastlines longer than the US and at a geographical location where two ocean currents meet, its cuisine is based on vast variety of fishes. Also, mountains that cover 70% of its land cut the country apart into numerous regions, each developing their own foodways to contribute to the diverse mix of the country. Its geographic features also resulted in a wide range of climate zones from subtropical to subarctic.

Hence, the country is splendid with indigenous ingredients and dishes particular to the regions. In addition to this, the mountains provide the country with a rich supply of water enriched with minerals, which also contributed to the cuisine centered on rice, fish, and other specialties that use ample amounts of water. Not only natural conditions, but combined with sophisticated philosophies and techniques that were developed by its people, the cuisine stands in a very unique place unseen in other countries. In more recent years its feature as a well-balanced, healthy diet collected the attention of people worldwide.

These characteristics led washoku to be nominated by UNESCO as a World Heritage in 2013. In accordance to its nomination, there came up the need to define what to include in the cuisine. Upon being nominated a World Heritage, the Japanese government agreed on the following four points as components of washoku [MAFF, 2016b]:

» "various fresh ingredients and using their natural tastes"

» "well-balanced and healthy diets"

» "emphasis of the beauty of nature in the presentation"

» "connecting to annual events"

These points became a good starting point for many efforts to follow on the study of the washoku culture. Many of them were government lead [MAFF, 2013, 2014a, 2015, 2016a], and among their works there were several that aimed to give structure to the washoku cuisine. Some are shown in the figure below.

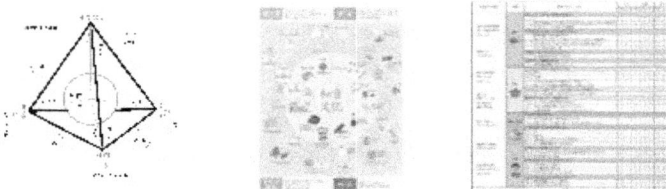

Figure: Past efforts to provide structure to the Japanese cuisine. Adapted from [Kumakura, 2011], [MAFF, 2014a], and [MAFF, 2015] respectively

These frameworks all point to somewhat the same point: the "washoku-ness" of a thing cannot be determined in a mere yes-no basis, but there is a whole gradient in between.

Though the point of the Washoku Language is not necessarily to analyze and/or define what exactly washoku is, the work can also be considered to fall on the same line of efforts as these frameworks to better understand the cuisine.

5.2. The Washoku Language

This section will introduce three of the actual cooking words from the Washoku Language in full text. Each cooking word will have a name and a photograph at the top of the subsection, , followed by the context — history — idea — application format. Below the picture, the cooking word will begin with the context. Then comes the separator "▼ In this context" followed by the history. After the history section comes the separator "▼ Therefore" followed by idea section. Finally, after the Idea section comes the separator "▼ For example" leading into the application section. At the end of each cooking word you can also find a list of related cooking words, which are cooking words that would co along well with the one on the page to enforce one another.

In addition to the selected ten, the rest of the cooking words will be shown as a list showing only the name, photo, and an abstract of its entity.

5.2.1. No.11: Sound of Taste

When choosing ingredients, especially vegetables to use in your dishes.

▼ In this context

Sound has historically been an important factor of taste in washoku.

We have the idea of shokkan, which is the sound and/or texture that the food provides us when bitten or chewed on. Without the shokkan, the taste of a dish will be incomplete. For example, rice is often considered good when there's the slight elasticity, koshi, when chewed (slightly close to the idea of al dente when cooking pasta). We have an infinite amount of onomatopoeias that express these different shokkan, where some sounds are almost specifically designated for certain food items, and in other cases the food item is sometimes named after the shokkan it provides (such as the hari-hari zuke pickles). [Koizumi, 2002]

▼ Therefore

Include a variety of ingredients that each provide a different shokkan, and enjoy the different sounds that they make when cooking and eating them.

▼ For example

By considering the use of Diverse Indigenous Ingredients or the Five Basic Colors, the variety in shokkan becomes easier to incorporate. No need to have bad manners and be loud when you chew, but just calmly enjoy the sound and texture when you chew. Also, sounds can be enjoyed at all phases of Japanese cooking: the sound of food simmering in the pot, or the sound of a sharp Japanese knife slicing different items are good examples.

▶ No.01 Diverse Indigenous Ingredients, No.24 Five Basic Colors

5.2.2. No.23: Contrast and Coexistence

This entity of form can be seen throughout the cooking process: when choosing colors, when flavoring, when arranging food on the dish, etc.

▼ In this context

Contrast is something we often see in washoku.

For example, dark and light colors, strong and light taste, thick and thin texture, front and back, circles and rectangles, etc. There is no concrete explanation for why, but we can see the thought embedded into our logic, for example with the concept of hon-ne (a person's true unspoken feelings) and tatemae (actions and explanations expressed to hide the hon-ne). The light, white, weak aspects can analogically be thought of the tatemae, while the thick, dark, strong tastes as the hon-ne. There is also an idea called the Inyo-Gogyo, which originated as a Chinese cosmology but then highly influenced the washoku cuisine, that thinks in terms of in (ying) and yo (yang) as two contradicting forces which are actually complementary. [Koizumi, 2002; Hata, 2009; Morikawa, 2013]

▼ Therefore

Include contradicting qualities in the same meal, or enjoy contrasting tastes of the same item for different occasions.

▼ For example

The most noticeable and often seen is where a rectangular piece of food is arranged on a circular plate (and vise-versa). Other examples include including dishes with a dark taste and a light taste in the same meal, creating a contrast in the colors used in a dish. You can also create contrast in the time axis by enjoying contrasting tastes of the same item in different occasions: for example, sweet vs. spicy (dry) sake, strong vs. light tea, dark and light shoyu, satsumaage vs. hampen, misoshiru vs. suimono, etc.

▶ No.15 Various Means of Cooking, No.20 Light Round Taste

5.2.3. No.39: Thankfulness for Nature

You are either at the start or the end of a meal.

▼ In this context

A Japanese meal starts and ends with a moment of thankfulness.

Though it is a rather new manner (resources say it started around the second world war) to say itadaki-masu before a meal, the Japanese people has long held nature in reverence, thankful for the blessings it provides us. Saying the phrase (which literally means "I will receive" in a humble manner) before the meal became one way to express this thankfulness.

In addition, preparing a meal requires the work of many people from farming to distribution to cooking to serving. to show appreciation for the hard work of these people, people in the Edo period started saying what eventually became the phrase gochiso-sama at the end of the meal, which is a phrase acknowledging all the running around that went into the meal. [Takahashi, 2015; Okumura, 2015; JECHI, 2011]

▼ Therefore

Take a moment before and after the meal to express your thankfulness for nature's blessings, and also to acknowledge the people who provided the food for you.

▼ For example

Taking a moment as a group to say "itadaki-masu" before the meal and "gochiso-sama" after are important aspects of a Japanese meal even today. Though it often tends to lose the true intent behind the words, it would be great if you could actually take the opportunity to thank nature and the people who took their time and effort to prepare the meal.

▶ No.01 Diverse Indigenous Ingredients

6. Cooking with the Cooking Language

Alexander's approach to attacking mass-housing was to create a new way of building that involves the families into the process, even if they were total novices in architecture. Getting involved does not merely mean just participating in the hammering and the sanding, doing whatever the architect tells you to do. In Alexander's sense, it meant that you and your family are the ones that decide and design how everything would be in your new home so that it fits your family's distinct needs.

In the same sense, the cooking language isn't just a tool that would help people learn how to cook, nor is it a how-to cookbook that the user can just follow directions just to be involved with the cooking process. The true goal of cooking languages is to give everyone a chance to first-handedly get involved in the cooking process so that they can feel a personal connection to the food they make and eat.

6.1. The Two Test cases

This section will introduce test cases of cooking using the Washoku Language. These cooking sessions were conducted to see how the cooking language will act as a tool to create this kind of a personal connection to the food we eat.

Two sessions of cooking were conducted, but due to space reasons, this paper will only introduce abstracts of each cases, and focus more on its results and synthesis. One of the two cases can be read in detail in appendix B.

6.1.1. Case 1: Planning and Cooking a Japanese Meal

In the first of the two cooking sessions, a group of four college undergrad students, all friends with each other, were collected to plan a dinner for the night. Since this was the first case ever of designing an actual menu using a pattern-like tool, I collected participants with at least moderate cooking experience/skills. They were told their goal was to collaboratively plan a menu together, and to each describe the dish they created at the end. In the planning process, they were given the list of 42 washoku words to help them plan the dinner. After they got a grasp of what they were going to cook, they went shopping for ingredients, and engaged in a cooking session to actually cook the menu. After cooking and eating as a group, the members were again handed the list of washoku words to engage in a collaborative reflection session.

Figure: Photos from the test cooking session

6.2. Case 2: Bridging the Skill Gap

The goal of the second case of cooking was to see if a cooking language will actually act as a tool to bridge the gap between people of significantly different skill levels of cooking. For this cooking session using the Washoku Language, two college undergrad students were told to collaboratively design and cook a dish. Of the two participants, one person had relatively high cooking skills, while the other rarely had experience with cooking. The goal of this experiment was to observe how the novice cook would interact with the experienced cook using the washoku language as a tool that potentially fills in the skill gap between the two.

The full case, including participant profiles, transcripts from the planning session, the reflection session, and their analyses can be read in Appendix B.

Figure: Photos from the second cooking session

6.3. Syntheses: Practical Uses of the Cooking Language

Below are the points that I found a cooking language to be actually be useful for. These are all points discovered from the test cases.

6.3.1.Framework for thinking of menus

Through the two cases of planning menus using the cooking language, I have discovered there to be two ways to provide a framework to help people devise a menu. First, there were certain cooking words that provided a framework by itself. The Kata of Meals and the Five Basic Colors, which happened to be used by both teams, are good examples. These cooking words worked by discovering existing frameworks from the cuisine, and modifying them so the essence is still there, but is more useable in daily contexts. Since these frameworks are ones that are used throughout the cuisine's history, menus planned using these framework cooking words most likely end up having qualities that remind us of the corresponding cuisine. In this sense, the other cooking words acted as sources for ideas on how to fill in and decorate the framework. In many cases, the cooking words acted as triggers for recalling past experiences of cooking/eating. These became good sources for ideas on what and how to cook during the planning session.

The other way a cooking language can provide us with a framework to help think of menus is a more global approach. In the second case, the participants were asked to choose at least five cooking words, and then think what to cook from there. This was a rather strict approach than in the first case where the participants were allowed to use the cooking language in whatever way they liked; this resulted in the participants not using the cooking words as much, resulting almost twice as long to agree on a menu. By taking the strict approach, the cooking language helped people think of menus easily yet creatively.

6.3.2. Topics to enhance conversations

This is a rather manifest use of a cooking language. Remembering the comments left by that participant from the first case (introduced at the end of section 5.1.5), the cooking words helps set a topic of conversation for reflecting on the cooking experience. In both sessions, participants retrospectively and surprisingly discovered cooking words they haven't considered in the preliminary planning to be present in the reflection session. This suggests another effect of a cooking language: retrospectively giving meaning to and therefore enhancing cooking and eating experiences by providing discoveries.

6.3.3. A tool to learn, discover, and experience the cuisine

Though this is a supplementary effect, it is also a manifest and important one. Especially during the reflection sessions, participants repeatedly mentioned how they learned something new about the Japanese cuisine. The first group of students repeatedly mentioned cooking words that provided them with new learnings, for example, Power of Fermentation, Contrast and Coexistence, and Eating Skills. Eating Skills seemed to be insightful for the second group too, considering the depth they went in discussing the cooking word. As I mentioned above, both groups discussed similar topics and reached similar conclusions on the Japanese cuisine. One future possibility is to focus more on these mere learnings about the cuisine, and develop a program to learn about it.

6.3.4. A collaboration tool that opens up the train of thought

When I was reading the script from the planning session for the first group, I discovered them talking about certain cooking words without being inspired by it. In other words, by using the cooking words, I was retrospectively able to discover reasonings for certain trains of thoughts used by the experienced cooks. For example, Student A and Student C, probably the two most experienced cooks from the first group, naturally headed towards a ichi-jyu-sansai meal (Kata of Meals), wanted to include a variety of colors (Five Basic Colors), and suggested to include seasonal items into the menu (Eating the Season). This leads into the next point: a cooking language will help notice the reasonings and/or the train of thought behind experienced cooks.

This aspect was highlighted even more in the second case. By using the cooking language as a tool that opens up the train of thought of experienced cooks, novice cooks can join in the cooking process without difficulty. We saw in the second case that the pair of participants was able to share the menu planning experience with no problem, the conversation driven by the cooking language. Then in the way they described the dish they cooked, we saw no significant difference in the way they understood the dish. From these points I think it is safe to say that the cooking language became a tool for collaborative cooking that allowed novice cooks to be included in the process.

7.   Conclusion

In the shadows of its glory of being nominated as a World Heritage and receiving world-wide fame, the washoku cuisine is recently facing some struggles. For example, in a large-scale, cross-generation survey conducted by a team from Japan's Ministry of Agriculture Forestry and Fisheries [MAFF, 2016c], only 29.8% of respondents said they were taught about the washoku culture at home, at school, etc.. Those who responded that they are teaching/ passing down the culture to future generations were as few as 16.8%. Results from the same survey shows repeated evidence that the washoku culture is having trouble making its way down to future generations. Indeed, with the golden arch and the green siren seen on the corner of every city, traditional Japanese foodways are always in combat against new cultures from western nations.

However, viewed with a broader, historical perspective, we can see that that this battle is nothing new. As the Harmony and Prodigious Development cooking word suggests, our country has a long history of incorporating foreign ways, naturalizing it, and then evolving it in an original, sophisticated ways. There is a reason the washoku culture is considered living culture that is able to, based on its tradition and technology that developed over the long history, supplely change itself based on what the age and environment may demand [MAFF, 2014].

There is an old Japanese phrase that reads onko-chishin. The phrase, scribed in four kanji, literally reads "to warm (to visit) the past to discover the new." This has been at the heart of the Japanese development: history and traditions are always respected, while never losing the faith to move forward to create new history. I believe the Washoku Language will become a tool for onko-chishin by guiding us to the past to provide us with new discoveries.

This is probably nothing limited to the Japanese cuisine: in the process of continuous evolution of any cuisine over time, a cooking language will help us to learn from historic roots, not only to protect and practice it, but also to inherit its essence to create new styles of cooking and eating that matches the demand of the fast-changing age.

Alexander had an underlying belief consistent throughout his series of works: the liveliness of humans would only result when there is good quality in the buildings that they live in. The inquiry for creating quality in towns and buildings was his approach to creating a community with a human feeling. Though he believed that it was the pattern of events (and not its physical geometry alone) that happens at a place that gives the place its life, he also believed that the physical environment was essential and inseparable from (though not exactly causing) the events.

In the same way, I believe the warm, welcoming, fun, human, creative, and sometimes mystic atmosphere that we experience in the kitchen and around the dining table is inseparable from its physical structures — both of the meal and the environment. Therefore, though a cooking language focuses on the physical entities of meals, its ultimate goal is to create a lifestyle with the special atmosphere.

8. References

[Akado et al., 2016] Akado, Y., Shibata, S., Yoshikawa, A., Sano, A., Iba, T. (2016). Cooking Patterns: A Pattern Language for Everyday Cooking. in Proceedings for 5th Asian Conference on Pattern Language of Programs 2016 (Asian PLoP 2016), Taipei, Taiwan, 2016.

[Ako, 2015] Ako, M. (2015). Washoku tte Nani [What is Washoku?]. Tokyo, Japan: Chikuma Primer Shinsho.

[Alexander, 1964] Alexander, C. (1964) Notes on the Synthesis of Form. Cambridge, MA: Harvard University Press.

[Alexander, 1979] Alexander, C. (1979). The Timeless Way of Building. New York, NY: Oxford University Press.

[Alexander et al., 1985] Alexander, C., Davis, H., Martinez, J., Corner, D. (1985). The Production of Houses. New York, NY: Oxford University Press.

[BKG, 2008] Bessatsu Katei Gaho (2008). Eikyu Hozon Reshipi Ichiryu Ryori-cho no Washoku Hoten [Recipes for Permanent Records Treasury of Washoku from a Top- Chef: 300 gifts of recipes for us]. Tokyo, Japan: Sekai Bunka-sha.

[Ehara, 2012] Ehara A. (2012). Katei Ryouri no Kindai [Modern Times for Home Cooking]. Tokyo, Japan: Yoshikawa Kobunkan.

[Eto, 2009] Eto, K. (2009). Pattern, Wiki, XP: Toki wo koeta souzou no gensoku [Pattern, Wiki, XP: The Timeless Principles of Creation]. Tokyo, Japan: Gijyutsu Hyoronsha.

[Grabow, 1983] Grabow, S. (1983). Christopher Alexander: The Search for a New Paradigm in Architecture. London, United Kingdom: Routledge Kegan & Paul.

[Guptill et al., 2013] Guptill, A., Copelton D., Lucal, B. (2013). Food & Society: Principles and Paradoxes. Malden, MA: Polity Press.

[Hata, 2009] Hata, K. (2009). Nihon Ryori: Kiso kara Manabu Utsuwa to Moritsuke [The Japanese Cuisine: Learning Plate Selection and Arrangements from the Basics]. Tokyo, Japan: Shibata Shoten.

[Hesse, 1970] Hesse, M. (1970). Models and Analogies in Science. Notre Dame, IN: University of Notre Dame Press.

[Iba, 2013] Iba, T. (2013). Pattern Language as Media for the Creative Society. paper presented at Collaborative Innovation Networks (COIN) conference.

[Iba, 2015] Iba, T. (2015). Pattern Languages as Pragmatic Media of Thinking, Communication, and Creation. Proceedings for Pursuit of Pattern Languages for Societal Change (PURPLSOC2015), July, 2015.

[Iba and Isaku, 2012a] Iba, T. and Isaku, T. (2012). Holistic Pattern-Mining Patterns: A Pattern Language for Pattern Mining on a Holistic Approach. Proceedings for the 19th Conference on Pattern Languages of Programs (PLoP2012)

[Iba and Isaku, 2012b] Iba, T. and Isaku, T. (2014), "Presentation Patterns: A Pattern Language for Creative Presentations, Part I," Paper presented at 10th Latin American Conference on Pattern Languages of Programs (SugarLoafPLoP 2014), Brazil, Nov., 2014

[Iba and Isaku, 2013] Iba, T. and Isaku, T. (2013). Collaboration Patterns: A Pattern Language for Creative Collaborations, Proceedings for 18th Conference on Pattern Languages of Programs (EuroPLoP 2013).

[Iba and Isaku, 2016] Iba, T. and Isaku, T. (2016), A Pattern Language for Creating Pattern Languages: 364 Patterns for Pattern Mining, Writing, and Symbolizing. Paper presented at 23rd conference on Pattern Languages of Programs (PLoP16), Arlington, IL.

[Iba and Kajiwara, 2012] Iba, T. and Kajiwara, F. (2016) Purojekuto Dezain Pattan Kikaku Purodhusu Shinki Zigyou ni Kakawaru Hito no tame no Kikaku no Kotsu 32 [Project Design Patterns: 32 Project Designing Tips for People who Work with Projects, Producing, and New Businesses]. Tokyo, Japan: Shoeisha.

[Isaku and Iba, 2014] Isaku, T., Iba, T. (2014) Towards a Pattern Language for Cooking: A Generative Approach to Cooking. Proceedings for 19th European Conference on Pattern Languages of Programs (EuroPLoP14). 12 pages.

[Isaku and Iba, 2015] Isaku T, Iba T (2015) Creative CoCooking Patterns: A Pattern Language for Creative Collaborative Cooking. Proceedings of the 20th European Conference on Pattern Languages of Programs, ACM, New York.

[Isaku et al., 2015] Isaku, T., Kubonaga E., and Iba, T. (2015) The Cooking Language: Applying the Theory of Patterns into Cooking. 1st Pursuit of Pattern Languages for Social Change (PURPLSOC).

[Isaku and Iba, 2016a] Isaku, T., Iba, T. (2016) Creative CoCooking Patterns: A Pattern Language for Creative Collaborative Cooking part 2. Paper presented at the 21st European Conference on Pattern Languages of Programs, Irsee, Germany — July 06 - 10, 2016.

[JECHI, 2011] Japan Education Centre for the Hotel Industry (2011). Washoku Kentei: Nyumon-hen [Washoku License Exam: Introductory Level]. Tokyo, Japan: Japan Education Centre for the Hotel Industry.

[JECHI, 2015] Japan Education Centre for the Hotel Industry (2015).Washoku Kentei: Nyumon-hen [Washoku License Exam: Basics Level]. Tokyo, Japan: Japan Education Centre for the Hotel Industry

[Kawakita, 1967] Kawakita J. (1967). Hassou Hou [The Abduction Method: For Creativity Development]. Tokyo, Japan: Chuo-Koron.

[Koizumi, 2002] Koizumi T. (2002). Shoku to nihonzin no chie [Food and the Intelligence of the Japanese]. Tokyo, Japan: Iwanami-Shoten.

[Kumakura, 2007] Kumakura I. (2007). Nihon Ryouri no Rekishi [History of the Japanese Cuisine]. Tokyo, Japan: Yoshikawa Kobunkan.

[Kumakura, 2011] Kumakura, I. (2011) . Nihon no Dentouteki Shokubunka toshite no Washoku (Washoku as Japan's Traditional Culinary Culture). in Ministry of Agriculture Forestry and Fisheries (MAFF)(2011) Nihon Shokubunka Tekisuto (Textbook on Japan's Culinary Culture) Retrieved from http://www.maff.go.jp/j/keikaku/syokubunka/culture/ (Retrieved Dec. 30, 2016).

[MAFF, 2013] Ministry of Agriculture Forestry and Fisheries (MAFF) (2013) Washoku Gaidobukku (Washoku Guidebook). Retrieved from http://www.maff.go.jp/j/keikaku/syokubunka/culture/ (Retrieved Dec. 30, 2016).

[MAFF, 2014a] Ministry of Agriculture Forestry and Fisheries (MAFF) (2014a) "Washoku" wo Mirai e ("Washoku" for the Future). Retrieved from http://www.maff.go.jp/j/keikaku/syokubunka/culture/ (Retrieved Dec. 30, 2016).

[MAFF, 2014b] Ministry of Agriculture Forestry and Fisheries (MAFF) (2014b). Heisei 26 nendo Shokuhin Rosu Toukei Chousa Houkoku (Setai Chosa) [2014 Food Loss Statistical Survey Report (By Household)] Retrieved from http://www.estat.go.jp/SG1/estat/List.do?lid=000001140357 (Retrieved Dec. 26, 2016).

[MAFF, 2015] Ministry of Agriculture Forestry and Fisheries (MAFF) (2015) Washoku wo Mamoru. Tsunagu. Hiromeru. (Protecting, Connecting, and Spreading Wshoku). Retrieved from http://www.maff.go.jp/j/keikaku/syokubunka/culture/ (Retrieved Dec. 30, 2016).

[MAFF, 2016a] Ministry of Agriculture Forestry and Fisheries (MAFF) (2016a) Washoku Bunka no Keishou no Torikumi ni Tsuite (On Initiatives for Passing the Washoku Culture Down). Retrieved from http://www.maff.go.jp/j/council/seisaku/syoku_vision/keishou.html(Retrieved Dec. 30, 2016).

[MAFF, 2016b] Ministry of Agriculture Forestry and Fisheries (MAFF) (2016b)Washoku: Traditional Dietary Cultures of the Japanese. Retrieved from http://www.maff.go.jp/j/keikaku/syokubunka/ich/ (Retrieved Dec. 26, 2016).

[MAFF, 2016c] Ministry of Agriculture Forestry and Fisheries (MAFF) Room of Food Cultures and Marketing Development.(2016). Washoku Bunka no Keishou ni Tsuite [On the Inheritance of the Washoku Culture]. Retrieved from http://www.maff.go.jp/j/keikaku/syokubunka/culture/ (retrieved Dec. 26, 2016)

[Miyazaki, 2009] Miyazaki, M. (2009). Shitte okitai "shoku" no nihonshi [The "Culinary" history of Japan you'll want to know] Tokyo, Japan: Kadokawa Gakugei Shuppan.

[Morikawa, 2013] Morikawa, H. (2013). Washoku no Kyokasho: Gion Kondate-cho [Washoku Textbook: Gion Menu-pad]. Tokyo, Japan: Sekai Bunka-sha.

[Nozaki and Okumura, 2015]Nozaki, H., Okumura, A. (2015). Nihon no Tashinami-cho [Notes on Enjoying Japan: Washoku]. Tokyo, Japan: Ziyu Kokumin-sha.

[Okamura, 2015] Okumura, A. (2015). Washoku no Kihon ga Wakaru Hon: Washoku Adobaiza Kentei Koushiki Tekisuto [A Book that tells you the basics of Washoku: Official Textbook for the Washoku Advisor License Exam]. Maebashi, Japan: Japan Business Ability Testing Association.

[Sasabe et al., 2016a] Sasabe, A., Isaku, T. Kaneko, T., Kubonaga, E., Iba, T. (2016a). Parenting Patterns: A Pattern Language for Growing with your Child. 5th Asian Conference on Pattern Language of Programs (AsianPLoP2016), 2016

[Sasabe et al., 2016b] Sasabe, A., Kaneko, T., Takahashi, K. and Iba, T. (2016b). Pattern Mining Patterns: A Search for the Seeds of Patterns. ACM PLoP'16

[Shibata, 2016] Shibata, S., Kogure, S.,Shimizu, H., and Iba, T. (2016). Pattern Symbolizing Patterns: Showing the content and value by expressions to encourage intuitive comprehension. ACM PLoP'16.

[Takahashi, 2015] Takahashi, T. (2015). Washoku no Michi [Tao of the Japanese Cuisine]. Tokyo, Japan: IBC Publishing.

[Takanashi, 2013]Takanashi, N. (2013) Hajimete no Shojin Ryouri: Kiso kara Manabu Yasai no Ryouri [Introduction to Shojin Cooking: Learning Vegetable Dishes from the Basics]. Tokyo, Japan: Tokyo Shoseki.

[Yoshikawa et al., 2016] Yoshikawa, A., Akado, Y., Shibata, S., Iba, T.. Cooking Life Patterns: A Pattern Language for Enjoying: Cooking in Everyday Life, 21st European Conference on Pattern Languages of Programs (EuroPLoP2016), Germany, Jul., 2016

[Johnston and Baumann] Johnston, J., and Baumann S. (2009). Foodies: Democracy and Distinction in the Gourmet Foodscape. New York: Talor & Francis.

[Kamp, 2006] Kamp D. (2006) The United States of Arugula: How we Became a Gourmet Nation. New York, NY: Broadway Books

[NPD Group, 2015] NPD Group (2015). Eating Patterns in America. retrieved from: https://www.npd.com/latest-reports/eating-patterns-america-consumer-consumptionbehavior/ (Retrieved Dec. 26, 2016).

Pattern Song: Auditory Expression For Pattern Languages

Iba, Takashi

Faculty of Policy Management, Keio University, Japan

iba@sfc.keio.ac.jp

Ueno, Mayu

Faculty of Environment and Information Studies, Keio University, Japan

Yoshikawa, Ayaka

Faculty of Environment and Information Studies, Keio University, Japan

This paper introduces the concept of the 'pattern song' as an auditory expression of a pattern language and presents the first such song. A pattern song is one in which the pattern language and its patterns are embedded into the lyrics. The song introduced in this study is 'Everyday World-Making,' which expresses patterns from 'Ways of Everyday World-Making', a pattern language for living well while working and parenting. Pattern song 'Everyday World-Making' tells the story of a parent who goes from being worn out by working and parenting to finding happiness and contentment in their everyday life. As the targets of this pattern language may have busy daily lives, auditory expression is an effective way to share these patterns. This paper discusses the auditory expression of a pattern language and analyzes the relation between lyrics and patterns, as well as feedback from listeners.

Pattern Language; Song; Music; Pattern Object

1. Introduction

Pattern language is a method for describing practical knowledge in ways that can be shared and used by others. A type of creative problem solving, it also functions as a common vocabulary that can be shared among a group of individuals in collaborative activities. Created in 1977 by Christopher Alexander in relation to the field of architecture (Alexander et al. 1977), the method has been adapted to a range of fields including software design (Beck and Cunningham 1987), education (Pedagogical Patterns Editorial Board 2012), welfare (Iba and Okada 2015), and social change (Shimomukai et al. 2015).

Pattern languages are generally presented as reading materials (e.g., books, papers, cards, and webpages). Many patterns have been published in book form (Figure 1). In the software community, patterns are shared as academic papers and submitted to pattern language conferences (PLoP and other PLoPs held all over the world). Patterns have also been shared via the Internet in locations such as Ward Cunningham's Portland Pattern Repository, which contains software design patterns in the first ever wiki or reader-modifiable web pages.

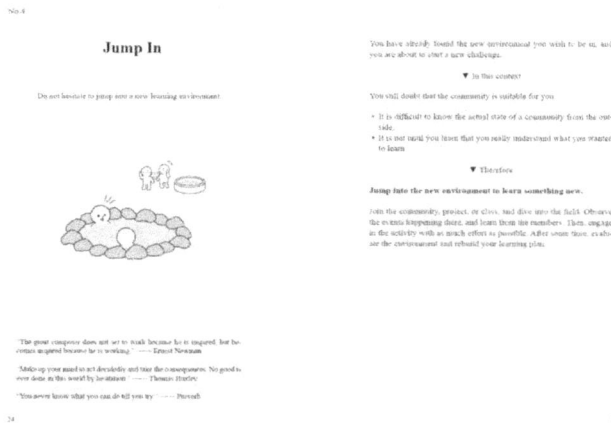

Figure 1: Book extract from 'Learning Patterns' (Iba and Iba Lab, 2014)

In recent years, pattern cards such as Iba Lab's 'Presentation Patterns Cards' (Figure 2) and 'Group Works'[1] have been introduced as tools for using pattern languages in collaborative settings, such as dialogue workshops (Iba, 2014, 2016). The `Learning Patterns Card Game' is a card game to become familiar with the Learning Patterns, a pattern language for

---

[1] *Group Works: a pattern language for bringing life to meetings and other gatherings. https://groupworksdeck.org*

creative learning (Okazaki, et al., 2011), and the 'Fearless Journey'[2] game cards allow users to learn about patterns on introducing new ideas within organizations (Manns and Rising 2005) in the form of a game. More recently, 'Pattern Objects' (Iba et al., 2016) have been introduced as a way to make patterns visible in everyday life (Figure 3).

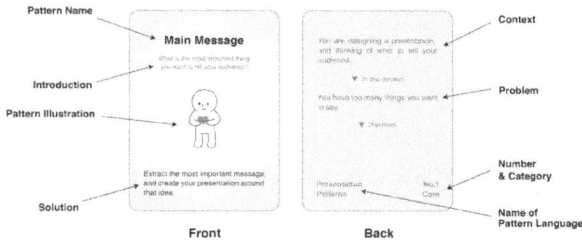

Figure 2: A pattern card from the 'Presentation Patterns'

Figure 3: Pattern objects that make patterns visible in everyday life (Iba et al., 2016)

As mentioned above, patterns are shared through visual media in the form of printed words. We wondered, however, whether patterns could be shared in a way that allows the audience to understand and internalize them in a more effortless, natural and non-visual manner. This led us to explore music and lyrics as a new form of pattern-sharing media. In this paper, we present the concept of the pattern song as an auditory medium for sharing pattern languages.

2. The function of 'songs' as media to foster empathy

Music is one way to convey a message to an audience in a way that is unobtrusive and easy to accept. The lyrics and associated melody functions to express the story of the song, which naturally evokes emotion and influences the listener's mood. Additionally, a song is a story being told by a person's unique voice, which gives a feeling of comfort to the listener. These comforting, melodic qualities allow a song to deliver its message naturally and smoothly. Songs and their lyrics are thus easily internalized. They are capable of moving the listener's emotions without the feeling that these have been 'forced' upon them by some outside force. Instead, the words create the feeling that the listeners arrived at the message by themselves, or that their hidden feelings were revealed and made explicit through the song. By giving rise to these thoughts, songs are able to positively empower listeners. Music can thus be thought of as a type of expression that is very close to the human soul, and a media that fosters empathy.

In the book The World in Six Songs (Levitin, 2008), Daniel J. Levitin states the following regarding the function and power of songs: "the demonstrated power of song-as-memory-aid has been known to humans for thousands and thousands of years" (Levitin, 2008, p.177). "Why does music have such power to move us?" he asks. To which the answer, with reference to Pete Seeger, is that it is due to "the way that medium and meaning combine in song, the combination of form and structure uniting with an emotional message."

Interestingly, songs were once a means of communicating important information in our daily lives. Before the development of print technologies, everyday know-how was shared and passed down through 'knowledge songs'.

> "Ubiquitous also in every culture are the kinds of knowledge songs that encode information vital to the survival of every member of the group, not just warnings about crocodile aggression, but day-to-day guides such as how to cook certain dark green leaves so that they are less bitter, or where to get fresh drinking water without invading the territory of a neighboring tribe." (Levitin, 2008, p.159)

However, these knowledge songs became obsolete with the invention of the printing press.

> *"With the invention of the printing press, the need for knowledge songs started to fade. In preliterate societies, they were the sole repository of cultural knowledge, history, and day-to-day procedures. They would have been fundamental to information transmission. Today knowledge songs are of a different stripe." (Levitin, 2008, p.151)*

Walter J. Ong called the modern electronic age an age of 'secondary orality' (Ong, 1982), in which knowledge songs may return in a new form. According to Ong, the age of orality was followed by the age of literacy (writing/print), which was followed by the current age of secondary literacy (videography, etc.). In other words, after writing and print became widespread, orality took on renewed importance through the development of the telephone, the radio, the television, and other electronic technologies.

> *"... with telephone, radio, television and various kinds of sound tape, electronic technology has brought us intro the age of "secondary orality". This new orality has striking resemblances to the old in its participatory mystique, its fostering of a communal sense, its concentration on the present moment, and even its use of formulas (Ong 1971, pp.284-303; 1977, pp.16-49, 305-41). But it is essentially a more deliberate and self-conscious orality, based permanently on the use of writing and print, which are essential for the manufacture and operation of the equipment and for its use as well." (Ong, 1982, p.133-134)*

The pattern song – an oral representation of a pattern language, a literary media – is an example of expression in this age of 'second orality'.

An important aspect of the pattern song is the fact that songs are a form of expression that is easy to be memorized.

> *"Songwriters know implicitly that setting something to music is the best guarantee that it will be remembered. In contemporary society, writing things down on paper, a PDA, or a computer may seem more practical, but it may not be more powerful. Songs stick in our heads, play back in our dreams, pop into our consciousness at unexpected times." (Levitin, 2008, p.153)*

The idea of expressing pattern language in the form of a song is also somewhat practical when considering 'art' in a broader context, as language and art have similar functions.

> *"Language and art both serve to represent the world to us in ways that are not exactly the world itself, but which allow us to preserve essential features of the world in our own minds, and to convey what our minds perceive to others." (Levitin, 2008, p.16)*

In other words, pattern language expressed linguistically, and pattern language expressed as a song both function in the same way. This is reinforced by Niklas Luhmann's Social Systems Theory, in which language and art are both defined as media for coupling physical systems of consciousness and social systems of communication (Luhmann, 1984, 1997). Language and art both function to aid thinking and communication.

3. Pattern song: 'Everyday World-Making'

This section will present the pattern song, 'Everyday World-Making'. We will describe the process of creating the song, as well as its relation to the original pattern language, 'Ways of Everyday World-Making' (Iba Lab and Lifestyle Research Center, 2016; Ogo, et al., 2017). 'Everyday World-Making' was created as a song that expresses the concepts of 'Ways of Everyday World-Making,' a pattern language about living well while working and parenting.

The pattern song is written from the perspective of possible readers of the pattern language, which, in this case, is people living busy lifestyles centered around working and parenting. This section will first present a short description of the pattern language, 'Ways of Everyday World-Making', followed by a description of the creative process and final output of the pattern song, 'Everyday World-Making'. Finally, the section will discuss the pattern song's relation to the pattern language.

4. 'Ways of Everyday World-Making' patterns

'Ways of Everyday World-Making' is the pattern language on which our pattern song is based. 'Ways of Everyday World-Making' is a human action pattern language (Pattern Language 3.0) that deals with how to live well while parenting and working. The underling concept to 'Ways of Everyday World-Making' is 'to create the everyday world in which we live'. 'Ways of Everyday World-Making' operates under the belief that the world in which we live, raise our children, work, and enjoy activities is a product of our individual efforts. That is, we make it for ourselves.

This pattern language consists of 34 different patterns that can be read by anyone, regardless of age or gender. The 34 patterns are organized into a core category, Own World-Making, and seven sub-categories: Original Color, Smart Juggling, Helping Hands, Turning Point, Growing with the Child, Thoughtful Gift, and Dear Future. The names and illustrations of patterns in each category are shown in Figures 4-11.

0. Everyday World

Figure 4: A pattern in the Own World-Making category

1. Natural Balance   2. Palette Mixing   3. Search for Style

Figure 5: Patterns in the Original Color category

4. Plenty Simple   5. Compose the Day   6. Good Stopping Point

7. Quality Chore Time   8. Favour for Future   9. Focus and Simplify

Figure 6: Patterns in the Smart Juggling category

10. Empathetic Friends

11. Ask for a Gift

12. Family News

13. Dinner Table Meeting

14. Tight-Knit Team

15. Parent Ally

Figure 7: Patterns in the Helping Hands category

16. Job with Joy

17. A Part of Me

18. Invent the Workstyle

19. Growing Strength

20. Follow the Gut

21. Brand New Start

Figure 8: Patterns in the Turning Point category

22. Share the View

23. Child in Charge

24. Take-off Chance

25. Journey of Parenting

26. Test for Fit

27. Ready for Chance

Figure 9: Patterns in the Growing with the Child category

28. Reflection Check

29. Time for Favourites

30. Gesture of Love

Figure 10: Patterns in the Thoughtful Gift category

31. Sketch of Future

32. Warm-up for the Hike

33. Precious Memories

Figure 11: Patterns in the Dear Future category

5. 'Everyday World-Making' and the song writing process

The pattern song 'Everyday World-Making' tells the story of a parent who goes from being worn out by working and parenting to finding happiness and contentment in their everyday life. Through the course of the song, the parent discovers the preciousness of everyday life and learns to appreciate to the people around him/her. In so doing, he/she is able to become more positive about him/herself.

The song was written following the Context, Problem, Solution structure, with the concept of 'creating our own world together' as the central message (as is the case in the 'Ways of Everyday World-Making' patterns). The song-writing process began with the chorus section, which reflects the main message of the pattern language. The A and B sections were written after the chorus. The A section comprises lyrics that introduce the context and the problem of the story, while the B section contains the episodes that lead into the chorus (resolution). The song was written to embody the overall message of the entire pattern language. After the initial draft was completed, the song was further revised through a series of collaborative feedback sessions with one of the authors of 'Ways of Everyday World-Making'. Concepts from additional patterns to the original pattern language were added to the song as part of this process.

'Everyday World-Making' is written from the perspective of a working parent. However, the song targeted a younger audience who may be thinking about become parents in the future. The music of 'Everyday World-Making' was created by MayuGene (Mayu Ueno), and the lyrics were written by MayuGene (Mayu Ueno) & Takashi Iba. The song was released on iTunes[3], Spotify[4], Google Play Music[5], Amazon Music[6] and other music platforms (Figure 12), and has been performed at various pattern language workshops and talks (see section 4).

Figure 12: Cover image of the pattern song 'Everyday World-Making'

6. Relation between the pattern song and the pattern language

As mentioned previously, 'Everyday World' was written to express the messages contained

3   https://itunes.apple.com/jp/album/id1271022854
4   https://open.spotify.com/album/2RmeBsS7tqKLuLbr9L69QQ
5   https://play.google.com/store/music/album?id=Bdnmej7yu32fy6ovofx3plr4e6q
6   https://www.amazon.com/dp/B074RD3WJP/

in the pattern language, 'Ways of Everyday World-Making'. Figures 13-15 show the lyrics of the song, and how these lyrics are related to the patterns. The left side of the figure shows the lyrics in Japanese (the song's original language). The right side gives a translation of the song and a list of patterns relating to certain parts of the lyrics.

These figures show that the beginning of the song tends to contain more Problem elements (written in blue, designated (P)), while the chorus and later parts consists of lyrics relating to Solutions (written in green, designated (S)), Categories (written in brown, with brackets [ ]), and Names (written in red, designated (N)). This gradual shift from Problem to Solution to Consequences was designed so that listeners can follow the transition from a problematic situation to a better, more buoyant quality of life.

『日々の世界』　　　　Everyday World　　　　No.0 Everyday World (N)

あのこはどんどん変わっていくのに　　Everyone seems to do it so well but me?　　No.2 Palette Mixing (P)
わたしはどうかしら？　はあ　　I can't say the same.
仕事も家事も君とのことも　　Work, home, and you:　　No.1 Natural Balance (P)
大切なのだけど　時間が足んない　　I care about them all but I just don't have the time.　　No.5 Compose the Day (P) / No.9 Focus and Simplify (P)

急ぐ帰り道　赤い信号　　Rushing home but a red light caught me.
いつまで待つのかな　もう　　Seems like I'm always waiting.
ため息飲んで　見上げた空の先　　Suppress a sigh and stare into the sky.　　No.5 Compose the Day (P)
早く行かなくちゃ　　Time to go again.

おかえり　ただいま　　When I get home, you're at the door.　　No.24 Take-off Chance (P)
に涙が溢れた　　Just that brings tears to my eyes.
おつかれ　ありがとう　　"My pleasure" and "Thank you"　　[Thoughtful Gift] (No.28-30)
特別な日じゃなくても　　maybe aren't just for special days.　　No.33 Precious Memories (S)

世界をつくろう　　We can make our world together.　　[Own World-Making](No.0) / No.0 Everyday world (S)
わたしたちなりの　　Let's do some.　　[Original Color](No.1-3)
日々の世界をつくって　　"Everyday World-Making"　　No.1 Natural Balance (S) / No.3 Search for Style (S)
らしくやっていこうよ　wow　　and be ourselves.　　No.0 Everyday World (N) / No.0 Everyday world (S)
悩めるのも　　Times of trouble
わたしたちだからこそのチャンス　　might be our hidden chance.　　No.2 Palette Mixing (S) / No.25 Journey of Parenting (S)
それでも悲しい夜は君に　　Even knowing that, the night can still be blue.　　No.28 Reflection Check (P)
愛を伝えよう　　So I'll give to you my "I love you".　　No.30 Gesture of Love (N)

Figure 13: Patterns and categories embedded in the lyrics of Pattern Song #1

わたしはいつも抱えてしまうけど	I can't help but to hold it in myself.	No.10 Empathetic Friend (P)
みんなどうしてるの? ねぇ	How does everyone else do it?	
打ち明けてみた 弱音が重なった	Shared my weak voice, there was a harmony of empathy.	No.10 Empathetic Friend (S)
まだ 行ける気がした	Made me think I'm still okay.	
やわらかい風吹き	Wind softly brushes me	
感じたよろこび	and gives me hope.	
いまここにいる意味	Why I'm here now.	
そうよ ひとりじゃないから	See, I'm not all alone.	[Helping Hands] (No.10-15)
		[Own World-Making] (No.1-3)
世界をつくろう	We can make our world together.	No.0 Everyday world (S)
わたしたちなりの	Let's do some	[Original Color] (No.1-3)
日々の世界をつくって	"Everyday World-Making"	No.1 Natural Balance (S)
らしくやっていこうよ wow	and be ourselves.	No.3 Search for Style (S)
試してくのも	Trial and error is	No.0 Everyday world (N)
新しいわたしたちのスタンス	our brand new style.	No.0 Everyday world (S)
今夜帰ったら 眠る君に	When I get home tonight,	No.26 Test for Fit (S)
愛をささやこう	I'll whisper love in your sleeping ear.	[Original Color] (No.1-3)
		No.3 Search for Style (S)
		No.30 Gesture of Love (S)

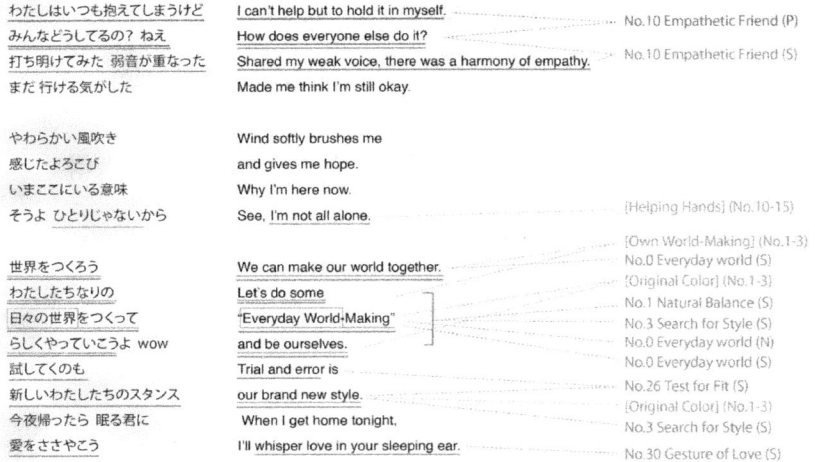

Figure 14: Patterns and categories embedded in the lyrics of Pattern Song #2

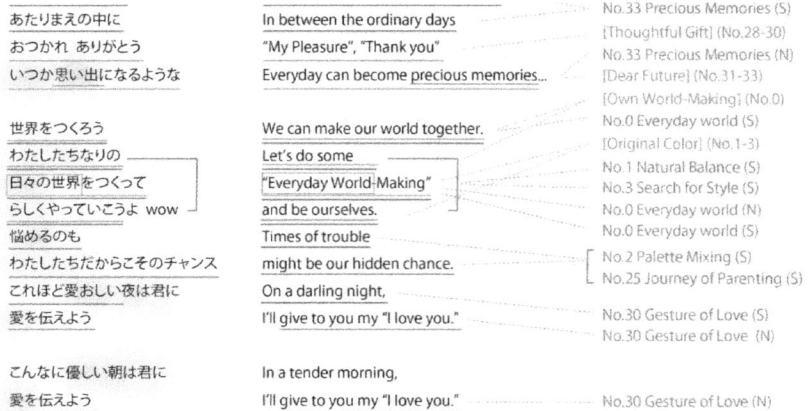

あたりまえの中に	In between the ordinary days	No.33 Precious Memories (S)
おつかれ ありがとう	"My Pleasure", "Thank you"	[Thoughtful Gift] (No.28-30)
いつか思い出になるような	Everyday can become precious memories...	No.33 Precious Memories (N)
		[Dear Future] (No.31-33)
		[Own World-Making] (No.0)
世界をつくろう	We can make our world together.	No.0 Everyday world (S)
わたしたちなりの	Let's do some	[Original Color] (No.1-3)
日々の世界をつくって	"Everyday World-Making"	No.1 Natural Balance (S)
らしくやっていこうよ wow	and be ourselves.	No.3 Search for Style (S)
悩めるのも	Times of trouble	No.0 Everyday world (N)
わたしたちだからこそのチャンス	might be our hidden chance.	No.0 Everyday world (S)
これほど愛おしい夜は君に	On a darling night,	No.2 Palette Mixing (S)
愛を伝えよう	I'll give to you my "I love you."	No.25 Journey of Parenting (S)
		No.30 Gesture of Love (S)
こんなに優しい朝は君に	In a tender morning,	No.30 Gesture of Love (N)
愛を伝えよう	I'll give to you my "I love you."	No.30 Gesture of Love (N)

Figure 15: Patterns and categories embedded in the lyrics of Pattern Song #3

7. Pattern song performances and listener feedback

The demo version of the pattern song 'Everyday World-Making' was shared on YouTube prior to its official release, and as of November 2017 had gained more than 2,000 views. The song has also been performed live at workshops.

The song was performed live at the SFC Open Research Forum 2016 (ORF2016, hosted by Keio Research Institute at SFC) at the end of a sponsored session with Kao Corporation about the pattern language in 'Ways of Everyday World-Making' (Figure 16). The song was performed by its creator, singer-songwriter MayuGene (a co-author of this paper), along with co-lyricist Takashi Iba (another co-author). The song was introduced as the first pattern song and performed before an audience who had just learned about the 'Ways of Everyday World-Making' patterns. Below are the comments of one female participant:

"Today I heard a beautiful song! It is a song called 'Everyday World-Making'. The song was created as the result of a collaborative research with Keio University and Kao Corporation, with the goal of supporting people who want to balance working and parenting in their lives. During the session we received booklets and cards that contained hints about parenting and working (organized using the method of pattern language), and the song was performed as a finale to the session.

Singer-songwriter MayuGene, one of the members of the Iba Lab, performed the song, and the whole audience stood up and clapped along. Professor Iba joined in the second verse as well. Such fun! But while it was fun, I had to keep trying to hold back my tears. I tried hard not to ruin the make-up I wore for the first time in a while (plus, it was a joint research with Kao Corporation)!

'Rushing home but a red light caught me. Seems like I'm always waiting.' I lost it then. Trust me, I'm enjoying my first time parenting, but there are just times when I can't help but cry. There are definitely some days when it's tough, painful. I feel from the bottom of my heart that I'm happy, but at the same time, I'm incredibly alone. Why do I feel this way? ...

This song really struck me in the midst of these thoughts. Everyday world. During days of parenting, it's easy to feel like I've been trapped inside the house and left behind by the rest of the world, but every action I take and every contact I make with my baby build up to make my own everyday world. Raising a child means that I'm raising someone who will eventually go out into the world. Creating your everyday world eventually leads to a bigger world. No, we are not alone. Every little thing in our lives has value. Me, you, everyone is valuable, and everyone is worthy. That's the message I got from this song.

I think many people in the same situation would appreciate this song. I want to sing this song with other parents too. It's a song that brings me hope and comfort. `Let's do some Everyday World-Making and be ourselves'."

This comment indicates that the pattern song is a powerful way to express the message of a pattern language. A convenient media by which to condense the concepts from a pattern language, it also has a 'catchy' quality and the power to speak to people's hearts.

Figure 16: Live performance of the pattern song at the ORF2016 session

The song was also performed at a workshop on 'Ways of Everyday World-Making' patterns at the Shonan Fujisawa Campus, Keio University (Figure 17). This workshop was held for university students who want to balance working and parenting in the future. The song was performed by MayuGene with Yuma Akado from Iba Laboratory, after participants learned about the patterns and wrote letters to their future selves using patterns from 'Ways of Everyday World-Making'. After the event, several participants posted comments on their social media pages, including, "The song was uplifting and makes me want to take on another day with more passion", and "This song is a great song for busy parents".

Figure 17: Live performance of the pattern song at the campus workshop

8. Conclusion

In this paper, we introduced the concept of the pattern song as an auditory medium to express and share patterns. Since their inception, pattern languages have been shared using different forms of visual media, such as books and cards. In an effort to shift to a more natural and creative medium that reflects modern society, we explored new forms of expression and came up with the concept of expressing patterns through 'auditory media'. To exemplify this, we examined the case of the pattern song for the pattern language 'Ways of Everyday World-Making'. We also considered its effectiveness in contributing to the creative shift in our society.

9. Acknowledgements

The 'Ways of Everyday World-Making' patterns were created also by the following project members: Alice Sasabe, Sakurako Kogure, Iroha Ogo, Kaho Takahashi, Rito Tajima from Iba Lab, and also Seiko Miyakawa, Chie Akita, Kimie Itou, Yumiko Imazu, and Nobuko Yoshida from Kao Corporation. We would like to thank the project members and interviewees for sharing their experiences of this project. We also extend our thanks to members of The Bandaids for arranging and playing the song.

10. References

Alexander C, Ishikawa S, Silverstein M, Jacobson M, Fiksdahl-King I, Angel S. (1977) A pattern language: towns, buildings, construction. Oxford University Press, New York.

Beck K, Cunningham W. (1987) Using pattern languages for object-oriented programs. the OOPSLA-87 workshop on the specification and design for object-oriented programming, Orlando, FL.

Iba T. (2014) Pattern language as media for creative dialogue: functional analysis of dialogue workshop. In: Baumgartner P., Sickinger R. (eds) PURPLSOC: the workshop 2014, Krems, pp 212–231.

Iba, T. (2016) "Pattern Language 3.0 and Fundamental Behavioral Properties", Baumgartner, P., Gruber-Muecke, T., and Sickinger, R. (Eds.) Pursuit of Pattern Languages for Societal Change. Designing Lively Scenarios in Various Fields. Berlin: epubli, pp.200-233.

Iba T, Iba Laboratory. (2014) Learning Patterns: A Pattern Language for Creative Learning. CreativeShift, Yokohama.

Iba T, Okada M. (eds) with Iba Laboratory, Dementia Friendly Japan Initiative (2015) Words for a journey: the art of being with dementia. CreativeShift, Yokohama.

Iba, T. Yoshikawa, A., Kaneko, T., Kimura, N., Kubota, T. (2016) "Pattern Objects: Making Patterns Visible in Daily Life" in Designing Networks for Innovation and Improvisation, eds by Matthäus P. Zylka, Hauke Fuehres, Andrea Fronzetti Colladon, Peter A.Gloor, Springer International Publishing, pp.105-1128.

Iba Lab and Lifestyle Research Center. (2016) Hibi no Sekai no Tsukurikata [Ways of Everyday World-Making], in Japanese, SFC Open Research Forum 2016 (ORF2016).

Levitin, D. J. (2008) The World in Six Songs: How the Musical Brain Created Human Nature, Penguin Random House.

Luhmann, N. (1984). Soziale Systeme: Grundriß einer allgemeinen Theorie, Frankfurt: Suhrkamp. (English translation: Social Systems, John Bednarz Jr., Dirk Baecker (translator), Stanford: Stanford University Press, 1995)

Luhmann, N. (1997) Die Gesellschaft der Gesellschaft, Frankfurt: Suhrkamp (English translation: Theory of Society, Volume 1 & 2, Rhodes Barrett (translator), Stanford: Stanford University Press, 2012 & 2013)

Manns M L, Rising L. (2004) Fearless change: patterns for introducing new ideas. Addison-Wesley Professional, Boston.

Ogo, I, Iba, T, Ito, K, Miyakawa, S. (2017) 'Ways of Everyday World-Making: Living well with Working and Parenting,' 2nd World Conference on PURPLSOC (Pursuit of Pattern Languages for Societal Change).

Okazaki, Y., Takaoka, A., Okabe, Y., Sakamoto, M., and Iba, T. (2011) "Learning Patterns Card Game," Artifacts, the 3rd International Conference on Collaborative Innovation Networks 2011.

Ong, W J. (1982) Orality and Literacy: The Technologizing of the World, Routledge.

Pedagogical Patterns Editorial Board (2012) Pedagogical patterns: advice for educators. Joseph Bergin Software Tools, San Bernardino.

Shimomukai E, Nakamura S, Iba T. (2015) Change making patterns: a pattern language for fostering social entrepreneurship. CreativeShift, Yokohama.

11. Appendix

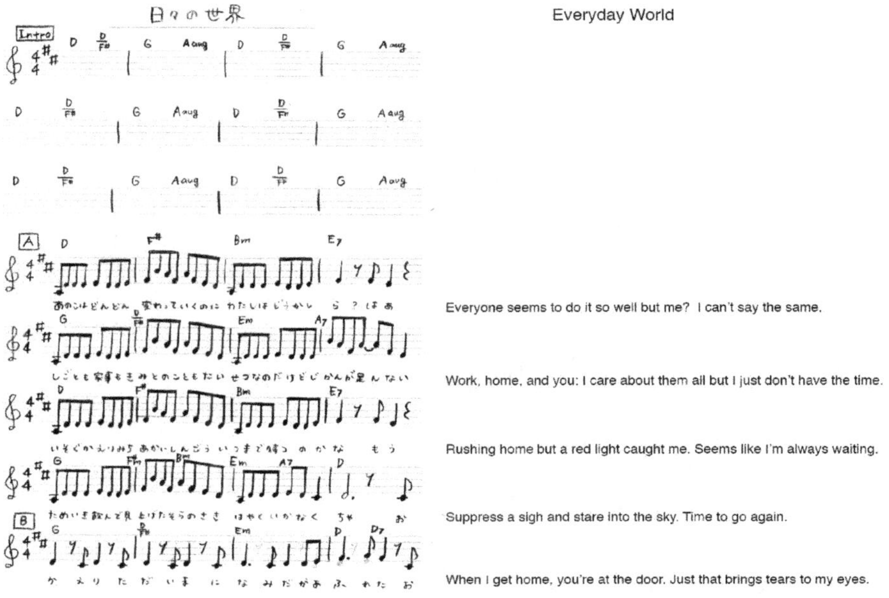

Figure 18: Score and lyrics of 'Everyday World' #1

"My pleasure" and "Thank you." maybe aren't just for special days.

We can make our world together.

Let's do some "Everyday World-Making" and be ourselves.

Times of trouble might be our hidden chance.

Even knowing that, the night can still be blue.

So I'll give to you my "I love you".

I can't help but to hold it in myself.

Figure 19: Score and lyrics of 'Everyday World' #2

How does everyone else do it? Shared my weak voice,

there was a harmony of empathy. Made me think I'm still okay.

Wind softly brushes me and gives me hope. Why I'm here now.

See, I'm not all alone.

We can make our world together. Let's do some

"Everyday World-Making" and be ourselves.

Trial and error is our brand new style.

When I get home tonight,

Figure 20: Score and lyrics of 'Everyday World' #3

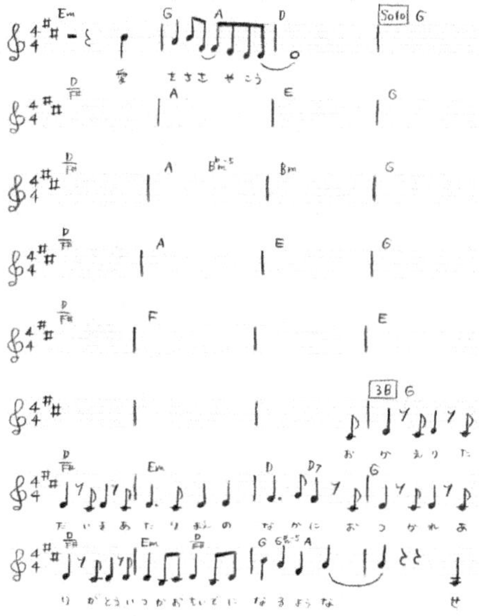

I'll whisper love in your sleeping ear.

When I get home you're at the door.

In between the ordinary days, "My Pleasure", "Thank you."

Everyday can become precious memories...

Figure 21: Score and Lyrics of 'Everyday World' #4

We can make our world together. Let's do some

"Everyday World-Making" and be ourselves.

Times of trouble might be our hidden chance.

On a darling night,

I'll give to you my "I love you."

In a tender morning.

I'll give to you my "I love you."

Figure 22: Score and lyrics of 'Everyday World' #5

Life Transition Patterns: A Pattern Language for Shaping Your Future

Iba, Takashi
Faculty of Policy Management, Keio University, Japan
iba@sfc.keio.ac.jp

Kubo, Tomoko
Department of Educational Planning and Development, Kawaijuku Educational Institution, Japan

This paper presents Life Transition Patterns, a pattern language that supports people in making life decisions about subjects such as school and career, to fabricate their own future. Twenty seven patterns in the pattern language enable high school and university students to think about their life path more thoroughly and put forward the notion that making career choices is a way to design your own style of living. Readers of this pattern language are able to search for the `right' place (school, company, etc.) to actualize their ideal lifestyle through the understanding of the given concepts. This pattern language was created as a result of interviews with a diverse group of university students and working adults, who have been searching for their ideal way of life throughout the course of their careers. The paper presents a summary of all 27 patterns and also provides examples of the usage of the pattern language.

Life Transition, Career Design; Creative Society, 100-year life, Pattern Language

1. Introduction

In Japan, choosing a life path has traditionally been defined as making choices about the school to attend, the major to study and the company where one wants to work. This thought process was shaped by a common value that existed up to the time of Japan's rapid economic growth: that happiness is attained by enrolling into a high ranking university and then being successful in attaining employment in a well-known company. In other words, a person's future is guaranteed to be a successful one as long as one is able to keep achieving these short-term goals.

However, much has changed in current Japanese society and that traditional value system is no longer valid. Existing jobs may become obsolete, and new ones may be created. More, people could even design their own jobs. Therefore, devising a life path is no longer the simple process of attending a prestigious school and working for a large company.

Therefore, we created a pattern language that enables high school and university students to think about the course of their life more thoroughly. This pattern language suggests that to make career choices is to design your own style of living. Readers of this pattern language are able to search for the right place (school, company, etc.) to actualize their ideal style of living through the understanding the concepts given forth.

2. Life Transition in a Creative Society

Social realities have changed drastically with the development of Information Technology. What direction will these changes take in the future? The transformations of our recent past can be classified as epochs pertaining to the three "C"s: Consumption, Communication and Creation (Iba, 2016a) (Figure 1).

More than a half-century ago, began the age mass consumption where one's capability to enjoy an array of products and services expressed the richness of that individual's life and became the symbol of happiness and success. Thus, people began to focus on these signs of status and attain this first "C" which stands for consumption.

In the latter half of the 1990s, the Internet and cell phones became popular, and the age of communication arrived. This technological advancement created our so-called "Information Society." In this era, relationships and communication with other people were the main concerns of people. Building fruitful relationships and engaging in the creation of online and offline communication networks (in the real world) began to represent the fullness of one's life. The second "C," of communication, thus, defined this time.

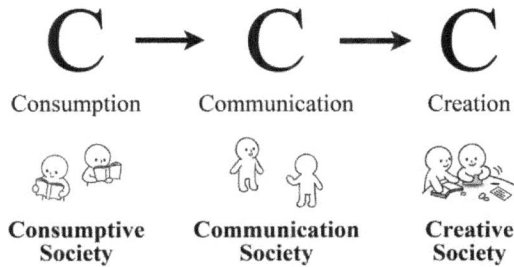

Figure 1: An overview of social change to a Creative Society

We are now entering the era of the third "C" of creation. Richard Florida described the positive trends of the world as stemming from the viewpoint of "creative economy" and "creative cities." Daniel Pink named the era following the "information age" as the "conceptual age" where design and sympathy become important. A "fab society" where everyone can make objects by themselves is held up as a vision in the context of personal fabrication (Commission on the General Planning of Fab Society, 2015). All of these are oriented to the same direction of creativity as the act of ,making' is performed by more and more people. Moving along this trajectory, the next iteration of society may be termed the "creative society."

People of this creative society will be able to design and make their own goods, tools, concepts, knowledge, mechanisms, and ultimately, they will shape their own future with their own hands. The production of goods would no longer be limited to just companies and organizations but would be undertaken by all people according to their own needs and tastes. In the forthcoming creative society, people would begin to put value in the act and process of conception. To be able to create what one desires will become the symbol of the wealth and fulfillment of a life. In this future creative society, devices such as 3D printers and laser cutters, and places like the Future Center and the Living Lab will underpin activities of production of structures, systems, methods, as well as goods.

Every human will become a designer and creator of objects to best suit particular lifestyle visions. Goods that are now bought will all become custom tailored by people for themselves. Hand in hand with the trend towards a creative age, society is transitioning to a time of longevity in lifespans. The development of medical technology has lengthened life expectancy, and it is becoming important to conceive of life-designs of 100 years or more. Lynda Gratton and Andrew Scott, in their book entitled The 100-year life, emphasize the change from a "three-stage life" to a "multi-stage life." To elucidate further, the 20th century conception of the first stage of education, followed by a career, and then by retirement comprised the "three-stage life." This life-design incorporated only two major transitions: "from education to employment," and "from employment to retirement." In the future, as human life is further lengthened, people will experience multiple stages and many life transitions.

> *"There are real opportunities to move away from the constraints of a three-stage life to a way of living that is more flexible, and more responsive - a multi-stage life with a variety of careers, with breaks and transitions." (Gratton & Scott, 2016, p.5)*

Simple judging criteria such as "a good school of a high rank" and "a well-known and stable workplace" will no longer suffice in such a society. People will need to become more aware of their personal strengths, desires, potential and will have to set themselves multiple goals accordingly. Also, in order to advance through various stages, they would also need to continually upgrade, enhance and shape themselves. They may intermittently need some time to concentrate on training and strengthening the skills in the form of investing for themselves, or sometimes practicing something to enhance yourself. Lynda Gratton and Andrew Scott says.

> *"The longer your life, the more your identity reflects what you craft rather than a reactive response to where you began...In a way that past generations simply didn't have to do, each one of us will need to think about who we are and how we construct our life and how this reflects our identity and values."(Gratton & Scott, p.20-21)*

In other words, living with shaping yourselves in various ways will be the basis of life in the emergent age. It would be necessary to think about the selection of career paths that adjust to the characteristics of this age. Therefore, in this research, we created a pattern language for designing careers and lives.

3. Creation Process of the Proposed Pattern Language

Life Transition Patterns was created using the standard process of creating a pattern language. The method contains three different phases (Iba and Isaku, 2016): Pattern Mining, Pattern Writing and Pattern Symbolizing (Figure 2).

Figure 2: Process of Creating a Pattern Language

3.1. Pattern Mining

In the phase of Pattern Mining, we first conducted a "Mining Dialogue" to extract knowledge of practice from some teachers, "Clustering" to find common patterns among the obtained data, and "Seed Making" for organizing them by writing down the ideas in a specific format".

In the mining dialogue, we interviewed students who all had different backgrounds and attended different universities. Every mining session lasted around 4 hours and was conducted with 2 to 4 students. In the end, 437 elements that they thought were important for selecting a school were collected and written down on sticky notes.

In the clustering phase, we classified the collected data in groups based on the KJ method (Iba and Isaku, 2016; Sasabe et al., 2016). 8 people collaborated together to figure out the essence of the contents written on individual sticky notes and arranged their positions according to their meanings (Figure 3). In this way, after 8 hours, groups of paper with similar meanings gradually began to materialize, and 437 fragments of data were classified into 68 groups.

In the seed making stage, every single group generated in the clustering phase was recorded according to a specific format known as the "Seed of Pattern" to summarize the context, problem and solution of each idea. Writing them down in simple form, helped us avoid the duplication of ideas and stop the leakage of important elements. It also made the step of

Structure Building much easier and faster. Structure Building is the process of figuring out the whole picture of good practices of career design from the similarities and relevancies seen among the 27 patterns (Figure 4). It starts with a bottom-up approach, but it is also important to consider the readers' perspectives, such as legibility and the heuristic level of each pattern. In the end, three main categories (A,B,C) were generated.

Figure 3: Clustering in the phase of Pattern Mining

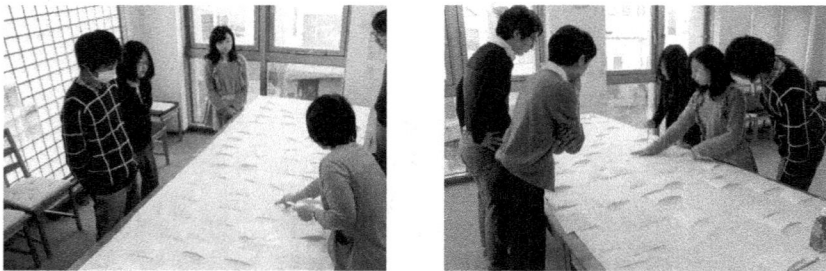

Figure 4: Structure Building in the phase of Pattern Mining

3.2. Pattern Writing

Pattern Writing is the next phase of creating a pattern language. At this stage, we noted down the full description of the Seed of Pattern: its context, problem, force, solution, action and consequence. It was necessary in this phase to consider the position of every single pattern with regard to the whole picture, as well as to review what was discussed in the mining dialogue.

First, to conduct the Pattern Review, we re-evaluated patterns recorded by individual writers using the method of group discussion (Figure 5). All the patterns were assessed from different perspectives to eliminate misunderstanding and to improve the quality of the description. Sometimes it was necessary to reconsider the relationships and positions of patterns and to re-structure them. In fact, this phase of revising and correcting was repeated over and over again, to make our patterns reach the expected level of quality.

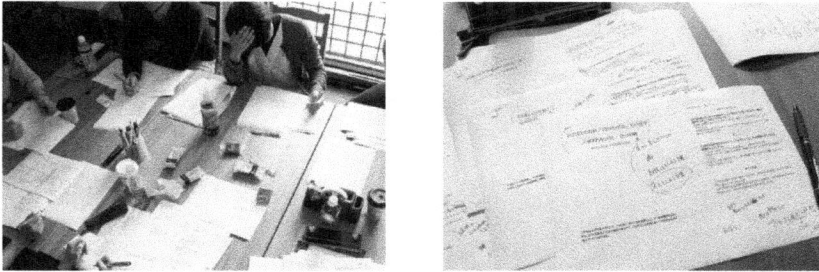

Figure 5: Pattern Review in the phase of Pattern Writing

3.3. Pattern Symbolizing

Pattern Symbolizing is the last phase of creating a pattern language, and it includes Pattern Naming and Pattern Illustration to symbolically express the patterns (Figure 6). This process remains exploratory and some of the pattern content may be improved further in this phase, since the essence of patterns has to be reconsidered to draw symbolic illustrations. The patterns were completed and collated into a designed booklet and onto cards.

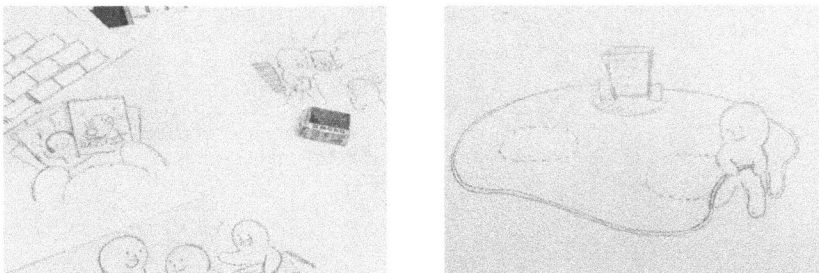

Figure 6: Pattern Illustrating in the phase of Pattern Symbolizing

4. Patterns

Life Transition Patterns comprise 27 designs which are classified into 3 categories: A, finding ways to shine; B, finding places that shine; and C, working toward the desired direction. Figure 7 demonstrates a journey map for Life Transition Patterns. Table 1-3 depicts the summary of the patterns in the category A-C respectively.

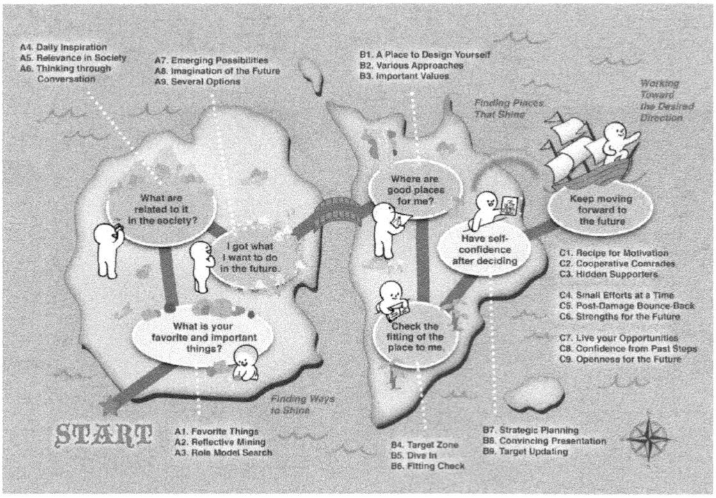

Figure 7: Journey Map for Life Transition Patterns.

A. Finding Ways to Shine			
No.	Pattern Name	Pattern Illustration	Context, Problem and Solution
A1	**Favorite Things**	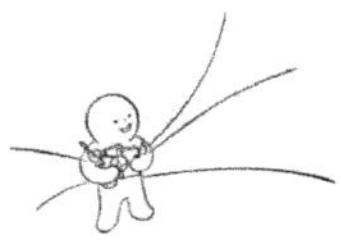	You are starting to think about your future direction. In this context, putting too much value on societal expectations and other people's opinions can hinder you from living your life as you like it. Therefore, start thinking about your future direction based on what you are passionate about and things that are important to you.
A2	**Reflective Mining**		You have activities that you enjoy doing. In this context, although you enjoy those activities, you cannot imagine a realistic future in which you could pursue them as a career. Therefore, discover the general direction of your interests by identifying the essential elements in the activities that you enjoy.
A3	**Role Model Search**		You are thinking about what kind of future direction would be good for you. In this context, if you base your imagination on your past experiences, you will limit your options to things that you already know. Therefore, find people whose lifestyle or work you admire; analyze the aspects of their thought or actions that impress you the most; and incorporate those into your life.

A4	Daily Inspiration		You want to incorporate your interests into your future career. In this context, if you put off thinking about it, you may not be able to find the opportunity to connect your interests to your career path. Therefore, when you encounter something that you find interesting in your daily life, and deepen your understanding of it.
A5	Relevance in Society		You want to incorporate your interests into your future career. In this context, you don't know how your hobbies are relevant to society or how they can be absorbed into a career. Therefore, learn how the activities that you like are used or practiced in society by exploring related news, books, etc.
A6	Thinking through Conversation		You are developing some ideas about your future path. In this context, reflecting on your own, you may not be able to reach the required depth of thought or you may overlook unconscious biases. Therefore, talk about your ideas with people whose interests are similar to yours, or with people who will encourage you.
A7	Emerging Possibilities		You are trying to make a certain decision about your life path. In this context, as you gain depth in your ideas and garner knowledge about various things, it becomes harder to make decisions. Therefore, instead of becoming anxious about making a quick decision, consider the process as a necessary approach and believe that good options will arise as a result.
A8	Imagination of the Future		You are faced with a decision between several options. In this context, you find all of your options attractive and do not know how to proceed with your decision-making. Therefore, for each option, imagine what your everyday life would be like and what kind of future it could bring, and think about which one would bring out your best qualities.
A9	Several Options		You have several visions of the future that are very attractive. In this context, when you narrow your choice to just one and give up the other options completely, you may regret it later. Therefore, consider the fact that you have various options to potentially broaden your future possibilities, and make efforts to stay in touch with all of them in some way.

Table 1: Patterns in Category A: Finding Ways to Shine

B. Finding Places That Shine			
No.	Pattern Name	Pattern Illustration	Context, Problem and Solution
B1	**A Place to Design Yourself**		You want to start listing up concrete options for your future. In this context, if you put too much emphasis on factors such as prestige or rank, you may make decisions without considering what you want to do at that place and how you would like to shape your future. Therefore, look at places that will enable you to work on what you would like and will thus bring you closer to achieving your future aspirations.
B2	**Various Approaches**		You want to look for places where you can pursue your interests. In this context, if you only look at places that are obviously related to your interest, you may overlook other possibilities. Therefore, extensively research what kinds of ways you can take to achieve your desired future, and choose the one that fits you the best.
B3	**Important Values**		You want to look for places where you can get closer to your desired future. In this context, you may either not be able to find the right places at all, or you may find too many of them. Therefore, come up with several options that interest you, compare them by looking into each in detail, and review what qualities/factors are important to you.
B4	**Target Zone**		You are beginning to understand what kinds of qualities you are looking for in a school/company. In this context, if you narrow your choices too much, you risk not getting into any of them and losing the benefit of options. Therefore, search for various places that meet the qualities/factors that are important to you and consider each of them as places that can help you get to your ideal future.
B5	**Dive In**		You are beginning to get an idea of specific schools/companies to which you want to apply. In this context, if you make decisions based on available information and your current understanding of the school/company, what you actually get may be different from what you had in mind. Therefore, get experiential knowledge of what you would actually do at each school/company.
B6	**Checking Suitability**		You are beginning to get firm ideas about specific schools/companies to which you want to apply. In this context, even if a place seems suitable to you in terms of your interests and other conditions, it may not turn out to be a comfortable environment for you. Therefore, visit the school/company and see for yourself whether the environment you will be spending a great deal of time at is actually a fit for you.

B7	Strategic Planning		You have a target school/company, but it seems like an unrealistic choice due to factors such as grades or tuition fees. In this context, you may feel as though your goal would be impossible for you to attain and give up. Therefore, instead of surrendering, think about getting to that goal through a different plan or approach.
B8	Convincing Presentation		You have decided where to apply, but people around you (such as family) do not support your decision. In this context, you thus begin to question whether you should listen to what others say instead of going with what you want, and begin to feel uncertain about your choice. Therefore, explain to your near ones why you want to go to a particular institution and how you are going to make it happen.
B9	Target Updating Target		You are starting to feel uncertain about the direction you had in mind and were originally happy about. In this context, if you stick to your original plan just because you have committed to it, you may be overlooking a newer or better option. Therefore, as you work toward your goals and discover that your way of thinking/perceiving is evolving, update your targets based on what you currently feel is best for you.

Table 2: Patterns in Category B: Finding Places That Shine

C. Working Toward the Desired Direction			
No.	Pattern Name	Pattern Illustration	Context, Problem and Solution
C1	Recipe for Motivation		You are working towards achieving the goal you have set for yourself. In this context, Although you know you must work hard, it is difficult to maintain your motivation consistently over a long span of time. Therefore, consider the inconsistencies in your motivation as an inevitable factor, and find your own methods for enthusing yourself.
C2	Cooperative Comrades		You are working toward achieving the goal you have set. In this context, it is difficult to go beyond your abilities if you are studying/preparing on your own. Therefore, create supportive relationships with people working towards a similar goal, or people who are going through the same situation as you.
C3	Hidden Supporters		You are working toward achieving the goal you have set and are going through a difficult time. In this context, you are coming close to giving up or compromising your goal. Therefore, think about the people who have helped you and all that they have done, and use that support as motivation for you to continue working hard.

C4	Small Efforts		There are things you are not good at and you want to do something about them. In this context, if you blindly try to improve in areas of weakness, your efforts are unlikely to bring actual results. Therefore, continue setting small goals that make you work a bit harder each time.
C5	Post-Damage Bounce-Back		While working toward achieving your goal, something didn't go as you had planned. In this context, it takes you time to absorb and accept the situation and to recover from the setback. These events prevent you from taking the next action. Therefore, keeping in mind that everything you experience is a valuable hint for the next step you must take, reflect on what happened and start working toward your next act.
C6	Strengths for the Future		You are working hard every day toward your desired goal. In this context, if your everyday life is a constant repetition of studying/preparing without any room for you to do the things you enjoy, you will start to feel a sense of purposelessness. Therefore, think about how studying/preparing for your goal is beneficial to your life as a whole in addition to the role it plays in the achievement of your desired goal.
C7	Live your Opportunities		You currently have other things that you are involved in, such as sports teams, student councils, and other extracurricular activities. In this context, you either commit too much to the things you are currently involved in and put off your preparations for the future, or give up on them completely. Therefore, find a balance and work hard on the things that you can only do now, but plan for the future so that you do not regret later.
C8	Confidence from Past Steps		You are working hard to realize your goal. In this context, things do not always work out even if you work hard, and you may be tempted to give up on the way to your goal. Therefore, look back on your efforts and progress you have made thus far and let that give you the confidence to keep going.
C9	Openness for the Future		You have entered the a new stage of your career. In this context, once you actually get there, despite feeling a sense of accomplishment and security for getting in, the future becomes somewhat predictable once you actually get there, causing you to lose your sense of excitement. Therefore, as you gain expertise in your new environment, also discover your personal strengths and your individuality and find potential future directions.

Table 3: Patterns in Category C: Working Toward the Desired Direction

5. Utilizing Patterns

The pattern language proposed in this paper is provided in the form of a booklet and a set of cards(Figure 8). The booklet is designed to be read by a single person, and the card set is primarily intended for use in dialogues. In the context of this paper, we would like to introduce this pattern language may be applied using the set of cards: in counseling, in dialogues for sharing experiences, and in the inquiry of meaning.

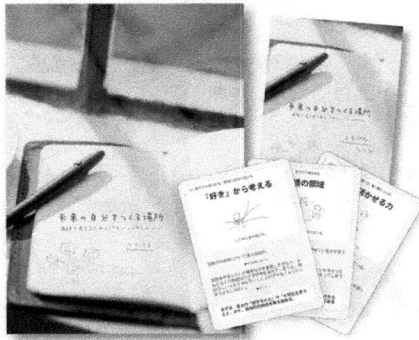

Figure 8: Life Transition Patterns Booklet and Cards

5.1. Counseling with Patterns

The first way to use the set of cards is to apply them in counseling sessions for people who are thinking about their career paths. The use of the cards can encourage them to think for themselves rather than taking advice based from others.

There are several ways to use the card in counseling. First of all, a counselor can talk while looking at the group of cards chosen according to the stage of the thought process. There is also a method called the "Pattern Concierge" (Mori et al., 2016) that introduces the cards that are deemed to be suitable for the problem the person is facing. A person may also pick up a card at random and talk about it.

Here, as in the last method displayed, we introduce the case of a college student from the Iba Laboratory counseled a younger sister who was thinking about her career (Figure 9). First, the cards were shuffled, turned over and placed on a table. They were flipped one by one and the pattern was read in the booklet. The pattern on the card was discussed in detail and the process was repeated with another card. When the number of cards added up to a certain extent, a cluster was created with cards that were related and the discussion completed so far was summarized. Then, the counselor moved on to the next card until all the cards on the table were ultimately set into and converged into appropriate clusters.

The sister who consulted felt, "It was a good experience because I had been reconsidering things about myself occasionally, but I had never reflected this deeply on myself. I think it was right for me to do this." She also said, "I thought most of the cards I drew were applicable to me and I even felt like something is leading the order of the cards I picked but I guess this was because I am suffering." Other remarks from her included the fact that "The contents of the cards were easy to understand because there are examples in the book." The pattern cards can be used as a counseling tool in this way.

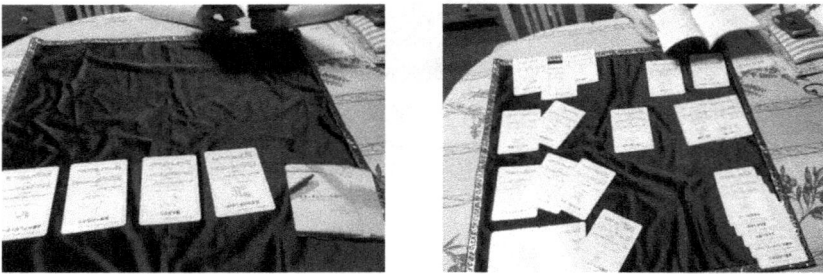

Figure 9: Counseling with the Life Transition Patterns

5.2. Dialogue for Sharing Experience with Patterns

Second, the pattern cards may be applied in dialogue workshops, which have been held with various pattern languages so far. In such modules, people talk about their own experiences based on the patterns (Iba, 2012, 2015, 2016b, 2017). In the paragraphs that follow, we present the method for conducting a dialogue workshop with college students using the Life Transition Patterns cards (Figure 10).

Make a team of 5-6 people seated around a table. Use only the 9 patterns of category (A) at the initial stage. Shuffle the cards, distribute a card to each person, and keep the rest on the table. Participants must read the card allocated to them, recall an experience related to the pattern displayed on the card, and then describe it in detail. Participants should take turns to introduce the content of the pattern on their card and to relate their story.. Participants are free to recount personal events or even occasions that may have occurred to others around them. They may share narratives that may or may not have yielded positive results for them. They may also say that they are getting no ideas from their card or that they have no experience to share with regard to that particular design. Generally speaking, all the participants would have something to share because as college students, each one would have had some experience of conducting some kind of course/career selection or would have done some decision making so as to participate in some groups or clubs at their educational institutions.

This cards get people to talk and the dialogue comes alive. Talking about the experiences they have already had leads to ideas about future career selection. Thus, the stories shared by participants become learning they can utilize in their future. When everyone has finished talking, list all the remaining cards on the tables and discuss them openly. When all the patterns in a particular category have been discussed, the participants are encouraged to simultaneously point at their favorite card saying "Three, two, one!" One segment of the dialogue workshop can now end after a short discussion about why the participants chose a particular card as their favorite. Now the facilitator may move on to the next category and repeat the same process.

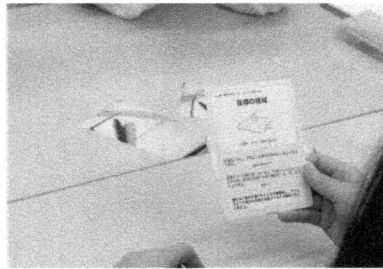

Figure 10: Dialogue Workshop for Sharing Experience

5.3. Inquiry of Meaning with Patterns

The third way of utilizing the pattern cards is through conducting meaning inquiry workshops. In such a session, a person reflects on why what the pattern is saying is important to make a better life. The point of asking why is the characteristic of this meaning inquiry workshop, whereas in the dialogue workshop above discussions were primarily hinged on the experience of how it was done and in what kind of context.

In his book Overcrowded regarding the "innovation of meaning," Roberto Verganti emphasized that "people search for meaning" (Verganti, 2016, p. 32) . He said, "the most distinctive change in our society: the shift from the search for solutions to the search for meaning" (Verganti, 2016, p. 27). Here, the meaning is "the purpose people try to achieve: why they do things" (Verganti, 2016, p.32). Based on this point, Takashi Iba, one of the authors, proposed to use the patterns as tools for exploring deeper meaning within ourselves rather than to merely support the practice of making sense of the world around us.

Here, we introduce the meaning inquiry workshop conducted at an online school (Figure 11). In a course offered by this online school, Takashi Iba introduced this pattern language as a lecturer and more than 250 people participated. The participants' remarks are displayed on the timeline in real time.

The first pattern introduced was "Favorite Things." The question asked to participants was: "Why is practicing `Favorite Things' important to the enhancement of the quality of life and to the creation of happy lives?" Some of the many observations tendered were :

» "Because the excitement continues to accelerate."

» "Because a person can find happiness in doing what one likes, and because it directs people to gain the ability to explore by themselves."

» " `Favorite Things' may correspond to potential abilities. "

» "It feels like I can be myself when I think from the perspective of `Favorite Things.' "

» "Although it depends on people when to feel happy, I believe no one feels unhappy when doing something they like."

» "I think selecting `Favorite Things' is linked with one's essential energy, which leads one to more humane activities."

Next, the following comments about "Relevance in Society" were shared. Participants said:

» "I think it is important to increase one's number of friends and to broaden the idea of what one likes."

» "You may feel like you are supported by meeting social requirements or considering the needs of other people."

» "When you have a connection to society, you can feel that you belong to it. This attachment is very important."

» "Because it makes you feel the significance of being more social."

» "Because I'm not living alone, it is important to think about society and about how I can help my society."

» "Through social connections, what I consider a desired outcome will lead to someone else's happiness and that would make me happy in turn, leading to a virtuous circle."

Remarks posted with regard to the meaning of the pattern "Hidden Supporters" were:

» "In order to advance without forgetting appreciation."

» "Because it will become a driving force to go a step further when you are discouraged."

» "When I think of someone who has supported or cheered me up to this moment, it makes me feel like I cannot give up so easily."

» "To always be modest."

» "Because people cannot survive alone."

» "I can feel that I'm happy to be alive."

Following such a meaning inquiry workshop, participants said: "Thinking about the meaning leads to the essence, bringing in a three dimensional perspective in the dialogue;" "There is a possibility that `the origin of one's life' can be found, and the field of vision could be accelerated to spread to people suffering from hesitation;" and "By seeking the meaning, more essential questions may be visualized."

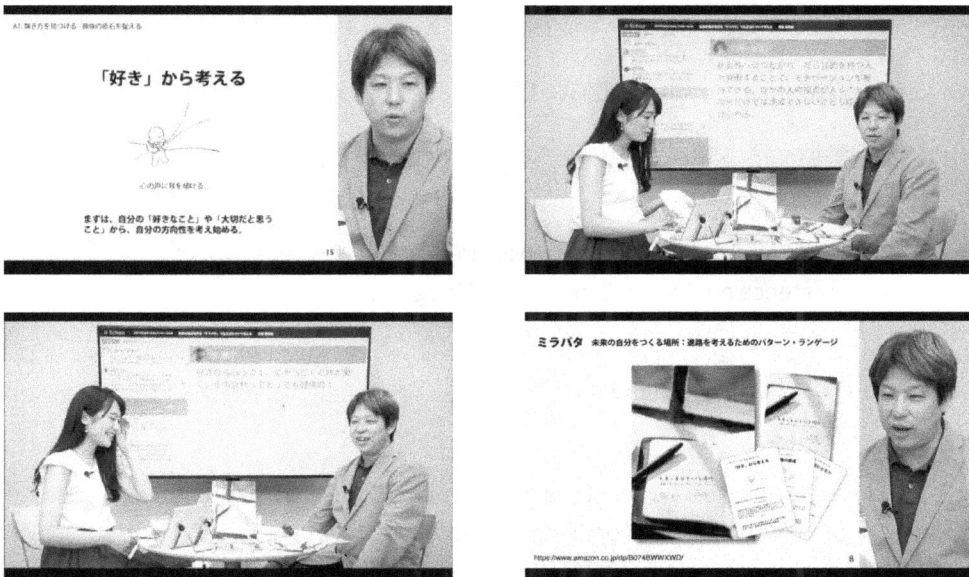

Figure 11: Meaning Inquiry Workshop in an Online School

6. Conclusion

The paper presented the content of the twenty-seven designs that comprise Life Transition Patterns, and also provided examples of some applications of the pattern language. We anticipate that there are many other ways of using this pattern language, and we would be happy to receive knowledge of other ways this pattern language could be put into practice.

7. Acknowledgement

We would like to thank our project members from CreativeShift Inc. and Kawaijuku Educational Institution. We would also like to express our appreciation to our interviewees. Our gratitude is also extended to Ayaka Yoshikawa for translating the patterns into English and to Haruka Mori for supporting us in the writing of this paper.

8. References

Bergin, J., Kohls, C., Köppe, C., Mor, Y., Portier, M., Schümmer, T., & Warburton, S. (2015). Assessment-driven course design foundational patterns. In Proceedings of the 20th European Conference on Pattern Languages of Programs (EuroPLoP ,15). ACM, New York, NY, USA, , Article 31 , 13 pages.

Commission on the General Planning of Fab Society (2015). Fab Society Declaration, http://www.soumu.go.jp/main_content/000361197.pdf [Accessed in Dec 2017]

Gratton, L. & Scott, A. (2016) The 100-year life: Living and Working in an Age of Longevity, Bloomsbury.

Iba, T. (2012) "A Pattern Language for Designing Pattern Dialogue Workshops," the 17th European Conference on Pattern Languages of Programs.

Iba, T. (2015) "Pattern Languages as Media for Creative Dialogue: Functional Analysis of Dialogue Workshops," Peter Baumgartner, Richard Sickinger (eds), PURPLSOC: The Workshop 2014, pp.212-231.

Iba, T. (2016a) "Sociological Perspective of the Creative Society" in Matth us P. Zylka, Hauke Fuehres, Andrea Fronzetti Colladon, Peter A. Gloor (eds.), Designing Networks for Innovation and Improvisation, Springer International Publishing, pp.29-42.

Iba, T. (2016b) "Pattern Language 3.0 and Fundamental Behavioral Properties" in World Conference on Pursuit of Pattern Languages for Societal Change, 2015, published in a book: Peter Baumgartner, Tina Gruber-Muecke, Richard Sickinger (Eds.), Pursuit of Pattern Languages for Societal Change. Designing Lively Scenarios in Various Fields. Berlin: epubli, pp.200-233.

Iba, T. (2017) "Peer Learning via Dialogue with a Pattern Language," in the 7th International Conference on Collaborative Innovation Networks.

Iba, T. and Iba Laboratory (2014a) Learning Patterns: A Pattern Language for Creative Learning, CreativeShift.

Iba, T. and Iba Laboratory (2014b) Presentation Patterns: A Pattern Language for Creative Presentations, CreativeShift.

Iba, T. and Iba Laboratory (2014c) Collaboration Patterns: A Pattern Language for Creative Collaborations, CreativeShift.

Iba, T. and Isaku, T. (2016) 'A pattern language for creating pattern languages: 364 patterns for pattern mining, writing, and symbolizing', In Proceedings of the 2016 Conference on Pattern Languages of Programs.

Kawakita, J. (1967) HassouHou [The Abduction Method: For Creativity Development], in

Japanese, Chuo-Koron.

Mori, H., Kimura, N., Ando, S., & Iba, T. (2016) "Pattern Concierge: Using Push and Pull Patterns to Help Clients Design Their Future," 23rd Conference on Pattern Languages of Programs.

Sasabe, A., Kaneko, T., Takahashi, K., an Iba, T. (2016) "Pattern Mining Patterns: A Search for the Seeds of Patterns," 23rd Conference on Pattern Languages of Programs.

Verganti, R. (2016) Overcrowded: Designing Meaningful Products in a World Awash with Ideas, The MIT Press.

Cook-That-Dish Patterns for Tacos: A Tool for Collaborative Cooking

Yoshikawa, Ayaka

Faculty of Environment and Information Studies, Keio University, 5322 Endo, Fujisawa, Kanagawa, Japan

t14595ay@sfc.keio.ac.jp

Shimizu, Hitomi

Faculty of Policy Management, Keio University, 5322 Endo, Fujisawa, Kanagawa, Japan

s15417hs@sfc.keio.ac.jp

Iba, Takashi

Faculty of Policy Management, Keio University, 5322 Endo, Fujisawa, Kanagawa, Japan

iba@sfc.keio.ac.jp

This paper proposes Cook-That-Dish Patterns for Tacos, a recipe-like collection of patterns that function as a participation-inducing tool in collaborative cooking sessions, as well as its application. The Cook-That-Dish Patterns for Tacos (Taco Patterns, for short) presented in this paper, is a collection of twenty-seven patterns, divided into five categories: Pico de Gallo, Guacamole, Meat, Condiments, and Tortilla. Each pattern describes a step in the process of making tacos, in a concise "context-problem-solution-consequence" format. The Taco Pattern cards have been used in cooking parties, in which participants with various cooking experiences broke off into teams and worked simultaneously on preparing their assigned part, which come together as one meal. Through this implementation, we found that the patterns are (1) an effective tool to involve all participants with varying experience levels, (2) a practical format to convey the implications behind cooking processes, and (3) a valid tool to enable cooking to be done in a flexibly distributed manner.

Pattern language; cooking; collaboration; recipes; workshops

1. Introduction

Cooking, the art of preparing food for consumption is an activity that has been an essential and familiar part of people's everyday lives. It is a practical method in which humans have learned to survive with over the course of history, turning resources into forms that we can consume. Moreover, cooking can be a highly creative activity that can give both the person engaged in the cooking as well as those who consume the product, a sense of pleasure, satisfaction, and a higher quality of life.

In modern times, it has become easier than ever for one to engage in the activity of cooking. Ingredients can be acquired without having to grow them or hunt for them, and there are an abundant amount of information that teaches us how to cook, such as recipes, web articles, books, etc. Thanks to many that came before us, methods, tools, and knowledge on cooking have been developed and fine-tuned.

However, despite the fact that cooking has become more accessible than ever, it has become less essential to people's lives. Because of the widespread availability of restaurants, take-out options, and ready-made foods, many people simply have fewer opportunities to cook. Therefore, they have less familiarity with the activity, and can consequently feel intimidated or reluctant about cooking. It is to remove this fear, and invite more people to enjoy cooking, that we conducted this research.

2. Background

Over the past few years, there have been several research efforts dealing the topic of cooking, and using the pattern language method to open up the activity to more people. For instance, there have been several researches, which use the pattern language method to share the general knowledge of the cooking process, such as the Generative Cooking Approach (Isaku & Iba, 2014) and the Cooking Patterns (Akado, et al, 2016). The Cooking Language method has also been created as a method to allow people to gain a better understanding of individual ingredients and their functions in a pattern-like format (Isaku, et al, 2015). On the more social side, there are the Co-Cooking Patterns, which contain pattern about how to enhance better communication in collaborative cooking sessions (Isaku & Iba, 2015). Lastly, there are also patterns on how to incorporate the activity of cooking into everyday life, called the Cooking Life Patterns (Yoshikawa, et al, 2016).

With these previous works in mind, the purpose of this research is to create a tool which functions as an on-the-spot support that directly affects people's actions in the kitchen.

While the other works were effective for more long-term growth in its readers/users, we wanted to create a new type of patterns that can engage people in the activity of cooking and induce prompt learning/growth in their cooking, especially for those who are beginners. Therefore, we came up the Cook-That-Dish Patterns, a type of patterns that describes the process of cooking a certain dish. As mentioned earlier, there are prior works that deal with the general practical knowledge of cooking using the pattern language method (Isaku, et al., 2015; Akado, et al., 2016); however, the Cook-That-Dish Patterns is the first attempt to focus on a specific dish and provide all description of its recipe using the pattern format.

3. Cook-That-Dish Patterns

Here we present the concept of Cook-That-Dish Patterns, a new type of patterns that describe the steps on how to cook a certain dish. This new genre of patterns was created as a tool to replace the role of recipes with a more comprehensive and informative guide, to allow even beginners to cook well. Cook-That-Dish Patterns are similar to recipes in that they provide step-by-step instructions on how to make a dish, but differ in that the patterns provide an insight on the meaning behind each cooking process, a factor that is commonly lacking in recipes. Each pattern explains a certain step in the cooking process in the following format: context (the timing in which one should perform the pattern), problem (what would happen if the pattern is not performed), solution (what to do to prevent the problem from happening), and a "pattern name" that captures the essence of the pattern.

Using the pattern format to describe cooking processes allow readers to understand the significance of performing a certain step. That is, the reader is able to see that an action (the solution) must be done to prevent an undesirable outcome (the problem). Not only does this make the information clearer, but also by understanding why a certain action must be taken, the reader is able to take in the information and use it to make decisions on his/her own discretion.

Cook-That-Dish Patterns can be created for just about any recipe in any genre of cuisine. Examples of Cook-That-Dish Patterns that we have created thus far are as follows: Taco Patterns, Miso Soup Patterns, and the Carbonara Patterns (Figure 1). For any recipe, one cooking step can be translated to one or two patterns. Therefore, a recipe with ten cooking steps may contain around ten to fifteen patterns, depending on the difficulty and sophistication of the dish.

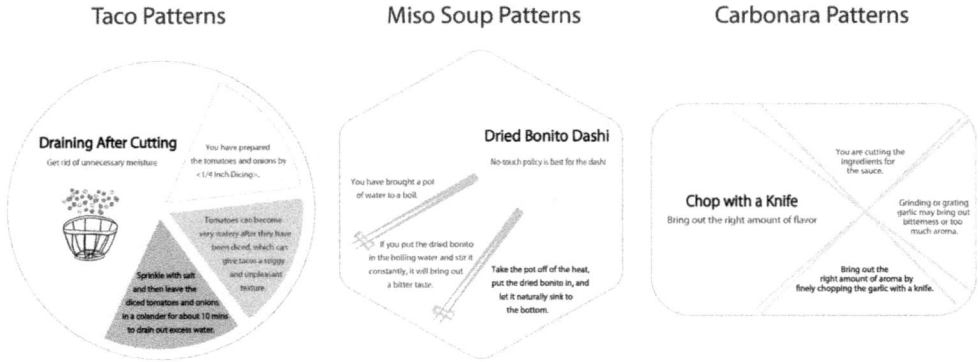

Figure 1: Examples of Cook-That-Dish Patterns (in card form)

3.1. Cook-That-Dish Patterns for Tacos (Taco Patterns)

The first example of Cook-That-Dish Patterns is the work we present in this paper; the Cook-That-Dish-Patterns for Tacos (hereinafter referred to as, Taco Patterns). The Taco Patterns is a collection of twenty-seven patterns that together describe the process of making tacos. For this particular collection of Cook-That-Dish Patterns, we intended for the patterns to be used in group cooking sessions, as tacos are a type of dish in which the cooking process can be broken down into several parts and cooked simultaneously by people in different teams. Furthermore, they can be served in a buffet style, allowing for people to assemble their tacos with whatever combination of toppings that suits their taste. As the patterns are designed to be used in collaborative cooking sessions in which people cook together, they are presented in the form of pattern cards that can be distributed among the participants and brought into the kitchen to refer to during the cooking process.

3.2. The Process of Creating the Taco Patterns

The collection of twenty-seven Taco Patterns was created through processes of data collection, pattern writing (Iba & Isaku, 2016) and pattern symbolizing (Shibata, et al, 2016).

In the beginning stage, we collected data on how to make tacos through examining various taco recipes, and extracted tips/methods that seemed to play a significant role in the cooking process of tacos. During this phase, we tested out the various cooking methods in the kitchen to see which tips/methods were useful and yielded good results. Through this process, we decided to narrow our patterns' focus on tacos comprised of five main components: a tortilla, minced meat (beef & pork), pico de gallo, guacamole, as well as other toppings (Figure 2). This type of taco is one that is a common variety, and is fairly simple to put together. We then created a recipe-like list of steps to take, in making each component of the taco.

Figure 2: Five components of a taco: tortilla, meat, pico de gallo, guacamole, and other toppings

Using the list as a general guide, we then wrote down each step in the pattern format (context, problem, and solution). We wrote each cooking step in the pattern format to show what should be done (the solution) at which timing (the context) to avoid an undesirable result (the problem). For instance, one of the steps in creating a good "pico de gallo" is to leave the tomatoes in a colander (strainer) after dicing them. In the pattern format, this step was documented as follows.

Context: You have prepared the tomatoes and onions by performing

<1/4-Inch Dicing>.

▼In this context

Problem: Tomatoes can become very watery after they have been diced, which can give tacos a soggy and unpleasant texture.

▼Therefore

Solution: After sprinkling with salt, leave the diced tomatoes and onions in a colander for about 10 mins to cut excess juice.

After all of the cooking steps were written in this manner, we then went through a symbolizing phase. During this phase, we assigned a "pattern name" and illustration to each pattern, and also designed the cards in which the patterns would be printed on. We also added an ingredient list card to each of the five categories, which show the ingredients/tools/number of people necessary, as well has the difficulty of the task represented by the number of stars. An example of a pattern card, "Draining After Cutting", and the category card for pico de gallo is shown in Figure 3.

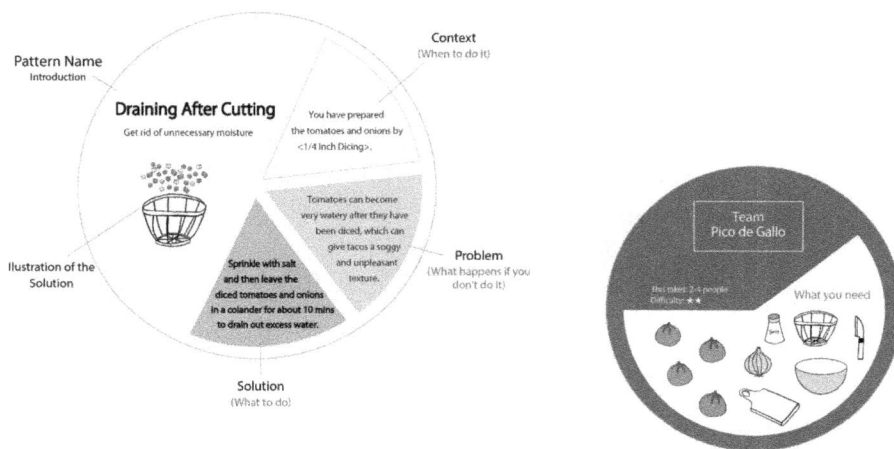

Figure 3: Example of a Taco Pattern Card (left) and Category Card (right)

A collection of twenty-seven Taco Patterns resulted from a three-month process of writing, revising, adding illustrations, and designing the cards. In order for the cards to be used in the kitchen by multiple people, the cards were laminated after printing. The entire Taco Patterns collection is shown in Figure 4.

Taco Patterns

Figure 4: The Taco Pattern cards collection

3.3. The Overview of the Taco Pattern Cards

The Taco Patterns are comprised of twenty-seven patterns in five categories: four patterns in Guacamole, four in Meat, four in Pico de gallo, five in Other Toppings, and ten in Tortilla. In Table 1 below, the pattern name, illustration, and contents of the patterns (context, problem, solution) are shown in the order in which they should be executed for each category.

	Pattern Name	Pattern Illustration	Context, Problem and Solution
Guacamole	Chunky but Consistent		You are preparing the guacamole. In this context, leaving large pieces of avocado in the guacamole may create an unpleasant texture. Therefore, halve and scoop out the avocado with a spoon, and use a fork to mash it into a relatively uniform consistency.
	A Sprinkle of Color		You have mashed the avocados until it is <Chunky but Consistent>. In this context, a guacamole with only avocados can be bland both in its taste and appearance. Therefore, add in some pico de gallo to make the texture and flavor more interesting.
	Tangy Finish		You have mashed the avocados and added <A Sprinkle of Color>. In this context, avocados have a mild flavor, which may be overpowered by the flavor of other ingredients. Therefore, sharpen and define the taste of avocados by mixing in salt and lemon, tasting and adjusting as you go.
	Double Wrap		You have finished making your guacamole. In this context, if the avocados are exposed to oxygen, it will start to brown and will not look as good as it was when you just made it. Therefore, press a double layer of plastic wrap onto the surface of the guacamole to protect it from oxygen and retain its color.

Meat	**Gentle Stir**		You are cooking the ground meat in a large pan. In this context, if you try to break up the meat and stir too much, the flavor of the meat will be damaged. Therefore, gently move around the meat with your spatula and evenly cook the meat.
	Oil Cut		You are cooking the meat by <Gentle Stirs>. In this context, as the meat cooks, the pan gets filled with excess oil from the meat. Therefore, as the meat starts to color and the pan gets oily, use a paper towel to absorb and remove excess oil.
	Water the Pan		You are cooking the meat by doing <Gentle Stirs>, and the meat is starting to color. In this context, if you continue to cook the meat without adding any moisture, the meat will become dry and hard. Therefore, after doing <Oil Cut>, add water to the meat and continue cooking it as it simmers.
	Enough Punch		The meat is starting to brown and you are ready to season the meat. In this context, if the meat is lightly seasoned, it may not have enough flavor when it's eaten together with other ingredients. Therefore, do a taste test with several people and season the meat so that it has enough punch.

Pico de Gallo			
	Specks of Onion		You are going to make some pico de gallo. In this context, if you put too much onion, the strong flavor of onions will kill the flavor of tomatoes. Therefore, as a rule of thumb, use 1 small onion for every 4 tomatoes, and then adjust the ratio as you taste.
	Mul-ti-axis Cutting		You are doing <1/4 Inch Dicing>. In this context, dicing tomatoes and onions little at a time can be time consuming and tiresome. Therefore, leaving the stem intact, cut in half, lay halves on its flat sides, make horizontal and vertical cuts almost all the way through, and then dice in its place.
	¼ Inch Dicing		You are cutting tomatoes and onions for the pico de gallo. In this context, unevenly sized pieces of tomatoes and onions will create an inconsistent texture in your mouth. Therefore, cut tomatoes and onions into relatively uniform 1/4 inch dices.
	Draining After Cutting		You have prepared the tomatoes and onions by <1/4 Inch Dicing>. In this context, tomatoes can become very watery after they have been diced, which can give tacos a soggy and unpleasant texture. Therefore, sprinkle with salt and then leave the diced tomatoes and onions in a colander for about 10 mins to drain out excess

Toppings	**Large Water Bath**		You are washing a delicate ingredient, in this case, lettuce. In this context, if you wash the lettuce directly under running water, it is hard to thoroughly clean it, and you also risk damaging the leaves. Therefore, fill a large bowl with water and wash the lettuce gently in the water bath.
	Dry Before Cutting		You have washed the lettuce leaves in a <Large Water Bath> and are going to cut them. In this context, if you cut and serve wet lettuce leaves, the taco will taste watery and soggy. Therefore, gently pat the lettuce leaves with paper towels to remove the beads of water.
	Several At Once		You have done <Dry Before Cutting> and are now ready to cut the lettuce. In this context, if you cut the lettuce leaves one piece at a time, it is inefficient and also makes it harder to cut evenly. Therefore, stack up a few lettuce leaves, gently roll them together, and cut into even, <1/4 Inch Strips>.
	¼ Inch Strips		You are ready to cut the lettuce <Several at Once>. In this context, if the lettuce is cut too large, it will be difficult to fit it into the taco shell with other ingredients. Therefore, cut the lettuce leaves into strips that are about 1/4 inch wide.
	Half & Half		You are going to make a sour cream sauce. In this context, sour cream on its own is not soft enough to evenly distribute onto the taco. Therefore, add the same amount of yogurt into the sour cream and mix together until it has no lumps.

Flours First		You are measuring the ingredients for the tortilla. In this context, if the ingredients are put into the bowl in a random order, it may not mix evenly. Therefore, start by mixing all of the dry ingredients first, before adding in the wet ingredients.
Mix with Chop-sticks		You have placed ingredients into the bowl starting with "Flours First". In this context, if you mix the mixture while the water is still hot, you may burn your hands. Therefore, mix evenly in a large motion with chopsticks until the dough is cool enough to touch.
Knead Until Smooth		The dough is starting to come together as you "Mix with Chopsticks". In this context, the dough will not become smooth if you keep mixing it with chopsticks. Therefore, use your hands to knead the dough until there is no loose flour remaining.
Rest the Dough		You have executed "Knead Until Smooth". In this context, if you cut and roll out the dough right away, the tortillas will not come out evenly. Therefore, cover the dough in plastic wrap and let it rest for about 10 minutes.
Roll and Rest		The time to "Rest the Dough" is over. In this context, if you cut and roll out the dough simultaneously, the tortillas will be deformed. Therefore, cut the dough and roll into balls with your hands and let rest for another few minutes.

Flour Tortillas

Flour Tortillas	**Keep Hydrated**		There are times in the cooking process where the tortillas are on "stand-by". In this context, if you leave the dough uncovered, it will slowly dry out and become brittle. Therefore, when you are not working with the dough, cover it with plastic wrap to lock in the moisture.
	Flour Barrier		You have done "Roll and Rest" and are ready to roll out the dough into tortillas. In this context, if you directly roll out the dough, it will stick to the rolling pin and the surface it's on. Therefore, lightly flour your surface and rolling pin to create a barrier between the dough.
	Constant Movement		You are rolling out the tortillas with enough "Flour Barrier". In this context, if you roll out the dough in only one direction, the tortillas will not be round. Therefore, constantly move the dough around, turning sideways and flipping, to roll it into an even circle.
	A Teaspoon of Oil		You have rolled out the tortillas, and are ready to cook them. In this context, if the oil is not evenly spread onto the pan or there is too much of it, the tortillas will get burned spots. Therefore, pour a teaspoon of oil into the pan and whirl the pan to spread evenly.
	45 Seconds per Side		You are cooking the tortillas with a "Teaspoon of Oil". In this context, if the temperature of the pan is too high or too low, the tortillas may get a bad texture. Therefore, adjust the temperature to where the tortillas look slightly puffy and golden at 45 sec. per side.

Table 1: Overview of the contents of the Taco Patterns

4. Using the Taco Patterns: Collaborative Cooking Sessions

We have used the Taco Patterns in cooking parties, in which university students (and occasionally teachers) get together and cook together in groups. The participants of the sessions have varying cooking experiences; there were some who cook for themselves every day, and some who have rarely used a knife in their entire lifetime. The aim of these cooking sessions was to see whether and how the pattern cards would allow such people with various cooking experience levels to successfully cook a meal *together*, without having the people who are more experienced take over the process and the others observing as bystanders. Up to present, we have conducted five workshops from with around fifteen to thirty-five people in each session, engaging more than a hundred participants in total. For this research, participants were students from Keio University SFC campus.

4.1. Cooking with the Pattern Cards

In our cooking sessions, we convened people in large kitchen spaces and asked them to cook tacos together, using the pattern cards. Each session began by showing participants the five categories from the Taco Patterns as well as their levels of difficulty/estimated number of people necessary and guiding them to self-organize the teams in which they would work in. After dividing into groups, we took some time for self-introductions and ice breaking.

Once the group members are comfortable with each other, we distributed each of the five teams with the corresponding pattern cards as well as the ingredients/tools necessary to complete the task. After each team has what they need, they take time to go over the pattern card with each other one by one and decide the order in which they will carry out the patterns.

Some teams assigned a member to each pattern, and each would be responsible for making sure that the pattern is carried out during the cooking process.

After the teams have established a common understanding of the process, each team cooks their part of the taco according to the patterns (Figure 6). During the cooking process, they could refer back to the patterns if necessary. In the end, the finished parts are served in individual dishes, and a buffet-style taco dinner is ready for everyone to enjoy.

Figure 6: Cooking session using Taco Patterns
(Photos taken April 21st, 2016 at a facility near Keio SFC)

4.2. Conversation Examples and Feedback from Participants

As explained above, the Taco Patterns were used as a guide for each team through the cooking process, and particularly played a role in functioning as common vocabulary for the participants. The following contain some examples of the conversations that took place during the sessions.

1. Conversation sample from Team Tortilla, regarding the patterns, "Teaspoon of Oil" and "45 Seconds Per Side":

» Participant A – "Okay, I think we should start cooking the tortillas. We need about a 'Teaspoon of Oil' for each tortilla, right?"

» Participant B – "Right, and make sure to cook them '45 Seconds Per Side'... I think the heat should be lowered since it's cooking a lot faster right now."

2. Conversation sample from Team Pico de Gallo during the buffet dinner, regarding the "Draining After Cutting" pattern.

» Participant C – "I now see why 'Draining After Cutting' was so important. Look at all the juice that came out! I guess we should have left them in the colander for longer."

3. Conversation sample from Team Meat, regarding the "Enough Punch" pattern.

» Participant D – "Hey, can you have a taste and see if it's okay? I feel like I may have made it too spicy."

» Participant E – "I think it's good! The 'Enough Punch' pattern said it should be slightly over seasoned, anyway."

(All conversation samples taken from session on May 24th, 2016)

In addition to the patterns function as a common vocabulary, we received feedback about its ability to cover information which are often missing in standard recipes, such as that "by taking the time to go over each pattern, [the participant] was able to learn about why each step had to be taken. [The participant felt] like the 'problem' section was the most insightful part." Furthermore, there were comments that the patterns encouraged collaboration among the teams, such as that "even though [the participant] had very little experience with cooking, [the participant] was able to partake in the cooking process because the patterns allowed everyone to be 'on the same page'". After the cooking sessions, there were three cases in which participants convened their own cooking sessions using the Taco Patterns, with a new group of participants.

4.3. The Function of the Patterns

Through the implementations, we found that the patterns are an (1) an effective tool to involve all participants with varying experiences, (2) a practical format to convey the meaning behind cooking processes, and (3) a valid tool to enable cooking to be done in a flexibly distributed manner. Firstly, it enables cooking to be an activity in which all participants are involved regardless of experience by having a common vocabulary to communicate about the cooking process. Secondly, by conveying the meaning behind cooking processes in a practical, concise manner, even beginners can grasp the good practices in cooking. After grasping the basic cooking steps, they can be adjusted and applied to create each persons' own variations. Lastly, its presentation as categorized pattern cards enables cooking to be done in a flexibly distributed manner, allowing for a relatively large number of people to cook simultaneously. Using this method, we anticipate that there can be future applications in which such collaborative cooking workshops can be held for various recipes and for various groups.

5. Conclusion

This paper presented Cook-That-Dish Patterns, a new type of patterns for cooking, and focused on the Taco Patterns as an example. The new type of cooking patterns, which was explored through this research, serves as an alternative method of documenting/sharing the knowledge behind cooking a certain dish, and is effective in communicating the intentions behind each cooking process. Furthermore, using the pattern card format in the cooking process allow for cooking to be done by groups of people simultaneously, suggesting new possibilities for large-group cooking sessions. We anticipate further research on opening up the knowledge behind cooking processes to involve more people to participate in the activity of cooking.

6. Acknowledgements

We would like to thank the participants of our cooking sessions for their contribution to this research, as well as those who provided valuable feedback about the patterns and the paper.

7. References

Akado, Y., Shibata, S., Yoshikawa, A., Sano, A., and Iba, T. (2016) "Cooking Patterns: A Pattern Language for Everyday Cooking," 5th Asian Conference on Pattern Languages of Programs (AsianPLoP2016), Taiwan, Mar., 2016

Alexander, C., Ishikawa, S., and Silverstein, M., Jacobson, M., Fiksdahi-King, I. and Angel, S. (1977) A Pattern Language: Towns, Buildings, Construction, Oxford University Press.

Iba, T., & Isaku, T. (2016). A pattern language for creating pattern languages: 364 patterns for pattern mining, writing, and symbolizing. In Proceedings of the 2016 Conference on Pattern Languages of Programs.

Isaku, T., Kubonaga, E., Iba, T. (2015). "The Cooking Language: Applying the Theory of Patterns into Cooking" pp.234-248

Isaku, T., Iba, T.Creative CoCooking Patterns: A Pattern Language for Creative Collaborative Cooking, 20th European Conference on Pattern Languages of Programs, 2015.

Isaku, T., Iba, T. (2014). Towards a Pattern Language for Cooking: A Generative Approach to Cooking, 19th European Conference on Pattern Languages of Programs, 2014.

Shibata, S., Kogure, S., Shimizu, H., & Iba, T. (2016) "Pattern Symbolizing Patterns - Showing the content and value by expressions to encourage intuitive comprehension," 23rd Conference on Pattern Languages of Programs (PLoP2016), USA, Oct., 2016

Yoshikawa, A., Akado, Y., Shibata, S., & Iba, T. (2016) "Cooking Life Patterns: A Pattern Language for Enjoying: Cooking in Everyday Life," 21st European Conference on Pattern Languages of Programs (EuroPLoP2016), Germany, Jul., 2016

Welfare Pattern Languages by a Local Government

Takiguchi, Kazuo
Economic and Labor Affairs Bureau, City of Kawasaki, Kawasaki Frontier Building 10th Floor. 11-2 Ekimae-Honcho, Kawasaki-ku, Kawasaki 210-0007, Japan
takiguchi-k@city.kawasaki.jp

Kitamura, Naohiro
Association of Hataraku Shiawase JINEN-DO, 5-10-11 Kami-Asao, Asao-ku, Kawasaki 215-0021, Japan
info@hatarakushiawase.net

Okada, Makoto
Fujitsu Laboratories Ltd, 4-1-1 Kamikodanaka, Nakahara-ku, Kawasaki 211-8588, Japan / Dementia Friendly Japan Initiative
okadamkt@jp.fujitsu.com

Iba, Takashi
Faculty of Policy Management, Keio University, 5322 Endo, Fujisawa 252-0882, Japan / CreativeShift Lab, Inc.
iba@sfc.keio.ac.jp

This paper presents two pattern languages, "Employment of the Disabled Patterns" and "Welfare Innovation Patterns", designed to enrich co-creative interaction relating to welfare issues among stakeholders. "Employment of the Disabled Patterns" generates working styles for persons with disabilities. It contains 30 patterns describing positive and practical wisdom to help individuals with disabilities to work within a company structure. The "Welfare Innovation Patterns" also contains 30 patterns and describes tacit knowledge for creating products and services that achieve more human-centric welfare. These pattern units were created by the City of Kawasaki, a local government organization in Japan. These two pattern languages are intended to work as a methodology and a process to encourage a supportive social environment. The role of the city is to connect the industrial arena and the welfare fields. In this paper, we describe the intentions of the City of Kawasaki, provide a detailed description of two pattern language, and discuss the benefits of using pattern language ideas in local government agencies.

Pattern Language; Local government, Achieve the Enforcement of Policy

1. Introduction

Although our society is heading towards improving welfare, it is not easy to create a supportive social environment. Some of the staff create a very positive environment, but their knowledge and actions are not shared with others. The City of Kawasaki recognizes that there is much tacit knowledge in this field, and that the sharing of such information would be very important in the creation of a more inclusive society. It also recognizes that the experiential know-how of welfare workers would be very helpful in preparing for the upcoming super aged Society in Japan (Cabinet Office, Government of Japan., 2017).

To promote and bring into reality a better, more inclusive, welfare society, it is necessary to enrich people belonging to different backgrounds. In 2014, the City of Kawasaki formulated the Kawasaki Welfare Promotion Plan (Kawasaki, Welfare Promotion Plan, 2014, 2017). It aims to advocate for a new vitality and inclusive social values through the fusion of the domains of industry and welfare. The city has started a forum involving about 300 companies to stimulate cooperation among people belonging to both domains.

One of the issues targeted by this plan is the employment of persons with disabilities. Although there are laws such as the "Act for Promotion of Employment of Persons with Disabilities" (Ministry of Health, Labor and Welfare, 2017) which encourages companies to sustain an employment rate of 2.0% or more of individuals suffering from disability, companies and persons with disabilities in reality do not know how to work together. It is necessary to share the tacit knowledge available in the welfare sector in the hiring, managing, and retention of persons with disabilities in workplaces.

Another goal of the plan is to promote the development of new products and services through cooperation between industrial organizations and welfare workers. This task is not as easy as it sounds, because the perspectives of the two sectors are very different. For the city of Kawasaki, the fusion of the two stakeholders is a big challenge as it faces a super aging society.

In order to disseminate knowledge widely and to share the wisdom of experienced care and welfare, the City of Kawasaki planned to use a pattern language which was proposed by Alexander (Alexander et al., 1977). We, including other members of the city of Kawasaki, developed two new pattern languages, followed by "Words for Journey", a pattern language for living with dementia (Iba, et al., 2015a), and the first pattern language in the welfare sector.

The two new pattern languages are designed to promote the city's intentions regarding welfare issues. Pattern languages should be useful and should stimulate mutual understanding through discussion. To achieve this aim, one must first fill the gap between the industrial norm and welfare sensitivity. Pattern language can be utilized as an appropriate tool to mitigate misunderstandings between industrial custom and the feelings of persons who need welfare support. Second, the role of local government must be broadened from merely encouraging dialogue to becoming an agency that creates opportunities and induces continuous positive change.

In the following sections, we present detailed descriptions of two pattern languages related to social inclusion and welfare: "Employment of the Disabled" and "Welfare Innovation" and present case studies of the use of these pattern language sets by the city.

2. "Employment of the Disabled Patterns"

2.1. Overview of the pattern language

"Employment of the Disabled" is a pattern language designed to build working styles for persons with disabilities. It comprises 30 patterns describing positive and practical wisdom to help individuals who face the challenges of disabilities to work within a company. These patterns were extracted from interviews about the experiences of three kinds of people: those that hire persons with disabilities and exploit their abilities productively in the workplace; staff members of a support agency that helps persons with disabilities to get jobs, and the persons with disabilities.

The main intent of these patterns is to empower both companies and the persons with disabilities to create a workplace where everyone can work enthusiastically. Therefore, these patterns are aimed at two different groups of readers. The first are members of companies that hire the persons with disabilities. The second are people who face the challenge of living their life with disabilities.

The contents of patterns are planned so as to draw positive motivation. The patterns do not impose an obligation to act in a particular manner. On the contrary, they are meant to encourage everyone to generate feelings such as "I can work well together with a person with disabilities in the same workplace". In addition, those with disabilities can solve problems they may face in work situations by looking back at the pattern name and reconsidering their behaviors objectively on their own. Furthermore, the pattern language itself can be the trigger that generates communication opportunities, when the communication is not generated in the workplace.

Each pattern is written in the Pattern Language 3.0 format: *Patten Name, Introduction, Pattern Illustration, Context, Problem, Solution, and Consequence* (Iba, T., 2015). The Pattern Name defines the pattern with a short memorable word or phrase for easy reference. The Introduction helps readers to imagine how patterns fit into their daily lives. Pattern Illustration shows the pattern's essence, and characters that express human movements and feelings. The Context describes the situations in which the pattern should be used. Next, a Problem that is likely to occur in the context is presented. Then, a Solution to the problem is described. Finally, the Consequence describes how things can be changed when this pattern is put into practice (Figure 1).

Please note that the *Pattern Name* is not just a headline or summary for the pattern but a new word or phrase that can be used in conversations (Shibata et *al.*, 2016). Furthermore, *Pattern Illustration* is not just a complementary figure illustrating the pattern but an important element which represents the essence of the pattern. Therefore, we elaborated on the name and illustration. Figure1 shows an example of the pattern *Welcome Sign* from the "Words for Employment of Companies" group.

Number & Category	A22 team communication
Pattern Name	**Welcome Sign**
Introduction	We create an atmosphere where we work together as members of a team in the workplace.
Pattern Illustration	
Context	The persons with disabilities have started working, but the workplace somehow makes an isolated atmosphere for those with disabilities. ▼ In this context

Problem	**If there are few greetings and little conversations in the workplace, it is dificult to enter the team and a psychological distance and feeling loneliness will be born.** Those with disabilities will feel there is no place in this company. If workers are unable to have a sense of belonging, even required communication on the job becomes difficult. Even if there is some trouble, it would be difficult to discover the problem in such an atmosphere. ▼ Therefore
Solution	**Express warm feelings by colleagues to make persons with disabilities feel comfortable and they can behave as usual.** For example, it is important to create an atmosphere that makes a new member feel welcome by preparing desks and lockers on the first day of assignment, to listen attentively to their questions, and to continue casual oral conversations on topics that do not cause stress such as hobbies, hometowns, favorite sports and subjects that build common ground. ▼ Consequently
Consequence	An anxiety is reduced, and the environment becomes light and they feel easy to talk to people at the workplace. Even when you want to consult about working, the mental barrier will be low, and you will be able to work forward with ease. By supporting informal communication, the atmosphere of the whole team will also improve.

Figure 1: Format and Content of the Welcome Sign

"Employment of the Disabled Patterns" is available as a booklet and as a set of cards (Figure 2) in Japanese. The booklet contains the full contents of the patterns. The card set consists of the same patterns but contains only the summary of each pattern. The card set is intended to be utilized in workshops where people talk about their experiences using patterns. Each pattern is printed on one side with the Pattern Name, Introduction, Pattern Illustration, Context, a key sentence of the Solution, and Pattern Number. The omission of the details is quite important because it makes people initiate conversations rather than merely read during workshops.

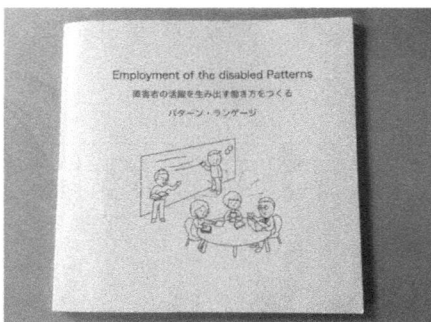

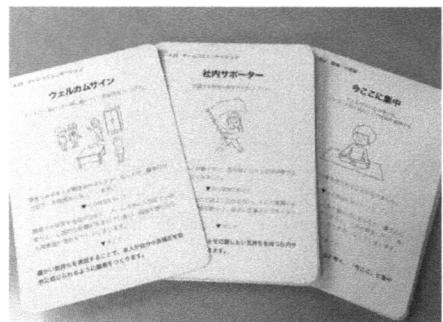

Figure 2: Book and Cards of "Employment of the Disabled Patterns"

2.2. Patterns in "Employment of the Disabled Patterns"

"Employment of the Disabled Patterns" is categorized into two different sets: Words for Employment of Companies, and Words for Those with Disabilities.

The first set of patterns, *Words for Employment of Companies*, contains 18 patterns: *Top Declaration, Understanding Seeds, Workplace Arrangement, Find a Discovery, Welcome Sign, Co-workers Supporters, Pride of Work, Confirming the Okay, Avoiding Weak Points, Transmitted Words, Objective Vision of Failure, Watching over as One, Top Boost, Accept Burden, Three-Legged Race of Dialogue, Refer to the External Viewpoint, Two Perspectives,* and *Pursuit of Open Workplace* (Table 1). These are patterns for companies to help people work successfully with colleagues who have disabilities.

The second set, *Words for the Persons with Disabilities*, contains 12 patterns: *Take a Step, Small Success Experience, Consideration List, Send a win-win Relationship, Concentrate Here Now, Accelerator and Brake, Box I Can Do, Snuggle Buddy, Release and Spread, Motivated Switch, My Recovery Method,* and *Choose the Way by Myself* (Table 2). These are patterns for the persons with disabilities to become more active and to help them contribute more to the workplace.

For Employment of Companies			
No.	Pattern Name	Pattern Illustration	Context, Problem and Solution
1	Top Declaration		You are hiring persons with disabilities as employees. In this context, when you hire to just follow the legal obligation, it will be a burden to work together when problems occur. **Therefore, managers change company policies to encourage the employment of persons with disabilities and create positive values within the whole company.**
2	Understanding Seeds		You decide the jobs to assign to persons with disabilities and prepare to work together. In this context, if you ask for too much consideration from your colleagues, their sense of burden and anxiety will increase, and they will not feel like working inclusively. **Therefore, select important points of consideration to transmit to your colleagues in order to make them ready to work with the persons with disabilities.**

3	Workplace Arrangement		You are thinking about how to work together with the persons with disabilities in the workplace. In this context, if you judge them with bias, the possibility of them working as a member of the company will be closed. **Therefore, arrange your workplace by knowing the prejudice so that the persons with disabilities can work together and use their own characteristics effectively.**
4	Find a Discovery		You start working with the persons with disabilities. In this context, having a prejudice about disabilities or denying consideration for those with disabilities will not provide opportunities for them to work actively. **Therefore, understand that there are differences in personality and position, so try to find the differences between you and those with disabilities.**
5	Welcome Sign		You start working with the persons with disabilities, but the workplace somehow makes an isolated atmosphere for those with disabilities. In this context, if there are few greetings and little conversations in the workplace, it is difficult to enter the team and a psychological distance and feeling of loneliness will be born. **Therefore, express a warm feeling to make your colleagues with disabilities feel comfortable and they can stay natural.**
6	Co-workers Supporters		You encounter situations where superiors and colleagues pointed out missing parts to the persons with disabilities while working together. In this context, it is difficult for you to work gradually if you do not pay attention to them due to the feeling of not knowing about those with disabilities". **Therefore, increase the number of in-house supporters who have the desire to support working with the person with disabilities.**

7	Pride of Work		You are thinking about how you can work positively with persons with disabilities. In this context, if you do not know how those with disabilities are contributing to the workplace, they will not know whether they can keep working, and their willingness to work will disappear. **Therefore, show their accomplishments and announce „for whom and for what" and make them proud of their work.**
8	Confirming the Okay		You feel it seems like the persons with disabilities continue to be doing well on track by themselves. In this context, when the situation in the workplace is busy, there is no time to talk. If you discontinue regular discussions, you will not be able to notice the fact that they are in trouble. **Therefore, make sure to spend time talking to those with disabilities regularly and to check their work, even if there is nothing wrong.**
9	Avoiding Weak Points		You are urging the persons with disabilities to work on various tasks. In this context, as the work increases, they may be entrusted with a task that they are not good at, and it becomes easy for them to feel stressed. **Therefore, devote thought to your way of working in the office. Organize the workplace in a manner that avoids causing of weakness as much as possible and try to not make your colleagues with disabilities feel stressed.**
10	Transmitted Words		You are trying to teach the persons with disabilities a new job. In this context, depending on how you tell it, you may not be able to proceed with your job because of misunderstanding. **Therefore, prepare to be able to imagine what you want to convey clearly. In addition, find a way to communicate clearly and create an understanding between you and those with disabilities.**

11	Objective Vision of Failure		You encounter a problem while the persons with disabilities are working. In this context, when you automatically assume that the problems are caused because of the disabilities, it would be impossible to find the real cause. **Therefore, analyze the factors of failure based on facts. Understand correctly whether or not it is due to the characteristics of the disabilities.**
12	Watching over as One		You try to get the persons with disabilities to work alone, but the results were not as positive as you expected. In this context, if you disturb their own pace of work, they will feel impatient and stress, make mistakes easily and cause trouble. **Therefore, try to create an environment where they can grow by deciding the period without hurrying the outcome.**
13	Top Boost		You are creating a structure capable of working positively with persons with disabilities. In this context, if there is a gap between the company policies and the workplace realities, the entire company will feel negatively about the employment of persons with disabilities when a problem occurs. **Therefore, create a place, including among top executives, to confirm the efforts of employment of persons with disabilities. Act as an organization by sharing the thought with the whole company.**
14	Accept Burden		You are encountering a situation where you work with persons with disabilities, and your colleagues are feeling a sense of burden. In this context, if colleagues are feeling weighed down, those with disabilities will not be able to work comfortably **Therefore, make opportunities for colleagues to talk and find out why they are feeling encumbered by working in an inclusive structure.**

15	Three-Legged Race of Dialogue		ou hesitate to ask persons with disabilities, „May I know about…?" In this context, just because there are obstacles, you cannot say what you want to say, and if you cannot ask what you want to know, your sense of discomfort in working together will increase. **Therefore, respect each other's position and listen and talk directly without setting taboos.**
16	Refer to the External Viewpoint		You start working with persons with disabilities and encounter various problems issues. In this context, when you try to determine actions without having adequate information, you cannot find the right way to exploit their abilities and you cannot find a solution. **Therefore, listen to the opinion from a person who has a new perspective and find the way you can productively use their abilities.**
17	Two Perspectives		You have figured out that the persons with disabilities get used to the workplace and want to work as much as other colleagues. In this context, those with disabilities lose opportunities to work better and if you do not adequately evaluate their accomplishments even when they do their best, their motivation to work may decrease. **Therefore, create opportunities without bias, evaluate everything based on results, and check their growth carefully.**
18	Pursuit of Open Workplace		You are thinking about the significance of hiring persons with disabilities. In this context, if you make judgments by just following the existing rules and obligations of the company, you will be unlikely to exploit their abilities. **Therefore, evaluate that you will continue to change your business and rules little by little, to make a comfortable and flexible workplace.**

Table 1: Patterns for Companies in "Employment of the Disabled"

For Those with Disabilities			
No.	Pattern Name	Pattern Illustration	Context, Problem and Solution
19	Take a Step		You want to work in a company. In this context, even though you desire work, if you do not act on that feeling, only time will pass and your goal will be lost. **Therefore, imagine what you want to be and try and move first.**
20	Small Success Experience		You want to work in a company. In this context, even though you desire work, if you do not act on that feeling, only time will pass and your goal will be lost. **Therefore, imagine what you want to be and try and move first.**
21	Consideration List		You are going to participate in a recruiting interview. In this context, you explain the things that you can do for the company and the aspects you would want the company to consider. If you cannot express them convincingly or take too much time to explain, it will be hard to tell your thoughts and feelings to others. **Therefore, prepare the necessary consideration for yourself so that you can explain yourself to others, and arrange for an easy transmission.**
22	Send a Win-Win Relationship		You have started working in a new workplace. In this context, you cannot ask for consideration and as a result, you are unable to demonstrate your strengths. **Therefore, ask for considerations that are feasible and that will be positive for the entire workplace and not just yourself. In addition, have a respectful dialogue with your opponent.**

23	Concentrate Here Now		You are assigned to the workplace. In this context, if you are doing work somewhat lazily or working distractedly, you will make mistakes or get results you didn't want. **Therefore, see that this work is important, try to focus on the „here and now" and work steadily.**
24	Accelerator and Brake		You are getting used to the workplace, and the number of tasks you are entrusted with have increased. In this context, you are in difficulty when you make a mistake in the pace of achieving results and you struggle to keep working. **Therefore, understand your characteristics of feeling stressed when you work too hard, and you will be extra careful.**
25	Box I Can Do		You have become accustomed to the workplace, so you would like to look back on your work. In this context, when you see eyes on your work, you feel depressed by seeing what you could not do rather than something you can do and you think that you are not suited for this job. **Therefore, enjoy finding what you can do and divide it into „Can do boxes" and „Challenge boxes".**
26	Snuggle Buddy		You are losing Positive feelings that you had on the first day of your employment. In this context, it is painful for you to hold your problem to yourself because you feel it would be difficult for your colleagues to understand the challenges those with disabilities face. **Therefore, find a good buddy who works efficiently in the workplace despite having disabilities and talk to each other.**

27	Release and Spread		You are wondering how you can work in your way. In this context, if you are stuck with the stereotype, such as; you should be like this and you will not be able to break down the current situation. **Therefore, try to separate from the situation that continues to worry you and think about improvement measures from a different perspective.**
28	Motivated Switch		You do not feel like going to work today. In this context, if you continue to work without motivation, you will tend to make mistakes and your relationship with your environment will get worse. **Therefore, practice telling yourself that you can switch your focus towards putting in more effort and to working hard.**
29	My Recovery Method		You feel tired of working. In this context, when your mind and body are tired, and if you do not understand the cause of the weariness, you will not be able to continue working at the requested pace from the company. **Therefore, try to regain your energetic feelings in your own way.**
30	Choose the Way by Myself		You are visualizing how to become an active figure in the workplace. In this context, if you just rely on someone's judgment without thinking yourself, you will only be able to move in passive mode. **Therefore, decide small things based on your own thoughts in order to keep yourself active.**

Table 2: Patterns for Those with Disabilities in "Employment of the Disabled"

2.3. Applications of the "Employment of Disabled Patterns"

"Employment of Disabled Patterns" was created in 2016, and the City of Kawasaki has already utilized these patterns in city events such as the "KAWASAKI Halloween". The Halloween event is held by the City of Kawasaki annually, and more than 1,000 people attend the parade. During this event, two patterns were utilized. The Welcome Sign helps the expression of a warm feeling so that the workplace projects a good atmosphere so that people with disabilities can naturally feel that they belong. Small Success Experience makes it possible for someone to feel a sense of accomplishment, confidence and joy from small successful experiences. The City of Kawasaki utilized Welcome Sign, by having persons with disabilities leading a long parade line and guiding a large number of attendants and everyone walked together to show the collaboration of citizens. It also utilized Small Success Experience and two boys, who had mental disabilities, led the long parade line. This small accomplishment made them feel proud of themselves, and they started to gain confidence (Figure 3).

Figure 3: Scenes from the Halloween event

Another example utilizing patterns is related to professional soccer games. There is a professional football team named "Kawasaki Frontale" and its games are held once in two weeks at the Todoroki Stadium in Kawasaki. As in the previous example, two patterns, Welcome Sign and Small Success Experience were utilized. All people, regardless of their circumstances, including the elderly, the youngsters and those with disabilities, were welcomed to work together for their hometown team. In addition, they work together to clean and organize their stadium every two weeks, so they always feel success and share the feeling of satisfaction. The purpose of Welcome Sign is to visualize social inclusion. The objective of Small Success Experience is to help persons with disabilities become more confident of working within society by having a daily successful experience (Figure 4).

Figure 4: Scenes from the football stadium

"Employment of the Disabled Patterns" is used at employee training seminars in Kawasa-ki. The seminars are free and have been held since 2016. The seminars utilize the World Café Method. The attendees include persons with mental disabilities and the staff members from Hataraku Shiawase JINEN-DO who work as facilitators in the discussions that are held. The patterns work as cases that often occur in workplaces. For example, through dialogues inspired from using the pattern, *Find a Discovery*, attendees understand that there are differences in personality and position. *Pride of Work* gives attendees the opportunity to reconsider that all jobs are valuable to those who do them. *Watching over as One* creates triggers to review their environment as workplaces, and let attendees notice how important people's growth is.

The purpose of holding these seminars is to make people aware of the importance of working along with persons with mental disabilities. Participants feel that there are many issues that they have to keep in mind when working with persons with mental disabilities. In the process, they discover the essence of hiring and managing workers regardless of mental disabilities because everything is basically founded on human relationships.

Over 170 people participated in the seminars that began in October 2016, and the average satisfaction rate was about 96%. Many participants said that they wanted to use similar training sessions with colleagues in their workplaces to support people with disabilities. In addition, they said that they felt they could conduct similar training sessions by utilizing pattern language in their workplaces. This means that *"Employment of the Disabled Patterns"* can be utilized even further in many areas and especially in the workplace (Figure 5).

Figure 5: Scenes from the employment seminar

3. "Welfare Innovation Patterns"

3.1. Overview of the Pattern Language

Welfare innovation aims to create new vitality and social value through the fusion of the fields of industry and welfare. It is necessary for Japanese society to create sustainable innovation in order to overcome the challenges stemming from factors such as a declining population, a fast-decreasing birth rate, an increasingly aging society and, at the same time, to realize sustainable economic growth. For the City of Kawasaki, preparing for a super aged society, promoting active and diverse participation, and promoting the employment of the persons with disabilities are very important issues.

"Welfare Innovation Patterns" delineates the tacit knowledge required to create products and services that achieve more human-centric welfare. The design is meant to stimulate cooperation between the domains of industry and welfare. Although there is much tacit knowledge in areas of developing products and services, especially for welfare purpose, such information is not shared with the industrial domain. This lack of cooperation causes much misunderstanding and friction between the two sides. Therefore, we interviewed people who are doing well in both fields, and summarized the tacit know-how of those people as a pattern language. The patterns are contributing well-designed products or services for welfare purposes, and promote superior processes by encouraging the accumulation of people involved in promoting welfare innovation.

The composition of each design in this set as well as in the *"Employment of the Disabled Patterns"* consists of the Pattern Language 3.0 format: *Pattern Name, Introduction, Pattern Illustration, Context, Problem, Solution, and Consequence* ".

"*Welfare Innovation Patterns*" is also available as a set of a booklet and cards. The purpose of combining the two methods is same as for the "*Employment of the Disabled Patterns*" and it encourages dialogue between companies and people who work in the welfare domain (Figure 6).

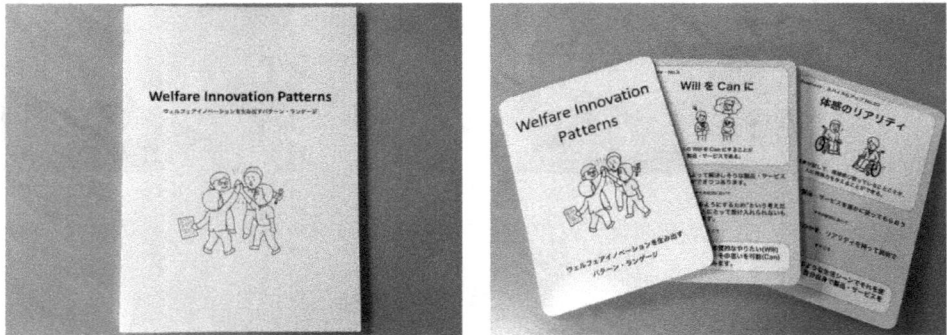

Figure 6: A booklet and cards of "Welfare Innovation Patterns"

3.2. Patterns for "Welfare Innovation"

In "Welfare Innovation Patterns," there are three Core patterns: *Value for Users, Sense of Unity with Everyday Life, and Will to Can*. Table 3 shows the summaries of *Core patterns: Pattern Name, Pattern Illustration, Context, Key Sentences of Problem and Solution*. The rest of the patterns are organized into three sets, each containing 9 patterns: *Exploring the Needs, Supporting Life with the Power of Business, and Pursuing Possibilities*.

The first category, *Exploring the Needs*, contains the following configurations: *Sense of the Place, Listen to the User, Partner on Site, Acquaint your User, Behavioral Background, Match Pace, Bring a Contribution, Point where the Feeling Moves, and A Story beyond Expectation* (Table 4). These are patterns for suppliers to understand the specific needs of users. This set focuses on the stage of grasping needs and of discovering further possibilities.

The second category, *Supporting Life with the Power of Business, includes: Communicating the Future You Want to Realize, Revisiting Strengths, The Other' Point of View, Revealing the Feeling, Convincing Data, Collaborating to Solve Problems, Familiar Consultant, Reality of Bodily Sensations, and Determining the Likeable* (Table 5). These are patterns for people trying to support life as a business. This set is intended to draw forward positive and active motivation to create new products and services. To achieve this, people can learn and discuss how to create positive relationships with those who work in the domain of welfare. These approaches make it possible to merge the thought processes of both the fields of industry and welfare.

The third category, *Pursue Possibility*, comprises: *If I were you, Watching Other Areas, Reserve Needs, Accommodative Design, Only What is Necessary, Delivery Speed, Point and Line, Ease of Use Feeling, and To be Loved* (Table 6). This set of patterns focus to pursue possibilities for a daily life.

CORE			
No.	Pattern Name	Pattern Illustration	Context, Problem and Solution
1	Value for Users		You are in charge of planning new products / services. In this context, you do not know how to proceed with the planning of the development of products and services based on thought processes of the care and welfare field. **Therefore, try to view the world from the point of view of the person using the products / services and think: "What kind of value can we create by the use of these products / services."**
2	Sense of Unity with Everyday Life		You are thinking about what kind of value you can add to the lives of people who will use your products / services. If you focus too much on the trouble they face in their daily lives and produce a product / service that your intended users will hesitate to utilize, people's feelings will be further depressed and their desire to be active will decrease. **Therefore, plan such products / services that can fit naturally into people's lives and will make people feel positive and active by using them.**

3	Will to Can		You think your products / services can solve problems. However, if you create products / services based just on the idea of „making possible things they cannot do", your products / services may become unacceptable to the end users. **Therefore, focus on the essential desire (Will) of people who will use your products / services, and develop products / services designed to achieve their desires (Can).**

Table 3: Patterns in the Core Category of Welfare Innovation

Needs			
No.	Pattern Name	Pattern Illustration	Context, Problem and Solution
4	Sense of the Place		You are gathering information in order to proceed with your project. In this context, you cannot understand the actual situation and the essential needs of your end users by being satisfied with only superficial impressions and information gained from the public. **Therefore, go to the sites where the products / services are regularly used and make your own first-hand evaluation.**
5	Listen to the User		You try to delve further into your end users' needs and consider the deeper questions you want to ask from your target consumers. However, you hesitate to ask your intended end users directly and try to understand their requirements by listening to their families and friends. **Therefore, meet directly with the persons who will use your products / services and talk to them in as much detail as possible.**

6	Partner on Site		You find that there are many people who want a regular engagement in site projects. If you vaguely gather information from many people, the plan will go out of hand, and cannot develop anything. **Therefore, find a working partner who can give you useful feedback and who is willing to create something together with you.**
7	Acquaint Your User		You have come to the site to find out the needs of your end users. It is difficult to get people to open their hearts to you immediately and this rectitude makes you unable to get the information you want. **Therefore, candidly share your purpose of intruding into the life and work of your consumer. In addition, you must respect the life and work style / pace / values of the individuals and reduce their feeling of discomfort of being in the spotlight.**
8	Behavioral Background		You are gathering information in order to judge people's needs by stepping into the context of your users' ground realities. However, you cannot quite grasp their real needs and desires. **Therefore, explore and deconstruct the background of the words you hear and you should carefully observe behavioral features, however small they may be.**
9	Match Pace		The user and the company are collaborating on the development of the products / services. However, it is becoming difficult to keep the collaboration going since the two sides are not quite in sync. **Therefore, share each other's circumstances and make progress by gradually adjusting to each other's pace.**

10	Bring a Contri-bution		You are operating your projects by including other members. However, if only some of the members are overloa-ded with things to do, the team relati-onships will become frayed. **Therefore, reconfirm each members' respective areas, express relative strengths and interdependencies, so all members can participate in the project with equal motivation and create a win-win relationship.**
11	Point Where the Feeling Moves		You are thinking about people who will use your new products / services. However, you have pushed the con-ceptions of the developer side, and you cannot connect to the active feelings of the end users. **Therefore, find the points of interest of your consumers and make a carefully considered connection between your products / services and your end users. It is important to give your consumers the opportunity to meet with the product / services being developed, so that they can try and discover what they really need and have the chance to gain a solution that will make a difference to their lives.**
12	A Story beyond Expectations		You are trying to get people to use your products and services at the prototype stage. In this context, even though you have attained an evaluation regarding your innovation, you cannot obtain the direct voice of intended users. **Therefo-re, reflect on both the direct changes that products and services can bring about and also the lifestyle trans-formations that the developers did not expect, and you must share that story with others.**

Table 4: Patterns in the Needs Category of Welfare Innovation Patterns

Business			
No.	Pattern Name	Pattern Illustration	Context, Problem and Solution
13	Communicating the Future You Want to Realize		You want to advance the creation of products and services by getting help from many people other than yourself. You think you have a good idea and that there are tasks you can accomplish, but other people are not interested in them. **Therefore, clearly and persuasively communicate your thoughts about the world you want to realize with your words.**
14	Revisiting Strengths		You are trying to create products and services that solve issues related to care and welfare. However, you cannot demonstrate the company's own original strengths and you cannot achieve your potential. **Therefore, eliminate your existing ideas about how you can make use of your company's strengths. Imagine a specific life scene from various perspectives in both vertical and horizontal directions.**
15	The Other Point of View		You want to talk to the people in the field of care and welfare about the technology you want to bring to reality for people to use. You find it difficult to build good relationships with the people in the domain of care and welfare because you cannot maintain adequate dialogue with them. **Therefore, try to understand the characteristics of the worksite, the values of the organization, the ideas and feelings that are not verbalized, and learn the perspective of the discipline while engaging in conversation with the people involved in the field.**

16	Revealing the Feeling		You have created a framework for what you want to do and have made a plan for the future you want to realize. In this context, you are proceeding with the plan by yourself and cannot clarify who uses the products and services or how to use them. **Therefore, ask your colleagues and family and also request a lot of people who have not worked with you to respond to a summarization of your ideas and projects and record their reactions.**
17	Convincing Data		You want to get approval for your project from the people who are involved in care and welfare situations. You illustrate to them the image of the future that you want to realize and demonstrate the positive features of the products and services. However, you cannot appeal to the emotions of the field workers in care and welfare. **Therefore, respond to their needs and prove that you can meet their requirements. In doing so, use your own data which you have gathered in the field.**
18	Collaborating to Solve Problems		You encounter problems that require solving as your plan advances. In this context, the more you try to impose your authority, the worse situation will become. **Therefore, do not try to solve issues forcibly. Find friends who can complement your plan, and collaborate to solve problems.**
19	Familiar Consultant		You are building a team of developers and users. There may be pitfalls that the team cannot determine on its own, and may overlook the potential areas where it can perform better. **Therefore, get opinions from someone who has a fresh perspective, or from experienced and trustworthy people.**

20	Reality of Bodily Sensations		You are trying to make someone to use the products / services which are ready to use. However, you cannot explain the real perspective of how useful it is in the area of care and welfare. **Therefore, try using the products / services yourself while thinking about who can use them and in what kind of life scenarios.**
21	Determining the Likeable		You test the product / service in the care and welfare field and receive good comments. If you are satisfied with just having a good review, your efforts towards growth and development will gradually stagnate. **Therefore, carefully consider how the empathetic element is connected to the future you want to realize, and keep improving.**

Table 5: Patterns in the Business Category of Welfare Innovation Patterns

Possibility			
No.	Pattern Name	Pattern Illustration	Context, Problem and Solution
22	If I were you		You want to provide new value in the field of care and welfare. In this context, you can think of an extension of the current product / service and cannot find the premise that you really want to work on. **Therefore, imagine what you would feel and which part of the product / service would feel unpleasant to you if you or someone close to you were to use the products / services of care and welfare.**

23	Observing Other Areas		You are trying to create valuable products and services in the field of care and welfare. However, you cannot discover breakthrough ideas for new developments if you only regard the features of the care and welfare field. **Therefore, have an interest in new technology applied to other fields or methods and think about whether you can link those products and services to the field of care and welfare.**
24	Reserve Needs		You have ascertained a lot of needs by delving into the circumstances of the people who need some kind of support. If the needs you have determined cannot be resolved immediately and have to be excluded from the scope of your effort, the potential of helping people achieve what they can accomplish will be lost. **Therefore, keep all the possibilities of resolution open, even if you cannot solve the problems in the short-term.**
25	Accommodative Design		You are designing the functions of products and services. If you try to satisfy the needs of all people, the products / services are likely to become over specified and in actuality, they will become difficult to handle for people who really need to use. **Therefore, design products and services with basic requirements that make them accessible to everyone's characteristics and abilities.**
26	Only What is Necessary		You are planning to develop products and services that complement the ability of the people. The excessive dependence on products / services in daily life would deprive users of maintaining what they can do and may cause them to lose their abilities. **Therefore, keep users' strengths intact, design products / services that support only and exactly what they really need.**

27	Delivery Speed		You are developing products and services steadily. In this context, it has become impossible to judge how much function can be added to services / products. **Therefore, expect that the lives of a certain number of people may be transformed by your pro-ducts / services, make the decision to deliver your products / services faster.**
28	Point and Line		You are trying to test your products and services at the prototype stage. You were told that it was hard to use the products / services in the context where they are actually used. **Therefo-re, think carefully about the usage circumstances before and after the product / service is used. To gene-rate products / services of value, design not only the change in one moment (point) of life, but also the transformation of the context (lines) before and after that point.**
29	Ease of Use Feeling		You want to make a product that can be used by many people. Even if it fulfils the function, people do not want to use it. **Therefore, make efforts to make it easier to use and to match the price and the desires of people who use the product in everyday life.**
30	To be Loved		You want to provide products and ser-vices that can be used by many people. Products should not be created by paying attention to superficial features, and you should not be satisfied with temporary attention or gradual usage. **Therefore, continue to pursue the comfort of use, build products with features that may be used for a long time, focus on quality so that ever-yone can enjoy your product with confidence.**

Table 6: Patterns in the Possibility Category of Welfare Innovation Patterns

3.3. Application of "Welfare Innovation Patterns"

"Welfare Innovation Patterns" were created by the City of Kawasaki in 2017, in the year following the development of the "Employment of Disabled Patterns". Right after the release of the "Welfare Innovation Patterns", the City of Kawasaki began to utilize it to create new services. They applied two patterns: *Point where the Feeling Moves and Bring a Contribution for a service using "WHILL"*.

"WHILL" is a so-called electric wheelchair that is very innovative. It is comfortable to ride and easy to handle. It has also received the Good Design Grand Award in 2015. This recognition is given to a product that is original in design and that enhances the quality of life of people. However, although this wheelchair is an innovative product, it is very expensive and is difficult for an individual to purchase and that is a huge problem. The city of Kawasaki felt there were more possibilities for this wheelchair and tried to figure out how to make the most of it.

The city of Kawasaki utilized the pattern, *Point where the Feeling Moves*. The city and the wheelchair company decided to cooperate with a nursing service for the aged people. They set a mini course at a gymnasium and asked the elderly to be test-riders at the course. They collected the real voices of the mature participants such as "It is so much fun to ride" or "I want to go outside riding on it". The city of Kawasaki then applied the next pattern, *Bring a Contribution*. The city arranged a collaboration with the wheelchair company and a universal design taxi company. They discussed how they could work together to make the vocalized desires of the test-riders come to life. They found that although it was difficult for the taxi company to buy expensive electric wheelchairs, if the wheelchair company rented its products to the taxi company, they could collaborate and start a new service such as Monitor Touring (Figure 7).

Figure 7: Application of Patterns to the Test-Ride Event and to the New Service.

4. Conclusion

In this paper, we presented two pattern languages, *"Employment of the Disabled"* and *"Welfare Innovation"* and introduced the ways in which the patterns language concepts may be used. In order for many people to be involved, it is necessary to reflect on how the pattern language programs may be employed in various situations; how such opportunities may be created and what actions can be undertaken. There will be possible opportunity to encourage further behavioral change. In addition, since we are looking for innovative words that can create tacit knowledge towards solving problems in the field of care and welfare, we will continue to work on creating pattern language solutions. We believe that this process itself is one of the activities to build a society in which people, especially individuals other than professionals in the field of care and welfare, support each other naturally. Last, we hope that our research will become a catalyst for the formation of a sustainable society in a super aged society.

5. Acknowledgements

We would like to acknowledge other members of our project: Motohiro Kanayama, Jun Katsuno, Taihei Ogi, Masaki Tomizawa, Yumi Ebata, Mayako Hoshino, Miho Masai, and Yuri Abe. We are also grateful to Kazuki Toba and Tomoki Kaneko for their support in writing this paper. Finally, we would like to say thank you to all the participants for their help and cooperation in the form of interviews and feedback and for providing us with the opportunity to examine real cases during the process of the creation of the patterns.

6. References

Alexander, C., Ishikawa, S., Silverstein, M., Jacobson, M., Fiksdahl-King, I. & Angel, S. (1977) A Pattern Language: Towns, Buildings, Construction. Oxford University Press.

City of Kawasaki, (2014, revised 2017). Kawasaki Welfare Promotion Plan. In Japanese.

Cabinet Office, Government of Japan. (2017). Annual Report on the Aging Society 2017. In Japanese.

Ministry of Health, Labor, & Welfare. (2017). Act for Promotion of Employment of Persons with Disabilities. In Japanese.

Iba, T. (2015). Pattern Language 3.0 and Fundamental Behavioral Properties. World Conference on Pursuit of Pattern Languages for Societal Change (PURPLSOC2015).

Iba, T., Okada, M., & Dementia Friendly Japan Initiative. (2015). Words for a Journey: The Art of Being with Dementia. CreativeShift.

Shibata, S., Sakurako, K., Hitomi, S., & Iba, T. (2016). Pattern Naming Patterns: Symbolizing the content and value by expressions to facilitate intuitive comprehension. 23th Pattern Languages of Programs (PLoP2016).

Closing the gap between concern and action: tools and lessons from working to develop a pattern language (on sustainable living)

Paine, Greg

City Futures Research Centre, University of New South Wales, Sydney, Australia
gregory.paine@bigpond.com

This paper describes research that explored the question: What might be a language that not only describes "the whole" of sustainability but is also generative of the solutions and actions we need? The research utilized the experiences of a group of individuals seeking to "live more sustainably", thus covering the full range of household needs and decisions. Interaction with these individuals was through the lens, and aspirations, of Alexander's "pattern language" model. Like the research, this paper interweaves these two components. Thirteen proto-Patterns were developed around one aspect of the participants' experiences – the need, and difficulty, in maintaining a "mindfulness" to the task.

The research also found a "how to" gap when applying Alexander's model, specifically the lack of a concise workbook. As such, a principal component of this paper is to detail:

(i) the purpose-designed "pattern-making" tool used to gather the experiences of the individual participants with the aim of generating a series of Patterns. The design is based on Alexander's notion of a Pattern as embodying a "resolved tension". It can be copied or modified for use in other projects.

(ii)lessons learnt from this work, to assist in the development of any future Pattern "workbook".

Sustainable living; patterns, pattern languages; research tools; mindfulness

1. Introduction

We now have a range of languages, scientific, managerial and political, to describe the imperative of "sustainable development". But invariably they fall short in encompassing the whole of the issue, and therefore also the necessary broad spectrum of required solution-actions; all too often preferencing only particular scientific, managerial and political parts. Critically, these languages have also failed to stimulate the necessary quantum and timeliness of required actions. What then might be a language that is not only descriptive of "the whole" of sustainability but also generative of the solutions and actions we need?

This paper describes research that explored this question. It utilized:

(i)   a household-based behavior-change project ("Living Waters-Living Communities") centered around sustainable development, and

(ii)   Christopher Alexander's participatory and lived experience-based pattern language model.

The research itself, and now this paper, "interweaved" these two foci. The choice to work with these two components was prompted by Alexander's own aspirations to develop just such a holistic and generative (pattern) language; in particular the need to both:

(i)   define the invariably daunting "large-ness" of the "whole" of any issue into manageable human-scaled "chunks" without, as is all-too-often the case, neglecting that whole (Alexander 2016), and

(ii)   collaborate closely and on an equal basis with existing practitioners of such (generally unwritten) languages and/or with those who will ultimately use the resultant (written) language(s) (Alexander 1979).

The tools and learning outcomes from the research will be of interest to practitioners involved in both the endeavor of sustainable development and the application of the pattern language model in this or in other fields.

The outcomes relating to "sustainability" dealt with in this paper principally comprise a description of the thirteen Patterns developed around one of the issues raised by the research participants – the need to maintain a constant "mindfulness" to the task.

The outcomes relating to Alexander's pattern language model are given more attention given it is hoped they will be of assistance to Pattern practitioners generally and because, as was discovered during the research, there is as yet no dedicated "workbook" to assist novice and aspiring practitioners. The outcomes comprise:

(i)   The design of a new "pattern-making" tool (the "Pattern game") to assist in gathering and analyzing data, and used in this research in the interviews with participants. This tool is easily transferrable, with any relevant modification, to other projects which aim to discern Patterns.

(ii)   The writing of an embryonic pattern language around one aspect of the participants' experiences (mindfulness).

(iii)   The subsequent lessons from the Pattern-writing process. A key finding was the necessity for a dedicated "Pattern writer" to complete the exercise.

(iv)   The possible applicability of the resultant Patterns on "mindfulness" to the Pattern process generally.

2. How might we live sustainably? Developing a language to assist

2.1. The Living Waters-Living Communities behavior-change project.

The Living Waters–Living Communities project established a series of "learning-circles" comprising participants who had volunteered to try and live "more sustainably" in their everyday lives and households. The participants met to support each other in addressing the practical dilemmas they then encountered. The project was conducted in the northern beaches area of Sydney, Australia between 2000 and 2001 by the local government authority and OzGREEN, a locally-based international environmental education organization (Figure 1). Funding was provided by the State government (see: http://www.environment.nsw.gov.au/stormwater/casestudies/livingwaters.htm).

Figure 1: Cover graphic: the Living Waters-Living Communities project booklet.

The project was based on the understanding that:

» making a commitment to something, particularly where as complex as global "sustainability", is often not in itself sufficient; on-going support and assistance to maintain this aspiration will still be required,

» many environmental education projects address only one or a limited range of issues (eg. water, or energy, or food waste); however "sustainability" requires addressing the full range of lifestyle patterns and these are invariably, and conveniently, evident at the household level, and

» effective "environmental education" is about instilling changes in behavior; it is not simply the dispensing of knowledge but must also address the difficult and often elusive factors implicit in personal and collective change.

2.2. The associated research: "closing the gap between concern and action".

The research was interested in not just the theoretical underpinnings of sustainability but the further understandings that arise from its *practice*, in particular the difficulties that then invariably arise – with the intention that these understandings, if expressed clearly, could then be used by others with similar aims.

The Living Waters-Living Communities project comprised a "good fit" with this objective. It allowed:

(i)   an exploration of the nature of sustainability from the perspective of the whole – here the multiple issues that arise within everyday household decision-making – rather than the more usual sectorial approaches (eg. building design, consumption, energy conservation, or economic systems), and

(ii)   the utilization of the actual experiences of a group of people committed to the practice sustainable development – again at this very immediate and encompassing household scale.

The research comprised (Paine, 2004):

·   observation of the group learning-circle discussions,

·   individual interviews with 29 participants, and

·   work with 10 participants as a group to generate a series of lessons around one aspect of their actions (the need for an on-going mindfulness).

The research drew on Alexander's pattern language work to design the tool used for the participant interviews and to develop the "lessons" themselves (as "proto" Patterns).

3. The "pattern game" interview tool: design and reflections from use

3.1. Conceptual background.

The interview tool was purpose-designed to address the limitations of the usual alternatives: structured questionnaires and un-structured discussion. The former tend to be closed, whereas the participants' approaches to their task, from the observations of their discussions, were wide open. The latter risked being too un-focused – the intention was to go beyond the realm of the individual participants and define replicable Patterns for use by others. Further, as with all research, the process also needed to include a rigor, able to "test" the interviewees' own descriptions and evaluations of their actions.

Conceptually, there were two main design influences:

(i)   Alexander's (1966, 1979) idea that Patterns comprise the resolution of a set of forces, and

(ii)   psychologist George Kelly's (1955) Personal Construct Theory.

These influences were not sequential but coalesced to form an initial structure subsequently refined through review. The tool:

» Establishes two "poles" which "prise apart" the "whole" as described in the linked pair of words that is the term sustainable development: "sustainable" (i.e. the abstract universal of ecologically sustainable living) and "development" (i.e. the concrete particular of our living impact).

» Creates a "dialogue space" between these two poles, stimulating discussion and revealing lessons about the inevitable tensions and ambiguities present within this whole (i.e. the actual practice of sustainable development) as experienced by the participants.

This space can also be seen as the "gap" between our *concern* for the need to live more sustainably and our current lack of sufficient *action* to address that concern. It was envisaged that the discussion here would reveal data that could then be used to generate a series of Patterns about what assisted (i.e. closing the gap) or hindered (i.e. maintaining the gap) participants' efforts.

As it turned out, the operation of the tool tended to resemble the playing of a game, as described below.

3.2. The pattern-game.

The pattern-game interview is formatted onto an A3-sized sheet of paper. Seven blank text boxes are aligned down each side, with a large area of blank space in the middle. The paper is folded so that it appears as A4 size, with the text boxes turned outwards. A question is added to each side above the two columns of boxes. There are six steps:

1. Participants are handed the folded sheet with the first question visible. It asks for 'seven things that, to you, best characterize sustainable living for the society in which you live.' Participants are requested to aim for a single word, or as few words as possible, and write each in a text box.

2. The participants are then requested to turn the page over. Here there is a similar arrangement. This time they are asked for 'seven things that best characterize your current living impact on the earth', also in a single word or as few words as possible.

3. Next, participants are requested to open the folded sheet (this was often the first time they knew it was larger than A4) and then draw lines between the boxes on either side of the page where they think there are links. Different colored pens are used for links showing ,a consistency', ,no current consistency', and for where the participants think the link does not fit these two categories.

4. Participants are then asked to describe the reasoning behind each of the lines (links), prompted by questions by the interviewer. The discussion is recorded.

5. When it appears that most of the information about the line has been obtained, the participant is requested to think of a word, or as few words as possible, to sum up the discussion and write it on the line.

6. When all the lines are discussed and key words allocated, the participant is requested to hold out the page in both hands (as if taking a deep breath, thus also assisting to "re-energize" themselves if necessary), think about all the key words and then summarize them in another word at the bottom of the page.

A completed pattern-game is at Figure 2. Most interviews took between one and two hours, with the average being 1¾ hours.

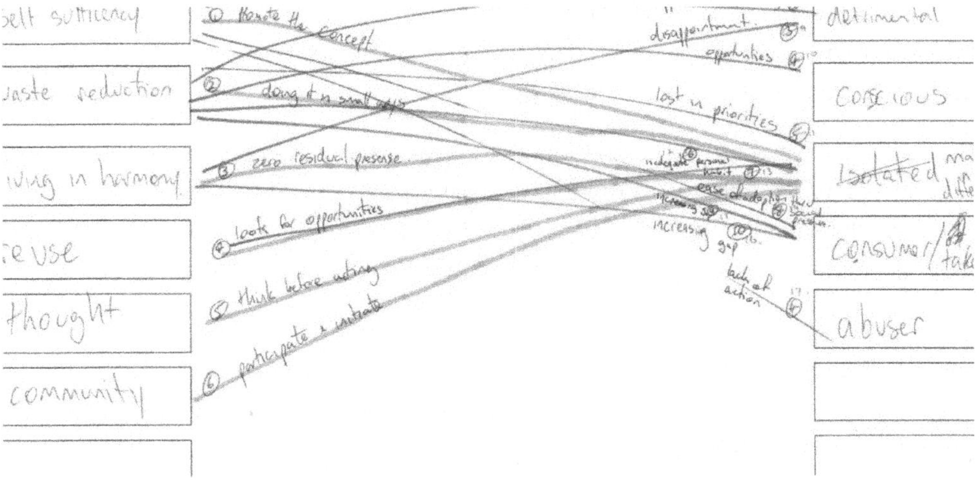

Figure 2: An example of a completed pattern-game.

3.3. The design concept: (i) Alexander's idea of patterns as a set of forces.

An initial task in any problem-solving is to accurately define the problem itself. But how to do this when the complex nature of contemporary, invariably "wicked", problems means they are not singular or linear, but made up of any number of forces pushing each other around? Alexander's solution was to conceptualize each discrete component of such problems as a "pressure pattern" generated by those forces. Each problem-component is properly defined (i.e. the "shape" of the pressure-pattern is correct) when these forces are accurately delineated and hence in static tension with each other (Figure 3). The problem can then be given due attention. The next step is to derive, from this pattern, a solution. Alexander also conceptualizes such solutions as a pattern, in effect embedded within the tensioned "problem" pattern. But this time the pattern comprises the resolution of those forces. As stated in Chermayeff & Alexander, 1965 (p.108): "Forces have a characteristic pattern and the good form [i.e. solution] is in equilibrium with the pattern, almost as if it was lying at the neutral point of a vector of a field of forces."

I realized that I too would need to discern such tensioned arrangements if I were to establish similar (Alexandrian) patterns. The research therefore aimed to establish with participants a similar set of forces operating within various discrete components of their efforts to live sustainably; and then discuss the attributes, helpful and hindering, of the resultant "tensioned field" (or pattern) – all without becoming overwhelmed by the otherwise immensity of the matter at hand (i.e. "living sustainably"). This became the main structural determinate of the interview tool:

(i)   The definition of the "whole" of the task adopted by each household into discrete "bite-sized" components was achieved by the request to nominate one "thing" in each of the seven boxes on either side of the page.

(There could have been any number of boxes. Seven was chosen on the basis that most participants would probably list three to five matters fairly quickly, but would need to, as intended, think more deeply about a sixth and seventh; and seven would still be a manageable number to discuss in detail. However participants could add further boxes if they wished).

(ii)   The "tensioned forces" are represented by the lines linking the various boxes on either side of the page. The discussion and summing-up key word relating to each line then yielded the very grounded experiences gained by the participants from tackling these tensions.

As an aside, one can suggest some resonance between this interview as a "game" and two other games: (1) Alexander's reference, early in his career, to Herman Hesse's glass bead game exercise, also played as a way to understand and work with the complexity of "the whole of things" (Alexander 1968); and (2) the active, storied "string-games" played between the fingers in many traditional societies (and by children as the "cat's-cradle"), and which in turn, though now in three-dimensions, also have resonance with Alexander's tensioned-forces diagram (Figure 3).[1]

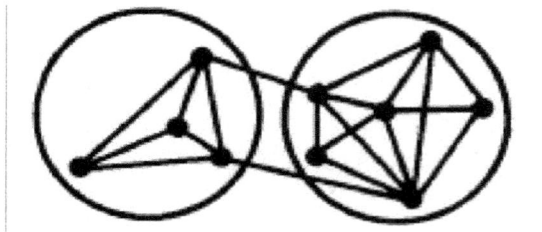

Figure 3: Issues as delineated fields of tensioned forces (Alexander 1964:65).

3.4. The design concept: (ii) George Kelly's Personal Construct Theory.

George Kelly (1955) proposed that we understand the world through dichotomous constructs. He designed a purpose-made tool, the Role Construct Repertory Test, to elicit from patients these dual perspectives they hold about particular matters. A "construct" and then a "contrast" are nominated as "polar" ends by patients in response to set questions, and

---

[1]   *Actually, string-games are effectively carried out in four dimensions – to include the dimension of time in relation to the playing of the game itself and often also in relation to the stories recited as part of the play.*

then discussed.

Kelly's theory and his associated Test provided a practical example of how to work with the research participants to elicit the particular "tensioned" forces they were experiencing. It was though not copied directly but used here more as a conceptual guide. There were a number of elements:

(i)   A difficulty in applying Alexander's idea of "tensioned forces" is that there can be any number of "poles" setting up these forces as applicable to the problem at hand. This generates a logistical problem in isolating each in order to discuss and seek resolutions, and in ensuring that none are missed. For the pattern-game it was thought a combination of Kelly's dual-pole spectrum and the request for participants to list a stipulated number of matters of interest (here, seven) would make the task of describing and discussing the enormity of "sustainable development" manageable.

(ii)   Kelly's interest is in the relative values patients place on the two poles, whereas Alexander is interested in the "shape" of the (tensioned) middle-ground. My research was also interested in this overall "shape" – not just in any negative tensions arising from opposites but, more importantly, in finding where "opposites" have come into some symmetry. The pattern-game therefore establishes not so much dualities but rather the nature of the tensioned links themselves, as identified by the participants – on the basis that it is here important "lesson patterns" would arise. (Here one can also note a similarity between this tensioned-link space and Chermayeff & Alexander's (1965) idea of a "lock" being a "realm" and "activity zone" rather than a barrier).

(iii)   A further element derives from comment (Bannister & Fransella 1971) that the structure of Kelly's tool has a close correlation with the underlying proposition (i.e. Personal Construct Theory) used to analyze responses, thus reducing the need (by the psychologist) for further "intermediate" work with that data. This idea prompted my search for a "pattern making" tool that would have similarly "close-ness" to Alexander's background theory – with the resultant data (i.e. the "ingredients" of the intended pattern language) being expressed as far as possible by the participants themselves without risking later "misinterpretation" by myself.

(iv)   Finally, there is Kelly's notion of the "enquiring man" – that we all actively experiment, in the nature of a scientist, with our predicaments. As such, individual constructs should be seen as fluid. This fitted well with the characteristics of the research participants who were engaged in a continuous process of practice and learning, and with Alexander's (1977) idea that patterns should be considered, at least initially, as hypotheses, open for review and improvement.

3.5. The pattern-game: a summary of attributes.

The objective that pattern languages inherently have a close-fit with user needs, coupled with Kelly's idea of a dynamic "enquiring man", generated a need for my interviews to be participatory and interactive. The design of the pattern-game means that both the participant and the interviewer have before them a visible summary of the evolving discussion, allowing for continuous feedback and stimulating further reflection. It also addresses a limitation often found in structured interviews in projects such as this – a lingering tendency by the researcher to want to impart information to the interviewees (in this case in relation to the all-important imperative of sustainable development) rather than maximizing opportunity for the participants to impart *their* experiential knowledge, in collaboration. As finally developed it:

(i)   was successful in maintaining a view of the whole while also opening up and exploring the intricacies of the "joints" of this whole.

(ii)   provides for both direct questioning and open discussion.

(iii)   establishes a neutral "middle ground" between the abstract and the concrete, being where resolutions to outstanding dilemmas will often be found.

(iv)   produces and records both "gut" reactions and more reflective discussion.

(v)   is challenging, thus generating thoughtful and creative responses.

(vi)   is graphic, meaning the results of the interview are immediately visible, allowing for reflection and addition.

(vii)   retains a visible participant ownership of the (their) information, thereby also reducing the possibility of subsequent misinterpretation.

(viii)   allows the data to be easily transcribed (in a 3-column format), assisting later analysis.

The pattern-game elicited positive, un-prompted comments as the interviews progressed (Box 1).[2]

2   A modified version of the pattern-game has since been used in a series of workshops to determine the health needs of residents of four residential estates and then how the design and management of those estates could assist. Here a dialogue space was established between the two poles of "the things I do (now) to keep healthy" and "the things I should be doing (but do not do) to keep healthy." For details, refer:

> » How did you think of it? It's a really good game. It really makes you think.
>
> » This is very interesting. Did you design this? You don't know as you are going along...
>
> » An incredible process. Very powerful. It's great. One of the reasons I like it – it deals with the visual side of stuff – everything is so text based in our society – it's interactive. And it doesn't alienate other learning styles. Prompts the subconscious as much as the conscious.
>
> » At the beginning I thought: uh oh, more paper work. Then it gave me the opportunity to think about the positive things. Thought provoking.
>
> » Well, I've found this therapeutic...challenging as well

Box 1: Some participant responses to the pattern-game tool

4. Translating the data into Patterns: process and lessons

4.1. Twenty patterns about the practice of household sustainability.

The interview data revealed some 20 patterns about participants' experiences. These were then distilled into a more manageable set of seven (although they are inherently inter-linked) (Figure 4). Note that the reference to pattern here is not to (Alexandrian) Patterns but to the conventional meaning of the word in analysis to denote a theme or repetitive occurrence that "stands out". They are:

» Time

» Community

» Consumption/guilt

» Mindfulness

» Knowledge/education

» Degree of control

» Personal development

Paine & Thompson, 2017.

Each are described in detail at: http://handle.uws.edu.au:8081/1959.7/664 (pages 191-198).

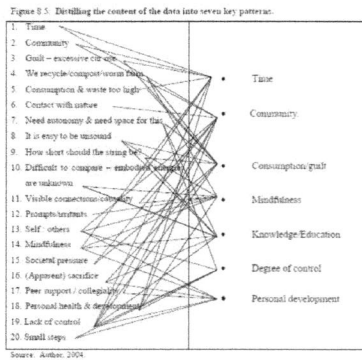

Figure 4: Distilling the 20 "sustainability" themes.

Conversion into Alexandrian Patterns of course necessitated further work. Consistent with Alexander's "grounded" approach this was initially undertaken via a workshop with the interview participants. As it turned out, final development required additional, and unexpected, work by myself as researcher. This section of the paper describes the process, and lessons learnt.

Limitations of the research meant only one of the seven "theme" patterns was chosen for the workshop – mindfulness. The reason for this choice is not critical here; in summary:

» participants often cited the need for an on-going effort to maintain concentration on the objective of "sustainability", blocking out competing considerations, even when making quite mundane everyday decisions.

» the attribute of mindfulness appeared to receive little explicit attention in the field of sustainable development and change management in general.

» it was thought the topic would be unusual, and thus interesting to the workshop participants.

» it was thought that from the view-point of also learning about the process of generating Alexandrian Patterns, this more challenging topic might yield some different insights into the Pattern-writing process.

4.2. The collaborative Pattern-writing workshop.

To help familiarize participants with the chosen theme the workshop began by "mind-mapping" the word "mindfulness". Responses were written on a whiteboard (Figure 5).

Figure 5: The "mindfulness" mind-map

A short background explanation of the intent and format of Alexandrian Patterns was then given. Here I was initially hesitant in using the word "pattern", choosing instead "sustainability principle" and "lesson". However, this turned out to be unnecessary. The participants appeared to quickly grasp the meaning and intent of Alexander's meaning, with one participant also commenting that "people feel secure with patterns". (This understanding was fortunate in that "lesson" is too closely associated with teaching, and sounds like an instruction rather than, as intended in Alexander's Patterns, something having a natural "good fit" to the needs of those who develop and use them).

Each participant was handed three cards. Thick notation cards were used to suggest substance and worth. Participants were asked to fill in each card with details about an discrete aspect of mindfulness of their choosing. The information sought was described on the cards (Figure 6):

» the description of a tension apparent within their chosen aspect of mindfulness; something needing resolution, a problem.

» a solution to that problem, described in an open manner such that it could be resolved in more than one possible way depending on the user.

» finally (though placed first on the card), a catchy title (something like a "T-shirt slogan" was suggested by one participant).

TITLE
Something catchy.
PROBLEM STATEMENT
A tension. Something needing resolution.
SOLUTION
Written so that it captures an "essence" so it can be achieved in many different ways.

Figure 6: The design of the Pattern-writing cards

Critical to an Alexandrian Pattern is a statement about context. For this project a context statement was not requested given this was already established and known – the endeavors of the participants themselves to live more sustainably within their own households and locality. It was thought it may be confusing to require such further statement. On reflection though, it may have been better to issue the cards with an additional section with this context already entered.

A Pattern also includes statements as to its relationship with other Patterns. The final part of the workshop therefore involved ordering the Pattern cards, and discussion of the result. Participants were requested to place their cards (on a wall) into three different categories comprising levels of scale: the individual, family, and society. These were identified in my earlier literature review as typical foci of sustainable development action. They also had resonance, I thought, with the hierarchies typical within Alexander's groupings of Patterns. Once categorized, participants were invited to draw lines between the cards to show any links. However the participants were reluctant to be constrained by these categories, and half of the total number of cards ended up being placed in an extra "open" category. This outcome, and the alternate orderings participants proposed, was important in itself (and further discussed below).

It was reassuring, in the context of the responses being potentially used by the community at large in the manner of a lingua franca, that the participants appeared to have no difficulty in understanding the Pattern concept. Most appeared more intrigued than daunted by the exercise. They appeared to enjoy the experience and were not in a hurry to leave the workshop event itself.

The workshop resulted in 30 responses in total. A sample is included in Annexure 1. The full set of cards is available at: http://handle.uws.edu.au:8081/1959.7/664 (pages 395-398).

However the responses also presented a dilemma. Most did not achieve the quality of an Alexandrian Pattern. There was often no particular "tension" within the stated problem that would then require resolution, and hence no sharp distinction between the problem statement and the solution. Further, some solutions were either too vague to be useful as day-to-day "rules", and more in the manner of descriptive ideas; or too specific, meaning they could not be implemented in different ways according to need.

4.3. A further necessary exercise involving synthesis by a "Pattern writer".

An initial response was to convene another workshop to iteratively develop what had been written in the first, prompted by comment by Alexander (in Shipsky 1984) that one should not expect the process to be necessarily easy, or quick. However, this option was not pursued. Alexander has also noted the process can take many years to learn (Alexander 1996). Instead, and for the purposes of the research, I undertook the second iteration myself.

In doing so I found my "intervention" became a necessary and therefore valid part of the process given I was the only holder of the combined information (from the literature review on sustainable development, my observations of the discussion groups, and *all* the interviews) necessary to derive the gestalts that would provide the Pattern content. In particular I found that by integrating the statements on the workshop cards with information from the other research components I could generate the tensions that were missing in many of the workshop responses.

Thirteen Patterns have been written in an abbreviated (or "proto") Alexandrian format. Others are possible. The 13 Patterns can be considered as a "sub-whole" of a larger language on sustainable development: complete and actionable in their own right, and part of a larger language still to develop. They give a "taste" of what such a pattern language might comprise, as well as allow conclusions about the process. The titles, many of which came directly from the workshop participants, are:

» Small steps, integrated with life.

» We don't know it all: make best guesses and then review.

» Count me in.

» The people who are there at the time are the right people.

» Extend the family.

» The air is in aware.

» Think with friends.

» Both sides of the coin: love the shadow as well as the light.

» Don't mess your nest: knowing where things come from and go to.

» Look ahead, look behind, think of humankind.

» Self as example: be seen being green.

» Earth=Life=Us. Love it or lose it.

» Humerosis (about the role of "trickstering" in inducing change).

The Patterns draw on and include where possible the actual words of the participants in the interviews and workshop, as well as external knowledge from my literature review.

The full text of the first Pattern is included at Figure 7. The full set of 13 Patterns can be accessed at: http://handle.uws.edu.au:8081/1959.7/664 (pages 245-270).

4.4. Lessons from the pattern writing process.

As the writing of the Patterns progressed it became evident the process is necessarily disciplined. There is as yet no dedicated workbook on how to develop Alexandrian Patterns. As such, initial assistance was gleaned from Alexander's writings and from published comment by others who have worked with or been taught by Alexander.[3] These sources plus my own reflection on the process generated a number of lessons, summarized into the six described below. They potentially form the basis of a future workbook on how to use Alexander's approach.

---

3   A summary list is included in Paine (2016) Choosing Life: learning from diverse fields about the agency of pattern in integrative decision-ma-
     king. Paper presented at The Regenerative City PUARL conference, San Francisco, October, 2016.

TITLE	1. SMALL STEPS, INTEGRATED WITH LIFE
PROBLEM	**The complexity of daily living does not allow us to consider ever-ything we do in one go: [Its] Complicated, everything connected; I would find it very difficult to go about my daily business if I thought about every single item. And yet, at some stage, we must.** This is also the dilemma of the systems perspective of 'everything connected': where do you start, and what should come first? It is the problem that Christopher Alexander addresses in the idea, from biological systems, of sequential growth [2]: take things one step at a time, but make each step in itself a whole that then contributes to a larger whole. *A continual process throughout our lives...One weekly goal. Doing what I can rather than thinking of everything in a whole mass.* By seeing environmental action as one and the same thing as our on-going everyday decisions about living, with each action comprising a 'holon', both whole in itself but also contributing to the larger whole [3], small steps can become cumulative actions supporting the overall sustainability endeavor. In turn, the natural dynamics of life will prompt the process to keep moving. *It's dynamic...If we can hold within ourselves the idea of a caring use of the environment that will determine our impact rather than a high minded 'I do this, I don't do that'.* Watch how your decisions change over time as you become more practiced, knowledgeable, and intuitive, so that the greater whole unfolds: *Not just in my own backyard, but worldwide. Helping in Third World communities. It's protecting the Amazon jungle. It's so many things. It is ethical investing. " • Learning and improving by doing. • Learning to be patient by working with the earth–solutions always bloom in their own time.*
RESPONSE	Approach environmental action as a set of small steps derived from and infused into everyday living -a caring use of the environment, rather than a series of 'external' instructions on what should or should not be done. Consider and take each step in its own time and watch as the range of matters addressed increases.
References	[1] Comment by Living Waters-Living Communities participants shown in italics. [2] Christopher Alexander: The Nature of Order (Vols. 1-4). (2001-5). [3] Arthur Koestler: The Ghost in the Machine. (1967).

Figure 7: 'Mindfulness" Pattern #1: Small Steps, Integrated with Life.

(1)   A required concentrated, and grounded, effort.

The process of defining a Pattern is not easy, even when already deeply immersed in the subject matter. Particular effort is required to:

» define the scope and thus boundaries of each Pattern so they are able to stand alone, not "muddled" by material better located in another, albeit related, Pattern.

» envisage a resolution (the "solution") to the tensioned relationships that define the prob-lem being dealt with in the Pattern.

» form that solution to be specific enough to be actionable, but open enough to allow it to be undertaken in different ways to suit the circumstance.

» provide sufficient background to explain the content (and give voice to the associated participant-users), but also maintain a concise format.

These difficulties are similar to those inherent in making phenomenological descriptions. This is not unexpected if one sees both processes as being about an "essence". As van Manen (1990, p.10) describes it, an essence (and, one could suggest, a Pattern) has a substantial task: "The essence or nature of an experience has been adequately described…if the description re-awakens or shows us the lived quality and significance of the experience in a fuller or deeper manner". In turn this will then meet the intention of a Pattern that it compel action (Alexander 1979).

All this requires Patterns to be grounded in the practical experiences of the language-participants: their hopes, experiences and dilemmas. Ideally this would be achieved via the participants themselves writing the Patterns. However, and as described above, although the participants in this project were willing the resultant work fell short of the intended nature of a Pattern and required extra work.

(2)   The necessary intervention of a "Pattern-writer".

The workshop raised the question: to what extent can – or should – a group of people write their own Pattern languages, or does there need to be outside assistance, acting somewhat like a mid-wife? The conclusion from this project is that a dedicated "Pattern-writer" is necessary, at least until participants themselves gain more experience in the task, given:

» the workshop outcome, where many of the responses were limited to the descriptive.

» the difficulty I myself found in writing the Patterns post-workshop, even given my immersion in the subject. It would take time for others to become as familiar with both the processes and the subject matter.

» tcomment by Alexander himself that the task requires the development of necessary skills, based on intuitive processes founded on a thorough knowledge of the subject matter (Alexander 2002).

» a realization, when thinking further about Alexander's work, that he himself appears to take on this role (while also working closely with the end-users).

To ensure substance and rigor, Patterns necessarily draw on a larger body of evidence. In this project this came from sources only I had immediate access to. One outcome was the addition by myself of two Patterns which came out of the interview material: *The people who are there at the time are the right people* and *Extend the family.* Although this material had not been raised again in the workshop it did appear to me, now as Pattern "mid-wife", to be relevant.[4]

Two other points are relevant. One is that the "mid-wife" role requires being an "honest-broker" with the other participants. The other is that, as in phenomenological work in general, it is not possible to fully "bracket" oneself to *only* record the experiences of others; an element of the self will always intrude (van Manen 1990). The research sought to minimize this by:

» writing the Patterns with constant reference to statements from the workshop and the interviews in order to call on, as much as possible, the participants' experiences rather than my own.

» requesting reviews of the resultant Patterns by others. In this project this was undertaken by colleagues given it was not possible at the time to further engage with the Living Waters-Living Communities participants.

(3)   Patterns as more than a homily.

As the Pattern-writer I did though have a lingering on-going concern: that I might merely be reporting, and repeating, information we already know. Could the Patterns be criticized as mere "homilies", lulling users into comfortable inaction when a key objective is to stimulate action and change?

However, and as addressed in the Pattern *Small steps, integrated with life* (Figure 7), the complex nature of sustainable development (and other "wicked" issues) can only be dealt with via smaller, more manageable but necessarily connected actions. Each Pattern therefore needs to address a bite-sized aspect. Further, in Alexandrian Patterns there is an overt and necessary valuing of everyday needs, behaviors and values. Bringing matters down to such scales can mean the subject matter may appear mundane. It needs to be remembered though that each Pattern is meant to be read and action-ed in reference to the larger group of connected Patterns within which it sits.

Another key attribute of a Pattern is that it should bring to the fore our felt understandings. This too can make Patterns seem, at least at first glance, ordinary or even trivial; particularly given our current tendency to de-value the role of such understandings. However neurolog-

---

4   The title *The people who are there at the time, are the right people,* is taken (with acknowledgement) from the Open Space Technology process for conducting workshops and meetings – see www.openspaceworld.org

ical mapping now confirms that we invariably make decisions, including where matters are quite complex, based on how we feel about something not simply on how we intellectualize it (McGilchrist 2009): established scientific method is now "catching up" with our inherent processes of "embodied cognition" (Claxton 2012) (and indeed with the overall role, within Alexander's oeuvre, of felt experience).

Full testing as to the usefulness of the Patterns from this research will not be obtained until feedback from users is received. In the meantime, reassurance that the Patterns have moved beyond the homily was taken from the reviews of colleagues and others.

(4)   An empathic approach, keeping the larger whole in mind.

Patterns are about identifying and stimulating holistic solutions to problems, many of which have arisen because of past partial or fragmented actions. The processes involved resonate with grounded theory, phenomenology, and action research methodologies. They generate certain requirements.

One is that the Pattern-writer (whether as an individual or a collective group) commit to this wider perspective through an understanding and valuing of contexts and factors beyond one's own field and time and place, and of the connections between things. In turn this requires diverse collaborative working arrangements with those extended fields of knowledge and experience (refer, for example, to Hocking, Brown & Harris 2016).

Another is to value both analytical and intuitive knowledge. Analysis gives us the intricate details of a problem; intuition gives us the contextual whole view. Alexander refers to the basis of such intuition as a felt awareness (Alexander 1979, 2002). In developing Patterns, asking what one feels about something can be more important than asking what one thinks about something. One test used in writing the Patterns here was whether they actually felt right, and (as was found when reviewed by others) likely to result in people reading or hearing it to nod in agreement or give a quiet smile of recognition.

(5)   Being open to different groupings and connections between Patterns.

An inherent part of any language is a clear relationship between its component elements. Alexander addresses this in his ordering of Patterns from coarse to fine-grained, and by including advice within each Pattern of how it connects with others. The ordering proposed in the workshop had a similar scale: society, family and individual. However, as noted, this proved unsuitable. Nevertheless, some arrangement was still needed. The experience of the workshop indicates that such arrangements should be tailored to each circumstance, and that one needs to be open to various possibilities.

The workshop participants made a number of suggestions. These tended to be complex, suggesting an understanding and acceptance of the complexity of the task: a Rubik's Cube, a corkscrew, and a "continuous spiral moving through awareness, responsibility, discipline on each [society, family, individual] level." The participant making this last suggestion added: "I like the spiral–it's seamless, you keep coming up against the same place you have seen before, but you are seeing it from a different perspective."

Prompted by these responses I subsequently set out to arrange the 13 Patterns produced by myself as Pattern-writer. Working with each Pattern title on a separate card, six groupings finally suggested themselves:

» the individual self

» others

» the wider human and non-human community

» process

» understanding, and

» somewhat out on its own, the "trickster" Pattern (*Humerosis*).

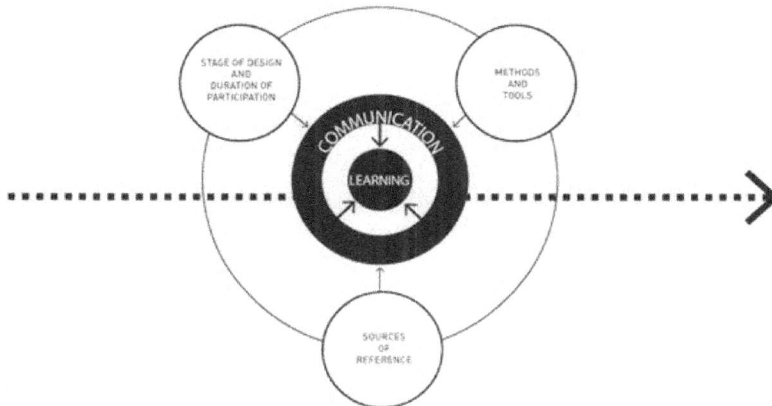

Figure 8: A possible grouping of the thirteen "mindfulness" patterns.

Looking further, it was found that other arrangements at different scales and levels of "hierarchy" were also apparent, including (Figure 8):

» the "individual self," "others" and "wider human and non-human community" groupings could be further grouped in various arrangements on the basis of inherent connections between the self and the wider community.

» the "process" and "understanding" groupings have a similarity, and interact with the more "people"-centered groupings (as listed above).

» two Patterns (Self as Example and Humerosis), although with some connection to others, also exhibit an autonomy.

This simultaneous autonomy and connection between groupings suggests a nested arrangement, with each element independent but also working collaboratively with others. Instructively, it is not at all consistent with the hierarchical arrangement I had suggested at the workshop.

(6)   Bringing Patterns to life: necessary practice, testing and feedback loops.

Ultimately, it is not the actual definition and presentation of a Pattern that is most important. Patterns come to life through their practice. They must relate to the head, the heart and the hand. The solution component must not only be inherently "do-able", it must also inspire and generate that "doing". Pattern languages therefore require equal attention to the means by which they can become known and action-ed, and subsequently reviewed and improved. Further, this generative quality is unlikely to be achieved after only one iteration.

This project was only able to deal with some of these requirements. The ultimate usefulness of the Patterns will, by definition, be improved through an on-going iterative process with users. However, although the completed Patterns were given to the participants, further comment was not sought as part of the formal research (research validation achieved by review by colleagues working within the field of sustainability).

As an example of this latter process, the Solution component as originally drafted for the Pattern: *Don't mess your nest: knowing where things come from and go to* read:

Make visible the invisible. Understand all actions, and describe and name (label) things, in terms of their connections–where they have come from, and where they might go to.

However, reviewers suggested this solution needed greater 'relativity', more 'sense of the interconnections within connections', and a 'notion of blurry boundaries'. Doubts were expressed as to whether one could "make visible the invisible" when links and feedbacks are often indirect, whether one could "understand all actions" when we cannot be comprehensive, and whether it was appropriate to "label" things because labeling is fixed and can prevent fluidity. As a result, the Pattern was amended to now read:

Bring what is hidden into greater consciousness. Think about all actions and describe and name things in terms of their connections—where they have come from, and where they might go to.

5. Possible application of the "mindfulness" patterns when writing Patterns

A (preliminary) final comment arises when considering the nature of mindfulness as suggested here in conjunction with various comments from Alexander suggesting the need, when developing a pattern language, for an inherent "attentiveness". Shipsky (1984, p.58) for instance notes Alexander emphasizing the necessity of "good observation" rather than "inventing", and the associated need to put oneself into a "receptive state, a completely non-pushing state", wary of the "active" ego "always trying to invent, to bring extraneous stuff into the situation."

There is also various critical comment by Alexander (for example, in his conversations with Grabow 1983 and Mehaffy 2004) when reviewing work by others using the Patterns in *A Pattern Language*. In what is almost a lament, Alexander notes that too-often the fundamental quality intended by the language is "only faintly showing through here and there" (Bhatt & Brand 2008), with users simply adopting the "look". In *A New Theory of Urban Design* (Alexander et al 1987) there is comment about an apparent "weirdness" to some of the resultant designs. More fundamentally, Alexander has expressed frustration about an apparent lack of "present-mindedness" to the underlying "value" objective of the pattern language process, and which is to generate an overall improved world (eg. Alexander 1996).

There are though different understandings of mindfulness. In Buddhist practice, mindfulness training seeks to increase the state of awareness of what one is doing, while actually doing it. Thera (1968) refers to the ultimate attainment of this as "bare attention": careful and factual observation unencumbered by emotional reaction, discriminative thought, reflection and purposeful action. There is resonance here with the attribute of the "reduction" in the process of developing phenomenological descriptions from observed data. Both ideas are consistent with the generation of Patterns. But only in part – the Pattern process also entails something more – a necessary active component including, as noted above, a recognition of value. Here, again, there is a similarity with the perceived need by some phenomenologists to move beyond the "mere" here-and-now of description and recognize societal needs for learning and change. It is something which van Manen (1990) for example seeks to address in the notion of a hermeneutic phenomenology. This need has also led Csikszentmihalyi (1995, in Caban et al 2000, p.67) to come to a more active view of mindfulness, defining it as: "a state of mind that results from drawing novel distinctions, examining information from new perspectives, being sensitive to context. An open, probabilistic state of mind in which the individual might be led to finding similarities among things thought different."[5] The final part of this comment in particular is worth noting given that it could be characterized as an overall "pattern" mindset, or consciousness.

All these notions have a similarity with the varied components of mindfulness distilled from the lived-experiences of the Living Waters-Living Communities practitioners. It may be then that the mindfulness Patterns developed here from these experiences (in relation to the task of "sustainable living") might also be useful in guiding the broader work of writing, and then implementing, Patterns and pattern languages (and as such could also comprise a valid part of any future Pattern workbook).

6. References

Alexander, C. (2016). Making the Garden. First Things. www.firstthings.com/article/2016/making-the-garden

Alexander, C. (2002). The Nature of Order. An Essay on the Art of Building and the Nature of the Universe. (Book 2: The Process of Creating Life). Berkeley, California. The Center for Environmental Structure,

Alexander, C. (1996). The Origins of Pattern Theory, the Future of the Theory, and the Generation of a Living World. Object-Orientated Programs, Languages and Applications Conference. San Jose.

Alexander, C., Neis, N., Anninou, A. & King, I. (1987). A New Theory of Urban Design. New York, NY: Oxford University Press.

Alexander, C. (1979). The Timeless Way of Building. Oxford, England: Oxford University Press.

Alexander, C., Ishikawa, S., Silverstein, M., Jacobson, M., Fiksdahl-King, I., & Angel, S. (1977). A Pattern Language. New York, NY: Oxford University Press.

5   Khautipalo (1979) also suggests an "active" component in the Buddhist notion of mindfulness in his reference to mindfulness as a way to both "root out" the "unwholesome" and cultivate the "wholesome" (and which is, again, consistent with the necessarily holistic stance within pattern languages).

Alexander, C. (1968). The Glass Bead Game Conjecture. Lotus 5, pp.151-154.

Alexander, C. (1964). Notes on the Synthesis of Form. Cambridge, USA: Harvard University Press.

Bannister, D., & Fransella, F. (1971). Inquiring Man. The Theory of Personal Constructs. London: Penguin.

Bhatt, R. & Brand, J. (2008). Christopher Alexander: A Review Essay. Design Issues. Vol.24 No.2.

Caban, G., Scott, C. & Sweica, R. (2000). Design Learning in Museum Settings. Form/Work: an Interdisciplinary Journal of Design and Built Environment. No.5, October: 61-69.

Chermayeff, S., & Alexander, C. (1965). Community and Privacy: Toward a New Architecture of Humanism. London: Anchor Books.

Claxton, G (2012) Turning thinking on its head: How bodies make up their minds. Thinking Skills and Creativity. Vol.7 No.2 (August 2012): 78-84.

Grabow, S. (1983). Christopher Alexander: The Search for a New Paradigm in Architecture. Northumberland: Oriel Press.

Hocking, V., Brown, V. A., & Harris, J. (2016). Tackling wicked problems through collective design. Intelligent Buildings International. 8:1, 24-36.

Kellehear, A. (1993). The Unobtrusive Researcher: Guide to Methods. Sydney, Australia: Allen & Unwin.

Kelly, G. (1955). The Psychology of Personal Constructs. New York, NY: Norton.

Khantipalo, P. (1979). Buddha Points to the Mind. The Wisdom of the East. Sydney: ABC Books.

McGilchrist, I. (2009). The Master and his Emissary: The divided brain and the making of the western world. New Haven, CT: Yale University Press.

Mehaffy, M. (2004). A Conversation with Christopher Alexander. Katarxis No.3: New Science, New Urbanism, New Architecture? (on-line publication).

OzGREEN & Warringah Council (2001) Living Waters Living Communities Sustainable Living-Community Education Program. Dee Why, NSW.

Paine, G. (2004). Wholes, patterns and sustainable development. Closing the gap between concern and action (Unpublished doctoral thesis). University of Western Sydney, Sydney, Australia. http://handle.uws.edu.au:8081/1959.7/664

Paine, G. & Thompson, S. (2017). Planning and Building Healthy Communities for Mental Health: Method, findings and reflections from a recent integrative study. Journal of Urban Design and Mental Health 2017;3:11.

Shipsky, J. (1984). Christopher Alexander, theory and practice. Architecture. 74, 54-63.

Thera, N. (1968). The Power of Mindfulness. Kandi: The Wheel Publication, Buddhist Publication Society.

van Manen, M. (1990). Researching Lived Experience. Human Science for an Action Sensitive Pedagogy. Albany, NY: State University of New York Press.

7. Acknowledgements

This paper is based on research assisted by a Hawkesbury Postgraduate Research Award from the Western Sydney University. Supervision by Emeritus Professor Valerie A. Brown, Professor Susan Thompson and Jeremy Dawkins, the contributions of the Living Waters-Living Communities project participants, and the support of OzGREEN is gratefully acknowledged.

Earlier versions of parts of this paper have been previously published in The Qualitative Report. See:

» Paine, G. (2015). A pattern-generating tool for use in semi-structured interviews. Vol. 20(4), 471-484: http://nsuworks.nova.edu/tqr/vol20/iss4/9/

» Paine, G. (2015). Converting Research Findings into Action-Able Pattern-Languages. Vol. 20(7), pp.1125-1140: http://www.nova.edu/ssss/QR/QR20/7/paine4.pdf

The mindfulness patterns were initially published in The Fifth Estate, an on-line newspaper promoting and supporting environmental sustainability within the built environment industries.

Wicked problems, systems approach, pattern language, ecological epistemology, hierarchy theory, interactive value: Multiparadigm inquiry generating service systems thinking

Ing, David

Aalto University and the International Society for the Systems Sciences, Toronto, Canada

coevolving@gmail.com

Systemic design methods in the 21st century have roots in systems theory developed in the 20th century, centering around prominent figures. Within the ecology of systems sciences, six schools of thought coevolved across a variety of domains.

- (i) Wicked problems and Issues-Based Information Systems were the focus of Horst Rittel, continuing as argumentation schemes.
- (ii) The systems approach with inquiring systems from C. West Churchman fed the interactive planning of Russell Ackoff.
- (iii) Pattern language originated in the built environment by Christopher Alexander, was cross-appropriated into information systems by members of the Hillside Group.
- (iv) Ecological epistemology in anthropology started by Gregory Bateson has been extended and refined by Tim Ingold.
- (v) Hierarchy theory in ecological systems by Timothy F.H. Allen is a foundation for the panarchy and resilience science of C.S. Holling and Lance Gunderson.
- (vi) Interactive value and theory of the offering from Richard Normann led to business orchestration by Rafael Ramirez and Johan Wallin.

During this period, the design profession has evolved with changes in technology. Building things and places centered on structuralism. Constructing experiences draws on phenomenology. The rise of information technology has resulted in a turn towards interaction and materiality.

Service systems thinking proposes a generative pattern language structured on (i) voices on issues (who + what), (ii) affording value(s) (how + why), and (iii) spatio-temporal frames (where + when). This approach comes through multiparadigm inquiry that builds on the history of systems theories developed from the 1960s into the 1990s. Paradigm interplay
leads to a philosophical turn for systemic design in the context of the 21st century.

Wicked problems; systems approach; pattern language; ecological epistemology; hierarchy theory; interactive value

1. Introduction

Generative pattern language, in its history, was originally intended for the domain of "town, buildings, construction" (Alexander, Ishikawa, & Silverstein, 1977). In an early specification for multi-service centers, the prototype design ...

> *... deals chiefly with the spatial organization; but since human and spatial organization cannot properly be separated, many of the specifications given in this report go into questions of human organization as well. [....]*
>
> *The ultimate purpose of a prototype design, then, is to provide guidelines which will generate a large number of specific buildings (Alexander, Ishikawa, & Silverstein, 1968, p. 1).*

The original charter for the Center for Environment Structure was clear in its emphasis on the built environment.

> *The pattern format is designed to express ideas about the physical environment in a clear way. In doing so, it opens these ideas up to exacting criticism and improvement (Alexander, Ishikawa, & Silverstein, 1967, p. 1).*

The PURPLSOC community acknowledges "invariant spatial patterns associated with the stability of human-environmental systems in both towns and buildings", with the pattern approach ...

> *... beyond architecture and urban design and ... in many other disparate fields, such as design, media, arts, IT, management, pedagogy, social activism, social innovation and diverse grassroots movements. [....] The PURPLSOC (In Pursuit of Pattern Languages for Societal Change) platform aims to substantiate the broad applicability and richness of pattern related work in all fields, and by sharing best practice examples from outside the scientific community to further raise awareness of this approach to encompass the wider public. Additionally PURPLSOC offers a platform to discuss and study Alexander's most recent research work ....*
>
> *(Baumgartner & Sickinger, 2014, p. 3)*

More generally, pattern language can be seen as an approach to ill-structured problems. In the domain emphasizing organizational ill-structured problems – "problems which involve more than one person in their formulation, solution, implementation and evaluation":

> *... an ideal of "pure type" ill-structured problem is defined as one which possesses one or more of the following characteristics (Rittel, 1971): (a) The problem is well-defined in the*

sense that it can be clearly stated but those charged with dealing with it cannot agree upon an appropriate solution or strategy; (b) they cannot agree on a methodology for developing such a strategy; or (c) they cannot even agree on a clear formulation (definition) of the problem (objectives, controllable variables and uncontrollable variables). Simply stated, ill-structured problems are who Ackoff (Ackoff, 1974) has termed "messes": they are complex mixtures of highly interdependent important problems that by definition cannot be formulated, let alone solve, independently of one another (Ian I. Mitroff & Emshoff, 1979, p. 1).

With pattern language, the work of Christopher Alexander is one approach towards dealing with ill-structured problems. Alternative approaches are not only in practice today, but were also in active development by the late 1960s.

Appreciating the variety of approaches may involve crossing paradigms. Giving due diligence, three questions are addressed in the text that follows.

1. What is multiparadigm inquiry?
2. Where have (and might have) (1960s-2010s) paradigms influenced generative
3. pattern language?
4. Why might a pattern language project or community pay more attention to its
5. paradigm?

This exposition serves as a prequel to a "Pattern Manual for Service Systems Thinking" (xxx, 2016) , in the same way that the "Pattern Manual" (Alexander et al., 1967) was a beginning for the work in built physical environments.

2. What is multiparadigm inquiry?

"Inquiry is an activity which produces knowledge" (Churchman, 1971, p. 5) . While a library can be a "collection of information", a pragmatic action conception of knowledge sees that "knowledge resides in the user and not in the collection" (Churchman, 1971, p. 10) .

Modern science is a creator of knowledge. A critical view of science surfaces some limits.

There will be the suggestion that science's mode of representing nature is very restricted, so that it cannot even talk about some of its most pressing problems and specifically its relationship to other social systems. For example, science has no adequate way of studying its own relationship to politics, to religion, or even to a system apparently quite close to its own interests, education. As a system, science cannot discuss social change (implementation) in any but a very restricted sense (Churchman, 1971, p. 18).

These issues with science lead us to philosophy. The philosophy of science studies what qualifies as science, the reliability of science, and the ultimate purpose of science. *The Structure of Scientific Revolutions* (Kuhn, 1967) is a well known and often cited work by graduate students across a broad spectrum of disciplines.

2.1. The structure of scientific revolutions is built on paradigms and shifts

The Oxford English Dictionary provides 4 major definitions of science, of which our interestfalls primarily on the fourth.

> *1. A pattern or model, an exemplar; (also) a typical instance of something, an example.*
>
> *2.*
>
> *a. Grammar. In the traditional grammar of Latin, Greek, and other inflected languages: a pattern or table showing all the inflected forms of a particular verb, noun, or adjective, serving as a model for other words of the same conjugation or declension. Also fig.*
>
> *b. Linguistics. A set of units which are linguistically substitutable in a given context, esp. a syntactic one.*
>
> *3. Rhetoric. A figure of speech in which a comparison is made by resemblance; = paradigma n. 1. rare.*
>
> **4. A conceptual or methodological model underlying the theories and practices of a science or discipline at a particular time; (hence) a generally accepted world view. 1962 T. S. Kuhn Struct. Sci. Revol. ii. 10 'Normal science' means research firmly based upon one or more past scientific achievements..that some particular scientific community acknowledges..as supplying the foundation for its further practice... I..refer to [these achievements] as 'paradigms'.**

Thomas Kuhn saw normal science under a paradigm, with revolutionary transitions to the next paradigm. This is depicted in Figure 1.

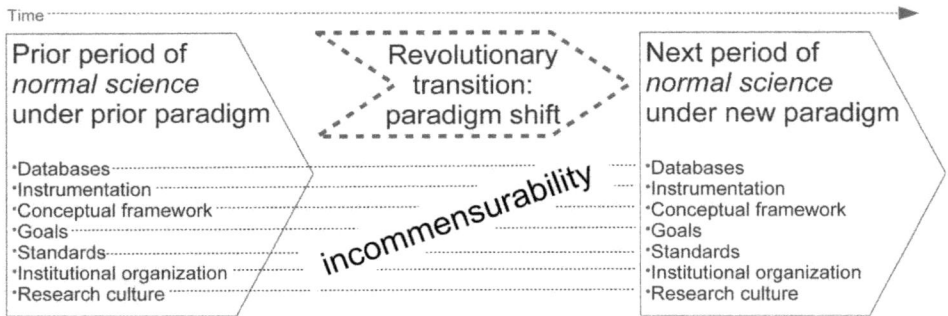

Figure 1: Normal science, scientific revolution, new paradigm

> *Kuhn modeled the history of a science as a succession of dogmatic periods of "normal science" under a "paradigm", separated by "revolutionary" transitions to the next paradigm. According to Kuhn such a break from the past rejuvenates a field that had stagnated under the weight of anomalies that it no longer seemed to have the resources to solve. A new paradigm introduces changes at all levels, from established databases and instrumentation to the conceptual framework, goals, standards, institutional organization, and research culture—so much so that some older practitioners can hardly recognize the new paradigm as their field. This disconnect produces "incommensurability" across paradigm change, ranging from communication failure to problems of rational choice between the two, since there exists no fixed measure of success (Nickles, 2017).*

If a fine distinction were to be made, a worldview is based on values and beliefs, whereas a paradigm relates to constructs that scientists count as knowledge. Individual human beings each have a world view. Groups of scientists can share a paradigm.

2.2. Multiple paradigms can be recognized in concurrent plurality

In the social sciences, theories of organization can be conceptualized with sets of assumptions related to ontology, epistemology, human nature and methodology. Mapping along the dimensions of (i) the nature of science as subjective or as objective, and (ii) the nature of society in terms of regulation or radical change, four paradigms are described: (a) a functionalist paradigm (with objective regulation); (b) an interpretive paradigm (with subjective regulation); (c) a radical humanist paradigm (with subjective radical change); and (d) a radical structuralist paradigm (with objective radical change), drawn in Figure 2. These define "very basic meta-theoretical assumptions which underwrite frame of reference, mode of theorising and modus operandi" of the theorists who operate within them (Burrell & Morgan, 1979, p. 23).

THE SOCIOLOGY OF RADICAL CHANGE

"Radical humanist"	"Radical structuralist"
"Interpretive"	"Functionalist"

SUBJECTIVE — — — — — OBJECTIVE

THE SOCIOLOGY OF REGULATION

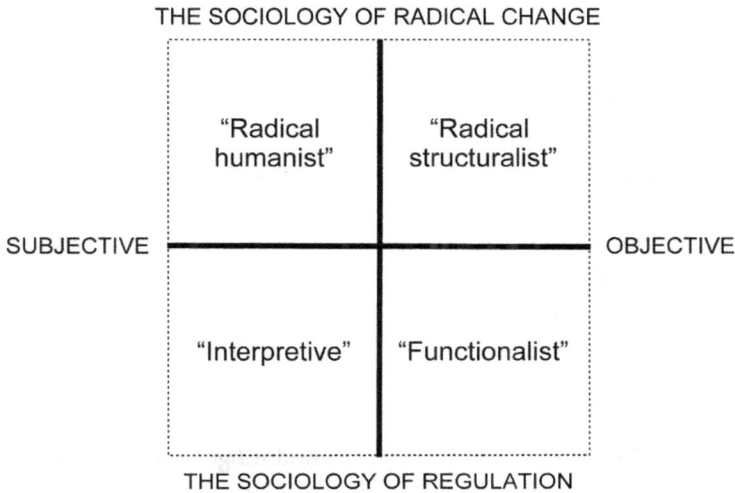

Figure 2: Four paradigms for the analysis of social theory (Burrell & Morgan, 1979, p. 22)

The Burrell-Morgan four paradigms often show up in organizational analysis. In the domain of management information systems, "from study to study, the indisputable consensus is that positivism dominates information systems research" (Goles & Hirschheim, 2000, p. 254), as in Figure 3.

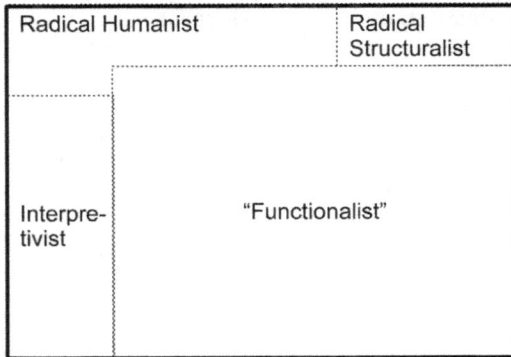

Radical Humanist	Radical Structuralist
Interpre- tivist	"Functionalist"

Figure 3: Proportional representation in IS research (Goles & Hirschheim, 2000, p. 254)

Creating a 2x2 matrix does not, however, constitute a paradigmatic framework. With a "linguistic turn" in social theory, an alternative view sees the dimensions of (i) the origin of concepts and problem statements as part of the constitutive process in research, ranging from "local / emergent" research conceptions to "elite / a priori" ones; and (ii) the relation of research practices to the dominant social discourses within the organization studies, from a "consensus discourse" (with reproductive practice in knowledge, social relations and identity) to a "dissensus" that works as a productive practice that disrupts the structures. These can be represented in a 2x2 matrix, but the "mistake" of labelling these as four paradigms is not taken (Deetz, 1996).

Researchers, rather than choosing to operate within a single paradigm, can investigate the variety of modes of rationality. Multiparadigm inquiry contrasts with modern and postmo ern stances in Table 1.

	Modern	Multiparadigm	Postmodern
Ideology	**Centering** Focus on authorship, promote chosen voices, beliefs and issues. Sharpen selective focus	**Accommodating** Value divergent paradigm lenses Explore paradox and plurality	**De-centering** Stress fluctuating and fragmented discourses Accentuate difference and uncertainty
Ontology	**Strong** States of being Entities are distinct, determinant and comprehensible	**Stratified** Multiple dimensions Expose interplay of entities and processes	**Weak** Processes of becoming Meanings are indeterminant, in constant flux and transformation
Epistemology	**Restricted** Employ paradigm prescriptions systematically Construct cohesive representations to advance paradigm development	**Pluralist** Apply divergent paradigm lenses Reflect organizational tensions and encourage greater reflexivity	**Eclectic** Use varied methods freely Deconstruct organizational contexts and processes to produce small stories or modest narratives

Table 1: Alternative approaches to inquiry (Lewis & Kelemen, 2002, p. 254)

Modern paradigms focus on cohesive and static representations. Postmodernism has fragmented and fluctuating discourses. Multiparadigm inquiry seeks to employ and link divergent perspectives with two goals: (i) to encourage greater awareness of theoretical alternatives and thereby facilitate discourse and/or inquiry across paradigms; and (ii) to foster greater understandings of organizational plurality and paradox (Lewis & Kelemen, 2002, p. 258).

3. Where have (and might have) (1960s-2010s) paradigms influenced generative pattern language?

A pattern language initiative may be as ambitious as the books that have taken a decade to complete, or as practical as a project language (Motohashi, Hanyuda, & Nakano, 2013). A group or community may implicitly or explicitly have a paradigm that is internally consistent and externally valid to varying degrees. The universe of works on pattern language – and its influences -- date back to the mid 1960s. Some notable books and journals articles published over that period are listed as exemplars of alternative views.

3.1. Over 50 years, Christopher Alexander and coauthors evolved concepts

Christopher Alexander was undoubtedly a chief driver behind the popularization of pattern language. As a researcher, however, his writing and language gradually evolved.

In 1964, Notes on the Synthesis of Form focused on the "process of design" and "goodness of fit" (Alexander, 1964).

In 1965, "A City is Not a Tree" described "natural cities" in contrast with "artificial cities" and introduced the mathematical form of a "semilattice" (Alexander, 1966).

In 1967, "Pattern Manual" was a charter for The Center for Environmental Structure (CES) at Berkeley, describing its activities in (i) publication, distribution and criticism of patterns; (ii) design and invention of patterns; and (iii) basic research. The immediate and future plans named initial staff and associates, with an expectation of two years for the center to become organized and self-sufficient. A pattern format was proposed as a hypothesis, with examples of (i) locating house numbers in a residential zone from a moving car, and (ii) encouraging the formation of social groups by organizing rooms around common lounges or corridors. "Each pattern statement contains a number of parts and describes the spatial relations among those parts" (Alexander et al., 1967, p. 11).

In 1968, "Systems Generating Systems" was published following a commission of the Systemat exhibit display for the Aspen Design Conference, written in 1967 as a monograph for Inland Steel. This article introduced the ties between systems thinking and its application to built environments.

> *1. There are two ideas hidden in the word system: the idea of a system as a whole and the idea of a generating system.*
>
> *2. A system as a whole is not an object but a way of looking at an object. It focuses on some holistic property which can only be understood as a product of interaction among parts.*
>
> *3. A generating system is not a view of a single thing. It is a kit of parts, with rules about the way these parts may be combined. 4. Almost every 'system as a whole' is generated by a 'generating system'. If we wish to make things which function as 'wholes' we shall have to invent generating systems to create them. [....]*
>
> *In a properly functioning building, the building and the people in it together form a whole: a social, human whole. The building systems which have so far been created do not in this sense generate wholes at all. (Alexander, 1968, p. 605)*

This 1967 writing on "Systems Generating Systems" can be fleshed out in the broader context of *The Timeless Way of Building* (Alexander, 1979) and the 1983 publication of interviews with Alexander (Grabow, 1983) in the distinctions between generative systems and non-generative systems (Steenson, 2014).

In 1968, *A Pattern Language which Generates Multi-Service Centers* demonstrates how a pattern language could become instantiated differently for a variety of sites and circumstances. These community facilities were to provide a variety of special services to citizens, particularly in low-income communities. Eight buildings generated the by pattern language were described for Hunts Point, San Francisco, Brooklyn, Bowery, Phoenix, Newark, and two in Harlem (Alexander et al., 1968).

In 1975, The Oregon Experiment was named as third volume from the Center for Environmental Structure, yet the first book released. The experiment was a master plan for the University of Oregon, presented as a practical manifestation. This community was unique, with a single owner (The State of Oregon) and a single, centralized budget. The book outline six principles of implementation:

> • *(i) organic order, with the whole emerging gradually from local acts;*
>
> • *(ii) participation, with decisions in the hands of the users;*
>
> • *(iii) piecemeal growth, with construction weighted overwhelmingly towards small projects;*

• *(iv) patterns, as communally adopted planning principles;*

• *(v) diagnosis of well-being of the whole, through annual detailing of spaces alive and dead; and*

• *(vi) coordination, through a funding process regulating the stream of individual projects put forward by users (Alexander, Silverstein, Angel, Ishikawa, & Abrams, 1975, p. 6).*

In 1977, *A Pattern Language: Towns, Buildings, Construction* was released as the second volume from the CES. The language starts with the largest scale patterns defining a town or community (1. Independent Regions ... 94. Sleeping in Public), then groups of buildings and individual buildings on the land (95. Building Complex ... 204 Secret Place), and lastly a building from the rough scheme of spaces (205. Structure Follows Social Spaces ... 253. Things from Your Life). Starting with 253 patterns, "Choosing a Language for Your Project" suggests "taking patterns from this language we have printed here, and then by adding patterns of your own" (Alexander et al., 1977, p. Xxxviii).

In 1979, *The Timeless Way of Building*, named as the first volume from the CES, was released after the other two. The Timeless Way "is a process which brings order out of nothing but ourselves; it cannot be attained, but it will happen of its own accord, if we will only let it" (Alexander, 1979, p. 3). *The Quality without a Name* "is the root criterion of life and spirit in man, a town, a building, or a wilderness. This quality is objective and precise, but it cannot be named" (Alexander, 1979, p. 19). The Gate is a living pattern language that must be built. The Way is the practice relating the pattern language common to a group of people "who adopt it as the basis for the reconstruction of their world" (Alexander, 1979, p. 353). *The Kernel of the Way* "has nothing, in the end, to do with languages", but instead "merely release the fundamental order which is native to us" (Alexander, 1979, p. 531).

In 1999, "The Origins of Pattern Theory" was published in IEEE Software (Alexander, 1999), based on a 1996 talk at the OOPSLA conference of the Association for Computing Machinery (Alexander, 1996b). Alexander described the pattern language for built environments has having three essential features: (i) a moral component; (ii) an aim of creating morphological coherence; and (iii) generativity to produce living structure. He saidthat he hadn't seen evidence of either the moral component nor generativity in software pattern theory. The content previewed work forthcoming in *The Nature of Order*.

From 2002 to 2005, the four volumes of *The Nature of Order* were released. Book One, *The Phenomenon of Life* described the phenomenon of life; wholeness and the theory of cen ters; and fifteen fundamental properties (i.e. "objects and buildings which have life all have certain identifiable structural characteristics. The same geometric features keep showing up inthem, again and again") (Alexander, 2002a, p. 144). Alexander's definition of the nature of order, "unites the objective and subjective, it shows us that order as the foundation of all things ... is both rooted in substance and rooted in feeling, is at once objective in a scientific sense, yet all also substantial in the sense of poetry, in the sense of feelings which make us human, which make us in secret and vulnerable thoughts, just what we are" (Alexander, 2002a, p. 298).

Book Two, *The Process of Creating Life*, proposes a dynamic view of order. Instead of being concerned with design as a static structure, becoming is an essential feature of the buil- ding process. Mentioning David Bohm, Alexander describes a process "which I mean by 'emergence of the wholeness' and by 'emergence of the configuration from the wholeness'" (Alexander, 2002b, p. 19) becomes described as "unfolding wholeness". Structurepreserving transformation preserves the balance as a system of centers modifies other centers within the whole. "The wholeness is changed, since the relative strength of centers has changed. The centers have not changed greatly, only slightly. Yet this slight change changes the who- leness of the entire configuration, and by our making the intensification, a new structure more highly differentiated that before has been created" (Alexander, 2002b, p. 53).

Book Three, *A Vision of a Living World*, shows examples of "buildings, neighbourhoods, gar- dens, public space, wilderness, house, construction details, color, ornament" (Alexander, 2005, p. 5).

Book Four, *The Luminous Ground*, deals with the inner meaning for the builder. "My hypothe- sis is this: that all value depends on a structure in which each center, the life of each center, approaches this simple, forgotten, remembered, unremembered "I" ... that in the living work of each center, in some degree, is a connection to this "I", or self ...." (Alexander, 2004a, p. 3). "I believe it is in the nature of matter, that it is soaked through with self or "I" (Alexander, 2004a, p. 8).

In 2003, a short overview for a scientific audience was released as "New Concepts in Com- plexity Theory", and released on natureoforder.com web site. "The beauty of naturally oc- curring patterns and forms has rarely been discussed by scientists as a practical matter, as something needing to be explained, and as part of science itself. Yet the fifteen trans- formations, if indeed they provide a primary thrust in the engine of evolution, and in the many engines of pattern formation, give us a way of understanding how beauty -- aesthetics -- plays a concrete role, not an incidental role, in the formation of the universe. (Alexander, 2003, p. 21).

In 2004, "Sustainability and Morphogenesis: The Birth of a Living World" was presented as a Schumacher Lecture in the UK. The speech asserted three empirical propositions:

> *(1) When environments are built by morphogenesis they will of their own accord become sustainable.*
>
> *(2) Among strategies for dealing with sustainability, morphogenesis alone can deal with ALL the issues of sustainability together.*
>
> *(3) This effort will reorient all our efforts, and achieve the deeper agenda of the sustainable movement, in a form that is more profoundly satisfying, and more in keeping with our social and cultural aspirations (Alexander, 2004b, p. 3).*

In 2005, version 17 of a draft of "Generative Codes" was posted on the livingneighborhoods. org web site. A "generative feature of urban codes – that the code must contain a description of the approximate sequence in which the elements of the code are best brought forth in order that a living while whole may unfold successfully from them – is natural and ordinary" (Alexander, Schmidt, Hanson, & Mehaffy, 2005, p. 3).

In 2007, "Empirical Findings from *The Nature of Order*" presented 59 "results that summarize 30 years of observation and experience", with 25 judged as both testable and tested marked as "demonstrated" (Alexander, 2007). In result 16, Alexander notes that as a replacement for the term "structure-preserving transformation" used in the Book 2, he has adopted "the more expressive term 'wholeness-extending'".

The 2015 publication of *The Battle for the Life and Beauty of the Earth: A Struggle Between Two World-Systems* describes the methods and experiences of building the Eishin School in Japan circa 1985. The practices of creating a pattern language, dealing with construction budget and then laying out the buildings on the land (rather than drawing blueprints) is a thick description of dealing with stakeholders and the physicality in the built environment.

Tracing through this long history of works, some general themes are consistent, yet the language to describe them evolves. The later work aimed towards developing stronger theoretical foundations raises questions about the implicit paradigm in Alexander's philosophy of science.

3.2. At Berkeley, Churchman, Rittel and Alexander taught in the 1960s-1970s

In the 1960s and 1970s, Christopher Alexander was not the only professor interested in the challenges of ill-structured problems. The Design Methods Movement was "the result of post war optimism and a belief that making design more scientific would help to produce a better world. However, it became clear that real world problems were 'wicked', requiring a different approach from the application of scientific techniques developed during World War II" (Langrish, 2016, p. 1). Centered on a "Conference on Design Methods" in London in 1962, the key figures were considered to be Bruce Archer, John Chris Jones, Christopher Alexander and Horst Rittel. By 1971, Alexander had resigned from the board of editors of the DMG Newsletter, because he felt that the intent to create well-defined procedures which would enable people to design better buildings had been lost. "I believe passionately in the idea that people should design buildings for themselves. In other words, not only that they should be involved in the buildings that are for them but that they should actually help design them" (Alexander & Jacobson, 1971).

At the University of California Berkeley, there were some other major figures just on campus. A student at that time could observe the interactions.

> *Both Alexander and Rittel were part of what at the time was called the „design methods'*
> *movement in architecture, worked and taught in the same building, and did talk and were*
> *seen walking off to have lunch together. Churchman was teaching in the Business School a*
> *few minutes down on the way to the center of campus (Mann, 2017).*

Christopher Alexander, Horst Rittel and West Churchman were all influential thinkers at the intersection of design and systems thinking, and on the faculty at Berkeley.

C. West Churchman (1913-2004) joined Berkeley in 1957, cofounding the graduate programs in Operations Research at the School of Business Administration (Ulrich, 2009). From 1964 to 1970, he was Associate Director and Research Philosopher at the Space Sciences Laboratory. That influence would show up in publications by his students, including *The Subjective Side of Science: A Philosophical Inquiry Into the Psychology of the Apollo Moon Scientists* (Ian I. Mitroff, 1974), Creating a dialectical social science: Concepts, methods, and models (Ian I. Mitroff & Mason, 1981), and *Challenging strategic planning assumptions: theory, cases, and techniques* (Mason & Mitroff, 1981). After his retirement in 1981, Churchman continued to teach Peace & Conflict Studies at the university.

Horst W.J. Rittel (1930-1990) came to Berkeley in 1963, into the College of Environmental

Design. That college had come together in 1959 with the three schools of architecture, landscape architecture and urban planning orchestrated into a single organization by dean William Wurster. Having previously taught at Hochschule für Gestaltung (HfG) Ulm, Rittel introduced cybernetics into operations research at Berkeley (Rith & Dubberly, 2007). Rittel was a key figure in the Design Methods Movement internationally, and was a cofounder of the Design Methods Group at Berkeley. By 1972, a second-generation design method was being proposed:

> *Protzen: Then the change in attitude calls for different procedures, and these procedures if developed you would call 'second-generation' procedures?*

> *Rittel: Yes. And these methods are characterized by a number of traits, one of them being that the design process is not considered to be a sequence of activities that are pretty well defined and that are carried through one after the other, like 'understand the problem, collect information, analyse information, synthesize, decide', and so on; and another being that you cannot understand the problem without having a concept of the solution in mind; and that you cannot gather information meaningfully unless you have understood the problem but that you cannot understand the problem without information without it – in other words that all the categories of the typical design model of the first generation do not exist any more, and that ll those difficulties that these phases are supposed to deal with occur all the time in a fashion which depends on the state of the understanding of the problem. The second feature of the second generation is that it is argumentative, as I explained before. That means that the statement made are systematically challenged in order to expose them to viewpoints of the different sides, and the structure of the process becomes one of alternating steps on the micro-level; that means the generation of solution specifications towards end statement and subjecting them discussion of their pros and cons. This process in turn raises questions of a factual nature and questions of a deontic or ought-to-be-nature. In the treatment of such factual or deontic questions in the course of dealing with an issue many of the traditional methods of the first generation may become tools, used to support or attack any of the positions taken. You might make a cost-benefit study as an argument against somebody else's deontic statements, or you might use an operations research model in order to support a prediction or argue against somebody's prediction. However, I wouldn't say that the methods are the same just in a different arrangement and with a different attitude, but that there are some methods particular to second generation, and that these are in particular the rules for structuring arguments, and that these are new, and not in the group of methods developed in the first generation (Rittel, Grant, & Protzen, 1972).*

In 1974, Rittel was appointed to the Institut für Grundlagen der Planung at Universität Stuttgart. He continued travelling back and forth between Germany and California as "an international commuter splitting his time between the two institutions" (Churchman, Protzen, & Webber, 1992).

Christopher Alexander (born 1936) joined the faculty of the College of Environmental Design at Berkeley in 1963, also at the invitation of dean William Wurster. In 1967, he cofounded the Center for Environmental Structure with the staff and associates listed as: Tamas I. Bartha, Alan M. Hershdorfer, Sara Ishikawa, Roslyn Lindheim, Marvin L. Manheim, Harris Savin, Murray Silverstein, Sim Van der Ryn, plus himself (Alexander et al., 1967, p. 6). In 1998, Alexander officially retired from the university. He received a grant from Bill Joy at Sun Microsystems to complete *The Nature of Order* (Brown, 2000).

While the majority of today's scholars read and cite Alexander, Rittel and Churchman as independent luminaries, the graduate students at Berkeley in the 1970s with an interest in planning could easily cross over from the colleges of environmental design and business administration. Those alumni went on to full careers, and the majority are in retirement. In the 21st century, we now have the opportunity to not start from scratch, but to stand on the shoulders of their continued learning.

An open system of knowledge should recognize (and potentially reconcile, adopt and/or embrace) parallel research in alternative streams of thought.

3.3. Architecture ~ problem-seeking; Design ~ problem-solving

Pattern language originated in the planning and construction of built environments. Thus, distinctions between architecture and design may clarify the premises on which conceptualization takes place.

In 1969, *Problem Seeking: New directions in architectural programming* described distinctions that were in use at an architecture firm in Texas, as drawn in Figure 4.

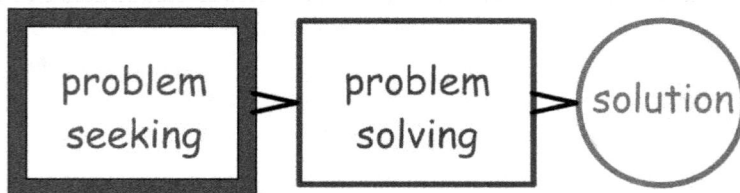

Figure 4: Programming is problem seeking; design is problem solving (Peña & Focke, 1969)

> *Programming is a specialized and often misunderstood term. It is "a statement of an architectural problem and the requirements to be met in offering a solution". While the term is used with other descriptive adjectives such as computer programming, educational programming, functional programming, etc., in this report, programming is used to refer only to architectural programming. Why programming? The client has a project with many unidentified sub-problems. The architect must define the client's total problem. Design is problem solving; programming is problem seeking. The end of the programming process is a statement of the total problem; such a statement is the element that joins programming and design. The "total problem" then serves to point up constituent problems, in terms of four considerations, those of form, function, economy and time. The aim of the programming is to provide a sound basis for effective design. The State of the Problem represents the essense and the uniqueness of the project. Furthermore, it suggests the solution to the problem by defining the main issues and giving direction to the designer (Peña & Focke, 1969, p. 3).*

The original illustration of a linear process may be unfortunate, as some circularity between problem solving and problem seeking may be conceptually interpreted between the lines.

In 1971, "Some Principles for Design of an Educational System for Design" outlines the kind of knowledge that guides architects and designers.

> *Instrumental knowledge relates three kinds of entities with each other. These three entities, which can be described as variable which can assume different values are:*
>
> *1. Performance variables, which express desired characteristics of the object under design, and in terms of which the object will be evaluated ("construction cost", "esthetic appeal", "overall quality" and the like).*
>
> *2. Design variables, which describe the possibilities of the designer, his range of choice, his design variables, the things he has some control over ("height of ceiling", "shape of door knob", "type of heating", and the like).*
>
> *3. Context variables, which are those factors affecting the object to be designed but not controlled by the designer "land price", "height of people", "likelihood of earthquakes", "type of eating habits", and so forth).*
>
> *If we call (O) a specification of the performance of an object O, (i.e. a statement aboutthe observed, desired, or predicted performance of O), if we write D(O) for a specification of design variables of O (as intended or actual), and if C(O) describes a particular constellation of the context of O, then the general format for an item of instrumental knowledge becomes (in the simplest case):*

"Under context C(O), design configuration D(O) will lead to performance P(O)". (Rittel, 1971, p. 20)

In addition, the design process and the structure of the designer's knowledge has some intellectual difficulties that recur.

1. To assess the worthwhileness of a project.

2. To determine the appropriate level of a problem.

3. To determine the nature of the solution.

4. To construct and evaluation system.

5. To anticipate the context of the object.

6. To identify a relevant solution space.

7. To constrain the solution space.

8. To construct a system of functional relationships which connect design variables, context variables and performance variables with each other.

9. To find an appropriate solution in the solution space.

10. To avoid undesired side- and after-effects of a planning.

11. To implement a solution proposal.

12. To test the results (Rittel, 1971, pp. 21–23).

As a basic dilemma of human existence, reasoning is challenged by anticipating action, and nonrational spontaneous action is irresponsible.

In 2006, a distinction between architecture and design in software has become a conventional wisdom.

The aforementioned Dick Gabriel posed a question to the Hillside Group: what is design? Here's my reply to him:

As a noun, design is the named (although sometimes unnamable) structure or behavior of a system whose presence resolves or contributes to the resolution of a force or forces on that system. A design thus represents one point in a potential decision space. A design may be singular (representing a leaf decision) or it may be collective (representing a set of other decisions).

As a verb, design is the activity of making such decisions. Given a large set of forces, a relatively malleable set of materials, and a large landscape upon which to play, the resulting decision space may be large and complex. As such, there is a science associated with design (empirical analysis can point us to optimal regions or exact points in this design space) as well as an art (within the degrees of freedom that range beyond an empirical decision; there are opportunities for elegance, beauty, simplicity, novelty, and cleverness).

A few related terms:

All architecture is design but not all design is architecture. *Architecture represents the significant design decisions that shape a system, where significant is measured by cost of change (Booch, 2006).*

In this paradigm of architecture and design, there are distinctions made between the two. In comparison, the Alexandrian paradigm doesn't emphasize the same distinction, although there is a gradient of abstraction from patterns in a language through to completion of the finished built environment.

3.4. Wicked problems led to IBIS and argumentation schemes

The phrase "wicked problems" was first related to social issues associated with planning that included urban environments.

In 1967, "Wicked Problems" were first surfaced in the journal Management Science as a result of conversations occurring at Berkeley.

Professor Horst Rittel of the University of California Architecture Department has suggested in a recent seminar that the term „wicked problem" refer to that class of social system problems which are ill-formulated, where the information is confusing, where there are many clients and decision makers with conflicting values, and where the ramifications in the whole system are thoroughly confusing. The adjective „wicked" is supposed to describe the mischievous and even evil quality of these problems, where proposed „solutions" often turn out to be worse than the symptoms. [....]

Rittel suggested that there are various attempts to „tame" these wicked problems, among which must be counted the efforts of operations research and management science. Sometimes the taming consists of trying to generate an aura of good feeling or consensus. Sometimes, as in OR, it consists of „carving off" a piece of the problem and finding a rational and feasible solution to this piece. In the latter case, it is up to someone else (presumably a manager) to handle the untamed part. [....]

The moral principle is this: whoever attempts to tame a part of a wicked problem, but not the whole, is morally wrong (Churchman, 1967, pp. B141–B142).

In 1970, "Issues as Elements of Information Systems" was published as a working paper from the Institute of Urban and Regional Development at Berkeley.

Issue-Based Information Systems (IBIS) are meant to support coordination and planning of political decision processes. IBIS guides the identification, structuring and settling of issues raised by problem-solving groups, and provides information pertinent to the discourse. It is linked to conventional documentation systems but also activates other sources. Element of the system are topics, issues, questions of fact, positions, arguments and model problems (Kunz & Rittel, 1970, p. 1).

In 1973, "Dilemmas in a General Theory of Planning" formalized wicked problems with goal formation and problem definition.

There are at least ten distinguishing properties of planning-type problems, i.e. wicked ones .... We use the term "wicked" in a meaning akin to that of "malignant" (in contrast to "benign") or "vicious" (like a circle) or "tricky" (like a leprechaun) or "aggressive" (like a lion, in contrast to the docility of a lamb). [....]

1. There is no definitive formulation of a wicked problem ....

2. Wicked problems have no stopping rule ....

3. Solutions to wicked problems are not true-or-false, but good-or-bad ....

4. There is no immediate and no ultimate test of a solution to a wicked problem ....

5. Every solution to a wicked problem is a „one-shot operation"; because there is no opportunity to learn by trial-and-error, every attempt counts significantly ....

6. Wicked problems do not have an enumerable (or an exhaustively describable) set of potential solutions, nor is there a well-described set of permissible operations that may be incorporated into the plan ....

7. Every wicked problem is essentially unique ....

8. Every wicked problem can be considered to be a symptom of another problem ....

9. The existence of a discrepancy representing a wicked problem can be explained in numerous ways. The choice of explanation determines the nature of the problem's resolution ....

10. The planner has no right to be wrong ....

What was once a clear-cut win-win strategy, that had the status of a near-truism, has now become a source of contentious differences among subpublics. [....]

Our point ... is that diverse values are held by different groups of individuals -- that what satisfies one may be abhorrent to another, that what comprises problem-solution for one is problem-generation for another. Under such circumstances, and in the absence of an overriding social theory or an overriding social ethic, there is no gainsaying which group is right and which should have its ends served (Rittel & Webber, 1973, pp. 160–169).

In 1980, "APIS: A Concept for an Argumentative Planning Information System" reported on progress on IBIS for planning.

APIS (Argumentative Planning Information System) ... is specifically tailed to a particular class of planning situations. It is meant to be useful to in the context of government planning, on local, state, national or international levels. It is not intended to support the treatment of problems of physical planning (such as the design of buildings, engineering design, or managerial planning. APIS is laid out for policy planning, the design of legislation, the development of government programs, and similar tasks (Rittel, 1980, p. 3).

In 1987, "gIBIS: A Hypertext Tool of Team Design Deliberation" extended Rittel's work with technology.

The IBIS model focuses on the articulation of the key Issues in the design problem. Each Issue can have many Positions, where a Position is a statement or assertion which resolves the Issue. Often Positions will be mutually exclusive of one another, but the method does not support this. Each of an Issue's Positions, in turn, may have one or more Arguments which either support that Position or object to it. [....]

There were three technological themes guiding our design of gIBIS. The first was an interest in exploring the capture of design rationale .... The second was an interest in supporting computer mediated teamwork, and particularly the various kinds of design conversations that might be carried on via networked computers, a la email or news .... Thirdly, we wanted an application in which we would have a sufficiently large information base to investigate issues regarding the navigation (i.e. search and browsing) of very large and loosely structured information spaces (Conklin & Begeman, 1987, p. 248).

In 2003, "Facilitated Hypertext for Collective Sensemaking: 15 years on from gIBIS" brought together researchers who had worked on Compendium for a reflection.

> *With the benefit of 15 years' hindsight, we can see the failure of so many DR [design ratio-nale] systems to be adopted as symptomatic of the more general problem of fostering new kinds of 'literacy' in real working environments. Pursuing Engelbart's goal of "augmenting human intellect", we describe the Compendium approach to collective sensemaking, which demonstrates the impact that a facilitator can have on the learning and adoption prob-lems that plagued earlier DR systems. We also describe how conventional documents and modelling notations can be morphed into and out of Compendium's 'native hypertext' in order to support other modes of working across diverse communities of practice (Conklin, Selvin, Shum, & Sierhuis, 2001, p. 1).*

In this paradigm on wicked problems, collaborative planning including political positioning has been structured with argumentation schemes and facilitated with graphical electronic technologies. In comparison, the Alexandrian paradigm uses rough sketches that are ma-terialized into physical environments that can be continually evaluated with stakeholders.

3.5. Systems approach led to assumption surfacing, postnormal science

The systems approach has its roots in the development of General Systems Theory, and has evolved with an appreciation of inquiring systems.

In 1956, "General Systems Theory: The Skeleton of Science" described model-building so-mewhere between generalized constructions (pure mathematics) and specialized theories (disciplines).

> *[The quest of General Systems Theory is] for a body of systematic theoretical constructs which will discuss the general relationships of the empirical world. It does not seek, of course, to establish a single, self-contained "general theory of practically everything" which will replace all the special theories of particular disciplines. Such a theory would be almost without content, for we always pay for generality by sacrificing content, and all we can say about practically everything is almost nothing. Somewhere however between the specific that has no meaning and the general that has no content there must be, for each purpose and at each level of abstraction, an optimum degree of generality (Boulding, 1956, pp. 197–198).*

In 1968, The Systems Approach described a shift from operations research, where the per-spective of scientists broadened.

> *Systems are made up of sets of components that work together for the overall objective of the whole. The systems approach is simply a way of thinking about these total systems and their components. We have already seen one essential feature of this way of thinking, na-*

mely, that thinking enters in at the very outset of dictating the manner in which we describe what it is we are planing to do (Churchman, 1968, pp. 11–12).

In 1971, The Design of Inquiring Systems was targeted at interests of philosophical issues of design, of inquiry, and of social systems.

> *We are specifically interested in the design of systems, i.e., of structures that have organized components. [....]*
>
> *Inquiry is an activity which produces knowledge (Churchman, 1971, pp. 7–8).*

In 1979, The Systems Approach and its Enemies tackled the challenges with improving systems as a whole.

> *Common to all these enemies is that none of them accepts the reality of the „whole system": we do not exist in such a system. Furthermore, in the case of morality, religion, and aesthetics, at least a part of our reality as human is not „in" any system, and yet it plays a central role in our lives.*
>
> *To me these enemies provide a powerful way of learning about the systems approach, precisely because they enable the rational mind to step outside itself and to observe itself (from the vantage point of the enemies). [....]*
>
> *We must face the reality that the enemies offer: what's really happening in the human world is politics, or morality, or religion, or aesthetics. This confrontation with reality is totally different from the rational approach, because the reality of the enemies cannot be conceptualized, approximated, or measured (Churchman, 1979, pp. 24–53).*

In 1981, *Challenging Strategic Planning Assumptions, where decision-making under conditions of uncertainty and turbulence are not only dealt with effectively, but potentially as opportunities.*

> *[Our] theory of real world problem solving attempts to incorporate each of these ideals:*
>
> *1. **Democracy** The ideal that all parties have a right and a capacity to participate in problem solving and to benefit from the result.*
>
> *2. **Scientific method** The ideal that the most appropriate scientific techniques should be used to produce knowledge for problem solving.*
>
> *3. **Empiricism** The ideal that all problem solving should have a grounded experiential referent in the real world.*

4. **Evolution** *The idea that all problems are couched in a dynamic context and that they change and evolve through time. Real world problem solving is eternally restless.*

Further, we draw on a fifth ideal, holism – the ideal that all problems are linked to others and must be dealt with as a whole. This does not mean that one must solve all problems simultaneously, clearly an impossible demand. Rather, it means that one must attempt to consider as large a problem set as possible in the formulation of any particular problem (Mason & Mitroff, 1981, p. 20).

In 1986, "Reflections on Systems and their Models" distinctions were drawn between different types of systems and different ways of representing them.

There are three basic types of systems and models of them, and a meta-system: one that contains all three types as parts of it (see Table [2]).

Systems and models	Parts	Whole
Deterministic	Not purposeful	Not purposeful
Animated	Not purposeful	Purposeful
Social	Purposeful	Purposeful
Ecological	Purposeful	Not purposeful

Table 2: Types of systems and models

(1) Deterministic: systems and models in which neither the parts nor the whole are

purposeful.

(2) Animated: systems and models in which the whole is purposeful but the parts are

not.

(3) Social: systems and models in which both the parts and the whole are purposeful.

These three types of system form a hierarchy in the following sense: animated systems have deterministic systems as their parts. In addition, some of them can create and use deterministic systems, but not vice versa. Social systems have animated systems as their parts. All three types of system are contained in ecological systems, some of whose parts are purposeful but not the whole. For example, Earth is an ecological system that has no purpose of its own but contains social and animate systems that do, and deterministic systems that don't (Ackoff & Gharajedaghi, 1996, p. 14).

In 2004, "The Post-Normal Science of Precaution" sees the scientific system as in a crisis of confidence, legitimacy and power.

> *Now we can discern the emergence of two approaches to the understanding and manage-*
> *ment of the scientific enterprise. The first is what might be called "mainstream science,"*
> *which carries on with inherited attitudes and assumptions of inevitable and irresistible*
> *progress, in spite of the drastic changes in the new conditions. It proudly maintains the*
> *reductionist tradition of Western science, in which complex systems are assumed to be*
> *capable of being taken apart, studied in their elements and then reassembled. In this old*
> *paradigm, systemic properties are deemed incapable of scientific study and are therefore*
> *to be ignored. [....]*
>
> *The contrasting approach to science, still in the very early stages of development, could be*
> *called 'precautionary', since it is usually concerned with reacting to the unintended harmful*
> *effects of progress. Its style is 'post-normal'; it lies at the contested interfaces of science and*
> *policy. It addresses issues where, typically, facts are uncertain, values in dispute, stakes high*
> *and decisions urgent (Ravetz, 2004, p. 349).*

In this paradigm around the systems approach, questions on methods for collectively designing systems and validating their appropriateness under changing conditions are brought
forward. In comparison, the Alexandrian paradigm takes a more idealized approach, and
relies on architectural expertise to facilitate the design and construction of a built environment.

3.6. Pattern language has rise in agile, groups, public sphere

Beyond built physical environments, the pattern language approach has been implemented
in a variety of other domains, with varying levels of adherence to the basic ideas.

In 1987, the first patterns were written by Ward Cunningham and Kent Beck at the Tekt-
ronix Semiconductor Test Systems group, and reported at the OOPLSA conference. Bruce
Anderson gave talks in 1990, and the four others that would become known as the Gang
of Four – Eric Gamma, Richard Helm, Ralph Johnson and John Vlissides – met at an OOPSLA
1991 workshop.

> *In August of 1993, KentBeck and GradyBooch sponsored a mountain retreat in Colorado*
> *where a group of us converged on foundations for software patterns. WardCunningham,*
> *RalphJohnson, KenAuer, HalHildebrand, GradyBooch, KentBeck and JimCoplien struggled*
> *with Alexander's ideas and our own experiences to forge a marriage of objects and pat-*
> *terns. We agreed that we were ready to build on ErichGamma's foundation work studying*
> *object-oriented patterns, to use patterns in a generative way in the sense that Christo-*
> *pherAlexander uses patterns for urban planning and building architecture. We then used*

> *the term generative to mean creational to distinguish them from Gamma patterns that captured observations.*

> *Bruce again held his workshop at OOPSLA ,93, this time with patterns in the workshop title and prominently on the agenda.*

> *The HillsideGroup met again in early April 1994 to plan the first PLoP conference. We wanted something really wacky and unusual, but most of us felt (and were willing to take) the risk that goes with new things. That was RichardGabriel's first time with us. He exhorted us all to go into PLoP with confidence and act as though we knew what we were doing (Cunningham, 2000).*

In 1994, the Portland Pattern Repository was created as the first wiki, enabling internal references that would map to hypertext links (Cunningham, 1994).

In 1995, Design Patterns: Elements of Reusable Object-Oriented Software was published, and became one of the best known works in computer science.

> *The purpose of this book is to record experience in designing object-oriented as design patterns. Each design pattern systematically names, explains and evaluates an important and recurring design in object-oriented systems. Our goal is to capture design experience in a form that people can use effectively. To this end, we have documented some of the most important design patterns and present them as a catalog.*

> *[....]*

> *For this book we have concentrated on patterns at a certain level of abstraction. Design patterns are not about designs such as linked lists and hash tables that can be encoded in classes and reused as is. Nor are they complex, domain-specific designs for an entire application or subsystem. The design patterns in this book are descriptions of communicating objects and classes that are customized to solve a general design problem in a particular context. (Gamma, Helm, Johnson, & Vlissides, 1995, pp. 2–3).*

The catalog is this book are considered "Gamma patterns", and thus a not strong adoption of the Alexandrian approach.

> *A generative pattern is one of the KindsOfPatterns. It is first a pattern; a solution to a problem in a context. In the early days of patterns, we used the term generative to mean creational. But a closer reading of Alexander shows that by generative, he means something that leads to emergent behavior.*

> *Generative patterns work indirectly; they work on the underlying structure of a problem (which may not be manifest in the problem) rather than attacking the problem directly. Good design patterns are like that: they encode the deep structure (in the Senge sense) of a solution and its associated forces, rather than cataloging a solution.*

> *We can contrast a Generative Pattern with a GammaPattern, which is not generative. (That doesn't make them bad, just different. Much of the software visualization work going on in the industry is all about Gamma patterns) (Coplien, 1995).*

In 1995, Pattern Languages of Program Design became the first in the series of proceedings from the meetings of the Hillside Group (Coplien & Schmidt, 1995).

In 1996, *Patterns of Software: Tales from the Software Community*, the foreword was written by Christopher Alexander, on first reading the article that became the chapter "The Bed Game, Rugs and Beauty".

> *What was fascinating to me, indeed quite astonishing, was that in his essay I found out that a computer scientist, not known to me, and whom I had never met, seemed to understand more about what I had done and was trying to do in my own field than my own colleagues who are architects (Alexander, 1996a, p. v).*

Encouraged by the cross-appropriation into software development, Alexander also recognized that the writing on The Nature of Order (which would not be officially published for another 6 years) would potentially be left to a subsequent book by Gabriel.

> *As I reached the end of Patterns of Software, I realized that my story as told by Richard Gabriel -- was incomplete in a number of important ways, which may have direct bearing on the computer scientists struggling with just these questions. Richard Gabriel focuses, very much, on unsolved problems, on the struggle and the path to almost ineluctable difficulties in architecture. He does not comment, perhaps enough, on the fact that these problems are solvable in practice, in fact are being solved right now. The geometry of life, in buildings, which I wrote about for 25 years, in order to attain it, is finally being attained, just now (Alexander, 1996a, p. vii).*

As an influential figure on the software development community, Richard Gabriel wrote and compiled a series of essays from the position of "critic-at-large".

> *One of my goals in writing these essays was to bring out the reality of commercial software development and to help people realize that right now software development -- except when a project essentially is creating a near variant of an existing program -- is in a state where the artifact desired is brand new and its construction is unknown, and therefore the*

means to approach its construction is unknown and possibly difficult to ascertain; and, furthermore, a group of people is trying to work together -- maybe for the first time -- to accomplish it (Gabriel, 1996a, pp. xv–xvi).

In trying to understand Alexander's writing, a strong contribution is made in the chapter on quality without a name.

Alexander proposes some words to describe the quality without a name, but even though he feels they point the reader in a direction that helps comprehension, these words ultimately confuse. The words are alive, whole, comfortable, free, exact, egoless, and eternal. I'll go through all of them to try to explain the quality without a name [....]

What is revolutionary about Alexander is that he is resuming the quest for an understanding of objective quality that science and philosophy abandoned in the modern era. In the seventeenth and eighteenth centuries, a tension developed in which mind and matter were separated by science and philosophy. From this came the separation of fact and value. After the separation, a fact had no value associated with it, a fact could not be good or bad, it just was. Science, then, tried to find theories that explained things as they were and no longer sought what was good or beautiful about things. That is, we no longer sought the objective characteristics of beauty, which is where Alexander started his quest (Gabriel, 1996b, pp. 36–39).

In 2001, the "Manifesto for Agile Software Development" was released by 17 signatories. They include key members at the dawn of the Hillside Group (e.g. Kent Beck, Ward Cunningham), an author of a position paper on Scrum Development Process at OOPSLA'95 (Schwaber, 1997), and the founding chairman of the Scrum Foundation in 2008 (Jeff Sutherland). The original document was published on the Internet, and continues to be available:

Manifesto for Agile Software Development

We are uncovering better ways of developing software by doing it and helping others do it. Through this work we have come to value:

Individuals and interactions over processes and tools

Working software over comprehensive documentation

Customer collaboration over contract negotiation

Responding to change over following a plan

That is, while there is value in the items on the right, we value the items on the left more

(Beck et al., 2001).

The manifesto included "Twelve Principles of Agile Software". Ten years later, a subsequent meeting produced a history with reflections (Cockburn, 2011), and proposals for a revision (Ambler, 2011).

In 2004, Organizational Patterns of Agile Software Development reflected a change in social style for developing software.

> *Our interest in this book is what software development has learned about itself from an organizational and social perspective. [...] Now we are in the fourth style: one that breaks down hierarchy, that features dynamic social structures and communication paths, and that values immediacy. This fourth style often bears the label "agile," but that is just one of many characterizations of a broad new way of developing software that has emerged over the past decade. [....]*

> *Patterns provide a way to capture both the broad, invariant practices of socially built artifacts as well as the specialized practices of individual disciplines, along with an understanding of how those practices build on each other (Coplien & Harrison, 2004, pp. 2–3).*

This work continued with a Scrum summit associated with the VikingPLoP conference in 2008 (Bjørnvig & Coplien, 2008). The Scrum Pattern Community has held official workshops every year since 2010, and collaborates on a wiki at scrumplop.org. By 2016, there were plans to formalize the web site content as a forthcoming A Scrum Book (Ramos, den Hollander, Heasman, & Coplien, 2016).

In 2008, Liberating Voices: A Pattern Language for *Communication Revolution* proposed a new model of social change, whereby information and communications could be used to address urgent social issues collaboratively.

> *This book presents the first draft of a language for a communications revolution. It is intended to be an everyday guide for people who are working to shape a better future. .... [The] objective of this book and the broader pattern language project is to characterize this unruly and uncoordinated revolution by integrating the totality of their efforts. [....]*

> *The structure of our language acknowledges the enormity of this world: a world that can be seen as comprising three deeply interconnected and enmeshed worlds of distinctive as well as shared characteristics. The first world is physical and measurable and ultimately*

provides our sustenance. It includes natural elements like air, sunlight, water and soil, as well as physical products of humankind like roads, buildings, books, pesticides and bombs. The second world is the world of individual and social communications and interpretation, a world also complex – and messy. Within this world, some people learn and grow wise; others may become banal, stupid, uncaring and brutal. The third world is the world of the knowledge that we collectively create and recreate over time, a world of theories, disciplines, data, language, policies, institutions, laws and taboos (Schuler, 2008, pp. 2–3).

This work began in 2001 with grants from the National Science Foundation, with the Public Sphere Project at publicsphereproject.org, drawing 85 contributors on the pattern language. In 2012, pattern cards based on the content in the 2008 book were released for free download. In 2014, a new research and action community network was formed focusing on "Collection Action for the Public Good", extended the principles from the prior work.

In 2012, the Group Pattern Language Project released the Group Works desk of 100 fullcolour cards (of 91 patterns, plus 9 category cards).

> *The Group Works deck ... names what skilled facilitators and other participants do to make things work. The content is more specific than values and less specific than tips and techniques, cutting across existing methodologies with a designer's eye to capture the patterns that repeat. The deck can be used to plan sessions, reflect on and debrief them, provide guidance, and share responsibility for making the process go well. It has the potential to provide a common reference point for practitioners, and serve as a framework and learning tool for those studying the field (Group Pattern Language Project, 2013).*

The project was started as "A Pattern Language for Group Conversation" in 2008 at we.riseup.net/pattern_language. This became the "Pattern Language for Group Process" at grouppatternlanguage.org through 2012, at which time the Group Works deck was released and the domain migrated to groupworksdeck.org.

The paradigm espoused by these projects aim to adopt the Alexandrian philosophy faithfully, despite the application of techniques beyond built physical environments. Christopher Alexander himself acknowledges the heritage and general spirit, while claiming limited knowledge about the domains.

3.7. Ecological epistemology led to interaction design + affordances

If taking pattern language beyond the built physical environment is to be seriously regrounded in the changing philosophy in the design profession, the impacts of shifts in ecological epistemology and interaction design should be recognized.

In 1972, Steps to an Ecology of Mind introduced many ideas that would only become label-led as ecological epistemology after the death of Gregory Bateson.

> *The essays, spread over thirty-five years, combine to propose a new way of thinking about ideas and about those aggregates of ideas which I call „minds." This way of thinking I call the „ecology of mind," or the ecology of ideas. It is a science which does not yet exist as an organized body of theory or knowledge. [....]*
>
> *The questions which the book raises are ecological: How do ideas interact? Is there some sort of natural selection which determines the survival of some ideas and the extinction or death of others? What sort of economics limits the multiplicity of ideas in a given region of mind? What are the necessary conditions for stability (or survival) of such a system or subsystem? [...]*
>
> *It was only in late 1969 that I became fully conscious of what I had been doing. With the writing of the Korzybski Lecture, „Form, Substance, and Difference," I found that in my work with primitive peoples, schizophrenia, biological symmetry, and in my discontent with the conventional theories of evolution and learning, I had identified a widely scattered set of bench marks or points of reference from which a new scientific territory could be defined. These bench marks I have called „steps" in the title of the book (Bateson, 1972, p. xvii).*

In 1979, The Ecological Approach to Visual Perception starts from the environment to be perceived by an animal, and leads into a philosophy that is neither objectivist or subjectivist, but instead in the complementary relation.

> *The affordances of the environment are what it offers the animal, what it provides or furnishes, either for good or ill. The verb to afford is found in the dictionary, but the noun affordance is not. I have made it up. I mean by it something that refers to both the environ-ment and the animal in a way no existing term does. It implies the complementarity of the animal and the environment. The antecedents of the term and the history of the concept will be treated later; for the present, let us consider examples of an affordance. [p. 127]*
>
> *If a terrestrial surface is nearly horizontal (instead of slanted), nearly flat (instead of convex or concave), and sufficiently extended (relative to the size of the animal) and if its substance is rigid (relative to the weight of the animal), then the surface affords support. It is a surface of support, and we call it a substratum, ground, or floor. It is stand-on-able, permitting an upright posture for quadrupeds and bipeds. It is therefore walk-on-able and run-over-able. It is not sink-into-able like a surface of water or a swamp, that is, not for heavy terrestrial*

animals. Support for water bugs is different.

Note that the four properties listed -- horizontal, flat, extended, and rigid – would be physical properties of a surface if they were measured with the scales and standard units used in physics. As an affordance of support for a species of animal, however, they have to be measured relative to the animal. They are unique for that animal. They are not just abstract physical properties. They have unity relative to the posture and behavior of the animal being considered. So an affordance cannot be measured as we measure in physics. [....]

In architecture a niche is a place that is suitable for a piece of statuary, a place into which the object fits. In ecology a niche is a setting of environmental features that are suitable for an animal, into which it fits metaphorically.

An important fact about the affordances of the environment is that they are in a sense objective, real, and physical, unlike values and meanings, which are often supposed to be subjective, phenomenal, and mental. But, actually, an affordance is neither an objective property nor a subjective property; or it is both if you like. An affordance cuts across the dichotomy of subjective-objective and helps us to understand its inadequacy. It is equally a fact of the environment and a fact of behavior. It is both physical and psychical, yet neither. An affordance points both ways, to the environment and to the observer (Gibson, 1979, pp. 127–129).

A 1999 report of "Putting It All Together – Towards a Pattern Language for Interaction Design: A CHI 97 Workshop" related the rationale, structure and process of the meeting.

Interaction design is becoming more diverse in that a wider range of people are becoming involved in it. Within CHI, it is well accepted that anthropologists, psychologists, and visual designers, as well as engineers and computer scientists, have roles to play in systems design. [...] While the multidisciplinary nature of interaction design brings much richness, it is also challenging because no common perspective, set of practices, or theoretical orientation can be assumed.

Another factor driving the diversification of interaction design is customization. As systems become increasingly customizable, more and more design -- in the sense of front end creation, application programming, and software configuration -- is being done in-house. [....] And, in many cases, these participants lack formal training in design, andhence any common perspective or language.

A Possible Solution: Pattern Languages

So, we have a rapidly expanding game: more players and more technology projected onto workplaces which we are learning more and more about. This increasing complexity and diversity can be source of richness, or of chaos. Thus, we need to explore ways of dealing with the increasing complexity and diversity of the interaction design field. This workshop explored one approach to putting it all together through a common language. Our model is the work of Christopher Alexander and his colleagues who over the last few decades have looked at what works and what doesn't work in architecture and urban design. The basic approach is to closely examine particular cases, attempt to identify recurring patterns and integrate them into a language of relatively concrete patterns (Bayle et al., 1998, p. 17).

In addition to the findings in the 1998 report, addition research was subsequently published as "Lingua Francas for design: sacred places and pattern languages" (Erickson, 2000).

In 1999, "Affordance, Conventions, and Design" traced the development of CHI (Computer Human Interaction) from the publication of *The Psychology of Everyday Things* in 1998, with a reissuing in the same year with the changed title of *The Design of Everyday Things*.

> *In POET, I argued that understanding how to operate a novel device had three major dimensions: conceptual models, constraints, and affordances. These three concepts have had a mixed reception.*
>
> *To me, the most important part of a successful design is the underlying conceptual model. This is the hard part of design: formulating an appropriate conceptual model and then assuring that everything else be consistent with it. I see lots of token acceptance of this idea, but far too little serious work. The power of constraints has largely been ignored.*
>
> *To my great surprise, the concept of affordance was adopted by the design community, especially graphical and industrial design. Alas, yes, the concept has caught on, but not always with complete understanding. My fault: I was really talking about perceived affordances, which are not at all the same as real ones.*

Perceived Affordance

POET was about "perceived affordance." When I get around to revising POET, I will make a global change, replacing all instances of the word "affordance" with the phrase "perceived affordance." The designer cares more about what actions the user perceives to be possible than what is true. Moreover, affordances, both real and perceived, play very different roles in physical products than they do in the world of screen-based products. In the latter case, affordances play a relatively minor role: cultural conventions are much more important. More on that in a moment. In product design, where one deals with real, physical objects, there can be both real and perceived affordances, and the two sets need not be the same.

In graphical, screen-based interfaces, the designer primarily can control only perceived affordances. The computer system already comes with built-in physical affordances. The computer, with its keyboard, display screen, pointing device, and selection buttons (e.g., mouse buttons) affords pointing, touching, looking, and clicking on every pixel of the screen. Most of this affordance is of little interest for the purpose of the application under design (Norman, 1999, p. 39).

Norman's interpretation of affordances as described by Gibson challenges definitions in an alternative paradigm.

" *The word affordance was coined by the perceptual psychologist J. J. Gibson to refer to the actionable properties between the world and an actor (a person or animal). To Gibson, affordances are relationships. They exist naturally: they do not have to be visible, known, or desirable.*

I originally hated the idea: it didn't make sense. I cared about processing mechanisms, and Gibson waved them off as irrelevant (Norman, 1999, p. 39).

The specification of "exist naturally" by Norman is counter to the recognition of "man's alteration of the natural environment" by Gibson.

" *In the last few thousand years, as everybody now realizes, the very face of the earth has been modified by man. The layout of surfaces has been changed, by cutting, clearing, leveling, paving, and building. Natural deserts and mountains, swamps and rivers, forests and plains still exist, but they are being encroached upon and reshaped by man-made layouts. Moreover, the substances of the environment have been partly converted from the natural materials of the earth into various kinds of artificial materials such as bronze, iron, concrete, and bread. Even the medium of the environment – the air for us and the water for fish-is becoming slowly altered despite the restorative cycles that yielded a steady state for millions of years prior to man.*

Why has man changed the shapes and substances of his environment? To change what it affords him. He has made more available what benefits him and less pressing what injures him. In making life easier for himself, of course, he has made life harder for most of the other animals. Over the millennia, he has made it easier for himself to get food, easier to keep warm, easier to see at night, easier to get about, and easier to train his offspring.

This is not a new environment -- an artificial environment distinct from the natural environment -- but the same old environment modified by man. It is a mistake to separate the natural from the artificial as if there were two environments; artifacts have to be manu-

factured from natural substances. It is also a mistake to separate the cultural environment from the natural environment, as if there were a world of mental products distinct from the world of material products. There is only one world, however diverse, and all animals live in it, although we human animals have altered it to suit ourselves. We have done so wastefully, thoughtlessly, and if we do not mend our to ways, fatally (Gibson, 1979, pp. 129–130).

This relational view of affordances is also consistent with "social affordances" in the CSCW (computer supported cooperative work) community (citing Gibson, but not Norman).

> *Our working definition of a social affordance is the relationship between the properties of an object and the social characteristics of a group that enable particular kinds of interaction among members of that group. For example, consider a door that opens out into a busy hallway. If a person opens the door quickly, it may strike someone entering from the other direction. One possible solution is to put a glass window in the door. The glass window addresses the problem at two levels. At the level of individual perception, the glass makes a person on the other side visible (i.e., the window affords seeing through it to a sighted person). At the social level, since people are socialized to not strike others with doors, they will refrain from doing so if given the chance. Furthermore, not only can the potential door opener see through the window, but the person on the other side can see as well, and thus there is shared knowledge of the situation (e.g., ‚I know that you know that I know'). As a consequence, the door opener will be held accountable for her actions. This accountability, which arises from the optical properties of glass, human perceptual abilities, and the social rules of the culture, is an example of what we call a social affordance (Bradner, Kellogg, & Erickson, 1999, p. 154).*

In 2000, Perception of the Environment: Essays on livelihood, dwelling and skill extended the work on ecological epistemology into ecological anthropology.

> *Gibson wanted to know how people come to perceive the environment around them. The majority of psychologists, at least at the time when Gibson was writing, assumed that they did so by constructing representations of the world inside their heads. It was supposed that the mind got to work on the raw material of experience, consisting of sensations of light, sound, pressure on the skin, and so on, organising it into an internal model which, in turn, could serve as a guide to subsequent action. The mind, then, was conceived as a kind of data-processing device, akin to a digital computer, and the problem for the psychologist was to figure out how it worked. But Gibson's approach was quite different. It was to throw out the idea, that has been with us since the time of Descartes, of the mind as a distinct organ that is capable of operating upon the bodily data of sense. Perception, Gibson argued, is*

not the achievement of a mind in a body, but of the organism as a whole in its environment, and is tantamount to the organism's own exploratory movement through the world. If mind is anywhere, then, it is not 'inside the head' rather than 'out there' in the world. To the contrary, it is immanent in the network of sensory pathways that are set up by virtue of the perceiver's immersion in his or her environment. Reading Gibson, I was reminded of the teaching of that notorious maverick of anthropology, Gregory Bateson. The mind, Bateson had always insisted, is not limited by the skin. Could not an ecological approach to perception provide the link I was looking for, between the biological life of the organism in its environment and the cultural life of the mind in society?

The issue for me, at the time, was to find a way of formulating this link that could also resolve what I felt to be a deep-rooted problem in my own work. Setting out from the complementarity thesis, I had argued that human beings must simultaneously be constituted both as organisms within systems of ecological relations, and as persons within systems of social relations. The critical task for anthropology, it seemed, was to understand the reciprocal interplay between the two kinds of system, social and ecological (Ingold, 2000, pp. 2–3).

In 2011, Being Alive: Essays on Movement, Knowledge and Description provided more of the philosophical background supporting an ecological approach to anthropology. In reflection of research conducted over the past decade:

> *I therefore had to leave the mainstream to find my answers. In psychology I turned to the work of James Gibson, whose ecological approach to perception, developed in 1950s and 1960s, was explicitly opposed to the prevailing paradigm of cognitivism. And in ethology I rediscovered the long neglected, pre-war writings of the Estonian-born pioneer of biosemiotics, Jakob von Uexküll. Both seemed to offer a radically alternative way of thinking about meaning, finding it not in the correspondence between an external world and its interior representation, but in the immediate coupling of perception and action. Yet, as I also found, behind this commonality lay significant differences (Ingold, 2011, p. 77).*

This stance would lead to positioning away from Martin Heidegger, and towards Gilles Deleuze.

> *Can there be any escape from this shuttling back and forth between enclosure and disclosure, between an ecology of the real and a phenomenology of experience? So long as we suppose that life is fully encompassed in the relations between one thing and another -- between the animal and its environment or the being and its world -- we are bound to have to begin with a separation, siding either with the environment vis-à-vis its inhabitants or with the being vis-à-vis its world. A more radical alternative, however, would be to re-*

verse Heidegger's priorities: that is, to celebrate the openness inherent in the animal's very captivation by its environment. This is the openness of a life that will not be contained, that overflows any boundaries that might be thrown around it, threading its way like the roots and runners of a rhizome through whatever clefts and fissures leave room for growth and movement .... Once again, we can take our cue from von Uexküll, who compares the world of nature to polyphonic music, in which the life of every creature is equivalent to a melody in counterpoint .... [....]

Life, for Deleuze, is lived not within a perimeter but along lines. He calls them 'lines of flight', or sometimes 'lines of becoming'. Such lines prise an opening, even as they bind the animal with its world. Every species, indeed every individual has its own particular line, or rather bundle of lines .... Critically, however, these lines do not connect ....

(Ingold, 2011, p. 83)

The term "meshwork" is borrowed from Henri Lefebvre, and contrasted with the actor network of Bruno Latour. The dissolution of boundary between organism and environment is consistent with anthropologist Gregory Bateson, as well as cognitive scientist Andy Clark.

In this paradigm based in an ecological epistemology, living in space is more fully appreciated as living in time, "On Human Correspondence" (i.e. co-responding) alongside each other (as well as animals and other trails in the world) (Ingold, 2017). This philosophy acknowledges, but goes well beyond "Building, Dwelling, Thinking" (originally in German as "Bauen Wohnen Denken" in 1951) (Heidegger, 1971). In the Alexandrian paradigm, time is better handled in The Timeless Way of Building than in *A Pattern Language*, but a different view of the world is taken in *The Nature of Order*.

3.8. Hierarchy theory led to panarchy and resilience science

In a pattern language, relations between patterns in the physical built environment typically begin from the largest scales, down to the smaller scales.

The patterns are ordered, beginning with the very largest, for regions and towns, then working down through neighborhoods, clusters of buildings, buildings, rooms and alcoves, ending finally with details of construction.

This order, which is presented as a straight linear sequence, is essential to the way the language works. [....] What is most important about this sequence, is that it is based on the connections between the patterns. Each pattern is connected to certain „larger" patterns which come above it in the language; and to certain „smaller" patterns which come below it in the language. The pattern helps to complete those larger patterns which are „above" it, and is itself completed by those smaller pat- terns which are „below" it (Alexander et al., 1977, p. xii).

In the systems sciences, this ordering is recognized through hierarchy theory, which has become a foundation for panarchy and resilience science.

In 1982, Hierarchy: Perspectives for Ecological Complexity recognized that theoretical work for ecological systems was not as well developed as those for biological systems.

> *... complexity is something that needs more than an ad hoc treatment. We see most important complexity as related to the interaction of different levels of organization; in order to give complexity proper account in our scientific models, those models are almost required to be hierarchical. We suggest that there is something about either our facility for observation or that which generates our observations which gives patterns that generally remain opaque unless we model using hierarchies. By hierarchy is understood a system of behavioral interconnections wherein the higher levels constrain and control the lower levels to various degrees depending on the time constants of the behavior. [....] Since bulkier structures in biology generally behave more slowly, not only do slow entities constrain fast, but also large entities usually constrain small. Sometimes the lower levels of the hierarchy are nested inside and in aggregate make up the higher levels (cells and tissues), but sometimes this is not the case (ecological consumers and resources). In the nested and non-nested cases, complexity comes from the nonlinearity and asymmetry of an entity affecting while also being affected by its environment. The environment is a higher level, and it responds more slowly that entities it constrains. For all hierarchies there is complexity associated with the relationship between the rate-independence of the constraint itself and the ratedependence of the dynamical interaction of the constrained entities (parts in a nested structure. In the non-nested case there is further complexity in spontaneous behavior coming from undefined extra degrees of freedom at both the higher and the lower levels. Complexity need have little to do with the number of variables (Allen & Starr, 1982, pp. xiii–xiv).*

While these definitions are centered for application in ecologies, they can also be applied to other types of systems.

> *The ideas collected here come from that part of general systems theory which is beyond the mechanistic cybernetic approach. [...] This approach views system theory not just as a tool for solving problems already defined, but as a conceptual framework within which one might develop new ideas about biology (Allen & Starr, 1982, p. 4).*

In 1984, How Buildings Learn: What Happens After They're Built extended the work based in hierarchy theory into a more popularized form with built environments.

> The leading theorist – practically the only theorist – of change rate in buildings in Frank Duffy .... He distinguishes four layers, which he calls Shell, Services, Scenery and Set.
>
> [...]
>
> I've taken the liberty of expanding Duffy's "four S's" -- which are oriented toward interior work in commercial buildings – into a slightly revised, general-purpose "six S's":
>
> • SITE – This is the geographic setting, the urban location, and the legally defined lot, whose boundaries and context outlast generations of ephemeral buildings. "Site is eternal," Duffy agrees.
>
> • STRUCTURE – The foundation and load-bearing elements are perilous and expensive to change, so people don't. There are the building. Structural life ranges from 30 to 300 years (but few buildings make it past 60, for other reasons).
>
> • SKIN – Exterior surfaces now change every 20 years or so, to keep up with fashion or technology, or for wholesale repair. Recent focus on energy costs has led to re-engineered Skins that are air-tight and better insulated.
>
> • SERVICES – These are the working guts of a building communications wiring, electrical wiring, plumbing, sprinkler system, HVAC (heating, ventilating, and air conditioning), and moving parts like elevators and escalators. They wear out or obsolesce every 7 to 15 years. Many builds are demolished early if their outdated systems are too deeply embedded to replace easily.
>
> • SPACE PLAN – The interior layout – where walls, ceilings, floors, and doors go. Turbulent commercial space can change every 3 years or so, exceptionally quiet homes might wait 30 years.
>
> • STUFF – Chairs, desks, phones, pictures; kitchen appliances, lamps, hair brushes; all the things that twitch around daily to monthly. Furniture is called mobilia in Italian for good reason.
>
> Duffy's time-layered perspective is fundamental to understanding how buildings actually behave. The 6-S sequence is precisely followed in both design and construction. [.....]
>
> The layering also defines how a building relates to people. Organizational levels of respon-

sibility match the pace levels. [....]

Buildings rule us via their time layering at least as much as we rule them, and in a surprising way. This idea comes from Robert V. O'Neill's A Hierarchical Concept of Ecosystems. O'Neill and his co-authors noted that ecosystems could be better understood by observing the rates of change of different components. [....] The insight is this: "The dynamics of the system will be dominated by the slow components, with the rapid components simply following along" (O'Neill, DeAngelis, Waide, & Allen, 1986, p. 98). Slow constrains quick; slow controls quick (Brand, 1994, pp. 12–17).

This book was complemented and popularized with a BBC television documentary series. These "shearing layers" of change would eventually be relabelled as "pacing layers" (Brand, 1999).

In 2003, Panarchy: Understanding Transformations in Human and Natural Systems would extend hierarchy theory to understand cycles of adaptive change.

The theory that we develop must of necessity transcend boundaries of scale and discipline. It must be capable of organizing our understanding of economic, ecological, and institutional systems. And it must explain situations where all three types of systems interact. The cross-scale, interdisciplinary, and dynamic nature of the theory has lead [sic] us to con the term panarchy for it. Its essential focus is to rationalize the interplay between change and persistence, between the predictable and unpredictable. Thus, we drew upon the Greek god Pan to capture an image of unpredictable change and upon notions of hierarchies across scale to represent structures that sustain experiments, test results, and allow adaptive evolution (Holling, Gunderson, & Ludwig, 2002, p. 5).

In 2004, "Resilience, Adaptability and Transformability in Social-ecological Systems" formalized some definitions that had been developed within the Resilience Alliance.

Resilience is the capacity of a system to absorb disturbance and reorganize while undergoing change so as to still retain essentially the same function, structure, identity, and feedbacks. As amplified below, the focus is on the dynamics of the system when it is disturbed far from its modal state. The notion of speed of return to equilibrium ... leads to what has been termed "engineering resilience" ... and, although related to one aspect of "ecological resilience," cannot be considered as the measure of resilience. Because of the possibility of multiple stable states, when considering the extent to which a system can be changed, return time doesn't measure all of the ways in which a system may fail -- permanently or temporarily -- to retain essential functions. It is also important to bear in mind that "systems" consist of nested dynamics operating at particular organizational scales -- "sub-systems," as it were, of households to villages to nations, trees to patches to landscapes (Walker, Holling, Carpenter, & Kinzig, 2004, p. 2).

In 2015, "Regime Shifts in the Anthropocene: Drivers, Risks, and Resilience" shifted research from theory into analyzing a scientific database at regimeshifts.org.

> *Research on regime shifts has typically focused on theoretical models ..., empirical evidence of regime shifts ..., or potential early warning signals ..... These approaches require in-depth knowledge of the causal structure of the system or high-quality temporal data, leading to a focus on the analysis of particular cases of regime shifts. Here we complement this work by synthesizing and comparing different types of regime shifts in terms of global change impacts and opportunities for management. Our aim is to understand: i) What are the main drivers of regime shifts globally? ii) What are their most common impacts on eco-system services? And, iii) what can be done to manage or avoid them? (Rocha, Peterson, & Biggs, 2015, p. 2)*

In this paradigm, relationships between hierarchy, resilience and regime shifts are apprecia-ted with cross-scale effects over time. These foundations in biology and ecology can expand the Alexandrian research into complexity based primarily in physics.

3.9. Interactive value is in the shift to a service economy

New insight into value has come as the world has moved from the economics of scarcity towards an economics of plenty.

In 1994, *Designing Interactive Strategy: From Value Chain to Value Constellation* portrayed changes in markets and in business. Co-produced value is a shift from the traditional view o value added.

> *In 1967 Thompson describe three types of relationships between parts of an organization. The most simple is one in what termed a 'pooled' relationship, in which the different parts each contribute to form a whole. The second type of relationship is what he called 'sequen-tial': sections of an organization produce parts which are then inputted into another part. The dynamics of this type of organizational relationship are very similar to the value chain process as described by Porter. Finally, Thompson described the 'reciprocal' relationship, the most complex of the three. In this case, the outputs of each section of the organization become inputs to the sections from which they get their own inputs. [....]*
>
> *Applying Thompson's categories to the system of value-creating actors, we can see that*

the value chain covers the fist two types of relationships. It does not, however, provide the conceptual framework to describe the more complex interaction among different actors which liquidification and density, through the removal of temporal and spatial constraint, have brought to bear upon their interfaces: the 'reciprocal relationship'. Co-production is the term we use to describe the 'reciprocal' relationships between actors which characterize the service economy (Normann & Ramírez, 1994, p. 30).

As an alternative to centering on products (or services) alone, a definition of offerings is proposed.

The distinction made in the industrial economy between 'products' and 'services' obeyed the following logic: activities packaged into physical goods were more readily amenable to the scale economics of mass production of that era. They were, in effect, an efficient way of storing activities by sharing the cost their creation represented among many price-carrying manifestations which could be matched by as many revenue-generating customers. Service activities were less easy to design so as to benefit from such economics; scale was achieved when they were 'productified', as in the case of trust or unit funds which were found to efficiently 'productivity' costly financial advice in many distinct (if identical) units which were price carrying, and which could be individually sold to many individual revenue-generating customers. [....]

... all relationships between economic actors are manifested in offerings. An offering engages each economic actor participating in a commercial relationship with others in multiple activities. Offerings organize activities along several dimensions:

(1) In time, as they store past activities and simultaneously entail a code for potential future activity;

(2) In space or location, geographically grounding the simultaneity of activities characteristic of the current technological era and the sequentiality of the past; and

(3) In terms of the relationships among actors involved in the co-production of value in the offering. It is in this sense that offerings create and define social systems. Offering designers must address the question of how different actors' activities are to be configured for optimum value creation: who does what, when, where, and with whom?

The total activity set which an offering assumes is constantly being 'unbundled' and 're-bundled' in innovative ways ... (Normann & Ramírez, 1994, pp. 50–53).

In 2004, "Evolving to a New Dominant Logic for Marketing" oriented towards the service economy with a shift from operand resources to operant resources.

> *Constantin and Lusch (1994) define operand resources as resources on which an opera-*
> *tion or act is performed to produce an effect, and they compare operand resources with*
> *operant resources, which are employed to act on operand resources (and other operant*
> *resources). [...] A goods-centered dominant logic developed in which the operand resources*
> *were considered primary. A firm (or nation) had factors of production (largely operand*
> *resources) and a technology (an operant resource), which had value to the extent that the*
> *firm could convert its operand resources into outputs at a low cost. Customers, like resour-*
> *ces, became something to be captured or acted on ....*
>
> *Operant resources are resources that produce effects (Constantin and Lusch 1994). The*
> *relative role of operant resources began to shift in the late twentieth century as humans*
> *began to realize that skills and knowledge were the most important types of resources. [....]*
>
> *Operant resources are often invisible and intangible; often they are core competences or*
> *organizational processes. They are likely to be dynamic and infinite and not static and*
> *finite, as is usually the case with operand resources. Because operant resources produce*
> *effects, they enable humans both to multiply the value of natural resources and to create*
> *additional operant resources. [....]*
>
> *The service-centered view of marketing implies that marketing is a continuous series of*
> *social and economic processes that is largely focused on operant resources with which*
> *the firm is constantly striving to make better value propositions than its competitors. In a*
> *free enterprise system, the firm primarily knows whether it is making better value proposi-*
> *tions from the feedback it receives from the marketplace in terms of firm financial perfor-*
> *mance. Because firms can always do better at serving customers and improving financial*
> *performance, the service-centered view of marketing perceives marketing as a continuous*
> *learning process (directed at improving operant resources) (Vargo & Lusch, 2004, pp. 2–5).*

In 2007, "Steps Towards a Science of Service Systems" proposed research and education oriented towards a world with information services growing rapidly.

> *The service economy refers to the service sector, one of three main economic categories,*
> *in addition to service activities performed in the extractive and manufacturing sectors. The*
> *growth of the service sector has resulted in part from the specialization and outsourcing of*
> *service activities performed inside manufacturing firms (for example, design, maintenance,*
> *human re- sources, customer contact specialists). According to a recent National Academy*
> *of Engineering report, the service sector accounts for more than 80 percent of the US gross*
> *domestic product, employs a large and growing share of the science and engineering work-*
> *force, and is the primary user of IT. [....]*

... we're cultivating an interdisciplinary effort called Service Science, Management, and Engineering -- the application of scientific, management, and engineering disciplines to tasks that one organization (service provider) beneficially performs for and with another (service client). SSME aims to understand how an organization can invest effectively to create service innovations and to realize more predictable outcomes. With information and business services the service economy's fastest-growing segments -- and with the rise of Web services, service-oriented architectures (SOA), and self-service systems -- we see a strong relationship between the study of service systems and the more established study of computational systems (Spohrer, Maglio, Bailey, & Gruhl, 2007, pp. 71–72).

In 2011, The Science of Service Systems was a volume of articles presenting multidisciplinary and multisectoral perspectives on the nature of service systems.

What types of entities interact to co-create value? Service systems are such entities, be they individuals, firms, or nations. Service science is a transdisciplinary approach to study, improve, create, scale, and innovate in service .... We think of service as value cocreation – broadly speaking, as useful change that results from communication, planning, or other purposeful and knowledge-intensive interactions between distinct service system entities, such as individuals, firms, and nations .... And so we think of service science as the systematic search for principles and approaches that can help understand and improve all kinds of value cocreation between interacting service systems .... Value cocreation interactions fall into two categories. Value-propositionbased interactions deal with access rights to resources that measurable benefit stakeholders, while governance-mechanism-based interactions deal with dispute resolution mechanisms needed to clean-up failures and debug shortcomings of the first type of interactions (Demirkan, Spohrer, & Krishna, 2011, pp. 1–2).

This paradigm sees value creation as an interaction beyond the coproduction of outputs (as offerings, products and/or services). In the Alexandrian philosophy, preferences are seen as objective, and therefore shared across a collection of individuals.

4. Why might a pattern language project or community pay more attention to its paradigm?

In The Nature of Order, Christopher Alexander sought to deepen the scientific foundations underlying his approach to architecting and constructing built physical environments. As others target the use of pattern language for alternative contexts – of which the social change of the PURPLSOC community is beyond Alexander's scope – the external validity and internal consistency within the espoused paradigm may break down.

4.1. Is an assumed paradigm leading you to making errors?

The application of pattern language beyond built physical environments can lead to errors in a variety of types, as shows in Table 3.

Type 1 error	False positive	Finding a (statistical) relation that isn't real
Type 2 error	False negative	Missing a (statistical) relation that is real
Type 3 error	Tricking ourselves	Unintentional error of solving the wrong problems precisely (through ignorance, faulty education or unreflective practice)
Type 4 error	Tricking errors	Intentions error of solving wrong problems (through malice, ideology, overzealousness, self-righteousness, wrongdoing)

Table 3: Types of Errors

The basic ideas behind the Type One and Type Two Errors are easy to grasp. Suppose one is interested in testing whether a new drug is better than an old one a treating headaches. In the process of giving the new drug and old drug to two evenly matched groups ... two errors can be made.

First, one can conclude wrongly that the new drug is better than the old one when actually the old one is better or equal to the new one. This is known as the Type One Error, or E1. E1 is akin to saying that there's a meaningful difference between the two drugs when there is not.

Second, one can also conclude wrongly that the old drug is better than the new one when in fact the new one is better. This is known as Type Two Error, or E2. E2 is akin to saying that there is not a meaningful difference between the drugs when there is. [...]

The Type Three Error is the unintentional error of solving the wrong problems precisely [The] Type 4 error is the intentional error of solving the wrong problems. [...]

The Type Three Error is primarily the result of ignorance, a narrow and fault education, and unreflective practice.

In contrast, the Type Four Error is the result of deliberate malice, narrow ideology, overzealousness, a sense of self-righteousness, and wrongdoing. ... [Every] Type Four Error is invariably political or has strong political elements ... (Ian I. Mitroff & Silvers, 2010, pp. 3–5).

Starting off a pattern language initiative without reflecting on the implicit assumptions (or presumptions) from the paradigm is a blindness.

If they can get you asking the wrong questions, they don't have to worry about the answers (Pynchon, 1973).

Without a strong appreciation of the underlying paradigm, the vector of progress on improving a pattern language will be ambiguous.

4.2. Learn from Christopher Alexander's later descriptions based on practices

The concepts and language presented by Christopher Alexander, since *Notes on the Synthesis of Form* in 1964, have evolved so that establishing a coherent paradigm is a challenge.

With The Nature of Order as a highly theoretical work that can be difficult to comprehend, another alternative is proposed. Rather than working from theory to practice, working from practice to theory may be fruitful. Christopher Alexander's latest (and potentially last) work may illuminate methods that can be used practically, as outlined in Table 4.

(i) Pattern language for the community	(a) *Interviewing on hopes and dreams*
	(b) *Making a first sketch of a pattern language*
	(c) *Making a first draft pattern from teachers' comments*
	(d) *Checking seven principles for the completeness of the languages*
	(e) *Refining the language*
	(f) *Creating pattern language as a list of key centers*

(ii) Construction budget	a) Making a record of all of the spaces and areas which were defined by the pattern languages
	((b) Trimming all space to available budget, as an average percentage reduction for allitems in interior space, and then exterior space
	(c) Asking faculty to re-allocate the spaces, keeping the same trimmed totals, conforming with the available resources
(iii) Reality of the land	(a) Laying out the site plan on the ground
	(b) Finding the two fundamental systems of centers, and combining them
	(c) Visualizing the evolving site plan with marks on the land (e.g. flags)
	(d) Fixing first hardline drawings of detailed positions on the site (position, orientation, dimension
	(e) Judging detailed building positions on the land (with flags)
	(f) Recording the site plan on paper

Table 4: Alexandrian methods for built environments

The larger perspective shows that writing the pattern language is only the first step towards producing a tangible outcome. Reflection on how these steps might or might not be appropriate for the domain chosen in the early stages of a pattern language community could lead members to try a different tack.

4.3. Dialectical assumption analysis is a generative approach

A technique for establishing a better approach to generative pattern language could use the Strategic Assumption Surfacing Technique, outline in Table 5.

Step	Activity	Means for accomplishing
1	Formation of Different Groups	• MAPS (Multivariate Analysis and Participative Structure) Design Technology
		• Personality Type Technology
		• Ad Hoc Group Technology
		• Vested Interests Technology

2	Assumption Surfacing	• Stakeholder Analysis
		• Assumption Sorting
3	Dialectical Debate bet-ween Group Policies and Synthesis	• Assumption Negotiation
		• Assumptional Decision Theory

Table 5: Steps towards assumption surfacing

... the environment is more often than not one of constantly changing conditions, uncer-tainty, and turbulence than that of certainty, stability and predictability. Little wonder that under these conditions problem forming and problem defining become as important, if not more so, than problem solving by means of conventional techniques.

[...]

Essentially the Dialectic is an adversarial problem forming methodology especially suited to treating intensely ill-structured, i.e., difficult-to-define, issues. It does this by attempting to set up at least two very different (antithetical) and maximally challenging views (definitions, policies) of a problem situation so that everything that one view takes for granted as a basic and reasonable assumption, the other challenges as intensely as it can. [....]

The intent is ... to allow the manager to take advantage of a turbulent environment and thereby to convert a problematic situation into an opportunity (I. I. Mitroff, Emshoff, & Kilmann, 1979, pp. 583–584).

Assumption surfacing is seen as a method for ill-structured problems. Incompatible pre-sumptions in the underlying paradigm for generative pattern language can be improved through a focus on the inquiring system.

4.4. Pattern Manual for Service Systems Thinking is explicit in its para-digm

In some respects, this paper serves as an assumption surfacing for the paradigm underlying the "Pattern Manual for Service Systems Thinking" presented at PUARL last year (xxx, 2016) . While other pattern languages may not select a similar paradigm, the project should be aware of potential blind spots.

5. References

Ackoff, R. L. (1974). Redesigning the future: a systems approach to societal problems. Wiley.

Ackoff, R. L., & Gharajedaghi, J. (1996). Reflections on Systems and their Models. Systems Research, 13(1), 13–23. https://doi.org/10.1002/(SICI)1099-1735(199603)13:1<13::AIDS-RES66>3.0.CO;2-O

Alexander, C. (1964). Notes on the Synthesis of Form (Paperback). Harvard University Press.

Alexander, C. (1966). A City is Not a Tree. Design, 206, 46–55.

Alexander, C. (1968). Systems Generating Systems. Architectural Digest, 38.

Alexander, C. (1979). The Timeless Way of Building. Oxford University Press.

Alexander, C. (1996a). Foreword. In Patterns of software (pp. v–xi). New York: Oxford University Press.

Alexander, C. (1996b, October). Patterns in Architecture. Presented at the OOPSLA '96, San Jose, California. Retrieved from https://www.youtube.com/watch?v=98LdFA-_zfA

Alexander, C. (1999). The origins of pattern theory: The future of the theory, and the generation of a living world. IEEE Software, 16(5), 71–82. https://doi.org/10.1109/52.795104

Alexander, C. (2002a). The phenomenon of life (Vol. 9). Center for Environmental Structure.

Alexander, C. (2002b). The process of creating life (Vol. 10). Berkeley, California: Center for Environmental Structure.

Alexander, C. (2003, May). New Concepts In Complexity Theory: A Scientific Introduction to the Concepts in the Nature of Order. Retrieved from http://www.natureoforder.com/library-of-articles.htm

Alexander, C. (2004a). The Luminous Ground (Vol. 10). Berkeley, California: Center for Environmental Structure.

Alexander, C. (2004b, October). Sustainability And Morphogenesis: The Birth of a Living World. Presented at the Schumacher Lecture, Bristol, UK. Retrieved from http://www.living-neighborhoods.org/ht-0/archive.htm

Alexander, C. (2005). A Vision of a Living World (Vol. 11). Berkeley, California: Center for Environmental Structure.

Alexander, C. (2007). Empirical Findings from The Nature of Order. Environmental & Architectural Phenomenology, 18, 11–19.

Alexander, C., Ishikawa, S., & Silverstein, M. (1967). Pattern Manual. Berkeley, California: Center for Environmental Structure.

Alexander, C., Ishikawa, S., & Silverstein, M. (1968). A Pattern Language which Generates Multi-service Centers. Center for Environmental Structure.

Alexander, C., Ishikawa, S., & Silverstein, M. (1977). A Pattern Language: Towns, Building, Construction. New York: Oxford University Press US.

Alexander, C., & Jacobson, M. (1971). The state of the art in design methods. DMG Newsletter, 5(3), 3–7.

Alexander, C., Schmidt, R., Hanson, B., & Mehaffy, M. (2005, November). Generative Codes: The Path to Building Welcoming, Beautiful, Sustainable Neighborhoods. Retrieved from http://www.livingneighborhoods.org/ht-0/generative.htm

Alexander, C., Silverstein, M., Angel, S., Ishikawa, S., & Abrams, D. (1975). The Oregon Experiment. Oxford University Press.

Allen, T. F. H., & Starr, T. B. (1982). Hierarchy: Perspectives for Ecological Complexity. University of Chicago Press.

Ambler, S. W. (2011, March 30). Agile at 10: What We Believe. Dr. Dobb's Journal. Retrieved from http://www.drdobbs.com/architecture-and-design/agile-at-10-what-webelieve-scott-ambler/229301128

Bateson, G. (1972). The Science of Mind and Order. In Steps to an ecology of mind (1987 reprint, pp. xvii–xxvi). Northvale, NJ: Jason Aronson.

Baumgartner, P., & Sickinger, R. (2014). Foreword. In P. Baumgartner & R. Sickinger (Eds.), PURPLSOC: The Workshop 2014 (pp. 3–5). Austria: Danube University Krems.

Bayle, E., Bellamy, R., Casaday, G., Erickson, T., Fincher, S., Grinter, B., … Thomas, J.

(1998). Putting It All Together: Towards a Pattern Language for Interaction Design: A CHI 97 Workshop. SIGCHI Bulletin, 30(1), 17–23. https://doi.org/10.1145/280571.280580

Beck, K., Beedle, M., van Bennekum, A., Cockburn, A., Cunningham, W., Fowler, M., … Thomas, D. (2001). Manifesto for Agile Software Development. Retrieved from http://agilemanifesto.org/

Bjørnvig, G., & Coplien, J. O. (2008, June 21). Scrum as Organizational Patterns. Retrieved September 23, 2017, from https://sites.google.com/a/scrumorgpatterns.com/www/

Booch, G. (2006, March 2). On Design [Blog]. Retrieved June 27, 2016, from https://web.archive.org/web/20160213001803/https://www.ibm.com/developerworks/community/blogs/gradybooch/entry/on_design?lang=en

Boulding, K. E. (1956). General Systems Theory -- The Skeleton of Science. Management Science, 2(3), 197–208.

Bradner, E., Kellogg, W. A., & Erickson, T. (1999). The Adoption and Use of 'BABBLE': A Field Study of Chat in the Workplace. In ECSCW '99 (pp. 139–158). Springer, Dordrecht. https://doi.org/10.1007/0-306-47316-X_8

Brand, S. (1994). How buildings learn: what happens after they're built. New York: Viking.

Brand, S. (1999). The clock of the long now: time and responsibility. Basic Books.

Brown, P. L. (2000, November 23). A Design Controversy Goes Cozy.com. The New York Times. Retrieved from https://www.nytimes.com/2000/11/23/garden/a-designcontroversy-goes-cozycom.html

Burrell, G., & Morgan, G. (1979). Sociological paradigms and organisational analysis: elements of the sociology of corporate life. Ashgate.

Churchman, C. W. (1967). Wicked Problems. Management Science, 14(4), B-141-B-146. https://doi.org/10.1287/mnsc.14.4.B141

Churchman, C. W. (1968). The systems approach. Delacorte Press.

Churchman, C. W. (1971). The design of inquiring systems: basic concepts of systems and organization. Basic Books.

Churchman, C. W. (1979). The Systems Approach and its Enemies. New York: Basic Books.

Churchman, C. W., Protzen, J.-P., & Webber, M. M. (1992). Horst W.J. Rittel, Architecture: Berkeley. In University of California: In Memoriam. Berkeley, California: University of California. Retrieved from http://texts.cdlib.org/view?docId=hb7c6007sj;NAAN=13030&chunk.id=div00053

Cockburn, A. (2011, January 2). It started in 2001 with the Manifesto. Retrieved January 11, 2014, from http://10yearsagile.org/it-started-in-2001-with-the-manifesto#more-483

Conklin, J., & Begeman, M. L. (1987). gIBIS: A Hypertext Tool for Team Design Deliberation. In Proceedings of the ACM Conference on Hypertext (pp. 247–251). New York, NY, USA: ACM. https://doi.org/10.1145/317426.317444

Conklin, J., Selvin, A., Shum, S. B., & Sierhuis, M. (2001). Facilitated Hypertext for Collective Sensemaking: 15 Years on from gIBIS. In Proceedings of the 12th ACM Conference on Hypertext and Hypermedia (pp. 123–124). New York, NY, USA: ACM. https://doi.org/10.1145/504216.504246

Coplien, J. O. (1995, May 28). Generative Pattern [Wiki]. Retrieved September 22, 2017, from http://wiki.c2.com/?GenerativePattern

Coplien, J. O., & Harrison, N. B. (2004). Organizational patterns of agile software development. Prentice-Hall, Inc.

Coplien, J. O., & Schmidt, D. C. (Eds.). (1995). Pattern languages of program design. ACM Press.

Cunningham, W. (1994). Portland Pattern Repository [Wiki]. Retrieved September 22, 2017, from http://c2.com/ppr/

Cunningham, W. (2000). History Of Patterns [Wiki]. Retrieved September 22, 2017, from http://wiki.c2.com/?HistoryOfPatterns

Deetz, S. (1996). Describing Differences in Approaches to Organization Science: Rethinking Burrell and Morgan and Their Legacy. Organization Science, 7(2), 191–207. https://doi.org/10.1287/orsc.7.2.191

Demirkan, H., Spohrer, J. C., & Krishna, V. (2011). Introduction of the Science of Service Systems. In The Science of Service Systems (pp. 1–11). Boston: Springer. https://doi.org/10.1007/978-1-4419-8270-4_1

Erickson, T. (2000). Lingua Francas for design: sacred places and pattern languages. In Proceedings of the 3rd Conference on Designing Interactive Systems (pp. 357–368). ACM Press. https://doi.org/10.1145/347642.347794

Gabriel, R. P. (1996a). Preface. In Patterns of software (pp. xiii–xviii). New York: Oxford University Press.

Gabriel, R. P. (1996b). The Quality Without a Name. In Patterns of software (pp. 33–44). New York: Oxford University Press.

Gamma, E., Helm, R., Johnson, R., & Vlissides, J. (1995). Design Patterns: Elements of Reusable Object-Oriented Software. Addison.

Gibson, J. J. (1979). The Theory of Affordances. In The Ecological Approach to Visual Perception (pp. 127–143). Boston: Houghton Mifflin.

Goles, T., & Hirschheim, R. (2000). The paradigm is dead, the paradigm is dead...long live the paradigm: the legacy of Burrell and Morgan. Omega, 28(3), 249–268. https://doi.org/10.1016/S0305-0483(99)00042-0

Grabow, S. (1983). Christopher Alexander: The Search for a New Paradigm in Architecture. Oriel Press.

Group Patern Language Project. (2013). Group Works: A Pattern Language for Bringing Life to Meetings and Other Gatherings. Retrieved September 23, 2017, from https://groupworksdeck.org/

Heidegger, M. (1971). Building Dwelling Thinking. In A. Hofstadter (Ed.), Poetry, Language, Thought (pp. 143–159). New York: Harper & Row.

Holling, C. S., Gunderson, L. H., & Ludwig, D. (2002). In Quest of a Theory of Adaptive Change. In L. H. Gunderson & C. S. Holling (Eds.), Panarchy: understanding transformations in human and natural systems (pp. 3–22). Island Press.

xxx (2016). Pattern Manual for Service Systems Thinking. In Proceedings of the 2016 International PUARL Conference. San Francisco: Portland Urban Architecture Research Laboratory. Retrieved from http://coevolving.com/commons/20161028-pattern-manualfor-service-systems-thinking

Ingold, T. (2000). General introduction. In The Perception of the Environment: Essays on Livelihood, Dwelling and Skill (pp. 1–7). Routledge.

Ingold, T. (2011). Point, line, counterpoint: From environment to fluid space. In Being Alive: Essays on Movement, Knowledge and Description (pp. 76–88). Routledge.

Ingold, T. (2017). On human correspondence. Journal of the Royal Anthropological Institute, 23(1), 9–27. https://doi.org/10.1111/1467-9655.12541 Kuhn, T. S. (1967). The structure of scientific revolutions. Chicago: University of Chicago Press.

Kunz, W., & Rittel, H. W. (1970). Issues as elements of information systems (Vol. 131). Institute of Urban and Regional Development, University of California, Berkeley.

Langrish, J. Z. (2016). The Design Methods Movement: From Optimism to Darwinism. In Proceedings of DRS 2016. Brighton, UK. Retrieved from https://drs2016.squarespace.com/222

Lewis, M. W., & Kelemen, M. L. (2002). Multiparadigm inquiry: Exploring organizational pluralism and paradox. Human Relations, 55(2), 251–275. https://doi.org/10.1177/0018726702055002185

Mann, T. (2017, April 17). Types of patterns a pattern science would study. Pattern Languages for Systemic Transformation. Response. Retrieved from https://www.facebook.com/groups/125513674232534/permalink/1240668896050334/

Mason, R. O., & Mitroff, I. I. (1981). Challenging strategic planning assumptions: theory, cases, and techniques. Wiley.

Mitroff, I. I. (1974). The Subjective Side of Science: A Philosophical Inquiry Into the Psychology of the Apollo Moon Scientists. Elsevier.

Mitroff, I. I., & Emshoff, J. R. (1979). On Strategic Assumption-Making: A Dialectical Approach to Policy and Planning. The Academy of Management Review, 4(1), 1. https://doi.org/10.2307/257398

Mitroff, I. I., Emshoff, J. R., & Kilmann, R. H. (1979). Assumptional analysis: A methodology for strategic problem solving. Management Science, 583–593. https://doi.org/10.1287/mnsc.25.6.583

Mitroff, I. I., & Mason, R. O. (1981). Creating a dialectical social science: concepts, methods, and models. D. Reidel.

Mitroff, I. I., & Silvers, A. (2010). Dirty rotten strategies: how we trick ourselves and others into solving the wrong problems precisely. Stanford University Press.

Motohashi, M., Hanyuda, E., & Nakano, H. (2013). From pattern languages to a project language: a shift proposal from existing pattern community. In Proceedings of the 20th Conference on Pattern Languages of Programs (p. 33). The Hillside Group. Retrieved from http://dl.acm.org/citation.cfm?id=2725669.2725708

Nickles, T. (2017). Historicist Theories of Scientific Rationality. In E. N. Zalta (Ed.), The Stanford Encyclopedia of Philosophy (Summer 2017). Metaphysics Research Lab, Stanford University. Retrieved from https://plato.stanford.edu/archives/sum2017/entries/rationality-historicist/

Norman, D. A. (1999). Affordance, conventions, and design. Interactions, 6(3), 38–43. https://doi.org/10.1145/301153.301168

Normann, R., & Ramírez, R. (1994). Designing interactive strategy: from value chain to value constellation. Wiley.

O'Neill, R. V., DeAngelis, D. L., Waide, J. B., & Allen, T. F. H. (1986). A Hierarchical Concept of Ecosystems. Princeton University Press.

Peña, W. M., & Focke, J. W. (1969). Problem Seeking: New directions in architectural programming (1st ed.). Houston, TX: Caudill, Rowlett and Scott.

Pynchon, T. (1973). Gravity's rainbow. Viking Press.

Ramos, C., den Hollander, M., Heasman, L., & Coplien, J. O. (2016, September 30). History of the Patterns. Retrieved September 23, 2017, from http://scrumbook.org/bookoutline/history-of-the-patterns.html

Ravetz, J. R. (2004). The post-normal science of precaution. Futures, 36(3), 347–357. https://doi.org/10.1016/S0016-3287(03)00160-5

Rith, C., & Dubberly, H. (2007). Why Horst WJ Rittel matters. Design Issues, 23(1), 72–91. https://doi.org/10.1162/desi.2007.23.1.72

Rittel, H. W. (1971). Some Principles for the Design of an Educational System for Design. Journal of Architectural Education, 26(1–2), 16–27. https://doi.org/10.1080/10464883.1971.11102482

Rittel, H. W. (1980). APIS, a Concept for an Argumentative Planning Information System (Vol. 324). Institute of Urban & Regional Development, University of California, Berkeley.

Rittel, H. W., Grant, D. P., & Protzen, J.-P. (1972). Second-generation Design Methods. The DMG 5th Anniversary Report, 1, 5–10.

Rittel, H. W., & Webber, M. M. (1973). Dilemmas in a general theory of planning. Policy Sciences, 4(2), 155–169. https://doi.org/10.1007/BF01405730

Rocha, J. C., Peterson, G. D., & Biggs, R. (2015). Regime Shifts in the Anthropocene: Drivers, Risks, and Resilience. PLoS ONE. https://doi.org/10.1371/journal.pone.0134639

Schuler, D. (2008). Liberating Voices: A Pattern Language for Communication Revolution. MIT Press.

Schwaber, K. (1997). SCRUM Development Process. In Business Object Design and Implementation (pp. 117–134). London: Springer. https://doi.org/10.1007/978-1-4471-0947-1_11

Spohrer, J., Maglio, P. P., Bailey, J., & Gruhl, D. (2007). Steps Toward a Science of Service Systems. Computer, 40(1), 71–77. https://doi.org/10.1109/MC.2007.33

Steenson, M. W. (2014). Architectures of Information: Christopher Alexander, Cedric Price, and Nicholas Negroponte and MIT's Architecture Machine Group (Doctoral dissertation).

Princeton University, Princeton, NJ. Ulrich, W. (2009, March 27). A Tribute to C.W. Churchman. Retrieved September 20, 2017, from http://wulrich.com/cwc.html

Vargo, S. L., & Lusch, R. F. (2004). Evolving to a New Dominant Logic for Marketing. Journal of Marketing, 68(1), 1–17. https://doi.org/10.1509/jmkg.68.1.1.24036

Walker, B., Holling, C. S., Carpenter, S. R., & Kinzig, A. (2004). Resilience, Adaptability and Transformability in Social–ecological Systems. Ecology and Society, 9(2), 5.

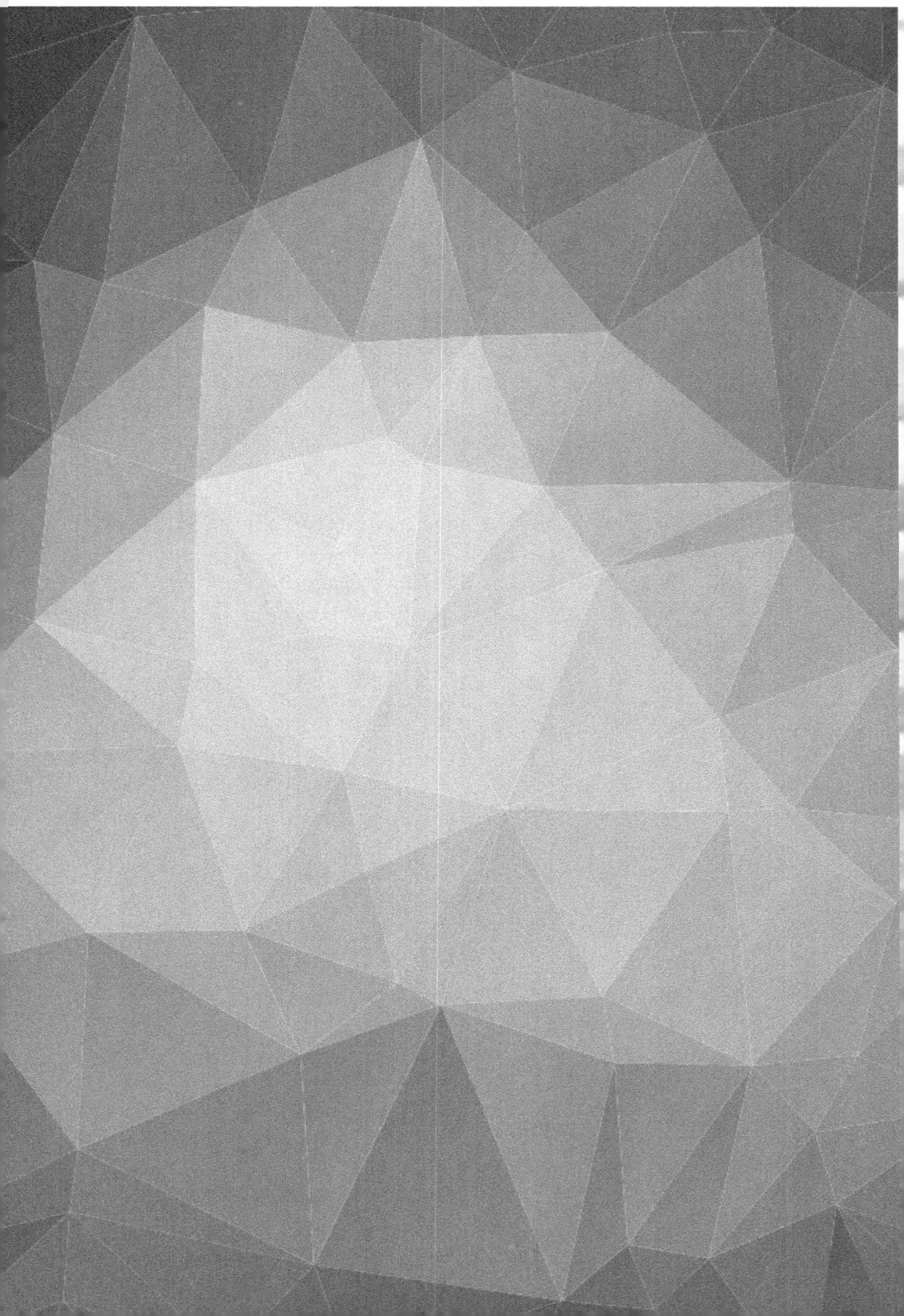

A Building is not a Turkish Carpet – Patterns, Properties and Beauty

Jacobson, Max
Retired
maxjacobson@yahoo.com

A review of the historical development of Christopher Alexander and his various associate's work with particular attention to the developing concept of "beauty" in the various books. While it is illustrated that the actual word rarely if ever appears in the bulk of the work, it becomes a central focus of the latest 4-volume The Nature of Order. This eventual concept of beauty, derived initially from an intense analysis of ancient Turkish carpets, turns out to constitute the characteristics of Nature. As such, this 'natural' form of beauty omits other forms, such as the Sublime, Euclidean geometry, and the beauty of noble social ideals expressed in architecture.

Alexander; Beauty; Nature; Patterns; 15 Properties

1. Introduction

Today I want to talk about one aspect of Chris Alexander's writing and built works - this with the understanding that most of this work was born with the help of the midwifery of many co-authors, associates, employees. and students. It constitutes a somewhat coherent field of thought that has grown, been modified, and refined over a period of over 50 years.

Specifically it will be an exploration of the relationship between the Alexander approach to architectural design, and the quality of beauty, focusing particularly on the *"A Pattern Language"* (APL) of 1977, and *"The Nature of Order"* (NOO) of 2002-2005. I believe that this approach is fundamentally a search for beauty in architecture, and in the entire man-made environment. This in spite of the fact that the Pattern Language presents practical solutions to functional problems, and does not explicitly discuss beauty, while Alexander's more recent The Nature of Order reverses this, and is primarily concerned with beauty, overshadowing functional concerns. Thus I feel these 2 works have quite different approaches to the goal of beauty, and describing these differences will be the main focus of my remarks. Secondly I will ask whether either work has the generative capacity to produce beautiful buildings. Finally I will try to point out some of the shortcomings of each.

2. Background

I need to characterize my role and experience in this area. I worked under Chris for 8 years, both as a grad student at Berkeley, as an associate at the Center for Environmental Structure, and finally as a co-author of the APL. For all of those years, he was my most important mentor, my guru if you will. He provided the foundation for most of my current views of the role and meaning of architecture. At the conclusion of our work on the APL, Murray Silverstein and I left the Center and started our own architectural practice. For the next 40 years, we committed ourselves to the practice, along with occasional teaching gigs, and writing 2 books on architecture. But our path diverged from Chris's subsequent practice and writing. The APL continued to be the backbone of our design approach, but we didn't closely follow Chris's later professional work and writing.[1] I retired a couple of years ago, and as a result of attending a couple of PUARL conferences, I began to take a renewed interest in what Chris and his associates were doing since 1975. Thus I am a relative newcomer to his work since then, including his teaching, built projects, and books. I approach this work with a fresh eye.

And since beauty is one of the main topics of my comments today, I think I need to define

---

1   Exceptions were my attendance at Chris's 1993 exhibition of his carpet collection, which was published as "A Foreshadowing of 21st Century Art", Oxford University Press, 1993, and his lecture at Berkeley in 2012.

how I understand the quality. My definition of beauty is historical and general. Culling historical definitions, it can be summarized by saying that a beautiful object is whole, meaning it is both complete and economical. It lacks nothing, and nothing can be removed without diminishing its beauty.[2] Beauty embodies a kind of truth,[3] exposing all, hiding nothing, embodying eternally valid relationships (such as geometry). Exquisite functional excellence leads to our sense of beauty.[4] A nd we demand that beauty not be evil, that it be on the side of the good.[5]

Beauty invariably generates pleasure, but many different kinds of pleasure.

Take physical pleasure. A smoothly polished hand rail gives pleasure to our skin, a well-proportioned table and chair gives comfort to our sitting, a sunny window alcove warms our body as we settle in to read a book.

Beauty affects our psychological experience. Beauty comforts our psychological pain, our fatigue, our negative attitudes of ennui, or angst. It increases our confidence in our own power of appreciation. It refreshes and strengthens our inner landscape.

Beauty can have a simple, immediate emotional impact that floods through us. We are touched by a beautiful story, musical passage, or building. We may be surprised by the force of the emotion, and not fully understand why we respond as we do.

Finally, we can derive intellectual pleasure from beauty, grasping its source, and its truth. This can range from awe and wonder, to a calmer understanding of its beauty. There are beautiful ideas, vistas, geometries, that mainly give us intellectual pleasure.

We seek out beauty for various kinds of pleasure, including comfort, satisfaction, stimulus, even excitement and challenge that can even embody fear.

3. Beauty and the Pattern Language

The work on the *APL* was an attempt to make a more beautiful built environment. But beauty wasn't directly addressed in the book. Instead, it presented hypothesized solutions to perceived problems in the environment. The word "beauty" simply doesn't exist in the text. But the book attempts to help create beautiful environments via the resolution of physical and psychological barriers to comfort.

2   "I strive for an architecture from which nothing can be taken away." (Helmut Jahn), and "Beauty is the purgation of the superfluous." (Michelangelo), and "The line of beauty is the result of perfect economy." (Emerson, from his essay "Beauty").
3   "Beauty is truth, truth beauty, - That is all Ye know on Earth, and all ye need to know." (Keats, from "Ode on a Grecian Urn"), and "Architecture is the reaching out for the truth." (Lou Kahn).
4   "The first principle of architectural beauty is that the essential lines of a construction be determined by a perfect appropriateness to its use." (Gustave Eiffel), and "True beauty and usefulness always go hand in hand." (from the "Institutio Oratoria of Quntilian").
5   "The beautiful consists in utility and the power to produce some good." (Plato)

I think this approach was partly due to the times, and to the relative lack of practical professional experience of those of us working with Chris at the Center for Environmental Structure (CES).

Many of us in the universities during the 60's were rejecting the Vietnam war, the boring work in the corporation, symbolized by crewcuts and martinis, suits and ties, cigarettes and plastics. And we rejected the bland, cold, spiritless architecture which reflected this atmosphere. We felt the buildings that were being put up around us were painfully ugly, and they often replaced earlier structures that were actually quite beautiful. As budding architects, we wanted to reverse this deadening atmosphere and to design beautiful buildings.

But most of us had little, if any, experience in putting a real building together – designing with a client, detailing and supervising construction.[6] We were not yet confident that we could produce a beautiful building.

So we started by going back to basics, trying to figure out what made sense in buildings and what didn't. What are the patterns that make us feel comfortable, that exist in the buildings we love? In this phase we were trying to heal, to comfort ourselves from the pain of the boring and oppressive architecture around us. We wanted an architecture that one could relax and feel at home in, that could counter up-tightness. We identified patterns from beautiful places, but we described them as solutions to functional problems.

Yet Chris made it clear early on that beauty lay at the heart of this effort, in spite of his reputation as a methodologist. In the architecture department at Berkeley there was a departmental group that published the Design Methods Newsletter, covering all the various approaches to rationalizing the design process – evaluation, client participation, statistical methods, computer programming, design and graphics, etc. In early 1971 I was asked by the group to interview Chris regarding his approach to design. In that interview he disavowed any interest in, or any value in, computer graphics, evaluation, brainstorming, or any "rational design methodology" which he felt removed one from the real process of designing good buildings. He stressed

> *"...I am definitely concerned with trying to make better buildings...the frame of mind that you need to be in to create a good building. Are you thinking about smell and touch, and what happens when people are walking about in a place? But particularly are you at peace with yourself?" And further, it became clear that "good" meant "beautiful" for him. In denying that the earlier Notes on the Synthesis of Form was a design method, he charac-*

---

6   *The exception was Sara Ishikawa who had worked in architectural offices for around 5 years before beginning work with Chris. Also, several faculty members at Berkeley served as consultants to the CES, including Sym van der Ryn, Sandy Hirshen, and Roz Lindheim.*

terized that effort as "I wanted to be able to create beautiful buildings..with the same kind of beauty that traditional architecture had...even the simple emphasis on function and requirements in "Notes" was, for me, merely a way of getting at beauty."[7]

This pursuit of beauty, and the need for the designer to be at peace with oneself, were to emerge full throated in Chris's later 2005 NOO, but interestingly submerged in the 1977 APL. As mentioned, there is scarcely a mention of the word "beauty" in the *APL* – instead the patterns are an approach to "humanize" the world – to make it more human, more comfortable, and, only by implication, more beautiful.

The design process using the book can be seen as rather simple, straight forward – select those patterns that seem relevant to your project, and go through them in the order suggested, applying them as you deem appropriate to your particular situation, retaining the core concept but as you see fit. In this sense, the *APL* is indeed a method, a "methodology" in spite of Alexander's dismissal of the idea, albeit a very relaxed and comforting method.

The *APL* does not give instructions regarding the proper attitude or emotional preparation required of the designer. One is not instructed be "at peace with oneself". The book does, however incidentally, produce a certain peace and relaxation in the mind of the user. The idea of inner peace lurks beneath the surface. No longer does one need to worry or consider fashion and current esthetic standards. Instead, if a pattern is accepted, then the natural instincts of the designer/user on how to apply it will be the most reliable and 'real'. This aspect is tremendously liberating, putting the center of a valid response into the heart of the designer. And this kind of free design process can be a beautiful experience.

This freedom from the need for professional correctness is why the *APL* remains so popular among the general readership. It is meant for anyone to use, though it was envisioned especially as a tool for laypeople creating a design for themselves, and for students seeking guidance in their design work.

For those not steeped in the design cannons of the schools and journals, it is natural and easy to accept a unique list of patterns appropriate to the need, reject any that seem wrong or weird, to feel that the process is founded on well-reasoned arguments that speak directly to one's physical and emotional needs, and in most cases echo one's own intuitions.

In fact, the word 'architect' is also never mentioned in the *APL*! This underscores the bias of the book, that most of modern architecture, architectural curricula in the schools, and virtually all published work, was producing an inhuman environment. Those architects and

7   *"Max Jacobson Interviews Christopher Alexander", Design Methods Newsletter, March 1971, Vol. 5, No. 3. The interview was republished in Architectural Design, December, 1971.*

students that reject the APL approach are typically devoted to individual architectural creativity, and this takes the form of intense focus on esthetics, what is currently viewed as the cutting edge of design, and a feeling that architecture requires study in an accepted institution and manner, not the instinctual responses of amateurs.

3.1. The physical book itself was carefully studied to be a beautiful object

The 1200 pages are assembled so that the book can be comfortably held in the hand, and carried around. The paper thin pages, combined with the deep red cloth cover, embossed in gold, all contribute to its biblical flavor – you know you are holding something valuable and beautiful.

The lead photographs which introduce each pattern were selected to be beautiful examples of the pattern, and the very informal sketches were economical distillations of the basic idea. Even the typeface was selected for clear and easy reading. Here's the intro example photo for the pattern "6 Foot Balcony".

Figure 1.

The structure of the APL embodies some of the traditional qualities of beauty mentioned earlier. The material is complete, whole, covering the entire range of building issues from the region, the city, the neighborhood, down to the buildings and their decorative details. And in this sense, nothing can really be omitted from the material without damaging the basic theory that any design act is both a completion of a higher order entity, and something that must be completed itself by the smaller scale patterns. So it is both complete and economical.

The book is clearly functional which is one of its most beautiful aspects. It was demonstrated by my grad school experiments with lay subjects, that they can start to design workable schematic house plans using the language. And this is true of my architectural students now when they are willing to give up some of their preconceptions. In short, it works as a design guide for those who want to use it.

Is the material true? I think that by and large the patterns address real problems, and recommend genuine solutions. There is an honest attempt to specify a level of confidence in each pattern, admitting that some are more well-founded than others. And we must remember that the patterns are only hypotheses, put forward with the best knowledge possessed at the moment, inviting criticism and further research to produce better material.

And is the book a force for the "good"? We certainly thought we were redirecting architecture into a healthier, more humane direction. But, of course, not everyone agreed. The majority of the architectural faculty at Berkeley at the time thought the material led students into a dangerous direction, since it was opposed to the safe established canons of the curriculum. Some thought it was intellectually weak in assuming what was good for some was good for all. Others felt the book simply presented a medieval esthetic rooted in Europe, not applicable to the modern world. On the other hand, the book was taken seriously at some schools of architecture, notably the U. of Oregon, Kansas State U., Darmstadt, and a new school in Naples. Nevertheless, while the lay community has largely embraced it, the profession has largely ignored it.

3.2. But does the *APL* have the capacity to produce beautiful buildings?

To the extent that it is used in design, it has produced mixed results. At one extreme are the people who pick one or two patterns, hire an architect to do the building, and then say that they "used the *APL*". These buildings in general don't reflect the wholeness intended, and look just like all other buildings. At the other extreme are the buildings done by the authors of the work as they tried to put into practice the principles of the book. And therein lies a tale.

As part of our work on *APL*, it was deemed important to include a specific building system, human-based, that was both buildable by all, and that resulted in humane structures.

The question of a human-based building system had been focused on for several years before the publication of APL in 1977. A conference on Responsive Housebuilding Technologies was held at MIT in 1972. Alexander and I presented two papers which attempted to lay out basic specifications for a human-based building system.[8] Chris's paper consisted of 24 Postulates governing a humane room shape. They included *polygonal room plan shapes*

---

8   *"An Attempt to Derive the Nature of a Human Building System from First Principles", C. Alexander, and "Specifications for an Organic and Human Building System", C. Alexander and Max Jacobson, both in The Responsive House, Ed Allen, ed., MIT Press, 1974.*

without acute inner angles, columns at the corners of spaces, walls to contain stiffening ribs, a grid of columns, continuous beans connecting columns, thickened openings, and angled joints between verticals and horizontals. He presented a sketch summarizing these basic points. At this point, a post and beam system was most naturally suggested by this paper.

Figure 2.

In our joint paper we added the notions of thick walls, easy repair, and the use of human scaled building components to allow easy construction. We offered the Japanese house tradition of design based on tatami mats as an example of a post and beam system that enabled user design and standard construction.

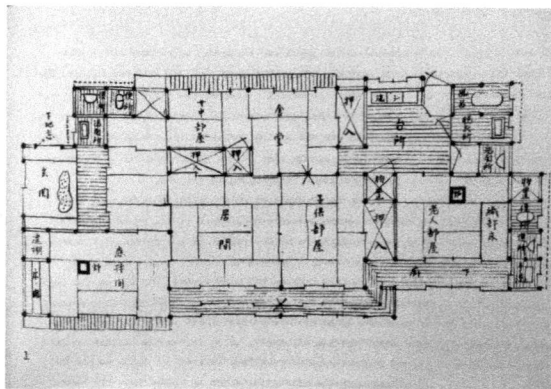

Figure 3.

In this joint paper, we presented a simple wooden post and beam model that I had built at the CES which embodied most of the principles we were proposing.

Figure 4

Figure 5

We then asked non-architect subjects to use both the APL and the post-and-beam rules to do a schematic house design for themselves. In our joint paper we then presented examples of how this combination of the patterns and the post-and-beam system enabled laymen to design reasonable schematic house plans for themselves. At this point we were not judging whether their work was beautiful, simply whether they were able to use the patterns and the post-and-beam system to produce reasonable first drafts of plans. Here is one of the better ones, a 2-story plan.

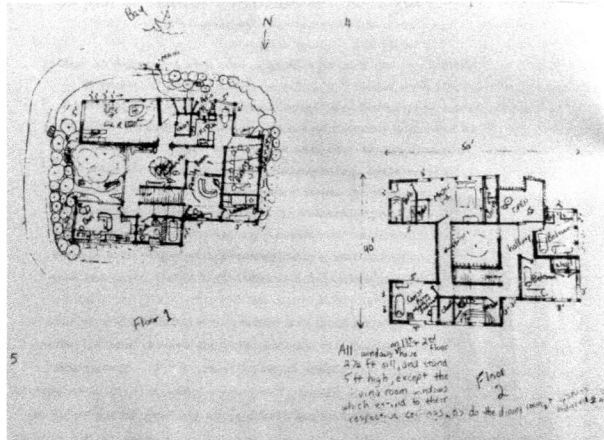

Figure 6.

However, as we worked on including a construction system in the *APL*, Chris decided to replace the wooden post-and-beam system with a system based on ultra-lightweight concrete poured into wooden forms. It was argued in the pattern "Good Materials" that large pieces of structural wood, such as 8X8s, weren't feasible given the state of the world's forests, but that smaller wood was appropriate for doors, windows, trim, even for wood and plywood forms. Left unexplored was the option of using small pieces of wood to build the whole structure, i.e., typical stud construction. The real objection to wood construction, I believe, was Chris's feeling that it produces thinness of structure, and that heft and mass are required for psychological comfort. From the pattern "Box Columns", we read

"Columns feel uncomfortable unless they are reasonably thick and solid. This feeling is rooted in structural reality. A long thin column, carrying a heavy load, is likely to fail by buckling: and our feelings, apparently, are particularly tuned in to this possibility."

A long thin column doesn't make sense in concrete construction, but this factor is less critical in a material like wood that can take tension. The irony is that the columns of light weight concrete were to be formed by four wooden 1X10 inch planks, more wood per foot of height than a 6X6 post.

I disagreed with this concrete building system from the start, in spite of the fact that I illustrated its application in the book. Chris – the European - felt that concrete had to be depended upon since the forests of the world were being depleted and not every country even had forests to tap. One can sympathize with this, but I – the Northern Californian - felt that wood construction shouldn't be eliminated because of its building ease, the potential re-invigoration of forests with ongoing fresh planting, and the basic ecological argument that sun, water, and soil grew the material automatically, while concrete involved mining and refining via lots of energy. Plus, I liked wooden buildings, especially since I thought I could build them.

At any rate, Chris was committed to pursuing the ultra-light weight concrete system, and a test structure was built in the backyard of the CES in Berkeley. Sarah Ishikawa and I half-heartedly helped a bit in the construction of the building. I found it quite "clunky" and was a bit embarrassed by its appearance. I didn't think it was beautiful at all. It felt heavy and oppressive.

Figure 7.

I had fallen in love with my little balsa wood post-and-beam model, and wanted to build a cabin for myself using the system. I followed the criteria that Chris and I had worked on some years earlier, finding I was able to incorporate them using rough wood 4X4's, plywood, and fiberglass, and using the labor skills of myself and friends.

Figure 8.

Figure 9.

These were the last days of the group that did the APL. We all left Chris to do our own teaching and practicing outside the CES. Murray and I formed an architectural practice on our own, much to the dismay of Chris. We never considered using the light-weight concrete system outlined in the APL, but worked only with wood construction. Chris then also went on to accept commissions for houses, doing both the design and the construction.

It is interesting to compare the earliest residential building that Chris did with the earliest that Murray and I did, each of us incorporating the appropriate patterns, each trying to create a beautiful building. But we started out in radically different directions. Chris's Sala House is shown in Figures 10a and 10b:

Figure 10a.

Figure 10b.

Murray and I first did the Kuperman House, shown below in Figures 11a and 11b.

Figure 11a.

Figure 11b.

Chris's Sala house wasn't built with the system proposed in the *APL*. Instead, he reverted to a wooden post-and-beam grid system (with 6X6 posts, and 6X8 beams), covered on the exterior with a 2 inch thick reinforced concrete layer, poured into levels shaped by 2X12 formboards, in alternating colors of red and grey. He was the general contractor, using the labor of his students and associates at the CES.

We, on the other hand, reverted to standard 2X4 wood framed walls and exterior wood siding. We produced complete drawings, and observed the construction process, but a normal contractor did all the construction, save some soji screens built by the owner.

Now the basic schematic design of each was informed by the *APL* and both buildings received very happy feedback from the satisfied clients. But were the authors of the APL able to use the patterns to create a beautiful building? That, after all, is why we were starting to work as architects. Looking back at these first projects after 35 years of distance, I would say that they each embodied some aspects of beauty (especially on the interiors), as well as some aspects of awkwardness and ugliness. But they were perhaps better than the current typical developer houses, and even some architect-designed houses. But not all. These two examples are the work of relatively inexperienced architects and they do not measure up to the beauty of work being done by some of the more experienced and talented architects in the Bay Area at that time such as Charles Moore, Bill Turnbull, Joe Esherick, George Homsey and many others. Of course, we both got better over the years.

Some other students and associates of Chris went on to start practices of their own, utilizing the APL, and many of the products were quite good. But none had the beauty of indigenous buildings, or of those by the architects mentioned above, much less than those by Frank Lloyd Wright, Bernard Maybeck, or Rudolph Shindler.

Overall, I feel that use of the *APL* has improved the work of architects, mediocre designers as well as the more talented. And it has helped the builders and laymen who have been willing to use it to produce better buildings, often good buildings that show many aspects of beauty. But in the end (I think Murray would agree with me), the APL has produced "good-enough beauty", enough to make happy clients and users, beautiful enough to bring some pride to the designers and builders who produced it. And that is a big step in the right direction.

4. Beauty according to The Nature of Order

Chris came to feel that the *APL*, by itself, was inadequate to create really beautiful buildings. Something else was needed. His answer appeared in his 4-volume *NOO*, sub-titled *"An Essay on the Art of Building and The Nature of the Universe"*. The word "essay" is defined as "a short piece of writing on a particular subject". I once devilishly weighed the volumes. While the *APL* came in at just over a pound, the *NOO* weighs almost 13 pounds!

I feel there are 3 major conceptual corner stones to this mega-work: The word Beauty is replaced with Life; it is described by The 15 Properties; and It is felt and verified by The Mirror of the Self.

4.1. The Life of an Object

In his much earlier The Timeless Way of Building (1979), Chris wrote about "The Quality Without a Name".

> "There is a central quality which is the root criterion of life and spirit in a man, a town, a building, or a wilderness. This quality is objective and precise, but it cannot be named".

He gives several words which approximately describe this central quality – alive, whole, comfortable, free, exact, egoless, eternal. This "quality without a name" appears 23 years later in Volume 1 of the NOO, where the best description of it is "the Life in things". This Life in things comes from Wholeness, and is further described as innocence, simplicity, truthfulness, wabi-to-sabi or rustic beauty.

Note how similar this "Life in an object" is to the Chinese concept of Chi, the life energy that is inherent in all things. It too is undefinable, but is approximately described as the spirit, the energy, the essence of an object.

I don't pretend to understand this quality completely, but it seems to me to aptly describe organic beauty, the kind of beauty that we see in nature, in the objects that we see as being natural. It excludes objects that have been primarily created out of a concept or idea. It includes those that age and are imperfect. For Chris's NOO the beauty of an object is the same as its degree of Life as defined by the 15 Properties.

4.2. The 15 Properties

Starting in the 70's Chris gradually built an important Turkish carpet collection, studying the ways that they created beautiful visual results. This continued during the next 25 years of his teaching, writing, and building. The secret of their beauty, he came to believe, lay in the principles that underlay their design, principles which he finally labeled "The 15 Properties". They emerged from tribal carpets woven by indigenous people, the earliest in time being the best, those freest of modern influences. These properties include Levels of Scale, Strong Centers, Boundaries between these Centers, Alternating Repetition, Local Symmetries, Deep Interlock, Contrast, Gradients, Roughness, and Simplicity.

These properties were first derived from 2-dimensional carpets, and do not, on the face of it, deal with the volumes of buildings or the experience of moving through them. Thus, the Properties are abstract. But Alexander posits that these properties lie at the heart of all beautiful objects – buildings, landscapes, tools, and paintings. In short, the Beauty of any object – its Life - is defined by the extent to which it embodies the 15 Properties.

It is surprising then that the Properties, derived from Turkish carpets, do indeed describe nature's organisms . The properties correspond to the characteristics of cells, animal and plant structures, even topographical features such as shorelines. For example, this organic cross section displays the properties of good shapes, strong centers, contrast, levels of scale, boundaries, roughness, echoes, simplicity, even a void.

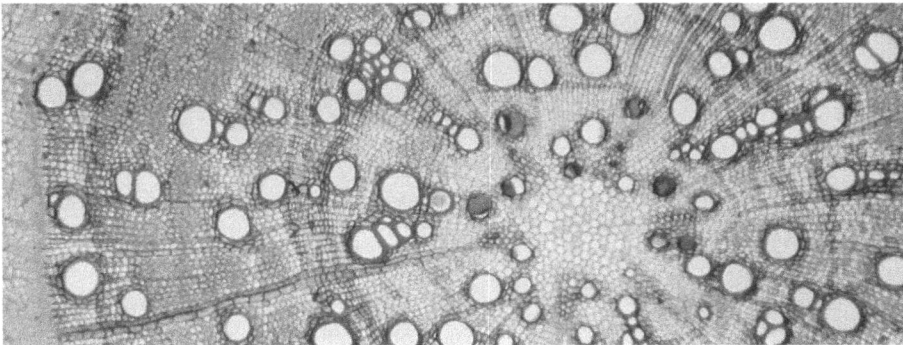

Figure 12.

This tree possesses the properties of levels of scale, alternating repetition, good shape, local symmetries, deep interlock, contrast, gradients, roughness, and echoes.

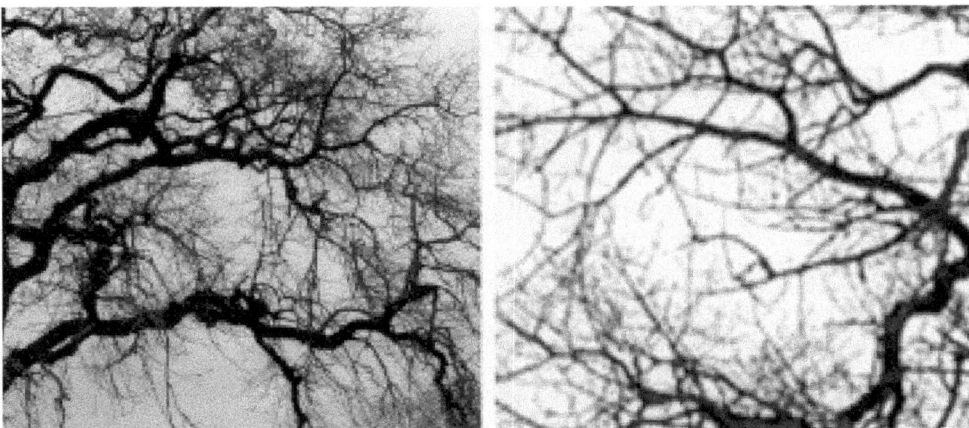

Figure 13.

It turns out that the properties do indeed describe the kind of beauty that we see in the organic natural world. I feel that these 15 properties constitute one of Chris's greatest insights. They enable us to not only identify the organic beauty of buildings, but also that kind of beauty in all human craft - our utensils, clothes, ordered landscapes - all our arts.

Chris goes on, in the *NOO*, to insist that the only way we humans can create this beauty is to act like nature ourselves, without the interference of ideas, opinions, and past learning, paying attention instead to our feelings. This can be difficult for the designer since our minds are abuzz with images, thoughts, memories, hopes and design goals. But Chris requires that we focus only on how to shape each new element in response to what is already there, in such a way that we can feel it increasing the life of the whole. If we succeed in this, we may create Natural or Organic Beauty, full of Life.

4.3. The Mirror of the Self

The *NOO* maintains that we can recognize the quality of Life in an object, its deep beauty, by comparing it to our inner selves, recognizing the extent to which it corresponds to our deepest core self.

Chris presents dual images of objects – buildings, parks, tea cups – one of which embodies more fully the 15 properties. He then asks (paraphrasing) "Which of the two is more like yourself, which captures your inner nature, which is a better image of yourself, which has more life?" "Not which you 'like' the most, or 'prefer', because that is too shaped by history, training, education, i.e., outer influences such as 'ideas', and 'conceptions'. These ideas and concepts take us away from making contact with our inner, deeper, more basic nature, our organic structure."

Since we humans are all of the same species, we share the same organic makeup. This probably explains why there is such a high degree of agreement among those who are asked to choose. Most people eventually choose the object that is richest in the 15 properties because it is most like their shared inner organic selves. But this will be a difficult judgement for many designers, who have developed strong preferences based on past experience and training.

But in short, the theory is that those objects which are the most accurate mirrors of our inner self - forgetting about ideas, preferences, theories, even what one thinks is most beautiful, are in fact the most beautiful.

4.4. Does the NOO have the capacity to produce beautiful buildings?

Of course, one must have a serious worry that no one except Chris Alexander (along with his staff members on the job) is capable of employing the design method proposed in the NOO. He sets such a high standard of almost religious fervor, total construction and budget control, of patience, of focus on a single attitude of design, that few others on their own will be able fully employ his method. His acolytes are able to partially work in this way, and produce admirable projects, but will rarely if ever do work that comes up to the level that Chris calls for. In fact, in the *NOO* he presents only his architecture as examples of current architect-designed buildings that have the quality of beauty, or Life, that he seeks, little or nothing from the work of his past students and associates[9], nothing from the work of other contemporary architects that have also tried to create the same type of beauty.[10]

So asking whether the *NOO* is capable of producing beautiful buildings is equivalent to asking whether Chris's buildings are beautiful. If we wanted, we could take his word for it: He does not hesitate to praise his work as being full of life, of being beautiful. He makes no critical comments to temper these judgements. We could take the words of his satisfied clients and users that he generously quotes. Or we could simply look at the photos of his work that he provides and apply the Mirror of the Self, asking whether the images correspond to our deepest selves, to who we want to be at the end of our lives. I find that if I apply this test to the images of his buildings I'm able to find many instances of beauty, but overall they don't fully represent my inner self. My inner self is in better correspondence with the work of Bernard Maybeck, Rudolf Shindler, or Frank Lloyd Wright. What about you?

Instead of looking at images in the book (Are many of the photos intentionally out of focus to create a mystical sense?), it would be preferable to visit his work in person, to walk around and through the actual buildings, which I haven't done. From the photos alone, I again see many areas of great beauty such as the large central building on the Eishen campus. But much of the beauty that I see in the bulk of the work is flavored with traditional European motifs that are part of Chris's background, instead of a universally envisioned architecture that we can all feel reflects our inner nature.

5. Limitations of APL beauty and NOO beauty

The *APL* implies that beautiful buildings emerge from the deep comfort that results from the solutions to problems, from the resolution of discomfort, both psychological, and physical.

9   Such as our work, or that of Howard Davis, Saul Picardo, Kyriakos, among others.
10   He does include the Ennis house by Frank Lloyd Wright as a good example in his later Battle book in 2012.

The *NOO* says that beautiful buildings come from the deep comfort we experience when we recognize that the Life and organic order of the place echoes the organic order of our own deepest inner selves.

Both of these visions have limitations and are incomplete.

The beauty that the *APL* generates from the comfort of satisfied needs, ignores desires. I don't mean the desire for a comfortable room or garden, I mean the desire for a transformation, a new vision of one's life. The importance of this kind of desire as an element in design was emphasized by Lou Kahn: *"Need is a current, everyday affair. But desire – that is something else again. Desire is the forerunner of a new need. It is the yet not stated, the yet not made which motivates."*[11] Any architect that has worked with a client is deeply aware of the role of clients' desires as well as their needs, both of which are important to satisfy. The APL necessarily focuses on general, universal patterns that apply to everyone, not the specific desires that any individual might express. The attitude of the book is that individual goals, desires, and eccentricities may lead one astray from the main design task of solving human needs.

Both the *APL* and the *NOO* ignore the sublime, the beauty of the overpowering, the beauty that says "I am overwhelming and larger than you and your petty needs." I'm not here referring to the current use of the word (the sublimeness of the cathedral or a rosy sunset), but rather the Romantic notion of the word as first expressed by Edmund Burke in 1757.[12] The sublime form of beauty awes and frightens us a bit, separating our limited selves from the inhuman power of nature, which has the power to destroy us. And yet, there is a part of us that is attracted to it. This form of beauty, and our tendency to seek it out, is famously

---

11   Quoted from *Light is the Theme*, Kimbell Art Museum, 2011.
12   *A Philosophical Enquiry into the Origin of Our Ideas of the Sublime and Beautiful*, Edmund Burke, 1757.

illustrated in Casper David Friedrich's painting of 1818, the "Wanderer Above the Mist".

Figure 14.

Alexander's work ignores a building's potential for the tantalizing danger, risky adventure, or thrill of the illegal, which so many "starchitects" today play with to energize their sometimes arbitrary, "fun" buildings (such as this glass floor in the Dutch Embassy in Berlin by Rem Koohlhaas).

Figure 15.

Take, for example, the APL's emphasis on physical and psychological comfort as the sine qua non of good architecture. Certainly the idea of making comfortable spaces seemed to us all-important during the late 60's and early 70's. In fact, the architecture that was being done then was, for the most part, causing emotional and physical pain. Most were cold, featureless, boring, ugly. The resultant pain was comforted by the kind of architecture urged by the patterns, almost like a medicinal treatment. But this "comfort beauty" can slip into a coziness, sometimes verging into quaintness (*gemütlichkeit*).

A part of us does want to feel that we are part of the organic world, to relax into the comfort that we are bound and held by natural order. That can be a beautiful feeling. But there is another part of us that recognizes our disconnectedness from nature, our fragility in the face of the overpowering and uncontrollable. We are occasionally lured by the experience of this vulnerability which feels deliciously dangerous, risky, and adventuresome, like Friedrich's Wanderer perched on an eyrie, gazing at the limitless, partly hidden world below. Architecture sometimes taps into the sublime. Such a building can offer the opportunity to expand our selves, to see a new possibility, to grow. But this hinges on a bit of discomfort, a jarring of our habitual expectations. Examples of sublime architecture include Louis Kahn's Salk Center in La Jolla, California, the Kimbell Art Museum in Dallas/Ft. Worth, and his National Assembly Building in Bangladesh.

Figure 16.

While the APL ignores the sublime, the *NOO* outlaws architectural ideas and concepts in the design process, assuming that they inevitably disturb our 'true' perception which is based ultimately more on intuitive and introspective feeling than on thinking. This approach shuts us off from another kind of beauty, that which emerges from geometry and mathematics, and from noble and revolutionary social ideas, all of which can be expressed beautifully in architecture.[13] Here are some geometrical, numerical, and structural examples of ideas

13   In spite of the warnings against "geometrical fundamentalism" by Salingaros and Mehaffy.

being incorporated and expressed in architecture that contribute to a kind of beauty:

a.   The circle in a square (sphere in a cube) geometrical idea embodied in the Pantheon;

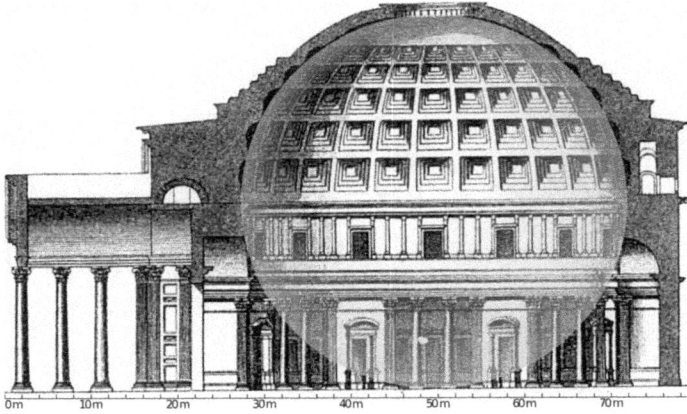

Figure 17.

b.   The repeating whole number ratios that harmonize the villas of Palladio;

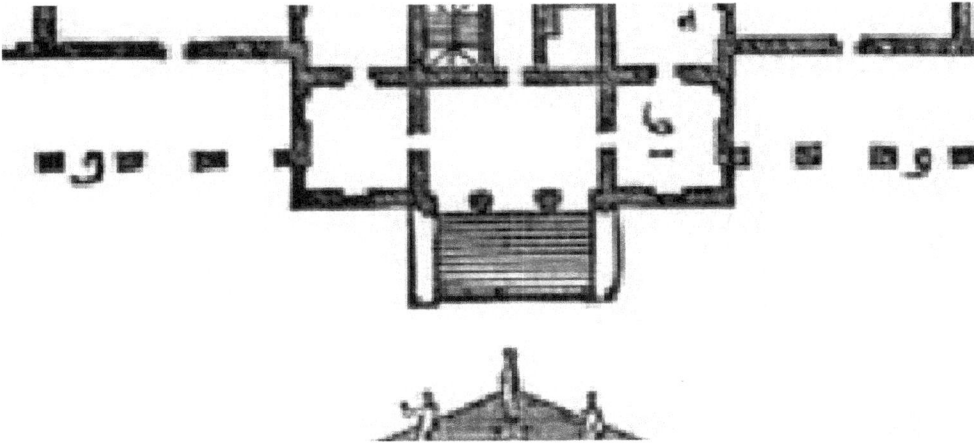

Figure 18.

c.   The Golden Proportion embodied in Corbu's Modular and in many buildings throughout history;

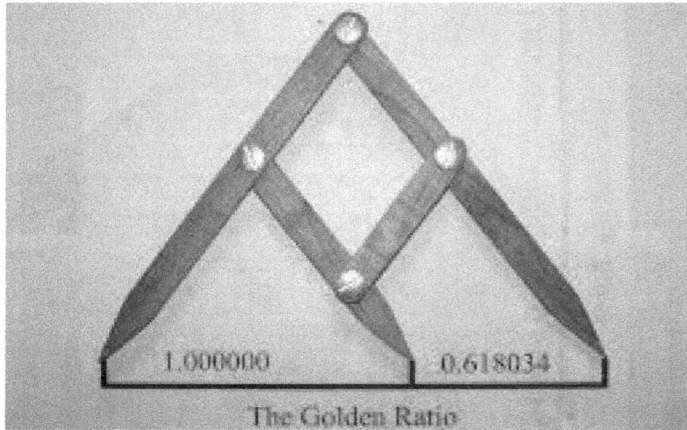

Figure 19.

d.   The cycloid which forms the vaults in Kahn 's Kimbell Art Museum;

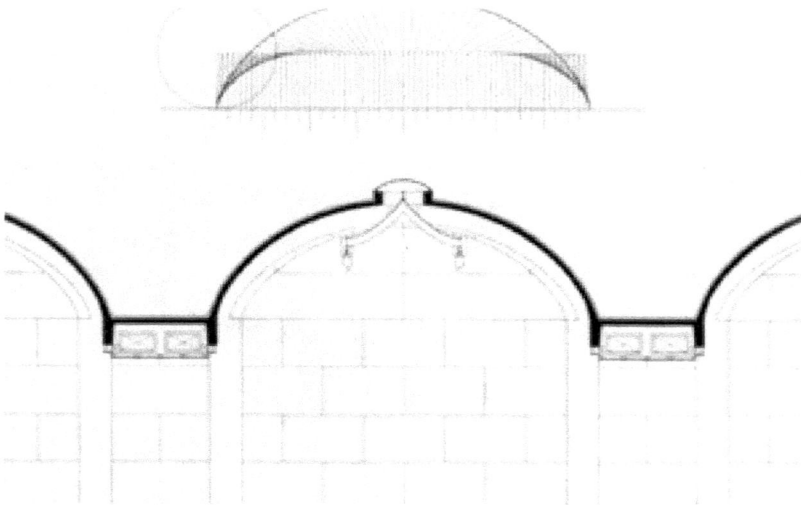

Figure 20.

e.   Or the catenary curve which Gaudi employed in Casa Milla and the Sagrada Familia cathedral.

Figure 21.

And here are a couple of social ideas that have led to another kind of architectural beauty:

f.   Jefferson's University of Virginia that expresses the centrality of the library, and the intimate relationship of students with their chosen professor;

Figure 22.

g.   Or Shindler's Kings Road House in LA that expresses the human complexities of human sharing and privacy, of the centrality of creative work, and the integration of nature and shelter.

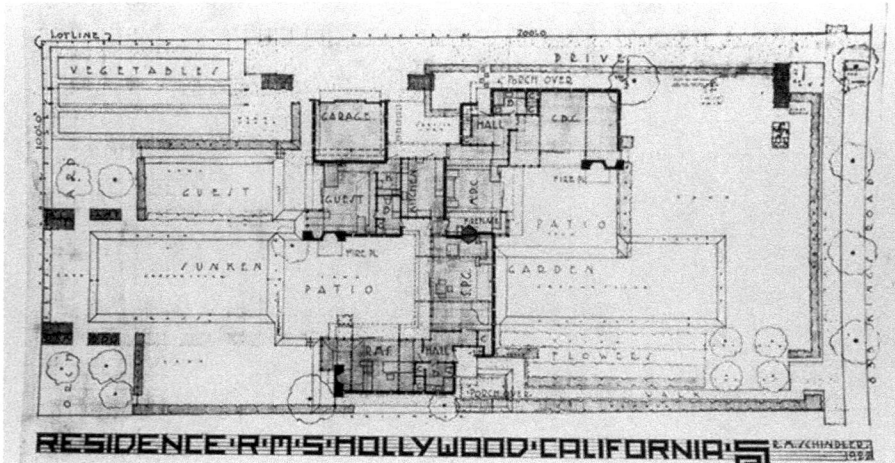

Figure 23.

6. Conclusion

The 15 properties themselves are a powerful tool in the recognition and production of organic form, a fundamental kind of beauty. But I think it is a mistake to insist that an object must contain all of them, or to be completely organic to be beautiful. We humans are more than just passive receptors of visual order. We are active problem solvers, seeking out puzzles, completing what is left out. This explains, I think, why the best architects invite us to visually play with their work, to sort out what is explicit and what is suggested.

As a final example, the façade of Gropius's own house in Dessau (now destroyed) plays with stated and unstated wholes, or centers. It contains Strong Centers, but they are not totally defined by *Boundaries*. It contains Levels of Scale, Alternating Repetition, Positive Space, but not *Local Symmetries* (intentionally), it contains Interlock, Contrast, Gradients, but not *Roughness* (again, intentional). This building asks us to do some work, to mentally fill in some of the suggested and implicit inter-relationships. And there is esthetic pleasure in this visual work.

Figure 24a.

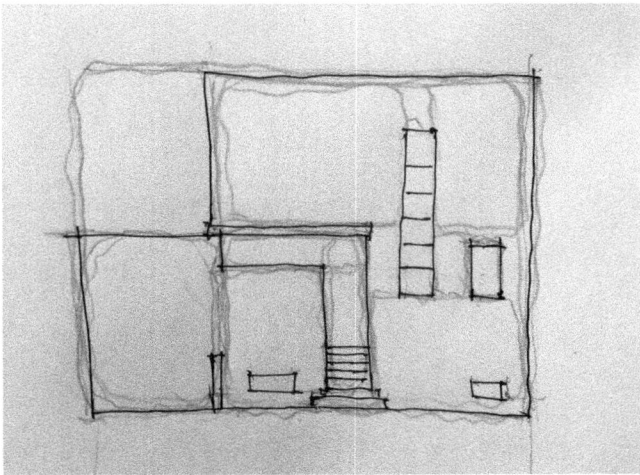

Figure 24b.

I think Chris's 15 properties gives us a fresh way to understand our 'guilty' appreciation of beauty in some of the work of other talented architects. Using the properties one can see that such buildings embody, to a degree, several of the organic elements, and take delight in ferreting them out. And this is similarly true for the patterns; the buildings we find beautiful likely embody many of them.

Alexander, and his many co-workers, have given us all very valuable insights and tools to aid the creation of beauty. But none of them guarantee it. It is possible to use the patterns and the 15 Properties and still create a "good enough" building. To do more requires maturity, talent, and empathy. And the modesty to help us recognize that beauty may come to us from unexpected sources and that we need to be open to receive it.

Watch this
keynote on
YouTube

We thank the following for their kind support in reviewing the contributions for this book:

Artemis Anniou
Peter Baumgartner
Anne Dörner
Tomoki Furukawazono
Tina Gruber-Mücke
Takashi Iba
Susan Ingham
Taichi Isaku
Hajo Neis
Ana Pinto
Richard Sickinger
Wolfgang Stark
Anne Stieger
Stefan Tewes
Christina Weber

www.ingramcontent.com/pod-product-compliance
Lightning Source LLC
Chambersburg PA
CBHW080127270326
41926CB00021B/4382

* 9 7 8 3 9 0 3 1 5 0 4 3 0 *